Studies in Natural Language Processing

Computational lexical semantics

T0382343

Studies in Natural Language Processing

Series Editor:
Branimir K. Boguraev, IBM T. J. Watson Research

Editorial Advisory Board
Don Hindle, AT&T Laboratories
Martin Kay, Xerox PARC
David McDonald, Content Technologies
Hans Uszkoreit, University of Saarbrucken
Yorick Wilks, University of Sheffield

This series publishes monographs, texts, and edited volumes within the interdisciplinary field of computational linguistics. It represents the range of topics of concern to the scholars working in this increasingly important field, whether their background is in formal linguistics, psycholinguistics, cognitive psychology, or artificial intelligence.

Also in this series:

Inheritance, defaults and the lexicon edited by T. Briscoe et al.
Challenges in natural language processing edited by M. Bates and
    R. M. Weischedel
Semantic processing for finite domains by Martha Stone Palmer
Memory and context for language interpretation by Hiyan Alshawi
The linguistic basis of text generation by Laurence Danlos
Natural language parsing edited by David R. Dowty, Lauri Karttunen, and
    Arnold Zwicky
Relational models of the lexicon by Martha Walton Evens
Computational linguistics by Ralph Grishman
Semantic interpretation and the resolution of ambiguity by Graeme Hirst
Reference and computation by Amichai Kronfeld
Machine translation edited by Sergei Nirenburg
Systemic text generation as problem solving by Terry Patten
*Text generation: Using discourse strategies and focus constraints to generate
    natural language text* by K. R. McKeown
Planning English sentences by D. E. Appelt

Computational lexical semantics

Edited by

PATRICK SAINT-DIZIER

Institut de Recherche en
Informatique de Toulouse –
CNRS

EVELYNE VIEGAS

Brandeis University

CAMBRIDGE
UNIVERSITY PRESS

CAMBRIDGE UNIVERSITY PRESS
Cambridge, New York, Melbourne, Madrid, Cape Town, Singapore, São Paulo

Cambridge University Press
The Edinburgh Building, Cambridge CB2 2RU, UK

Published in the United States of America by Cambridge University Press, New York

www.cambridge.org
Information on this title: www.cambridge.org/9780521444101

First published 1995
This digitally printed first paperback version 2005

A catalogue record for this publication is available from the British Library

Library of Congress Cataloguing in Publication data
Saint-Dizier, Patrick, 1954–
    Computational lexical semantics / Patrick Saint-Dizier, Evelyne
Viegas.
        p.   cm. – (Studies in natural language processing)
    Includes index.
    ISBN 0-521-44410-1
    1. Semantics – Data processing. 2. Computational linguistics.
    3. Artificial intelligence. I. Viegas, Evelyne. II. Title.
    III. Series.
    P325.S25   1995
    401′.43′0285–dc20   93-47127
                                                         CIP

ISBN-13 978-0-521-44410-1 hardback
ISBN-10 0-521-44410-1 hardback

ISBN-13 978-0-521-02320-7 paperback
ISBN-10 0-521-02320-3 paperback

Contents

Contributors

HOCINE ABIR   Laboratoire d'Informatique de Paris-Nord, Institut Galilée, Université Paris-Nord

GABRIEL G. BÈS   Université Blaise Pascal

SABINE BERGLER   Computer Science Department, Concordia University

TED BRISCOE   Computer Laboratory, University of Cambridge

GERRIT BURKERT   Institut für Informatik, Universität Stuttgart

MARC CAVAZZA   CISI Advanced Methods

ANN COPESTAKE   Computer Laboratory, University of Cambridge

D. A. CRUSE   Department of Linguistics, University of Manchester

BONNIE J. DORR   Department of Computer Science, University of Maryland

PETER GERSTL   IBM Germany, Gmbh, IWBS, Computer Science Department, University of Hamburg

DIRK HEYLEN   OTS TRANS 10 Rijksuniversiteit Utrecht, Utrecht

NANCY IDE   Department of Computer Science, Vassar College

JACQUES JAYEZ   EHESS, Paris

DANIEL KAYSER   Laboratoire d'Informatique de Paris-Nord, Institut Galilée, Université Paris-Nord

ADAM KILGARRIFF   Longman Group Ltd.

GUY LAPALME   Département d'Informatique et de recherche operationnelle, Université de Montréal

ALEX LASCARIDES   Human Communication Research Centre, University of Edinburgh

ALAIN LECOMTE   Université Blaise Pascal

JEAN-FRANÇOIS LE NY   Institut des Sciences Cognitives et de la Communication, Université de Paris-Sud, Orsay

MARTHA PALMER   Department of Computer and Information Science, University of Pennsylvania

ALAIN POLGUÈRE   Department of English Language and Literature, National University of Singapore

JAMES PUSTEJOVSKY   Computer Science Department, Brandeis University

MARGARITA ALONSO RAMOS   Département de linguistique et de philologie, Université de Montréal

PATRICK SAINT-DIZIER   IRIT – CNRS, Université Paul Sabatier

AGNES TUTIN   Département de linguistique et de philologie, Université de Montréal

JEAN VÉRONIS   Groupe Représentation et Traitement des Connaissances, Centre National de la Recherche Scientifique

EVELYNE VIEGAS   Computer Science Department, Brandeis University

PIERRE ZWEIGENBAUM   DIAM-INSERM U.194

Preface

This volume on computational lexical semantics emerged from a workshop on lexical semantics issues organized in Toulouse, France, in January 1992. The chapters presented here are extended versions of the original texts.

Lexical semantics is now becoming a major research area in computational linguistics and it is playing more of a central role in various types of applications involving natural language parsers as well as generators.

Lexical semantics covers a wide spectrum of problematics from different disciplines, from psycholinguistics to knowledge representation and to computer architecture, which makes this field relatively difficult to perceive as a whole. The goal of this volume is to present the state of the art in lexical semantics from a computational linguistics point of view and from a range of perspectives: psycholinguistics, linguistics (formal and applied), computational linguistics, and application development. The following points are particularly developed in this volume:

- psycholinguistics: mental lexicons, access to lexical items, form of lexical items, links between concepts and words, and lexicalizing operations;
- linguistics and formal aspects of lexical semantics: lexical semantics relations, prototypes, conceptual representations, event structure, argument structure, and lexical redundancy;
- knowledge representation: systems of rules, treatment of type coercion, aspects of inheritance, and relations between linguistics and world knowledge;
- applications: creation and maintenance of large-size lexicons, the role of the lexicon in parsing and generation, lexical knowledge bases, and acquisition of lexical data;
- operational aspects: processing models and architecture of lexical systems.

The workshop from which this volume was produced and the production of the volume itself have been supported by the GDR-PRC communication Homme-Machine, under contract with the French Ministry of Research and Space and the Centre National de la Recherche Scientifique (CNRS). We thank them for their substantial support. We also thank anonymous reviewers for their comments and the publisher for its cooperation in helping us prepare this volume.

Patrick Saint-Dizier and
Evelyne Viegas

1 An introduction to lexical semantics from a linguistic and a psycholinguistic perspective

PATRICK SAINT-DIZIER AND EVELYNE VIEGAS

1.1 Introduction

In this chapter, we present a synopsis of several notions of psycholinguistics and linguistics that are relevant to the field of lexical semantics. We mainly focus on the notions or theoretical approaches that are broadly used and admitted in computational linguistics. Lexical semantics is now playing a central role in computational linguistics, besides grammar formalisms for parsing and generation, and sentence and discourse semantic representation production. The central role of lexical semantics in computational linguistics can be explained by the fact that lexical entries contain a considerable part of the information that is related to the word-sense they represent.

This introduction will provide the reader with some basic concepts in the field of lexical semantics and should also be considered as a guide to the chapters included in this book. We first present some basic concepts of psycholinguistics which have some interest for natural language processing. We then focus on the linguistic aspects which are commonly admitted to contribute substantially to the field. It has not, however, been possible to include all aspects of lexical semantics: the absence of certain approaches should not be considered as an a priori judgment on their value.

The first part of this text introduces psycholinguistic notions of interest to lexical semantics; we then present linguistic notions more in depth. At the end of this chapter, we review the chapters in this volume.

1.2 Contribution of psycholinguistics to the study of word meaning

Results from psycholinguistic research can give us a good idea of how concepts are organized in memory, and how this information is accessed in the mental lexicon. Besides, the study of the relevant information that is retrieved from the mental lexicon, in the cases of recognition and production, can give us good clues regarding the information to be found in computational lexicons. The importance of ideas in psycholinguistics may be illustrated by its influence on artificial intelligence, in particular in knowledge representation: psycholinguistics played a leading role in the design of a number of models of knowledge representation.

We would like to thank the GDR-PRC Communication Homme-Machine of the French Ministry of Research and Space for funding the seminar from which this book has emerged. We also thank Bran Boguraev and anonymous reviewers for supporting the publication of this book.

Psycholinguistics is largely integrated in the field of cognitive psychology, and more precisely in the field of cognitive science. The approach and vocabulary of psycholinguistics are less and less structural, and more and more functional.

Psycholinguistics can be defined as the experimental study of the psychological processes by which human beings learn and put into practice a natural language system (Caron, 1989).

In this chapter, we focus on lexical access. The concern of lexical access studies is to answer two different types of questions with regard to the nature of the internal or mental lexicon, and to the access of processing. A mental lexicon should draw up an inventory of lexemes which are known and stored in our brain, so that we might be able to:

- name and describe persons, objects, places, events and feelings,
- convey our thoughts through lexicalization and grammaticalization,
- recognize or produce words that we hear, read or pronounce.

The processing of lexical access goes so fast that there is almost no space for introspection, as it is mostly unconscious. According to Brown and McNeill (1966), the case of 'the word on the tip of the tongue' cannot give us reliable indications of how a word should be represented in memory. This is the reason why analysis techniques are based on real-time techniques, so that processes can be apprehended as they process: most of the experiments use such an approach, and essentially techniques of lexical decision tasks.

We first present the models on memory organization, plus the different approaches to the access of the mental lexicon. Then we present an overview on different approaches or theories on word meaning.

1.2.1   *The model of Collins and Quillian*

The model developed by Collins and Quillian (1972) is represented as a network, with type nodes (PLANT), occurrence nodes (STRUCTURE, LIVING, . . .), and associative relations connecting the nodes to each other (AND, OR). Each occurrence node refers itself to a type node, sketched in the following diagram by means of dotted arrows. Basically a semantic network is based on the notion of *graphs*, with *nodes* representing the concepts, and *edges*, which are binary relations between the nodes. In this model, words (or concepts) are not primitive. We give as an example in Figure 1.1 the meaning representation of the word *plant*: a living structure which is not an animal, which often has leaves, taking its food from either air, water or earth.

This type of model focuses on *encyclopedic knowledge* (or in other terms, the contents of some *long-term memory* store), while other models distinguish between *long-term memory* (Tulving, 1972) and *current memory* (or in other terms *working memory* or *short-term memory*).

The model designed by Collins and Quillian is based on a principle of economy of storage, a postulate which does not seem to apply all the time. According to Conrad (1972), memory organization is ruled instead by a principle of *efficiency*

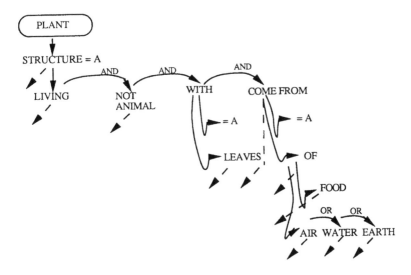

Figure 1.1

rather than *economy*, with multiple paths and redundancies allowing flexibility of access.

1.2.2   *The model of Miller and Johnson-Laird*

Miller and Johnson-Laird were essentially interested in the relation between perception and language. They worked on finding the processes which allow objects and events to be associated to lexical labels. From their viewpoint, perception is a structured activity, the result of which enables us to extract distinctive characteristics from an object (e.g., form, color, dimension, orientation). Perception is viewed as an activity of conceptualization for it refers to schemas, i.e., to a representation of relevant perceptual information attached to a concept. The explicative theory of the organization of the mental lexicon was given by Miller and Johnson-Laird (1976) by means of the following diagram:

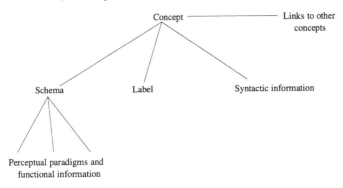

The conceptual level acts as a link between perceptual schemas and lexical items. A lexical concept consists of a label (for instance, *table*), a schema, and rules governing the syntactic behavior of the label. The schema integrates functional and perceptual information. It is also possible for the schema to include memory information that has no direct perceptual consequences. The linguistic meaning of lexical items is derived from the different relations which occur between them, via sub-routines such as *isa, has-a, is-in*. According to the authors, the mental lexicon would have two components:

1. a lexical component with relations between lexemes such as class inclusion, whole-part relations, syntagmatical and paradigmatical relations, and
2. a conceptual component which includes various perceptual features, minimal syntactic information, plus mnesical information (emotion, functionality).

Recent research on memory suggests that there is no distinction between *long-term* and *short-term memories*, and that *perception* is not the input of the «processing black box» and *memory/knowledge* the output. Rather, it seems that memory capabilities involve every aspect and level of activity within the «black box», and that *perception* and *memory/knowledge* are interlinked with each other. Memory seems to be organized in terms of *distributed memory*, highlighting the sensory and motor aspects, as well as the higher cognitive aspects (Allport, 1985).

In the two following sections we look at how the memory is accessed, depending on whether we are dealing with recognition or production.

1.2.3 *Lexical access in recognition*

The issue of lexical access in recognition, can be summarized in the following way:

- how can we read or hear a lexical item, whether simple or compound, as being a simple or compound item which we know?
- how are we then able to retrieve it from our mental lexical «storage»?

When understanding multi-word utterances we have access not only to individual words but we must also take into account the relations between them, in terms of lexical semantics and sentence meaning.

What the models discussed now have in common is the aim to set up a word-detector system: (Forster, 1976; Morton, 1982; Marslen-Wilson, 1984). There are two hypotheses, one requiring a serial retrieval, as when we consult a dictionary (Forster), and another requiring parallel retrieval, which can be performed thanks to an automatic activation of words within an interactive treatment of language (Morton, Marslen-Wilson).

Another result of much interest that provides some clues of how to structure lexicons comes from Forster's *semantic priming:* the reaction time for the recognition of a stimulus is lowered when a lexical item has been presented after another item that is semantically and contextually related to it. It takes less time to recognize the word *nurse* than to recognize the word *lawyer*, if *doctor* has already been encountered.

Another quite interesting result comes from the works of Morton (1982) and Marslen-Wilson (1984). The former, who developed the «logogen model», introduced the notion of *logogens*, which are associated with lexical items, and remain activated during the whole process of retrieval. He first considers that, to be operational, a word-detector system needs all the information coming from the context; second, that the retrieval of items is performed in parallel. The latter, in cooperation with Welsh, developed the «cohort model», a system in which identification of words is not the result of a selective activation of a logogen, but the result of a progressive elimination of logogens. Besides, Marslen-Wilson considers that the elaboration of the meaning of a sentence starts as soon as the sentence begins.

1.2.4 *Lexical access in production*

The issue of lexical access in production can be summarized, in the following way:

- how do we associate a given object or event with the appropriate lexical label?
- how does the process of lexical retrieval within the context of utterances production work?

Most of the works in psycholinguistics have dealt with language recognition, and most of the time the models which present a component to treat production are, to a large extent, rather hypothetical, as they have been very rarely experimented. However, it must be pointed out that in this domain the experimentation is quite uneasy. Most of the data belong to observation rather than experimentation. Today, it seems that it is better to try to apprehend the processes involved during the production of lexical items by looking at the speakers' errors.

The best-known model is that presented by Garrett concerning «lapsus analysis» (Garrett, 1982). Other studies are concerned with performance errors produced by aphasics, with two main distinctions that can be roughly described as: Broca's aphasia, which involves the loss of grammatical morphemes, and Wernicke's aphasia, which involves the loss of lexical items. The production component is very often described as involving two sub-components, often called the «what-to-say» and «how-to-say» components.

The «what-to-say» component

The «what-to-say» component involves an activity of planning at a pre-linguistic level where the speaker, willing to fulfill the communication and situation goals, decides, in accordance with the representation he has of his co-speaker(s) and the content of the message he wants to convey, how to cut out and order his «what-to-say».

At the linguistic level, planning is essentially concerned with the ordering and the train of utterances, plus the construction of the corresponding phonological sequence. Garrett showed that some regularities could be derived from the analysis of errors in a corpus produced by «normal» speakers (Garrett, 1982) by positing two levels in the stage of planning:

- a *functional* level, where items are found in an abstract form bearing only grammatical and semantic information, and
- a *positional* level, where grammatical morphemes and phonological form are inserted, and where the order of production is provided.

Another interesting orientation was that taken by Butterworth, who analyzed *pauses* in spontaneous speeches (Butterworth, 1980). His results can be summarized as follows:

- the frequency of pauses is dependent on the complexity of the planning of the semantic content of a discourse, thus stressing that semantic programming is not entirely unconscious but is partly controlled;
- the frequency of pauses seems to be unaffected by the syntactic complexity, thus showing that syntactic programming partly involves automatic processes;
- the frequency of pauses is high during the lexical selection of words which have a high degree of uncertainty.

The results of these psycholinguistic studies can be applied to a computational perspective in terms of some heuristics.

The «how-to-say» component

The «how-to-say» component is concerned with the «translation» of «the mental lexicon» into an utterance and requires various choices which have to be taken into account: word choice (e.g., specific denomination), order of enunciation (e.g., theme, rheme), speech act (e.g., illocutionary). This component reminds us that for a given semantic content, there are various linguistic realizations, hence we hardly have a one-to-one correspondence between a semantic content and its production.

As far as lexical selection is concerned, there are various parameters to be taken into account, which can be summarized as follows:

- the *automatic activation effect*, which will present the «word we have in mind». This effect is very often linked to the frequency of use, and corresponds to the «basic level» of Eleanor Rosch (1975). For instance, when naming in a broad context, we use more easily the word *dog* rather than a more general one like *animal* or a too specific one such as *alsatian;*
- the *priming effect*, which selects a word pre-activated by the context. For instance, we shall select more easily the word *client* in the context of a lawyer's waiting room rather than *patient;*

- the choice of the order of enunciation and of the speech act will determine whether we use an assertion or a question, for instance, whether or not we use modalities, such as *I think that*, and the order in which we will present the argumentation.

1.2.5   *Automatic or controlled processes? Parallel or serial treatments?*

Psycholinguists do not give a definite answer to the question of knowing whether we are dealing with controlled processes (implying an active and conscious retrieval) or automatic ones concerning lexical access. Experiments on visual stimulus showed that context effects do not rule out the existence of an automatic level of word recognition, which is relatively indifferent to contextual information. Marslen-Wilson disagrees with these results, when applied to speech. Besides, it seems that the access to different components is not performed in a serial way in a data-driven mode, in which each component (e.g., phonological, lexical, syntactic) would be considered autonomous, receiving information from the immediate upper level and giving information to the immediate lower level. Rather the different components are accessed in parallel, with at least part of the treatment performed in a concept-driven mode, with semantic analysis guiding, for instance, phonological and syntactic analyses.

Rumelhart, Smolensky, McClelland and Hinton (1986) claim that both treatments are needed, depending on the cases under consideration: *We believe that processes that happen very quickly – say less than 0.25 to 0.5 seconds – occur essentially in parallel and should be described in terms of parallel models. Processes that take longer, we believe, have a serial component and can more readily be described in terms of sequential information-processing models.*

As linguists or cognitivists using the results of psycholinguistic studies, we should keep in mind Morton's words when talking about the different systems proposed by psycholinguists, including Morton's own model: *don't become too attached to any of them.*

The mental lexicon is essentially subjective (as a product of individual experiences), and it is handled by a principle of efficiency, rather than economy, with multiple access paths enabling great flexibility and the coherence of its good functioning.

The ways lexicons are structured and organized have a great impact on the ways they should be accessed. We tackle this question in the next section paragraphs, by looking at some of the most well-known theories.

1.2.6   *Componential semantics*

In componential analysis, the sense of a word is defined as a set of *features* that distinguish it from other words in the language. Inaugurated by Hjelmslev, componential analysis was essentially developed by Katz and Fodor (1963).

Here is an example for the word *duck*, with the following notation: syntactic markers, (semantic markers), [semantic differentiators], <syntactic or semantic contextual delimitation>:

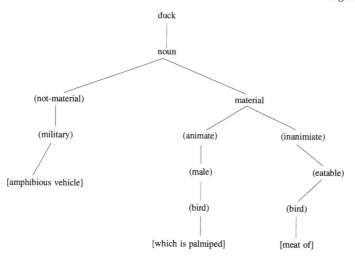

The meaning of a lexical item is analyzed in terms of atoms of senses (the terminal elements of the tree-structure).

Other works have added the notion of prototypicality, which gives the most typical word in a family of words (*orange* or *apple* are prototypes for *fruit*, in most Western communities, for instance), and the most typical values in terms of the properties of a word. Here is an example of prototypical attributes for the words *tower* and *piano* (Le Ny, 1979):

Tower	Piano
Height	Acoustics
Age	Shape
Beauty	Color
Strength	Beauty
Price	Price
Profitability	Material
. . .	. . .
Weight	Weight
. . .	. . .
Chemical	
Composition	
. . .	

The notion of prototype is also extended to the different values of the attributes, for instance, the attribute value for *color*, for the word *piano*, varies among speakers from *black* to *brown* to *white*.

1.2.7   *Procedural semantics*

The theory of procedural semantics was essentially developed by Miller and Johnson-Laird (1976). It consists of defining the meaning of a word by the procedures involved in its usage. The word is not considered as a static entity (a set of features or propositions) but as a *sub-routine*, which is called by the running program, whether it be in a phase of recognition or production. Therefore, the sense of a sentence can be considered analogous to a computer program. This model takes into account both production and recognition using the same set of rules, which is certainly an advantage for an artificial intelligence model, but which, on the contrary, does not seem to be in line with the results of most psycholinguistic research.

Here is an example of the analysis of the utterance *did Lucy bring the dessert?* in the following context: a person A participated to an episode Ep which he remembers, and the memory of this episode is called M(Ep). Another person B was not present, but knows that Ep took place and learns what happened by talking to A. When the question *did Lucy bring the dessert?* is asked, the episode Ep is identified as the conversation topic for both protagonists. B asked the question *did Lucy bring the dessert?* and A can answer «*Yes*», «*No*», «*Yes, she brought chocolate cake*», «*I don't remember*», «*I think so*», etc.

The following is an extract of the set of instructions in the program by Miller and Johnson-Laird:

- find in memory an episode where $F(x,y)$;
- assign to F the value «bring», assign to x the value «Lucy», assign to y the value «dessert»;
- if the description is found, then answer «yes»; if nothing is found, answer «I don't know»; if an information contradicting the description is found, then answer «no».

From a lexical viewpoint, «bring» will call a *sub-routine* which consists in:

- finding in the domain under consideration an event *e* where $COME(x)$;
- verifying if, during *e*, $BRING(x,y)$, etc.

In this perspective, a word is seen neither in isolation nor independently of context, and its meaning is seen as a sub-routine within a program. However, it seems that little is said, if anything, on the proper semantics or syntax of words.

1.3 Lexical semantics in linguistics

In this section, we survey several leading areas of lexical semantics in linguistics: argument structure, thematic roles, selectional restrictions, lexical semantics essential relations, ontologies, lexical conceptual representation, event structure and qualia structure.

1.3.1 *Argument structure*

To every predicate is associated an argument structure (Grimshaw, 1990) which specifies the number of arguments it requires. The arguments represent those elements which must necessarily be involved in the action or state described by the predicate. Adjuncts are not a priori included in an argument structure, even if they contribute in a significant way to the description of the action or state. Verbs as well as some nouns, adjectives and prepositions have an argument structure. There are two basic theories for describing the relations between a predicate and its arguments: a logical theory, in which arguments are ordered and have a rigid underlying meaning and a thematic role distribution system that labels a sequence of arguments by means of thematic roles.

An argument structure is often associated with the notions of sub-categorization frame and thematic role distribution, but an argument structure itself does not say anything about the syntactic category of arguments (which is often not unique) or about their thematic roles. It specifies only in a very abstract way the arity of a predicate, i.e., the number of actors which participate in the definition of the predicate. This approach allows us to abstract away from syntactic classifications such as transitivity or di-transitivity verb to state simply that, for example, a certain verb is of arity 2, namely, that it has an external argument (the subject, which is compulsory in a number of languages like English and French, but not in Spanish or Italian) and an internal argument (the object).

The argument structure of a verb defines the arguments that must be present, in one way or another, in any syntactic construction involving that verb. For example, we have the following argument structures for verbs:

>*give: 3*   (or, alternatively: give: X, Y, Z)
>*think: 2*
>*argue: 2*
>*sleep: 1.*

Adjuncts to verbs add information to the predicate such as time, place or manner; they do not appear in the argument structure. In some cases, some arguments may be left implicit, as in give and buy:

>*Jane gives a book.*

It should also be noticed that the argument structure associated to a verb may not be unique.

As in the case of verbs, a number of nouns, adjectives and prepositions may have an argument structure. However, arguments are usually optional and may not be realized in a sentence. Nominalized verbs in particular fall in this class. We have, for example:

>*destruction: noun, 1 (destruction of the city)*
>*attempt: noun, 2 (X's attempt to leave)*
>*arrival: noun, 1 (X's arrival)*
>*envious: adjective, 2 (X is envious of Y)*
>*outside: preposition, 2 (X is outside location Y)*
>*between: preposition, 3 (X is between Y and Z).*

Arguments in an argument structure are differentiated by the relation they have with the predicate. This allows the identification of natural classes of arguments which may be realized in the syntax in a number of different ways. As we shall see later, the properties of these relations can be expressed in various ways, such as thematic roles or combined primitive elements.

1.3.2 *Thematic roles*

Thematic roles have motivated much research in formal and applied linguistics and have attained a relatively high degree of sophistication. We review here major aspects that may be relevant to computational lexical semantics.

Thematic role assignment

The relationships between arguments and a predicate can be represented by thematic roles. We can say, for example, that in the case of the verb give, of arity 3, its first argument bears the thematic role *agent*, the second argument bears the role *patient* and the latter, the role *theme*. The definitions of thematic roles remain, however, very sketchy. For example, the number of thematic roles depends on authors. Their exact definition is also relatively fuzzy and in some cases there is a kind of continuum between them. Consequently, the way arguments are assigned a thematic role can be controversial.

A syntactic constraint is that, in any syntactic realization, an argument bears one and only one thematic role and different arguments are assigned different thematic roles. However, it should be noted that thematic roles are only conceptual lexical labels which do not project in the grammatical representation.

The most prominent thematic roles, for which we propose a generally admitted definition, are the following:

Agent: the participant designated by the predicate as doing or causing the action (e.g., first argument of eat, hit, watch, give);

Patient: the participant undergoing the action and who is affected by it (e.g., second argument of kill, eat);

Theme: the participant changing location, condition, or state or being in a given state or position (e.g., the second argument of give, the argument of walk and die);

Experiencer: the participant that is informed of something or that experiences some psychological state expressed by the predicate (e.g., first argument of love, second argument of annoy);

Source: the object from which movement occurs (e.g., second argument of leave);

Goal: the object toward which a movement is directed (e.g., second argument of reach, arrive), or the motivation of an action;

Location: the place in which the action or state described by the predicate takes place (e.g., second argument of fall);

Beneficiary: the participant that benefits from the action expressed by the verb (e.g., second argument of grant).

Thematic roles can be defined in a much more refined way, in particular from an empirical basis when modeling an application domain. Thematic roles are then decomposed and structured according to their detailed semantic contents. Common characteristics to a given thematic role form a thematic role type (Dowty, 1989). Some thematic roles may also be considered as sub-types of others. Finally, at the level of thematic role assignment, the previous definition can be made more flexible by considering that some roles may be major or minor for a given participant. For example, in the case of the verb *to buy*, the major source is the participant who gives the object, while a secondary source could be the other participant who gives the money for the object being bought.

Hierarchical organization of thematic roles

Arguments are often structured by means of a prominence relation along two dimensions: a thematic and an aspectual dimension (Grimshaw, 1990). The most prominent thematic role is the agent, followed by the experiencer and the patient, and, at the same level goal, source and location, and finally, theme. This can be represented as follows:

(Agent (Experiencer (Goal / Source / Location (Theme / Patient))))

The deeper embedded arguments are first assigned a thematic role, and the external argument is the one which is marked last. This marking respects the hierarchy of thematic roles. For example, for the verb *to give* we have the following marking:

give (Agent (Goal (Theme)))

Because of their implicit meaning, agents are necessarily external arguments. Agents may also be replaced by Causes.

Although simpler, the aspectual dimension also structures arguments. An event can basically be considered as the sequence: activity-subsequent state. Then, the argument participating to the first element of the sequence, the activity, is more important than the others. It is thus, in general, realized as the subject of the predicate. In agentive transitive verbs such as *meet*, the agent is the most prominent from the aspectual point of view:

meet: (Agent (Theme))
       1   2   : aspectual hierarchy

similarly for psychological state verbs like fear:

fear: (Experiencer (Theme))
      1   2

but we have a symmetric situation for causative verbs like frighten:

frighten: (Experiencer (Theme))
      2   1

because in *fear*, the first argument is the target of the emotion while in *frighten*, it is the cause of the emotion.

So far, we have examined only verbs. Nouns, adjectives and prepositions also have similar thematic roles. In the case of nominalizations, nouns preserve the thematic role distribution of their corresponding verbs. Prepositions usually have clear thematic roles, depending on their semantics. For example, the preposition *to* has, in its spatial meaning, one argument which is marked as Goal.

Toward thematic proto-roles

Thematic roles turn out to be too general in many cases, and, thus, of little practical interest. The idea proposed in Dowty (1991) is to define thematic roles by means of clusters rather than by means of criteria. The problem, then, is to decompose in an adequate way a thematic role into fragments of meaning. A. Cruse (1986) proposes the following decomposition for the notion of agent:

Agent: + volitional, + agentive, + effective, + initiative.

In Dowty (1991), the notion of theme is decomposed into three kinds of themes according to the aspectuality of the sentence. We have the following sub-roles for theme, related to different aspectual values:

incremental theme: affected object or incrementally affected objects (e.g., write a paper, play a concerto);

holistic theme: there is a change of location (concrete or abstract), but the goal is not necessarily reached (e.g., go to Paris, walk 2 kilometers);

source theme: the object is not affected, but an underlying object, such as a diskette or a photograph (e.g., copy a file on a diskette, make a picture of a landscape) is affected.

The definition of sub-roles also permits us to preserve the principle of thematic unicity by allowing different sub-roles to be assigned to different syntactic constituents.

The status of the roles Agent and Patient is more complex. There is indeed a kind of continuum between them: some patients, for example, may have a small degree of agentivity. Dowty (1991) views these two roles as proto-roles and defines them by means of several properties. The definitions for the proto-roles Agent and Patient are the following:

Agent:
+ volition (John is working)
+ sentience or perception (John knows it)
+ causes event to occur (Phone calls cause interruptions)
+ movement (The wind blown down the house)

Finally, the referent exists independently of the action described by the predicate.

Patient:
+ change of state (John opened the window)
+ incremental theme (Ann writes a book)
+ causally affected event (Smoking causes cancer)
+ stationary, relative to movement of proto-agent (The bus entered the garage)

Finally, the referent may not exist independently of the action described by the verb, or may even not exist at all.

We can now introduce the Argument Selection Principle. In a sentence, the role Agent will then be assigned to the syntactic constituent which has the highest degree of agentivity, and similarly for the role Patient. The argument of a predicate having the highest number of properties of the proto-agent role is realized as the subject. If two arguments have the same number of proto-agent properties, then they can be either subject or object. For a predicate with three arguments, the non-subject argument which has the smaller number of proto-patient properties will be realized as the oblique or PP. As can be seen, there is a kind of competition between roles for the assignment of the subject position.

1.3.3   *Selectional restrictions*

Selectional restrictions introduce more pragmatic (or domain-dependent) criteria on the semantic content of arguments. Selectional restrictions are extensively used in Natural Language Processing applications and are often based on AI (artificial intelligence) knowledge representation techniques. The basic principle is to associate to each argument of a predicate a list of semantic features F_i that express constraints on the semantic nature of the arguments. This list of restrictions may have different forms:

- [F_i]: a single semantic feature, e.g., human, animate, eatable, etc.;
- [F1 ∧ F2 . . . ∧ Fn]: a conjunction of elements expressing a conjunction of constraints that must be met;
- [F1 ∨ F2 . . . ∨ Fm]: a disjunction of constraints: one of these constraints must be met;
- a combination of conjunctions and disjunctions.

For example, the verb *drink* requires its object to have (at least) the following two semantic features: [liquid ∧ eatable]

Selectional restrictions are often defined on an empirical basis. Recently several research efforts have tended to define principle-based methods to define them. An interesting result for our present purpose is the organization of the semantic types used as selectional restrictions into a tree or a lattice of types. These types are structured by means of the type/sub-type relation where, for example, a human is a sub-type of animate entities. Here is a small sample, purely empirical, of a structure of semantic types:

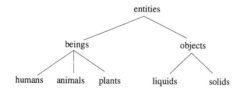

A way of structuring semantic features into trees and lattices is described in detail in Cruse (1986) and in several AI systems such as KL-One (Brachman and Schmolze, 1985). Besides structural properties like coherence that are associated to structuring types, this kind of structure allows a much more flexible use of selectional restrictions. If an argument is indeed required to be of semantic type F, then the realization can be of any type G which is a sub-type of F. For example, a verb such as *buy* requires an object as its second argument. This object can be either a liquid or a solid, according to the tree just shown.

The major problem with selectional restrictions is the definition of semantic features, their granularity, their organization, their maintenance and their exact uses in predicates. They also have deep relations with the description of ontological knowledge associated to a domain that we will explore in the section on ontologies.

1.3.4   *Lexical semantics relations*

In this section, we consider a more global level of lexical organization and different well-known relations that structure lexical items. Lexical semantics relations play an essential role in lexical semantics and intervene at many levels in natural language comprehension and production. They are also a central element in the organization of lexical semantics knowledge bases. Most of the material presented here is borrowed from Cruse (1986).

Congruence relations

Two words W1 and W2 denoting respectively sets of entities E1 and E2 are in one of the following four relations :

- identity: E1 = E2,
- inclusion: E2 is included into E1,
- overlap: E1 and E2 have a non-empty intersection, but one is not included into the other,
- disjunction: E1 and E2 have no element in common.

These relations support various types of lexical configurations such as the type/sub-type relation.

Hierarchical relations

There are basically three major types of hierarchical relations: taxonomies, meronomies and proportional series.

Taxonomies.   The taxonomy relation is the well-known isa relation which associates an entity of a certain type to another entity (called the hyponym) of a more general type. Taxonomy introduces a type/sub-type relation which can be characterized by one of the following linguistic tests:

X is a sub-type of Y if the following expressions are correct:

- X is a kind of Y or X is a type of Y for nouns and
- X-ing is a way of Y-ing for verbs.

Taxonomies have up to seven levels that correspond to different levels of genericity (natural taxonomies usually have five levels, technical taxonomies may have more than seven levels). It is also important to note that in some cases, certain nodes do not have any corresponding word in a given language, whereas they have one in another language. A taxonomy may thus have holes. Taxonomic decomposition corresponds to a kind of 'point of view', for example the term *human* can be decomposed into sub-types according to physical or to mental properties. As a consequence a given word-sense may enter into different taxonomies. The main property of a taxonomy is transitivity of properties from the type to the sub-type. This property can also be viewed as a well-formedness criterion for taxonomies.

Most levels of a certain degree of genericity have a large number of sub-types; each of them has different possible realizations as words. The notion of sub-type is, however, difficult to qualify in a homogeneous way. There is indeed a problem of prototypicality which is raised: some sub-types are more prototypical than others of their hyponym (the type above them). Let us recall the famous example of the blackbird which is more prototypical of a bird than a hen, which is itself more prototypical of that same class than a penguin.

Meronomies. Meronomies describe the part-whole relation. It is a fairly complex relation that attempts to take into account the degree of differentiation of the parts with respect to the whole and also the role that these parts play with respect to their whole. For example, elements such as spatial cohesion and spatial differentiation, and functional differentiation and the nature of the links between the parts are crucial elements for determining meronomies. In fact, depending on the quality of these elements, we may have different kinds of meronomies, with different types of properties.

Meronomies can be characterized, maybe in a slightly too restrictive way, by the following linguistic tests. A is a part of B if one of these sentences is correct:

> B has A (or B has a A),
> B is part of A.

The meronomy relation has itself some properties (or attributes) which must be taken into account in any realistic model:

- optionality of a part, and
- cardinality of a part with respect to the whole, e.g., a human has 2 legs, a car has 4 wheels.

Winston and Chaffin (1987) distinguish 6 kinds of meronomies that differ according to the functionalities, the spatial cohesion and the degree of dissimilarity between the parts and their whole. We have the following classes:

- component / integral object: there is a clear structural and functional relation between the whole and its parts, e.g., handle/cup, phonology/linguistics;
- member / set or group: parts do not necessarily have a structural or functional relation with respect to the whole, parts are distinct from each other. Included in this class, for example, are tree/forest, student/class;
- portion / mass: there is a complete similarity between the parts and between parts and the whole. Limits between parts are arbitrary and parts do not have any specific function a priori with respect to the whole. We have in this class, for example: slice/bread, centimeter/meter. This sub-relation is often called a mereology;
- object / material: this type of relation describes the materials from which an object is constructed or created, or the constitutive elements of an object, e.g., alcohol/wine, steel/car.
- sub-activity / activity or process: describes the different sub-activities that form an activity in a structured way, for example, in a temporally organized way. Examples include: pay/buy, give exams/teach;
- precise place / area: parts do not really contribute to the whole in a functional way. This sub-relation expresses spatiality, as in: oasis/desert, Alps/Europe.

Similar to taxonomies, the meronomy relation cannot really be conceived between two elements, but should be conceived with respect to the set of all the parts forming the whole. This also permits us to introduce a kind of point of view in a meronomic description. Meronomies do not, in general, allow transitivity at logical and linguistic levels. However, some authors tend to allow transitivity at the linguistic level between elements which are linked by the same sub-type of meronomic relation just described. Finally, interestingly, meronomies may have a very restricted form of transitivity of properties from parts to the whole. This transitivity does not, however, obey any general principle and should be indicated in each description. For example, the property color associated to the body of a car is usually inherited by the whole, i.e., the car. This example is somewhat general; it is also valid for bicycles, planes, trains, buses etc. However, a general statement of the form: the whole inherits the color of its largest part (largest with a spatial meaning) is not always true.

Non-branching hierarchies. Non-branching hierarchies allow for the ordering of elements that correspond to different levels of organization or of dimensionality. The structure does not correspond to a type/sub-type organization, but could have in somes cases some similarity with a meronomic relation. Non-branching hierarchies are often related to a spatial, a temporal or an abstract notion of dimensionality.

We can distinguish among three kinds of non-branching hierarchies:

- a continuous hierarchy where limits between elements are somewhat fuzzy, as in: frozen-cold-mild-hot; small-average-large, and in most topological relations;
- a non-continuous and non-gradable hierarchy, in general not based on any measurable property such as institutional hierarchies and technical hierarchies: sentence-proposition-phrase-word-morpheme;
- a non-continuous and gradable hierarchy, organized according to a given dimension, such as units of measure.

In some cases, non-branching hierarchies may reflect a more linguistic than common-world knowledge.

Non-hierarchical relations

Among non-hierarchical relations we mainly distinguish among synonymies and the different forms of opposition. These relations, as we shall see it, are either binary or ternary. The ternary character reflects the context-dependence of some of these relations.

Synonyms. Two words are synonyms if they have a significant similar semantic content. Synonyms have a significant semantic overlap, but the degree of synonymy is not necessarily related to that overlap. There are very few absolute synonyms, if any, in a language, but words may be synonyms in given contexts. Therefore we view the synonymy relation as a ternary relation: W1 and W2 are synonyms in the context C. Synonyms often do not depend on the degree of precision of the semantic descriptions, but their degree of synonymy may however change at different levels of granularity (Spark Jones, 1986).

For example, within the context of computer science, we can say that a directory and a *repertoire* are *synonyms* even if the former belongs to the Unix world while the latter belongs to the Macintosh world. Similarly, in the more abstract context of *state*, we can say that *remember* and *memorize* are synonyms.

To refine the notion of synonymy, some authors tend to make a distinction between essential features and secondary features associated to a word. This distinction is certainly empirically motivated, but it is extremely difficult to use it in practice.

Synonymy, in a lexical knowledge base, can play the role of a kind of integrity constraint about the feature-values that may be assigned to two words stated as synonyms. It can also play a very interesting role in natural language generation, where terms can be replaced by their synonyms in some contexts.

Antonyms and opposites. Antonyms and opposites cover a very large variety of phenomena, more or less clearly defined. A basic definition could be that W1 and W2 are antonyms or opposites if they have most semantic characteristics in common but if they also differ in a significant way on at least one essential semantic dimension. Like synonyms, antonyms and opposites are highly contextual and thus introduce a kind of ternary relation. There also various degrees of opposition, as some pairs of word-senses are more prototypically opposites than others. Antonyms refer to gradable properties and opposites to non-gradable ones.

For example, with respect to the context '*to start*', to *keep on* and *to stop* are opposites. Similarly, *good* and *bad* are generally admitted as antonyms, and are more prototypical than the opposition between father and mother.

Antonyms do not necessarily partition the conceptual space into two mutually exclusive compartments which cover the whole conceptual domain. Some overlap or space in between is possible, as in good and bad, since it is indeed possible to say that something is neither good nor bad, or, possibly, to say that something is both good and bad. A special class of antonyms is made up of complementaries, which divide the whole conceptual space into two non-overlapping compartments. In Cruse (1986) several classes of complementaries are defined, such as the class of interactives, which represent a relation of the type stimulus-response, as in: *grant–refuse*, with respect to the context of *request*.

Another interesting class among opposites consists of directional opposites. They represent either basic, topological, or conceptual (metaphorical) directional oppositions. In this class, which is conceptually relatively simple, fall examples such as: *start–finish, top–bottom, descend–ascend*.

The role of opposites in a lexical semantics knowledge base is somewhat difficult to define. Like synonyms, opposites and antonyms may certainly play the role of integrity constraints. Their use in natural language generation, for example, to avoid the use of too many negations, is somewhat hard to make explicit, because of numerous pragmatic factors that may intervene, such as the polarity of an element in a pair of opposites or antonyms. We can say, for example, '*how expensive is this book?*' but probably not '*how cheap is this book?*'. Finally, the linguistic tests or the analytic methods for defining exactly and to what degree if two elements are opposites or antonyms remain to be defined precisely.

1.3.5 *Ontologies*

Ontologies are a vast domain in lexical semantics and in artificial intelligence whose boundaries are somewhat fuzzy. Basically, an ontology is a formal system that aims at representing for a given domain by means of basic elements, the different concepts and their related linguistic realizations. A larger view of ontological knowledge can also include various forms of encyclopedic knowledge about the domain, and common-sense knowledge as well as rhetorical and metaphorical knowledge and expressions.

Ontological descriptions are used in a number of situations and classes of applications. In terms of application, several systems tend to incorporate ontological knowledge to improve their quality and generality. Ontological knowledge can be particularly crucial for applications such as intelligent user-front ends in natural language and automatic retrieval of documents. Ontological knowledge is used implicitly in a number of practical and theoretical approaches such as: semantic

networks and conceptual graphs, lexical conceptual structure, generative lexicons, scenarios and scripts and discourse management systems. Some general
domains like space and tense have already originated the development of very
detailed ontological systems.

The definition of an ontology is a very delicate task. The main point is to be
able to define real primitive or basic elements of knowledge associated to the
domain. This definition depends on several factors, among which are:

- the degree of granularity one wants to attain in the system;
- the reference to already existing partial ontologies which must homo-
  geneously be integrated into the system (e.g., spatial or temporal
  ontologies);
- the reference to theories of linguistic knowledge representation, such
  as the Lexical Conceptual Structure (LCS) (Jackendoff, 1990) or the
  Conceptual Graphs framework.

An ontology is based on a formal language composed of:

1. sets of entities, often structured and typed
2. a set of relations and operations and their related properties
3. a finite set of basic predicates describing primitive states and actions of
   the domain, their formal semantics being simply defined by their respective domains of interpretation within the application and
4. a set of functions operating on the entities. These functions are usually
   defined from a corpus analysis.

This language is usually a sub-set of first-order logic and it is used to represent
linguistic as well as application-dependent knowledge at various levels of generality. Here is a simplified ontology for a portion of the banking domain. We have
the following entities:

I: individuals, including 2 sub-types:
- human beings (further sub-divided into: customers and staff),
- institutions (further sub-divided into: banks, companies and national
  or private institutions).
A: concrete amounts of money. Topological space with positive rational
    numbers with two decimal digits has a complete order relation <, equal-
    ity and the classical arithmetic operations.
M: concrete materials, such as paper, plastic and metals (for coins).
S: supports, of a more or less abstract nature; e.g., a check and a coin are
    supports for money.
T: set of instants, oriented line of reals with a total ordering.

Variables I, A, M, S and T will be used to represent the type of an entity or of an
argument in a predicate.

Primitive actions, states and relations are represented by *predicates*. Arguments
may be polymorphic. We have, for example, the following predicates:

belong_to(individual: I, money: A, date: T).
abstract_support_for(support: S, what_it_represents: A and possibly I)
introduces a relation between a support and what it stands for.
store(who: I, what_is_stored: A or S or M, date: T).

With these predicates it is, for example, possible to represent the notion of a movement of money (as would be represented in the Lexical Conceptual Structure discussed in section 1.3.6) from an account to another account as follows:

$$movement(of\_possession, i1, i2, amount) = belong\_to(i1, amount, t1)$$
$$\wedge\ belong\_to(i2, amount, t2) \wedge different(i1,i2) \wedge t2 > t1.$$

Similarly, *functions* can be defined, for example, to determine the interest of a loan.

The methods for defining these data are rather empirical and intuitive. Corpus analysis can be helpful for that task. Other informative elements can be the primitive notions used in the domain if it is a more or less formalized domain, as is often the case in a computerized application such as a database. Roots of hierarchies can also be considered as primitive elements. Finally, predicates describing states should be preferred to those describing actions since most actions simply entail a change of state.

There are relations between ontologies and selectional restrictions. We can say that it should be possible to characterize any term used in the selectional restrictions by a formula defined from ontological elements. These definitions should also preserve the type hierarchies.

1.3.6   *The lexical conceptual structure*

Basic concepts

The Lexical Conceptual Structure (LCS for short) (Jackendoff, 1988, 1990) aims at establishing a formal correspondence based on a notion of primitive concept between the external language on the one hand and the internal language on the other hand. Basic concepts are lexical and the meaning of a sentence is constructed from lexical meanings. The LCS establishes the following basic postulates:

- any syntactic constituent has a conceptual representation
- any conceptual category encodes one or more linguistic units
- most of these categories make the difference between type and object
- these categories are also quantifiable
- the conceptual structure of a lexical item is an entity with zero or more arguments.

These statements can be summarized by the three following representational dimensions:

1. entity --> Event / Thing / Place / . . .
2. entity --> Token / Type
3. entity --> $F(Arg_1, Arg_2, \ldots, Arg_n)$.

Let us consider a syntactic construction XP which describes an entity, and has a corresponding conceptual constituent that can be defined as follows:

$$[_{x_0} \_ <XP < YP >>] \equiv [_{\text{Entity}} F(E_1 , E_2 , E_3)].$$

Where E_1, E_2 and E_3, respectively, represent the subject, the XP and the YP.

The LCS has a strong connection with the notion of thematic roles, but it goes deeper into the specification and the representation of these roles. It also develops the necessity of topological systems to represent a number of dimensions in a refined way. For example, a topological system should allow the represention of the difference between *run* and *jog;* it should also be able to represent the spatial differences between, for example, a *car* and a *bus*, or between *run* and *tiptoe*. These differences are, however, extremely difficult to represent in an accurate way.

Introduction to LCS

In the LCS, the basic structures represent the relation between a predicate (or a function) and its arguments. Arguments represent parts of speech such as object, event, state, action, place, path, property and quality. These parts of speech type the entity they are associated to. They are usually represented as indices:

$$[_{\text{Part of Speech}} \quad <\text{entity}>]$$

Each of these parts of speech is combined with 'labels' which are primitives. They often have the form of a preposition, but must not be confused with them. These labels represent semantic properties in an unambiguous way. For example, for Path, we may have the following types of representations:

$$[\text{Path}] \dashrightarrow [\{\text{TO, FROM, TOWARD, AWAY-FROM, VIA}, \dots \}$$
$$[\{\text{OBJECT, PLACE}\}]].$$

where the symbols { and } represent a disjunction of possibilities.

Parts of speech and semantic labels allow for the representation of different syntactic objects. For example, here are the representations of the preposition *into* and the verb *run* (where we give the category, the indexed sub-categorization frame and the semantic representation):

$$\text{into: preposition, } \_ NP_j , [_{\text{Path}} \text{TO} ([_{\text{Place}} \text{IN} ([_{\text{Object}} \quad]_j)])].$$
$$\text{run: verb, } \_ NP_j , [_{\text{Event}} \quad \text{GO} ([_{\text{Object}} \quad]_i , [_{\text{Path}} \quad]_j)].$$

The indexes i and j represent the argument positions as given in the sub-categorization frame. Traditionally, the index i is reserved for the external argument (the subject).

Words do not necessarily correspond to fully instantiated constituents – they have the form of open structures. The LCS representations also allow the introduction of selectional restrictions to make the meaning of parts of speech more precise. For example, the object of the verb *drink* can be represented as follows:

$$[_{\text{Object}} \quad \text{LIQUID}]_j$$

Constituents may also have implicit arguments which are not realized in the syntax. In that case, a non-indexed argument is created in the conceptual representation. This is the case for example for the verb *butter*, where the notion of butter is 'incorporated' into the verb itself:

[$_{Event}$ CAUSE ([$_{Object}$] $_i$), [$_{Event}$ GO ([$_{Object}$ BUTTER],
[$_{Path}$ TO ([$_{Place}$ ON ([$_{Object}$] $_j$)])])])].

Multiple and optional arguments

Some constituents like NPs may play several roles, some being more prominent than others (see the previous section on thematic roles). For that purpose, the LCS allows two positions to bear the same index in the conceptual representation. This could be viewed as a kind of semantic binding relation, similar to the syntactic binding of co-referents. For example, the verb *buy* is represented as follows, where there is a double exchange: an object and a certain amount of money:

buy: verb, _ NP $_j$, from NP $_k$,
[GO$_{Poss}$ ([   ] $_j$, [FROM [   ] $_k$ TO [   ] $_i$]),
EXCH [GO$_{Poss}$ ([MONEY], [FROM [   ] $_i$ TO [ ] $_k$])]]]].

Notice that in this example the primitive GO, which is very general, has been further specialized in a GO of possession. Other specializations are possible such as the GO of location or time (see Dorr, this volume).

The LCS also allows for the specification of optional structures. These elements can be underlined in the LCS representation. Also a given word may be represented in a number of different ways depending on pragmatic factors. For example, in:

John climbed the mountain.

a representation will state that he has reached the top, whereas a second one will simply say that he is climbing the mountain.

Finally, the LCS also has some specific operators that express a conceptual modification of the clause they dominate. Among these operators, we have change of a state into an event, causal relations, accompaniment and exchange (see the representation of the verb *buy*).

Besides the introduction of operators, some of which are already familiar to the artificial intelligence community, the LCS introduces a deep relationship between the syntax and the semantic representation of lexical items. It also gives a principled account of how to construct these representations. LCS representations are now starting to be used in a number of application areas such as the basis of an interlingua for machine translation (see Dorr, this volume). The primitives presented in the theory often have, however, to be made more precise for given application domains. Some systems propose, for example, hierarchies of operators where these is a general concept, such as GO, and a full range of possible instantiations of it, depending on the type of the arguments (e.g., objects, places, etc).

1.3.7   *Event structure and temporal lexical information*

An event structure permits the identification of a particular type of event (Vendler, 1967) associated to a word or to a phrase, e.g., achievement, accomplishment, state. Basically, a word or a phrase may denote a state, a process or a transition.

A state is an event that is fully evaluated relative to no other event. The following words usually denote states: sleep, believe, white, employee. A process can be analyzed as a sequence of identical events. For example, the event of running can be decomposed into a (possibly infinite) set of sub-events corresponding to the running of a shorter distance. At the very limit, this event is decomposed into the basic gestures related to running. Finally, transitions are predicates which are evaluated relative to an opposition. Transitions describe the transformation of a state into another state by means of a process (Pustejovsky, 1991, 'The syntax of event structure, Cognition'). To illustrate the notion of transitivity, let us consider the verb *open*. The basic idea is that before opening a door, it is closed (original state), and when the action of opening has been performed, the door is in the subsequent state of being opened.

Closely related to the notion of event structure are the notions of tense and aspect. They allow the localization of events in a temporal space. They also allow the organization of events. We have, for example, the following temporal relations: precedence without any overlap, precedence with the first event ending exactly when the second begins, precedence with partial overlap, and complete inclusion of one event into another. These situations are identified at the discourse analysis level, but their exact meaning or their global organization may depend on temporal information which is lexical. Besides aspectual values associated to verbs, temporal adverbials are probably the most important lexical elements for determining the temporal organization of the states, processes and transitions found in a statement.

Let us illustrate the temporal lexical semantics of adverbials. They have first a feature that represents their associated reference function:

- *deictic:* the adverbial establishes a temporal relation within the enunciation, e.g.: tomorrow, last week, next semester;
- *anaphoric:* the adverbial refers to an already given antecedent, directly or indirectly, e.g.: then, two hours after;
- *autonomous:* the adverbial states a direct reference, as in a date;
- *polyvalent:* the adverbial can be either a deictic or an anaphoric, e.g., at noon.

Adverbials have a second feature that describes the orientation of the two events they organize:

- *equality or overlap:* now, meanwhile
- *posteriority:* then, three minutes after
- *anteriority:* an hour ahead, the year before

Finally, a feature introduces the contrast between *punctuality* of the described event (at 2 PM, now) and the notion of *durativity* (during 5 hours). Punctuality is clearly dependent on the granularity of the representation: it introduces a type of non-monotonic variable-depth representation schema (Abir and Kayser, this volume).

1.3.8   The qualia and inheritance structures

James Pustejovsky is developing the «generative lexicon», which is a highly organized and structured lexicon. Pustejovsky works on a theory of lexical meaning that tries to identify the core meaning of lexical items. He provides, for that purpose, a method for the decomposition of lexical categories, augmented with a theory of lexical semantics that embodies a notion of co-compositionality and type coercion. The latter notions are generative devices that operate between four levels of semantic description, which can be roughly presented as follows (Pustejovsky, 1991):

- *argument structure:* it represents the predicate structure for a word; giving the minimal specification of the lexical semantics of the word,
- *event structure:* it identifies a particular event type, including a sortal distinction between three classes of events (state, process or transition);
- *qualia structure:* it provides the essential attributes of an object, distributed among four aspects of the meaning of the word, captured through the following roles:
  - formal role, contains that which distinguishes it within a larger domain
  - constitutive role, essentially giving the relation between the lexical item and its constituents or proper parts
  - telic role, which defines its purpose and goal
  - agentive role, which gives the information about whatever brings it about
- *inheritance structure:* it involves two inheritance mechanisms
  - fixed inheritance, which can be said to be the «traditional» *is-a* relation enriched with the qualia structure.
  - projective inheritance, which gives the conclusion space for a concept, or in other words creates for that concept its relational structure for ad hoc categories which are usually said to belong to commonsense knowledge.

We now focus on the two last structures, namely, the qualia and the inheritance structures; through some type examples, they will be given in an informal way. The information to be found in the qualia structure is provided by corpora analyses plus information from dictionaries. Here are examples of qualia structures for *book* and *dictionary:*

book (*x*)
        [Formal: book-shape (*x*)]
        [Constitutive: {pages, covert, ...}]
        [Telic: read(T,y,*x*)]
        [Agentive:artifact(*x*), write(T,z,*x*)]
dictionary (*x*)
        [Formal: book(*x*), disk(*x*)]
        [Constitutive: alphabetized-list(*x*)]
        [Telic: reference(P,y,*x*), consult(T,y,*x*)]
        [Agentive:artifact(*x*), compile(T,z,*x*)]

We now show an example of lexical inheritance, for the words *novel* and *dictionary*: In order to be able to build the correct inheritance structures, Pustejovsky explains that we should be able to find in the qualia the paths that allow us to answer the following questions:

	novel is a book	dictionary is a book
read	yes	?
buy	yes	yes
consult	?	yes

Figure 1.2 shows the inheritance structure for *novel* and *dictionary*, where F, T, A stand for Formal, Telic and Agentive, respectively. From the representation we can derive, for instance, that *dictionary* is a formal *book*, and is a telic *reference*, so that it inherits the *consult* predicate avoiding the inheritance of the *read* predicate, which would be wrong in the case of *dictionary*. Pustejovsky rejects the notion of a fixed set of primitives, assuming that there is rather a fixed number of generative devices which construct the semantic expressions.

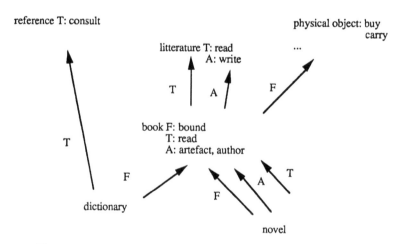

Figure 1.2

We believe the «generative lexicon» is today one of the most promising computational lexicons, for the following reasons:

- it takes into account the lexical semantics of a word, and its creative usage
- it explicitly formulates the link between the syntax and the semantics of the word
- it defines the links between the concepts in the lexicon

For a discussion between Mel'čuk's Meaning-Text-Theory and Pustejovsky's Generative Lexicon Theory, see Kilgarriff (this volume).

1.3.9   *Lexical functions in the meaning-text theory*

The work of Mel'čuk on Meaning-Text-Theory (MTT) (Mel'čuk, 1988) is by and large taken into account in the field of computational linguistics. Meaning-Text-Theory describes a set of possible models, the Meaning-Text-Models (MTMs), relating texts to their meaning representations. An MTM describes the (bidirectional) mapping between meanings and natural language texts. There are seven levels of description:

1. semantic representations (SemR)
2. deep syntactic representations (DSyntR)
3. surface syntactic representations (SSyntR)
4. deep morphological representations (DMorphR)
5. surface morphological representations (SMorphR)
6. deep phonetic representations (DPhonR)
7. surface phonetic representations (SPhonR)

We are interested here in the first three levels of description: SemR is represented as a semantic network, DSyntR and SSyntR as trees. The syntactic levels use dependency trees: the grammatical relations are explicitly labeled on the branches, whereas lexemes and grammatical words are labeled on the nodes.

Lexical information in the MTM is presented in the Explanatory Combinatorial Dictionary (ECD). The ECD attempts to cover all the linguistic knowledge (as opposed to world knowledge). Lexical entries are divided into three zones, namely, the semantic zone, the syntactic zone and the lexical combinatorial zone:

- the semantic zone specifies a semantic network which defines the meaning of the lexical entry in terms of simpler meaningful elements. In other words the meaning of a word is paraphrased through a minimally complex locution. For instance the lexeme *forbid* is defined as X forbids Y Z.
- the syntactic zone specifies the entry's syntactic class, the syntactic features used to identify specific constructions which accept the lexeme, plus government patterns which show how the semantic actants of the lexical entry are manifested on the two syntactic levels (DSyntR and SSyntR).

- the lexical combinatorial zone specifies semantically related lexemes as the values of "lexical functions" (LFs): A lexical function F is a correspondence which associates a lexical item L, called the key word of F, with a set of lexical items F(L) – the value of F (Mel'čuk, 1988).

Mel'čuk defined about 60 LFs. LFs can also be composed to define certain functions and lexemes. There are two kinds of LFs:

- paradigmatic LFs, which compute synonyms, superordinate terms, converse terms; they identify semantically related words of the same syntactic class. For instance, Syn(forbid): prohibit
- syntagmatic LFs, which calculate the values of collocational words co-occurring in the same sentence in specified syntactic relationships with the entry words. For a more comprehensive description of LFs, see (Ramos, Lapalme and Tutin, this volume). The work of Mel'čuk is very useful, as it provides a large amount of descriptive data, taking into account collocations, the study of which has been given little attention so far.

Contents of this volume

This introduction has provided the reader with basic results and references to some of the main trends of lexical semantics both from the perspective of linguistics and psycholinguistics. The elements presented are meant to serve as a basis for the chapters presented in this book.

The chapters included in this volume cover a large spectrum of the domain of computational lexical semantics. They can be divided into six different topics: psycholinguistic aspects of lexical semantics, linguistic issues, constructions of lexical semantic knowledge bases, lexical semantics and inference, applications and advanced computational aspects. These different fields are presented in their respective parts in this book where a short introduction is provided.

References

Allport, D. A. (1985). Distributed Memory, Modular Subsystems and Dysphasia, in *Current Perspectives in Dysphasia*, Newman, S., Epstein, R. (Eds.). Edinburgh: Churchill Livingstone.

Brachman, R. J., Schmolze, J. G. (1985). An Overview of the KL-One Knowledge Representation System, *Cognitive Science*, 9:171–216.

Brown, R., McNeill, D. (1966). The 'tip of the tongue' Phenomenon, *Journal of Verbal Learning and Verbal Behaviour*, 5, pp. 325–337.

Butterworth, B. (1980). Evidence from Pauses in Speech, *Language Production: Speech and Talk, Vol. I*. London: Academic Press, pp. 155–176.

Caron, J. (1989). *Précis de psycholinguistique*, Paris: Le Psychologue, Presses Universitaires de France.

Collins, A. M., Quillian, M. R. (1972). How to Make a Language User, in *Organization of Memory*, Tulving, Donaldson (Eds.), New York: Academic Press, pp. 309–351.

Cruse, A. (1986). *Lexical Semantics*, Cambridge University Press.

Dowty, D. (1989). On the Semantic Content of the Notion of Thematic Role, in *Properties, Types and Meaning*, G. Cherchia, B. Partee, R. Turner (Eds.), Kluwer Academic Press.
Dowty, D. (1991). Thematic Proto-roles and Argument Selection, *Language*, vol. 67–3.
Forster, K. I. (1976). Accessing the Mental Lexicon, in *New Approaches to Language Mechanisms*, R. J. Wales and Walker (Eds.), Amsterdam: North Holland, pp. 257–287.
Garrett, M. F. (1982). Production of Speech: Observations from Normal and Pathological Language Use, in *Normality and Pathology in Cognitive Functions*, Ellis, A. W. (Ed.), London: Academic Press.
Grimshaw, J. (1990). *Argument Structure*, MIT Press.
Jackendoff, R. (1987). The Status of Thematic Relations in Linguistic Theory, *Linguistic Inquiry*, 18, 369–411.
Jackendoff, R. (1988). *Consciousness and the Computational Mind*, MIT Press.
Jackendoff, R. (1990). *Semantic Structures*, MIT Press.
Katz, J. J., Fodor, J. A. (1963). The Structure of a Semantic Theory, in *Language*, 39, pp. 170–210.
Le Ny, J.-F. (1979). *La sémantique psychologique,* Paris: Presses Universitaires de France, Le psychologue, 257 pp.
Marslen-Wilson, W. (1984). Function and Process in *Spoken Word Recognition: A Tutorial Review*, in Bouma and Bouwhuis (Eds.), pp. 125–150.
Mel'čuk, I. A. (1988a). Paraphrase et lexique dans la théorie linguistique sens-texte. Vingt ans apr s (2 me partie), Cahiers de lexicologie, 53, 2, pp. 5–53.
Mel'čuk, I. A. (1988b). *Dependency Syntax: Theory and Practice*, State University of New York Press.
Miller, G. A., Johnson-Laird, P. N. (1976). *Language and Perception*, Cambridge, Mass.: The Belknap Press of Harvard University Press.
Morton, J. (1982). Disintegrating the Lexicon: An Information Processing Approach, in Mehler, Walker and Garrett (Eds.) (1982), pp. 89–109.
Pustejovsky, J. (1991). The Generative Lexicon, in *Computational Linguistics*, vol. 17, no. 4, pp. 409–441.
Quillian, M. R. (1967). Word Concepts: A Theory and Simulation of Some Basic Semantic Capabilities, *Behavorial Science*, 12, pp. 410–430, 637–673.
Rosch, E. (1975). Cognitive Representations of Semantic Categories, in *Journal of Experimental Psychology:* General, 104, pp. 192–233.
Rumelhart, D. E., Smolensky, J. L., McClelland, J. L., Hinton, G. E. (1986). Schemata and Sequential Thought Processes in PDP models, in *Parallel Distributed Processing: Explorations in the Microstructure of Cognition, Volume I: Foundations*, Rumelhart, D. E., McClelland, J. L. (Eds.), Cambridge, Mass.: MIT Press.
Spark Jones, K. (1986). *Synonymy*, Edinburgh University Press.
Vendler, Z. (1967). *Linguistics and Philosophy*, Ithaca, NY: Cornell University Press.
Wilks, Y. (1977). *Good and Bad Arguments about Semantic Primitives*, Rapport de recherche no. 42. Department of Artificial Intelligence, University of Edinburgh.
Winston, M.E., Chaffin, R., Hermann, D. (1987). A Taxonomy of Part-Whole Relations, *Cognitive Science*, 11, 417–444.

PART I

Psycholinguistics for lexical semantics

The first topic, psycholinguistic and cognitive aspects of lexical semantics, is addressed in the first two chapters. This area is particularly active but relatively ignored in computational circles. The reasons might be a lack of precise methods and formalisms. This area is, however, crucial for the construction of well-designed semantic lexicons by the empirical psychologically based analysis introduced in the domain of computational lexical semantics.

"Polysemy and related phenomena from a cognitive linguistic viewpoint" by Alan Cruse surveys the ways in which the contribution of the same grammatical word makes to the meaning of a larger unit depending on the context. Two main explanatory hypotheses that account for contextual variation are explored: lexical semantics and pragmatics. Alternatives to this approach are studied in the other parts of the volume.

The second chapter, "Mental lexicon and machine lexicon: Which properties are shared by machine and mental word representations? Which are not?" by J.-F. Le Ny, sets language comprehension and interpretation within a general cognitive science perspective. Properties common to natural and artificial semantic units (e.g., denotation, super-ordination, case roles, etc.) are first explored. Then, problems related to activability and accessibility in the memory are addressed in both a theoretical and experimental way.

2 Polysemy and related phenomena from a cognitive linguistic viewpoint

D. A. CRUSE

2.1 Introduction

One of the fundamental problems of lexical semantics is the fact that what C. Ruhl (1989) calls the 'perceived meaning' of a word can vary so greatly from one context to another. In this chapter I want to survey the ways in which the contribution the same grammatical word makes to the meaning of a larger unit may differ in different contexts. There are two main sources of explanatory hypotheses for contextual variations in word meaning: lexical semantics and pragmatics. While there are probably no contexts where each of these is not involved in some way, their relative contributions can vary. For instance, in the following examples the difference between 1 and 2 in respect of the interpretation of the word *teacher* (i.e., "male teacher" and "female teacher", respectively) can be accounted for entirely by differential contextual enrichment of a single lexical meaning for *teacher* (in other words, pragmatically):

1. The teacher stroked his beard.
2. Our maths teacher is on maternity leave.

The only involvement of lexical semantics here is that the specification of the meaning of *teacher* must somehow make it clear that although it is unspecified for sex, it is, unlike, say, *chair*, specifiable for sex. Examples 3 and 4 exemplify a slightly different type of contextual enrichment, in that the extra specificity in context is of a meronymous rather than a hyponymous type:

3. John washed the car.
4. The mechanic lubricated the car.

The different actions performed on the car allow us to infer that the agents were occupied with different parts of the car in each case. Here the different readings are not even clearly conceptualizable, and one can envisage numbers of verbs each evoking a slightly different portion of the car. Lack of distinctness is confirmed by the impossibility of zeugma:

5. The mechanic washed and lubricated the car.

Another case of apparently different interpretations arising from inferential enrichment on the basis of contextual clues is provided by 6 and 7:

6. The ostrich is a strange bird.
7. I wish I could fly like a bird.

Obviously the class of birds referred to in 7 does not include ostriches, but only prototypical birds. There is, however, no reason to believe that different senses of *bird* are involved:

8.   An ostrich is a bird, but it cannot fly like one.

Probably similar to these are the loose as opposed to precise uses of words, as in 9 and 10:

9.   A circle is the locus of a point equidistant from a given point.
10.   The mourners stood in a circle around the grave.

There may be some dispute in this case as to which is the unmarked use and which the contextually modulated use; whatever the answer, it seems clear that we are dealing with differential contextual modulation and not with polysemy.

By contrast, the difference between 11 and 12 in respect of the interpretation of *bank* has an important semantic component. Associated with the word form *bank* are two pre-existing bundles of semantic properties; in addition to their usual role of enrichment (for instance, the bank in 12 is unlikely to be one of the so-called clearing banks), contextual factors must first select one of these bundles:

11.   We moored the boat to the bank.
12.   I need to go to the bank to cash a check.

It is necessary to distinguish two separate (although interrelated) notions that are often conflated in discussions of contextual variation of word meaning. The first is the degree of distinctness of two (or more) readings; the second is the extent to which separate entries in the lexicon are justified. The first type of distinctness will be referred to by the traditional term polysemy; the second type will be called polylexy. It is assumed that until a certain degree of polysemy has been demonstrated, questions of polylexy do not arise (i.e., polylexic variants are a sub-class of polysemic variants). In examples 1 and 2, *teacher* displays neither polysemy nor, a fortiori, polylexy, merely contextual modulation; *bank* in 11 and 12 displays both polysemy and polylexy (in addition to contextual modulation); *omelette* in 13 and 14 is polysemic, but not polylexic:

13.   Mary ordered an omelette.
14.   The omelette left without paying.

In many accounts (Nunberg, 1979, is typical), the difference between the readings of *omelette* in 13 and 14 would be attributed to pragmatics rather than semantics. It is undoubtedly true that one of the readings is generated from the other by a general rule of sense-transformation triggered by context. However, the important point for present purposes is that there is a kind of selection by context from distinct alternatives (although these are potential, rather than pre-existing, as with the readings of *bank* in 11 and 12) and not merely differential contextual enrichment. Many recent studies of contextual variation in word meaning have concentrated on what I call polylexy, often with the avowed aim of minimizing the number of lexical entities and maximizing the role of pragmatic factors. This chapter, however, concentrates on types and degrees of distinctness of meaning variants insofar as these can be established by linguistic criteria. No attempt is made to describe or predict recurrent patterns of variation, as, for instance, in Apresjian (1972), Lehrer (1990) or Pustejovsky (1991), although, of course, these are important matters. The present work does, however, raise questions concerning the relationship between the semantic nature of readings and their polysemic status, but these are not pursued here. A preliminary attempt will be made to accommodate the facts concerning polysemy within the framework of cognitive semantics as represented by, for instance, Lakoff (1987), Taylor (1989) and Cruse (1990).

2.2   Antagonistic readings

There is a considerable variety of ways in which meaning variants of some distinctness can occur, and I shall attempt to survey the whole range (excluding those associated with syntactic differences). A major dichotomy within this range is effected by means of the feature of antagonism. Some variants are competing alternatives, in the sense that the choice of one of them excludes the others. Variants with this mutual property I shall describe as antagonistic. A clear example is provided by *bank* in examples 11 and 12. Each of these contexts of course favors one reading over the other, but the readings can be seen in direct conflict in a context such as 15:

15.   We finally reached the bank.

Just as with the well-known visual ambiguity produced by the so-called Necker cubes, a processing constraint prevents us from attending to the two construals simultaneously. This does not mean that both readings of 15 cannot be simultaneously true, nor even that they cannot both be intended by the utterer to be picked up by the receiver. But in the latter case there is a penalty: the utterance is a marked one, and produces a sense of punning or zeugma, perhaps arising from the necessity to alternate rapidly from one construal to the other. In normal language use, only one sense at a time is intended to be operative.

In contrast to antagonistic readings are discrete clusters of semantic properties which normally co-exist and co-operate within the meaning of a word. A paradigm example of this is provided by *book*, which is simultaneously a physical object and an abstract text. These distinct units of meaning are not normally in competition, in that when they both occur, there is no sense of markedness or punning:

16.   Mary is reading a book.

In the event described in 16, Mary is (probably) holding an object in her hands, turning the pages and so on, and at the same time attending to and processing a text. It is only in non-prototypical occurrences that these two components (in a non-technical sense) of the meaning of *book* are not simultaneously operative. The properties of antagonism and co-operation create two families of relationships between meaning variants. I shall deal first with the antagonistic type. (The traditional distinction between homonymy and polysemy, that is, between accidental and motivated multiplicity of readings, will be ignored in what follows: in respect of the criteria for distinctness discussed here, there is no difference between accidental variants and the most distinct motivated variants.)

One of the main points to be made in this chapter is that the traditional sharp dichotomy between polysemy and monosemy is misleading: there is, in fact, a continuum of degrees of distinctness ranging from not distinct at all (as with the two readings of *teacher*), to fully distinct (as with the two readings of *bank*). (There may, in fact, be two continua, one, a continuum of antagonism, ranging from discrete and antagonistic to discrete and co-operative, and the other, a continuum of discreteness.) I shall begin by looking at the highest degree of distinctness – what is traditionally regarded as full ambiguity of sense.

2.2.1   *Full ambiguity*

Fully ambiguous senses are characterized by (a) discreteness and (b) antagonism. It is worth noting that the standard ambiguity criteria of an identity constraint in co-ordination and independent truth conditions do not reliably discriminate between the <u>bank</u> type of variation and the <u>book</u> type. Consider 17:

17.   Mary likes the book; so does Sue.

This would be a very unusual, if not actually an anomalous way of describing a situation in which Mary liked the text, but found the cover design, typography and so on to be of poor quality, whereas Sue liked the book as an object, but considered the contents to be rubbish. Perhaps the identity constraint here is not quite so strong as it is in 18:

18.   Mary was wearing a light coat; so was Sue.

But I do not believe the difference is great enough to make the test reliable for ambiguity. What the identity test diagnoses is discreteness; it is indifferent to the distinction between antagonism and co-operation. The same is true of the independent truth condition criterion. Clearly, if Mary is wearing a coat which is light in color, but heavy in weight, 19 could be truthfully answered either 'Yes' or 'No':

19.   Is Mary wearing a light coat?

This is usually considered to be diagnostic of ambiguity, but consider 20 and 21:

20.   A: Do you like the book?
       B: (i) Yes, it's one of my favorite novels.
          (ii) No, it looks ghastly – and yet it's one of my favorite novels.
21.   A: Do you like the book?
       B: (i) No, I find the sentimentality nauseating.
          (ii) Yes, it's magnificently produced – a pity the poems are such rubbish.

The crucial point is the normality of a negative answer when one of the readings would justify an affirmative answer. Contrast 20 and 21 with 22, where the presence of a teacher of either sex forces an affirmative answer:

22.   A: Were you accompanied by a teacher?
          B: (i) Yes, it was Mrs. Smith, the maths teacher.
             (ii)? No, it was Mr. Jones, the geography teacher.

It seems that this test, too, responds to discreteness, but is indifferent to antagonism or co-operation between readings.

One of the clearest indices of antagonism is the potential to form puns as in 23:

23.   I love the banks of the Thames – Barclays, NatWest . . .

This correlates closely with the zeugma which results when one attempts to use the word in a superordinate sense:

24.   ?The north side of the Thames at Richmond and Barclays are my two favorite banks.
25.   ?John and his driving license expired last Thursday.
26.   ?The omelette was not properly cooked and left without paying.

It should be noted that zeugmatic effects cannot be produced with *book*:

27.   This book is difficult both to read and to carry around.

The same is true of *teacher*. Although it is true that the notions "male teacher" and "female teacher" are in a sense mutually exclusive, this is not a property of the word *teacher*, which in the plural form can refer to male and female teachers simultaneously without anomaly:

28.   A third of our teachers are either on maternity leave or paternity leave.

It has already been mentioned that discreteness is a characteristic, but not uniquely diagnostic feature of truly ambiguous words. Two further similar features are worth mentioning. The first is that it is not possible to use such a word without an implicit commitment to one (more rarely more than one) of its senses. In using the word *teacher*, for instance, one can leave it undetermined whether reference is to a male or a female teacher; a similar indeterminacy with regard to the two meanings of *bank* is impossible. This feature is not uniquely diagnostic of ambiguous items because it is, for instance, true also of *play* (a musical instrument). Thus 29 is normal only when a specific instrument can be retrieved from the context, and cannot be used to ask whether Mary plays some unspecified instrument or other:

29.   Does Mary play?

However, *play* shows no signs of antagonism between readings: if Mary is playing the piano and Sue is playing the violin, there is nothing odd about saying *Don't they play well?* The second characteristic feature of ambiguous words is that they display what Geeraerts (1989) calls 'definitional polysemy', that is to say, more than one meaning definition is required to cover the full range of their uses. This feature correlates well with the lack of a superordinate use, but not perfectly, because (a) some words are 'autohyponymous', that is, one of their senses is hyponymous to the other, and (b) some monosemic words require a disjunct definition of the form 'A or B'. It is arguable that, for instance, *princess* is of the latter type, since separate definitions are required for princesses 'of the blood' and princesses by marriage. However, *princess* differs from *bank* in that simultaneous reference to the two types of princess is quite normal.

A slightly more controversial type of ambiguity is the so-called autohyponymous type, where one reading is hyponymous to the other, as in the case of *dog* ("canine"/"male canine") and *drink* ("ingest liquid"/"imbibe alcoholic beverage"). It is often claimed that ambiguity cannot be demonstrated in such cases (see, for instance, Kempson, 1977); Ruhl (1989) states that it is pointless to postulate a separate hyponymous sense, since the hyponymous reading can always be explained by contextual modulation. I am prepared to concede that a polylexic analysis may in some cases be unjustified, especially where, as in the case of *dog* (but not *drink*), the existence of the more specific reading can be predicted by general rule. But there can be no doubt about the polysemy of *dog* and *drink*. The separate nature of the specific reading shows up in contexts like 30 and 31, where the superordinate reading would give rise to contradiction:

30.   I like bitches, but I don't like dogs.
31.   John doesn't drink – he'll have an orange juice.

In spite of Ruhl's claims, contextual modulation cannot explain the appearance of a specific reading in these cases. If Ruhl were correct, it ought to be possible to interpret *children* in 32 to mean "boys", but it clearly is not possible:

32.   ?I'm glad it's a girl – I can't stand children.

The antagonism between the two readings of *dog* can be felt intuitively when for instance *That's a dog* is used to refer to a male dog (both readings are applicable). Witness also the zeugmatic nature of 33:

33.   ?Dogs can become pregnant at the age of 12 months, but mature later than bitches.

(For a fuller discussion see Cruse, 1986: 58–65.)

2.2.2   *Semi-distinct readings*

The examples of polysemy that have been considered so far have involved readings which are fully antagonistic and fully discrete. I now want to consider two types of case where the readings must be considered antagonistic rather than co-operative, but where antagonism and/or discreteness are weaker. The first type of case involves what in Cruse (1986) were called 'local senses' on a 'sense spectrum'. The example given there was **mouth**, as in *a horse's mouth, the mouth of a bottle, the mouth of a cave, the mouth of a river*, etc. I argued that there is not a determinate number of such local senses: if less-than-fully-established instances of such senses are taken into account, they form a kind of continuum of meaning, without fully discrete separation of senses. This state of affairs seems to be typical of sets of metaphorical extensions of a common ontological type based on a similar relational correspondence. Local senses which are contiguous on the continuum do not give rise to zeugma:

34.   The mouth of the cave resembled that of a bottle.

This suggests that we have local superordinates. More distantly separated points on the continuum, however, do give rise to zeugma:

35.   ?The poisoned chocolate entered the mouth of the Contessa just as her yacht entered that of the river.

Contiguous local senses, although their distinctness is in a sense incomplete, do not give rise to problems in use, because they are kept apart by being restricted to different domains; within its own domain, each local sense plays the part of a fully distinct sense. The basic, or literal, reading of *mouth* (judging by its relative contextual freedom) is "mouth of animal/human". The extensions of this are relatively fragile in the sense that they require fairly precise conditions for their appearance. Only the base sense appears in a neutral context such as *We did a project on mouths*; the reading "mouth of a river" is scarcely possible unless the lexical item *river* occurs in the near vicinity within the previous discourse. Even given the contextual setting of a boating trip on a river, I would judge 36 to be more normal than 37 if no recent mention of the word *river* has occurred:

36.   Shall we go down to the mouth of the river?
37.   Shall we go down to the mouth?

In some ways further removed from fully-fledged polysemy are what I call sub-senses. These, like local senses, are protected from mutual competition by being domiciled in different domains; one of the ways in which they differ from local senses, however, is that there exists a fully functional superordinate sense. An example of a word with sub-senses is *knife*, as in 38 and 39:

38.   When you set the table, make sure that the knives are clean.
39.   The intruder threatened me with a knife.

The superordinate sense of *knife* can be observed in 40:

40.   The drawer was full of knives of various sorts – items of cutlery, pen-knives, hunting knives, etc.

Why is it not sufficient to say that the readings of *knife* in 38 and 39 are simply the result of contextual enrichment of the superordinate sense, like those of *teacher* in 1 and 2? There are several reasons. First, consider the following scenario. A young boy is sitting at a table in front of a plate of sausages and chips. He has been given a fork, but no knife. On the table beside him is a pen-knife that he has been playing with. He picks up a sausage and tears it into two with his fingers. His mother says: 'Johnny, use your knife to cut your sausage'. Johnny replies: 'I haven't got one.' (Had he been asked whether he had a knife to sharpen a pencil with he would have answered 'Yes'.) This needs to be contrasted with another scenario. Two schoolgirls are discussing their respective teachers. Sue says that she dreams of marrying her teacher, and asks Beth: 'Would you like to marry your teacher?' Now Beth's teacher is a woman. Although it is contextually clear that Sue's question concerns a male teacher, Beth cannot answer: 'I haven't got one.' There is therefore a crucial difference between the *knife* case and the *teacher* case: the "cutlery" reading of *knife* has a significantly greater degree of discreteness than the "male" or "female" readings of *teacher*. A second point of difference between *knife* and *teacher* is that the "cutlery" reading of *knife* has its own lexical relations, and participates in certain lexical fields independently of other readings:

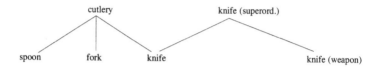

Nothing comparable can be observed in the case of the specific readings of *teacher*. Third, within its home domain, the "cutlery" reading of *knife* needs no qualifying adjective – indeed, it is not obvious which adjective would be appropriate. Within the taxonomy of items of cutlery, *knife* shows all the signs of being a basic level item: it is used for neutral reference, and represents the highest taxonomic level with which distinct behavior patterns and visual images can be associated. Fourth, the superordinate sense is marked and appears only under contextual pressure; the unmarked readings of *knife* are specific ones, but they vary from domain to domain. In a neutral context, the dominant reading of teacher is sex-neutral: *You would do better with a teacher, rather than trying to learn on your own*; *knife*, on the other hand, like *bank* (only less so) is somewhat uneasy in a neutral context: *I want you to go out and buy a knife.* One has a need to know what kind of knife. Clearly it would be misleading simply to describe *knife* as polysemous (there would be an embarrassing question of how many senses to recognize); on the other hand, it would be inappropriate to relegate it to the level of *teacher*. It seems, therefore, that a sharp dichotomy between polysemy and monosemy is untenable, and *knife* must be assigned an intermediate status.

Before leaving the topic of antagonistic readings to consider co-operative ones, some mention should be made of another phenomenon, which shades imperceptibly into polysemy with no clear dividing line, and that is syntactic metonymy. There are two varieties of syntactic metonymy: in one variety, the ellipted element is invariable; in the other variety, the ellipsis is 'open' and the missing element must be recovered from the context. In both cases we find a continuum from zero to full lexicality, the main features determining position on the continuum being the identifiability and determinateness of the missing elements, and their acceptability when overtly expressed. I shall first discuss instances of latency, that is, cases where the deleted elements are recoverable from the context, and I shall begin with examples from the non-lexical end of the continuum.

I take the term 'latent' from Matthews (1981), who used it to designate a particular type of ellipsis. Consider 41 and 42:

41. We'd better stop – John's watching.
42. Mary is reading.

Zero object realization with the verb *watch* acts as a signal of definiteness: in 41, the hearer is required to recover a specific direct object from the context. This type of ellipsis is a property of certain lexical items in English (see Fillmore, 1986, where a number of examples of this phenomenon are discussed). Notice that the absence of an overt direct object for *read* in 42 has a different effect; here, the object is not latent, and there is no implicit instruction to the hearer to identify a specific deleted item. The patterns of occurrence of latency are language specific. In Turkish, for instance, the direct object of any transitive verb, if not overt, is latent; in a Turkish translation of 42, an overt indefinite direct object expression must be supplied. Now consider 43 and 44:

43. John is watching. [He is watching a football match on TV.]
44. John is watching the parade.

Do we say that *watch* displays polysemy here? Or do we say that the same interpretation of *watch* occurs in 43 and 44, but that 43 has a covert direct object? One observation that might seem to favor a lexical (i.e., polysemic) solution is that *watch* behaves in some respects like an ambiguous word. For instance, in 45, John and Mary have to be watching what is in some sense the same thing:

45. John is watching; so is Mary.

This stands in clear contrast to 46, where there is no identity constraint:

46. John is reading; so is Mary.

However, the arguments against a lexical solution for watch are more weighty. First, there would be the embarrassment of an indefinitely large number of readings. Second, the deleted elements are easily identifiable and can be overtly expressed without loss of normality. Thus, corresponding to 41 we find:

47. We'd better stop – John's watching us.

Third, the identity constraint in 45 and the lack of it in 46 can be attributed entirely to the properties of the deleted items, i.e., to the fact that the deleted item in 45 is definite, while that in 46 is indefinite, Thus, the identity constraints in 48 and 49 parallel those in 45 and 46:

48. John is watching it; so is Mary.
49. John is reading something; so is Mary.

Two other words which behave in a similar way to *watch*, but with some differences, are *patient* and *cub* (in the sense, respectively, of "recipient of medical treatment" and "young animal"). Both take complements, which, if not overtly expressed, are latent. Thus, 50 cannot be used to mean that Mary is undergoing some unspecified form of medical treatment, and 51 is odd if there is no intention to refer to some specific animal species that the hearer can readily identify:

50.   Mary is a patient.
51.   I saw three cubs this morning.

Patient must be understood as "patient of X", where X is something like Doctor A, Dentist B, Clinic C, or whatever, and if none of these is overtly expressed, then the missing item must be recovered from the context. Here again, a lexical solution is disfavored: the number of possible readings is indefinitely large, and the latent complements are normally readily identifiable and can be overtly expressed without abnormality.

I would now like to discuss three examples which take us nearer to polysemy, but without leaving the realm of latency. The first concerns the use of *heavy* in expressions such as *heavy rain, a heavy smoker, a heavy prison sentence, a heavy work load, heavy responsibilities*, and so on. How are these instances of *heavy* related? Is *heavy* polysemous? One approach is to say that *heavy* means "having a high value on scale X", where X is latent. This has a certain plausibility. But there are some pointers against a non-lexical latency analysis. It is not difficult to produce zeugma:

52.   ?John's prison sentence and the rain on the courtroom roof were both
         heavier than expected.

More important, perhaps, is that the missing elements, although usually identifiable, cannot usually be expressed overtly without producing a stilted and clumsy effect:

53.   John received a heavy prison sentence (?in terms of length).
54.   The picnic was ruined by heavy rain (?in terms of rate of precipita-
         tion).

The somewhat indeterminate number of possible readings would count against a lexical analysis; however, unlike, say, *watch*, there are unpredictable restrictions, which makes it more lexical: **heavy wind, *a heavy famine*. Similar observations are valid for my second example, the verb *like*, as in 55 and 56:

55.   John likes blondes.
56.   John likes marshmallows.

As Lyons (1977) points out, a co-ordination of these is somewhat odd:

57.   ?John likes blondes and marshmallows.

In this case we can gloss *like* as "find pleasing in respect of property X", where X is again latent, needing to be recovered from the context. Notice that overtly specifying the relevant properties in 57 removes the zeugma:

58.   John likes marshmallows for their taste and blondes for their beauty.

This makes the readings of 55 and 56 more like contextual enrichments of a superordinate. On the other hand, such overt specification of properties is in general less normal than leaving them unspecified, and their identification in particular instances is somewhat uncertain (have we identified the appropriate property in respect of which John likes blondes?).[1] My third example concerns the French verb *sentir* as in *Ça sent l'ail*, which can be translated into English, according to context, as either *That smells of garlic* or *That tastes of garlic*. Is *sentir* ambiguous (in respect of these two readings) or is it simply that English lacks a verb with the required range of generality? There is some evidence for ambiguity. For instance, 59 must be interpreted in such a way that Jean and Marie are both doing the same thing, i.e., either both smelling or both tasting (although I understand the former would be the default reading):

59.   Jean peut sentir l'ail; Marie aussi.

Also, my French informants tell me that in the use of *sentir* they feel themselves to be committed to one reading or the other. Notice, however, that provided the sensory modalities are made explicit, the two readings can co-ordinate quite normally:

60.   Jean sentait l'odeur du citron et le goût de l'ail.

Here again we can appeal to latency and say that if the sensory modality is not overtly specified with *sentir*, then it is latent. In all three cases – *heavy*, *like* and *sentir* – we have something which is not-quite-polysemy, not-quite-syntactic-metonymy and not-quite-contextual-modulation.

The examples discussed in the previous paragraph raise the question of whether a similar analysis is not possible for *knife,* i.e., *knife* = "knife of type X", where X is latent. There are certainly many resemblances to the former cases. If this analysis were adopted, *knife* would be situated near the polysemy end of the continuum, because of the difficulty of identifying, and the abnormality of overtly expressing, the deleted material.

A similar continuum can be observed in those cases of syntactic metonymy where the deletions are specific and not to be sought in the context. At one extreme we find examples like *Mary is expecting*, where the deleted item is readily identifiable and is fully normal if overtly expressed: *Mary is expecting a baby*. Here the argument for polysemy is weakest. The same is probably true of *engaged* in the sense of "engaged to be married", although in this case the full form is slightly less common. Moving further along the continuum toward polysemy, we must ask whether for instance *drink* in *I gave up drinking when I got married* should be analyzed as a syntactic metonym. The arguments for polysemy in this case would be the usual ones, namely, the difficulty of precisely identifying the deleted item, and the relative abnormality of overtly expressing it.

2.3   Cooperative readings

Turning now to non-antagonistic bundles of semantic properties associated with a single word form, we can recognize two types according to whether the distinct bundles are related paratactically or hypotactically. Within each type a range of degrees of discreteness is found. I shall not deal here with the hypotactic sort (related to classical semantic components like [MALE] and [HORSE] of <u>stallion</u>) as this would take us too far from polysemy. The most discrete of the paratactic sort are those to which I give the name 'facet' (a facet is a discrete component of a single sense). Facets are well represented by the example of *book*, whose facets I shall refer to as [TOME] and [TEXT]. Facets have the following properties:

    (a)   They are non-antagonistic.

We have seen how this applies to *book* (see the discussion of example 16).

    (b)   They are autonomous.

There are two criteria for autonomy, a strong one and a less strong one. The stronger criterion is that the word form can be used in connection with one of the meaning-bundles, in explicit contrast to the other, in expressions such as *the X itself* and/or *the real X*. Sentences 61 and 62 illustrate this with the [TEXT] and [TOME] facets of *book*, respectively:

61.   I am not interested in the cover design, lay-out, typography and so on; I am interested in the book itself.

62.   I am not interested in the contents; I am interested in the book itself.

Example 63 shows that the [BIRTH-GIVER] facet of *mother* is autonomous:

63.   Mary brought me up, but Sue is my real mother.

A weaker indication of autonomy is that the word form may be used to refer to an entity which possesses properties corresponding only to one of the meaning-bundles. For instance, a set of blank pages between two covers may be referred to as a book: *I have a book to write the minutes of the meeting in*, as can a text which has a purely mental existence but is not yet physically embodied: *I have composed the book in my mind, but I have not yet committed it to paper*. Likewise a woman who adopts a child can count as the child's mother.

    (c)   They give rise to identity constraints and the possibility of independent sets of truth conditions (see the discussion of examples 12 and 13).

    (d)   Multi-faceted words are not themselves ambiguous, but they may give rise to ambiguous phrases.

For instance, *a long book* can mean either a long text, as in *This book is too long to read in one day*, or a long physical object, as in *This book is too long to fit between those two shelves*; these two readings of the phrase are fully antagonistic. There are similarly two antagonistic readings of *a new book*, depending on whether *new* modifies [TEXT] or [TOME]. More generally, predicates can focus on one facet to the exclusion of the other(s): thus, in *a difficult book, difficult* focuses on [TEXT], whereas in *a thick book, thick* focuses on [TOME]. This is not the same as autonomy. An adjective in an NP, for instance, can take a single facet of a multi-faceted word as its scope, but the NP as a whole may still refer normally. For example, in *That's a friendly shop, friendly* describes the personnel in the shop, but the phrase *a friendly shop* does not refer uniquely to the personnel, but to the whole establishment in which they are employed.

(e) Each facet may be independently involved in lexical relations.

Both *It's a novel* and *It's a hardback* entail *It's a book*, from which we may conclude that *novel* and *hardback* are hyponyms of *book*. However, they are not straightforward co-hyponyms in the way that *cat* and *dog* are of *animal*. For one thing, they are not incompatibles, as co-hyponyms of the same superordinate prototypically are: *It's a hardback* does not entail *It's not a novel*. This is because each represents a specification of a different facet of *book*. If we assume that *novel* has the facets [NOVEL] and [TOME], it can be seen that all the extra specificity of *novel* as compared to *book* arises through a specification of the [TEXT] facet of *book*: the two [TOME] facets are identical. In the case of *hardback*, the [TEXT] facet is shared with *book*, and the additional specificity comes from a narrowing down of the [TOME] facet.

(f) The different facets of a word sense form a gestalt.

Typically there is no taxonomic superordinate notion which covers a set of facets; nor is there anything to which they stand in a meronymic relation. But there is a kind of global notion, whose components are felt to go together naturally.[2]

The detailed properties of facets and facet-like semantic bundles display considerable variation. For instance, what was assumed above to be the [TOME] facet of *novel* fails both the tests of autonomy, in spite of the normality of 64, which shows that a novel has weight:

64. A: Why is this suitcase so heavy?
     B: I packed all those novels you brought from the library.

For instance, although 61 is still well-formed semantically if *book* is replaced by *novel*, 62 becomes unintelligible:

65. ?I am not interested in the contents, I am interested in the novel itself.

Also, whereas an as yet unembodied text could be referred to as a novel, a textless tome could not. Some facets satisfy the weaker criterion of autonomy, but not the stronger one. Consider the [PERSONNEL] facet of *shop* and *factory*. We can use *factory* and to a lesser extent *shop* to refer only to the personnel:

66. The whole factory/?shop came out on strike.

However, *the shop itself* and *the factory itself* could never refer to the personnel, but only to the buildings and other physical installations. This is a little-explored area. Why is it that the first interpretation of *a long book* that comes to the mind of an English speaker is a long text, the other reading being much more contextually restricted, whereas the first interpretation of *ein langes Buch* to a German is a long tome? Perhaps this is because *Buch* has a relatively weak [TEXT] facet, like the [TOME] facet of *novel*. It cannot be quite as weak as that, however, because although *?a green novel* is a trifle odd, *ein interessantes Buch* is perfectly normal. Why is *a friendly shop* normal, but not *?a well-trained shop* or *?a pretty shop* (in the sense of having pretty assistants)? Also, why is *a friendly shop* not matched by *?un magasin aimable* or *?eine freundlicher Geschäft*, whereas *ein freundlicher Laden* is normal, and has the same interpretation as the parallel English construction? I assume that the answers to at least some of these questions lie in the way the meanings of the words are represented in the cognitive system.

2.4   Polysemy and cognitive linguistics

The framework within which I want to consider the facts that I have just described is that of cognitive linguistics. One of the main tenets of this approach is that the meanings of linguistic expressions do not have their being in some autonomous linguistic domain, but arise by the evocation of patterns of conceptual content in the cognitive system. I start out with a somewhat simplistic model of the cognitive system. I assume that in the human mind there is a set of established, more-or-less discrete concepts forming a highly interconnected network. Every concept is connected directly or indirectly with every other concept in the network. The direct links are of specific kinds, such as "-is a-", "-is a kind of-", "-is a part of-", "-is used for-", and so on. Much of what we think of as the properties of a concept will thus be represented in terms of linkages with other concepts; these links will be of varying strengths, reflecting degrees of centrality or necessity according to some appropriate measure or measures. The identity of a concept does not necessarily consist entirely of relational links with other concepts; at least some concepts must have a substantive core of some kind, perhaps a complex of sensory-motor images. A concept also has an inner coherence; it forms a unified gestalt. A typical concept has some sort of prototype representation, or, at least, a representation from which the so-called prototype effects follow naturally. I shall not attempt to be more precise about the nature of prototypes, but I shall assume that a prototype forms a kind of working unit of the cognitive system. The established concepts (finite in number) are not the only conceptual units available to us. An unlimited number of ad hoc concepts can be generated from patterns of combination of established concepts.

A natural language possesses an inventory of word forms, and these are mapped onto the concept network. In the simplest cases, a word serves only to activate a concept. This gives access at the same time to all the connections that the concept has with other concepts. For some words, for instance, basic level items, the mapping onto the associated concept constitutes the whole of their meaning. So, for example, if we hear the word *horse*, this gives immediate access to the concept [HORSE]. The semantic connections between the concept [HORSE] and other related concepts such as [ANIMAL], [MARE], [COW], [HOOF], [STABLE], [JOCKEY], etc. will be represented in the concept network, and there will be no direct connections between these and the word form *horse*. This means that many meaning relations, such as hyponymy, incompatibility, meronymy and so on are, on this view, primarily conceptual relations, and only secondarily lexical relations.

The mapping relations between lexical forms and concepts are not always one-to-one (perhaps they are only rarely so). Obviously many word forms will map onto more than one concept: for instance, *bank*. Another possibility that must be catered for is the mapping of several word forms onto the same concept. An example of this would be: *die, kick the bucket, decease, pass away, snuff it*, etc. Like many synonym clusters, this group contains a neutral, basic term, namely, *die*, and we may surmise that this derives all its meaning from the fact that it is mapped onto the concept [DIE]. The stable meaning properties which distinguish the other members of the group from *die* and from each other can then be viewed as properties of the individual lexical items, as distinct from properties of the common concept (although these properties, too, must have some sort of representation in the cognitive system). Word-specific properties will include such things as emotive coloring, evaluative features, and various sorts of contextual affinities, such as allegiance to particular dialects, registers, or domains of discourse such as medical, legal and ecclesiastical. These properties will have the power to modulate the central concept.

We may now turn to a consideration of what sort of account of polysemy and its relatives is possible within the framework outlined in this chapter. No more than a beginning can be made here. I would like to take as a starting point Taylor's proposal (1989) that polysemy should correspond to multiple prototype representation. I accept the implication that a prototype representation is a significant cognitive unit; furthermore, I do not deny that in many cases, polysemy corresponds to multiple prototypes. But there are two aspects of the proposal that I would like to take up. First, Taylor's proposal has more merit if it is taken to refer to polylexy rather than polysemy. It seems reasonable to me to require that separate entries in the lexicon should correspond to discrete, permanently laid down, conceptual representations. Polysemous variants, at least as I have characterized them, can correspond to concepts which are completely ad hoc, or only partially established. The second aspect of Taylor's proposal that I wish to question is that it takes no account of the distinction between antagonistic and cooperative interpretations. There seems little doubt that *book*, for instance, corresponds to two separate prototype structures, yet is not truly ambiguous. This raises a number of questions, perhaps the most obvious of which concerns the nature of antagonism and cooperation: how is the difference between these two to be accounted for?

Presumably the answer will lie in the nature of the mapping from word form to concept. Antagonistic readings will have separate mappings to each prototype, whereas for co-operative readings there will be a single mapping, with two prototypes somehow included within the same conceptual envelope. A mechanism to produce antagonism is not too difficult to envisage: cases of 'lateral inhibition' are well known in psychology and physiology, where out of a battery of elements, the one responding most strongly to some stimulus inhibits the responses of the others. What is more difficult, perhaps, is to explain the ontogenesis of the two arrangements: what contextual features lead to the setting up of facets rather than polysemes?

Within non-antagonistic readings, the major problem is to explain the different statuses of, for example, the [TOME] facets in *book*, *Buch* and *novel*. There are two possible ways of picturing the differences of status. One is to say that the two prototypes corresponding to a word like *Buch* are not equally accessible: it may take more cognitive work to activate one rather than the other. This might account, for instance, for the difference in preferred reading between *a long book* and *ein langes Buch*. Something more radical seems to be needed for the difference between *book* and *novel*, though. I suggest that for *novel*, only the [TEXT] prototype is established, while the [TOME] facet is generated ad hoc as and when the context demands it.

Antagonistic sub-polysemic readings pose a number of problems. I shall consider only the case of *knife*. I am not sure whether the notion of latency is helpful in connection with *knife*, but if it is, it is difficult to see how it can be a property of a concept: it must be a property of the lexical item (this applies also to *watch* and the rest). Taylor suggests that the prototype model is most appropriate for basic level items like *chair* and *table*, superordinate categories like *furniture* often being vaguer and more loosely organized. Perhaps this is a helpful way of looking at the readings of *knife*: the basic level knives are represented by prototypes, while the superordinate is a more diffuse structure. We might then think not of the contextual enrichment of a superordinate, but of the contextual impoverishment of a basic level term, or even of the superordinate being generated on an ad hoc basis.

Notes

1. A monosemic solution would be possible within Qualia Theory (see Pustejovsky, 1991), with *heavy* and *like* selecting suitable roles in the semantic specifications of their associated nouns to modify. However, as far as I can see, there is nothing in Qualia Theory that would predict the zeugma in 52 and 57.

2. There would seem to be some correspondence between what are here called facets and what Pustejovsky (1991) calls qualia roles. However, facets are defined on linguistic criteria as a particular degree of distinctness, or polysemic status, without regard to their semantic properties. Qualia theory (at least as expounded in the work cited) does not make predictions as to the polysemic status of variant readings. It remains to be discovered what the precise correspondences are between polysemic status and qualia structure.

References

Apresjian, J. D. (1972) Regular Polysemy. *Linguistics,*124, 5–39.

Cruse, D. A. (1986) *Lexical Semantics*. Cambridge: Cambridge University Press.

Cruse, D. A. (1990) Prototype theory and lexical semantics. In Tsohatzidis, S. L. (ed.), *Meanings and Prototypes*. London: Routledge.

Fillmore, C. J. (1986) Pragmatically controlled zero anaphora. *BLS*, 12, 95–107.

Geeraerts, D. (1989) Prospects and problems of prototype theory. *Linguistics* 27, 587–612.

Kempson, R.M. (1977) *Semantic Theory*. Cambridge: Cambridge University Press.

Lakoff, G. (1987) *Women, Fire and Dangerous Things*. Chicago: University of Chicago Press.

Lehrer, A. J. (1990) Polysemy, conventionality and the structure of the lexicon. *Cognitive Linguistics*,1, 2, 207–246.

Lyons, J. (1977) *Semantics*. Cambridge: Cambridge University Press.

Matthews, P. H. (1981) *Syntax*. Cambridge: Cambridge University Press.

Nunberg, G. (1979) The non-uniqueness of semantic solutions: polysemy. *Linguistics and Philosophy* 3, 143–184.

Pustejovsky, J. (1991) The generative lexicon. *Computational Linguistics* 17,4, 409–441.

Ruhl, C. (1989) *On Monosemy*. New York: SUNY Press.

Taylor, J.R. (1989) *Linguistic Categorisation: Prototypes in Linguistic Theory*. Oxford: Clarendon Press.

3 Mental lexicon and machine lexicon: Which properties are shared by machine and mental word representations? Which are not?

JEAN-FRANÇOIS LE NY

Language comprehension and interpretation[1] can be set within a general cognitive science perspective that encompasses both human minds and intelligent machine systems. This comprehensive view, however, must necessarily entail the search for compatibility between various types of concepts or models subsuming classes of facts obtained through specific methods, and hence belonging to various scientific domains, from artificial intelligence to cognitive psychology, and ranging over linguistics, logics, neurosciences, and others.

No sub-domain of cognitive science is more fascinating for the exploration of such functional identities between artificial and natural processing or representation and none deserves more to be comparatively worked out than language comprehension or interpretation. The purpose of this chapter is to highlight some of these identities, but also some differences, in particular as concerns lexical semantics.

A large number of concepts are obviously shared by computational semantics and cognitive psychology. I will approach them in this chapter mainly in the form of relational properties, belonging to lexical-semantic, or lexical-conceptual,[2] units, and will classify them according to whether they can be attributed, or not, to both mental and machine representations. For the sake of simplicity I will often restrict this comparison to consideration of lexical units that are expressed by nouns in most natural languages and which, as a rule, denote classes of objects or individuals. But other kinds of lexical-conceptual units, expressed in these natural languages by verbs, adjectivals, prepositions, function words, etc., and which denote events or actions, properties, various sorts of relations, etc., could also be submitted to this type of analysis and comparison.

Several levels of description concerning lexico-semantic units can be considered in a cognitive science framework, all being objective, i.e., not based on conscious, phenomenological properties. At the lowest level, which is also the most

This research was supported by a grant from the Institut des Sciences Cognitives et de la Communication, Orsay, which is funded by the Cognisciences Program of the C.N.R.S. (National Center of Scientific Research, France). I thank two anonymous reviewers for helpful comments on a first version of the manuscript, and Connie Greenbaum for a thorough revision of the English version.

highly abstract one, the lexico-semantic units are nothing else than physical objects, which involve very deep differences between the natural and the artificial ones: machine symbols are states of the computer physical components, whereas mental symbols consist of, or are based on, states of the neural tissues in brains – whatever philosophical stance one chooses on the brain/mind issue. At the second lowest level, if we consider the local organization of the symbols rather than their matter, differences are also very deep: some are sets of bits, whereas the others are presumably structured sub-networks of neurons and synapses. But properties existing at these very low levels are sub-cognitive and are beyond the scope of this chapter since one major general assumption of cognitive science is that they are (or can be made) largely irrelevant to intelligent processing. The only relevant issue here is the extent to which these basic differences place constraints on higher levels of cognitive properties. Hence the distinction between the properties shared by natural and artificial representations and those that are not is an important task in this domain.

At the cognitive level, a lexical unit is commonly considered (de Saussure, 1916) as being composed of two parts, the *signifiant* and the *signifié*, that is, the representation of the morphological aspects, i.e., the phonological, orthographic and motor components of the corresponding word (or phrase) and its meaning or semantic (conceptual) content. I will focus exclusively on the latter part.

Properties common to natural and artificial semantic units

The first section lists the sets of properties that are customarily attributed to semantic units in computational semantics or knowledge representation as well as in cognitive psychology. All are relational. These properties often have several realizations or denominations, which may differ according to the particular cognitive science theory considered. My presentation is intended to encompass them within a common abstract schema, expressed in a formal way. These properties need not be elaborated at length, and will be presented in abbreviated form.

The list is divided into three parts, according to an apparent decreasing degree of agreement in the cognitive community. The first and second parts contain well-known properties, or relations, which are widely accepted in several domains (computational semantics or knowledge representation, linguistics, cognitive psychology, logics, and philosophy of mind) in a common form, despite minor divergencies between authors in their formulation. They will be presented as basic and derived properties, respectively. The third part of the list contains additional properties of mental representations, which have been recently specified in cognitive psychology and debated among cognitive scientists (see Le Ny, 1989a, for a detailed discussion), but are more rarely taken into account in computational semantics.

In the following sections, I will introduce another property that can be assigned to semantic units: *activability*. This is directly related with a mental form of information processing, *activation*, which apparently has considerable impact in langage comprehension. This will lead directly to the issue of whether it would be useful for the future development of machine interpretation to mimic this property, or some of its aspects, in an appropriate way. The response need not be affirmative in all cases, but in some it seems that this enhancement could bring artificial interpretation closer to human use of language and could be better adapted for applications involving man–machine dialog.

A.   Basic properties

The list of properties is presented below with a corresponding example and a formula that can be considered common to various sciences, via an appropriate interpretation: formal and syntactic in computational semantics, linguistic and social in non-formal linguistics, mental in cognitive psychology and, possibly, neural in cognitive neurobiology. In the formulas, *L* represents the semantic content of a particular lexical unit.

1. *Denotation* – or *categorization* – which can be expressed as "D(*L*,a)", i.e., "*L* applies to a", "*L* takes a as one of its instances", in which a is an element of a determined set (*extension* of the concept or meaning associated with *L*).

This property is used in all explicit statements such as: "a is an *L*", "a is an instance of *L*", "a belongs to the *L*s" and in various other cases, such as anaphor; examples: "Socrates is a man", "Coco is a robin", "this is a paper", "the philosopher. . . " (Socrates having been mentioned previously). This same property is involved in all mental activities involving categories or concepts: perception, judgment, verbal predication, reasoning, internal thought, etc. In logical terms, this property is expressed by terms having the functional role of natural predicators (Carnap, 1947) or predicates: "*L*x", "*L*xy", etc.

2. *Superordination/subordination*, which can be expressed as Z(*L*,S), and corresponds to: "*L* is a sub-category of S", or "S is a super-category of *L*"; usually, "*L* is a sort of S", "a *L* is-a S"; examples: "men are mortal", "a robin is a kind of bird", "a robin is-a bird". Several relations of this type create a hierarchy of categories (for example: "a robin is a bird, a bird is an animal"), and several coordinated hierarchies can be organized in a categorial (conceptual) tree, i.e., a taxonomy. Multiple such relations generate lattices.

3. *Attribution*, i.e., assignment of attributes (or attribute-value pairs), properties, semantic features or semantic relations, etc., to a category, which can be expressed as A(*L*,p). The second argument, p, in this assignment can be viewed in various ways, and expressed in various forms, according to the particular cognitive theory or formal language chosen by an author. This is illustrated by a few simple examples.

a. "involves the property (*L*,p)", or "has the property (*l*,p)" – in which *l* is any individual denoted by *L* – or "involves the feature (*L*,f), "has the feature (*l*,f)", in which f is a reformulation of p. The same relation can also be expressed in predicative terms, "P*l*" or, for relations, "P*l*,b", etc. Examples: "the concept of 'orange' involves the attribute 'round'", or "oranges have the property of roundness", "oranges are round", "for any orange. ROUND(orange)".

We can incorporate some sub-relations that take arguments considered as being similar enough to properties into this general relation of attribution, as meronymic (or part-whole) sub-relations.[3] In M(L,p), M is taken as representing 'PART-OF', and p the relevant part. Examples are: "chairs have a back", "for any chair, PART-OF (chair, back)", etc.

b. More complex expressions can be formulated in terms of attributes/value(s): A(L,U,v), U being the attribute and v its value, that is, "involves the attribute U with the value v" or "has the attribute/value U/v".[4] Examples are: "the concept 'orange' involves 'form' with value 'round' ", or "oranges have a round form" or "for any orange, Form-of (orange, round")).

c. Still more complex relations can be introduced on this previous basis with the addition of:

- disjunction: (example: "an apple has green, or yellow, or red colors, etc.");
- sketchy frequencies of values: (example: "the color of reinettes du Mans apples is usually grey, sometimes yellow, seldom green, and never red"), etc.

As stated earlier, use of the various versions of attribution outlined in 3. a, b, c, basically depends on theoretical choices. Nevertheless, what is common to all are the basic relation, namely attribution, and the basic content of the arguments it takes (attributes, attribute/values pairs, features, relational features, part-whole, etc.) These latter elements are also present in one form or another in all theories, and differ from object categorization.

4. Filler requirement in *case roles* (Fillmore, 1968) or *actanciation* (Tesnière, 1959) of verbs or verb nominalizations, C(L,G,H,I), with possible specification of the fillers, C(L,G,M,H,N,I,O). This relation concerns, for example, verbs having two necessary case roles, for which G represents an agent, H a patient, I being empty, such as in "the boy pushes the girl", or three case roles, for which G represents an agent, H a receiver, I an object, such as in "the boy gives the girl an apple".

Specification involves semantic restriction of the possible fillers in the predetermined case roles. For example, M and N, which represent categories of possible fillers for G and H, respectively, could be restricted to human beings, whereas O, which represents a category of possible fillers for I, would be restricted to non-human objects. A concrete example is the concept 'to give', which primarily (i. e. typically) takes human beings as fillers in both the roles of 'giver' ('agent') and 'receiver', and a physical, non-human, object in the role of 'given'. Similarly, the verbal concept 'to cure' (in the sense of item 1) takes doctors, or some other members of the caring professions, as 'agents', sick people as 'patients', and 'medicine' as 'instrument'. As in 3., the detailed list of case roles or acting entities ("actants", according to Tesnière, 1959), and the precise specification of their filler ranges, primarily depend on theoretical or pragmatical choices. But existence of the general relation is common to all.

5. Semantic or conceptual *structures*, involving sets of relations (of first, second, third order, etc.) and roles, which correspond to various types of semantic schemas, frames, scripts or scenarios, scientific concepts, etc., with their own categories of slots and fillers. For example, the semantic unit 'restaurant' involves the concepts 'food', 'tables', 'to eat', 'to pay', etc. Similarly, 'compilation' (in computer science) involves 'program', 'source', 'programming language', 'machine code', 'duration', etc. I will not elaborate on this point.

B.   Second-order, or derived, properties

These correspond to the capacity for semantic units to enter into various conceptual and logical transformations.

6. *Entailment*, derived from items 1. and 2.: E(L,B), or "entails (implies) (L,B)"; $\forall$x L(x) --> B(x). Examples: "if x is a robin, it is a bird", "a robin is a bird".

7. *Inheritance*, derived from 1. and 3.:

a. I (L,S,{U}), or "inherits from (L,S,{U})", where S is a superordinate unit, and {U} a set of attributes or properties transferred from S to L. An example is: "a robin has all the properties of a bird".

b. I (L,S,(t1,t2,t3, . . .)), or "inherits (L,S,(t1,t2,t3, . . .))", where (t1,t2,t3, . . .) is a specified list of features or attribute values, which set appropriate restrictions on the values inherited from S. Example: "a Canadian apple is green" (but has no other color value from 'apple');

c. I (L,S,(f1,f2,f3, . . ., with p1,p2,p3, . . .)), or "L inherits from S the features (f1,f2,f3, . . . with their respective probabilities p1, p2, p3, . . .)", and various types of additional complexities. The example mentioned in 3.c, concerning the relation between the "reinettes du Mans" and "apples" in general, is also relevant to this point.

C.   Well-known psychological properties

In addition to the basic or derived properties already listed, which are common to both computational and psychological semantics, some others are primarily psychological, but sometimes are also used in knowledge representation.

8. *Similarity*, primarily expressed as S(L,B) or "similar to (L,B)", or S(L,B,g), i.e., "similar to (L,B) as concerns the dimension or attribute g"; examples are: "a shell is similar to a house", "the Ukraine is similar to France as concerns population".

Similarity is viewed in this framework as a basic relation, regardless of the possibility to reduce it to proximity in a hierarchy of categories through the relations mentioned previously.

Similarity can be ordered: "L is more similar to B than it is to C", or "L is more similar to B than C is"; similarity can also accept approximate assessments (whose validity has been demonstrated by psychological experiments): "if the degree of similarity between L and B is set at approximately 5, the degree of similarity between *L* and B is set at approximately 5, the degree of similarity between *L* and C is approximately 2".

9. *Typicality (or representativity),* expressed as: T(*L*,S), "typical of (L,S)", where S is a superordinate of *L*, and *L* a hyponym of S more typical than the others; or "typical of (*L*,a)", "is a prototype of (*L*,a)", where a is an instance of *L*. Examples: "sparrows are typical of birds"; "Médor is typical of spaniels".

Typicality is defined here in Rosch's framework (Kleiber, 1988; Mervis, Catlin and Rosch, 1976; Le Ny, 1989a; Rosch and Lloyds, 1977; Rosch and Mervis, 1975). It is useful to distinguish typicality of sub-categories, first introduced above (*L* is typical of its superordinate S, or some infraordinate I of *L* is typical of *L* itself) from typicality of instances (one instance is typical of *L*): compare the examples concerning sparrows and Médor.[5] Typicality can be ordered and graded. For example: "if the degree of typicality of sparrows relative to birds is 7 (on a 7-degree scale), the corresponding degree of typicality of chickens is 1".

10. Basic level in hierarchies, expressed as: BL(*L*,S,I), "is at the basic level in hierarchy (L,S,I)", where S is the highest unit, and I one unit at the lowest level, defining this level. For example: "'dog' is at the basic cognitive level in the hierarchy of animals (from 'animal' to 'Irish setters')".

A basic difference in processing mechanisms

After this review and evaluation of common relational properties attributable to lexico-semantic units, this section focuses on a different sub-set of cognitive properties. They come from cognitive psychology and have not been taken into account by most authors in computational semantics. I will introduce them as belonging to a general class, summarized by a general property that can be termed *activability* of mental lexico-semantic units, according to my choice of a comprehension model. In an alternative family of models, this property would be termed *accessibility* to stored information, but translation from one denomination to the other can be done without much difference, as I will show.

I will briefly present the major concepts used in two broad classes of models of language comprehension that are employed in cognitive psychology today. They are based on two different views of processing mechanisms: the first relies on the metaphor of the computer, the second is closer to neurobiology.

Both share the same general view of comprehension. In short, during language comprehension, an oral or written message, i.e., a structured physical input information, is transformed into a semantic representation, which is conserved for a short time in transient memory. This semantic representation is the compound result of successive processes that run step by step, combining information from two distinct sources, the input message and the stored long-term memory knowledge, mainly the lexicon and the grammatical rules. This same view is also the theoretical basis for most automatic interpreters. For present purposes, the subsequent course of this transient semantic representation, in particular its consolidation in long-term memory or transfer to it, or the decay and forgetting process that can take place instead, can be partially ignored. What follows views the representation built in recent memory from the input message as the end of the comprehension process per se.

A major difference between these two classes of psychological models lies in the nature and location of the semantic representation. In the first it is assumed to be built in some kind of special memory store, viewed as *containing* the output of the comprehension process: models of this class will be termed store models hereafter. The basic functional mechanism of information processing associated with this view is information transfer.

This mechanism is viewed as being basically the same in humans as in computers, and hence in all types of artificial language interpreters. Pieces of information are repeatedly transferred from some location in some physical memory store to another location in the same or another physical memory store. The basis of this transfer is the *copy* operation, in association with the *rewrite* operation.

For example, a language interpreter recognizes a word in a sentence and immediately writes down a particular copy of it in a partial, provisional, sub-representation, for instance the sub-representation of a time adjunct from the current sentence, which is stored in a particular store, for example, the one labeled *time adjunct*. The interpreter simultaneously copies the grammatical and semantic information for this particular word found in the lexicon under the corresponding lexical entry, possibly after selection if the system opts for this. Later, the system will recopy all the information contained in this time adjunct sub-representation in the whole sentence representation.

However there is no reason to believe that the role of memory in mental comprehension also originates from such *copy* or *rewrite* mechanisms: no evidence of these has been found in the brain, where processing is presumably brought about by neural activation. Apparently this sub-cognitive property of the brain tightly constrains the nature of mental processes, including comprehension and, hence, the corresponding representations.

The second family of models (Anderson, 1983; Collins and Loftus, 1975; Kintsch, 1988; Le Ny, 1989a, 1991a, 1991b) is precisely based on this activation process and its negative form, inhibition. One major assumption in these is that there is no structural difference between long-term and working memory, and thus no need for copying. The substitutive basic property is that symbolic representations conserved in long-term memory are in one of several activity states at any given time, ranging from inactivity (or in fact, very low activity) to very high activity, where level of activity, or *level of activation* is a major variable to take into consideration.

Discourse, in particular, is a source of activation of the lexico-semantic representations corresponding to the words, such that what is termed a *semantic representation in recent memory* is nothing more than the momentarily active part of long-term memory. In other words, a particular semantic representation is viewed in these models as stemming directly from both the message and the representations in long-term memory – mental lexicon and mental grammatical structures –

by activation/inhibition of their relevant parts. These assumptions characterize activation models in language comprehension.

This sense of the word activation (with its inhibitory form), as a positive or negative *graded* variable, obviously differs from the one in which the same word is used in computer science, where it refers to a *binary* option (for a rule or, possibly, a lexical unit) between two states of a system.

Specific properties of units in the lexicon

I will now return to the lexicon and focus on the property of the lexico-semantic mental representations previously mentioned, *activability*. I will consider two aspects of it, which will apply to different facts. The general, abstract form of activability is the dynamic capacity of lexico-semantic units to permanently receive various amounts of fresh activation or inhibition and to change their momentary levels of activation accordingly. Hence any unit in any speaker must be viewed as having an activation value – a level of activation – associated with it at any time. If we represented the organization of the mental lexicon as forming a semantic network, with nodes corresponding to the lexico-semantic units drawn on a horizontal plane as small circles (rather than dots), we could represent activation levels as values on an Y-axis, i.e., as vertical pikes above these nodes. If we added time to this representation, the cognitive activity of a speaker would be dynamically shown as an ever changing mountain landscape, with continuously growing and shortening pikes. However, a dimension of invariance can be introduced in this view: the degree of *basic activability* of every particular lexico-semantic unit, which is the second aspect of activability. We can define this as a property determining the *way* and *extent* a unit that is now in a basic state of rest will be *later activated*. To be in a basic state of rest here means that the current processing does not involve this particular unit.

Two empirical criteria can be stated for assessment of this degree of basic activability. The first is the observed facility with which the considered unit can be, or not at all, activated by relevant conditions, for example, perceptual presentation of the corresponding word, or associated information. The second is the speed with which this unit will attain a given level of activation, for example the one required by a given decision. Experimental methods allow operationalization of these criteria: techniques using reaction times, and in particular decision times, which will be presented in the following paragraphs, are very powerful tools for the determination of speeds of activation up to a given level, which can yield an assessment of a basic degree of activability.[6]

Abundant experimental data shows that lexico-semantic units cannot be equivalently retrieved from memory (under similar conditions) during cognitive processes, when retrieval is defined from appropriate classes of behavioral data – typically, measures of chosen parameters in perception, recall or recognition. These variations in retrieval affect all representations stored in memory and, hence word representations present in the mental lexicon as a part of long-term memory.

For example, cognitive tasks concerning rapid access to mental lexico-semantic units – word identification, lexical decision on strings of letters, etc. – have evidenced a priority effect as a function of frequency of use of the corresponding words (Allen, McNeal and Kvak, 1992; Carr and Pollatsek, 1985; Howes and Salomon, 1951; Morton, 1969; Scarborough, Cortese and Scarborough, 1977). In lexical decision tasks, subjects must decide whether a sequence of letters presented on a video screen are, or not, words from their language. Experiments show that the more frequent the words are, the shorter their corresponding decision times, which can be interpreted as showing that "perhaps the lexicon is coded as a function of word frequency" (Allen et al., 1992). Word frequency effects have been shown to be a major factor in language processing,[7] but other objective factors such as word length, phonemic composition, pronounceability, orthographic proximity with other words, etc. also have similar effects on response times and can, thus, be considered as factors of activability.

Activability and accessibility in man and machine: Disambiguation

Man and machine can now be compared for activability and accessibility. The two words are associated in this discussion since theoretical stances are irrelevant here. In computers, information accessibility depends exclusively on two rather different sets of factors: first, hardware factors concerning computer and memory physical and systemic properties, and second, software factors depending on organization of the lexicon and algorithms implemented for access to words, for example hashing. But nothing like a differential functional access to various words exists there, and, apparently, there is no need for it.

The paradoxical fact is, however, that physical access from computer memories is nowadays very fast, and upgrading steadily, whereas basic brain operations that achieve retrieval from human long-term memory are very slow, but lexical access in language processing is both fast and fairly accurate in man in spite of these differences. This can be observed, for example, in laboratory experiments and, empirically, in immediate disambiguation of ambiguous words in the context of everyday discourse.

To better comprehend this fact, it is useful to consider not only activability of a lexico-semantic unit, taken as a whole, but activability of its meaning, conditionally on the morphological representation. This point has been discussed in more detail elsewhere (Le Ny, 1989b). This amounts to decomposing lexical activation or access into two main phases: the first resulted in recognition of the form of the word, with its relevant flexional cues, and, the second in activation of, or access to, the meaning of this word after its form has been recognized. A major point is then that activation of a meaning unit in the mental lexicon can be brought about not only from activation of the corresponding morphological information (for example, the meaning unit 'doctor' from the word form "doctor", i.e., bottom-up) but also from activation of other meaning units (for example the meaning 'doctor' from the meaning 'nurse', no matter how this has been previously activated). This point can be illustrated by the psychological phenomenon of *seman-*

tic priming (Meyer and Schvaneveldt, 1971; Neely, 1991, for a review): the situation is based on the simple lexical decision task described earlier, but two sequences of characters are presented this time in succession. The subjects must decide on the second. In case it is actually a word, "yes" decision times are shorter if this second word is preceded by a semantically related word (as in the pair "nurse-doctor") than by a neutral word or sequence of letters (as in the pair "xxxxx-doctor"). This main fact is usually interpreted as a result of preactivation of the semantic unit 'doctor' by the unit 'nurse', whereas xxxx preactivates nothing. Observe that activation of a semantic unit by another semantic unit is not at all *top-down*.

Another point of particular interest is the way activability of competing readings can play a significant role in processing and automatic disambiguation of ambiguous words. Let us assume an ambiguous word has only two distinct readings: there is a conditional frequency of use for them, i.e., not the conventional frequency of this particular word form, but of this particular reading given this word form, pR_1/W vs pR_2/W, where W is the word, R_1 and R_2 its readings. Experimental evidence shows that this conditional frequency is an important factor in immediate, automatic disambiguation (Marquer, 1988; Marquer, Lebreton, Léveillé, & Dionisio,1990; Simpson and Burgess, 1985).

Recent psychological models dealing with disambiguation have paid particular attention to this fact. The two readings can be close to one another in frequency, and the two readings can be equiprobable, or they can be far apart, with one reading dominating. Experimental data show that the process of disambiguation differs in these cases. In case of two readings very far apart in frequency, the primary, dominant reading seems to be activated automatically, whereas the secondary reading is not, which is interpretable as due to different degrees of activability. In the other case, the two readings are apparently activated simultaneously, and a decision process is required. This strongly suggests that readings of ambiguous words are stored in memory with different degrees of activability, mainly depending on semantic frequency factors.

A related, but remote, property can be found in some versions of an artificial lexicon: the priority order in which the different readings are stored under a lexical ambiguous entry – assuming that the system uses a unique entry for ambiguous words. However, such a priority is in no way comparable to an activability value such as the one just described, since it makes true computation on different strengths of the readings practically impossible, and all the more in context (see the following discussion). Would it be useful to implement such a property in a machine lexicon, for example, on a probabilistic basis? This may be an interesting topic for computational semantics.

Contextual activability and pre-activation

Let us now consider an important aspect of activation, context effects, on the same basis. These effects are known to be of particular importance for any theory of comprehension, or implementation of language interpreters. Activation models present assumptions and facts that are possibly able to account for a large set of context effects in human comprehension, and deserve analysis with respect to computational semantics. According to these models, many context effects can be accounted for by claiming that the momentary activation level of a lexico-semantic unit L, or more interestingly of its meaning part M, when released by an input word W, is higher if W is processed in a favorable than an unfavorable context, C. Characterization of this intuitive opposition, *favorable vs. unfavorable*, shows that it is related to the degree of semantic similarity between the word and its context or, in a finer analysis, to the part of the information conveyed by the word that has been previously activated by the context. *Pre-activation* is thus the key concept in this field.

I will examine three main situations in which the context modifies the momentary activation level of a meaning unit in the lexicon. The first situation I want to consider is a simple one: let us assume that we have a simple *repetitive* context, i.e., context C of word W is simply a previous token of W. Thus, according to the theory, the processing of the first token, say W_1, produces an activation of the corresponding word form representation and word meaning, such as later processing of the second token W_2 takes place as this whole word representation is in a higher state than the basic level. The representation L of W has then been pre-activated before the occurrence of W_2.

A more interesting form of this phenomenon takes place if W_1 and W_2 are different words (different word forms), but have the same meaning: the words then activate separately their respective morphological representations, but these activate one and the same meaning unit, and hence refer to one and the same set of individuals (or particular individual, in case of a name or definite description). A clear exemplification of this appears in the processing of anaphors. The cognitive mechanism of anaphor in this view is a mental device that allows activation of a unique instantiated meaning from two different word forms. The second often belongs to a closed list (pronouns), or is a synonymous, or superordinate, of the first. For example: "Socrates came to the agora. He said . . . ", or: "Socrates came to the agora. The philosopher said . . ."

Anaphor is known to be a difficult issue for artificial interpretation. In fact, another difficulty here consists in the process of identification of the co-referent – which is not examined here, and may also be a complex task in some sentences for a human comprehender. But given this identification, nothing like a pre-activation exists in machine interpretation.

An even more interesting case is when the context is different from W, for example, another word V, or a whole sentence, S. Experimental data show that pre-activation also takes place in this case, provided there is a cognitive similarity, in particular a semantic one between the meaning of the previous unit V, or the previous sentence S, and that of W. For example, after comprehension of a paragraph such as: "A daring robbery took place at Bastia airport last night. Four men arrived in a helicopter, grabbed booty of seven million Francs and escaped successfully", recognition times were collected on a word from the paragraph, such as *booty*. They were shorter than the recognition times concerning the same word after comprehension of a similar paragraph containing a different first sentence such as: "The weather was very pleasant at the Bastia airport last night. Four men arrived in a helicopter, grabbed booty of seven million Francs and escaped successfully" (Duclos, 1990, unpublished results). This difference was apparently due to a pre-activation brought about by the first, contextual sentence present in the first paragraph, not in the second.

These effects of increase of the momentary activation level of a lexico-semantic unit by a previous context, i.e., of pre-activation, can be best modeled by incorporating an appropriate model of the mental lexicon *organization*. A simple version of this is a semantic network having degrees of semantic similarity on its links, i.e. variable semantic distances between its nodes. In such a network, activation can then be viewed as spreading from a node when it is activated, to another semantically similar node that is close to it in the network (Anderson, 1984; Collins and Loftus, 1975). In short, when presented with a word or a sentence, the human processor first activates the relevant node or nodes, corresponding to the physically present information, and simultaneously pre-activates other related nodes, thus preparing in this way for the processing of similar, or semantically related, upcoming information. The phenomenon mentioned above, semantic priming, yields another broad class of evidence in support of this view.

This is assumed to be the basis for contextual effects in language processing, i.e., the form anticipation takes, and the way the mental system uses the structural organization of its mental lexicon, based on similarity and previous learning, to meet various requirements in comprehension. One of these is disambiguation, as already discussed briefly: an additional fact is that the secondary, less activable reading can be pre-activated by a favorable, relevant context, and then produce response times that are shorter than the other reading.

These problems, of course, cannot be dealt with in detail here. Note however, that this family of activation model can be made fairly compatible with neurobiology on a distributed basis. Some caveats in the comparison with AI systems are of particular importance here. First, functional distances in a representational semantic network must obviously not be confused with metric distances in the brain. Moreover, the difference between semantic networks of this type and the ones frequently used in computational semantics must be emphasized. The relations represented by the links in the network do not represent abstract-logical relations – those listed earlier under items 2. and 3. – as in conventional semantic networks, but relations of psychological similarity – listed under 8. Compatibility between the two types of networks is beyond the scope of this chapter. Finally, it is interesting to compare pre-activation, viewed as a major form of the anticipation process in human mind or brain activity, with some methods of anticipation used or usable in interpreters.

Human anticipation is very different from the one used in deterministic interpreters (Sabah, 1990) in the form of a *looking forward* mechanism. No natural mechanism that could be considered as similar to this can be found in human comprehension. One is proposed by some (non-German) authors: reasoning on reading, they believe that mental comprehension in German must involve looking forward, which would be allegedly requisite, for example, to understand sentences in which the main form of the verb, or a separable particle, is at the end of the clause. This is, in my opinion, a misconception of the way people whose mother tongue is German process their language, in particular the way anticipation takes place in their processing: the notion of pre-activation proposes a better account of this. But there is no fact, for example, from the study of eye movements in reading, showing anticipated search of information and skipping forward in human readers, including Germans. In addition, there is obviously no possibility of hearing forward in the flow of oral speech.

However, another type of anticipation, closer to pre-activation, could be achieved to a certain extent in machine processing. When an interpreter uses very large lexicons, and is implemented in a computer using two or more physical memories, one of which is faster, it may be advantageous to mimic pre-activation of a sub-set of this large lexicon, by transferring such a sub-set, according to pre-determined rules – for example, based on the concept of text theme and, generally, probability of use – to an intermediate, faster, memory. If such an anticipation device could be updated on line, it would be still closer to human pre-activation, even though still largely different by nature. But the programming cost of this device would presumably outstrip its advantages.

Activability of semantic features

Let us now briefly apply the preceding view to a specific problem, that of semantic features. It is well known that this is a controversial issue, and there is no agreement among theories on the existence of this type of cognitive entity. Nevertheless, models of this type are in fairly good agreement with the facts, and can be extended. My line of reasoning will thus be: to postulate the existence of semantic features in word representations, namely, in their meaning part. How could we enrich this hypothetical view with the property of activability, and the role of activation in context effects?

I do not commit myself to a particular theory of semantic features here – although my private preference is basically for an attributes/attribute-values/probabilistic-distribution-of-attribute-values concept of features. My present postulate is, on the contrary, a weak one, which states merely that lexical units, in particular their meaning parts, can be analyzed into smaller pieces of meaning, sub-units, which can be (in set conditions) separately processed by the speaker. This postulate is not equivalent to an ultra-computational view of meaning, that is, it in no way implies that token lexico-semantic units are constructed on-line from features during comprehension.

The analysis presented here can then be extended to features: activability and related processes can be viewed as identical as concerns semantic features to those described for ambiguous word readings. The additional specific assumption is only that the property of activability is extended to semantic features in word representations. It turns out that another property, termed *salience* or *saliency*, is often used in conventional descriptions pertaining to cognitive psychology, to designate the capability of elements of a perception or a problem to catch attention. In this framework, salience is by no means different from activability as I have presented it. Thus, the postulate takes the form that a particular value of basic activability is associated with any semantic feature in any word representation.

The following assumptions can then be formulated for contextual effects: during language processing, the momentary activation levels of any semantic feature in a lexical meaning unit vary from moment to moment as a function of input information. In addition, pre-activation of the features is brought about by activation of related features or lexical units. For example, after comprehension of a simple sentence such as: "a beggar was in front of the church and held out his hand to people coming out of the mass", these assumptions predict that the activation level of the value *porch* on the attribute *part-of-object* in the representation of *church* becomes higher than the value *steeple* (in the same representation, same attribute), whereas *steeple* takes on a higher activation value after comprehension of a sentence such as: "when we arrived at Cormainville, the first thing we saw was the church above the old roofs". An experimental study based on response time comparisons shows that this is actually the case (Denis and Le Ny, 1986). Observe that neither "porch" nor "steeple" was mentioned in the sentences.

The role of context can thus be accounted for in a sharp and elegant way if we assume that appropriate semantic features are permanently pre-activated before the presentation of the target lexical unit in the discourse or text. This assumption is similar to that proposed earlier, namely that a secondary reading of an ambiguous word can be pre-activated. A major difference between ambiguity and features processing is apparently that opposite readings in an ambiguous word are in competition more than different features in comprehension. However, if we consider features as attribute values, we see that they are also in opposition, thus in a form of competition – such as *porch* and *steeple*. The notion of *opposition*, as used here, is congruent with so-called *structural* theories in linguistics.

The cognitive mechanism of feature pre-activation allows for delicate tuning of lexical meaning: it is able to account for several major phenomena such as modification of typicality according to a given context, disambiguation of complex lexico-semantic configurations, comprehension of analogies and metaphors, etc. It may be used, for example, for highly polysemic words, which have many very close meanings, rather than two simple, disjoined and opposed readings: an example is the verb "to take". As concerns metaphor, if it is assumed to be based on an analogy, a result of an intersection of shared features between two words or phrases, activation of these shared features can account for many examples. They include the ones where the analogy is initially concealed from the speaker, and recognized, i.e., activated, only at the time of metaphor processing, and even new metaphors, in which the analogy is suddenly *discovered* (rather than *created*, Indurkhya, 1992).

Finally, activability of features may apply to any instantiation of a given representation in comprehension: interpretation of every new token word in discourse or text requires tuning of the lexico-semantic knowledge associated with it in long-term memory and, as a rule, adjunction to it of particular, text-dependent information. Activation and pre-activation apparently afford this function.

Use of this mechanism in computational semantics is infrequent, presumably because it involves two problematic and very complex hypothetical properties: a basic one, attribution of features, debatable as concerns its nature, and a second-order one, applied to the first, activability of such features. Schank's work (Schank, 1975, 1982; Schank and Abelson, 1977) can be considered as involving an approximation of this, but on a speculative and personal basis: implementation of the properties discussed above would presumably require a large empirical investigation of representation analysis, and more consideration of psychological results. As has been suggested, use of these properties would also be made easier by conjunction of standard computational processing and techniques of neuromimetic networks (McClelland and Kawamoto, 1986), provided they admit a symbolic level.

Conclusion

This conclusion raises the questions presented in the introduction, but with a number of caveats. I have tried to describe a set of properties of lexico-semantics, some that have been implemented in interpreters and some that have not. The major question concerning the latter can be reformulated as follows: is it useful, or possible, to make an implementation of the second ones? As concerns possibility, an obvious answer is that this task certainly would require the creation not only of new tools enabling processing in an appropriate way, but also the ability to store and organize a huge amount of knowledge in the lexical base of the interpreter. But human lexical knowledge is huge. As concerns usefulness, the question remains open: some may claim they can do without. My opinion, notwithstanding the obvious necessity to know more, much more on these issues from a psychological and linguistic point of view, is that the properties mentioned last are the touchstone of the most complex effects in language such that it is impossible to carry out full language comprehension without mastering them. This is why these properties, in particular those based on activability, and all the related questions concerning disambiguation, fine context effects, feature activation, etc., deserve interest from scientists working in computational semantics.

Notes

1. I will use *language comprehension*, in this chapter, as an equivalent of *language understanding*, i.e., as referring to the mental activity by which a fragment of discourse is processed in a human mind, and produces a *semantic representation* as its output. A semantic representation is an individual realization of the meaning. *Language interpretation* will refer to machine processing, i.e., to a class of programs

(*interpreters*) designed to emulate the human function of comprehension, in mimicking the *external* behavior of a human speaker. However, I take it for granted that machine interpretation presently always involves an intermediate stage: building an internal machine representation, intended to be used later in various ways. The symmetrical sub-domains of natural or machine *language production* can be associated with the previous ones in research, as they raise similar problems. However, they will not be specifically dealt with in this chapter.

2. No distinction is made here between *semantic* and *conceptual*, both referring to the mental meaning associated with a word or phrase. In using a finer grain of analysis, *concept* and *conceptual* would be restricted to the semantic units that are well defined, for example, the ones used by experts in the domains of mathematics, philosophy, natural sciences, etc.

3. Meronymic relations can themselves be analyzed into finer sub-relations (Winston, Chaffin and Herrmann, 1987).

4. Attributes can be sub-divided into several categories with respect to various criteria, in particular the number of values: two-valued attributes as *gender* or *sex* (male/female) are different from many-valued ones, as *color* names, or continuous ones, as *length*.

5. A slightly different variable derived from the same facts can be used in the family of activation models: *initial level of activation*, from which prediction of facility and speed of activation is also possible. In addition, an alternative variable is used in the context of store models, *accessibility* to lexico-semantic units. This notion is also an operational equivalent of the degree of activability and is based on the analogy of accessibility from machine memories and knowledge bases. I will not discuss the respective merits of these notions in this chapter.

6. This property is presumably the expression of a causal relation in learning: repetition and overlearning make all representations more activable (or more accessible from memory), such that the differences in basic activability of lexical representations can be a result of the more or less frequent occurrence and processing of the corresponding words in the linguistic environment of every speaker (and their referents in the physical environment). From this point of view, this property of the lexicon is a functional property stemming from general rules of learning and memory.

7. An inversed form of typicality – where one superordinate of a unit is considered more typical than the others – has been assumed by Charniak and McDermott (1985). Reinterpretations of typicality effects in reasoning, which are sometimes based on concepts fairly different from the primary one, have been given in the frameworks of default logic (Reiter, 1980), fuzzy semantics or logic (Zadeh, 1970, 1975), non-monotonic logic (McDermott and Doyle, 1980).

References

Allen, P. A., McNeal, M., & Kvak, D. (1992). Perhaps the lexicon is coded as a function of word frequency, *Journal of Memory and Language, 31*, 826–844.

Anderson, J. (1983). *The Architecture of Cognition*, Cambridge, Mass.: Harvard University Press.

Anderson, J. (1984). Spreading activation. In J. R. Anderson & S. M. Kosslyn (Eds), *Essays in Learning and Memory*, New York: Freeman.

Carnap, R. (1947). *Meaning and Necessity*. Chicago: The University of Chicago Press.

Carr, T. H., & Pollatsek, A. (1985). Recognizing printed words: A look at current models. In D. Besner, T. G. Waller, & G. E. McKinnon (Eds.), *Reading Research: Advances in Theory and Practice* (Vol. 5). New York: Academic Press.

J.-F. Le Ny

Charniak, E., & McDermott, D. (1985). *Introduction to Artificial Intelligence*. Reading, Mass.: Addison-Wesley.

Collins, A., & Loftus, E. (1975). A spreading activation theory of semantic processing, *Psychological Review*, *82*, 407–428.

de Saussure, F. (1916). *Cours de linguistique générale*. Paris: Payot.

Denis, M., & Le Ny, J. F. (1986). Centering on figurative features during the comprehension of sentences describing scenes. *Psychological Research*, *48*, 145–152.

Fillmore, C. J. (1968). The case for case. In E. Bach & R. T. Harms (Eds.), *Universals of Linguistic Theory*. New-York: Holt, Rinehart & Winston, 1–90.

Howes, D. H., & Solomon, R. L. (1951). Visual duration thresholds as a function of word-probability. *Journal of Experimental Psychology*, *41*, 401–410.

Indurkhya, B. (1992). *Metaphor*. Cambridge: Cambridge University Press.

Kintsch, W. (1988). The role of knowledge in discourse comprehension: A construction-integration model. *Psychological Review*, *95*, 163–182.

Kleiber, G. (1988). Prototype, stéréotype: un air de famille, *DRLAV*, *38*, 1–61.

Le Ny J.-F. (1983). Le temps de réponse à des mots-sondes considéré comme un indicateur des processus de compréhension. *Le Travail Humain*, *45*, 109–118.

Le Ny, J.-F. (1989a). *Science cognitive et compréhension du langage*. Paris: Presses Universitaires de France.

Le Ny, J.-F. (1989b). Accès au lexique et compréhension du langage: la ligne de démarcation sémantique. *Lexique*, *8*, 65–85.

Le Ny, J.-F. (1991a). A psychological description of semantic representation in working memory after text comprehension, *Zeitschrift für Psychologie*, *11*, 129–136.

Le Ny, J.-F. (1991b). Compréhension du langage et représentations sémantiques. In J. Montangero et A. Tryphon (Eds.), *Psychologie génétique et sciences cognitives*. Gen ve: Fondation Archives Jean Piaget, 125–142.

McClelland, J. L., & Kawamoto, A. H. (1986). Mechanisms of sentence processing: assigning roles to constituents in sentences. In McClelland, J. L., Rumelhard, D. E., & the PDP Research Group, *Parallel Distributed Processing. Explorations in the Microstructure of Cognition, Vol. 2: Psychological and Biological Models*, 272–325. Cambridge, Mass.: MIT Press.

McDermott, D. V., & Doyle, J. (1980). Non-monotonic logic I. *Artificial Intelligence*, *13*, 41–72.

Marquer, P. (1988). Le traitement des homographes dépend-il de la fréquence relative de leurs acceptions? In C. Fuchs (Ed.), *L'ambiguïté et la paraphrase*. Caen: Centre de Publications de l'Université de Caen, 299–303.

Marquer, P., Lebreton, M., Leveillé, M., & Dionisio, C. (1990). A quel moment du traitement des homographes intervient la fréquence relative de leurs acceptions? *Année Psychologique*, *90*, 489–509.

Mervis, C. B., Catlin, J., & Rosch, E. (1976). Relationship among goodness-of-example, category norms and word frequency. *Bulletin of the Psychonomic Society*, *7*, 268–284.

Meyer, D. E., & Schvaneveldt, R. W. (1971). Facilitation in recognizing pairs of words: Evidence of a dependence between retrieval operations. *Journal of Experimental Psychology*, *90*, 227–234.

Morton, J. (1969). Interaction of information in word recognition. *Psychological Review*, *76*, 165–178.

Neely, J. H. (1991). Semantic priming effects in visual word recognition: A selective review of current findings and theories. In D. Besner and G. W. Humphreys (Eds.), *Basic Processes in Reading: Visual Word Recognition*, 264–236, Hillsdale, NJ: Erlbaum.

Reiter, R. (1980). A logic for default reasoning. *Artificial Intelligence*, *13*, 81–132.

Rosch, E., & Lloyds, B. (Eds) (1977). *Cognition and Categorization*. Hillsdale, NJ: Erlbaum.

Rosch, E., & Mervis, C. B. (1975). Family resemblances: Studies in the internal structure of categories. *Cognitive Psychology*, *3*, 382–439.

Rumelhart, D. E., McClelland, J. L., & the PDP Research Group. (1986). *Parallel Distributed Processing. Explorations in the Microstructure of Cognition, Vol. 1: Foundations.* Cambridge, Mass.: MIT Press.

Sabah, G. (1990). CARAMEL: A computational model of natural language understanding using a parallel implementation. Stockholm, *ECAI*, 563–565

Scarborough, D. L., Cortese, C., & Scarborough, H. S. (1977). Frequency and repetition effects in lexical memory. *Journal of Experimental Psychology: Human Perception and Performance*, *3*, 1–17.

Schank, R. C. (1975). *Conceptual Information Processing.* Amsterdam: North-Holland.

Schank, R. C. (1982). *Dynamic Memory: A Theory of Learning in Computers And People.* Cambridge: Cambridge University Press.

Schank, R. C., & Abelson, R. P. (1977). *Scripts, Plans, Goals and Understanding.* Hillsdale, NJ: Erlbaum.

Simpson, G. B., & Burgess, C. (1985). Activation and selection processes in the recognition of ambiguous words. *Journal of Experimental Psychology: Human Perception and Performance*, *11*, 28–39.

Tesnière, L. (1959). *Eléments de syntaxe structurale.* Paris: Klincksieck.

Winston, M. E., Chaffin, R., & Herrmann, D. (1987). A taxonomy of part-whole relations. *Cognitive Science*, *11*, 417–444.

Zadeh, L. A. (1970). Quantitative fuzzy semantics. *Information Science*, *1*, 1–17.

Zadeh, L. A. (1975). Fuzzy logic and approximate reasoning. *Synthese*, *30*, 407–425.

PART II

Foundational issues in lexical semantics

The next part in this book concerns linguistic issues for lexical semantics. The main issues addressed are based on the notion of Generative Lexicon (Pustejovsky, 1991) and its consequences for the construction of lexicons.

The first chapter, "Linguistic constraints on type coercion," by James Pustejovsky, summarizes the foundations of the Generative Lexicon which he defined a few years ago. This text investigates how best to characterize the formal mechanisms and the linguistic data necessary to explain the behavior of logical polysemy. A comprehensive range of polymorphic behaviors that account for the variations in semantic expressiveness found in natural languages is studied.

Within the same formal linguistic paradigm, we then have a contribution by Sabine Bergler, "From lexical semantics to text analysis," which illustrates several issues of the Generative Lexicon using data from the *Wall Street Journal*. This chapter addresses in depth an important issue of the Generative Lexicon: what kind of methods can be used to create Generative Lexicon lexical entries with precise semantic content for the Qualia roles of the Generative Lexicon, from linguistic analysis. Special attention is devoted to the production of partial representations and to incremental analysis of texts.

The next chapter, "Lexical functions, generative lexicons and the world" by Dirk Heylen, explores the convergences and divergences between Mel'čuk's analysis of lexical functions and the generative lexicon approach. The author then proposes an interesting and original knowledge representation method based on lexical functions mainly following Mel'čuk's approach.

"Semantic features in a generic lexicon," by Gabriel Bes and Alain Lecomte, starts from the observation that it is not possible to elaborate a unique theory that would organize the representation of lexical information in a uniform and canonical way. This chapter suggests the adoption of a polytheoretic conception exhibiting a hierarchy of pieces of information, and outlines the numerous convergences of the current semantic theories. It first reviews ways to organize semantic information hierarchically, and then examines the way semantic features can be organized and treated within a formal semantics system based on Montague semantics.

4 Linguistic constraints on type coercion

JAMES PUSTEJOVSKY

4.1 Degrees of polymorphism

In order to help characterize the expressive power of natural languages in terms of semantic expressiveness, it is natural to think in terms of semantic systems with increasing functional power. Furthermore, a natural way of capturing this might be in terms of the type system which the grammar refers to for its interpretation. What I would like to discuss in this chapter is a method for describing how semantic systems fall on a hierarchy of increasing expressiveness and richness of descriptive power and investigate various phenomena in natural language that indicate (1) that we need a certain amount of expressiveness that we have not considered before in our semantics, but also (2) that by looking at the data it becomes clear that we need natural constraints on the mechanisms which give us such expressive systems. After reviewing the range of semantic types from monomorphic languages to unrestricted polymorphic languages, I would like to argue that we should aim for a model which permits only a restricted amount of polymorphic behavior. I will characterize this class of languages as semi-polymorphic.

I will outline what kind of semantic system produces just this class of languages. I will argue that something like the generative lexicon framework is necessary to capture the richness of type shifting and sense extension phenomena.

Let me begin the discussion on expressiveness by reviewing how this same issue was played out in the realm of syntactic frameworks in the 1950s. When principles of context-free and transformational grammars were first introduced, one of the motivations for the richness of these new systems was the apparent inadequacies of finite-state descriptions for the different natural language constructions that were being discovered (Chomsky, 1955, 1957). That is, wherever the structuralists did not appreciate that a particular construction was not sufficiently characterizable by finite-state description, the power of a more expressive grammar became necessary. When Chomsky and others argued that natural languages appeared to be not even context-free, but in fact appeared to require mechanisms moving out of the family of context-free languages, the motivation was clearly data-directed and seemed warranted by the most prevalent interpretations of what CFGs were.

I would like to thank Bob Ingria, Noam Chomsky, Bran Boguraev, Patrick Saint-Dizier, Scott Waterman, Paul Buitelaar, Federica Busa, and Sabine Bergler for useful comments and discussion.

An analogous situation holds in the semantics of natural language today. We have reached a point where we are discovering phenomena in language that are beyond the range of explanation, given the current makeup of our lexical semantic systems. I will give some examples of what the current view of lexical semantics seems to be, and why this approach is unable to capture the richness of lexical creativity.

I think that one of the most difficult issues in semantics is that of lexical ambiguity. It seems clear that ambiguity essentially falls into two types, following a perceptive distinction that Weinreich made back in the 1960s (Weinreich, 1964), that of the distinction between *contrastive* and *complementary* ambiguity. This distinction classifies homonymous nouns such as *bank* as having the two contrastive senses of a lending institution and a river's edge. The same noun *bank* has complementary senses of the institution and the building as well as the people in the organization (Pustejovsky, 1991). The point is that current theories of lexical semantics, and by virtue of their incorporating these theories, theories of compositional semantics, are unable to account for the expressive and creative power of word sense. Words generally have fixed meanings in these frameworks, such as seen in the lexicons for classical Montague grammars (Dowty, 1979) as well as certain lexicalist frameworks (Levin, 1985). The ability to change the sense of a word in these systems is arrived at only by virtue of creating a new sense or lexical item, or by some sort of unconstrained meaning postulate.

If we think of this view in terms of its generative capacity, we have what might be characterized as a *monomorphic language* (cf. Strachey, 1967). In a monomorphic language, lexical items are given a single meaning, that is, one type and denotation. Lexical ambiguity is handled by having a multiple listing of the word. For example, the word *door* refers both to a physical object as well as an aperture for passage (cf. Nunberg, 1979). These two meanings must be represented as independent lexical items. Thus, for sentence (1), *paint* applies to physical objects, and the selectional constraint is satisfied by the lexical entry $door_1$ being marked with the appropriate feature.

(1)   John painted the $door_1$.
(2)   John walked through the $door_2$.

For sentence (2), however, reference is made to an aperture, since the verb selects for a space. This requires a second entry, $door_2$, which satisfies just that feature. What is missing here is the obvious connection between the two senses of the word *door*. Within monomorphic approaches to lexical meaning, the connection is captured at best by meaning postulates or lexical redundancy rules of some sort. Similar examples exist with an entire range of nominal types in natural languages, all of which seem to be logically polysemous, e.g., *fireplace, pipe, room*, etc. All of these have the meaning of both physical object and spatial enclosure (Pustejovsky and Anick, 1988).

Something is clearly being missed in this approach, namely, the logical relationship that a door is an aperture defined by a physical object in a particular way.

This particular definition leads us to view such nominals not as simply sets of individuals, but rather as essentially *relational*, albeit quite distinct in behavior from conventional relational nouns, such as *brother* or *edge* (cf. Pustejovsky, in press).

This kind of ambiguity does not exist with just noun types, but rather exists in all categories in language. Another example, not normally construed as lexical ambiguity, involves the type ambiguity of cases of multiple subcategorization. This is a case of ambiguity because, given the mapping between semantic and syntactic representations, there must be some correspondence between semantic type and syntactic expression. For the verbs in (3) and (4), the lexicon will have multiple entries, each representing a unique syntactic type. For example, for the verbs *believe, persuade, begin*, there are different subcategorizations corresponding to separate entries for the word, necessitated by syntactic uniqueness at surface structure.

(3)   a. John began$_1$ to read the novel.
       b. John began$_2$ reading the novel.
       c. John began$_3$ the novel.
(4)   a. Mary believes$_1$ John to have left.
       b. Mary believes$_2$ that John left.
       c. Mary believes$_3$ John.
       d. Mary believes$_4$ the story.

Most syntactic approaches to lexical representation as well as formal semantic schools have taken the approach of multiple listings of forms.[1] As mentioned before, there is no natural way to relate the senses of the verbs in these examples. This kind of type ambiguity is ubiquitous in language, and there must be some systematic way of relating structural forms to the semantic type selected by the verb, if we wish to do more than simply describe syntactic co-occurrence.

Consider next the ambiguity and context-dependence of adjectives such as *fast* and *slow*, where the meaning of the predicate varies depending on the head being modified. Typically, a lexicon requires an enumeration of different senses for such words, in order to account for the kinds of ambiguity in this example:

(5)   a. *a fast plane*: a plane that is inherently fast.
       b. *a fast book*: one that can be read in a short time.
       c. *a fast reader*: one who reads quickly.

As discussed in Pustejovsky and Boguraev (1993), there are at least three distinct word senses for *fast* involved in these examples: to move quickly; to perform some act quickly; and to do something that takes little time.

Upon closer analysis, each occurrence of *fast* in the last example predicates in a slightly different way. In fact, any finite enumeration of word senses will not account for creative applications of this adjective in the language. For example, *fast* in the phrase *a fast motorway* refers to the ability of vehicles on the motorway to sustain high speed. As a novel use of *fast*, we are clearly looking at a new sense that is not covered by the enumeration. I will outline a semantic theory in which such senses are generated by the semantic system rather than listed in a static lexicon.

Another logical polysemy involving adjectives, discussed in Ostler and Atkins (1992), is the ability of certain psychological predicates to apparently change type. For example, adjectives like *sad* and *happy* are able to predicate of both individuals (6a) and (6b), as well as event-denoting nouns (6c).

(6)   a. The woman is sad.
       b. a sad woman
       c. a sad day/event/occasion
(7)   a. The president is afraid.
       b. *the afraid president
       c. *an afraid day/event/occasion
(8)   a. The man is frightened.
       b. a frightened man
       c. *a frightened day/event/occasion

We need to explain two things with such apparently polysemous adjectives: first, assuming these adjectives select for animate objects, what licenses the modification of a nonselected type such as a temporal interval? And second, what constraints explain the inability of the adjective classes in (7) and (8) to operate in a similar fashion? Within the standard treatment of lexical semantics, these data would suggest two separate senses for each of these adjectives, one typed as predicating of animate objects, and the other predicating of intervals. Yet even with this solution, we must somehow explain that "a sad day" is still interpreted relative to a human judging the events of that interval as sad.

Summarizing our discussion of polysemy so far, it seems clear that the standard theory of lexical ambiguity can be characterized as a *monomorphic language* (ML) of types, with the following properties:

Monomorphic languages: A language where lexical items and complex phrases are provided a single type and denotation. In all these views, every word has a literal meaning. Lexical ambiguity is treated by multiple listing of words, both for contrastive ambiguity (Weinreich, 1964) and logical polysemy (Pustejovsky, 1991). Treating the lexicon as an enumerative listing of word senses has been the predominate view, and adherents include Montague (1974), Levin, (1985), and Levin and Rappaport (1988). Dowty (1979) has a more complex view of word senses which is still monomorphic, but the meaning postulates are more clearly defined than in Montague's model.

Although we will not discuss it here, the inverse of a restrictive theory such as that just described would be a theory denying the role of literal meaning entirely. Such a view is held by Searle (1979), for example. Viewed from the perspective we have adopted in this chapter, such a theory might be termed an *unrestricted polymorphic language* (UPL) since the meaning is determined more by the context than any inherent properties of the language lexicon. Briefly, the properties of such a system are:

Unrestricted polymorphic languages: No restriction on the type that a lexical item may assume. No operational distinction between subclasses of polymorphic transformations. Although not explicitly lexically based, Searle's theory (1979) is polymorphic in a fairly unrestricted form. The contribution of "background knowledge" acts as the trigger to shift the meaning of an expression in different pragmatically determined contexts, and there is nothing inherent in the language that constrains the meaning of the words in context.

From our brief discussion, I believe it is clear that what we want is a lexical semantic theory which accounts for the polysemy in natural language while not overgenerating to produce semantically ill-formed expressions. Furthermore, if our observations are correct, then such a theory must be in part lexically determined and not entirely pragmatically defined. Such a theory would generate what I will term *semi-polymorphic languages* (SPLs). Several lines of research have pointed to capturing the flexibility of word meaning and semantic interpretation, from early observations made by Katz (1964), Wilks (1975), and Nunberg (1979) to the work reported in Klein and van Benthem (1987). The properties of such a system would be at least the following:

Semi-polymorphic languages: All lexical items are semantically active, and have a richer typed semantic representation than conventionally assumed; semantic operations of lexically determined type changing (e.g., type coercions) operate under well-defined constraints. Different subclasses of polymorphic operations are defined, each with independent properties and conditions on their application.

As with the increasing generative capabilities of families of grammars, the range of sense extensions for a lexicon (and with them the subsequent semantic expressions) increases as restrictions on generation are lifted. What natural language data seem to require is a semantic system falling outside of monomorphic languages (ML), but well below the language of unrestricted polymorphic languages (UPL), what we have called semi-polymorphic languages (SPL):

$$ML \subseteq SPL \subseteq UPL$$

This is the view of semantics that I will present in the remainder of this chapter. I will describe the varieties of coercion types, and then outline an approach within generative lexicon theory of how best to constrain the application of coercion operations. The presentation of each phenomenon will be somewhat brief, in order to give a broader picture of how all categories participate in generative processes giving rise to logical polysemy.

4.2 The semantic type system

For our purposes here, I will assume a general familiarity with the framework of Generative Lexicon theory, and the mechanisms employed by the theory, as outlined in Pustejovsky (1991, 1993), Pustejovsky and Boguraev (1993), Copestake and Briscoe (1992), and Copestake (1992). Briefly, a generative lexicon can be characterized as a system involving at least the following four levels of representations:

1. *Argument structure:* Specification of number and type of logical arguments.
2. *Event structure:* Definition of the event type of a lexical item. Sorts include *state, process,* and *transition.*
3. *Qualia structure:* Composed of FORMAL, CONST, TELIC, and AGENTIVE roles.
4. *Lexical inheritance structure:* Identification of how a lexical structure is related to other structures in the type lattice.

A set of generative devices connects these four levels, providing for the compositional interpretation of words in context. The most important of these devices for our discussion is a semantic transformation called *type coercion* which captures the semantic relatedness between syntactically distinct expressions. As an operation on types within a λ-calculus, type coercion can be seen as transforming a monomorphic language into one with polymorphic types (cf. Milner, 1978; Cardelli and Wegner, 1985; Klein and van Benthem, 1987). Argument, event, and qualia types must conform to the well-formedness conditions defined by the type system and the lexical inheritance structure when undergoing operations of semantic composition. Lexical items are strongly typed yet are provided with mechanisms for fitting to novel typed environments by means of type coercion over a richer notion of types.

The method of fine-grained characterization of lexical entries, as proposed here, effectively allows us to conflate different word senses into a single *meta-entry*, thereby offering great potential not only for systematically encoding regularities of word behavior dependent on context, but also for greatly reducing the size of the lexicon. Following Pustejovsky and Anick (1988) we call such meta-entries *lexical conceptual paradigms* (LCPs). The theoretical claim here is that such a characterization constrains what a possible word meaning can be, through the mechanism of well-formed semantic expressions.

The notion of a meta-entry turns out to be very useful for capturing the systematic ambiguities which are so pervasive throughout language. For example, an apparently unambiguous noun such as *newspaper* can appear in many semantically distinct contexts, functioning sometimes as an organization, a physical object, or the information contained in the articles.

(9)   The newspapers attacked the President for raising taxes.
(10)   Mary spilled coffee on the newspaper.
(11)   John got angry at the newspaper.

Rather than treat these as distinct senses, we will analyze these senses as the logical expression of different "logical parameters" to the meta-entry for *newspaper*; i.e., the different qualia.

If lexical items are to be thought of as carrying several parameters (or dimensions) of interpretation, then the question immediately arises as to how a particular interpretation is arrived at in a given context. This question is answered in part by the semantic operation of *type coercion*. Intuitively, the process works as follows. In the construction of a semantic interpretation for a phrase or sentence, a lexical item is able to coerce an argument to the appropriate type only if that word or phrase has available to it, an interpretation of the expected type. Assuming that objects are represented within a typed λ-calculus, we can state type coercion as follows:

Type coercion: A semantic operation that converts an argument to the type which is expected by a predicate, where it would otherwise result in a type error.

Each expression α has available to it, a set of shifting operators, Σ_α, which operate over an expression, changing its type and denotation.[2] By making reference to these operators directly in the rule of function application, we can treat the operation of function application polymorphically, as below:

> *Function application with coercion (FA$_C$)*: If α is of type $<b,a>$, and β is of type c, then

(i)   if type $c = b$, then $\alpha(\beta)$ is of type a.
(ii) if there is a $\sigma \in \Sigma_\beta$ such that $\sigma(\beta)$ results in an expression of type b, then $\alpha(\sigma(\beta))$ is of type a.
(iii) otherwise a type error is produced.

We will consider specific subcases of coercion, involving most of the major categories. In the next section, we turn to the semantics of the nominal system and how logical ambiguity can be represented in a systematic and explanatory way, using the generative devices available to us in the theory.

4.2.1   *Nominal semantics*

Following Pustejovsky (1991), Pustejovsky and Boguraev (1993), and Copestake and Briscoe (1992), I will assume that nouns can be categorized semantically in terms of a system of qualia roles. For example, the noun *book* has the following lexical structure:[3]

$$\begin{bmatrix} \textbf{book(x)} \\ \text{CONST} = \textbf{pages(z)} \\ \text{FORMAL} = \textbf{physobj(x)} \\ \text{TELIC} = \textbf{read(P,y,x)} \\ \text{AGENTIVE} = \textbf{write(T,w,x)} \end{bmatrix}$$

This states that the noun *book* carries information regarding its constitution (CONST), its function (TELIC), its origin (AGENTIVE), and its basic form (FORMAL). The values of these qualia are typed and are accessible to semantic operations in composition with other phrases, as we will demonstrate in section 4.3.

One aspect of nominal representation that we hope to capture with this formalism is the paradigmatic behavior of a lexical item in the syntax. Briefly, this is achieved by type coercion over a Lexical Conceptual Paradigm's (LCP) qualia structure. Among the alternations captured by LCPs are the following:

1. Count/Mass alternations; *lamb.*
   a. The lamb is running in the field.
   b. John ate lamb for breakfast.
2. Container/Containee alternations; *bottle.*
   a. Mary broke the bottle.
   b. The baby finished the bottle.
3. Figure/Ground Reversals; *door, window.*
   a. The window is rotting.
   b. Mary crawled through the window.
4. Product/Producer diathesis; *newspaper, Honda.*
   a. The newspaper fired its editor.
   b. John spilled coffee on the newspaper.
5. Plant/Food alternations; *fig, apple.*
   a. Mary ate a fig for lunch.
   b. Mary watered the figs in the garden.
6. Process/Result diathesis; *examination, merger.*
   a. The company's merger with Honda will begin next fall.
   b. The merger will produce cars.
7. Place/People diathesis; *city, New York.*
   a. John traveled to New York.
   b. New York kicked the mayor out of office.

Similar alternations have been proposed for verbs as well, cf. Levin (1993). Others who have worked on regular alternations of the meanings of lexical forms include Ostler and Atkins (1992) and Apresjan (1973).

What lexical conceptual paradigms illustrate very clearly is that syntactic information is also inheritable between lexical items. To illustrate this point, consider the class of process/result nominals such as *merger, joint venture, consolidation,* etc. These nominals are ambiguous between an event interpretation (the *act* of merging) versus the resulting entity or state (the merger which *results*). This is a property of the whole paradigm, indicating that the alternation should be captured in qualia representation of the LCP itself (cf. Pustejovsky, in press for details).

Establishing whether a noun's polysemous behavior is due to the relational structure of the noun or a coercion rule can be difficult. One test, however, is that of *co-predication*. In (12), both predicates apply to different senses of the noun *door*, while in (13) a similar construction with *newspaper* is ill-formed.[4]

(12)   John painted and then walked through the door.
(13)   *The newspaper fired its editor and fell off the table.

The representation for *door*, for example, indicates a relational structure where both senses logically project without coercion rules being necessary.

$$\begin{bmatrix} \textbf{door}(x,y) \\ \text{CONST} = \textbf{aperture(y)} \\ \text{FORMAL} = \textbf{physobj(x)} \\ \text{TELIC} = \textbf{walk\_through(P,w,y)} \\ \text{AGENTIVE} = \textbf{artifact(x)} \end{bmatrix}$$

On the basis of this diagnostic, we would conclude that, although *newspaper* carries a qualia structure of equal complexity as *door*, it projects a single argument, and is not truly relational in nature. The sentence in (13) is a case where there is a type clash from the two predicates in the conjunction, and coercion is not available to one without being available to the other. This, then, is at least one diagnostic for determining whether a logical polysemy arises from a relationally structured object or from coercion.

4.2.2 *Verbal semantics*

In Pustejovsky (1989, 1993), it is suggested that the qualia structure might be usefully extended to the verbal system.[5] In this section, I will present an integrated representation of argument and event structures, seen as orthogonal parameter sets constrained by the qualia structure.

It has become quite standard to acknowledge the role of events in verbal semantics. Conventionally, the event variable for a verb within an event-based semantics is listed as a single argument along with the logical parameter defined by a particular predicate or relation. For example, a fairly conventional Davidsonian lexical representation for *build* might be:

$$\lambda y \lambda x \lambda e[build(e,x,y) \wedge \theta_1(e,x) \wedge \theta_2(e,y)]$$

This assumes an atomic view on event structure, where internal aspects of the event referred to by the single variable are inaccessible (Parsons, 1990). The role definitions for the parameters to the predicate are typically identified by thematic identifiers of some sort, e.g., θ_1 and θ_2 in the example above. Pustejovsky (1991b) and Moens (1992) argue that finer-grained distinctions are necessary for event descriptions in order to capture the phenomena associated with aspect and Aktionsarten. I will assume this is the case and introduce the mechanism of *Orthogonal Parameter Binding*, which allows us to bind into an expression from independent parameter lists. The logical arguments of an expression are separated by type, where logical arguments are distinct from the event structure arguments defined by a particular Aktionsart of a lexical item.[6] Given a listing of logical arguments and an event structure represented as a listing of event types,

[ARGS = ARG_1, ARG_2, . . . , ARG_N]
[EVENTSTR = $EVENT_1$, $EVENT_2$, . . . , $EVENT_M$]

we can view the semantics of the verb as being centrally defined by the qualia, but constrained by type information from the orthogonal bindings of the two parameter lists. The predicates in the qualia refer directly to the parameters:

$[\text{QUALIA} = [Q_i = \text{PRED}(\text{EVENT}_j, \text{ARG}_k)]]$

We furthermore introduce a distinction between three types of logical parameters for lexical items (here exemplified for verbs):[7]

1. *Arguments:* Syntactically realized parameters of the lexical item;
2. *Default arguments:* Parameters which participate in the logical expressions in the qualia, but which are not necessarily expressed syntactically, e.g., "John built the house *with bricks*".
3. *Shadow arguments:* Logical parameters which are semantically incorporated into the lexical item. They can be expressed only by operations of subtyping, e.g., "Mary buttered her toast *with an expensive butter*".
4. *Optional arguments:* Parameters which modify the logical expression, but are part of situational or propositional interpretation, not any particular lexical item's semantic representation. These include adjunct expressions of temporal or spatial modification.

This classification is a first attempt at refining the classification between argument and adjunct phrases. It is not just the lexical properties of a single item which determine the logical status of a phrase as a certain argument type. Compositional operations may create an argument or shadow an argument at a non-lexical projection, by virtue of compositionality in the phrase. In other cases, however, a logical argument is defaulted by virtue of a complement's semantics. For example, in *show a movie* the goal argument is defaulted by the semantics of the complement, and becomes an optional argument (see Pustejovsky, 1992). Furthermore, default arguments when realized in certain ways, can mimic the behavior of shadow arguments. For example, in the sentence

Mary built a wooden house with pine.

the default argument has effectively been saturated indirectly by a modifier in the direct object, and the further specification *with pine* is licensed in the same manner as in shadow arguments.

To illustrate how Orthogonal Parameter Binding structures a lexical entry, consider the verb *build* (see Figure 4.1). Following Pustejovsky (1991b), we assume it is typed as a transition with two subevents, a **process** of building followed by the **state** of the thing constructed. Furthermore, since it is logically a transitive verb, it has two arguments, with all the syntactic and semantic information entailed by that class (cf. Sanfilippo, 1993).[8] In addition, we add a *default argument* D-ARG, which participates in the qualia but is not necessarily expressed in the syntax. This is the material or substance being used in the building process.

The process is the AGENTIVE event involving both the syntactic subject, ARG1, and the default argument, D-ARG1, which gives rise to the event expressed in the FORMAL. This is the state of there being an individual, ARG2, defined as being made of the material from the default argument.

There are several consequences of this representation which we will not explore in this chapter. One result is that the binding problem in the imperfective

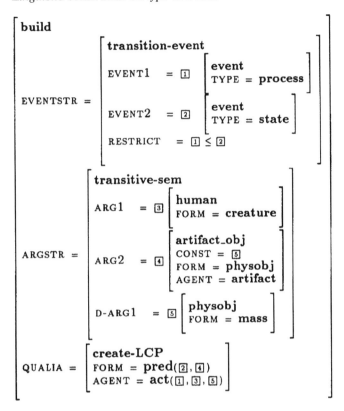

Figure 4.1.

is overcome in a fairly natural way. That is, in a sentence such as *John is building a house*, there is no assertion that a house exists in this atelic form of the event. Rather, this representation asserts no more than that the substance making up some (future) house has been acted upon.

4.2.3 Adjectival semantics

In order to describe the behavior of adjectival modification discussed in section 4.1, such as *the fast car*, we need to make reference to qualia structure once again. To illustrate how, consider the feature-based lexical definition for **car**.

$$\begin{bmatrix} \textbf{car(x)} \\ \text{CONST} = \{\textbf{body,engine,} \ldots\} \\ \text{FORMAL} = \textbf{physobj(x)} \\ \text{TELIC} = \textbf{drive(P,y,x)} \\ \text{AGENTIVE} = \textbf{artifact(x)} \end{bmatrix}$$

Given as a typed lambda-expression, it can be expressed as:

$\lambda x \, [\, car(x) \wedge Const = \{body, engine, \dots \}$
$\qquad \wedge \, Formal = physobj(x)$
$\qquad \wedge \, Telic = \lambda y, e \, [\, drive(x)(y)(e) \,]$
$\qquad \wedge \, Agentive = \lambda y, e \, [\, create(x)(y)(e) \,] \,]$

For our present purposes, we abbreviate these functions as Q_F, Q_C, Q_T, Q_A. When applied, they return the value of a particular qualia role. For example, the purpose of a car is for driving, it comes about by being created, and so on.

$Q_{T(car)} = \lambda x \lambda y [\, drive(x)(y) \,]$
$Q_{A(car)} = \lambda x \lambda y [\, create(x)(y) \,]$

Certain modifiers can be seen as modifying only one or a subset of the qualia for a noun, resulting in a type of restricted modification. Formally, we can accomplish this by making reference to the system of subtyping mentioned earlier; that is, an element is actually a set of type features structured as a semi-lattice.

This allows us to go beyond treating adjectives such as *fast* (see Figure 4.2) as intersective modifiers, for example, $\lambda x [car'(x) \wedge fast'(x)]$. Let us assume that an adjective such as *fast* is a member of the general type $<[N],[N]>$, but can be subtyped as applying to the *Telic* role of the noun being modified, as already argued. That is, it has as its type, $<[N \, Telic],[N]>$. The interpretation of the partial noun phrase, *fast car* can now be given as:[9]

$\lambda x \, [\, car(x) \wedge Const = \{body, engine, \dots \}$
$\qquad \wedge \, Formal = physobj(x)$
$\qquad \wedge \, Telic = \lambda y, e \, [\, drive(x)(y)(e)$
$\qquad \wedge \, fast(e) \,]$
$\qquad \wedge \, Agentive = \lambda y, e \, [\, create(x)(y)(e) \,] \,]$

Given that types can refer to type features, we can treat restrictive modification as a function application with coercion in the following manner. Following our previous discussion, we assume that a function can coerce its argument into a specified type just in case there is an alias σ which, when applied to the argument, gives the desired type. Notice from the previous example discussed, *fast car*, that the *Telic* interpretation of *fast* is available only because the head has a *Telic* value

$$\begin{bmatrix} \textbf{fast} \\ \\ \text{ARGSTR} = \begin{bmatrix} \textbf{event-modifier} \\ \\ \text{ARG1} \quad = \; \boxed{1} \begin{bmatrix} \textbf{event} \\ \text{TYPE} = \textbf{process} \end{bmatrix} \end{bmatrix} \\ \\ \text{QUALIA} = \begin{bmatrix} \textbf{event-mod-LCP} \\ \text{TELIC} = \textbf{fast}(\boxed{1}) \end{bmatrix} \end{bmatrix}$$

Figure 4.2.

specified. This indicates that for the noun type N, a type feature $[N\ Telic]$ is available as an inclusion polymorphism. Therefore, we can treat the semantics of such restrictive modification as follows: if α is of type $<[N\ Q],N>$, and β is of type N, then $[\![\alpha\beta]\!]=\beta \cap \alpha(Q_\beta)$. Thus, the role played by a type features is to allow a composition to be well formed, while restricting the scope of the denotation of the adjective.

4.3   Varieties of coercion

In this section I describe the range of coercion types in natural language. This is certainly not an exhaustive listing, but it gives an indication of just how languages may express polymorphic behavior through the application of coercion rules.

Type shifting, discussed in Geach (1972), and later in Partee and Rooth (1983), Partee (1992), Klein and Sag (1985), and Chierchia (1984), was first proposed as a way of allowing an NP, or any expression in general, to change its type (and hence its denotation) depending on the context. Briefly, we can imagine an expression being assigned a default typing, where the model defines what the well-defined and undefined type shiftings allowed for that expression are. The types for an expresssion are related by what Partee and Rooth call a *type ladder*. The utility of this proposal is obvious. It allows us to maintain a compositional semantics while also accounting for the different manifestations of an expression in a fairly principled way.

Some examples of type shifting will make this point clear. In sentence (14), *John* is originally typed as an individual, that is, e.

(14)   John and every woman arrived.

Yet the NP *every woman* is a generalized quantifier, and hence of type $<<e,t>,t>$. According to standard restrictions on coordination, the conjuncts must be of like type, which they are not. But there is an interpretation of *John* as a generalized quantifier, namely, $\lambda P[P(j)]$. Therefore, in this type of context, we see a kind of mutual constraint satisfaction occurring where the conjuncts sort it out, and arrive at a mutually compatible type; namely, $<<e,t>,t>$.

(15)   a.   John and every woman arrived.
        b.   *every woman*; type $<<e,t>,t> = \lambda P\ \forall\ x[woman'(x) \rightarrow P(x)]$
        c.   *John;* type e shifts to $<<e,t>t>$: $j \Rightarrow \lambda P[P(j)]$.

Type shifting has also been useful for bringing together two distinct approaches to the semantics of interrogatives, as proposed recently by Groonendijk and Stokhof (1989).

4.3.1   *Parametric polymorphisms*

Perhaps the most direct type shifting phenomenon in natural language involves what Strachey (1967) calls parametric polymorphism. Leiß (1991) and Shieber (1992) treat conjunction operators as true polymorphic operators taking *any* type as argument. For this reason, such lexical items are said to be parametric polymorphic. For example, *and* is able to conjoin almost any category X at any bar level in English. There are very few types of lexical items which have this behavior. As we shall see, the polymorphism witnessed by most words is of a very different nature.

4.3.2   *True type coercion*

Unlike parametric polymorphism, true type coercion involves the strict shifting of one type to another specified type, licensed by lexical governance. Furthermore, the shift is not arbitrary, but embeds the existing type into the resulting type by the proper coercion operation. Let us return to the paradigm mentioned in section 4.1:

(16)   a. Mary wants **a beer**.
        b. Mary wants **a cigarette**.
(17)   a. Mary enjoyed **the movie**.
        b. Mary enjoyed **watching the movie**.
(18)   a. John began **a novel**.
        b. John began **reading a novel**.
        c. John began **to read a novel**.

In order to capture the semantic relatedness of these different verb forms (as well as the similarity of the complement denotations), we will need to invoke a coercion rule to ensure that the semantic type of the verb is satisfied in all these cases, regardless of syntactic form.

The rule of function application with coercion (FA$_c$) given in section 4.2 describes just how the semantic transformation comes about. For a lexical structure such as *begin*, see Figure 4.3; the typing on the second argument is explicitly given as an event. Where that type is not satisfied, a coercion results. The coercion is, of course, successful only if the NP has available to it an alias of the appropriate type (Pustejovsky and Boguraev, 1993).

Given the representation of *novel* in section 4.2, the composition results in the following derivation for the sentence in (18a).

(19)   a. John began a novel.
        b. **begin'** $(Q_T(\text{a novel}))(\text{John}) \Rightarrow$
        c. **begin'** $(\lambda x, e^T[read(\text{a novel})(x)(e^T)])(\text{John}) \Rightarrow$
        d. **John**$\{\lambda x[\text{begin'}\ (\lambda x, e^T[read(\text{a novel})(x)(e^T)](x^*))(x^*)]\} \Rightarrow$
        e. **John**$\{\lambda x[\text{begin'}\ (\lambda e^T[read(\text{a novel})(x^*)(e^T)])(x^*)]\} \Rightarrow$
        f. **begin'** $(\lambda e^T[read(\text{a novel})(\text{John})(e^T)])(\text{John})$

This is equivalent to the feature structure form shown in Figure 4.4.

What are the constraints on the application of this kind of coercion? Intuitively, it appears that an event interpretation is available for an object only if it has a specific kind of qualia structure. In particular, one where either the TELIC or AGENTIVE roles are specified. For any object with QUALIA = $[q_a, q_t, q_c, q_f]$, where the base type is some q_i, there are alias types for q_i derived by *pumping*

$$
\begin{bmatrix}
\textbf{begin} \\[4pt]
\text{EVENTSTR} = \begin{bmatrix}
\textbf{transition-event} \\[4pt]
\text{EVENT1} \quad = \boxed{1} \begin{bmatrix} \textbf{event} \\ \text{TYPE} = \textbf{state} \end{bmatrix} \\[10pt]
\text{EVENT2} \quad = \boxed{2} \begin{bmatrix} \textbf{event} \\ \text{TYPE} = \text{inch}(\boxed{4}) \end{bmatrix}
\end{bmatrix} \\[30pt]
\text{ARGSTR} = \begin{bmatrix}
\textbf{transitive-sem} \\[4pt]
\text{ARG1} \quad = \boxed{3} \begin{bmatrix} \textbf{human} \\ \text{FORM} = \textbf{creature} \end{bmatrix} \\[10pt]
\text{ARG2} \quad = \boxed{4} \begin{bmatrix} \textbf{event} \\ \text{TYPE} = \textbf{transition} \end{bmatrix}
\end{bmatrix} \\[30pt]
\text{QUALIA} = \begin{bmatrix} \textbf{inchoate-LCP} \\ \text{FORM} = \text{pred}(\boxed{2}, \boxed{3}) \end{bmatrix}
\end{bmatrix}
$$

Figure 4.3.

$$
\begin{bmatrix}
\textbf{begin} \\[4pt]
\text{EVENTSTR} = \begin{bmatrix}
\textbf{transition-event} \\[4pt]
\text{EVENT1} \quad = \boxed{1} \begin{bmatrix} \textbf{event} \\ \text{TYPE} = \textbf{state} \end{bmatrix} \\[10pt]
\text{EVENT2} \quad = \boxed{2} \begin{bmatrix} \textbf{event} \\ \text{TYPE} = \text{inch}(\boxed{4}) \end{bmatrix}
\end{bmatrix} \\[30pt]
\text{ARGSTR} = \begin{bmatrix}
\textbf{transitive-sem} \\
\text{ARG1} \quad = \boxed{3} = \text{John} \\[4pt]
\text{ARG2} \quad = \boxed{4} \begin{bmatrix} \textbf{read} \\ \text{ARG1} \; = \boxed{3} \\ \text{ARG2} \; = [\text{a} - \text{novel}] \\ \text{QUALIA} = [\ldots] \end{bmatrix}
\end{bmatrix} \\[30pt]
\text{QUALIA} = \begin{bmatrix} \textbf{inchoate-LCP} \\ \text{FORM} = \text{pred}(\boxed{2}, \boxed{3}) \end{bmatrix}
\end{bmatrix}
$$

Figure 4.4.

the type, creating ad hoc types dynamically. We will refer to this generative device as *type pumping*. Pumping a type to create aliases for an object will follow from the semantic classification of an object. For example, objects with a TELIC value in addition to a base type of q_f will have an alias denoting the event value of the TELIC. Similarly, objects with both TELIC and AGENTIVE values (e.g., artifacts) will have two aliases, denoting the distinct event values of these qualia. The information that an NP of type physobj can be coerced into an event comes from the set of aliases associated with the noun *book*. The aliases derive from the pumping mechanism just mentioned.

In the verb phrase *begin a novel*, the verb *begin* expects a phrase whose semantic type is an event. Because the NP *the book* does not satisfy this type, the verb coerces the NP into an event denotation, one which is available from the head's own qualia structure. Thus, formally, each qualia aspect is a partial function from noun denotations into one of their subconstituents (cf. Pustejovsky, 1993, for details). The verb *begin*, therefore, can be said to semantically select for an argument of type event, instead of requiring three syntactic subcategorization frames.

Notice that there are two event types associated with *book* through the qualia roles TELIC and AGENTIVE. Aliases for a lexical item are inherited from particular qualia structures for that object. For example, any lexical structure with a TELIC constraint specified will inherit the type of that constraint as an alias. This, then, gives us a truly polymorphic treatment of verbs such as *begin*, due to coercion and qualia structure.[10]

Concealed questions

Another true type coercion can be seen with the construction known as "concealed questions". This construction has been studied by Grimshaw (1979), Heim (1979) and others. The phenomenon is illustrated in (20) – (23), where the verb's complement can be paraphrased by an indirect question:

(20)   a. John's favorite drink is obvious.
           = *What John's favorite drink is* is obvious.
       b. That John is silly is obvious.
(21)   a. They revealed the winner of the contest.
           = They revealed *who the winner of the contest is*.
       b. They revealed that John is the winner.
(22)   a. John understands the problem.
           = John understands *what the problem is*.
       b. John understands that there is a problem.

It is useful to think of this alternation in terms of coercion, as it explains which noun classes participate in this particular "metonymic extension". Under a generative lexical analysis, coercion would account for the multiple subcategorizations available in these examples. That is, these verbs would be typed as taking an argument of an interrogative type, while also allowing a simple propositional interpretation. Following Groenendijk and Stokhof (1989), we can assume that embedded interrogatives can be typed as <s,t>. Then the type for *understand* and *reveal* as used above would be <<s,t>,<e,t>>. The verb *know* would presumably also be so typed, but without some further remarks on syntactic constraints on coercion, we might expect all of the following sentences to be well formed, which of course they are not.

(23)　　a.　John knows that Mary bought a car.
　　　　b.　John knows what Mary bought.
　　　　c.　*John knows Mary's buying the car.
　　　　d.　*John knows the purchase of the car.
　　　　e.　John knows the answer.

Thus, for coercion to apply in a completely unconstrained fashion in these cases overgenerates and leaves unexplained why (23c) and (23d) are ungrammatical. This problem awaits further research, and a solution should prove helpful in determining how syntactic effects can contribute to limiting the application of semantic coercion.

4.3.3 *Subtype coercion: Inclusion polymorphism*

The question here is one of determination of the level of type specificity by a function. Within our typing system, we need to ensure that if a function selects for type *a* and input is actually type *a'*, which is a subtype of *a*, it too should be accepted by the function. This is a true polymorphism, and is handled directly by the rules of coercion mentioned in section 4.2. I will not explore the range of this phenomenon, but merely illustrate by example, to point out its relation to the other forms of polymorphism. The relationship between *car* and a subtype of *car*, *Honda*, is shown, where the subtyping relation is indicated by inheritance through the FORMAL role.

$$
\begin{bmatrix}
\textbf{car(x)} \\
\text{CONST} = \{\textbf{body,engine, } \ldots\} \\
\text{FORMAL} = \textbf{physobj(x)} \\
\text{TELIC} = \textbf{drive(P,y,x)} \\
\text{AGENTIVE} = \textbf{artifact(x)}
\end{bmatrix}
$$

As with other lexical inheritance mechanisms, the more specific value for the AGENTIVE role in the following structure supersedes the more general value of artifact in *car*, while still inheriting the values for the other qualia.

$$
\begin{bmatrix}
\textbf{Honda(x)} \\
\text{FORMAL} = \textbf{car(x)} \\
\text{AGENTIVE} = \textbf{create(Honda–Co,x)}
\end{bmatrix}
$$

　Beierle et al. (1992) and others have explored in some detail the formal mechanisms of reasoning over sort hierarchies, and I will not explore the issue any further here.

88   *J. Pustejovsky*

4.3.4   *Package and grind coercion*

Another well-studied type of logical polysemy which can be usefully categorized as coercion is the dual pair of *package* and *grind* operations. In (24) – (26), mass nouns have been packaged by definite articles, while (27) and (28) have mass nouns that are packaged by the Aktionsarten of the proposition.

(24)   Mary loves the wine.
(25)   Mary ate the cheese.
(26)   John drank the beer.
(27)   Sand drifted into the tent (for hours).
(28)   The senator spoke to the people.

Examples involving count nouns which have been ground by a term explicitly typed as applying to mass nouns (i.e., *more*) are (30) and (31). Sentences (29) and (32) involve a particular kind of fruit-grinding, and can be captured as a subtype of a more general grinding mechanism.

(29)   Mary put apple in the yogurt.
(30)   We should add some more wall to this side of the room.
(31)   The ensemble is playing more Mozart this year.
(32)   Adding banana to your diet will lower heart attack risks.

Following Copestake and Briscoe (1992), the lexical semantics for an individual count noun such as *haddock* is shown in Figure 4.5. Although their type system differs in some respects, this is essentially a generative lexical representation as described in section 4.2. Copestake and Briscoe (1992) argue for generative principles of sense derivation, and propose that a lexical rule such as the grinding operation in Figure 4.6 accounts for the "edible mass" sense of individual animals.

$$
\begin{bmatrix}
\textbf{count-noun} \\
\text{ORTH} = \textbf{``haddock''} \\
\text{SYNTAX} = \begin{bmatrix} \text{COUNT} = + \end{bmatrix} \\
\text{RQS} = \begin{bmatrix}
\textbf{animal} \\
\text{SEX} = \textbf{gender} \\
\text{AGE} = \textbf{scalar} \\
\text{EDIBLE} = \textbf{boolean} \\
\text{PHYSICAL-STATE} = \textbf{solid} \\
\text{FORM} = \begin{bmatrix} \textbf{physform} \\ \text{SHAPE} = \textbf{individuated} \end{bmatrix}
\end{bmatrix}
\end{bmatrix}
$$

Figure 4.5.

$$
\text{animal\_grinding} \quad
\begin{bmatrix}
\textbf{grinding} \\[4pt]
1 = \begin{bmatrix} \text{RQS} = \begin{bmatrix} \textbf{animal} \\ \text{EDIBLE} = + \end{bmatrix} \end{bmatrix} \\[10pt]
0 = \begin{bmatrix} \text{RQS} = \textbf{food\_substance} \end{bmatrix}
\end{bmatrix}
$$

Figure 4.6.

This derives the sense of *haddock meat* from the individual fish. Seen in a larger context, this lexical rule is a type coercion operation applying with very specific constraints. Copestake and Briscoe's arguments for generating the mass sense through coercion are convincing, especially since the coercion operation is necessarily available for creative grindings, such as those in (33):

(33)   a. Mary fixed shark for dinner.
        b. The carpenter ants are eating table.
        c. My people don't eat elephant.
        d. There's cat all over the highway.

Within the framework of the generative lexicon, however, a slightly different approach is also possible, one still involving coercion, but with a relational representation for objects such as *haddock*.

$$
\begin{bmatrix}
\textbf{haddock(x,y)} \\
\text{CONST} = \textbf{substance(y)} \\
\text{FORMAL} = \textbf{animal(x)} \\
\text{TELIC} = \textbf{eat(P,w,y)}
\end{bmatrix}
$$

One test we used in section 4.2 for determining the relational status of nominals was the co-predication test, which shows the ability to conjoin where conjuncts express distinct senses, and therefore require different types. As sentence (21) illustrates, co-predication is not a property for nouns such as *haddock* and *lamb*:

(34)   *John fed and carved the lamb (Copestake and Briscoe, 1992).

Since this co-predication results in a zeugma, the formal parameter list for the noun is most likely a single type, where the noun takes only one argument. The ungrammaticality of this sentence indicates that the logical polysemy of animal grinding is indeed due to an explicit application of a coercion rule rather than to a selection operation over a relational noun. Thus, the previous qualia structure is most likely spurious and the one proposed by Copestake and Briscoe is correct.

4.4   Bilateral coercion: Cocompositionality

In this section we discuss those cases of verbal logical polysemy involving *cocomposition* (Pustejovsky, 1991). Briefly, cocomposition describes a structure which contains more than one function application. Studying the polysemy of baking verbs will illustrate our point. For example, in (35), the verb *bake* has two meanings, both a *change of state* sense and a *create* sense (Atkins et al., 1988).

(35)   a. John **baked** the potato.
        b. John **baked** the cake.

Similarly, the verbs in (36) – (39) are ambiguous between a process reading and a transition reading, depending on the presence of a resultative adjectival. Normally, lexicons would have to enter both forms as separate lexical entries (Levin and Rappaport, in press).

(36)   a. Mary wiped the table.
        b. Mary wiped the table dry.
(37)   a. John hammered the metal.
        b. John hammered the metal flat.
(38)   a. Mary waxed the car.
        b. Mary waxed the car clean.
(39)   a. Mary ate.
        b. Mary ate herself sick.

In order to capture the logical polysemy in all these cases and obviate the need for multiple listings of words, Pustejovsky (1991) proposed that the complements carry information which acts on the governing verb, essentially taking the verb as argument and shifting its event type. Here we will make this proposal more explicit and describe what mechanism makes such an operation available.

Let us assume that the lexical structure for a verb such as *bake* is given in Figure 4.7, in terms of orthogonal parameter binding. We wish to claim that there is only one sense for *bake*, and that any other readings are derived through generative mechanisms in composition with its arguments. What we need to explain is why nouns such as *cake*, *bread*, *cookie*, etc. 'shift' the meaning of the verb *bake*, while other nouns (such as *potato*, *garlic*) do not. Intuitively, we would like to capture the fact that the former objects are prototypically brought about by the activity they are in composition with, something that the qualia structure should be able to express. Assume that the qualia for *cake* makes reference to [AGENTIVE = *bake*]. There are natural relations between the qualia. For example, the AGENTIVE refers to the coming about of something which is formally expressed as the FORMAL role.

We will employ another aspect of the type pumping mechanism mentioned earlier; namely, the ability to express relations between the qualia. Assume, as

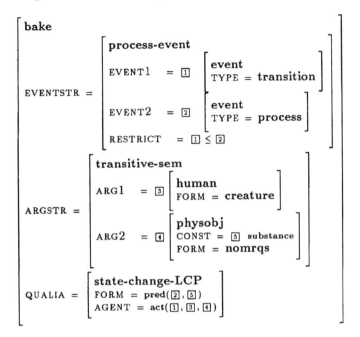

Figure 4.7.

before, an object with QUALIA = $[q_a, q_t, q_c, q_f]$, with base type q_i. Type pumping can also generate aliases which will act applicatively in the semantics. For example, for q_f we have the resulting types $\langle q_a, q_f \rangle$, $\langle q_t, q_f \rangle$, $\langle q_c, q_f \rangle$, $\langle q_a, q_t \rangle$, and so on. Some of these are obviously not meaningful types, but we can imagine the generative expansion of an object's type through this sort of pumping operation. What this operation makes available is a set of aliases for a finer contextual determination of what a word denotes in a specific context. In the context of the example above, it makes the type $\langle q_a, q_f \rangle$ available, which operates over a process to give the formal state denoted by *cake*.

Assuming that the qualia structure for *cake* is given as:

$$\begin{bmatrix} \textbf{cake(x)} \\ \text{CONST} = \{\textbf{flour(z)},\textbf{egg(z')}, \dots \} \\ \text{FORMAL} = \textbf{physobj(x)} \\ \text{TELIC} = \textbf{eat(P,y,x)} \\ \text{AGENTIVE} = \textbf{bake(P,w,x)} \end{bmatrix}$$

We can represent the semantics for the VP *bake a cake* as the feature structure in Figure 4.8. Besides the function application of *bake* to its internal argument, there is function application where a specific alias type of the complement operates over the event type of the predicate *bake* to create a new event type, i.e., a transition. This together with the fact that the AGENTIVE for the complement is iden-

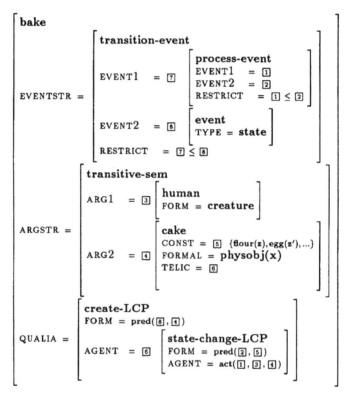

Figure 4.8.

tical to the qualia structure in the verb gives rise to the 'create' sense of *bake*, not
lexically, but *generatively*.[11]

4.5   Conclusion

I have attempted to accomplish two goals in this chapter. First, to point out that
natural language semantics must be viewed in the context of increasingly expressive systems. I suggested that one helpful way to do this is through the notion of
degrees of polymorphism. Second, I have attempted to outline what the range of
coercion types is, and how to think about natural constraints over the application
of these rules. Some of the proposals are incomplete and others merely sugges-
tive, but the thrust of the argument is very clear: we need a semantics with semi-
polymorphic power, and this can be accomplished only by (a) admitting the existence of type coercion phenomena, and (b) studying the constraints applying to
particular coercion types. Only through such an approach can we hope to gain a
better understanding of the creative power of natural language semantics as a distinct process from commonsense understanding and pragmatic inferencing.

Notes

1. One important exception, of course, is Klein and Sag, 1985, who argue for a type-shifting solution for many of these cases. I return to this in section 4.3.3.
2. These shifting operators are generated by an operation called *type pumping*.
3. I will assume a representation within a typed feature structure notation, following Carpenter (1990) and Copestake (1993).
4. Co-predication seems to have a stricter requirement on well-formedness than other (semantically equivalent) constructions, such as relative clauses:

   (i) John used to work for the newspaper that you're reading (cf. Nunberg, 1979).

   One possible explanation for this interesting contrast might be an inherent distinction between predication of the noun within the NP itself versus predication of the entire NP. That is, *newspaper* is unable to take the two predicates in (13) because it is not relationally typed, but internal to the NP, the qualia provide implicit relational opportunities for co-attributions.
5. In fact, Bergler (1992) explores one possible extension to verbal semantic representation, particularly in the context of *reporting verbs*. Bergler's attempt can be seen as a preliminary effort toward an integrated semantic representation for both verbs and nouns within generative lexicon theory. With the introduction of the mechanism of *Orthogonal Parameter Binding*, we can achieve a greater degree of expressiveness relating the semantics of all categories.
6. For details of this proposal, see Pustejovsky (in press).
7. The grammatical consequences of this distinction are analyzed in Pustejovsky (in press).
8. For the purpose of exposition, I adopt the feature notation and style of HPSG (Pollard and Sag, 1987). Furthermore, I am ignoring certain aspects of syntactic variation and verbal alternations as discussed in Sanfilippo (1993). These are addressed more fully in Pustejovsky (in press).
9. Bierwisch (1983) proposes a system of contextual shifts which highlight certain information about an NP while backgrounding other information. See Pustejovsky (in press) for discussion of how these systems differ.
10. What actually drives the type coercion is not entirely clear. For example, since *begin a book* seems to be able to refer to either the 'reading' or the 'writing' events, it may, in fact, be merely event type-satisfaction and not qualia satisfaction.
11. There is a very similar operation taking place with resultative constructions. For details of this proposal see Pustejovsky (in press). The result of this bilateral function application is what I have termed cocomposition.

References

Aït-Kaci, H. (1984). *A Lattice-Theoretic Approach to Computation Based on a Calculus of Partially Ordered Types*. Ph.D. thesis, University of Pennsylvania.

Apresjan, J. (1973). "Regular Polysemy", *Linguistics*, 142.

Atkins, Beryl, Judy Kegl, and Beth Levin, (1988). "Anatomy of a Verb Entry", *Journal of Lexicographic Research*, 1.

Bach, Emmon, (1986). "The Algebra of Events", in *Linguistics and Philosophy* 9, 5–16.

Beierle, C., U. Hedtstück, U. Pletat, P. H. Schmitt, and J. Siekmann, (1992). "An Order-Sorted Logic for Knowledge Representation Systems", *Artificial Intelligence*, 55:149–191.

Bergler, Sabine. (1992). *Evidential Analysis of Reported Speech*, Ph.D. Thesis, Brandeis University.

Cardelli, L. and P. Wegner. (1985). On Understanding Types, Data Abstraction and Polymorphism, *ACM Computing Surveys*, pp. 471–522.

Carpenter, B. (1992). "Typed Feature Structures", *Computational Linguistics*, 18:2.

Chierchia, G. (1984). *Topics in the Syntax and Semantics of Infinitives and Gerunds*, Ph.D. thesis, U. of Massachusetts, Amherst.

Chomsky, Noam. (1955). *The Logical Structure of Linguistic Theory*, University of Chicago Press.

Chomsky, N. (1957). *Syntactic Structures*, Mouton, The Hague.

Chomsky, Noam. (1981). *Lectures on Government and Binding*, Foris Publications, Dordrecht, Holland.

Copestake, Ann. (1992). "The ACQUILEX LKB: Representation Issues in Semi-Automatic Acquisition of Large Lexicons", *Proceedings of Third Conference on Applied Natural Language Processing*, Trento, Italy, pp. 88–95.

Copestake, Ann. (in press). "Defaults in the LKB", in T. Briscoe and A. Copestake (Eds.) *Default Inheritance in the Lexicon*, Cambridge University Press.

Copestake, A. and E. Briscoe. (1992). "Lexical Operations in a Unification-Based Framework", in J. Pustejovsky and S. Bergler (Eds.), *Lexical Semantics and Knowledge Representation*, Springer Verlag, New York.

Croft, William. (1986). *Categories and Relations in Syntax: The Clause-Level Organization of Information*, Ph.D. Dissertation, Stanford University.

Cruse, D. A. (1986). *Lexical Semantics*, Cambridge University Press.

Dowty, David R. (1979). *Word Meaning and Montague Grammar*, D. Reidel, Dordrecht, Holland.

Dowty, David R. (1985). "On Some Recent Analyses of Control", *Linguistics and Philosophy* 8: 1–41.

Dowty, David R. (1989). "On the Semantic Content of the Notion 'Thematic Role'", in *Properties, Types, and Meaning Volume II*, edited by Gennaro Chierchia, Barbara Partee, and Raymond Turner, Kluwer Academic Publishers, Dordrecht.

Evans, Roger and Gerald Gazdar. (1990). "The DATR papers: February 1990." Cognitive Science Research Paper CSRP 139, School of Cognitive and Computing Science, University of Sussex, Brighton, England.

Fillmore, Charles. (1968). "The Case for Case", in *Universals in Linguistic Theory*, E. Bach and R. Harms (Eds.). New York, Holt, Rinehart, and Winston.

Fillmore, Charles. (1985). "Construction Grammar", ms.

Fodor, Jerry. (1975). *The Language of Thought*, Harvard University Press, Cambridge.

Gazdar, G. , E. Klein, G. Pullum, and I. Sag. (1985). *Generalized Phrase Structure Grammar*, Harvard University Press.

Geach, P. (1972). "A Program for Syntax", in D. Davidson and G. Harman (Eds.), *Semantics of Natural Language*, Dordrecht, Reidel.

Goodman, Nelson. (1951). *The Structure of Appearance* , Reidel Publishing, Dordrecht.

Grice, H. P. (1971). "Meaning", in *Semantics: An Interdisciplinary Reader in Philosophy, Linguistics, and Psychology*, D. Steinberg and L. Jacobovits (Eds.), Cambridge, Cambridge University Press.

Grimshaw, Jane. (1979). "Complement Selection and the Lexicon", *Linguistic Inquiry* 10: 279–326.

Grimshaw, Jane. (1990). *Argument Structure*, MIT Press, Cambridge, MA.

Groenendijk, J., and M. Stokhof. (1989). "Type-Shifting Rules and the Semantics of Interrogatives", in G. Chierchia, B. Partee, and R. Turner (Eds.), *Properties, Types, and Meaning*, Dordrecht, Reidel.

Heim, I. (1979). "Concealed Questions", in R. Bäuerle, U. Egli, and A. von Stechow (Eds.), *Semantics from Different Points of View*, Springer, Berlin.

Hirst, Graeme. (1987). *Semantic Interpretation and the Resolution of Ambiguity*, Cambridge University Press, Cambridge.

Hobbs, Jerry. (1987). "World Knowledge and Word Meaning", in *Proceedings of TINLAP-3*, Las Cruces, New Mexico.

Hobbs, Jerry, William Croft, Todd Davies, Douglas Edwards, and Kenneth Laws. (1987). "Commonsense Metaphysics and Lexical Semantics", *Computational Linguistics*, Vol. 13, No. 3–4.

Hobbs, Jerry, Mark Stickel, Paul Martin, Douglas Edwards. (1988). "Interpretation as Abduction", in *Proceedings of the 26th Annual Meeting of the Association for Computational Linguistics*, Buffalo, published in Morristown, N.J.

Ingria, Robert and James Pustejovsky. (1988). "Active Objects in Syntax and Semantics", in C. Tenny (Ed.), MIT Working Papers in Parsing.

Jackendoff, Ray. (1972). *Semantic Interpretation in Generative Grammar*, MIT Press, Cambridge, MA.

Jackendoff, Ray. (1983). *Semantics and Cognition*, MIT Press, Cambridge, MA.

Katz, J. (1964). "Semantic Theory and the Meaning of 'Good'", *Journal of Philosophy*, 61:739–66.

Katz, Jerrold J. (1972). *Semantic Theory*, Harper and Row, New York.

Katz, Jerrold J. and Jerry Fodor, "The Structure of a Semantic Theory", *Language,* 39.2: 170–210.

Karttunen, Lauri. (1971). "Implicative Verbs", *Language* 47: 340–58, 1971.

Keenan, Edward, and Leonard Faltz. (1985). *Boolean Semantics for Natural Language*, Reidel Publishing, Dordrecht.

Klein, E. and I. Sag. (1985). "Type-Driven Translation", *Linguistics and Philosophy*, 8, 163–202.

Klein, E. and J. van Benthem. (1987). *Categories, Polymorphism, and Unification*, Centre for Cognitive Science, University of Edinburgh, and Institute for Language, Logic and Information, University of Amsterdam.

Lakoff, George. (1970). *Irregularity in Syntax*. Holt, Rinehart, and Winston.

Lakoff, George. (1987). *Women, Fire, and Dangerous Objects*, University of Chicago Press, Chicago.

Leiß, H. (1991) "Polymorphic Constructs in Natural and Programming Languages", *Semantics of Programming Languages*, Springer, Berlin.

Levin, B. (1985). (ed.). Lexical Semantics in Review, Lexicon Project Working Paper 1, Center for Cognitive Science, MIT Press, Cambridge, MA.

Levin, B. (1993). *Towards a Lexical Organization of English Verbs*, University of Chicago Press, Chicago, IL.

Levin, B. and T.R. Rapoport. (1988). "Lexical Subordination", *Proceedings of CLS 24*, 275–289.

Levin, Beth and Malka Rappaport. (1986). "The Formation of Adjectival Passives", *Linguistic Inquiry*, 17.4.

Levin, Beth and Malka Rappaport. (1988). "On the Nature of Unaccusativity", in *Proceedings of NELS 1988*.

Levin, Beth and Malka Rappaport. (in press). *Unaccusatives*, MIT Press, Cambridge, MA.

Lloyd, G.E.R. (1968). *Aristotle: The Growth and Structure of His Thought*, Cambridge University Press.

McKeon, Richard. (1941). *The Basic Works of Aristotle*, Random House.

Miller, G. (1991). *The Science of Words*, Scientific American Press.

Milner, R. (1978). "A Theory of Type Polymorphism in Programming", *Journal of Computer and System Science*, 17: 348–375.

Moens, M. (1992). "Review of *Events in the Semantics of English*", Language.

Montague, Richard (1974). *Formal Philosophy: The Collected Papers of Richard Montague*, Richard Thomason (Ed.), New Haven, Yale University Press.

Moravcsik, J. M. (1975). "Aita as Generative Factor in Aristotle's Philosophy", *Dialogue*.

Mourelatos, Alexander. (1981). "Events, Processes, and States", in *Syntax and Semantics: Tense and Aspect*, P. Tedeschi and A. Zaenen (Eds.), Academic Press, New York.

Nunberg, G. (1978). *The Pragmatics of Reference*. Indiana University Linguistics Club: Bloomington, Indiana.

Nunberg, G. (1979). "The Non-Uniqueness of Semantic Solutions: Polysemy", *Linguistics and Philosophy* 3: 143–184.

Ostler, N. and B. T. S. (1992). Atkins, "Predictable Meaning Shift: Some Linguistic Properties of Lexical Implications Rules", in J. Pustejovsky and S. Bergler (Eds.), *Lexical Semantics and Knowledge Representation*, Springer Verlag, New York.

Parsons, T. (1990). *Events in the Semantics of English*, Bradford Books / MIT Press, Cambridge.

Passonneau, Rebecca J. (1988). "A Computational Model of the Semantics of Tense and Aspect", *Computational Linguistics*, 14.2.

Partee, Barbara. (1992). "Syntactic Categories and Semantic Type", in M. Rosner and R. Johnson (Eds.), *Computational Linguistics and Formal Semantics*, Cambridge University Press.

Partee, B. and M. Rooth. (1983). "Generalized Conjunction and Type Ambiguity", in *Meaning, Use, and Interpretation of Language*, Bäuerle, Schwarze, and von Stechow (Eds.)., Walter de Gruyter.

Pollard, C. and I. Sag. (1987). *Information-Based Syntax and Semantics 1: Fundamental*, Center for the Study of Language and Information, Stanford, CA.

Pustejovsky, James. (1989). "Type Coercion and Selection", in *Proceedings of West Coast Conference on Formal Linguistics*, Vancouver.

Pustejovsky, James. (1989). "Issues in Computational Lexical Semantics", in the *Proceedings of the Fourth European ACL Conference*, April 10–12, 1989, Manchester, England.

Pustejovsky, James. (1992). "The Generative Lexicon", *Computational Linguistics*, 17(4).

Pustejovsky, J. (1992). "Principles versus Criteria: On Randall's Catapult Hypothesis", in Weissenborn, J., H. Goodluck, and T. Roeper (Eds.), *Theoretical Issues in Language Acquisition*, Kluwer Academic Publishers, Dordrecht.

Pustejovsky, James. (1993). "Type Coercion and Lexical Selection", in J. Pustejovsky (Ed.), *Semantics and the Lexicon*, Kluwer Academic Publishers.

Pustejovsky, James. (in press). *The Generative Lexicon: a Theory of Computational Lexical Semantics*, MIT Press.

Pustejovsky, James. (unpublished ms.). "Verbal Semantics in a Generative Lexicon".

Pustejovsky, James and Peter Anick, "On the Semantic Interpretation of Nominals", in *Proceedings of COLING-1988*, Budapest, 1988.

Pustejovsky, James and Bran Boguraev (1993). "Lexical Knowledge Representation and Natural Language Processing", *Artificial Intelligence* 63: 170–210.

Sag, I. and C. Pollard. (1991). "An Integrated Theory of Complement Control", *Language*, 67: 1, 63–113.

Sanfillipo, Antonio. (1993). "The LKB: A System for Representing Lexical Information extracted from Machine-Readable Dictionaries", in T. Briscoe and A. Copestake (Eds.), *Default Inheritance in the Lexicon*, Cambridge University Press.

Scha, Remko J. H. (1983). "Logical Foundations for Question Answering", Ms. 12.331 Philips Research Laboratories, Eindhoven, the Netherlands.

Searle, J. (1979). *Expression and Meaning*, Cambridge, Cambridge University Press.

Shieber, S. (1986). *An Introduction to Unification-Based Approaches to Grammar*, Center for the Study of Language and Information, Stanford, CA.

Shieber, S. (1992). *Constraint-Based Grammar Formalisms: Parsing And Type Inference for Natural and Computer Languages*, MIT Press, Cambridge, MA.

Sowa, J. (1992). "Logical Structures in the Lexicon", in J. Pustejovsky and S. Bergler (Eds.), *Lexical Semantics and Knowledge Representation*, Springer Verlag, New York.

Strachey, C. (1967). "Fundamental Concepts in Programming Languages", Lecture Notes for International Summer School in Computer Programming, Copenhagen.

Talmy, Len. (1975). "Semantics and Syntax of Motion", in J. P. Kimball (Ed.), *Syntax and Semantics 4*, Academic Press, New York.

Talmy, Len. (1985). "Lexicalization Patterns", in *Language Typology and Syntactic Description*, Timothy Shopen (Ed.), Cambridge, 1985.

Touretzky, David S. (1986). *The Mathematics of Inheritance Systems*, Morgan Kaufmann, Los Altos, CA.

Vendler, Zeno. (1967). *Linguistics and Philosophy*, Cornell University Press, Ithaca.

Weinreich, U. (1959). "Travels through Semantic Space", *Word* 14: 346–366.

Weinreich, U. (1963). "On the Semantic Structure of Language", in J. Greenberg (Ed.), *Universal of Language*, MIT Press, Cambridge, MA.

Weinreich, U. (1964). "*Webster's Third*: A Critique of its Semantics", *International Journal of American Linguistics* 30: 405–409.

Weinreich, U. (1972). *Explorations in Semantic Theory*, Mouton, The Hague.

Wilks, Yorick. (1975). "A Preferential Pattern Seeking Semantics for Natural Language Inference", *Artificial Intelligence*, 6, 53–74.

Wright, Georg H. von. (1963). *Norm and Action: A Logical Inquiry*, Routledge and Kegan Paul, London.

5   From lexical semantics to text analysis

SABINE BERGLER

5.1   Motivation

One of the major challenges today is coping with an overabundance of potentially important information. With newspapers such as the *Wall Street Journal* available electronically as a large text database, the analysis of natural language texts for the purpose of information retrieval has found renewed interest. Knowledge extraction and knowledge detection in large text databases are challenging problems, most recently under investigation in the TIPSTER projects funded by DARPA, the U.S. Department of Defense research funding agency. Traditionally, the parameters in the task of information retrieval are the style of analysis (statistical or linguistic), the domain of interest (TIPSTER, for instance, focuses on news concerning micro-chip design and joint ventures), the task (filling database entries, question answering, etc.), and the representation formalism (templates, Horn clauses, KL-ONE, etc.).

It is the premise of this chapter that much more detailed information can be gleaned from a careful linguistic analysis than from a statistical analysis. Moreover, a successful linguistic analysis provides more *reliable* data, as we hope to illustrate here. The problem is, however, that linguistic analysis is very costly and that systems that perform complete, reliable analysis of newspaper articles do not currently exist.

The challenge then is to find ways to do linguistic analysis when it is possible and to the extent that it is feasible. We claim that a promising approach is to perform a careful linguistic *preprocessing* of the texts, representing linguistically encoded information in a task independent, faithful, and reusable representation scheme.

We propose a representation scheme, MTR[1] (for Minimal Text Representation) that does not constitute a text interpretation (nor does it "extract" or "detect" any particular information) but rather forms a common intermediate representation that must be further processed with the particular domain, task, and representation formalism in mind. The benefit of an intermediate representation at the level of MTR is that certain computationally expensive linguistic analyses do not have to be reduplicated for different tasks.

The introduction of an intermediate representation (which has to be further evaluated) that also supports *partial* representation and thus *incremental* analysis of texts enables the cooperation of independent and specialized analysis modules that can be developed partly independently.

Recent research in robust partial parsing points in the same direction. SPARSER (McDonald, 1992), for instance, is able to determine names of corporations, institutions, positions, and persons based on linguistic heuristics even when the words involved are unknown to the system. The correct determination of proper names in newspaper articles is an important step in information retrieval. Used as a preprocessor, SPARSER's linguistic knowledge about names can therefore be useful even to information retrieval based on statistical methods.

It is the goal of this chapter to suggest that similar modules of partial linguistic analysis can be defined for different problems. These modules can be helpful only if they are sufficiently general to be adopted in different systems with different parameter settings and they have to yield a cumulative result when used together in one system.

One requirement for modular partial analysis is a clear delimitation of the task and the problem addressed. Our task domain here is newspaper text. Regularities in newspaper style have to be exploited when the task is bound to newspaper articles. Let us call the characteristics of a particular text type and style a *substyle* in analogy to the term *sublanguage*. In order to define a substyle, stylistic and even pragmatic information about the domain has to be linked to basic linguistic knowledge, such as word meaning, in a systematic, modular way.

Here we claim that such a systematic linking of lexical semantics and stylistic/pragmatic knowledge in fact provides the basis for a solution of the problem of analyzing reported speech in newspaper articles.

Reported speech[2] is a very frequent phenomenon. Especially in the American newspaper tradition we find articles where 90% of the sentences are instances of reported speech. Without a treatment of reported speech we cannot arrive at a general treatment of newspaper texts.

Reported speech has been discussed in the linguistic literature mostly under the aspect of *intentionality* (Quine, 1940, Davidson, 1968). Like verbs of belief and verbs of cognition, the reporting verb introduces an embedded statement that does not necessarily have to be asserted by the speaker of an instance of reported speech. Worse, the references contained in the embedded statement do not have to be "de re", that is, understandable or accurate out of the context of the original utterance situation. Reported speech is even harder to handle than belief contexts, because reporting what somebody else said does not necessarily imply the original speaker's attitude toward the statement; he or she may well have lied, a fact of which the reporter may be aware.

This theoretical complexity of the phenomenon of reported speech may be the reason why most computational models of text analysis do not account for it or subsume reported speech under the larger category of *propositional attitudes* (Nirenburg and Defrise, 1992). A careful study of reported speech as it occurs in newspaper articles, however, reveals that reported speech plays a very specific role in newspaper articles and does not exhibit the full range of complexity that has been discussed in the literature (Bergler, 1992).

In this study we found that the function of reported speech in newspaper articles is to provide *evidence* for the embedded statement by citing the source, in fact providing an *evaluative environment* for the *interpretation* of the reported statement.[3] It is, in fact, the lexical semantics of the matrix clause that sets up proper evaluation of the reported statement by supplying necessary background information. The lexical semantics *enables* but does not *determine* this evaluation; individual readers will supply their individual views for full evaluation.

5.2   Reported speech in newspaper texts

We recognize newspaper style, even out of the context of a newspaper, immediately and without hesitation. Yet the syntactic structures used are so varied that even part of speech determination presents a real problem for automatic analysis. The distinct style of newspaper articles is therefore not due to a simplified set of syntactic constructions. It is in fact so characteristic because it employs complex constructions, such as embedded sentences (among them reported speech) and heavy noun phrases, disproportionately more often than is usual in spoken language or fiction. To a human reader this extra level of complexity is, however, not an obstacle but often a useful tool for efficient knowledge extraction. Heavy noun phrases, for instance, provide a compact characterization of a discourse entity, usually at the beginning of a sentence, *at the level relevant for the article.*

Conventionalized patterns, no matter how complex, help the reader to navigate through the information presented. Newspaper articles exhibit highly conventionalized patterns at all levels.

One convention is to validate the accuracy and reliability of information presented by identifying the source of the information, usually in form of *reported speech.* Reported speech thus embeds factual information, called *primary information*, within the scope of a source and the circumstances of the original utterance, called *circumstantial information.*

The New York Times, December 8, 1990

The Ford Motor Company and Volkswagen A. G. of Germany are nearing agreement on a joint venture for European production of mini-vans. The vehicles' popularity is growing rapidly in Western Europe.

Volkswagen's supervisory board approved plans for the factory on Nov. 16, and the tentative agreement will go to Ford's board of directors next week. The British newspaper *The Financial Times* said the plant was expected to have a production capacity of 150,000 to 200,000 vehicles a year and could involve an investment of $2.5 billion to $3 billion. Ford and Volkswagen would not comment on those figures.

Figure 5.1. Text 1.

Consider the use of reported speech in Text 1. The sentence *The British newspaper The Financial Times said the plant was expected to have a production capacity of 150,000 to 200,000 vehicles a year and could involve an investment of $2.5 billion to $3 billion.* is certainly surprising: if the two companies involved do not want to disclose their estimates of the volume of the proposed production, how can The Financial Times have that information? And, more important, what is the status of this information?

The information attributed to *The Financial Times* is *hearsay* and it is marked as such. It is therefore of a lesser authority than the information that is not modified. However, it cannot be discarded off hand. The reporter has deemed the information pertinent enough to include it in the article and has chosen a description of the source that attributes some reliability: *The Financial Times* is a respected newspaper that would not risk its reputation if it didn't have an excellent source for this information. The embedded information therefore does not have a determined status of reliability; this assessment has to be made by the reader under consideration of the types of inferences that are to be drawn from it.[4]

An *evidential* analysis[5] preserves this role of the matrix clause as evidence for the reliability of the primary information of the complement clause. It does not provide the assessment of reliability for the primary information, just as the text does not. For any given purpose this assessment has to be made under the set of beliefs and the point of view of the reasoning system that wants to make use of the primary information; this step is thus beyond linguistic analysis.

5.3   Argumentative structure

The role of the reported speech in Text 1 is to present some information that is illustrative of the size of the planned project even though it was not confirmed by the involved parties. The use of reported speech then clearly attributes this information to a different source, marking it as less reliable. But not all use of reported speech indicates less reliability. Frequently, the whole story comes from one source (a press release, an interview) or is a mosaic of statements by different sources. In the latter case it is important to understand the *argumentative* structure (Cohen, 1987) of the statements made by different sources, i.e., whether they support and complement each other or whether they oppose each other.

We can distinguish three different cases depending on the topic of the article, namely

1. A single source is responsible for all the attributed statements.
2. Several sources contribute to the same point.
3. Two or more sources support different or opposing points.

Let us illustrate the importance that the position of a reported statement in the argumentative structure plays in the interpretation and evaluation of that statement with an example.

Who's News: Pacific Enterprises Chooses Ukropina As Chief Executive
By Jeff Rowe

(S₁) Pacific Enterprises named its president, James R. Ukropina, as chairman and chief executive, succeeding Paul A. Miller and ending a century of family leadership at the utility holding company.

(S₂) Analysts said the naming of Mr. Ukropina represented a conservative move by an unusually conservative utility concern. (S₃) Unlike some companies, Pacific Enterprises has "made no major errors moving outside their area of expertise," said Craig Schwerdt, an analyst with Seidler Amdec Securities Inc. in Los Angeles.

(S₄) "Each of the company's businesses are positioned to do well in the coming year," said Paul Milbauer, an analyst with C.J. Lawrence, Morgan Grenfell in New York. (S₅) Most of the company's retail operations are in the fast-growing West, and the gas unit will benefit from tightening environmental regulations, he said. (S₆) He added that more-stringent pollution controls are expected to increase demand for gas, which is relatively clean-burning.

Wall Street Journal, 10/5/89

Figure 5.2. Text 2

Consider Text 2 from the *Wall Street Journal*. Sentence S_1 introduces the topic of the article. In accordance with the observations of Lundquist (1989), the first sentence of an article in the *Wall Street Journal* usually summarizes the salient information of the article, and most important, introduces the individuals, companies, institutions, or products that form the *topic* of the article. Sentence S_2 presents an evaluation of S_1 (the gist of the evaluation becomes clear only after the third sentence, however). Sentences $S_3 - S_6$ serve to elaborate (and support) S_2. The support comes from two independent sources that offer complementary information. This simplified coherence structure for Text 2 is represented in Figure 5.3.

The two analysts provide complementary information, thus implicitly strengthening each other's statements.[6] This makes the interpretation easy: the reporter wants to indicate that the fact reported in (S_1) is considered positive. Note that the endorsement is stronger coming from two independent analysts rather than an employee of the enterprise, as illustrated in Variation 1.

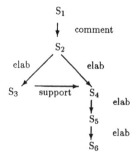

Figure 5.3. Simplified coherence structure for Text 2.

Variation 1

(S$_1$) Pacific Enterprises named its president, James R. Ukropina, as chairman and chief executive, succeeding Paul A. Miller and ending a century of family leadership at the utility holding company.

(S$_2'$) Pacific Enterprises said the naming of Mr. Ukropina represented a conservative move. (S$_3'$) Unlike some companies, Pacific Enterprises has "made no major errors moving outside their area of expertise," said Craig Schwerdt, a spokesman for Pacific Enterprises.

Figure 5.4. Variation 1 of Text 2.

(S$_2'$), slightly shortened, is now a statement attributed to the company itself, elaborated by Craig Schwerdt, now identified as a spokesman for Pacific Enterprises. While not different in content, the strength of the endorsement is somewhat weaker in this case, illustrating that statements made by employees of the company under discussion are not always stronger; they tend to be stronger for factual statements and negative evaluations or comments but weaker in the case of positive comments.

A case where the level of endorsement depends entirely on the judgment of the reader is when the reporter presents two (or more) differing opinions without any bias toward one or the other. These cases are not as frequent as the simpler cases where a bias becomes clear and a differing opinion is added for completeness but they do occur. Let us illustrate this case with a second variation of Text 1.

In Variation 2 the statements of the two independent analysts have been changed to oppose each other by changing the underlined items. Note that for minimal coherence we had to change more than the positive words in the second analyst's statements; we had to oppose the matrix clauses minimally by introducing polarization. We achieved that by changing (S$_2''$) to read *one analyst*, which sets up polarity between the statements of the two analysts. This is complemented

Variation 2

(S$_1$) Pacific Enterprises named its president, James R. Ukropina, as chairman and chief executive, succeeding Paul A. Miller and ending a century of family leadership at the utility holding company.

(S$_2''$) One analyst said the naming of Mr. Ukropina represented a conservative move by an unusually conservative utility concern. (S$_3$) Unlike some companies, Pacific Enterprises has "made no major errors moving outside their area of expertise," said Craig Schwerdt, an analyst with Seidler Amdec Securities Inc. in Los Angeles.

(S$_4''$) "None of the company's businesses are positioned to do well in the coming year," insisted Paul Milbauer, an analyst with C. J. Lawrence, Morgan Grenfell in New York. (S$_5''$) Most of the company's retail operations are in the fast-growing West, and the gas unit will suffer from tightening environmental regulations, he said.

Figure 5.5. Variation 2 of Text 2.

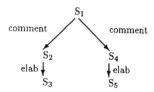

Figure 5.6. Simplified coherence structure for Variation 2 of Text 2.

by changing the reporting verb in (S_4'') to *insisted*, a verb that incorporates an opposition lexically (see Bergler, 1991, for details on *insist*).

Variation 2 displays a different coherence structure from the original text. Both S_2'' and S_4'' are independent comments on S_1 elaborated by S_3 and S_5'' respectively. The simplified coherence structure for Variation 2 is given in Figure 5.6. The coherence structure indicates that the statements of the two analysts do not elaborate on any common statement.

Unless a newspaper article conveys a simple announcement, the reporter will usually present different viewpoints on the same issue in order to balance the report. The reporter therefore implicitly constructs a possible argument. To detect the structure of the argument is a major component in the understanding of these articles, as Cohen (1987) points out. Variations 1 and 2 of Text 2 make this point obvious.

While the variations are not as felicitous as the original article in Text 2, they still demonstrate that almost identical factual material can be used to make very different points and can receive vastly different interpretations by different readers depending on the source of the information. The different texts also showed that the matrix clause of reported speech has a strong influence on the role the reported statement plays in the overall text. The next section will investigate the role of one component of the matrix clause, the source, in more detail.

5.4   The source

The matrix clause of reported speech contains two mandatory roles, namely, the source of the information in subject position and the reporting verb. We claim that the function of the matrix clause of reported speech in newspaper articles is to index the embedded statement with an *evaluative environment*, i.e., to provide the basic information necessary to evaluate the *reliability* or *credibility* of that statement (Bergler, 1991, 1992).

The last section demonstrated that the source is a major evaluation criteria for a reported statement. We distinguish three aspects that contribute to a source's reliability, namely

(1)   (a) Identity and personal attributes of the source.
         (b) Official position or role of the source.
         (c) Relevance of the source to the topic.

Note that these aspects are not necessarily all known or disclosed to the reader of a newspaper article. The reader might have some prior knowledge about the source but in general has to rely on the description given by the reporter. Examples for descriptions addressing just one of these aspects are given in (2):

(2)   (a) Here is the mature Abraham Lincoln uttering a trim three paragraphs – that eventually filled an entire wall of the Lincoln Memorial – at the dedication of a military cemetery in Gettysburg.
        (b) Finally, a referee confronted the cameras, crowd and official score-keepers, pressed the little button on his belt that cued him into the P.A. system, and uttered these words: "There was no infraction."
        (c) The stocks of banking concerns based in Massachusetts weren't helped much by the announcement, traders said, because many of those concerns have financial problems tied to their real-estate loan portfolios, making them unattractive takeover targets.

These examples illustrate the three aspects of source descriptions in turn, using a name, *Abraham Lincoln*, in (2a), a position, *referee*, in (2b), and a description of the relevant aspects, *traders*, in (2c). Classification of the different aspects is sometimes ambiguous; *referee* is not only a position but also the description of the relevance of that person to the reported speech act, i.e., that he was legitimately calling "no infraction" and in doing so settling the matter. Moreover, most source denoting noun phrases (source NPs for short) combine different aspects, as in example (3), where all three aspects are present:

(3)   The country's hard-line Communist leadership reaffirmed the nation's commitment to socialism, but said demands for the types of changes sweeping much of Eastern Europe "are open to discussions."

There is an implicit ordering of the importance of the three aspects mentioned above, roughly glossed as relevance > position > identity, or the relevance of the source to the topic is most important, the identity and personal characteristics are of least importance.[7]

Examples (2) and (3) show that the lexical semantics of the source NP contributes importantly to the evaluation of reliability but cannot determine reliability entirely.

5.5   Lexical semantics

Lexical semantics has grown into an independent field of research – independent from both syntactic theories (and their special requirements) and from application programs (and their special biases). This recent trend has brought us large dictionary databases (Proctor, 1978), lexicon building tools (Boguraev and Briscoe, 1989; Boguraev, 1992), corpus analysis tools (Church, 1988; Church and Hanks, 1990; Hindle, 1990), and formalisms for lexical semantics (Mel'c̆uk, 1988b,

Pustejovsky, 1991a) that greatly enrich computational linguistic research. There lies, however, a danger in considering lexical semantics as an entirely separate field of investigation.

In particular, lexical semantics has to take into account representational issues. A lexicon for general use has to contain information that allows the lexical items to contribute to a compositional analysis of general texts, including complex constructions, specialized terminology or style, and metaphorical use.

Traditional lexicons implement an assumption about representation that is so deeply engrained that there seems to be no alternative. The representation of sentences as embellished predicate argument structures is a case in point. Used mainly as an abstraction for a more elaborate representation formalism, the assumption underlying the predicate argument approach is that verbs function as predicates and nouns as arguments. As has been recently pointed out by Pustejovsky (1991a), however, this assumption is misleading not only for the obvious counterexamples such as predicative nouns, but also in a more subtle way. Reconsidering the passive role that nominal arguments play in traditional semantic accounts, Pustejovsky was able to suggest a very straightforward explanation for *coercion* (Pustejovsky, 1992b). Nouns in Pustejovsky's Generative Lexicon have a more elaborate structure that allows them to *cospecify* the semantics together with the verb. This can reduce the necessity for different word meanings for verbs, as illustrated in Example (4):

(4)   (a) John baked a cake.
         (b) John baked a potato.

Here the fact that a cake is an artifact that is brought about by baking, represented in the lexical entry for *cake* as a defining feature, selects for a create sense and hence an achievement reading for (4a), whereas the definition of *potato* as natural kind forces the reading of *bake* to be that of a process (see also Pustejovsky, 1991b for details on the event structure implied). One word sense for *bake* will be sufficient for both cases if the argument is allowed to cospecify the predicate.

The different angle under which the Generative Lexicon approaches traditional problems yields an elegant solution to a semantic problem. Here we go one step further and suggest how the Generative Lexicon can be used to set up and influence a pragmatic problem, namely, text analysis.

The previous section illustrated some requirements for the representation of reported speech. It is important to develop basic ideas about text representation and lexical semantics in conjunction to avoid a gap in the expressiveness of the two different representation levels. Meteer (1991) discusses the *Generation Gap* as the mismatch between the expressive power of the language of a text planner and a generation system. We see a similar gap between traditional lexicons and the analysis and representation of complex constructions as they occur in newspaper articles. It is the role of the lexicon to provide the basis for semantic composition, which in turn provides the basis for representation. Thus a lexicon has to contain the seeds for representation. This is the reason why lexicons have been custom tailored to one analysis system in the past, often specialized to a degree that made it hard to extend the coverage even within the same system, let alone transfer the lexicon to another task. With the new tools available to build large general lexicons, this reduplication of effort is no longer justified. The task is now to design appropriate analysis techniques that allow explicit expression of what the interface between a general lexicon and the pragmatic information required for a particular analysis looks like. The basic pragmatic function of reported speech that we developed in Section 5.4 is a case in point: while not supported by traditional lexicons, we show that this analysis is possible given the explicit linking of substyle information with general lexical entries in the next section.

5.5.1   *Layered lexicon design*

It is not contradictory to call for a linguistic preprocessing of texts as a first step toward interpretation to allow different interpretation by different user systems and to call for a lexicon that links lexical entries with pragmatic information. The pragmatic information we associate with lexical items has to be linguistic in nature. Thus the fact that reported speech shifts the responsibility for the correctness of the related information from the reporter to the quoted source is linguistic knowledge, yet it is about pragmatics. This section will introduce the explicit linking of lexical items with pragmatic knowledge. The next section shows how this lexicon structure interacts with an interpretation-neutral representation mechanism.

We assume here a *layered* lexicon, where subsequent layers are increasingly specific to text analysis and can be replaced or amended as a module.

The basis of this layered lexicon design is the "word lexicon", a list of words with definitions and some hierarchical structure, resembling loosely the information that we can find in very good printed dictionaries. Electronic lexicons for machine use are under development at different sites. We assume here a Generative Lexicon format (see Pustejovsky, 1992a, for an actual lexicon developed in this format).

Over the word lexicon we define several different meta-lexical layers of knowledge. The theory of the generative lexicon already provides for one meta-lexical construct, the so-called *Lexical Conceptual Paradigm*, or LCP (Pustejovsky and Boguraev, 1991). An LCP links the lexical entity to a mapping from syntactic patterns to semantic interpretation. Thus the fact that the concept of a *union* as the joining of two entities can be expressed syntactically with different patterns (*a union of X and Y, X's union with Y, . . .*) can be inherited to the different lexical items that actually lexicalize the concept of *union*, such as *merger*. This meta-lexical layer of LCPs does not change the word lexicon itself – it adds certain conceptual information at a higher level. Note that the LCP layer can be changed without affecting the word lexicon.

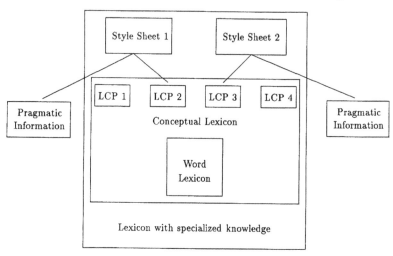

Figure 5.7. Layered lexicon design.

LCPs encode basic lexical knowledge that is not associated with individual entries, but with sets of entries, or concepts. The next layer above LCPs encodes specialized lexical knowledge, such as the particular meaning or function of words in a particular *style.*[8]

Figure 5.7 shows the idea of a layered lexicon design. This design has the advantage that outer layers can be changed without affecting inner layers. Thus the same word lexicon can be used with different conceptual groupings and specialized language information. Care has to be taken in designing the outer layers in a way that allows for easy extension of inner layers without introducing inconsistencies.

Figure 5.7 also shows that the outermost layer acts as an interface to pragmatic knowledge. The next section will introduce in detail how the meta-lexical construct *style sheet* links the particular interpretation that reported speech has in newspaper contexts to the LCP REPORTED-SPEECH. The same LCP would be linked to a very different interpretation schema by a style sheet THEATER or a style sheet GOTHIC-NOVEL. Style sheets select interpretations for the context at hand, as indicated by the style of the text. The explicit linking of pragmatic information with lexical concepts and lexical entries not only makes extending and maintaining a lexicon easier, it also facilitates experimentation with different interpretations for a given construct.

Research in commonsense reasoning has suggested that specialized and pragmatic information cannot be separated from basic lexical information (Hobbs et al., 1987). The layered lexicon, in contrast, assumes that a systematic linking of linguistic knowledge on one side and pragmatic information on the other is not only possible, but advantageous.

5.5.2   *Meta-lexical structures*

Let us illustrate the layered lexicon with some specific meta-lexical structures as needed for the interpretation of reported speech in newspaper articles.

In order to support an evidential analysis of reported speech we need to associate the pragmatic function that a source carries with the lexical items used to describe sources.

The three aspects introduced in Section 5.4, identity and personal attributes, official position, and relevance to the topic, have to be linked with source denoting nouns. This information is largely pragmatic and valid only for the analysis of reported speech in newspaper articles. Thus the concept *source denoting noun* has to be mapped through a style sheet to the appropriate pragmatic information.

LCP SOURCE – LCP

We will first describe an LCP that covers the concept of a source denoting noun, called SOURCE-LCP. An LCP consists of two parts, the lexical structure associated with the concept and the "syntactic realization patterns for how the word and its arguments are realized in text" (Pustejovsky and Boguraev, 1991). The basic semantics of the concept 'source' is: a source is any human or document that discloses some information. The lexical structure of the concept "source" is shown in (5):

$$
(5) \quad \begin{bmatrix} \text{SOURCE–LCP}(x, y) \\ \text{CONST: } information(y) \\ \text{FORMAL: } (human(x) \text{ \& metonymically extends to } z, \\ \quad \text{where: } represents(x,z)) \text{ or:} \\ \quad document(x) \\ \text{TELIC: } disclose(x,y) \end{bmatrix}
$$

The concept SOURCE-LCP applies to all humans and documents but is not part of their core definition. It is a concept that can apply to these lexical items. Notice the specification of a particular metonymic extension that occurs particularly frequently in source NPs in conjunction with utterance verbs, namely the metonymic extension of a human source to a company or institution which the source represents (see Bergler, 1991, for details).

Associated with the SOURCE-LCP are the syntactic patterns a source NP can have. Based on the analysis of a corpus of TIME magazine articles, a small grammar for source denoting NP was developed. The grammar is partial. Source NPs, like all NPs, can be adorned with modifiers, temporal adjuncts, appositions, and relative clauses of any shape. The important observation is that these cases are very rare in the corpus data and must be dealt with by general (i.e., syntactic) principles.

Style Sheet NEWSPAPER–RS

The SOURCE-LCP does not specify how to interpret a source NP. In particular, our intuitions about reliability factors are not represented. The LCP only connects lex-

source ⟶
    [quant] [mod] descriptor ["," name ","] |
    [descriptor | ((a | the) mod)] [mod] name |
    [inst 's | name 's] descriptor [name] |
    name "," [a | the] [relation prep] descriptor |
    name "," [a | the] name 's (descriptor | relation) |
    name "," free relative clause
descriptor ⟶
    role |
    [inst] position |
    [position (for | of)] [quant] inst name ⟶
    [title] [first] [middle] last ["," spec] ["," age ","]
position ⟶
    minister | *official* | *chief* | *president* | *neurosurgeon* | . . .
inst ⟶
    [location] [allegiance] [institution]
institution ⟶
    U.N. | *police* | *governement* | *city water authority* | . . .
location ⟶
    country | *city* | *state* | *region*
allegiance ⟶
    political party | *religion* | . . .

Figure 5.8. A partial semantic grammar for source NPs.

ical entries with semantic concepts and their syntactic realizations. We formulate pragmatic information separately.

Style sheets (Bergler, 1992) are collections of pragmatic information associated with a particular style or substyle (possibly restricted to one particular context). In our case, the three factors in reliability assessment from (1) are expressed as follows:

(6)
$$
\begin{bmatrix}
\text{RELIABILITY–FACTORS}(x, y) \\
\text{INDIVIDUAL1: } [x] \\
\text{POSITION: } profession(x) \text{ or } title(x) \\
\text{RELEVANCE: } access(x,y)
\end{bmatrix}
$$

This pragmatic information provides hooks for a commonsense reasoner. By itself, it does not provide the means for reliability assessment; it requires an interpretation function. The information provided shows access to the relevance factors determined for this style; *relevance* can be computed from the access of the individual to the information, *position* (and authority) can be computed from the profession or title of the individual, and personal features of the *individual* can be computed from any information associated with the individual. It is important to remember that that is exactly what the text provides: a basis for reliability assessment, not an interpretation.

The style sheet NEWSPAPER – RS links this pragmatic knowledge about reliability factors with the SOURCE-LCP.[9]

(7) **Style Sheet**
NEWSPAPER–RS
SOURCE–LCP(A, B) & RELIABILITY–FACTORS(X, Y)
where A = X, B = Y.

5.6   Source representation

Having discussed the role of lexical semantics, let us look at an adequate representation mechanism for source information in reported speech.

5.6.1   *Profiles*

In Bergler and Pustejovsky (1990), a representational device was introduced that collected all properties that a text ascribes to an entity. This device was called a *profile*. Here we modify the concept of a profile to include a collection of the statements of an entity:

(8)   A profile is a collection of all properties that a text asserts or implies about a particular discourse entity. In particular, the profile contains all statements made by or attributed to the entity.

We will depict profiles[10] here as a box containing essentially two sections. The first section presents an identifier for the profile, the name of the entity and any properties known. The second part consists of a list of statements introduced by the reporting verb used to introduce the reported statement.

Consider, for instance, the profile for the entity *The Financial Times* in Text 1, which would be represented graphically as in Figure 5.9. Different discourse entities may be connected in a text in different ways. Individuals map very easily to profiles, one profile for each individual. Looking at abstract entities, such as *companies*, however, it becomes clear that profiles also have to stand in some structured relation to each other reflecting the relations of the entities, about which they contain information.

One frequent relationship made explicit in newspaper texts is that of *representation*, where one entity represents another. Certain *employment* relationships are examples: *spokesman, spokeswoman, official, president, attorney* are examples of words that lexically specify a representation relationship between the entity and some employer.

Consider for instance S_2' and S_3' of Variation 1 of Text 2, repeated here as (9):

(9)   (S_2') Pacific Enterprises said the naming of Mr. Ukropina represented a conservative move. (S_3') Unlike some companies, Pacific Enterprises has "made no major errors moving outside their area of expertise," said Craig Schwerdt, a spokesman for Pacific Enterprises.

Here S_3' is a further elaboration of S_2'. Moreover, the word *spokesman* lexically specifies that the statement reported in S_3' has been made on behalf of the employer company, in our case *Pacific Enterprises*. This fact is reflected in the TELIC role[11] of the lexical entry for *spokesman*, given in (10).

financial-times

         name: The Financial Times
     business-type: newspaper
        country: Great Britain

said: the plant was expected to have a production capacity of 150,000 to 200,000 vehicles a year and could involve an investment of $2.5 billion to $3 billion.

Figure 5.9. Profile for entity *Financial Times* in Text 1.

pacific-enterprises
     name: Pacific Enterprises

said: the naming of Mr. Ukropina represented a conservative move.

craig-schwerdt

        name: Craig Schwerdt
     position: spokesman
     employer: Pacific Enterprises

said: Unlike some companies, Pacific Enterprises has "made no major errors moving outside their area of expertise."

Figure 5.10. Profiles for unemployment relationship in Variation 1.

$$\left[\begin{array}{l} \textbf{spokesman(x, y)} \\ \text{CONST}: \mathit{individual}(x) \\ \text{FORMAL}: \mathit{human}(x), \mathit{default}: \mathit{organization}(y) \\ \text{TELIC}: \mathit{speak\text{-}for}(x, y), \mathit{represent}(x, y, \mathit{public}) \\ \text{AGENTIVE}: \mathit{INH}(y), \mathit{default}: \mathit{hire}(y, x) \end{array} \right]$$

(10)

Here the predicate INH indicates that the value is inherited from the entry corresponding to the argument.

A representation relation has to be reflected in the structure of the profiles that represent the two discourse entities. Figure 5.10 adopts the convention of embedding the profile of a representative in the profile of the employer (for similar notions see Fauconnier, 1985; Kamp, 1988; Ballim and Wilks, 1991).

The convention of embedding the profile of the spokesman within a profile for the enterprise is licensed by the focus of newspapers on corporate structure. The metonymy used in S_2', *Pacific Enterprises* <u>said</u> . . . , constitutes an example of a pervasive use of metonymy, where the metonymic term describes more relevant information (or describes the same information more concisely) than the literal term (for detail see Bergler, 1991). It is by far more important to know that S_3' contains a statement made on behalf of *Pacific Enterprises* than it is to know that the spokesman's name is *Craig Schwerdt*. Our embedding scheme thus acknowledges the meaning of the use of one particular kind of metonymy.

5.6.2 *Supporting groups*

When an article cites several people in favor of the same issue, possibly contrasting their statements with several other people's who are not in favor of this issue, there is often no employment or membership relation that would allow us to embed one profile into another. Yet for the sake of the argumentation in the article at hand, these profiles form a group, where the statement of one individual holds in some sense for the whole group. The statements *support* one another and we call the resulting grouping a *supporting group*.

Text 1 exhibits such a supporting group where the analyst's statements support each other. The representation of supporting groups is a box containing all supporting profiles as illustrated in Figure 5.11.

Supporting groups mirror the argumentative structure of a text. To represent supporting group structure explicitly is therefore an expedient for summarizing an argument or when assessing the context of a statement. Supporting groups define a *local context* for the reported statements. Within this local context, coherence and reference questions are simplified to a certain degree; we can assume that statements that fall into the same supporting group refer to the same set of events and entities.

We speak of *opposing supporting groups* when different sources differ on the topic at hand, as is the case in Variation 2 of Text 2. Figure 5.12 shows the two opposing supporting groups.

SG1

analysts

Position:	analysts

said: the naming of Mr. Ukropina represented a conservative move by an unusually conservative utility concern.

craig-schwerdt

name:	Craig Schwerdt
position:	analyst
employer:	Seidler Amdec Securities Inc. in Los Angeles

said: Unlike some companies, Pacific Enterprises has "made no major errors moving outside their area of expertise."

paul-milbauer

name:	Paul Milbauer
position:	analyst
employer:	C. J. Lawrence, Morgan Grenfell in New York

said: "Each of the company's businesses are positioned to do well in the coming year."

said: Most of the company's retail operations are in the fast-growing West, and the gas unit will benefit from tightening environmental regulations.

added: More-stringent pollution controls are expected to increase demand for gas, which is relatively clean-burning.

Figure 5.11. Supporting group of analysts in Text 1.

OSG1

a1

    position: analyst
    quant: one

said the naming of Mr. Ukropina represented a conservative move by an unusually conservative utility concern.

craig-schwerdt

    name: Craig Schwerdt
    position: analyst
    employer: Seidler Amdec Securities Inc. in Los Angeles

said: Unlike some companies, Pacific Enterprises has "made no major errors moving outside their area of expertise."

OSG2

paul-milbauer

    name: Paul Milbauer
    position: analyst
    employer: C.J. Lawrence, Morgan Grenfell in New York

insisted: "None of the company's businesses are positioned to do well in the coming year."

said: Most of the company's retail operations are in the fast-growing West, and the gas unit will suffer from tightening environmental regulations.

Figure 5.12. Opposing supporting groups of Variation 2.

We do not expect members of opposing supporting groups to necessarily refer to the same events and persons; in fact it is very likely that they focus their attention on very different topics and that it is that difference, that opposes them. If the same events or entities are discussed in opposing supporting groups, we cannot assume the resulting characterization of the event or entity to be cumulative over opposing supporting groups. This is an important point for information extraction purposes. Blindly accumulating a characterization across opposing supporting groups might result in inconsistencies.

5.7   Deriving supporting group structure

The previous sections outlined lexical semantic structures to account for source NP interpretation and representational devices to structure statements according to their sources (profiles, supporting groups). Here, we show how lexical semantics and text representation interact in the process of deriving the supporting group structure of a text.

We have chosen an article that reports opposed statements in order to show that the resulting supporting group structure facilitates the assessment of the overall article. But the major focus of this section is on illustrating the interaction of lexical information and the process of grouping profiles. In particular, we suggest that a partial grouping can be obtained based on the analysis of the matrix clause alone. The benefit of a rough supporting group structure based on partial analysis lies in the fact that local contexts facilitate certain difficult problems of reference resolution within the complement clauses.

Text 3 is a collection of several paragraphs of a much longer text from the *Wall Street Journal.* Let us assume that some rudimentary parse has provided us with analyses of the matrix clauses. Identifying subsequent reference for the sources is then straightforward in this text. Regional thrift regulators and the regional officials refer to the same group, a single discourse entity. Mike Patriarca, acting principal supervisory agent with the Office of Thrift Supervision will have a separate profile, as will Leonard Bickwit, a Washington attorney for Lincoln, a Lincoln spokesman, and a spokesman for Arthur Andersen. Figure 5.14 illustrates the profiles.

The profiles fall into two opposing supporting groups, as S_1 already specifies: the thrift officials on one side and Lincoln and Andersen and their spokesmen and attorneys on the other. We can approximate this supporting group structure without analyzing the complement clauses. The lexical semantics of the source NPs and the reporting verbs provide enough information.

Let us first consider the profiles **P1** and **P3**. The heads of the relevant source NPs are *regulators*, *officials*, and *agent*. Note that the grouping of (S_1) and (S_3) is clear from coherence: In S_3 the definite article and the use of *also said* indicate that (S_3) is a continuation of (S_1). Here we consider the lexical semantics of *agent* and *regulators*, *officials* that allows us to group **P1** and **P3**.

Regulators Cite Delays and Phone Bugs
By Paulette Thomas and Brooks Jackson

(S_{1a}) Regional thrift regulators charged that phone calls were bugged during the examination of Lincoln Savings & Loan Association and (S_{1b}) that federal officials in Washington delayed Lincoln's seizure until its $2.5 billion cost made it the most expensive thrift failure ever.

(S_2) A Lincoln spokesman said its management "never authorized or participated in any bugging of anyone."

(S_3) The regional officials also said that Arthur Andersen, a Big Eight accounting firm, backdated data to support loans that were made with no underwriting standards. (S_4) Over two years, until April 1986, $1 billion in loans were approved, even though Lincoln had no written loan standards, said Mike Patriarca, acting principal supervisory agent with the Office of Thrift Supervision. (S_5) Fifty-two loans were made in March 1986, he said, and none had credit reports or other background work completed.

(S_6) "At a later time, the files looked good because they had been stuffed," Mr. Patriarca said. (S_7) Leonard Bickwit, a Washington attorney for Lincoln, conceded that some memos had been written after the fact. (S_{8a}) He said that "memorialization of underwriting activities that had been undertaken at an earlier time" did occur, but (S_{8b}) that Lincoln believed it adhered to lending standards superior to the industry average.

(S_{9a}) A spokesman for Arthur Andersen denied any improprieties, (S_{9b}) adding, "At the request of our then-client, we provided staff personnel to work for a limited period of time under the direction of client personnel to assist them in organizing certain files."

Figure 5.13. Text 3, from the *Wall Street Journal*, 10/27/89

The definition of *official* in the American Heritage Dictionary (Berube, 1987) is:

official n 1. One who holds an office or position.
office 3. A position of authority given to a person, as in a government or other organization.

The main meaning of the word *official*, when used as a source description in reported speech, is to convey that the source holds a position of authority or trust and that the reporter wants the reader to accept this for the sake of the article even though he or she might not give any more justification for that trustworthiness than the description *official*.

Agent is defined as:

agent n 1. One that acts or has the power to act.
2. One that acts as the representative of another.

The dictionary definition of *agent* is very similar to that of *spokesman*, except that where a *spokesman* speaks for somebody, an *agent* acts. Thus the lexical entries for *official* and *agent* are as follows:

P1

position: regional thrift regulators, officials

charged:

also said:

P2

position: spokesman
employer: Lincoln

said:

P3

name: Mike Patriarca
position: acting principal supervisory agent
employer: the Office of Thrift Supervision

said:

said:

said:

P4

name: Leonard Bickwit
position: attorney
employer: Lincoln
location: Washington

conceded:

said:

P5

position: spokesman
employer: Arthur Andersen

denied:

adding:

Figure 5.14. Profiles for Text 3.

(11) **Lexical Entries**

$$
\begin{bmatrix}
\textbf{official(x, y)} \\
\text{CONST: } individual(x) \\
\text{FORMAL: } human(x),\ organization(y), \\
\quad position(z),\ in(z, y),\ hold(x, z), \\
\quad has\text{–}authority(z),\ trust(y, x) \\
\text{TELIC: } INH(z) \\
\text{AGENTIVE: } INH(y), \\
\quad default:\ hire(y, x)
\end{bmatrix}
\qquad
\begin{bmatrix}
\textbf{agent(x, y)} \\
\text{CONST: } individual(x) \\
\text{FORMAL: } human(x) \\
\text{TELIC: } represent(x, y) \\
\text{AGENTIVE: } INH(y), \\
\quad default:\ hire(y, x)
\end{bmatrix}
$$

Resolving that *regional thrift regulators* and *regional officials* work for the *Office of Thrift Supervision*, we can establish that both **P1** and **P3** work for the same employer, suggesting that they fall into the same supporting group.[12]

P2 and **P4** similarly share an employer, *Lincoln Savings and Loan*. Again, the lexical entries reveal that both *spokesman* and *attorney*, are positions of representation, suggesting that these two profiles form another supporting group.[12]

(12) **Lexical Entries**

$$
\begin{bmatrix}
\textbf{attorney(x, y)} \\
\text{CONST: } individual(x) \\
\text{FORMAL: } human(x) \\
\text{TELIC: } fact\text{–}for(x, y), \\
\quad represent(x, y, legal\ domain) \\
\text{AGENTIVE: } hire(y, x)
\end{bmatrix}
\qquad
\begin{bmatrix}
\textbf{spokesman(x, y)} \\
\text{CONST: } individual(x) \\
\text{FORMAL: } human(x), \\
\quad default:\ organization(y) \\
\text{TELIC: } speak\text{–}for(x, y), \\
\quad represent(x, y, public) \\
\text{AGENTIVE: } INH(y),\ default:\ hire(y, x)
\end{bmatrix}
$$

The opposition of these two supporting groups, **(P1, P3)** and **(P2, P4)**, and the grouping of **P5** with the latter is encoded in the reporting verbs.

The key terms here are *charge, concede,* and *deny*. Definitions from the American Heritage Dictionary are:

charge	3. To blame or accuse.
concede	1. To admit as true or real; acknowledge.
deny	1. To declare untrue; contradict.
	3. To refuse to recognize or acknowledge; disavow.

The lexical entries for these three reporting verbs are:

(13)

$$
\begin{bmatrix}
\textbf{charge(x, y, z)} \\
\text{FORMAL: } human(x), \\
\quad human(y), \\
\quad wrongdoing(z) \\
\text{TELIC: } say(x, commit(y, z))
\end{bmatrix}
\begin{bmatrix}
\textbf{deny(x, y)} \\
\text{FORMAL: } human(x), \\
\quad proposition(y) \\
\text{TELIC: } say(x, not(y)), \\
\quad presupposed(y)
\end{bmatrix}
\begin{bmatrix}
\textbf{concede(x, y)} \\
\text{FORMAL: } human(x), \\
\quad proposition(y) \\
\text{TELIC: } say(x, true(y)), \\
\quad presupposed(y), \\
\quad bad\text{–}for(x,y)
\end{bmatrix}
$$

Charge is a polarizing word. If one person charges another with some wrongdoing, they will fall automatically into opposing supporting groups. Thus the first sentence in Text 3 already implies that there are two opposing supporting groups and that **P1** falls into the accusing supporting group. It is relatively straightforward to see that *concede* triggers the characterization of the supporting group containing **P4** as opposed: While *concede* lexically specifies agreement, it also specifies a reluctance, encoded in the entry as *bad-for*, suggesting that the *agent* of the *conceding* event is also the *patient* of the *charging*.

Without analyzing the complement clauses it is much harder to see that **P5** groups with **P4** rather than opposing it. When we look at the phrase *deny any improprieties*, however, the opposition to *charge* suggests itself much more strongly. In any case, the realization that **P5** is opposed to some other profile already constrains the options to be verified by a full analysis of the sentence.

The resulting supporting group structure is shown in Figure 5.15. Supporting groups provide a basis for the interpretation of the text. In the context of court proceedings, for instance, the supporting group around the defendant will contain statements that minimally implicate the defendant. Thus the interpretation of the statement embedded in (S₂) of Text 3, namely that *Linclon's management never authorized or participated in any bugging of anyone*, does not rule out that the management *knew about* and *tolerated* the bugging of the phone line, in violation of the rules of everyday discourse (Be informative. Be cooperative.) (Grice, 1967).

That supporting group structure is largely determined by the matrix clauses in our example is encouraging. Partial analyses of newspaper texts, concentrating on the matrix clauses, can already give an insight into the argumentative structure of the text and constrain the further processing of the complement sentences within the local contexts of profiles and supporting groups.

5.8   Conclusion

We have demonstrated here that it is possible to give an adequate representation of reported speech in newspaper articles without addressing the pragmatic problems involved in giving an interpretation. To find a linguistically motivated level of text representation that precedes text interpretation increases the reusability of the results of linguistic processing of texts. Newspaper texts in particular can serve as resources for many different applications, highlighting different aspects of the text.

This chapter does not aim to outline a full text representation formalism. Instead, we have focused on one representational device, *profiles,* and their resulting *supporting group structures.* Profiles were shown to capture the essence of reported speech without forcing an interpretation. The grouping of profiles into supporting groups does not necessarily require a full analysis of the sentences; the matrix clause often contains enough information to group profiles.

The representation for reported speech suggested here can be *interpreted* in different ways. We developed a *meta-lexical* structure that systematically maps pragmatic information to lexical entries, thus defining an explicit interface between semantics and pragmatics.

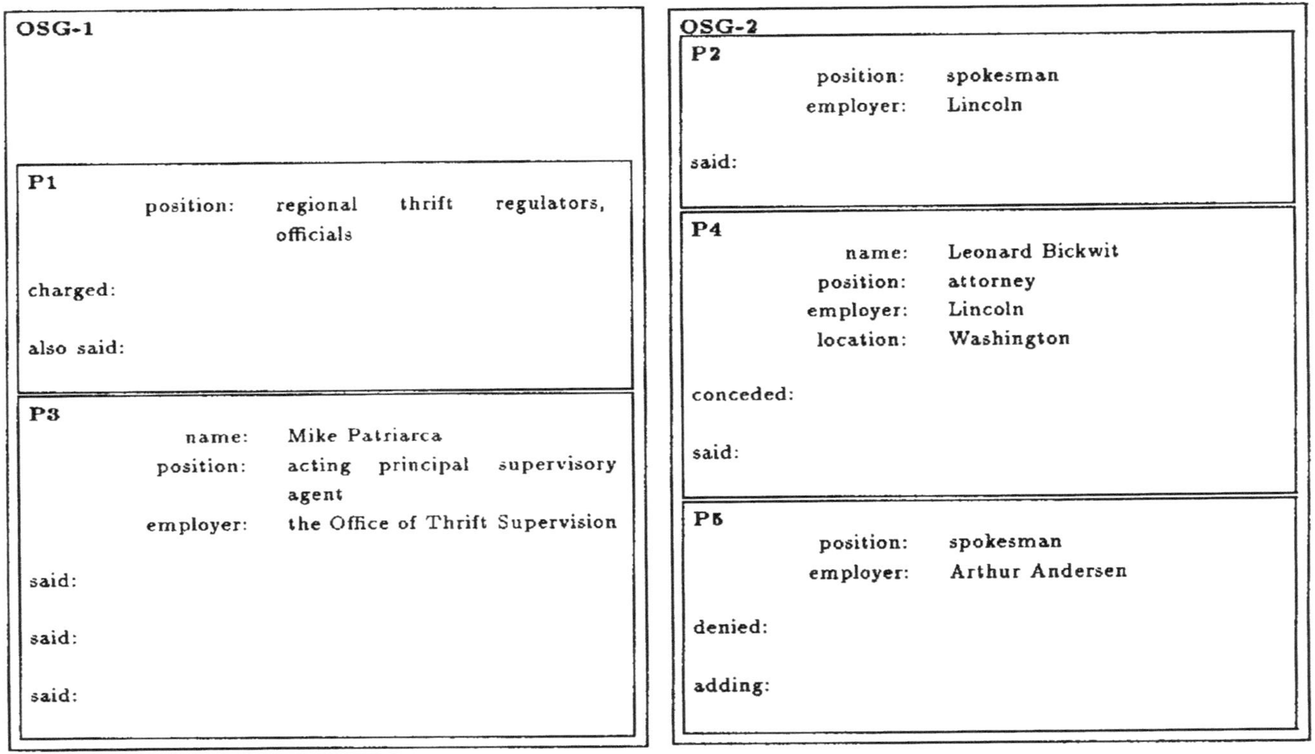

Figure 5.15. Opposing supporting group structure for Text 3.

Considering lexical semantics and text representation issues together avoids a mismatch between the two, leading to a more general solution for difficult problems than would otherwise be possible.

Notes

1. MTR is described in more detail in Bergler (1992). Here, we will only describe one aspect, profile structure.
2. See Quirk et al., (1985) and Jespersen (1924) for detailed descriptions of the grammatical features of reported speech.
3. Much information in newspaper articles is "second hand", i.e., information that the reporter has no direct access to. One of the crucial factors in evaluating reported speech is therefore the source of the information.
4. Note that this is quite different from the problems discussed in the literature in connection with opacity in the embedded constructs. See Bergler (1992) for a discussion why those problems do not arise in newspaper articles.
5. For more detail see Bergler (1992).
6. Note that this cannot necessarily be assumed to be the intention of the analysts but is an interpretation of their possibly totally independent statements through the reporter.
7. This assumes straightforward interpretation; if the source is known to be a pathological liar this knowledge overrides other considerations. The ordering is particular to newspaper style.
8. The layer of specialized lexical knowledge also includes the particulars of *sublanguage* and other special contexts. We will only be concerned with style.
9. This is of course only one aspect of NEWSPAPER – RS, another aspect is the link between reporting verbs and the associated pragmatic knowledge as described in Bergler (1992).
10. Profiles and the resulting profile structure are one aspect of a text representation formalism currently being developed by us. For the sake of simplicity we will not present the other devices or the philosophy behind the representation formalism, called MTR. See Bergler (1992) for more detail.
11. The TELIC role contains some crucial event associated with the defined word; for artifacts this is their *purpose*, for the job descriptions under consideration here this is the predominant *duty* associated with that job.
12. We do not suggest that this a trivial matter. The complexity of NP resolution forces us to develop heuristic methods to approach this problem. In newspaper articles we find that the different descriptions of an entity are either linked through definite articles or certain key terms that reoccur, as illustrated by the descriptions grouped into the same profile for Figure 5.14. We are currently working on this problem.

References

A. Ballim and Y. Wilks. (1992). *Artificial Believers*. Lawrence Erlbaum Associates, Hillsdale, New Jersey.

S. Bergler. (1991). The semantics of collocational patterns for reporting verbs. In *Proceedings of the Fifth European Conference of the Association for Computational Linguistics*, Berlin, Germany.

S. Bergler. (1992). *Evidential Analysis of Reported Speech*. PhD thesis, Brandeis University.

S. Bergler and J. Pustejovsky. (1990). Temporal reasoning from lexical semantics. In B. Endress-Niggemeyer, T. Herrmann, A. Kobsa, and D. Rösner, editors, *Interaktion und Kommunikation mit dem Computer*. Springer Verlag.

M. S. Berube, editor. (1987). *The American Heritage Dictionary*. Dell Publishing Co., Inc., New York. Paperback edition based on the Second College Edition, 1983, Houghton Mifflin Co.

B. Boguraev. (1992). Building a lexicon: The contribution of computational lexicography. In L. Bates and R. Weischedel, editors, *Challenges in Natural Language Processing*. Cambridge University Press.

B. Boguraev and T. Briscoe, editors. (1989). *Computational Lexicography for Natural Language Processing*. Longman, Harlow, Essex.

K.W. Church. (1988). A stochastic parts program and noun phrase parser for unrestricted text. In *Proceedings of the Second Conference on Applied Natural Language Processing, Austin, Texas, 1988*.

K.W. Church and P. Hanks. (1990). Word association norms, mutual information, and lexicography. *Computational Linguistics*, 16(1).

R. Cohen. (1987). Analyzing the structure of argumentative discourse. *Computational Linguistics*, 13(1–2).

D. Davidson. (1968). On saying that. *Synthèse*, 19:130–146. Reprinted in D. Davidson, *Inquiries into Truth and Interpretation*, Clarendon Press, Oxford.

G. Fauconnier. (1985). *Mental Spaces*. Bradford Books. MIT Press, Cambridge, MA.

H. P. Grice. (1967). Logic and conversation. Unpublished ms. of the William James Lectures, Harvard University.

D. Hindle. (1990). Noun classification from predicate-argument structures. In *Proceedings of the 28th Meeting of the Association for Computational Linguistics*.

J. Hobbs, W. Croft, T. Davies, D. Edwards, and K. Laws. (1987). Commonsense metaphysics and lexical semantics. *Computational Linguistics*, 13(3–4).

O. Jespersen. (1924). *The Philosophy of Grammar*. Allen and Unwin, London.

H. Kamp. (1988). Discourse Representation Theory: What it is and where it ought to go. In A. Blaser, editor, *Natural Language at the Computer*. Springer Verlag, Berlin.

L. Lundquist. (1989). Modality and text constitution. In M.-E. Conte, J. S. Petöfi , and E. Sözer, editors, *Text and Discourse Connectedness. Proceedings of the Conference on Connexity and Coherence, Urbino, July 1984*. John Benjamins Publishing Co., Amsterdam.

D. McDonald. (1992). An efficient chart-based algorithm for partial-parsing of unrestricted texts. In *Proceedings of the Conference on Applied Natural Language Processing*, Trento, Italy, April.

I. Mel'cuk. (1988). Semantic description of lexical units in an explanatory combinatorial dictionary: Basic principles and heuristic criteria. *International Journal of Lexicography*, 1(3).

M. Meteer. (1991). Bridging the 'generation gap' between text planning and linguistic realization. *Computational Intelligence*, 7(4).

S. Nirenburg and C. Defrise. (1992). Lexical and conceptual structure for knowledge-based machine translation. In J. Pustejovsky, editor, *Semantics and the Lexicon*. Kluwer, Dordrecht, NL.

Paul Procter, editor. (1978). *Longman Dictionary of Contemporary English*. Longman, Harlow, U.K.

J. Pustejovsky. (1991a). The Generative Lexicon. *Computational Linguistics*, 17(4).

J. Pustejovsky. (1991b). The syntax of event structure. *Cognition*, 41:47–81, 1991.

J. Pustejovsky. (1992a). The acquisition of lexical semantic knowledge from large corpora. In *Proceedings of the Speech and Natural Language Workshop*, pages 243–248, Morgan Kaufmann, San Mateo, CA.

J. Pustejovsky. (1992b). Type coercion and lexical inheritance. In J. Pustejovsky, editor, *Semantics and the Lexicon*. Kluwer, Dordrecht, NL, 1992.

J. Pustejovsky and B. Boguraev. (1991). Lexical knowledge representation and natural language processing. *IBM Journal of Research and Development*, 45(4).

W. V. O. Quine. (1940). *Mathematical Logic*. Harvard University Press, Cambridge, MA.

R. Quirk, S. Greenbaum, G. Leech, and J. Svartvik. (1985). *A Comprehensive Grammar of the English Language*. Longman, London.

6   Lexical functions, generative lexicons and the world

DIRK HEYLEN

6.1   Introduction

The connections between the study of natural language semantics, especially lexical semantics, and knowledge representation are manifold. One of the reasons why lexical semantics holds this place is obvious when one looks at compositional denotational theories of meaning. Here, one tries to account for the meaning of expressions in terms of a relation between linguistic expressions and the world. The *dictionary* makes explicit what part of the world each basic item refers to, whereas the *grammar rules* are associated with general instructions to combine the meanings of parts into the meanings of wholes. Most natural language understanding systems cannot relegate the interpretation function of basic items (as contained in the dictionary) to some mysterious interpretation function, say 'as in the case of Montague semantics, but have to be more explicit about the world and the substantive relation between basic expressions and the assumed ontology. Actual explanatory dictionaries can be viewed as stating complex relationships between natural language *expressions*. This perspective focuses on the fact that definitions are stated in language. The other perspective is focused on what is described: one could also say that a definition is the representation of a constraint on the world/model or the specification of the (now less mysterious) interpretation function for basic expressions.

Although it may not be realistic to argue that knowledge representation problems can be totally equated with problems of lexical semantics, there is enough reason to take notice of the latter when dealing with the former. Certainly this is the case where one deals with knowledge representation for natural language understanding. Within this general perspective we take the following position.

- Ontologies should be built in a principled way.
- There should be a close fit between linguistic knowledge and knowledge of the world. The linguistic system and the knowledge base should be attuned to one another as much as possible.
- If we use the knowledge bases for NLP applications, and suppose that the NLP system and the KB should be attuned somehow, the construction of the KB should rely on linguistic data.

This research was carried out while the author was working on the project 'Collocations and the Lexicalisation of Semantic Operations' (ET-10/75), which is sponsored by the CEC, Oxford University Press and the 'Association Suissetra' (Switzerland).

In a sense, this position elaborates the Montagovian perspective on the relation between language and the model in which it is interpreted. But whereas in formal semantics one is concerned only with the abstract structure of the model, there is more interest in the details of the actual inhabitants of the world in lexical semantics and knowledge representation systems. In trying to find ways to make more substantive claims about the 'world' on the one hand, but to stick to the methodological principle of 'linguistic motivation' on the other, we came across Mel'čuk's analysis of collocations in terms of lexical functions. These lexical functions bear a close resemblance to the semantic primitives or conceptual categories proposed in the literature on knowledge representation, while still being motivated by the analysis of collocations and other aspects of linguistic structure. This chapter will thus revolve around the following questions.

- Can we use linguistic data to construct adequate ontologies?
- Do collocations offer this kind of data?
- More particularly, does the analysis of collocations in terms of lexical functions à la Mel'čuk constitute a foundation for the construction of a linguistically motivated knowledge base?

The underlying motivation behind these questions is that if lexical semantics and knowledge representation have intricate connections, then it might well be worthwhile to inspect existing theories about lexical semantics as to their applicability in knowledge representation systems.

In this chapter we present some of the possibilities to extend the use of lexical functions to other domains besides the description of collocations. More particularly, we will attempt to interpret the concept of lexical function in a knowledge representation perspective. What we want to achieve is sufficient motivation to investigate the usefulness of lexical functions for knowledge representation and to indicate basic questions and problems which this kind of research should address.

This discussion consists of two major parts, each focusing on a specific level of interpretation of the lexical function – knowledge representation connection. In the first part we try to show how the network of lexical entries connected through lexical functions as defined in the Explanatory Combinatory Dictionaries (ECD) from Mel'čuk and his followers, relates to Pustejovsky's proposals concerning an encompassing theory of lexical semantics which is claimed to be useful for knowledge representation as well. In the second part we have a closer look at the exact 'epistemological' status of the ECD conceived of as a 'semantic' network.

6.2   Lexical functions and the generative lexicon

Overall, the approach to lexical semantics and knowledge representation as proposed by Pustejovsky looks technically similar to the one we are proposing. To put lexical functions in this general perspective, we point out the various connections one can establish between components of Pustejovsky's theory on the generative lexicon and aspects of the concept of lexical functions.

This section consists of three parts. The first is a presentation and classification of the LFs presented by Mel'čuk et al., (1984). The second part reviews some of the work by Pustejovsky on the generative lexicon. In the third part we relate the two theories.

6.2.1 *Lexical functions*

In the Extended Combinatory Dictionaries (ECD) as proposed by Mel'čuk, the 'truly linguistic restrictions on lexical cooccurrence' are systematically described by means of lexical functions. A typical case of such a linguistic restriction is the choice of the appropriate support verb selected by the noun (Mel'čuk and Polguère, 1987, p. 271).

Eng.	(to) ASK a question	(to) LET OUT a cry
Fr.	POSER (litt. 'put') une question	POUSSER ('push') un cri
Sp.	HACER ('make') una pregunta	DAR ('give') un grito
Russ.	ZADAT' ('give') vopros	ISPUSTIT' ('let out') krik

Lexical functions are not invoked, however, for restrictions on cooccurrence which are of a non-linguistic nature, but which derive from the meanings of lexemes and 'our knowledge of the world'. Such a restriction is illustrated by the example 'The telephone was drinking the sexy integrals' (ibid.). Lexical functions are defined as follows.

A lexical function **f** is a dependency that associates with a lexeme L, called the argument of **f**, another lexeme (or a set of (quasi-)synonymous lexemes) L' which expresses, with respect to L, a very abstract meaning (which can even be zero) and plays a specific syntactic role. For instance, for a noun N denoting an action, the lexical function **Oper₁** specifies a verb (semantically empty – or at least emptied) which takes as its grammatical subject the name of the agent of said action and as its direct object, the lexeme N itself.

Lexical functions express various semantic relations between lexical items. Most of these are relations which appear in collocational constructions. But morphological, syntactic and other constructions can provide relevant input for the inventory of lexical functions as well.

In the first article in Mel'čuk et al., (1984) we find the description of 37 functions. They clearly do not form a homogeneous group.[1] Although Mel'čuk claims that the lexical functions are used to describe lexical cooccurrence restrictions, he presents some lexical functions which have no bearing on lexical combinations but rather describe paradigmatic relations. An initial grouping of lexical functions could therefore be into *paradigmatic* and *syntagmatic* functions.[2]

- *Paradigmatic* SYN, CONV, ANTI, S_0, V_0, A_0, ADV_0, S_1, S_2, S_3, S_{instr}, S_{med}, S_{loc}, S_{mod}, S_{res}, $ABLE_1$, $ABLE_2$, . . . IMPER
- *Syntagmatic* SING, MULT, CULM, GENER, FIGUR, A_1, A_2, A_3, . . . , MAGN, VER, BON, POS_1, POS_2, . . . , ADV_1, ADV_2, LOC_{in}, LOC_{ab}, LOC_{ad}, PROPT, $OPER_1$, $OPER_2$, . . . , $FUNC_0$, $FUNC_1$, $FUNC_2$, . . . , $LABOR_{ij}$,

INVOLV, INCEP, CONT, FIN, CAUS, LIQU, PERM, REAL, FACT$_{0,1}$..., LABREAL, MANIF, DEGRAD, EXCESS

Paradigmatic relations

We partition the paradigmatic relations into the following classes.

- Sense relations: SYN, ANTI
- Morphologically derived words: S$_0$, V$_0$, A$_0$, ADV$_0$,
- Perspective alternation (diathesis): CONV
- Circumstantial relation (both arguments and adjuncts): S$_1$, S$_2$, S$_3$, S$_{instr}$, S$_{med}$, S$_{loc}$, S$_{mod}$, S$_{res}$,

The first category of sense relations are those that are typically listed in thesauri such as Roget's. The second group consists of morphological operations: nominalizations, verb formation, etc.[3]

The third class is exemplified by Mel'čuk with the following instances.

- CONV$_{21}$(être derrière) = être devant
- CONV$_{21}$(plus) = moins
- CONV$_{21}$(craindre) = effrayer

The subscripts indicate that when we replace the argument of the lexical function with its value and switch around the subject ($_1$) and the object ($_2$), we get synonymous expressions.

Syntagmatic relations

There are a number of ways to classify further the various lexical functions. The following are some possible modes of classification.

- semantic relatedness of function
- syntactic category of argument
- syntactic category of value

The first distinction we shall make is between *grammatical* and *lexical* combinations. This we do on the basis of the syntactic category of the value of a function. We distinguish between closed class values and open class values.

Grammatical combinations. These are lexical functions that yield prepositions (or other closed-class items) as values. These are ADV$_{1,2}$, LOC, PROPT.

Lexical combinations. As far as their syntactic construction is concerned, the lexical combinations are either modifier-head combinations or argument-head combinations. In the first case it is the head which typically restricts the lexical choice of its modifier. In terms of lexical functions the head is the argument of the function and the modifier is the resulting value. We say that the head is the 'base' of the collocation and the modifier is the 'collocate'. In the second case, the syntactic argument selects the lexical form of the head.

The lexical collocations are further divided according to the syntactic categories of their components. There are three types to distinguish, as exemplified by the following collocations: 'comble de la joie' (noun-*noun*); 'désir ardent' (*noun*-adjective); 'donner conseil' verb-*noun* combination.

Let's consider each type of combination in turn. The first type (N+N) is instantiated by the following functions.

- SING(riz) = grain [de riz]: an *instance* of
- MULT(abeille) = essaim [d' abeille]: a *collection* of
- CULM(joie) = comble [de la joie]
- FIGUR(fumée) = rideau [de fumée]
- GENER(colère) = sentiment [de colère]

Semantically speaking, SING and MULT are converses. CULM is similar in meaning to MULT but they select different arguments (countable nouns versus abstract 'mass-like' nouns) and the first also carries the meaning "highest degree of". These functions have clearly a *quantificational* meaning in common.

The second type (A+N) consists of the functions MAGN, VER, BON, POS. These express degree (MAGN is often paraphrasable by "very") or *quality* ("correct", "good" and "positive") of the noun. Some examples.

- VER(peur) = justifiée
- BON(conseil) = précieux
- POS(opinion) = favorable

The third type (V+N) constitutes the class of support and aspectual verbs.

- $\text{OPER}_1(\text{attention})$ = faire
- $\text{FUNC}_0(\text{vent})$ = souffler
- $\text{FINOPER}_1(\text{influence})$ = perdre

6.2.2 The generative lexicon

The generative approach to lexical semantics derives its name from the use of generative devices instead of a fixed set of primitives. Much of the theory consists of structuring and integrating a number of well-known proposals on specific topics in lexical semantics and knowledge representation into one coherent theory. According to Pustejovsky (1991) the lexical semantic description should consist of the specification of four components. In the *qualia structure* for nouns "the essential attributes of an object as defined by the lexical item" are specified. The *event structure* (for verbs) defines the event type as either a state, a process, or a transition, whereas the *argument structure* characterizes the predicate argument structure for a word. Finally, the *lexical inheritance structure* defines the relation between a word and other concepts in the lexicon. Pustejovsky says of these components:

The important difference between this highly configurational approach to lexical semantics and feature-based approaches is that the recursive calculus defined for word meaning here also provides the foundation for a fully compositional semantics for natural language and its interpretation into a knowledge representation model. (1991, pp. 12–13)

This decomposition of information and the interaction between the parts is motivated amongst others by aspects of the problem of logical polysemy. The interaction, for instance, between the event-structure of a verb and the qualia-structure of a noun is essential to Pustejovsky's account of the logical polysemy of verbs. This account suggests a more intricate notion of composition. The basic idea is that arguments are not merely passive objects to their functions but they actively determine part of the meaning of the structures in which they are involved (Pustejovsky, 1991, p. 21). One of the examples given to illustrate this point is the difference in event type between *bake potato* and *bake cake*. Pustejovsky assumes that 'bake' only has the *change-of-state* reading but that 'cake', being an artifact, projects an event type of its own. The systematic difference in meaning is attributed to specific principles of semantic composition.

Nominal structure

The appeal to the difference between artifacts and natural kinds to account for the ambiguity of the 'bake' case is also systematized in the qualia structure of a noun. The qualia information is divided into four groups. The account of this kind of information is constantly ambivalent between 'a semantic description of a noun' and 'basic knowledge about the object'.

1. The constitutive role describes the relation between an object and its constituents or parts: *Material, Weight, Parts.*
2. The formal role "distinguishes the object within a larger domain": *Orientation, Magnitude, Shape, Dimensionality, Color, Position.*
3. The telic role describes the *Purpose, Function* of an object.
4. The agentive role describes "the factors involved in the origin or 'bringing about' of an object: *Creator, Artifact, Natural Kind, Causal Chain*".

Lexical inheritance structure

Besides a traditional (AI) inheritance network relating concepts by hyponymy and similar relations, Pustejovsky also introduces the notion of projective transformation and projective conclusion space to relate predicates. These transformations include ¬ (negation), ≤ (temporal precedence), ≥ (temporal succession), = (temporal equivalence) and *act* (agency). To explain, for instance, why the relation between *prisoner* and *escape* is tighter than that between *prisoner* and *eat*, one can use these transformations on the qualia structure of 'prisoner', thereby defining the projective conclusion space. In this case, the telic role is paraphrasable as 'being confined in a prison'. Generalizing this to 'being confined'; applying the negation operator to get the opposition between *not-confined* and *confined*; applying some temporal operators to generate two states *free before capture* and *free after capture*; and applying the operator *act* one gets *turn in, capture, escape,* and *release* (varying the agent). 'Escape' is thus in the 'projective conclusion space' for the Telic role of 'prisoner' whereas 'eat' is not.

6.2.3 *Lexical functions and the generative lexicon*

In this part we point out some connections and combinations of Pustejovsky's and Mel'čuk's approach to lexical semantics and lexicography.

Event structure

The information on event structure of a lexical item consists of three components: its *event type*, the *focus* of the event and the rules of *event composition*. Event types are defined as typical structural relationships between events. For instance a State is made up of one event "evaluated relative to no other event" (Pustejovsky, 1991, p. 14), whereas a Process is a *sequence* or *set* of events, and a Transition is an event evaluated relative to its opposition or negation. Using labeled bracketing instead of trees, we can translate Pustejovsky's examples as follows.

State $[e]_S$	The door is closed: $[\text{closed(door)}]_S$
Process $[e_1, \ldots, e_n]_P$	Mary ran: $[\text{move}(e_1,m), \ldots, \text{move}(e_n,m)]_P$
Transition $[[E_1][E_2]]_T$	The door closed: $[[Q(x) \ \& \ \neg\text{closed(door)}]_P$
	$[\text{closed(door)}]_S]_T$

These event structures are enriched in several ways. Pustejovsky points out that *aspectual verbs* select complements that are events which they embed into their own event structure. He also describes some examples of how the composition of event structures is guided and bounded by general principles and constraints.

What does Mel'čuk's theory of lexical functions add to this perspective on event structures? There are two ways to view the combination of the two theories.

Incorporating Pustejovsky's proposals into a Mel'čuk-like framework, we can say that the application of the relevant functions should be made sensitive to the event structure of the argument. This is precisely what is argued for[4] in Nakhimovsky (1992) on the basis of the aspectual differences between 'The man walked' and 'The man took a walk'.

The other way round, we can use the lexical functions as predicates in and operations on event-structures. We are thinking here more particularly of functions such as OPER, FUNC, LABOR (roughly paraphrasable as DO), INCEP, CONT, FIN (BEGIN, CONTINUE, STOP) and CAUS, INVOLV.

Note that some of the lexical functions express the same meanings as aspectual verbs. In general it would be worthwhile to see in what ways such general semantic operations and types as 'causation' and 'accomplishment' are realized in language. In this case we see that there are three linguistic constructions which encode such general operations: syntactic alternation, a specific class of verbs (aspectual verbs) and a reflex in collocational patterning. Another interesting topic for research would be to find out how elements of event structure are reflected in an ECD lexicon by considering the network of lexical items related through various lexical functions and their compositions.

Qualia structure

The qualia structure for nouns groups together certain information on the objects denoted. Again it is interesting to observe how some of these aspects also pop up in the description of collocations. We could therefore ask whether the study of this kind of expression and the analysis of the structures in terms of lexical functions could lead to a reasonable inventory of such features, specifically by looking at what may restrict or condition the application of certain functions. On the other hand, it should be carefully investigated how the qualia structure of nouns may restrict or condition the application of certain functions.

Examples of some relations that one can expect between lexical functions and aspects of qualia structure are the following.

Constitutive role. Aspects such as Material, Weight and Parts will affect values for functions such as SING and MULT and CULM. Looking at the various lexical functions or collocations may lead us to more detailed (motivated) proposals concerning this role.

Formal role. Quite interesting with respect to features such as Orientation, Shape, Dimensionality etc. are LFs such as MAGN, DEGRAD and EXCESS. The general function MAGN paraphrasable by "très" or "intense(ment)" can apply to many facets of the object denoted by its argument. Mel'čuk notes: "La FL MAGN peut être précisée par un indice sémantique ou actantiel. Les écritures comme MAGN^{quant}, MAGN^{temp}, etc., signifient qu'il s'agit, respectivement d'une intensification quantitative ou bien temporelle, etc." (Mel'čuk et al., 1984, p. 8).

Telic role. Although there are no specific functions that yield the purpose and function of their arguments as such, some functions do specify certain actions typically performed with the objects, which in some cases might indeed express their purpose or "a built-in function or aim which specifies certain activities". An example could be a function such as OPER which when applied to *question* yields *poser*.

Agentive role. A role such as creator may be linked to the argument structure of the verbs that are the values of such functions as OPER, FUNC etc. For instance, S_1(OPER(conseil)) = conseiller; adviseur . . .

We do not want to raise the impression that the qualia structure of a noun should be filled with its collocates, but rather that some types of slots can also be related to some lexical function, give rise to instances of collocational behavior, or may affect it in other ways. This collocational behavior may lead us to suggestions for refining the qualia structure.

Argument structure

Pustejovsky does not devote much attention to the theory of argument structure. He refers to work by Grimshaw and others. In the work of Mel'čuk, there is a dependency theory of argument structure in terms of the Meaning Text Model. In the dictionary this information is coded in that part of the lexical entry which is called "le schéma de régime".

> Le schéma de régime est un tableau qui présente explicitement tous les actants syntaxiques du lexème, en spécifiant pour chacun, d'une part, sa forme de surface (infinitif, syntagme prépositionnel avec telle préposition, etc.) et, d'autre part, son interprétation sémantique (c'est-à-dire l'actant sémantique qui lui correspond). De plus, le schéma de régime mentionne toutes les restrictions sur la cooccurrence des différents actants syntaxiques du même lexème. (Mel'čuk et al., 1984, pp. 5–6)

These arguments also figure in the lexical functions in the form of subscripts. For instance, S_1, S_2, S_3 are the typical names for the first, second and third 'actant' of the argument of the function. This function shows that argument structure also figures as a typical lexical relation (possibly morphologically related) between words. In this case the lexical functions are not primarily derived from collocational data of course.

Lexical inheritance structure

Pustejovsky deals in the subtheory on lexical inheritance with how semantic information (of lexical items) is organized as a global knowledge base (Pustejovsky, 1991, p. 31). He distinguishes between two types of inheritance relations. The first of these is a static one, similar to the traditional networks assumed in AI and lexical research. The second mechanism is a dynamic one "which operates *generatively* from the qualia structure of a lexical item to create a relational structure for *ad hoc* categories" (1991, p. 31).

Both of these types of inheritance relations can be related to the work on lexical functions. In general, the information specified by the ECD in terms of lexical functions can be thought of as the specification of a semantic network where nodes are lexemes which are the argument and the value of the lexical function labeling the (directed) association between these nodes.

As for the first (Pustejovsky-) type of inheritance relation, many of the paradigmatic lexical functions correspond to links which are familiar from AI-networks and other work on Lexical Knowledge Bases (such as ISA, hyponym, hypernym, synonym). Among these are SYN, ANTI, GENER.

The dynamic kind of inheritance makes use of projective transformations which map predicates onto others. These transformations are comparable to lexical functions. It seems (at first sight) that their function can be "simulated" by using lexical functions (which are more or less independently motivated). The 'projective conclusion space' generated for a certain predicate (that is, the set of projective expansion which result from the application of the projective transformations on the predicate) can be compared to nodes which are reachable in a

Mel'čuk-like network by traversing several associations, i.e., by composing functions. Above we have presented Pustejovsky's analysis of the relation between 'prisoner' and 'escape'. An analysis in terms of lexical functions might use the following functions to relate the two items.

- S_2(emprison) = prisoner
- ANTI(CONV(emprison)) = escape

Again, we can think of the lexical functions as generating a network of lexical items connected by these semantic operations.

Conclusion

We have addressed the question 'how do lexical functions fit into a knowledge representation scheme' by relating the theory of lexical functions to another approach to lexical semantics (the generative lexicon) in which connections with knowledge representation issues have been made explicit. It is obvious that both theories are different in scope and intention. The purpose of the comparison was to establish the potential use of lexical functions outside their native habitat (the Explanatory Combinatory Dictionaries). The confrontation of the two theories viewed from this perspective results in two complementary issues which have repeatedly been touched upon in the discussion above: (1) the sensitivity of the lexical functions to aspects of the representation structures posited in the generative lexicon; (2) the possibility of using lexical functions as some kind of 'primitive instruction set' to be integrated in the generative lexicon set up.

We shall now discuss the epistemological nature of lexical functions and the semantic networks they give rise to.

6.3   Knowledge representation with lexical functions

In this section we 'assume' some interpretation of the ECD as a kind of knowledge representation model. We relate the LF-approach to more general issues of knowledge representation (KR) and situate this approach in terms of others. Some of the questions we will touch upon include: How do the lexical functions and the entries in the ECD relate to knowledge bases? In what sense would they constitute a linguistic basis for KR?

Pioneering work on knowledge representation by Quillian (1985) shows the intimate connection it has with lexical semantics and lexicography. One of the key concepts in KR, that of 'semantic network', is generally accredited to Quillian. The model described in the article consists of a recoding of definitions from a dictionary into a network of concepts/words. The associative links between the 'words' Quillian mentions are of different kinds: subclass-superclass, modification, disjunction, conjunction, and an open-ended category "by means of which all the remaining kinds of relationships are encoded".[5] Furthermore, in Quillian's network parameters are associated with certain 'words'.

[T]he parameter symbols are of three kinds, corresponding to certain ways that other words in the text may be related to the word to which the parameters belong. *S* is the parameter symbol whose value is to be any word related to the present word as its subject; D is the parameter symbol whose value is to be any word related to the present word as its direct object; and M is the parameter symbol whose value is to be any word that the present word directly modifies. (Quillian, 1985, p. 108)

Another feature of the network is the inclusion of information concerning 'selectional restrictions' on the value of the parameters. In this general set-up the following more detailed issues can be raised amongst others.

- The nature of objects that constitute the nodes/links.
- The precise inventory of objects inhabiting the nodes/links.
- The organization of the network.[6]
- The relation between the network, language, the mind and the world.
- The distinction between types and tokens.

From the ECD we can construct two kinds of semantic networks: the one representing definitions (the *definition network*), the other information encoded by lexical functions (the *LF network*). The following quote describes the former kind of network (which we didn't mention before).

An ECD definition is a decomposition of the meaning of the corresponding lexeme. It is a semantic network whose nodes are labeled either with semantic units (actually, lexemes) of L, or with variables, and whose arcs are labeled with distinctive numbers which identify different arguments of a predicate. A lexical label represents the definition (the meaning) of the corresponding lexeme, rather than the lexeme itself. (Mel'čuk and Polguère, 1987, p. 13)

Nature of nodes and links

Before we consider the nature of the elements making up the ECD-networks, we summarize the analysis of the status of semantic networks by Brachman (1985). Here, he describes five levels on which semantic networks can be viewed. On the *implementational* level a network is simply conceived of as a certain data-structure. Viewed from a *logical* level, nodes represent predicates and links represent logical relationships. On the *conceptual* level the nodes are word-senses and links represent semantic or conceptual relationships.

Networks at this level can be characterized as having small sets of language-independent conceptual elements (namely, primitive object- and action-types) and conceptually primitive relationships [. . .] out of which all expressible concepts can be constructed. (Brachman, 1985, p. 205)

Whereas "a general characteristic of this level is that it should be language-independent" (ibid.), on the *linguistic* level the elements are language specific and the links "stand for arbitrary relationships that exist in the world being represented" (ibid.). Brachman also considers a fifth level, which he places between the logical and the conceptual level. On this *epistemological* level, the formal structure and configuration of the elements making up the network are described. Although these distinctions may not be very clear-cut and the specification of each level a bit vague, we get at least some idea of the issues that are involved. Let us now turn to the ECD networks.

The lexemes making up the <u>nodes</u> in a network are defined as follows.

Un LEXÈME est un mot pris dans une seule acception bien déterminée et muni de toutes les informations caractérisant le comportement de ce mot justement lorsqu'il est utilisé dans cette acception. (Mel'čuk et al., 1984, p. 4)

From this we can infer that the network proposed is defined on a linguistic level. The words are taken from some specific language. Of course, the particular position taken on the matter of whether readings can be viewed as language-independent objects can influence the tendency toward a more conceptual interpretation of the objects. In any case, the linguistic level dominates. The nodes are made up from specific words from a specific language in a specific reading. Words from different languages with the same reading (sense) – assuming a position at which we can say this – would still constitute a different node.

In the definition network the <u>links</u> "are labeled with distinctive numbers which identify different arguments of a predicate". The level of analysis we are talking about is SemR (semantic representation) in MTT terms. The representations on this level are based on predicate argument relations. In terms of Brachman's classification the links reside on the logical level.

The associations between nodes in the LF-network induced by the lexical functions are of a more heterogeneous and obscure nature. Mel'čuk says that grossly speaking, a lexical function is a fairly abstract 'sense' or a certain 'semantico-syntactic' role. In the latter case we are dealing clearly with Brachman's conceptual level. As it is not explicitly defined what the ontological nature of 'senses' is, we can be guided only by examples and compare them with other proposals. We then see that the lexical functions proposed are most like the examples Brachman gives of other conceptual relations besides cases, viz., the primitives proposed by Schank and his followers. Mel'čuk notes the following about definitional networks in other frameworks.

In various computational or formal approaches, lexicographic definitions are written in terms of a small set of prefabricated elements. It looks as if the researcher's goal was to make his definitional language as different as possible from his object language (cf. conceptual dependencies in Schank, 1972, logical representations in Dowty, 1979, and the like). [. . .] In sharp contrast to this, the ECD defines a lexeme L of language L in terms of other lexemes L_1, L_2, . . . ,L_n, of L [. . .]. (Mel'čuk and Polguère, 1987, p. 265)

Indeed, we have seen that the nodes of the network are lexemes, of the language, but the labels on the arcs are not. Whereas one group of these derives from the general linguistic theory (Deep Semantics), another group is also named by symbols from some artificial (latinate) language different from the object language.

Inventory

The ultimate ECD for some language L contains (as nodes) all lexemes L, i.e., all words of L in all their senses. The labels on the arcs in the definitional network are fixed by the underlying linguistic theory. These are probably expected by Mel'čuk to be few in number and assumed to be universal. This is at least explicitly stated about the deep syntactic relations (Mel'c̆uk and Polguère, 1987, p. 262). As it is unclear where the abstract senses related to the lexical functions come from, the exact basis for the inventory of these is unknown. The inventory derives from the observation of recurrent patterns in an observable linguistic domain, mainly collocation patterning. This at least defines an empirical basis. From a methodological point of view, one should try to find ways to answer questions such as the following.

- How can we identify the relevant empirical data? Can we establish a representative sample?
- How can we find the correct analysis of the linguistic data in terms of the lexical functions?
- How can we identify the correct functions?

Suppose we are given some syntagm which we know counts as a collocation. Can we find out what lexical function is expressed? Do we have intuitions? Can the functions be described adequately? Are instances clear? Can we define tests?

Answers to these questions would help to decide on the adequacy of taking a lexical function perspective on knowledge representation.

Network, language, mind, world

There are many ways to view the relations between language, the world and the semantic network. In the TACITUS approach, for instance, one attempts first to construct commonsense theories about the world, i.e., build ontologies relative to which lexical items are defined. Most of the leading principles of this work are in direct contrast with Mel'c̆uk's views. To list a few of these we take some quotes from Hobbs (1985).

We use words to talk about the world. Therefore, to understand what words mean, we must have a prior explication of how we view the world.

It is easier to achieve elegance if one does not have to be held responsible to linguistic evidence. Predicates that *are* lexically realized are then pushed to the periphery of the theory. A large number of lexical items can be defined, or at least characterized, in terms provided by the core theories.

An old favorite question for lexical theorists is whether one can make a useful distinction between linguistic knowledge and world knowledge. The position I have articulated leads one to an answer that can be stated briefly. There is no useful distinction.

In contrast to Hobbs' view, which can be characterized as 'world first, word later', Mel'c̆uk starts from linguistic evidence and explictly states that the analysis is merely a linguistic one.

As we have already said, the SemR in the MTT is aimed at representing the **linguistic** meaning, i.e., the common core of all synonymous utterances [...]. Therefore, the full-fledged description of linguistic behavior should include another representation – the representation of the state of affairs in the real world, and another model – the Reality-Meaning Model. The latter ensures the transition between the results of perception etc. and the SemR, which is the starting/end point of linguistic activity proper.

We insist on distinguishing the SemR from the real world/knowledge representation because we feel that the description of linguistic activity in the strict sense of the term is very different from the description of perceptual or logical activity.

The SemR is not an ideal interlingua – although it can be effectively used to bring closer the source and the target languages – because a SemR, by definition, reflects the idiomatic characteristics of the language in question. (Mel'čuk and Polguère, 1987, pp. 268–269)

Types and tokens

I would like to interpret the difference between types and tokens using a Montagovian perspective. One can say of a certain linguistic expression that its denotation is of a certain *type* (in the case of Montague semantics, an individual, a truth-value, a function from individuals to truth-values, etc). The exact denotation, which depends on the specific model chosen, defines the token value of a specific expression (for instance 'John' could refer to a specific person when used by some speaker in some context, with a specific model in mind). In Montague grammar the aim is not to specify the token-models for linguistic expressions, but rather to characterize the structure of models in general insofar as they are constrained or determined by linguistic structure. This is why Emmon Bach talks about 'natural language metaphysics'.

Knowledge representation systems in some cases will specify both the abstract ontology of the 'world' and the specifics of some actual world, what is actually true and false in that world, which entities inhabit the world, etc. In this respect, the ECD network also deals with the first kind of specification only. The difference between the approaches to meaning in MTT and Montague are therefore perhaps not as different as Mel'čuk himself likes to think.

6.4   Conclusion

In the previous sections we have seen that the semantic networks constructable from an ECD resemble in many respects proposals for such networks in knowledge representation circles. Contrary to the spirit of Mel'čuk's interpretation, we could imagine that Mel'čuk's analysis can serve as a linguistic basis for knowledge representation. The evaluation of the suitability of lexical functions as linguistically motivated bases for knowledge representation should at least address the following questions.

- Are lexical functions linguistically motivated?
- Are they a proper basis for knowledge representation?

These questions presuppose one of our initial assumptions that ontologies should be linguistically motivated. We can imagine a number of arguments supporting this assumption. The most obvious reason for the assumption is that the knowledge bases we are considering are to be used by natural language processing applications. An adequate system should know what the assumptions about the world are that are encoded in linguistic structure. There is a more general argument conceivable – but one which leaves room for a less strict variant of this claim. In general one could say that the ontology should not be arbitrary but needs external motivation, or independent evidence. Both language and the world are open-ended systems, but whereas the open-endedness of language has been (at least conceptually) controlled by defining recursive systems called grammar there is yet no viable suggestion of defining a grammar of the world.

These arguments are certainly not conclusive. But we can also take a proper linguistic position and have as our main research objective the articulation of the structure of the world as assumed in linguistic structures, regardless of whether this structure is useful for other areas of science and engineering (say KR). In this perspective, the arguments merely point to potential motivations for taking into account the linguistic structure of the world when trying to structure the knowledge for some other purpose.

What about the claim that lexical functions are an appropriate foundation for filling in more ontological details? The evidence for this is difficult to establish as it is unclear why there is such a thing as collocational behavior. At the moment, we can only make hypotheses guided by such observations as the following. A large number of collocations can be fitted into a small number of categories (assigned some function): a large variety of expressions is used to express the same meaning. Collocations seem to appear frequently as well. Next, there is the observation that many of these functions/operations figure in other types of constructions as well and are useful in varying domains. Two other applications are, for instance, the use of lexical functions as a heuristic tool in the field work by Grimes (1992) to elicit lexical information from naive informants; and the use of lexical functions in the analysis and generation of cohesive texts (see Lee and Evens, 1992, and references cited therein).

Lexical functions were introduced by Mel'čuk to describe collocational patterns in natural language. A number of areas in knowledge representation models assume (primitive) operations which closely resemble such functions. The question then arises whether we can use collocations as an empirical basis and lexical functions as theoretical constructs as foundations for substantive analyses in KR. In this chapter we have tried to point out some justification for this approach, and many of the research questions which arise.

Notes

1. For a more detailed classification we would like to refer to Ramos and Tutin, (1992) and references cited there.
2. We have excluded from this list a small number of supportive functions. These are functions that never seem to be used on their own, but always appear in combinations: *Plus*, *Minus* and *Pred*. We did not include the atypical *Imper* and *Sympt* either.
3. These are commonly signaled in dictionaries by means of what Vossen et al., (1989, p. 179) call *Shunters*. Examples are the italic parts of the following definitions.

   • adornment: "an *act* which consists of adorning"
   • actuality: "a *state* which consists of being real"

4. Though not specifically for the Pustejovsky analysis.

5. "This is necessary because in natural language text almost anything can be considered as a relation, so that there is no way to specify in advance what relationships are to be needed [. . .]." (Quillian, 1985, p. 106).
6. We will not discuss this with respect to ECD networks.

References

Ronald J. Brachman. (1985). On the epistemological status of semantic networks. In Brachman and Levesque, editors, *Readings in Knowledge Representation*, pages 192–215. Morgan Kaufmann Publishers, Los Altos.

Joseph E. Grimes. (1992). Lexical functions across languages. In *International Workshop on the Meaning-Text Theory*, pages 123–132, Darmstadt.

Jerry R. Hobbs. (1985). World knowledge and word meaning. In *Theoretical Issues in Natural Language Processing 3*, pages 20–27. Association of Computational Linguistics.

Wonogjae Lee and Martha Evens. (1992). Generating cohesive text using lexical functions. In *International Workshop on the Meaning-Text Theory*, pages 207–214, Darmstadt.

I.A. Mel'čuk and A. Polguère. (1987). A formal lexicon in the meaning-text theory. *Computational Linguistics*, 13(3–4).

Igor Mel'čuk, Nadia Arbatchewsky-Jumarie, Léo Elnitsky, Lidija Iordanskaja, and Adèle Lessard. (1984). *Dictionnaire explicatif et combinatoire du français contemporain*. Les Presses de l'Université de Montréal, Montreal.

Alexander Nakhimovsky. (1992). The lexicon, grammar and commonsense knowledge: the case of aspectual polysemy. In *International Workshop on the Meaning-Text Theory*, pages 67–78, Darmstadt.

James Pustejovsky. (1991). The generative lexicon. *Computational Linguistics*, 17(4), October–December.

M. Ross Quillian. (1985). Word concepts: A theory and simulation of some basic semantic capabilities. In Brachman and Levesque, editors, *Readings in Knowledge Representation*, pages 98–118. Morgan Kaufmann Publishers, Los Altos.

M. Alonso Ramos and Agnès Tutin. (1992). A classification and description of the lexical functions of the explanatory combinatory dictionary. In *International Workshop on the Meaning-Text Theory*, pages 187–196, Darmstadt.

P. Vossen, W. Meijs, and M. den Broeder. (1989). Meaning and structure in dictionary definitions. In Boguraev and Briscoe, editors, *Computational Lexicography for Natural Language Processing*. Longman, New York.

7   Semantic features in a generic lexicon

GABRIEL G. BÈS AND ALAIN LECOMTE

7.1   Introduction

7.1.1   *Some approaches to semantics*

Various theories[1] are nowadays used in linguistic analysis, particularly in syntax, and it does not seem reasonable to expect a reduction of their number in the near future. Nor does it seem reasonable to expect that one theory will cover them, as a kind of meta-theory. Nevertheless, all these theories have in common the need for a lexicon which would include the necessary and sufficient information for combining lexical items and extracting a representation of the meaning of such combinations.

If it is not possible to propose a canonical theory to organize the storage of the lexical information, it is necessary to adopt a *"polytheoretic"* conception of the lexicon. (Hellwig, Minkwitz, and Koch, 1991). A point shared by different theories concerns the need for some *semantic* information even for a syntactic parsing of a sentence (and a fortiori, beyond this level, for the parsing of a text).

During a first period, the semantic information required was above all concentrated on the *thematic roles* (Gruber, 1965; Jackendoff, 1972). These thematic roles were introduced because the grammatical functions were insufficient for discriminating between various interpretations and for describing the similarities of sentences. For instance, in:

(1)   *The door opened*
(2)   *Charlie opened the door*

the door is considered as having the same semantic function but not the same grammatical function – subject for (1) and object for (2). Gruber (1965) gives to *the door* in the two sentences the same thematic role of *theme*. A similar objective was assigned to the *case-theory* (Fillmore, 1968). This trend is still dominating the work done in the framework of the GB-(Government Binding) theory, under the aspect of *theta-roles*.

But, at the same time as the Chomskyan Generative Theory was developed, the theory of Montague proposed a very integrated theory of syntax and semantics. So, during a second period, the semantic information required has consisted of functional structures which are combined at the same time that the signs that denote them are syntactically combined. These structures are matters for the *typed lambda-calculus* and the *intensional logic*. The semantic information required

141

involves semantic categories assigned to words, which can be translated into *logical types*. A high level of integration between the generative model and the theory of Montague was reached by the GPSG (Generalized Phrase Structure Grammars) approach (Gazdar et al., 1985).

In a third period, so-called *post-Montagovian* theories were developed in order to solve questions the theory of Montague could not deal with: for instance, the questions of the *ambiguity of quantifier-scopes,* of the *de re/de dicto* ambiguity, and the question of the *dynamic scope of quantifiers* (linked to the problems of coordination between sentences, as in "Peter has a donkey. He beats it.").

The semantic information required is then more complex. It involves some kind of rules which determines what kind of semantic categories a word can belong to (for instance: rules of *type-lifting*). The *Flexible Montague Grammar* (Hendricks, 1989) is so-called because categories are not rigidly assigned to words. For instance, it is well known that since Montague's PTQ (Montague, 1973), it has assigned to NPs a semantic category $<<e,t>,t>$ rather than merely **e** (in order to deal with the quantification phenomena). A consequence is that even a proper name is a functor over a predicate. This assignment is not necessary if we admit a type-raising rule according to which any unity of type **a** is also of type $<<a, b >,b>$ for all **b**, and if we use this rule only if necessary.

In Categorial Grammars, the type-lifting of an argument corresponds to a unary rule. The question arises whether it is syntactic or semantic. But numerous works (mainly Dowty, 1988) have suggested that the type-raising of categories, being constrained by lexical types, must appear as a lexical rule. Other approaches consider that families of categories or categories with variables must be assigned to words in the lexicon. This opens the way to *polymorphism* (Moortgat, 1988; Calder, 1987; Klein, Zeevat, and Calder, 1987).

Among the post-Montagovian theories, much attention must be paid to the *Theory of Discursive Representations* of Hans Kamp, and to its linearized version by Zeevat, called *InL* (Zeevat, 1991). This theory requires assigning to lexical entries expressions with an *index* (corresponding to *referent markers* in the DRS theory), such that expressions can be combined by the operation of unification with a control on the index-type. It has been shown that the DRS (Discourse Representation Structure) theory has several possible translations into other formalisms. For instance, it can be expressed in the Montagovian framework (with some rather small extensions, like the notions of *states* and *state-switching*) (Groenendijk and Stokhof, 1990; Dekker, 1990). It can be expressed, too, in the *Constructive Type Theory* (Ahn and Kolb, 1990). But it is still an open question whether these various theories are only variants of each other, or if they constitute something specific of their own.

This last point leads us to the polytheoretic approach. We have to enter enough information into a lexicon to provide each of the previous theories with what it needs to work, even if specific modules of translation are required to transform the generic information into a specific one.

Otherwise, many recent approaches to the lexicon have shown how to integrate a semantic information consisting in *aspectual features* into the syntax (Dowty, 1979; Pustejovsky, 1990). They have insisted, too, on the possibility of solving questions of *metaphor, metonymy* and *polysemy* (Sowa, 1989; Boguraev and Pustejovsky, 1991; Boguraev, Briscoe, and Copestake, 1991). Dealing with these questions requires considering lexical entries as providing much more information than was previously assumed. We shall see later, for instance, how we can conceive a lexical entry for a *common noun*, the point being that several viewpoints on the "piece of reality" denoted by it are always possible.

Finally, if we wish to include semantic information in the lexicon for different uses, it seems necessary to introduce a *hierarchy of pieces of information.* This hierarchy will come from an *observational level,* and will be based on a description of a language, paying attention to what constructions are permitted and to what are not. That seems to be a preliminary question for any processing of metaphors and polysemy. In a perspective of parsing a sentence, it allows the parser to eliminate impossible sentences at a first glance, just as human readers do. The *first* part of this communication will thus be devoted to this question of *hierarchization.* The *second* part will be concerned by a level of *meta-description* of the semantic information, linked to the level of phenomenological description of the syntax. In the third part, we shall try to look at *nouns,* and how the descriptions of meanings can be arranged in order to solve questions of *metaphor* and *polysemy.*

7.1.2   *Methodological requisites*

We insist on the fact that we try here to present neither any new theory, nor any kind of meta-theory. We try only to introduce a *meta-language* of description of the *word meanings,* in order that special algorithms may perform the transformation of this kind of description into formulas and terms used in an appropriate theory. We do not think that these descriptions could be directly usable in a meta-theory because such a theory would probably be untractable. Specific theories are used to deal with specific processings of sentences and texts. They are designed to be tractable. To put them altogether in only one device would provoke an explosion in complexity.

Furthermore, the semantic information we seek to include in the lexicon must be the most "concrete" possible (cf. Hellwig et al., 1991). That is, it must be related systematically to observations on meaning. These, in their turn, must be founded, at least in principle, on operational tests and must be reproducible and intersubjective.

Lastly, this information must be systematically associated with linguistic forms, particularly syntactic frames (see the following section), with a large coverage. In the ideal case, it should tend toward exhaustivity.

7.2   Hierarchization of the semantic information in the lexicon

Semantic features included in the lexicon refer to an implicit structure (cognitively interpretable or not) which:

1. gives them a structural meaning (a meaning obtained by a position in a structure rather than an intrinsic meaning) and
2. must allow us to derive the kind of semantic entities we want to use in different approaches.

Minimal ingredients are necessary to build those formulas these approaches require. This program must be performed by stages and these stages reflect an implicit hierarchical organization of the semantic information.

We assume that the semantic information is organized in three systems: a grammatical system, as included in the grammar, a conceptual system and an encyclopedic system.

The grammatical system

The semantic information included in this part is the minimal semantic information required in order for the rules of grammar to construct, concurrently with the syntactic information (and other grammatical information) a minimal semantic representation. It is formally related to linguistic forms. It allows us:

1. to know whether an interpretation is obtainable from a given utterance
2. to construct the part of the semantic interpretation which is determined by the syntactic construction.

The conceptual system

The semantic information included in the conceptual system expands the grammatical information. It is founded in some more or less conventional and explicit classificatory or definitional system. It is not related to syntactic forms, by definition.

The encyclopedic system

The semantic information in the encyclopedic system reflects a state of knowledge at a given instant. Consider the following examples:[2]

(3)   (a) *Jacques tourne la poignée*
         (b) *La poignée tourne*
         (c) *Jacques tourne la terre*
         (d) *La terre tourne*
         (e) *La terre tourne autour du soleil*
         (f) *Le soleil tourne autour de la terre*

At the first level, the grammar will assign a non-deviant semantic representation to sentences from (a) to (f). At this level, (3)(c) differs from (3)(a) only with respect to the denotation of *la poignée* (*the door-handle*) and *la terre* (*the earth*).

At the second level, the anomaly of (3)(c) is indicated. At the third level, (3)(f) is considered true before Galileo and false after him, (3)(e) being considered false before and true after. As another example, let us consider the sentence:

(4)   *"La lune tombe continuellement sur la terre"*
        ("The Moon is continually falling down to the Earth")

Here, the grammatical system can recognize this sentence as a meaningful sentence: that means a sentence which has a constructible interpretation. The syntactic construction associated with the verbal lemma *tomber* is sufficient to do that. We have: NP_0 surNP_1 as such a construction (where NP_i denote nominal phrases, complements of rank i in the sentence). Nevertheless, the conceptual system can recognize it as an anomaly because the denotation of the argument in the NP_0-place is a mobile entity, the movement of which is expressed by the verb. This movement is essentially *terminative* and requires a *termination point* located at the denotation of the argument which occurs at the NP_1-place. And the feature *terminative* is contradictory with the denotation of the adverb "continuellement". Thus, a metaphoric interpretation will necessarily be produced.

Lastly, the encyclopedic system could define *"tomber"* as *"to obey the gravitation law"* thus eliminating the iterative interpretation linked to the adverb.

These three levels are required if we want to avoid several pitfalls:

1. the pitfalls of a notion of lexicon assumed to exhaust the present knowledge,
2. the pitfalls of a definitional system based on necessary and sufficient conditions which immediately eliminates any seemingly deviant utterance, and
3. the pitfalls of a confusion between syntax and semantics which would lead us to a conception where "everything would be semantic", a conception which does not seem desirable in the present state of our knowledge.

7.3   The model

7.3.1   *Two kinds of semantic features*

We assume that a sentence must be described by a syntactic representation, a semantic representation and a mapping between them. Syntactic representations are built from syntactic constituents (NP, PP and the like). A semantic representation is a thematic structure where we distinguish thematic nodes. Syntactic constituents are mapped onto thematic nodes, and the semantic representation of the sentence is calculated from the semantic values (denotations) directly associated with the constituents, or transmitted by thematic nodes. A lexical entry presents typically a thematic structure, one or more syntactic frame(s) (subcategorization) and mappings between the former and each of the latter ones. In certain cases, the mapping function can be evaluated in terms of syntactic information alone. See for instance:

(5)   (a) *Le prisonnier dort*[3]
       (b) *La chaussée dort*
       (c) *Isabelle a volé un bijou à Marie*
       (d) *Isabelle a volé Pierre à Marie*
       (e) *Isabelle a volé une pierre à ce bijou*

In (5)(a) to (e) a semantic representation is constructible by a mapping from the syntactic representation. In the thematic structure of *dormir,* the thematic node, associated with the subject will require some feature-value as [+*animate*], but this information is not needed to calculate the mapping. Compare with:

(6)   (a) *Isabelle a volé Pierre*[4]
       (b) *Isabelle a volé ce bijou*
       (c) *Pierre rassemble ses habits*
       (d) *L'armoire rassemble ses habits*
       (e) *Le maire a élargi le prisonnier*
       (f) *Le maire a élargi la chaussée*

In (6)(a), *Pierre* must be mapped to the same thematic node as *Marie* in (5)(d) and in (6)(b), *ce bijou* (*jewel*) must be mapped onto the same thematic node as in (5)(c). *Pierre* in (6)(a) and in (5)(d) is not mapped onto the same thematic node. That of *ce bijou* in (6)(b) cannot be the same as the one in (5)(e). Depending on their denotation, *Pierre* and *l'armoire* (*the cupboard*) must be mapped onto different thematic nodes in (6)(c) and (6)(d) (cf. Fradin, 1990). The same is true for *le prisonnier* (*the prisoner*) and *la chaussée* (*the roadway*) in (6)(e) and (6)(f) but for this latter case, two different thematic structures will be used because one thematic node is required for the first sentence and another is required for the second, and it does not make sense to have both together in the same thematic structure. Thus we are able to say that there are at least two lexical meanings for the verb *élargir* (one corresponding to *to release,* the other to *to widen*).

We distinguish thus crucially between denotational semantic features of the first level, which will affect the constituents of a syntactic frame, and denotational semantic features of the second level which will be represented in the semantic nodes of the thematic structure. The first are relevant to the mapping function and they occur as distinctive features in many situations (as for (6)(c) and (6)(d), for instance). In such situations, a semantic feature is required when pairing a particular syntactic frame and the thematic structure associated with the given verb. This is not the case for the second ones.

It follows from these considerations that it is impossible (and not only inelegant, non-explicative or redundant) to calculate semantic representations from an "autonomous syntax". In some cases, syntactic frames enforce the construction of some semantic representation (even if deviant) while, in other cases, the semantic features associated with particular constituents in given frames eliminate mappings which would be otherwise possible with other linguistic forms. Any model of the lexicon must carefully account for these two different kinds of situations.

Little will be said here about syntactic frames.[5] We assume a list of constituents and of syntactic functions, and we require that they be defined in purely syntactic terms, without any kind of symbol belonging to the semantic representations. Such indices are only added for the pairing operation between syntactic frames and thematic structures. We discuss hereafter thematic structures and this operation of pairing.

7.3.2   *Thematic roles and thematic structures*

Recently, many authors (Rappaport, Laughren and Levin 1987; Jackendoff, 1990; Ravin, 1991; Pustejovsky, 1990) advanced solid arguments in favor of derived thematic roles. For instance, Rappaport et al. point up the fact that lexical entries cannot merely consist in lists of theta-roles (so-called theta-grids). One of the reasons is that there is no one-to-one mapping between argumental positions (our "syntactic positions") and semantic notions such as: agent, patient, theme or goal. They prefer to describe the theta-roles assignment by means of linking rules dictating a particular association of variables in "Lexical Conceptual Structures" with variables in the "Predicate-Argument Structure" of a given verb. Concurrently, Pustejovsky (1990) calculates these roles by starting from a system with *aspectual values*. Our conception is very similar except that we are not bound to a particular theoretical framework (such as GB) and thus we express this association in our meta-language of description, rather than in generative terms.

We shall assume here a denotational universe U, and a set of relations *Rel* over U. <U,Rel> is exactly what we call a *structure* in mathematical logic.

> *Definition 1: a thematic structure,* for a verb v, is a subset of <U, Rel> selected by v.

The thematic structure expresses the kind of semantic information a verb brings to us in the language use. In a cognitive perspective, we can say that such verbal structures give access to a certain denotational universe, or that this latter universe is the "real universe" when filtered by verbal structures.

> *Definition 2:* we shall call a *thematic node* or thematic position a node in a thematic structure.

It is important to note that the relations over U are primitive entities.

7.3.3   *Associations between syntactic frames and thematic structures*

> *Definition 3:* we shall call *a reading* of an utterance e any association of a syntactic frame $\{P_i\}_{i \in I}$ belonging to the verbal entry, with a sub-structure <U, Rel>.

This association must be a morphism:

$$\phi: <U, Rel> \rightarrow \{P_i\}_{i \in I}$$

That means: if d associates with each P_i its denotation in the universe of reference, we have:

for each R and $\rho \in$ *Rel:* for all T_i and $T_k \in U$, $R(T_i, T_k) \Rightarrow R(d(\phi(T_i)), d(\phi(T_k)))$

and $\rho(T_i) \Rightarrow \rho(d(\phi(T_i)))$

This condition entails that the denotations of constituents must be compatible with the relations included in the thematic structure of the entry. The morphism is not necessarily an isomorphism because some relations can be missing in the syntactic frame and some syntactic positions can be missing, too.

As an example, we take the verb *rassembler* (Fradin, 1990) in the sentences (6) (c) and (d) recalled here in (7)(a) and (b), to which we add (7)(c).

(7)   (a) *Pierre rassemble ses habits*[6]
        (b) *L'armoire rassemble ses habits*
        (c) *Pierre rassemble ses habits dans l'armoire*

L'armoire (*the cupboard*) in (7)(b) is associated with the same thematic role as *dans l'armoire* in (7)(c). Syntactically, (7)(a) and (7)(b) are associated with the same syntactic frame N_0VN_1. To make the necessary distinction, we have only to introduce the feature [*Nhum*+] as necessary for a syntactic frame:

N_0[Nhum+] V N_1

In doing so, we get a first-level feature which will be necessary to identify the appropriate reading of *l'armoire rassemble les habits*. [*Nhum*+] is a first-level feature which must be associated with the frame of (7)(a) and not with the frame of (7)(b). The denotation of *armoire* does not normally accept this feature because armoire denotes a physical non-animate entity. This situation triggers a necessary association with the syntactic frame which does not require this feature. This situation can be illustrated by the following figure, where SF_1, SF_2 and SF_3 correspond respectively to the syntactic frames of (7)(a), (b) and (c).

In Figure 7.1, the relations over the universe are represented by labeled arrows. Some of these are arcs joining two distinct vertices, and some are just loops. The former are binary relations and the latter unary ones (i.e., properties). The labels belong to a set of primitives such as: *loc, mobile,* or ©. This last label comes from the work of Desclés (cf. Desclés, 1990) where it is defined as an operator of intentional control. These relations give to their sources and goals specific interpretations which can receive appropriate names. For instance, many researchers will desire to interpret as **agent** the source of the ©-arrow. On the other hand, the status of the goal of such an arrow may depend on the kind of arrow it is composed with. For example, if it is composed with a *mobile* entity which is a physical object, the interpretation can be that of **theme**, if it is composed with a non-mobile entity that of a **patient,** etc.

There is another important feature of our meta-language: arrows can join not only a vertex to another one, but also a vertex to another arrow or even arrows between them. The best way to represent these situations is to make use of the recursively defined notion of *type*, as is done in the theory of semantic categories.

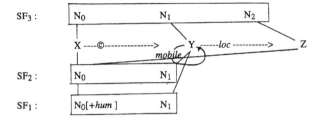

Figure 7.1.

Assigning an atomic type to the elements of U, and to the possible sorts of sentences, we define complex types in the following traditional manner:

if **a** and **b** are types, **a**→**b** is a type

We define the *composition of types* such as in the typed lambda-calculus by:

if **a** and **a**→**b** are types, the composition of objects inhabiting these types gives an object of type **b**.

We assume now the existence of atomic types for sentences, depending on what kind of entity it denotes: events, states or processes. We can use: **e**, **s** and **pr**. Elements in the universe U are assigned an atomic type **t**.

A thematic structure is given by a collection of *variables,* belonging to an atomic type, and a collection of *typed functors.* For instance, the thematic structure of *rassembler* contains:

$$©^{t\to(t\to(s\to e))}, \texttt{mobile}^{t\to t} \text{ and } \texttt{loc}^{t\to(t\to s)}$$

These functors have appropriate types in order to be combined in convenient ways. For instance, the last one (loc) must take as argument the result of the previous one (mobile). It is the reason why loc will be defined as a λ-function: $\lambda V.\texttt{loc}^{t\to(t\to s)}(V)$, which must take its argument *among* the results of the other functors. The thematic structure also contains variables, occurring as *parameters* of the functors: X, Y, Z . . . distinguished from other variables by the nature of punctuation signs surrounding them (brackets [. . .] instead of parentheses (. . .)) in order that the complete representation of the components of the thematic structure are:

$$\lambda U.©^{t\to(t\to(s\to e))}[X][Y](U), \texttt{mobile}^{t\to t}[Y] \text{ and } \lambda V.\texttt{loc}^{t\to(t\to s)}(V)\,[Z]$$

We call these functors: *parametrized functors.*

The associations of syntactic frames with thematic structures may be represented as *sets of equations* linking the parameters inside the parametrized functors and the variables denoting the syntactic positions in the frames. Finally, we will assume that a thematic structure is a λ-*scheme,* like:

$$\lambda X.\ \lambda Y.\ \lambda Z\ [\lambda U.©^{t\to(t\to(s\to e))}[X[\text{Nhum+}]][Y](U);$$
$$\texttt{mobile}^{t\to t}[Y];$$
$$\lambda V.\texttt{loc}^{t\to(t\to s)}(V)[Z]]$$

Parameters (X, Y, Z, . . .) are implicitly typed according to the typing of the functors, for instance, X is of type **t** and Y, too. Types may be feature-types. Some
(semantic) features are inherited from the syntactic frames via the equations. Features inherent to objects bound to the parameters must unify with these inherited
features. In a given grammatical construct, this necessary condition permits the
appropriate selection of the relevant component of the λ-scheme. Other semantic
features are licensed directly on the parameters (see the following discussion).
The components of a λ-scheme are reduced in parallel according to classical β-
reduction in the λ-calculus. Results are objects of single or complex type. If of
complex type, they are *ground* functors and may be applied to other components
in order to give terminal objects expressing a meaning.

    rassembler:

    Them:: λX. λY. λZ [λU.©$^{t\rightarrow(t\rightarrow(s\rightarrow e))}$[X[Nhum+]][Y](U);
              mobile$^{t\rightarrow t}$[Y];
              λV.loc$^{t\rightarrow(t\rightarrow s)}$(V)[Z]]

    SF1: N_0[Nhum+] V N_1
             N_0=X; N_1=Y

    SF2: N_0 V N_1
             N_0=Z; N_1=Y

    SF3: N_0 V N_1 prep_loc N_a
             N_0=X; N_1=Y; N_a=Z

A semantic feature occurring in a syntactic frame takes priority over any other
semantic feature. This is a preemption principle. It ensures that if some constituent in a sentence has a first-level feature, it must be assigned to the constituent in
a frame which has this feature. A syntactic frame which does not require it is
selected only if the sentence constituent does not possess it. This kind of preemption principle seems to have a high potential of generalization (cf. Lehrer, 1990).
We can conclude that first-level features are *more salient* than others.

    The semantic information can always be completed. For instance, in this exam-
ple, we must accept sentences like: *l'anniversaire de Marie a rassemblé la famille
dans la grande salle,*[7] even if the subject does not have the feature [Nhum+]. In
this case, the thematic part of the lexical entry must be completed by another relation: a causation relation, which is of type **t**→(**s**→**e**), with parameters: X and S:
cause$^{t\rightarrow(s\rightarrow\ e)}$(X, S), expressing that the event called *anniversaire,* linked to X, is
the cause for Y (identified with *the family*) being located in *the big room* (linked
to Z), this location being a state linked to the variable S. In this case, too, we have
to define a variant of the first syntactic frame, which includes the feature [Nev-
ent+] in place of [Nhum+]. We can express this information by means of a disjunctive syntactic frame:

rassembler:

Them:
$\lambda(X, Y, Z)[\lambda U.\copyright^{t\to(t\to(s\to e))}[X[Nhum+]][Y](U);$
$\quad\quad mobile^{t\to t}[Y];$
$\quad\quad \lambda V.loc^{t\to(t\to s)}(V)[Z];$
$\quad\quad \lambda U.cause^{t\to(s\to e)}[X[Nevent+]]\,(U)]$

SF1: $N_0[Nhum+] \vee [Nevent+]\; V\; N_1\; (prep\_loc\; N_a)$
$\quad\quad N_0=X;\; N_1=Y;\; (N_a=Z)$

SF2: $N_0\; V\; N_1$
$\quad\quad N_0=Z;\; N_1=Y$

Let us remark that adding this disjunctive frame necessitates adding semantic features to the parameters in the thematic structure, in order to perform the appropriate selection. A thematic structure is *not* a conjunctive set. That means that we do not interpret it as a conjunction of relations between the entities denoted by X, Y, Z and so on. All components of a λ-scheme are not necessarily realized in an utterance. (Let us recall that the mapping from thematic structures to syntactic frames is not an isomorphism.) Some components may be obligatory and conjunctively realized, but others are selected only by means of a sort of "case of".

From the point of view of the lexicographer, a particular interest of this kind of conception lies in the ability it provides to check the *coherence* of a lexical entry. A thematic structure will be coherent if there exists at least one way of combining components of the λ-scheme in order to get an object of a definite type. For instance, the functor $mobile^{t\to t}$ takes an argument of type **t** and gives a result of type **t**, otherwise, $loc^{t\to(t\to s)}$ takes two arguments of type **t** and gives an object of type **s** (a *state*), so for instance, *Peter* and *Paris* may be used as arguments for loc and give the location (*state*): *Peter in Paris*. In the same way, takes two arguments of type **t** and gives an object of type (s→e) which requires another argument, of type **s**, in order to give an object of a single type: **e** (an *event*). This typing thus requires the presence of the previously calculated location (it is an obligatory role in the thematic structure).

Furthermore, it is possible to express the meaning by starting from various components of *Them*. Various orders of enumeration of these components give rise to various expressions, and to various types of reality described. For instance, from the lexical entry for *rassembler,* we can get:

(8) *l'anniversaire de Marie rassemble la famille dans la grande salle*
$\quad\quad$ (type: **event**)

(9) *la grande salle rassemble la famille*[8]
$\quad\quad$ (type: **stative**).

(10) *la famille se rassemble dans la grande salle*[9]
$\quad\quad$ (type: **event**)

The ways of composition are:

First stage: for (8) we apply the λ-scheme to variables instantiated by the appropriate syntactic frame.

> X = *anniversaire_de_Marie*
> Y = *famille*
> Z = *grande_salle*

this yields:

$$\lambda(X,Y,Z)\ [\lambda U.©^{t \to (t \to (s \to e))}\ [X[\text{Nhum}+]][Y](U\ ;$$
$$\text{mobile}^{t \to t}[Y]\ ;$$
$$\lambda V.\text{loc}^{t \to (t \to s)})(V)[Z]\ ;$$
$$\lambda U.\text{cause}^{t \to (s \to e)}[X[\text{Nevent}+]](U)]\ (\textit{anniversaire\_de\_Marie}\ ,$$
$$\textit{famille, grande\_salle}\ )$$

Since X has not the feature [Nhum+], the component $\lambda U.\text{cause}^{t \to (s \to e)}[X[\text{N-event}+]]\ (U)$ is selected.

Second stage: "outer"-reduction. We obtain:

> [mobile^t[*famille*];
> $\lambda V.\text{loc}^{(t \to s)}(V)$[*grande_salle*];
> $\lambda U.\text{cause}^{(s \to e)}$[*anniversaire_de_Marie*] (U)]

Third stage: "inner"-reduction. The only appropriate argument for loc is: mobile^t[*famille*]. We thus obtain:

> [$\lambda V.\text{loc}^{(t \to s)}(V)$[*grande_salle*]] [mobile^t(*famille*))
> = loc^s(mobile^t[*famille*])[*grande_salle*]

This term is of type s and is thus appropriate to be an argument for cause:

> [$\lambda U.\text{cause}^{(s \to e)}$[*anniversaire_de_Marie*](U)](loc^s(mobile^t[*famille*])
> [*grande_salle*])
> = cause^e(*anniversaire_de_Marie*]((loc^s(mobile^t[*famille*])
> [*grande_salle*]))

and we get finally a term of type **e** (event).

First stage: for (9) we apply the λ-scheme to variables instantiated by the appropriate syntactic frame.

> Y = *famille*
> Z = *grande_salle*

this yields:

$$\lambda(X,Y,Z)\ [\lambda U.©^{t \to (t \to (s \to e))}\ [X[\text{Nhum}+]][Y](U);$$
$$\text{mobile}^{t \to t}[Y]\ ;$$
$$\lambda V.\text{loc}^{t \to (t \to s)}(V)[Z]\ ;$$
$$\lambda U.\text{cause}^{t \to (s \to e)}[X[\text{Nevent}+]](U)]\ (X,\textit{famille, grande\_salle})$$

Since X is not instantiated, all terms containing X are excluded from the structure.

Second stage: "outer"-reduction. We obtain:

[mobile^t[*famille*];
λV.loc$^{(t\rightarrow s)}$(V)[*grande_salle*];

Third stage: "inner"-reduction.

The only appropriate argument for loc is: mobile^t[*famille*]. We thus obtain:

[λV.loc$^{(t\rightarrow s)}$(V)[*grande_salle*]] (mobile^t[*famille*])
= loc^s(mobile^t[*famille*])(*grande_salle*)

and we get finally a term of type **s** (state).

First stage: for (10) we apply the λ-scheme to variables instantiated by the appropriate syntactic frame.

X = *famille*
Y = *famille*
Z = *grande_salle*

this yields:

λ(X,Y,Z) [λU.©$^{t\rightarrow(t\rightarrow(s\rightarrow e))}$ [X[Nhum+]][Y](U) ;
        mobile$^{t\rightarrow t}$[Y] ;
        λV.loc$^{t\rightarrow(t\rightarrow s)}$(V)[Z] ;
        λU.cause$^{t\rightarrow(s\rightarrow e)}$[X[Nevent+]](U)] (*famille, famille,*
        grande_salle)

Since X has the feature [Nhum+], the component λU.©$^{t\rightarrow(t\rightarrow(s\rightarrow e))}$ [X[Nhum+]]
[Y](U) is selected.

Second stage: "outer"-reduction. We obtain:

[mobile^t[*famille*];
λV.loc$^{(t\rightarrow s)}$(V)[*grande_salle*];
λU.©$^{s\rightarrow e}$[*famille, famille*](U)]

Third stage: "inner"-reduction.

The only appropriate argument for loc is: mobile^t[*famille*]. We thus obtain:

[λV.loc$^{(t\rightarrow s)}$(V)[*grande_salle*]] (mobile^t[*famille*])
= loc^s(mobile^t[*famille*])[*grande_salle*]

This term is of type s and is thus appropriate to be an argument for ©:

[λU.©$^{s\rightarrow e}$[*famille, famille*](U)](loc^s(mobile^t[*famille*])[*grande_salle*])
= ©^{e}[*famille, famille*]((loc^s(mobile^t[*famille*])[*grande_salle*]))

and we get finally a term of type **e** (event).

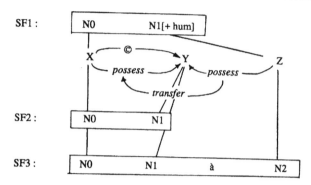

Figure 7.2.

7.3.4   *Other examples*

Let us look at other examples. For instance, the verb *voler* (to steal) has various syntactic frames:

(11)   SF1: N_0 V N_1[Nhum+]:   (a) *Pierre vole Marie*[10]
            SF2: N_0 V N_1:   (b) *Pierre vole un livre*
            SF3: N_0 V N_1 à N_2:   (c) *Pierre vole un livre à Marie*

The thematic structure is shown in Figure 7.2, expressed by the following simplified set of terms:[11]

$$\lambda U.©^{t \to (t \to (s \to e))}[X][Y](U),$$
$$\text{transfer}^{t \to (s \to (s \to s))}[Y]$$
$$(\text{possess}^{t \to (t \to s)}[Y][Z])(\text{possess}^{t \to (t \to s)}[Y][X])$$

These descriptions give the following simplified entry:

    voler:

    Them:
$$\lambda(X, Y, Z) [\lambda U.©^{t \to (t \to (s \to e))}[X][Y](U),$$
$$\text{transfer}^{t \to (s \to (s \to s))}[Y]$$
$$(\text{possess}^{t \to (t \to s)}[Y][Z])(\text{possess}^{t \to (t \to s)}[Y][X])]$$

    SF1: N_0 V N_1[Nhum+]
               N_0=X; N_1=Z
    SF2: N_0 V N_1
               N_0=X; N_1=Y
    SF3: N_0 V N_1 à N_2
               N_0=X; N_1=Y; N_2=Z

which gives respectively for (11)(a), (b) and (c):

$\copyright^e[Pierre][\Delta](\texttt{transfer}^s[\Delta]$ $(\texttt{possess}^s[\Delta][Marie])$
$(\texttt{possess}^s[\Delta][Pierre])^{12}$
$\copyright^e[Pierre][un\_livre](\texttt{transfer}^s[un\_livre]$
$(\texttt{possess}^s[un\_livre][\Delta])(\texttt{possess}^s[un\_livre][Pierre])$
$\copyright^e[Pierre][un\_livre](\texttt{transfer}^s[un\_livre]$
$(\texttt{possess}^s[un\_livre][Marie])(\texttt{possess}^s[un\_livre][Pierre])$

Movement verbs are described with a relation of transfer, too. For instance:

envoyer:

Them:[13]
$\lambda(X, Y, S, T) [\lambda U.\copyright^{t\to(t\to(s\to e))}[X][Y](U),$
$\qquad\qquad \texttt{i\_state}^{t\to(t\to s0)}[Y][S],$
$\qquad\qquad \texttt{f\_state}^{t\to(t\to s1)}[Y][T]$
$\lambda V.\lambda W.\texttt{transfer}^{t\to(s0\to(s1\to s))}[Y] (V)(W)]$

SF: N_0 V N_1 (de N_a à N_b)
N_0=X; N_1=Y; N_a=S; N_b=T

The composition of arrows inherent to a sentence like:

(12)   *Pierre envoie une lettre de Rome à Paris*[14]

gives the following expression:

$\copyright^e[Pierre][une\_lettre](\texttt{transfer}^s[une\_lettre](\texttt{i\_state}^{s0}[une\_lettre]$
$\quad [Rome])(\texttt{f\_state}^{s1}$
$[une\_lettre][Paris]))$

and results in a sentence of type **e**.

In such an entry, properties like initial_state or final _state are used to transform a *term* to a *state* (for instance the term denoting a city: "Paris" into the state of "being in Paris"). By the transfer relation, a term like "a letter" gives, via the states produced by initial_state and final_state, a new state (being in transfer from Rome to Paris), which can be an argument for the control relation, which transforms the arguments into an event.

It is worthwhile to notice here that these informations are able to determine the type of an index associated with an expression of the *InL* language. This formal language, due to Zeevat (1991) consists in linear formulations of Discourse Representation Structures (Kamp, 1981) and has been embedded in Unification Categorial Grammars (Klein, Zeevat, and Calder, 1987). Representations are made with formulas applying to other formulas, each of them being selected by an index. This kind of index is similar to discursive markers in DRS. And it corresponds to types of entities and events. The representation of (10) in *InL* would be:

[e][ENVOIE ([t][PIERRE], [t][LETTRE], [s][DE (s,[t]ROME),
    A(s, [t]PARIS)])]

making apparent that the result is of type **e**, and is made with: entities of type **t** (*Pierre* and *une_lettre*) and an entity of the **s** type, resulting from entities of the **t** type (*Rome* and *Paris*).

We must take into account that if the verb *envoyer* is taken in another syntactic frame, as in:

(13)   *Pierre envoie une lettre à Marie* (or *à la Sécurité Sociale,* or even: *à Paris*)[15]

the final state: *Marie,* or *la sécurité Sociale,* or *Paris* expresses not only the destination, but the "real goal", or the receiver (the one(s) to whom Pierre intended to send his letter). *Paris,* for instance is not assigned to the same thematic node as in (12). It will be necessary to interpret *Paris* as meaning: *some group of people,* or *some official living in Paris.* It would be unsatisfactory to deliver such roles as coming merely from a list, it is better to calculate them. Here, the lexical frame for *envoyer* must be completed in the following way:

envoyer:

Them:
$$\lambda(X, Y, S, T)\, [\lambda U.©^{t\to(t\to(s\to e))}[X][Y](U),$$
$$\text{i\_state}^{t\to(t\to s0)}[Y][S],$$
$$\text{f\_state}^{t\to(t\to s1)}[Y][T]$$
$$\lambda V.\lambda W.\text{transfer}^{t\to(s0\to(s1\to s))}[Y]\,(V)(W)]$$

SF1: $N_0\ V\ N_1$ de N_a à N_b
$N_0=X;\ N_1=Y;\ N_a=S;\ N_b=T$

SF2: $N_0\ V\ N_1$ à N_2
$N0=X=S;\ N1=Y;\ N2=T$

As we can see, the thematic structure is preserved. The distinction comes only from the fact that special constraints, in the association of variables of the syntactic frame and variables of the thematic structure, make some semantic variables identical. The coincidence of the source of © with the initial state makes the final state become a receiver. The appropriate combination of the relations gives:

$$©^e[Pierre][une\_lettre](\text{transfer}^s[une\_lettre](\text{i\_state}^{s0}[une\_lettre]$$
$$[Pierre])(\text{f\_state}^{s1}[une\_lettre][Paris]))$$

7.4   The construction of an interpretation in the case of an anomaly

If requisites on the first-level semantic features are fulfilled (and, above all, if there are none) a syntactic frame must be paired with the thematic structure. The identification of secondary features is sufficient to produce an effective interpretation. But it may happen that secondary features are not satisfied. Such cases are called *anomalies.* Anomalies are interpretable from the design of lexical entries for nominals. Pustejovsky has defined *Qualia Structures* for nominals (cf.

Pustejovsky, 1989; Boguraev and Pustejovsky, 1991; Boguraev, Briscoe, and Copestake 1991; Anick and Pustejovsky, 1991). A *Qualia Structure* is a structured representation. This structure specifies four aspects of a noun's meaning: its constituent parts, its formal structure, its purpose and function (i.e., its Telic Role); and how it comes about (i.e., its Agentive Role). For example, *book* might be represented as containing the following information:

> **book** (X, Y)
> [**Const**: information (Y)]
> [**Form**: bound-pages(X) or disk(X)]
> [**Telic**: read(T, w, Y)]
> [**Agentive**: artifact(X) & write(T, z, Y)]

(cf. Anick and Pustejovsky, 1991).

This information is used to display different aspects of the meaning of *book,* as in the following sentences:

(14)   *This book weighs four ounces*

(Formal Structure)

(15)   *John finished this book*

(Telic Role: John finished READING this book)

(16)   *This is an interesting book*

(Constituent Structure)

It seems, however that the telic component is actually not very well specified. How must we interpret, for instance, sentences in which a book refers to an instant of time, as in: "at the time of this book, people thought that it was right"? We are not quite sure that we must select a *reading* event or a *writing* event or even a *publishing* event. In fact, the thing denoted is not very well specified as a particular event. And it would not be economic to enumerate all the potential actions concerning a given object. In many contexts, a noun (like *book*) may be used merely as designating a temporal entity without making any precise reference to a particular action which concerns it; it then designates a kind of interval, here the interval of time during which the book in question was discussed, read, sold or in fashion. It must then be convenient to attribute *topological entities* to nominals. These entities are, for instance, intervals or other kinds of sets referring to periods during which the object denoted is active. This is particularly relevant in case of a noun like *conseil* studied by Kayser and Levrat (1990). These authors show the difficulty of encompassing all the contextual meanings of this kind of nominal. It is true that we can find the word *conseil* in many contexts such as:

(17)   (a) *le conseil est composé de trente-six membres*[16]
      (b) *le conseil a voté une motion*
      (c) *le conseil est élu tous les cinq ans*
      (d) *on ne peut joindre Paul durant le conseil*
        (and many others)

and it is true, too, that in every context, the nominal *conseil* belongs to a particular semantic category: a set, an individual agent, an entity associated with some discrete time and an entity associated with an interval of time. We suggest that all these possibilities are considered as viewpoints on the concept denoted by the word. That means that we consider substantives as kinds of spaces over which many topologies can be defined. The selection of one topology dictates the kind of entity we consider under a given word. Such a selection is analogous to the selection of one aspect in the Qualia Structure. We can have, for instance, the following representation for *conseil:*

conseil:
  [**Ext**: $\{member_1, member_2, \ldots, member_n\}$]
  [**Tcont**: $\{[t_1, t_2]; t_1, t_2 \in {}^+\}$]
  [**Tdiscr**: $\{t_i; t_i \in R^+\}$]
  [**Int**: $\{int_1, int_2, \ldots, int_p\}$]

(where **Ext** means the extensional viewpoint – membership – **Tcont** a topology on continuous time, **Tdiscr** a topology on discrete time and **Int** an intensional viewpoint – roles defining precisely for what the council is made).

When the identification of a sentence with a syntactic frame has been made (thanks to first-level semantic features), secondary semantic features, belonging to the conceptual system, are used to operate the correct selection of an aspect or a topology in the lexical entries for nominals. This selection is performed by means of a *mechanism of coercion* (see Pustejovsky, 1991).[17] We give the following example of the sentence:

(18)   *le congrès s'amuse*[18]

In this example, it is assumed that the word *congrès* has received a lexical entry similar to that of *conseil*. The syntactic frame associated with the verb *s'amuser* is: N_0 Vref. No special first-level semantic feature is required to make the identification of a thematic structure with this frame. But there is a secondary feature ([+animate]), handled by the parameter, which enforces the N_0 to be interpreted as something animate.[19]

  s'amuser

  Them:
  $\lambda U.©^{t \to (t \to (s \to e))}[X[+animate]][X](U)$;
  SF: N_0 V
  $N_0 = X$

The resulting category is: $s \to e$. This makes it possible to predict utterances like:

(19)   *le congrès s'amuse à imiter son président*[20]

The second-level features are introduced on the semantic parameters, in order to distinguish them from the first-level features (see note 18).

When faced with the sentence (19), the feature [+*animate*] is used to extract from the so-called Qualia-Structure of the word *congrès,* the extensional viewpoint, consisting of a set of members, each of which being [+human], because the entity *member[+human]* can be unified with X[+animate].

7.5 Conclusion: A work in progress

We have outlined a compositional framework attempting to provide a generic lexicon with semantic features. Genericity is a crucial constraint because it requires that features may be used by a system based on any particular theory (provided that there exists some translation module from the formal representations here involved to the desired ones). This constraint implies a theory-independent characterization of the semantic content of the lexicon. Among other things, it requires using abstract primitive relations that are not necessarily the ordinary thematic roles (the terminology of which being very dependent on a particular theory). On another hand, there must be a mechanism by which meanings are generated, depending on syntactic constructions and primitive relations. We introduce a grammatical system as opposed to a conceptual system in order that sentences are primarily assigned to existing syntactic frames, and then interpreted on the basis of such an assignment. Thus syntax and semantics are deeply interrelated: the syntax appears as almost a component of semantics, and reciprocally, the semantics provides features necessary to syntax. The system proposed here has not been implemented yet, although plans are currently underway to develop a prototype. It will consist of a Knowledge Base, where the units will be expressed by *typed feature structures* and will be hierarchically organized, as in an Inheritance Network. The particular entries for verbs must be built with templates which express generalizations. For instance, a Movement Verb like *marcher* is the result of a combination (by a &-operator) of templates: *movement, intentional control, way* (instantiated by *earth*) and *manner* (instantiated by *foot*). It will be very interesting to go further on this kind of example and to show how preliminary assigned constants in templates may be changed or neutralized according to another instance of coercion mechanism in order to take into account sentences like: *le train marche à bonne allure,*[21] and to explain why *avec des chaussures neuves*[22] in *Pierre marche avec des chaussures neuves*[23] is necessary as an adjunct and is not contradictory with the feature corresponding to 'on foot' as a manner in the template corresponding to *to walk.*

Notes

1. The first version of this chapter was written (January 1992) before the authors were aware of Pustejovsky (1991). There are actually many similarities between the two papers. What is expressed here in terms of compositionality may appear to be said in Pustejovsky's paper in terms of generativity. Nevertheless, our framework is slightly distinct from Pustejovsky's in that (1) emphasis is put on a hierarchical typology of semantic features such that some features are necessary for an interpretable

construction and others are relevant only for a "normal" interpretation, (2) it does not take the denomination of thematic roles (agent, object, . . .) for granted, (3) the mapping from the lexicon to syntax is theory-independent (and based only on observations collected in tables), (4) elementary meanings are not predicates, but functions and allow one to compute resulting types according to combinations driven by the syntactic frames, and (5) Qualia Structures are enriched with Topologies.

2. (a) *Jacques turns the door-handle*
   (b) *The door-handle turns*
   (c) *Jacques turns the earth*
   (d) *The earth turns*
   (e) *The earth turns around the sun*
   (f) *The sun turns around the earth*
3. (a) *The prisoner sleeps*
   (b) *The roadway is asleep*
4. (a) *Isabelle stole from Pierre*
   (b) *Isabelle stole this jewel*
   (c) *Pierre gathers his clothes together*
   (d) *The cupboard keeps all his clothes together*
   (e) *The mayor released the prisoner*
   (f) *The mayor widened the roadway*
5. A notation similar to the LADL-tables (e.g., Gross, 1975) is used, but this is only a notational device.
6. (a) *Pierre gathers his clothes together*
   (b) *The cupboard keeps all his clothes together*
   (c) *Pierre gathers his clothes together in the cupboard*
7. *Mary's birthday gathers the family together in the big room*
8. *The big room is the gathering place for the family*
9. *The family gathers in the big room*
10. (a) *Pierre steals from Marie*
    (b) *Pierre steals a book*
    (c) *Pierre steals a book from Marie*
11. The semantic distinction between *voler, acheter, emprunter* . . . is not here taken into account – it is the reason why we speak of a simplified representation.
12. We assume here that when a variable is not instantiated in a component where another parameter is, it is replaced by a dummy constant like Δ.
13. s0 and s1 are projections of a state s. We assume that projections of states are still states. This gives an account to the fact that in some circumstances, a state may be considered as a pair <s0, s1>: it expresses for instance the colocalization of an entity (independently of time). The same solution could have been used in the previous example.
14. *Pierre sends a letter from Rome to Paris*
15. *Pierre sends a letter to Marie (the Social Security, Paris, . . .)*
16. (a) *The council consists of thirty-six members*
    (b) *The council carried a motion*
    (c) *The council is elected every five years*
    (d) *One can't reach Paul during council meetings*
17. Pustejovsky (1991) gives the following definition of Type Coercion: A semantic operation that converts an argument to the type that is expected by a function, where it would otherwise result in a type error.
18. *The congress has fun*
19. Features handled by parameters serve two purposes: one is just selection of the appropriate component in the thematic structure, thanks to a similar feature handled

by the nominal argument, and this merely results from *unification,* the other is transmission of the feature to the nominal argument by means of *coercion.* The first mechanism has priority on the second one.

20. *The congress has fun imitating its chairman*
21. *The train goes at a great speed*
22. *with new shoes*
23. *Pierre is walking with new shoes*

Bibliography

P. Ahn and P. Kolb, 1990: Discourse Representation Meets Constructive Mathematics in *Papers from the Second Symposium on Logic and Language,* eds. L. Kalman & L. Polos, Akademiai Kiado, Budapest.

P. Anick and J. Pustejovsky, 1991: An Application of Lexical Semantics to Knowledge Acquisition from Corpora, *Meeting of the ACL, 1991.*

B. Boguraev, T. Briscoe and A. Copestake, 1991: Enjoy the Paper: Lexical Semantics via Lexicology, *Meeting of the ACL, 1991.*

B. Boguraev and J. Pustejovsky, 1991: Lexical Ambiguity and The Role of Knowledge Representation in Lexicon Design, *Meeting of the ACL, 1991.*

J. Calder, 1987: Typed Unification for NLP in *Categories, Polymorphism and Unification,* eds. Klein and van Benthem, Centre for Cognitive Studies, Edinburgh and ITLI, Amsterdam.

J. Dekker, 1990: Dynamic Interpretation, Flexibility and Monotonicity, in Stokhof and Torenvliet, *Proceedings of the 7th Amsterdam Colloquium.*

J. P. Desclés, 1990: *Langages applicatifs, langues naturelles et cognition,* Hermes, Paris.

D. Dowty, 1979: *Word Meaning and Montague Grammar,* D. Reidel, Dordrecht.

D. Dowty, 1988: Type Raising, Functional composition and non-constituent conjunction, in *Categorial Grammars and Natural Language Structures,* eds. Oehrle, Bach & Wheeler, D. Reidel, Dordrecht.

J. Fillmore, 1968: The case for case, in *Universal in Linguistic Theory,* eds. Bach and Harms, Holt, Rinehart and Winston, New York.

J. Fradin 1990: in Centre d'Etudes Lexicales, *La Définition,* Larousse, Paris.

G. Gazdar, I. Klein, G. Pullum and I. Sag, 1985: *Generalized Phrase Structure Grammar,* Blackwell, London.

J. Groenendijk and M. Stokhof, 1990: Dynamic Montague Grammar, in *Papers from the Second Symposium on Logic and Language,* eds. L. Kalman & L. Polos, Akademiai Kiado, Budapest.

M. Gross, 1975: *Méthodes en syntaxe,* Herman, Paris.

Gruber, 1965: *Studies in Lexical Relations,* thesis, University of Indiana.

Hellwig, Minkwitz and Koch, 1991: *Standards for Syntactic Descriptions,* EUROTRA-7 report.

J. Hendricks, 1989: Flexible Montague Grammar, *First European Summer school on NLP, Logic and Knowledge,* Groningen.

R. Jackendoff, 1972: *Semantic Interpretation in Generative Grammar,* MIT Press, Cambridge, Mass.

R. Jackendoff, 1990: *Semantic Structures,* MIT Press, Cambridge, Mass.

H. Kamp, 1983: Evénements, représentations discursives et référence temporelle, *Langage,* vol. 64, pp. 39–64.

D. Kayser and H. Levrat, 1990: in Centre d'Etudes Lexicales, *La Définition,* Larousse, Paris.

I. Klein, F. Zeevat and J. Calder, 1987: Unification Categorial Grammar, in *Categorial Grammar, Unification Grammar and Parsing,* eds. Haddock, Klein and Morrill. Centre for Cognitive Science, Edinburgh.

Lehrer, 1990: Polysemy, conventionality and the structure of the lexicon, *Cognitive Linguistics* **1–2**, pp. 207–246.

R. Montague, 1973: The Proper Treatment of Quantification in Ordinary English, in *Approaches to Natural Language,* eds Hintikka et al., Reidel, Dordrecht.

Moortgat, 1988: *Categorial Investigations*, Foris Publications, Dordrecht.

J. Pustejovsky, 1990: Semantic Function and Lexical Decomposition, in *Linguistic Approaches to Artificial Intelligence,* eds Schmitz, Schütz & Kunz, Peter Lang, Bern.

J. Pustejovsky, 1991: The Generative Lexicon, *Computational Linguistics*, vol. **17**, no. 4 , pp. 409–441.

J. Rappaport, K. Laughren and B. Levin, 1987: Levels of Lexical Representation, *Lexicon Project Working Papers,* Center for Cognitive Science, MIT, Cambridge, Mass.

T. Ravin, 1991: *Lexical Semantics without Thematic Roles,* Clarendon, Oxford University Press.

J. Sowa, 1989: Lexical Structures and Conceptual Structures, in *Semantics in the Lexicon,* ed. Pustejovsky, Kluwer, Dordrecht.

M. Steedman 1988: Combinators and Grammar, in *Categorial Grammars and Natural Language Structures,* eds. Oehrle, Bach & Wheeler, D. Reidel Pub, Dordrecht.

F. Zeevat, 1991: *Aspects of Discourse Semantics and Unification Grammar,* thesis, University of Amsterdam.

PART III

Lexical databases

Another current major issue in lexical semantics is the definition and the construction of real-size lexical databases that will be used by parsers and generators in conjunction with a grammatical system. Word meaning, terminological knowledge representation and extraction of knowledge in machine readable dictionaries are the main topics addressed. They really represent the backbone of a lexical semantics knowledge base construction.

The first chapter, "Lexical semantics and terminological knowledge representation" by Gerrit Burkert, shows the practical and formal inadequacies of semantic networks for representing knowledge, and the advantages of using a term subsumption language. In a first stage, this document shows how several aspects of word meaning can be adequately described using a term subsumption language. Then, some extensions are proposed that make the system more suitable for lexical semantics. Formal aspects are strongly motivated by several examples borrowed from an in-depth study of terminological knowledge extraction, which is a rather challenging area for lexical semantics.

"Word meaning between lexical and conceptual structure", by Peter Gerstl, presents a method and a system to introduce world-knowledge or domain-dependent knowledge in a lexicon. The meaning of a word is derived from general lexical information on the one hand and from ontological knowledge on the other hand. The notion of semantic scope is explored on an empirical basis by analyzing in a systematic way the influences involved in natural language expressions. This component has been integrated into the Lilog system developed at IBM Stuttgart.

In "The representation of group denoting nouns in a lexical knowledge base", Ann Copestake reports a new evolution of the Acquilex project, a project aimed at developing a theoretically motivated and computationally tractable multilingual lexical knowledge base. This chapter is a complement to existing results on structuring lexical knowledge bases by means of relations such as isa, part-of, synonymy, etc. It introduces a representation of group denoting nouns (e.g., band, orchestra, crowd) and explores in depth the relations between groups and their individual elements. Besides well-known semantic features, this work makes an extensive and insightful use of principles of the Generative Lexicon advocated in earlier chapters. This new component is integrated into a system that also treats complex phenomena such as logical metonymy and sense extension.

Martha Palmer and Alain Polguère, in "Preliminary lexical and conceptual analysis of BREAK: a computational perspective", bring into perspective a combination of lexical analysis and conceptual analysis to study in great detail the meaning of a verb: *break*. Defined within Mel'čuk's framework of the meaning-text theory, criteria for building a conceptual description are associated to factors from the "real-word" uses. The necessary conditions that allow the action indicated by a verb and, conversely, the effects of the use of a given verb on the environment are analyzed to motivate the underlying conceptual representation associated to that verb, which accounts for the different uses of it. Thus, the goal is not to capture the full meaning of the verb, but simply to account for the criteria that make the distinction between uses.

The same kind of problematics guides the next chapter, "Large neural networks for the resolution of lexical ambiguity", by Jean Véronis and Nancy Ide, but settled in a very different perspective. The research starts from the observation that in texts on unconstrained domains the potential meanings of a word are extremely numerous. Several kinds of information may contribute to the resolution of lexical ambiguity: morphological information, semantic features, primitive representations, syntactic role, etc. The difficulty with this approach is that it requires a prior construction of a complex lexical knowledge base. This chapter presents an approach that directly makes use of ready-made lexical information sources such as machine-readable versions of everyday dictionaries. A method is presented that elaborates on the connectionist model and works by Lesk and Wilks. It allows for the construction of a large network of words that describes co-occurrences of words and their modes. This network covers almost all terms of standard English (90,000 terms). This information may then be potentially used to disambiguate unrestricted texts.

8 Lexical semantics and terminological knowledge representation

GERRIT BURKERT

8.1 Introduction

Knowledge representation and reasoning are central to all fields of Artificial Intelligence research. It includes the development of formalisms for the representation of given subject matters as well as the development of inference procedures to reason about the represented knowledge. Before developing a knowledge representation formalism, one must determine what type of knowledge has to be modeled with the formalism. Since a lot of our knowledge of the world can easily be described using natural language, it is an interesting task to examine to what extent the contents of natural language utterances can be formalized and represented with a given representation formalism. Every approach to represent natural language utterances must include a method to formalize aspects of the meaning of single lexical units.[1]

An early attempt in this direction was Quillian's *Semantic Memory* (Quillian, 1968), an associational model of human memory. A semantic memory consists of nodes corresponding to English words and different associative links connecting the nodes. Based on that approach, various knowledge representation systems have been developed which can be subsumed under the term *semantic network*. Common to all these systems is that knowledge is represented by a network of nodes and links. The nodes usually represent concepts or meanings whereas the links represent relations between concepts. In most semantic network formalisms, a special kind of link between more specific and more general concepts exists. This link, often called IS-A or AKO (a kind of), organizes the concepts into a hierarchy in which information can be inherited from more general to more specific concepts. A serious problem with most of these semantic network formalisms is their poor semantic foundation. Often, there has been much imprecision about the meanings of the nodes and links (Woods, 1975; Schubert et al., 1979) and even the well-known IS-A link was used with a great variety of interpretations (Brachman, 1983).

Some approaches to representing natural language utterances in network-like structures rely on a small set of semantic primitives and complex conceptualizations are composed from this set of primitives. An example is Schank's *Concep-*

I would like to thank P. Forster, U. Heid, E. Lehmann, C. Rathke, B. Tausend, and two anonymous reviewers for many helpful comments on this chapter.

tual Dependency representation (Schank, 1972). It is doubtful, however, whether a universal set of semantic primitives can be given.[2]

In another approach, knowledge is represented in structures called frames (cf. Minsky, 1975), which emphasize the internal structure of the represented objects. There are a number of similarities between semantic networks and frame systems, e.g., in most frame systems the frames are interconnected by links and a special link, called IS-A link, which organizes the frames hierarchically. The problems associated with an insufficient semantic foundation also apply to frame systems.

Elements of different semantic network systems as well as elements of the frame theory influenced the development of the knowledge representation system KL-ONE (Brachman, 1979; Brachman and Schmolze, 1985). KL-ONE was an attempt to tackle a number of deficiencies of semantic network systems concerning their semantic foundation. Since it is difficult to define a general set of semantic primitives, such primitives are not part of the suggested formalism. The formalism rather allows us to introduce the primitives needed for modeling a certain domain and to define new concepts based on these primitives. New concepts are described by specifying one or more superconcepts, i.e., more general concepts, and a set of restrictions that constitute the differences between the new concept and its superconcepts. Based on this description, a new concept can be inserted automatically into the taxonomy at the correct place. This important inference mechanism of KL-ONE and similar knowledge representation systems is called *classification*.

Knowledge representation systems based on KL-ONE have been used in a variety of applications, including natural language processing systems. However, several modifications and extensions to KL-ONE are necessary for modeling the background knowledge of natural language processing systems (cf. Allgayer and Reddig, 1990).

The objective of this chapter is to investigate whether KL-ONE-like knowledge representation formalisms, especially so-called *term subsumption languages* (TSLs), can be used to represent aspects of the meaning of lexical units, in order to make the representation system a useful component of a natural language processing system. Subsequently, we will assume a (simplified) model of the knowledge base of a natural language processing system consisting of the following parts (Fig. 8.1):[3]

- the lexicon holding information about words,
- syntactic and semantic rules that are used to analyze the structure and contents of sentences,
- the terminological component holding a hierarchy of concepts representing word meanings,
- the assertional component, used to store information about instances of concepts (e.g., episodic knowledge),
- additional world or background knowledge that is necessary to understand the contents of natural language utterances.

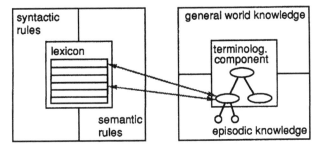

Figure 8.1. Model of the knowledge base of a NLP system

For the terminological component, a KL-ONE-based representation formalism is used. A concept in KL-ONE comprises the primitive components of more general concepts and the relations to other concepts. Therefore, the analysis incorporates aspects of decompositional semantics as well as relational aspects.

In the next section, the term subsumption language TED is presented. Since word meanings are also the subject of dictionary definitions, several dictionary definitions for nouns, verbs, and adjectives will be examined. The goal of this examination is to establish a list of requirements a representation formalism has to meet in order to be useful in natural language processing applications and to find out which extensions to current term subsumption formalisms are necessary. Finally, we summarize the results and give an overview of our current work.

8.2   TED – A term description language

A number of knowledge-based systems used KL-ONE or some of its successors as their knowledge representation basis. It turned out, however, that the semantics of some of KL-ONE's notions, e.g., the distinction between individual concepts and individuals of the assertional component, was rather unclear. Term subsumption languages are knowledge representation formalisms based on KL-ONE with semantically well-defined representational elements. The semantics is usually described by giving a mapping into first order predicate calculus or by providing a direct model-theoretic semantics which emphasizes an extensional view of concepts and subsumption. Based on such a semantic description, the inference algorithms, e.g., subsumption determination, can be analyzed with respect to soundness, completeness, and complexity. Unfortunately, it turns out that sound, complete, and efficient classification algorithms can be provided only for very restricted formalisms (cf. Nebel, 1990; Hollunder and Nutt, 1990).

For a knowledge representation system to be useful in the area of natural language processing, a restricted expressiveness cannot be tolerated and a formalism with extended expressive power is needed. Thus, in the expressiveness-tractability trade-off we have to decide for higher expressive power and in order to have a tractable representation system, we have to confine to sound but not necessarily complete inferences.[4]

An example for a restricted terminological representation formalism is TED (term description language, [Forster et al., 1991]) complemented by an assertional component called ALAN (assertional language). The representational constructs and inference algorithms of TED and ALAN are based on the formalism described in (Nebel, 1990).

In the following, the features of the terminological component TED are summarized. Basic elements are the *concepts*, organized in a concept taxonomy. The topmost concept in the taxonomy is anything. Relations between concepts are specified using *roles*. Similar to the concepts, the roles are organized hierarchically, the most general role being anyrole. Single-valued roles (functions) are called *attributes*.[5] Concepts are described by reference to one or more super-concepts and a set of role or attribute restrictions giving the distinguishing features of the new concept. Role restrictions can either be value or number restrictions, the former specifying the range and the latter the minimum and maximum number of role fillers of the concept for a given role. Attributes can be composed to attribute chains. Attributes or attribute chains can be restricted to a certain type or to a specific value that has to be an individual of the assertional component ALAN. Furthermore, two attributes or attribute chains can be restricted using the predicates equal or unequal. If a new concept is marked to be defined, the description is interpreted as necessary and sufficient for the concept, whereas if it has only necessary specifications it is marked primitive.[6] In the following, a BNF specification of the syntax of TED is given:

<concept-introduction> ::=
    (**defconcept** <concept-name> (<super-concepts>)
      <primitive-flag> <restriction>*)

<super-concepts> ::=
    <concept-name>*
  | **anything**

<primitive-flag> ::=
    :primitive
  | **:defined**

<role-introduction> ::=
    (**defrole** <role-name> (<super-roles>))

<super-roles> ::=
    <role-name>*
  | **anyrole**

<attribute-introduction> ::=
    (**defattribute** *<attribute-name>*)

<restriction> ::=
    <value-restriction>
  | *<number-restriction>*
  | *<attribute-restriction>*

<value-restriction> ::=
    (**:all** *<role-name>* *<concept>*)

<concept> ::=
    <concept-name>
  | *<concept-expression>*

<concept-expression> ::=
    (**concept** (*<super-concepts>*) *<primitive-flag>* *<restriction>**)

<number-restriction> ::=
    (**:atleast** *<number>* *<role-name>*)
  | (**:atmost** *<number>* *<role-name>*)
  | (**:exactly** *<number>* *<role-name>*)
  | (**:one** *<role-name>*)
  | (**:some** *<role-name>*)
  | (**:no** *<role-name>*)

<attribute-restriction> ::=
    (**:type** *<attribute-exp>* *<concept>*)
  | (**:value** *<attribute-exp>* *<instance>*)
  | (**:equal** *<attribute-exp>* *<attribute-exp>*)
  | (**:unequal** *<attribute-exp>* *<attribute-exp>*)

<attribute-exp> ::=
    <attribute-name>
  | (*<attribute-chain>*)

<attribute-chain> ::=
    <attribute-name>
  | *<attribute-name>* **:of** *<attribute-chain>*

A more detailed description of TED including a model-theoretic semantics is given in Forster et al. (1991). In the following example, the role member and the

concepts community, musician, music-group, and quartet are introduced into
the terminology:

```
(defrole member (part))

(defconcept community (set)
    :primitive
    (:all member human)
    (:atleast 2 member))

(defconcept musician (human)
    :primitive)


(defconcept music-group (community)
    :primitive
    (:all member musician))

(defconcept quartet (music-group)
    :defined
    (:exactly 4 member))
```

The role member is introduced as a subrole of a more general role called part.
The concept community is described as a subconcept of set with at least two
human members. It is marked primitive because the given restrictions do not constitute a sufficient description of community. That is, the introduction of community as a primitive concept can prevent every instance of the concept set satisfying the restrictions from automatically becoming an instance of the concept
community. The concept music-group is described as a subconcept of community
with the restriction that all elements being in a member relation with it must be
instances of the concept musician. Finally, the concept quartet is defined as a
music-group with exactly *four* members. The fact that the members of a quartet
are instances of musician is inherited from quartet's superconcept music-group.
Figure 8.2 shows the example terminology in a KL-ONE-like graphical notation.

Instances of concepts are introduced in the assertional component ALAN using
the definstance operator, e.g.,

```
(definstance beatles music-group
    (member (john paul george ringo)))
```

TED and ALAN have been implemented in Common Lisp and CLOS[7] and are
installed on several platforms.[8] The next section examines whether TED has sufficient expressive capabilities to represent the contents of simple dictionary definitions.

8.3   Trying to represent dictionary definitions

In this section, some aspects of a paradigmatic analysis of word meanings with
regard to possibilities to represent the relevant concepts and relations in a term

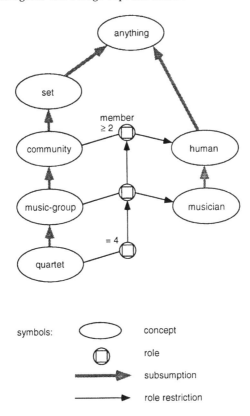

Figure 8.2. A small TED terminology.

subsumption language will be discussed. We do not, however, go into details of any semantic theory, nor do we treat aspects of the composition of the meaning of single lexical units to the contents of complete utterances.

The analysis of word meanings is also the subject of dictionary definitions. Since definitions in dictionaries as well as terminological representation formalisms are usually based on the principle of *genus proximum et differentia specifica*, it seems to be useful to analyze to what extent the contents of simple dictionary definitions can be represented using a terminological representation language. Furthermore, such an analysis can serve to give some idea whether terminological knowledge bases can be created by automatic extraction from machine-readable dictionaries. We must be aware of some deficiencies concerning the use of dictionary definitions for this purpose, however. First, dictionary definitions are intended for human users and require some background knowledge to be understandable. In addition, dictionary definitions are often not very precise or the dictionaries contain cyclic definitions. Despite those problems concerning dictionary definitions, it will be assumed in the following that definitions can be helpful to assess the suitability of a terminological representation formalism and to set up a list of further requirements for such a formalism.

First, we will have a look at some nominal definitions from the Elementary Dictionary of English (EDE, 1976), the machine-readable version of the Oxford Advanced Learner's Dictionary, third edition (OALD, 1988), and the Longman Dictionary of Contemporary English (LDOCE, 1987). The EDE (1976) is a small dictionary with about 7,500 entries for use in schools. The OALD (1988) and the LDOCE (1987) are monolingual dictionaries designed for learners of English as a second language. Let us start with a definition for the word *bicycle*:

bicycle [e]:[9] two-wheeled machine for riding

This definition suggests that *bicycle* can be represented as a subconcept of a concept representing *machine* that has two parts which are *wheels*:

```
a bicycle is a machine
    with 2 wheels
    for riding[10]
```

Prior to formalizing the contents of a definition, the words occurring in the definition have to be disambiguated. If a new concept bicycle[11] with this description is to be inserted into the taxonomy, the suitable concepts for *machine*, *wheel*, and *to ride* have to be found or must be created. The concept bicycle – if introduced with the given description – is primitive because its description is necessary but not sufficient: an object with this description could also be a motorcycle.

The investigation of nominal definitions reveals that in addition to the subsumption relation other relations occur quite frequently, e.g., the relation between an object and its parts or the relation between an object and its typical uses or functions.[12] These relations are not predefined in the representation formalism and have to be defined prior to more specific relations and concepts. It has to be decided which concepts and relations should be the foundation on which the description of new concepts and relations can be based. In other words, an ontology of basic concepts and relations has to be defined.[13] In the following, a relation between an object and its parts will be called part and a relation between an object and its typical uses or functions will be called function. It is important to note that there exist a number of different part and function relations and that part and function have to be specialized appropriately.[14] These basic concepts and relations are primitive, i.e., they have no sufficient description in terms of expressions of the representation formalism. Since these basic terms must nevertheless be used consistently throughout the terminological knowledge base, a general agreement about their meaning is essential. Consequently, the meaning of many general concepts and roles should be documented in detail using natural language texts, pictures, etc. This could be supported by the user interface of the representation system.

Returning to the description of bicycle: if we use the relations part and function, we can describe a bicycle as follows:

```
a bicycle is a machine
    with 2 part wheel
    with function riding
```

If this description is to be transferred into a formal representation language, further decisions have to be made, e.g., whether a bicycle has exactly two wheels (or at least two?) or whether there are other uses of a bicycle in addition to riding. When these decisions are made and the concepts for *machine, wheel* and *to ride* are identified as machine, wheel and to-ride respectively, a first attempt to represent the description in TED is possible:

```
(defrole has-wheel (part))
(defrole for-riding (function))
(defconcept bicycle (machine) :primitive
    (:exactly 2 has-wheel)
    (:all has-wheel wheel)
    (:one for-riding)
    (:all for-riding to-ride))
```

First, two subroles of part and function are introduced, namely, has-wheel and for-riding. The role has-wheel should be interpreted as relating an object exactly to those parts that are wheels. Next, the concept bicycle is introduced as a subconcept of machine with appropriate value and number restrictions for the roles has-wheel and for-riding. The restricted expressive capabilities of TED force us to introduce the subroles of part and function resulting in a rather awkward description of bicycle, a problem that arises with most other term subsumption formalisms, too.

We can avoid the introduction of these subroles if our formalism supports so-called *qualifying number restrictions* (Hollunder and Baader, 1991). In an extended version of TED, bicycle can be represented using qualifying number restrictions as follows:

```
(defconcept bicycle (machine) :primitive
    (:exactly 2 part wheel)
    (:one function to-ride))
```

The term (:exactly 2 part wheel) expresses the fact that exactly two of the elements standing in a part relation to bicycle are wheels.

Qualifying number restrictions have been integrated into TED extending the syntax description of TED by the following expressions:

<restriction> ::=
  <value-restriction>
  | *<number-restriction>*
  | *<qualifying-number-restriction>*
  | *<attribute-restriction>*

<*qualifying-number-restriction*> ::=
   (:**atleast** <*number*> <*role-name*> <*concept*>)
   | (:**atmost** <*number*> <*role-name*> <*concept*>)
   | (:**exactly** <*number*> <*role-name*> <*concept*>)
   | (:**one** <*role-name*> <*concept*>)
   | (:**some** <*role-name*> <*concept*>)
   | (:**no** <*role-name*> <*concept*>)

A sound and complete algorithm for subsumption determination for a term subsumption language extended by qualifying number restrictions is given in (Hollunder and Baader, 1991).

If we have sufficient information to describe the concept `bicycle` and if the concept taxonomy already contains an adequately described concept for vehicle, `bicycle` can be automatically classified as a subconcept of `vehicle`. The more special superconcept of `bicycle` is mentioned in the following definition:

> bicycle [1]: a two-wheeled vehicle which one rides by pushing its pedals with the feet

This definition suggests that a number of further `part` relations have to be added to the description of `bicycle`, e.g., a relation between a `bicycle` and its `pedals`. An adequate representation of a bicycle must also contain a description of how all the parts have to be combined to form a bicycle.[15] Furthermore, the fact that the bicycle is propelled by the person who is riding on the bicycle by using the pedals has to be included into the description. This leads to complex relationships between the concepts `bicycle`, `to-ride` and the concept representing the person who is riding on the bicycle. These relationships cannot be investigated in detail here. However, it is evident that for a concept description to be useful in natural language processing, usually additional information is needed that cannot be found in dictionary definitions. In addition, the expressive power of TED is not sufficient to express all these relationships.

Up to here we have described a bicycle as having exactly two wheels and one of its uses (perhaps the most important one) is riding. What about a bicycle with one wheel missing? Probably it will be called a bicycle anyway. If we had the expressive capabilities, we would better describe a bicycle as having *typically* two wheels. There is good reason to suppose that most `part` relations do not contribute to a concept description as necessary conditions but rather as typical information. Therefore, a suitable representation formalism must provide a possibility to specify part of a description as defeasible. There are, however, several problems with such kind of default information, e.g.,

- What effects do the defaults have on classification?
- What about concepts that inherit contradictory defaults from their superconcepts?
- How to deal with defaults in the assertional component?

Since many dictionary definitions contain words like "often", "usually" or "typically", defaults seem to be essential for the description of many concepts. It is evident that a suitable terminological representation formalism has to allow the specification of typical in addition to necessary and sufficient information. Apparently, we should not interpret all concept specifications as defeasible as is usually done in frame systems, because we would lose any kind of definition capability (Brachman, 1985). Nevertheless, defaults could be used as an additional means of specification. A concept specification could be subdivided into three parts:

definition – a number of restrictions making up sufficient and necessary conditions for the described concept – if this part is missing, a primitive concept is described;

assertions – restrictions that are necessarily true for all instances of the concept;

defaults – restrictions that are typically true for instances of the concept.

Dealing with defaults and nonmonotonic reasoning is an important subfield of knowledge representation and reasoning and a number of theories have been developed in this area (e.g., Reiter, 1980; Etherington and Reiter, 1983). The introduction of defaults into a terminological representation system leads to several problems, e.g., to what extent can default information be used by the classification mechanism? It is advantageous to carry out most of the default reasoning on the assertional level. A truth maintenance system will be needed to retract inferences that have been drawn based on default assumptions that turn out to be invalid.

Let us have a look at some more nominal definitions related to the description of *bicycle*:

> pedal [l]: barlike part of a machine which can be pressed with the foot in order to control the working of the machine or to drive it
> pedal [e]: the part of an instrument or a machine which we move with the foot
> wheel [l]: 1. a circular object with an outer frame which turns round an inner part to which it is joined (the hub), and is used for turning machinery, making vehicles move, etc. [. . .]
> wheel [o]: 1. circular frame or disc which turns on an axle (as on carts, cars, bicycles, etc and for various purposes in machines) [. . .]

The definitions of pedal do not refer to a more general term. A pedal is described using the inverse relation of part:

```
a pedal is a thing
    is part-of machine
    . . .
```

The introduction of inverse relations or, more general, of dependencies between relations into term description languages is desirable but leads to problems with subsumption determination. In TED, a role hierarchy can be created by means of the subsumption relation between roles. But all roles are primitive and no further role specification operators are available. Our current approach to describe dependencies between roles is by means of simple rules which are applied only on the assertional level. The fact that part-of is the inverse relation of part can be expressed as follows:

```
part(x,y) → part-of(y,x)
```

The introduction of an object of type bicycle with an instance of pedal as a part into the assertional component will result in the assertion of the inverse relation part-of from pedal to bicycle.

Rules of this kind can also be used to express transitivity of certain roles, e.g.,

```
component(x,y) ∧ component(y,z) → component(x,z)
```

A closer look at the definitions of *pedal* and *wheel* reveals further requirements. One of the definitions links pedal to the disjunction of the concepts instrument and machine.

Disjunction of concepts is currently not supported by TED and most other term subsumption languages because it is contradictory to the goal that concepts should be defined only by reference to their superconcepts. A possible solution to the problem is to find a common superconcept of the two concepts (maybe anything) or to introduce two concepts for pedal – pedals that are parts of instruments and pedals that are parts of machines.[16]

In the description of bicycle, we have introduced two general relations: part and function. While part is a relation between nominal concepts, the function relation links nominal concepts to concepts representing verbs. The definitions of *wheel* show that the relation between an object and its properties is a third important relation for the description of nominal concepts. Subsequently, relations of this type will be subsumed under a relation called property:

```
a wheel is an object
     with property round
     with function turning
```

Approaches to the representation of nominal concepts cannot easily be adopted for the representation of the contents of verbs and adjectives. The representation of verb and adjective meanings is the topic of the next section.

8.4   Dealing with verbs and adjectives

Verbs play a central role in sentences. Many linguistic approaches to lexical semantics are approaches to the representation of verb meanings and the representation of sentence contents is usually based on verb meanings. One problem is that verbs are usually more ambiguous than nouns and that the most frequent verbs are the most ambiguous. In the object-centered paradigm of terminological representation languages, verbs generally do not play a major role. This is possibly due to the fact that the predicate-argument-structure of many verbs with more than two argument positions cannot be easily represented by concepts and roles which describe unary and binary predicates respectively. Some verbs that can be described by a binary predicate usually are represented by roles in terminological representation formalisms. For example, the sentence *John needs the book* would be represented by a role needs of the object John with the book, e.g., book1, as a filler. This approach to representing the sentence has several deficiencies. First, all the information is represented in the instance John, i.e., the fact that book1 is needed by John is represented only implicitly. In addition, this approach is unsuitable for the representation of predicates with more than two arguments. One possibility is to represent these predicates as concepts with special roles describing their arguments. A consequence of this approach is that there are two ways to represent binary predicates.

Subsequently, we examine the question whether the predicate-argument-structure of verbs can adequately be represented in a terminological representation formalism.[17] The meaning of verbs often depends heavily on the fillers of so-called *case relations* or case roles that link the verb to its arguments (Fillmore, 1968). Since these case relations have at most one filler, attributes can be used for their description in TED. The description of a verb can comprise, among other things, the possible ranges for these attributes – represented by a :type-restriction in TED. Let us examine some definitions of verbs. Some of the definitions of bicycle contain the verb to ride:

> to ride [e]: to travel on a horse, or in a carriage, or on a bicycle
> to travel [e]: [. . .] 2. to move; to go
> to move [e]: 1. to go from one place to another. [. . .]

The definition of *to ride* suggests that riding is a kind of traveling. The relation between *to ride* and *to travel* resembles hyponymy between nouns. It is called troponymy in (Fellbaum, 1990) and is described by the formula *to v1 is to v2 in some particular manner*. Because of the similarity between hyponymy and troponymy, we will use the subsumption relation also for the representation of troponymy.

The difference between a verb concept and its superconcept can often be described by restricting one or more of its case relations. According to the definition of *to ride*, the concept has an attribute that can be filled by objects of type horse, carriage or bicycle. We will call this attribute means-of-transportation. Apparently, the given definition of *to ride* has some deficiencies: the type restriction is inadequate for the representation of *to ride* because it excludes motorcycles, camels, etc. We can introduce a concept that means *to travel on or in a vehicle* as follows:

> to ride is to travel
>   with means-of-transportation vehicle

In TED-notation, we first have to introduce the attribute means-of-transportation. We are then able to describe to-ride as a subconcept of to-travel with means-of-transportation restricted to objects of type vehicle:

> (defattribute means-of-transportation)
> (defconcept to-ride (to-travel)
>   :defined
>   (:type means-of-transportation vehicle))

Other examples for troponymy between verb concepts are the pairs *to stroll – to walk* and *to whisper – to speak*:

> to stroll [e]: to walk slowly, without hurrying
> to whisper [e]: to speak with the breath only, not with the voice

In addition to the subsumption relation and the case relations, other relations, including temporal relationships, can be used to describe verb meanings. Methods for reasoning with temporal relationships generally are not supported by term subsumption languages. If representation formalisms are to be extended by constructs for temporal modeling, several problems are to be tackled. Among these is a decision whether time should be represented as a set of points or as a set of intervals, about the needed granularity, and how to deal with uncertain temporal information. A possibility to describe temporal relationships in terminological representation formalisms is to understand time intervals as a *concrete domain* and to define a set of predicates for this domain. An approach to integrate concrete domains into term subsumption languages is presented in Baader and Hanschke (1991). Based on these ideas, relationships between time intervals can be described and used to enhance the specification of concepts representing verbs.

In the following, we will assume that concepts representing activities or events have an attribute `time` representing the time interval in which the activity or event takes place and that the concrete domain `time-interval` is defined with the relations introduced in Allen (1984) as predicates `:meets`, `:overlaps`, `:during`, etc.

Every activity inherits a type restriction of the attribute `time` to instances of the domain `time-interval`:[18]

```
(defconcept activity (anything)
    :primitive
    (:type time time-interval))
```

Obviously, two concepts representing activities can only be in a hyponymy relation if they exhibit the same time interval, i.e., the two activities take place simultaneously.

It has been shown that the subsumption relation, a set of case relations, and temporal relationships play an important role in the representation of verb meanings. However, additional relations between concepts representing verbs exist which are rarely mentioned in dictionary definitions. In Fellbaum (1990) all these relations are derived from a general entailment relation. They differ mainly in the underlying temporal relationships. For example, there is an entailment relation and a relation of temporal inclusion between the concepts representing *to snore* and *to sleep*:

```
to snore is to breathe
    entailed-activity is to sleep
    is temporally-included-in entailed-activity
```

In the syntax of TED:

```
(defattribute entailed-activity)
(defconcept to-snore (to-breathe)
    :primitive
    (:type entailed-activity to-sleep)
    (:during time (time :of entailed-activity)))
```

A drawback of the use of attributes for modeling entailed activities is that each activity can have at most one entailed activity.

The entailment relations and the temporal relationships could (and should) be used to draw a number of further inferences. For example, if a person is involved in some activity *a1* he/she is also involved in all entailed activities of *a1*. Most of these inferences cannot be carried out on the terminological level. This is another indication of the need for a separate component for the representation of rule-like formulas and inferences with these rules.

To summarize some of the topics concerning the representation of verb meanings: As a first approach, the subsumption relation can be used to build up hierarchies of verb concepts. The hierarchies will be relatively flat and are attached to nominal concepts as for example `activity` or `event`. Additional relations, e.g., entailment and temporal relationships, can be represented using attributes, roles, and predicates over attributes and attribute chains.

We will now turn to the representation of adjectives. Adjectives and adverbs are used to modify the meaning of nouns and verbs. Let us begin with some adjective definitions, all from EDE (1976):

> round: 1. shaped like a wheel [. . .]
> wet: not dry; having water on the surface, or inside the material
> fast: 1. quick(ly) [. . .]
> quick: taking little time; swift; active
> loud: easily heard; noisy; not quiet
> warm: 1. pleasantly hot; not cold [. . .]
> hot: 1. very warm [. . .]
> cold: 1. not hot; very cool [. . .]

Adjectives seem to be more difficult to describe than nouns and verbs. The investigation of adjective definitions revealed many cyclic definitions in the dictionaries we analyzed. The definitions show that similarity of meaning and contrast are important relations to describe the meaning of adjectives.[19] Other important relations exist between many adjectives and the attributes they describe, e.g., size, temperature, and between the adjective and the nouns or verbs they can modify. Unfortunately, these relations usually are not mentioned in dictionary definitions.

In term subsumption languages, adjectives can be represented as primitive individuals without further description. However, a more detailed description seems to be desirable, based at least on the already mentioned relations `similarity` and `contrast`. Some adjectives can be arranged on a scale, e.g., *cold - cool – warm – hot*. The representation of adjectives with term subsumption languages causes even more problems than the representation of nouns and verbs. This is mostly due to the fact that the subsumption relation does not seem to make sense for adjective descriptions. Furthermore, if adjectives are represented as concepts, what are suitable individuals of these concepts?

As a first approach, adjectives could be represented as subconcepts[20] of a concept `quality` with suitable relations, for example:

- `modifies` – the type of objects that can be modified by the concept
- `attr` – the attribute that is described
- `similar-to` – a relation to similar qualities
- `contrast` – concepts that stand in an antonymy relation to the described concept

Example:

```
(defconcept cold (quality)
    :primitive
    (:type attr temperature)
    (:type modifies thing-or-entity)
    (:type contrast hot))
```

The symmetry of `similar-to` can be represented using a rule:

```
similar-to(x,y) → similar-to(y,x)
```

A weaker version of `contrast` could be deduced with appropriate rules by using `contrast` and `similarity` relations.

This approach to representing adjectives has several drawbacks that partially result from the difficulty of deciding whether adjectives should be represented as concepts or individuals. Often, the meaning of adjectives depends heavily on the modified object – a fact that seems to be better captured by a representation of adjectives as concepts.

The disadvantage of this approach is that the only way to refer to a property on the assertional level is to create an instance of the property and to refer to this instance. For example, if a small bicycle has to be introduced into ALAN, instances of `bicycle` and `small` have to be created:

```
(defconcept small (quality) :primitive)
(instance-of bicycle
    (property (instance-of small)))
```

8.5   Summary and outlook

We have discussed approaches to the representation of some aspects of the meaning of nouns, verbs and adjectives with the expressive capabilities of term subsumption languages. For that purpose we have analyzed a number of dictionary definitions and tried to represent their contents in a terminological representation formalism called TED. This analysis revealed that term subsumption languages are partially suitable for applications in lexical semantics.

To summarize the features of TED that proved to be useful in this area: The subsumption relation as the main organizing principle of nominal concepts and concepts representing verbs allows for inheritance of properties and the description of more specific concepts. If a complete description of concepts is available, the description can be used to insert a new concept at the correct place into the taxonomy, i.e., to find the suitable super- and subconcepts. Roles can be used to describe relations between concepts, for example different `part` and `function` relations. Differences between a concept and its superconcept(s) are specified by means of role restrictions, namely value restrictions and number restrictions. It turned out that value restriction, i.e., the restriction of the range of a role or an attribute is frequently used to specialize concepts. General number restrictions are less frequently used except for some special cases, e.g., *at least 1*, *exactly 1* or *at most 0*. For that reason, abbreviations for these special cases have been included in TED (`:some`, `:one` and `:no`).

A number of additional expressive elements, however, turned out to be necessary. The possibilities to restrict roles of more general concept descriptions had to be extended by qualifying number restrictions.

Another important requirement is a possibility to describe concepts by means of typical features or defaults. As mentioned earlier, not every part of a concept specification should be defeasible. Instead, the formalism should support the separation of a concept description into definitions, assertions and defaults.

A more thorough investigation of the role of subsumption and classification in the field of lexical semantics seems to be necessary. In this chapter, we are confined to a paradigmatic analysis of word meanings. Actually, what has to be discussed more thoroughly is how instances of the concepts represented in a term subsumption language can be combined to complex structures that represent the contents of whole utterances.

The meaning of a word can vary considerably depending on the context. The representation also has to be useful to deal with the "creative use of words" (Boguraev and Pustejovsky, 1990). For example, to understand the meaning of *a fast motorway*, we probably find that `motorway` itself cannot be modified by the property `fast`. Inferences then have to find suitable concepts to modify by taking into consideration concepts that are in a `function` relation to `motorway`.

In addition to extended expressive capabilities, a set of basic concepts, roles and attributes has to be given on which the description of new concepts and roles can be based. Furthermore, aspects of knowledge acquisition and maintenance have to be addressed. These include graphical user interfaces and further knowledge management tools. Since a general agreement about the meaning especially of primitive concepts is essential, the representation system should allow for concept descriptions enhanced with natural language definitions, examples and pictures. For the creation of large terminological knowledge bases, approaches to the automatic extraction of information from machine-readable dictionaries seem to be promising (e.g., Montemagni and Vandervende, 1992; Farwell et al., 1992). It has to be taken into account, however, that not all the relevant information about a concept can be found in dictionary definitions.

The current implementation of TED supports concept descriptions by means of role or attribute restrictions, qualifying number restrictions, and the specification of default restrictions. Its algorithms for subsumption determination are sound but not complete. The assertional component ALAN is used to introduce instances of concepts and relations between instances. Currently, a small natural language question answering system for a geographical domain is developed based on a terminology represented in TED and geographic facts represented in ALAN.

Notes

1. We will use the term *lexical unit* for the union of a lexical form and a single sense (cf. Cruse, 1986).
2. The claim here is not that the semantic description of natural language is possible without referring to some kind of primitives. What is asked for is a level of representation with "knowledge-structuring primitives, rather than particular knowledge primitives" (Brachman, 1979). Thus, the set of semantic primitives can be extended at any time.
3. Actually, such a clear-cut distinction between these knowledge types is not possible, e.g., many recent developments question a strict separation of lexicon and grammar. Also there is no general agreement about the borderline between linguistic and extralinguistic knowledge.
4. However, the inferences of a formalism with higher expressive power can still be complete with respect to a notion of structural subsumption instead of extensional subsumption. In structural subsumption, the subsumption criterion is formally specified dependent on the structure of the concepts (cf. Woods, 1991).
5. In some terminological representation formalisms the term *feature* is used for single-valued roles. It is important to note that there is some similarity between terminological representation formalisms and feature-based unification systems mostly used in computational linguistics, although their reasoning capabilities are quite different (cf. Nebel and Smolka, 1989).
6. For a detailed introduction to term subsumption formalisms see Nebel (1990). A concept language extended by single-valued roles is described in Hollunder and Nutt (1990).
7. Common Lisp Object System (Keene, 1989).
8. TI Explorer, Sun, and Apple Macintosh.
9. The definitions are marked with [e], [o], or [l] for EDE (1976), OALD (1988), or LDOCE (1987) respectively.
10. This description does not follow the syntactic rules of any formal representation language. Rather, it should be viewed as a first step toward a formal specification.
11. In order to distinguish between words and elements of the representation, i.e., concepts and roles, the latter are printed in typewriter style.
12. These relations correspond to the constitutive and telic roles of the Qualia Structure described in Pustejovsky (1991).
13. An example for such an ontology is the Upper Model (Bateman et al., 1990).
14. Possible subrelations of part could be component, member, and material.
15. For that reason, a picture of a bicycle is included in LDOCE (1987).
16. Here, the former solution seems to be more adequate since the concepts for instrument and machine are closely related and certainly not disjunct.
17. This examination is partly based on approaches to the representation of verb meanings in WordNet (cf. Beckwith et al., 1991; Fellbaum, 1990).
18. Actually, the concept activity will have a more detailed description to be inherited by its subconcepts.
19. Here, only adjectives that modify a certain attribute of nouns or verbs are examined. In Gross and Miller (1990), these are called *ascriptive adjectives*.
20. The representation of adjectives as individuals of a concept quality could also be taken into consideration.

References

J. Allen. (1984). Towards a General Theory of Action and Time. *Artificial Intelligence*, 23(2):123–154.

J. Allgayer and C. Reddig. (1990). What KL-ONE Lookalikes Need to Cope with Natural Language – Scope and Aspect of Plural Noun Phrases. In K. H. Bläsius, U. Hedtstück and C.-R. Rollinger (Eds.), *Sorts and Types in Artificial Intelligence*, pp. 240–285. Springer-Verlag.

F. Baader and P. Hanschke. (1991). A Scheme for Integrating Concrete Domains into Concept Languages. Technical Report RR-91-10, Deutsches Forschungszentrum für Künstliche Intelligenz.

J. A. Bateman, R. T. Kasper, J. D. Moore and R. A. Whitney. (1990). The General Organization of Knowledge for Natural Language Processing: the Penman Upper Model. Technical Report, Information Science Institute.

R. Beckwith, C. Fellbaum, D. Gross and G. A. Miller. (1991). WordNet: A Lexical Database Organized on Psycholinguistic Principles. In U. Zernik (Ed.), *Lexical Acquisition: Exploiting On-Line Resources to Build a Lexicon*, pp. 211–232. Lawrence Erlbaum.

B. Boguraev and J. Pustejovsky. (1990). Lexical Ambiguity and Knowledge Representation. In N. V. Findler (Ed.), *Proceedings of the Thirteenth International Conference on Computational Linguistics*, Helsinki.

R. J. Brachman. (1979). On the Epistemological Status of Semantic Networks. In N. V. Findler (Ed.), *Associative Networks: Representation and Use of Knowledge by Computers*, pp. 3–50. Academic Press, New York, N.Y.

R. J. Brachman. (1983). What IS-A Is and Isn't: An Analysis of Taxonomic Links in Semantic Networks. *IEEE Computer*, 16(10):30–36.

R. J. Brachman. (1985). "I Lied about the Trees" or, Defaults and Definitions in Knowledge Representation. *AI-Magazine*, 6(3):80–93.

R. J. Brachman and J. G. Schmolze. (1985). An Overview of the KL-ONE Knowledge Representation System. *Cognitive Science*, 9(2):171–216.

D. A. Cruse. (1986). *Lexical Semantics*. Cambridge University Press.

EDE. (1976). *Elementary Dictionary of English*. Langenscheidt-Longman, München.

D. W. Etherington and R. Reiter. (1983). On Inheritance Hierarchies With Exceptions. In *Proc. AAAI*, pp. 104–108, Washington, D.C.

D. Farwell, L. Guthrie and Y. Wilks. (1992). The Automatic Creation of Lexical Entries for a Multilingual MT System. In *Proceedings of the Fifteenth International Conference on Computational Linguistics (COLING)*, pp. 532–538.

C. Fellbaum. (1990). English Verbs as a Semantic Net. *International Journal of Lexicography*, 3(4):278–301.

C. Fillmore. (1968). The Case for Case. In E. Bach and R. Harms (Eds.), *Universals in Linguistic Theory*. New York: Holt, Rinehart, and Winston.

P. Forster, O. Eck and G. Burkert. (1991). Wissensrepräsentation mit TED und ALAN. Bericht 10/91, Institut für Informatik, Universität Stuttgart.

D. Gross and K. J. Miller. (1990). Adjectives in WordNet. *International Journal of Lexicography*, 3(4):265–277.

B. Hollunder and F. Baader. (1991). Qualifying Number Restrictions in Concept Languages. Technical Report RR-91-03, Deutsches Forschungszentrum für Künstliche Intelligenz, 1991.

B. Hollunder and W. Nutt. (1990). Subsumption Algorithms for Concept Languages. Technical Report RR-90-04, Deutsches Forschungszentrum für Künstliche Intelligenz.

S. E. Keene. (1989). *Object-Oriented Programming in COMMON LISP: A Programmer's Guide to CLOS*. Addison-Wesley.

LDOCE. (1987). *Longman Dictionary of Contemporary English*. Longman Group.

M. Minsky. (1975). A Framework for Representing Knowledge. In P. H. Winston (Ed.), *The Psychology of Computer Vision*, pp. 211–277. McGraw-Hill, New York.

S. Montemagni and L. Vandervende. (1992). Structural Patterns vs. String Patterns for Extracting Semantic Information from Dictionaries. In *Proceedings of the Fifteenth International Conference on Computational Linguistics (COLING)*, pp. 546–552, Nantes.

B. Nebel. (1990). *Reasoning and Revision in Hybrid Representation Systems*. Lecture Notes in Artificial Intelligence. Springer Verlag.

B. Nebel and G. Smolka. (1989). Representation and Reasoning with Attributive Descriptions. IWBS Report 81, Wissenschaftliches Zentrum, Institut für Wissensbasierte Systeme.

OALD. (1988). *Oxford Advanced Learner's Dictionary Electronic Version*. Oxford University Press, Oxford, 3rd edition.

J. Pustejovsky. (1991). The Generative Lexicon. *Computational Linguistics*, 17(4):409–441.

M. Quillian. (1968). Semantic Memory. In M. Minsky (Ed.), *Semantic Information Processing*. The MIT Press, Cambridge, MA.

R. Reiter. (1980). A Logic for Default Reasoning. *Artificial Intelligence*, 13(1):81–132, April.

R. C. Schank. (1972). Conceptual Dependency: A Theory of Natural Language Understanding. *Cognitive Psychology*, 3(4):552–631.

L. K. Schubert, R. R. Goebel and N. J. Cercone. (1979). The Structure and Organization of a Semantic Net for Comprehension and Inference. In N. V. Findler (Ed.), *Associative Networks – The Representation and Use of Knowledge by Computers*, pp. 121–175. Academic Press, New York.

W. A. Woods. (1975). What's in a Link: Foundations for Semantic Networks. In D. G. Bobrow and A. M. Collins (Eds.), *Representation and Understanding: Studies in Cognitive Science*, pp. 35–82. Academic Press, New York, N.Y.

W. A. Woods. (1991). Understanding Subsumption and Taxonomy: A Framework for Progress. In J. F. Sowa (Ed.), *Principles of Semantic Networks*, pp. 45–94. Morgan Kaufmann, San Mateo, California.

9   Word meaning between lexical and conceptual structure

PETER GERSTL

9.1   Introduction

The lexical component of a large language understanding system has to cope with phenomena which may go beyond the scope of traditional linguistic investigation. The integration of theories about different aspects of language understanding suffers from cases which either fall out of the responsibility of specific theories or which are not covered in detail since they are treated as marginal problems. One of these cases is the 'interface' between discourse semantics and world knowledge. Despite a lot of activity in this area there still is no systematic way of coordinating these two knowledge sources.[1] The organization of lexical knowledge is one of the domains in which a proper coordination of semantics and world knowledge needs to be explicitly stated. The problem may be illustrated by the following set of examples, based on an analysis of the words "left" and "school" in a simple one- or two-sentence discourse.

(1)   "Mary turned right and John left".

(2)   "The painter left the school $\left\{ \begin{array}{l} untidy \\ drunk \\ grey \end{array} \right\}$ ".

Sentence (1) is an example in which "left" is ambiguous between a verbal and an adverbial reading. Although argument saturation in (2) definitely selects the verbal reading, the sentence is still ambiguous, dependent on whether the adjective "untidy" is associated with "the painter" or, in case of a small-clause analysis, with "the school". The former interpretation leads to the reading of "left" as completion of movement involving a statement about the painter's physical appearance. The latter interpretation informs us about a state of the school, which the painter did not change (the state of being untidy).

(3)   "John left the school".
(4)   "John left Mary".

I would like to thank Patrick Saint-Dizier and Evelyne Viegas for inviting me to the workshop. This encouraged me to further evaluate and make explicit the ideas presented in this chapter and gave me the opportunity to present them to an interested, insightful, and critical public. I would also like to thank Zuzana Krifka Dobeš and Rob van der Sandt for a number of helpful discussions and suggestions regarding an early version of this chapter. Thanks to Bryan Booth for helpful advice concerning style and readability. Finally, I am grateful to the Scientific Center of IBM Germany for supporting this research.

Examples (3) and (4), both of which select the reading of movement, are still in a sense semantically unspecific, though not in the same way ambiguous as (2). As Bierwisch (1983) points out, sentences such as (3) are unspecific with respect to the interpretation of "school" as referring to a building or to an institution. In general, words of a certain semantic class, such as, for example, "school", "opera", "church", are capable of referring to one out of a set of possible alternative interpretations. The result of what Bierwisch calls a *conceptual shift* has an impact on the interpretation of the event of movement denoted by "left", since leaving a building is of a different inferential quality than abandoning 'membership' in an institution. This influence on the interpretation of "left", in Bierwisch's terminology a case of *conceptual differentiation*, occurs in the interpretation of (4) as well, even though it is triggered by a different instance of conceptual shift. Parallel to the unspecificity in (3), the interpretation of "left" in (4) varies between a momentary event and the end of a certain period in the agent's life, thus giving rise to a set of far-reaching inferences on the basis of world knowledge. However, this is not a case of conceptual differentiation since the argument is not subject to a conceptual shift.

9.2   The architecture of a NLP System

The LILOG project ('**L**inguistic and **Log**ical Methods for Text Understanding) was initiated in April 1985. The first running prototype of the system was presented in March 1988 followed by the second prototype LEU/2 (LILOG Experimenting Environment) in July 1990. The project is supported and managed by IBM Germany.[2] It integrates research in artificial intelligence, natural language processing and theoretical linguistics. Partner projects are carried out at five German universities. The system is not intended to be a full-blown dialogue system but to serve as an environment in which theories about aspects of text understanding can be tested, and in which experiments about NLP strategies can be carried out. The experimental character of the system gives rise to a modular architecture that makes it possible to replace components, or to add new modules in order to change local parameters without the need of major modifications of the whole system. Figure 9.1 shows a block diagram of the overall architecture of the LILOG system.

The two-level approach to natural language semantics as proposed by Bierwisch and Lang (1989) is realized by the two main databases of the system: the lexicon belonging to the linguistic level and the knowledge base on the level of the domain model. The processes of language analysis and generation make use of these data by controlling the operation of the lexicon manager and the inference engine. The results of these operations are recorded in dialogue memory which keeps track of all the different types of information that arise in the course of language processing.

From a more practical point of view such a modular architecture may also have its drawbacks. Problems arise if theories about different aspects of text understanding do not fit well into the organization of modules. In these cases the mod-

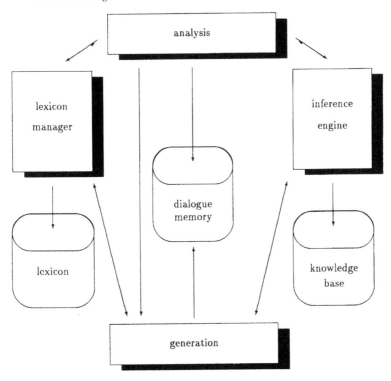

Figure 9.1. The architecture of the LILOG system

ular approach poses unnatural boundaries between aspects of text understanding that might require a closer interaction. This is reflected in the tendency of interfaces between modules either to become increasingly complex or to introduce a notable amount of redundancy with respect to functionality.[3] Interfacing problems frequently occur in the *vertical axis* of the system architecture since it traverses several boundaries between modules and passes through 'territories' of various theoretical interest. The vertical axis, a term derived from the geometry of Figure 9.1, constitutes the relation between *natural language expressions* (henceforth simply *expressions*) and *individuals*, i.e. representations of elements of the domain.

The vertical axis integrates two fundamental views of text understanding: language *analysis*, leading from expressions to individuals, and *generation*, mapping individuals onto expressions. Expressions are related by means of a concatenation operation that mirrors the sequential flow of language input. Individuals are linked by a network of properties and relations that are constrained by information coded in the knowledge base. In the following, we concentrate on that component of the vertical axis which links *occurrences of words*[4] as subparts of expressions to *discourse referents*, i.e., the individuals, which phrasal projections of words

P. Gerstl

Levels	LINGUISTIC KNOWLEDGE		NON-LINGUISTIC KNOWLEDGE	
Specific Knowledge	Discourse Knowledge		Episodic Knowledge	
General Knowledge	Categorial Knowledge		Conceptual Knowledge	
	TERMINOLOGICAL	ASSERTIONAL	TERMINOLOGICAL	ASSERTIONAL
	Lexical	Grammatical	Ontological	Inferential

Figure 9.2. The classification of knowledge types.

introduce and refer to. In our terms, the *referential potential* of a word is its property to qualify for reference to different elements of the domain according to the actual discourse context.[5] The referential potential of a word may be conceived of as the set of those possible referents which are associated with the expressions at different stages of the interpretation process during the analysis of a piece of discourse.

Although based on this architecture, the approach favored in this chapter aims toward balancing the computational load more evenly throughout the system. One point of departure leads to a shift of 'semantic responsibility' toward the non-linguistic level. The other more fundamental way in which this approach diverges from the LILOG architecture is the degree to which world knowledge influences language processing. From the point of view adopted here, the system architecture shown in Figure 9.1 can be transformed into a hierarchical scheme that reflects the arrangement of representational levels suited for a description of word meaning. The classification of knowledge types shown in Figure 9.2, which serves as the basis of our model, realizes this idea and constitutes a central idea of our approach.

The approach is based on the fundamental distinction between linguistic and non-linguistic knowledge following the idea of two-level semantics as proposed by Bierwisch and Lang, 1989. The distinction is motivated first by the modular architecture of the system, which allows us to treat different domain models on the basis of the same discourse model. Second, linguistic and non-linguistic knowledge can be distinguished with respect to a whole range of properties. Apart from this distinction, both linguistic and non-linguistic knowledge is further subdivided according to a uniform set of criteria which correspond to properties of the representation formalism. Morphosyntactic rules governed by principles of grammar and rules of inference constitute *assertional* knowledge representing regularities of language use and of the domain model respectively. Terminological knowledge, i.e., categorial and conceptual knowledge, provides the basic building blocks for all declarative representations of knowledge in the system. Terminological knowledge needs to be globally consistent; assertional knowledge does not. Only those partitions of assertional knowledge, which occur in the course of interpreting a natural language expression, are required to be (locally) consistent. The interpretation process has to keep track of not using inconsistent sets of rules, and therefore includes a powerful repair strategy for dealing with inconsistencies that cannot be avoided at first glance. One possible solution is a knowledge-packaging mechanism (Wachsmuth, 1989), which makes it possible to restrict the set of accessible knowledge elements to ensure local consistency by integrating only those packets which do not conflict with those already available. Another strategy involves an adequate treatment of defaults which allows the inference engine to maintain consistency by a proper arrangement of those defaults which might introduce conflicting information. This is what the truth maintenance module of the LILOG inference engine does (Lorenz, 1990).

The elements of terminological knowledge are partially ordered by means of the subsumption relation which licenses the inheritance of attributes between sorts and subsorts. Assertional and terminological knowledge together constitute what is called *general* knowledge. The following feature structures illustrate the lexical entries directly accessible through the surface form "left".

$$
\text{left}_{adverb}
\begin{bmatrix}
\text{mor:} & \begin{bmatrix} \text{root:} & \textit{'left'} \end{bmatrix} \\
\text{syn:} & \begin{bmatrix} \text{HEAD:} & \begin{bmatrix} \text{major:} & \text{a} \\ \text{aform:} & \text{norm} \end{bmatrix} \end{bmatrix} \\
\text{sx:} & \begin{bmatrix} \text{sort:} & \text{LEFT\_ORIENTATION} \end{bmatrix}
\end{bmatrix}
$$

$$
\text{left}_{noun}
\begin{bmatrix}
\text{mor:} & \begin{bmatrix} \text{root:} & \textit{'left'} \end{bmatrix} \\
\text{syn:} & \begin{bmatrix} \text{HEAD:} & \begin{bmatrix} \text{major:} & \text{n} \\ \text{nform:} & \text{count} \end{bmatrix} \\ \text{SUBCAT:} & <> \vee < \begin{bmatrix} \text{syn:} & \text{NP[gen]} \\ \text{sx:} & \_1 \end{bmatrix} > \end{bmatrix} \\
\text{sx:} & \begin{bmatrix} \text{sort:} & \text{POLITICAL\_LEFT} \end{bmatrix} \vee \begin{bmatrix} \text{sort:} & \text{LEFT\_HAND} \\ \text{poss:} & \text{PERSON}(\_1) \end{bmatrix}
\end{bmatrix}
$$

The entries are presented using the HPSG-style format of the LEU/2 lexicon. Uppercase feature names represent *feature paths* abbreviating a preceding 'local' attribute.[6] The value $C(\_1, \ldots, \_n)$ is a discourse marker representing a discourse referent. C is the concept which determines the non-linguistic properties of the discourse referent. The $\_1, \ldots, \_n$ are variables which may be instantiated by discourse markers of argument expressions. The term $C(r_1, \ldots r_n)$ refers to an instance of concept C, the ontological definition of which makes use of the discourse referents $r_1, \ldots r_n$. How this works will be illustrated in the following discussion.[7]

Despite the fact that we have two lexical entries representing the nominal and adverbial variants of "left" it is important to notice that they must not necessarily be considered homonymous because they may represent different linguistic realizations of the same underlying concept LEFT_ORIENTATION. The further refinement of the nominal variant into the subconcepts POLITICAL_LEFT and LEFT_HAND in the entry of left_{noun} is justified by the assumption that the interrelation between these subconcepts is not transparent in ordinary language use, and thus need not be modeled by rules of inference. This is the reason why both readings are realized as separate lexical entries as if it were an instance of 'true' homonymy. The decision whether the (sometimes purely historical) relation between two readings should be made explicit is generally dependent on the inferential capabilities the system has to provide. If the system is intended to model actual language use, then this is a matter of empirical investigation as in traditional dictionary design.

    The lexical entry with the base form "leave" is accessible through the application of a morphological rule f_{3rdsng} that is triggered by the occurrence of complements of a specific sort. It contains a disjunction of subcategorization lists that corresponds to the range of polysemous variants according to differences in argument structure. The association of theta-roles (values of the SUBCAT-feature) with the corresponding semantic roles (values of the SX-feature) is not explicitly stated in the lexical entry but follows from principles which prefer the selection of more specific alternatives to less specific ones. Elements of the list which are put in parentheses may, but need not, be realized syntactically.

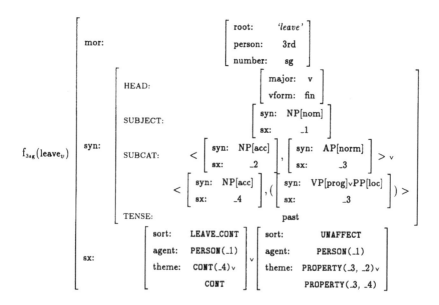

The feature-value pairs in the disjuncts of the SX feature represent *selectional constraints* which need to be fulfilled in order for a literal interpretation to be available. The following section gives an example of how a selectional constraint gets superimposed onto the conceptual type of a syntactically related expression. In case of argument saturation, selectional constraints are the formal counterpart of selectional restrictions.

General knowledge on the non-linguistic level is represented by entries of a terminological knowledge base. Concepts are represented by means of sortal definitions which relate sort names A to names of supersorts B by means of the subsumption relation ($\sqsubseteq$).[8] The formal expression $A \sqsubseteq B$ with sort names A,B expresses the fact, that 'B subsumes A', which is equivalent to saying 'the concept A represents is a subconcept of the concept represented by B'. In this case A inherits all the attributes of B. An attributive definition '$Q : C$' below the sortal definition of A means that Q names an attribute of A the range of which is restricted to instances of C. The attribute Q may be inherited from some superconcept $D \sqsupseteq A$ if it contains an attributive definition '$Q : E$'. In this case C is required to be subsumed by E. If A does not inherit Q, it is introduced as an attribute representing a *characteristic property* of A. In any case, all subsorts of A further inherit Q. Sortal names preceded by an asterisk represent sets of entities of the respective concept. A semicolon introduces a comment. The sample entries of our terminological knowledge base are presented using a simplification of the syntax of the L_{LILOG} language, which is a member of the KL-ONE family of knowledge representation languages (Pletat, 1991).

```
sort   STATE        ⊑  ...

       TIME_SPEC    :   TIME_INTERVALL  ; the temporal extension

       PLUS         :   *PROPOSITION    ; propositions valid in this state

       MINUS        :   *PROPOSITION    ; propositions not valid in this state


sort   EVENT        ⊑  ...

       SX.AGENT     :   ENTITY

       SX.THEME     :   $TOP$           ; $TOP$ is the upper bound of the sort lattice

       TIME_SPEC    :   TIME_POINT


sort   TRANSITION   ⊑  EVENT

       PRECOND      :   STATE

       POSTCOND     :   STATE


sort   LEAVE_CONT   ⊑  TRANSITION  ; 'leave a container'

       SX.THEME     :   CONT
```

Inference rules of a sorted first-order predicate logic are responsible for the proper instantiation of variables with values. They are represented as first-order formulas with restricted quantification. The occurrence of instances which fit the premise of a rule triggers its application,[9] i.e., rules are applied in a forward manner. As a result of the application of a rule containing an implication, instances of literals in the conclusion with appropriately bound variables become part of the currently accessible segment of episodic knowledge.[10]

$$\forall \, x : \text{TRANSITION} \, (\, \exists \, y,z : \text{STATE};$$
$$y = \text{PRECOND}(x) \wedge z = \text{POSTCOND}(x) \,)$$

$$\forall \, x : \text{TRANSITION};$$
$$t_x : \text{TIME\_POINT};$$
$$y,z : \text{STATE};$$
$$t_y, t_z : \text{TIME\_INTERVALL} \, (\quad y = \text{PRECOND}(x) \wedge$$
$$z = \text{POSTCOND}(x) \wedge$$
$$t_x = \text{TIME\_SPEC}(x) \wedge$$
$$t_y = \text{TIME\_SPEC}(y) \wedge$$
$$t_z = \text{TIME\_SPEC}(z) \rightarrow \text{meets}(t_y, t_x) \wedge \text{meets}(t_x, t_z) \,)$$

$$\forall \, x : \text{LEAVE\_CONT};$$
$$y,z : \text{STATE};$$
$$a : \text{ENTITY};$$
$$c : \text{CONT} \, (\quad y = \text{PRECOND}(x) \wedge$$
$$z = \text{POSTCOND}(x) \wedge$$
$$a = \text{SX.AGENT}(x) \wedge$$
$$c = \text{SX.THEME}(x) \wedge$$
$$\text{in}(a, c) \notin \text{MINUS}(y) \rightarrow \text{in}(a, c) \in \text{PLUS}(y) \wedge \text{in}(a, c) \in \text{MINUS}(z)$$

Specific knowledge consists in instances of categories or concepts which are structured by means of functions and relations. Specific linguistic knowledge is called *discourse knowledge*. Its elements are natural language expressions which correspond to instances of categories. Discourse knowledge is structured by an ordering relation that reflects the sequential character of natural language input together with various discourse relations. These control the flow of information, thereby forming a basis for referent accessibility and coherence. The logic underlying the rules of grammar has to deal with the concatenation of expressions. Specific non-linguistic knowledge is called *episodic knowledge*. Its elements are individuals, which uniquely correspond to instances of (set theoretic combinations of) concepts. Episodic knowledge is organized by functions and relations which may be extracted from conceptual knowledge by applying rules of inference. In the following section we introduce our model of word meaning on the basis of this classification.

9.3 The components of word meaning

According to our classification of knowledge types we distinguish three components of word meaning. Under the perspective of language analysis the first component (leftmost on the vertical axis), *categorization*, maps expressions onto partially instantiated categories. Word-level expressions are thus mapped onto categories representing lexical units. The second component, *lexical meaning*, maps partially instantiated categories onto partially instantiated concepts. *Individuation*, the last component, maps partially instantiated concepts onto individuals or sets of individuals, represented by discourse referents.[11] All three components are higher order functions, mapping sets of knowledge elements onto sets of their respective domain.

Lexical meaning is a complex many-to-many relation that results from the proper arrangement of two subcomponents: *categorial* and *conceptual selection*. Categorial selection is responsible for the choice of a disjunct from the set of polysemous alternatives provided by the semantic entry of a lexical unit. An example of categorial selection is the choice between the NP+A argument structure of "left" as in "John left the school grey" and the single NP complement as in "John left Mary". The set of polysemous alternatives consists of only those readings which differ in their linguistic properties. In drawing this distinction we relieve the strain on categorial selection by increasing the disambiguation potential of conceptual selection. We follow this strategy with the same goal in mind that guides the design of *generative lexicons* as proposed by Pustejovsky (1991), namely approaching a model of word meaning that 'spreads the semantic load more evenly' throughout different representational levels of the system. *Conceptual selection* guides the transition from one concept to a related concept on the basis of a fixed set of metonymical relations.[12] An example of conceptual selec-

	CATEGORIZATION	LEXICAL MEANING		INDIVIDUATION
Origin	application of morphosyntactic rules	categorial selection	conceptual selection	application of rules of inference
Domain	expressions	(partially) instantiated categories	(partially) instantiated concepts	(partially) instantiated concepts
Range	(partially) instantiated categories	(partially) instantiated categories	(partially) instantiated concepts	individuals

Figure 9.3. Components and their properties.

tion is the choice between the 'institutional' and 'locational' reading of "school" as in "John left the school when he was sixteen" versus "John left the school through the classroom window". The results of conceptual and categorial selection are linked by a set of semantic attributes bundled under the SX-feature of categories. This feature, which reappears as a functional attribute of concepts by means of *structure sharing*, provides information that transcends the boundary between linguistic and non-linguistic knowledge and thus makes up an integral part of lexical meaning.

In general, categorization is the result of applying morphosyntactic rules to an expression, but it may be affected up to a considerable degree by non-linguistic information that is accessible only via lexical meaning. Individuation plays a similar role with respect to rules of inference and individuals. In the course of interpreting an expression, individuation establishes links from partially instantiated concepts to referents in one of two possible ways, depending on whether or not an appropriate referent is available. Principles of discourse coherence force individuation to prefer links to those individuals which are currently in the focus of attention and thus qualify for reference by means of their thematic salience. The *set of accessible referents* is a subset of all the individuals introduced during the discourse. The accessibility of referents depends on various phenomena according to the organization and structuring of linguistic information such as: 'binding conditions', 'syntactic focusing', 'presuppositions', etc. (Asher and Wada, 1988). If no accessible referent is compatible with the requirements of the linguistic analysis, coherence can still be achieved if there is a way to establish a *conceptual link* between an element or a subset of the set of accessible referents and a concept in the semantic scope of the word at issue. Consider the following example:

(5)   "John left the school while it was being renovated.
         He jumped through one of the windows on the second floor
         climbing down the scaffolding.
         At the very moment he reached the street, the director came
         through the back door . . . "

Mentioning the "director" in a context where the reading of "school" as a building is already present makes a new aspect of its meaning explicit which is not identical but conceptually related to the meaning of "school" in the previous sentence: the meaning of "school" as the institution that is located in the building. According to the terminology of Clark and Haviland (1977) expressions such as "school" and "director" are linked by means of *bridging*. In our model, the bridging relation in (5) results from the combination of two relations at the level of specific knowledge: the metonymical relation between the instances representing the 'locational' and 'institutional' interpretation of "school", and the relation between the 'institutional' interpretation of "school" and the individual representing its "director".

An interesting consequence of the compositional view is that each of the components of word meaning can be further analyzed as the result of set-theoretic operations over *factors*. Factors, which are binary relations connecting knowledge elements, are often functional in nature. We can thus speak about the *domain* and the *range* of a factor. Some factors are explicitly represented by attributes of categories or concepts. Others are established 'on demand' at certain stages of the interpretation process by the backward application of rules. The following partially instantiated knowledge elements illustrate the nature of factors and components as intermediate results of the interpretation process. The focus is on the occurrence of "left" in sentence (4) of Section 9.1 which is repeated below for the sake of convenience.

(4)   "John left Mary".

Categorization as the result of the morphological analysis maps the expression "left" onto partial instances of lexical units with the appropriate phonological or orthographic specification. This leads to the partially instantiated category representing the third-person singular form of the verbal entry for "leave". Categorial selection further specifies the parameters of this entry by reducing the set of available disjunctions. The following feature structure shows the result of categorization and categorial selection.[13]

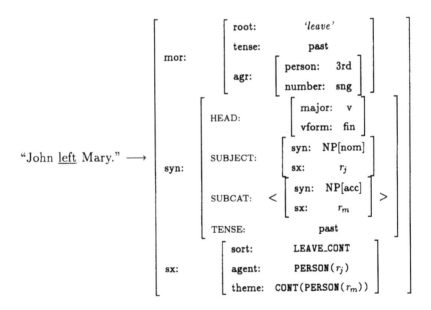

The value of the 'theme' attribute realizes the appropriate selectional restriction by means of the *conceptual constraint* CONT(PERSON(. . .)). Conceptual constraints call for a justification by means of the structure of conceptual knowledge. The evaluation of a conceptual constraint corresponds to the search for an individual which it may refer to. This is usually done by scanning the set of accessible referents using the inferential capabilities of background knowledge. Technically speaking, to evaluate the conceptual constraint A(B(r)) means to carry out the proof that a sufficiently salient metonymical relation between A and B is available in a currently accessible section of episodic knowledge. In case of A $\sqsubseteq$ B, the relation is trivially evaluated to the identity r = A(B(r)). Otherwise the inference engine may need to construct an instance of a metonymical relation f which maps *r* onto an instance *s* of type A. The termf(r) then systematically replaces A(B(r)). This is what happens in our example, where the concept PERSON, which classifies the referent of the syntactic argument ('Mary'), remains unchanged. The shifting operation leads to the accommodation of an instance of the concept SOCIAL_RELATION to which the selectional restriction for the thematic argument of the concept ABANDON applies. This instance relates two contextually salient individuals one of which is the referent of the expression instantiating the subject ('John') and one of which is the referent of the expression instantiating the syntactic position of direct object, thereby realizing the 'theme' ('Mary'). In the analysis of "John left the school grey" the situation is different. Normally conceived of as an instance of the concept COLOR, the concept associated with the word "grey" here is shifted to the informationally richer proposition representing the fact of 'being painted in grey'. The inference engine realizes this correspondence by scanning the attributes of the concept associated with the noun in object position (school$_{BUILDING}$) for an appropriate attribute that is compatible with the concept associated with "grey". In case of a rich conceptual structure this might lead not only to the information that the color of the school is grey but that it is, strictly speaking, a sufficiently representative part of the building's face that is assumed to be grey if no conflicting information is available.

The SX attribute as a common substructure of lexical and ontological knowledge represents the static aspect of lexical meaning. This claim corresponds to the view that argument structure can be thought of as an abbreviation for the part of conceptual structure that is visible to syntax (Jackendoff, 1987, pp. 404–405; Bresnan, 1982, p. 151). Since we strictly distinguish the syntactic aspects from the semantic representation of argument structure by keeping the SUBCAT and SX attributes distinct, our model accounts for the fact that one and the same theta grid may be associated with different distributions of thematic role structure (Jackendoff, 1987).[14]

$$
\left[
\begin{array}{ll}
\text{morph:} & \cdots \\
\text{syn:} & \cdots \\
\text{sx:} & \left[
\begin{array}{ll}
\text{sort:} & \text{LEAVE\_CONT} \\
\text{agent:} & \text{PERSON}(r_j) \\
\text{theme:} & \text{CONT(PERSON}(r_m))
\end{array}
\right]
\end{array}
\right]
\quad \rightarrow \quad
\begin{array}{lll}
\text{sort} & \text{LEAVE\_CONT} & \sqsubseteq \quad \text{TRANSITION} \\
& \text{SX.AGENT} & : \quad \text{PERSON}(r_j) \\
& \text{SX.THEME} & : \quad \text{CONT(PERSON}(r_m)) \\
& \text{PRECOND} & : \quad \text{STATE} \\
& \text{POSTCOND} & : \quad \text{STATE}
\end{array}
$$

The concept LEAVE_CONT is associated with a set of rules including those listed in the previous section. These rules assure that the agent is 'in the container' at t_1

and 'not in the container' at $t_2 > t_1$. Depending on the nature of the respective instance of CONT, the relation of 'being in a container' may represent a spatial relation, an entailment property, a set of social commitments, etc. Assuming that "left" in "John left Mary" is intended to refer to an act of desertion, the evaluation of the conceptual constraint CONT(PERSON(r_m)) involves both a semantic shift from CONT to SOCIAL_RELATION, and the introduction of a new referent r_{jm} instantiating a binary relation MARRIAGE or PARTNERSHIP with the arguments r_m and r_j.[15]

sort	LEAVE_CONT	⊑	...		sort	ABANDON	⊑	...
	SX.AGENT	:	PERSON(r_j)			SX.AGENT	:	PERSON(r_j)
	SX.THEME	:	CONT(PERSON(r_m))	→		SX.THEME	:	SOCIAL_RELATION(r_{jm})
	PRECOND	:	STATE			PRECOND	:	STATE
	POSTCOND	:	STATE			POSTCOND	:	STATE

We still have to close a gap in the description of our analysis. The conceptual attributes PRECOND and POSTCOND represent the characteristic properties of the concept TRANSITION in the domain model which are responsible for the inferences that can be drawn whenever instances of this concept show up. Conceptual selection is responsible for mapping semantic attributes onto those representing characteristic properties of a concept analogous to the way in which categorial selection maps subcategorization features of a lexical unit onto its semantic specification. Conceptual selection needs to take care of the fact that the values of both PRECOND and POSTCOND apply to the value of the AGENT role in case of 'leave$_{MOVE}$' and to the value of the THEME role in case of 'leave$_{UNAFFECT}$'. However, the fact that both conditions apply to the same entity is part of the characteristic properties of TRANSITION independent from its linguistic realization, thus making it a genuine element of non-linguistic knowledge. Furthermore, the information represented by the SX feature must be converted into propositional form since the conceptual attributes PRECOND and POSTCOND require their values to be subsumed under the concept STATE. What is needed here is a type changing operation similar to the *type coercion* mechanism of Pustejovsky (1991). The basic idea behind type coercion is that the lexical entry of a noun in object position contains information about how its semantic type may be changed in order to fit the requirements of the verb that controls it. This approach can be generalized to cases of ordinary predication as described in Pustejovsky and Anick (1988). In a generative lexicon, the lexical entry of a noun contains information which is characteristic of its meaning such as constituent parts, distinguishing properties, functional aspects and modes of origin. One difference between our approach and the position taken in Pustejovsky and Anick (1988) is that we handle these shifting operations exclusively on the basis of conceptual knowledge, whereas it belongs to lexical information (the *qualia structure*) in Pustejovsky's generative lexicon. In our example the evaluation of the conceptual constraint CONT(PERSON(r_m)) leads to an instance of the binary relation MARRIAGE which serves as the proper argument for the THEME attribute of ABANDON, complying with the selectional constraints of PRECOND and POSTCOND. The list of referents shown below summarizes the result of individuation:[16]

$r_a \leftarrow$ ABANDON $\quad \wedge \quad$ SX.AGENT(r_a) = $r_j \quad \wedge \quad$ SX.THEME(r_a) = $r_{jm} \quad \wedge$
$\qquad\qquad\qquad\qquad\qquad$ PRECOND(r_a) = $r_{pre} \quad \wedge \quad$ POSTCOND(r_a) = r_{post}

$r_j \leftarrow$ PERSON $\quad \wedge \quad$ SX.GENDER(r_j) = masc $\quad \wedge \quad$ NAME$(r_j,$ 'John'$)$

$r_{pre} \leftarrow$ STATE $\quad \wedge \quad r_{jm} \in$ PLUS(r_{pre})

$r_{post} \leftarrow$ STATE $\quad \wedge \quad r_{jm} \in$ MINUS(r_{post})

$r_{jm} \leftarrow$ MARRIAGE $\quad \wedge \quad$ ARG1(r_{jm}) = $r_j \quad \wedge \quad$ ARG2(r_{jm}) = r_m

$r_m \leftarrow$ PERSON $\quad \wedge \quad$ SX.GENDER(r_m) = fem $\quad \wedge \quad$ NAME$(r_m,$ 'Mary'$)$

In order to find the most plausible path along the 'vertical axis' of our system architecture, the procedure which balances linguistic and non-linguistic information needs to be further constrained, such that it provides a tractable solution to the problem of semantic variability. For a clear and systematic approach to the nature of this procedure we need to reconsider our compositional model of word meaning on the basis of its minimal building blocks, i.e., on the basis of factors.

9.4 The productive and restrictive force of factors

In approaching a universal notion of word meaning we have to take into account the fact that the term 'word meaning' itself is understood differently by different branches of linguistic research (lexicography, philosophy of language, computational linguistics, etc.). According to the two-level style semantics underlying our model, 'word' is the term we associate with the linguistic level and 'meaning' is what we associate with the non-linguistic level. So, the most extensive notion of word meaning is that of *reference* and the most restrictive one is that of *lexical meaning*. Between both of these extremes there is a whole range of notions that can be specified on the basis of the set of factors that are taken into account.

In order to understand the notion of a factor we need to reconsider the examples of Section 9.1. This section sheds light on phenomena which are responsible for establishing the range of non-linguistic entities a word can refer to. In our model these phenomena are represented by what we call the *productive force* of factors. The productive force of meaning components is responsible for the referential potential a word has and thus for its range of semantic variability. The following table shows the parallelism between components of word meaning and the variability effects introduced by their productive forces. Lexical meaning is subdi-

CATEGORIZATION	LEXICAL MEANING		INDIVIDUATION
	categorial selection	conceptual selection	
homonymy	unsystematic	systematic	referentiality
polymorphism	polysemy	polysemy	vagueness
		metonymy	indexicality

Figure 9.4. The productive force of components.

vided into its two subcomponents, categorial and conceptual selection, as shown in Figure 9.4.

The productive force of categorization derives from the coincidence of the surface realization of different lexical entries. Examples are the morphological ambiguities of "left" (noun, adverb or verb) and of "leaves" (verb or plural of "leaf"). In general, the distinction between homonymy as accidental coincidence of form, and polymorphism as category change without surface effects, can be made only if additional non-linguistic information is taken into account.[17]

Lexical meaning, as mentioned before, integrates two factors: categorial selection, operating on the lexicon and conceptual selection, operating on the ontology. Both of these subcomponents contribute their productive forces to the semantic scope of a word. This influence explicitly derives from information that is represented by certain attributes of terminological knowledge. The productive force of categorial selection is represented by the disjunction of readings in a lexical entry. In our examples, the intransitive and transitive cases represent different results of categorial selection. As Lehrer (1990) notices, many instances of polysemy do not behave in a predictable and systematic manner but are fixed by convention and thus need to be captured by separate lexical entries. Even examples of *unsystematic polysemy* that may be related on the basis of etymological arguments are represented as different categories if their meaning has developed independently from its etymological roots and if the connection is not apparent in the kind of language use the system is intended to model.

The productive force of conceptual selection results from conceptual relationships such as those proposed by Norrick (1981), which are represented explicitly by relational attributes between concepts. Conceptual relationships, a subset of which are the aforementioned metonymical relations, are responsible for many of the effects that have been called systematic or regular polysemy in the literature.

Finally, individuation provides an enormous productive force that leads to effects which are covered by the term *contextual relativity*, i.e., the property of referential expressions to be applicable to a potentially indefinite number of entities. Special cases of contextual relativity are introduced by indexical or deictic expressions which refer to elements of the discourse situation, and by vague expressions, the applicability of which depends on a whole range of contextual

CATEGORIZATION	LEXICAL MEANING		INDIVIDUATION
	categorial selection	conceptual selection	
	selectional restrictions		
morphology of surface form	conceptual requirements		
syntactic constraints on	domain specific properties		
type and argument structure	the set of accessible referents		

Figure 9.5. The restrictive force of components.

parameters (Bosch, 1983). All variability effects introduced by the productive force of individuation have in common extreme dependence on aspects of the discourse situation or, on whatever the discourse is about.

The influence of productive forces counteracts the influence of restrictive forces as a fundamental prerequisite for successful communication. We made extensive use of the restrictive forces of factors in describing the plausible interpretations of the example sentences (1) – (5). Figure 9.5 lists components of word meaning with their corresponding restrictive forces.

The form of the expression under consideration contributes a strong restrictive force since it rules out the vast majority of lexical units leaving only a small set of lexical alternatives. The requirements of syntactic well-formedness provide further restrictive forces by constraining the lexical unit to be of a certain type, thereby reducing the productive force of polymorphic variation. Other syntactic constraints which require the identity of certain features between constituents narrow down the semantic scope even further. When crossing the boundary between the linguistic and the non-linguistic level by following the semantic specifications of lexical meaning we find constraints, the nature of which is continuously discussed in the linguistic literature: *selectional restrictions*. Coinciding with the restrictive force of lexical semantics in our model, these restrictions integrate linguistic and non-linguistic properties. The final example of a factor providing a substantial amount of restrictive force is the set of accessible referents introduced in Section 9.3. As the primary productive force of individuation, this factor provides the most efficient means to keep the theoretically indefinite productivity of individuation tractable by constraining the set of accessible referents. In case of co-specification the most important influence on the interpretation derives from the restrictive force of individuation. Co-specification may take place either on the level of conceptual knowledge or on the level of episodic knowledge as the following examples illustrate:

- *Conceptual:* Non-identity of Referents/Identity of Concepts
  (6) "Sue takes [her money]$_{m_i}^{MONEY}$ to the bank, Joe keeps [it]$_{m_j}^{MONEY}$ under his pillow".

- *Episodic:* Non-identity of Concepts/Identity of Referents (Deane, 1988)

(7) "He jumped through [the window]$_{w_i}^{GROUND}$, which broke [it]$_{w_j}^{FIGURE}$ ".

(8) "[The game]$_{g_i}^{SET\_OF\_RULES}$ was hard to learn but [it]$_{g_j}^{SITUATION}$ only lasted an hour".

If the assumption of co-reference leads to a conflict at the conceptual level, the expressions need to be reanalyzed semantically in order to adjust the requirements they impose onto the joint referent. This generally involves the proper exploitation of all available productive forces from the selection of a specific semantic alternative to the evaluation of a conceptual constraint. It follows, that even though we presented the restrictive forces in what can be considered the most natural order under the viewpoint of language analysis, the order of application depends on the way the interpretation process makes use of them. There is no general law which forces the elimination of polysemous variants by the application of morphosyntactic constraints to precede the examination of selectional restrictions. There are, however, natural preferences for the order of application, since the information available for a certain reductive step often depends on the previous application of a certain factor.

Productive and restrictive forces can be considered opponents in the 'game' of constituting reference. Since they are functional in nature, one can speak of the application of a productive or restrictive force to a knowledge element. The application of a factor presupposes that the knowledge element belongs to its set of input values, and maps it onto an element of its set of output values. If relational factors associate different input values with the same result and provide multiple output values for the same input, they carry productive as well as restrictive forces at the same time. For the purpose of explanation we have sometimes simplified a relational factor to its productive or restrictive force in order to focus on certain phenomena. It is, however, important to notice that factors which have a productive force from the perspective of language analysis reveal a restrictive force when viewed from the perspective of language generation and vice versa.

Since deriving the referential potential of a word involves the integration of productive and restrictive forces, both perspectives cannot be described in isolation. This brings us back to the discussion of the LILOG architecture in Section 9.2, where we argued in favor of a stronger integration of common sense reasoning into language processing. This argument now follows as a natural consequence from the compositional model of word meaning. Instead of favoring the view of world knowledge as a service component for linguistic processing, we give the same status to the components which deal with non-linguistic information as to the components which are involved in language processing.[18] The priority of linguistic knowledge over non-linguistic knowledge giving reason for the unbalanced view of language analysis results from the enormous restrictive force of

P. Gerstl

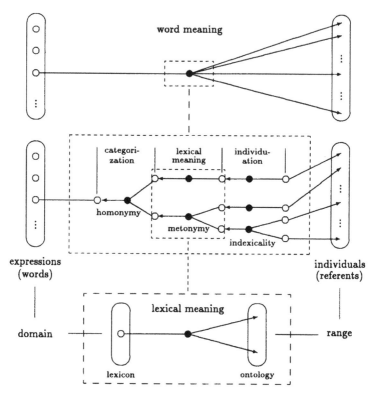

Figure 9.6. Variability as restrictive force under the viewpoint of generation.

categorization, which makes it a natural choice to start the interpretation of expressions on the linguistic side.

From this perspective, the goal of interpretation is to reach an equilibrium of productive and restrictive forces by picking out the individual which an expression is most plausibly intended to refer to. This may be achieved by minimizing the number of additional assumptions which neither are supported by the context nor can be inferred from background knowledge. In a system based on an architecture which resembles the one shown in Figure 9.1, aiming toward this goal requires the application of a smart control strategy which guides the close interaction of the operational parts of the system, i.e., of the parser/compositional-semantics module on the linguistic side and the inference engine on the non-linguistic side. Therefore, the next step in our approach is a detailed characterization of the procedural aspect of our model making explicit the way in which the interpretation process may be realized as a set of interacting procedures. This requires a precise definition of the formal properties of contexts including a well-defined set of operations over factors. In order for these computations to mirror the strategies we applied during our informal analysis in Sections 9.1 and 9.3, it must be possible to assess the results of applying productive or restrictive forces. On the basis of estimations about the result to be expected, the interpretation process is in the position to choose different strategies for the exploitation of factors in order to minimize the amount of computation needed and simultaneously maximize the plausibility of the interpretation result. This general background strategy bears a certain similarity to the theory of inference to the best explanation as used in plan ascription and diagnostics (Hobbs et al., 1990). Since our model is based on a system architecture which integrates different formal mechanisms, a necessary prerequisite for the application of this sort of reasoning to our domain is a systematic account to the notion of best explanation and to costs and weights of inference steps with respect to the mechanism used.[19]

9.5   Conclusion

In the preceding sections we have shown that though we are still far from a detailed characterization of word meaning in general, a systematic analysis of the influences involved in the interpretation of natural language expressions allows us to break down the complexity of this task considerably. By classifying the phenomena, which are assumed to extend the referential potential of a word, we singled out a small set of components that can be associated with certain parts of the architecture of a natural language understanding system. Finally, these components could be shown to be derivable from still more fine-grained elements which directly correspond to elements of the representation formalism, namely, factors. The discussion thus leads us from a rather abstract notion of referential meaning down to the minimal building blocks of the formalism. Since factors have fairly narrow ranges of applicability, each of them behaves in a predefined and predictable manner when evaluated in isolation. It is the way of interaction and mutual influence that renders word meaning as the result of the integration of a large number of different factors such a complex phenomenon. A flexible mechanism for controlling the interaction between factors on the basis of a cost/gain analysis makes it possible to exploit their productive and restrictive forces such that the system is able to derive the contextually most plausible interpretation of an expression with a minimum of processing effort. The central task of lexical semantics remains to provide a methodology for the actual formulation of lexical and ontological entries together with a discipline for the specification of their interdependence. As an anonymous referee correctly pointed out, there may be language-specific restrictions as to whether certain lexical items cover certain senses, i.e., the French verb 'quitter' which is very similar to 'laisser' does not allow for certain readings of movement since they are superseded by very specific interpretations. So 'quitter un travail' does not allow for a 'locational' reading in the sense of "[?]J'ai quitté ce travail parce que je devais partir" which is easily available with 'laisser'. What this shows is that a design methodology for lexical entries may not exclude the possibility to provide quite specific readings for certain combinations of lexical items. In this case computational lexical semantics is in fact very close to methods of traditional dictionary design. The main task of computational lexical semantics should be to provide the formal tools, together with a design methodology that represents senses, either as disjunctions of alternatives or, as a core meaning which leads to the individual interpretations by means of conceptual reasoning, or both. The general goal could then be to keep the semantic specifications as general as possible. This can be achieved by representing as much relevant information as possible within the conceptual model by reducing the formulation of lexical alternatives to those cases where the conceptual interrelation cannot be derived from the knowledge base. The example shown gives an idea of how the application of this design methodology to a concrete problem might look like.

Notes

1. See Pustejovsky (1991) for a recent collection of work in this territory.
2. Herzog and Rollinger (1991) contains a detailed description of the project.
3. Experiences of this kind are discussed in Klose et al. (1992).
4. The division between a vertical and a horizontal axis resembles the traditional dichotomy of a paradigmatic and a syntagmatic dimension though it covers representational aspects here.
5. In the following, 'word' is meant to refer to a word occurrence in a discourse and not to an abstract linguistic entity.
6. The notion of the referential potential of a word differs from the notion of the semantic scope of a word in that it refers to meaning in relation to those individuals which are available from the discourse context.
7. E.g., HEAD represents $local: | head:$.
8. NP[q] with q = nom,gen,acc,dat abbreviates $\left[HEAD: \begin{bmatrix} major: & n \\ case: & q \end{bmatrix} \right]$.

   XP[q] with q = norm,prog, . . . abbreviates $\left[HEAD: \begin{bmatrix} major: & x \\ xform: & q \end{bmatrix} \right]$.

9. In fact the supersort may be represented by a complex sortal expression which comprises set theoretic operations on sorts.
10. This is of course a simplification in terms of descriptive economy which disregards evaluation efficiency and strategies ensuring the termination of proofs.
11. 'Meet' and 'in' are constants of the semantic representation language which are mapped onto the appropriate concepts according to their actual argument assignments.
12. Partially instantiated in all these cases means that attributes may have constants or variables as values.
13. A systematic approach to these relations can be found in Norrick (1981). Examples are: 'actor-action', 'instrument-purpose','part-whole', . . .
14. r_j and r_m are discourse markers identifying the referents of the expressions "John" and "Mary" respectively.
15. SX.Y is a shortcut for the concatenation of the attributes SX and Y, which looks differently in pure L_{LILOG} syntax.

16. A certain instance of ABANDON may of course additionally involve a change of location but this is a matter of inferential knowledge and need not be stated as part of the concept definition.
17. $A \leftarrow B$ represents '*A* is an instance of *B*'.
18. It is important to note that polymorphism is defined on a purely linguistic basis. It is thus possible that two lexical entries which belong to different syntactic categories refer to the same concept (as illustrated by the polymorphism of 'left' in Section 9.3).
19. We should therefore better avoid speaking of the linguistic and non-linguistic *level* in order not to suggest a subordination relation between the two. With respect to the figure 9.1 we may equally well speak of the two *sides* (of the architecture).

References

Asher, Nicholas and Wada, Hajime. (1988). A Computational Account of Syntactic, Semantic and Discourse Principles for Anaphora Resolution. *Journal of Semantics*, 6:309–344.

Bierwisch, Manfred and Lang, Ewald. (1989). *Dimensional Adjectives. Grammatical Structure and Conceptual Interpretation*. Springer, Berlin, Heidelberg, New York.

Bierwisch, Manfred. (1983). Semantische und konzeptuelle Repräsentation lexikalischer Einheiten. In Růžička, R. and Motsch, W., editors, *Untersuchungen zur Semantik*, pages 61–99. Akademie Verlag, Berlin. [Studia Grammatica XXII].

Bosch, Peter. (1983). Vagueness is Context-Dependence. A solution to the sorites paradox. In Ballmer, T. T. and Pinkal, M., editors, *Approaching Vagueness*, pages 189–210. Elsevier Science Publishers, New York.

Bresnan, Joan. (1982). Poliadicity. In Bresnan, J., editor, *The Mental Representation of Grammatical Relations*. The MIT Press, Cambridge, Mass. and London.

Clark, H. H. and Haviland, S. E. (1977). Comprehension and the Given-New Contract. In Freedle, R. O., editor, *Discourse Production and Comprehension*. Ablex Publishing Company, Norwood, New Jersey.

Deane, Paul D. (1988). Polysemy and Cognition. *Lingua*, 75:325–361.

Herzog, Otthein and Rollinger, Claus, editors. (1991). *Text Understanding in LILOG: Integrating Computational Linguistics and Artificial Intelligence*. Lecture Notes in Artificial Intelligence. Springer, Berlin, New York.

Hobbs, Jerry, Stickel, Mark, Appelt, Douglas, and Martin, Paul. (1990). Interpretation as Abduction. Technical note 499, SRI International; Artificial Intelligence Center; Computing and Engineering Science Division.

Jackendoff, Ray. (1987). The Status of Thematic Relations in Linguistic Theory. *Linguistic Inquiry*, 18(3):369–411.

Klose, Gudrun, Lang, Ewald, and Pirlein, Thomas, editors. (1992). *Die Ontologie und Axiomatik der Wissensbasis von LILOG*. Informatik Fachberichte 307. Springer, Berlin, New York.

Lehrer, Adrienne. (1990). Polysemy, Conventionality, and the Structure of the Lexicon. *Cognitive Linguistics*, 1–2:207–246.

Lorenz, Sven. (1990). Nichtmonotones Schließen mit Ordnungssortierten Defaults. IWBS Report 100, IBM Germany GmbH, Scientific Center.

Norrick, Neal R. (1981). *Semiotic Principles in Semantic Theory*. Amsterdam Studies in the Theory and History of Linguistic Science IV. John Benjamins.

Pletat, Udo. (1991). The Knowledge Representation Language l_{LILOG}. In Herzog, O. and Rollinger, C., editors, *Text Understanding in LILOG: Integrating Computational Linguistics and Artificial Intelligence*, Lecture Notes in Artificial Intelligence, pages 357–379. Springer, Berlin, New York.

Pustejovsky, James and Anick, Peter G. (1988). On the Semantic Interpretation of Nominals. In *Proceedings of the 12th International Conference on Computational Linguistics*, pages 518–523.

Pustejovsky, James. (1991). The Generative Lexicon. *Computational Linguistics*, 17(4).

Wachsmuth, Ipke. (1989). Zur intelligenten Organisation von Wissensbeständen in künstlichen Systemen. IWBS Report 91, IBM Germany GmbH, Scientific Center.

10   The representation of group denoting nouns in a lexical knowledge base

ANN COPESTAKE

10.1   Introduction

The work reported here is part of research on the ACQUILEX project[1] which is aimed at the eventual development of a theoretically motivated, but comprehensive and computationally tractable, multilingual lexical knowledge base (LKB) usable for natural language processing, lexicography and other applications. One of the goals of the ACQUILEX project was to demonstrate the feasibility of building an LKB by acquiring a substantial portion of the information semi-automatically from machine readable dictionaries (MRDs). We have paid particular attention to lexical semantic information. Our work therefore attempts to integrate several strands of research:

- Linguistic theories of the lexicon and lexical semantics. In this chapter we will concentrate on the lexical semantics of nominals where our treatment is broadly based on that of Pustejovsky (1991), and in particular on his concepts of the *generative lexicon* and of *qualia structure*.
- Knowledge representation techniques. The formal lexical representation language (LRL) used in the ACQUILEX LKB system is based on typed features structures similar to those of Carpenter (1990, 1992), augmented with default inheritance and lexical rules. Our lexicons can thus be highly structured, hierarchical and generative.
- Lexicography and computational lexicography. The work reported here makes extensive use of the Longman Dictionary of Contemporary English (LDOCE; Procter, 1978). MRDs do not just provide data about individual lexical items; our theories of the lexicon have been developed and refined by considering the implicit organization of dictionaries and the insights of lexicographers.

In this chapter we will show how these strands can be combined in developing an appropriate representation for group nouns in the LRL, and in extracting the requisite information automatically from MRDs.

10.1.1   *Qualia structure*

Our treatment of the lexical semantics of nominals is ultimately based on Pustejovsky's approach, and, in particular, his description of *qualia structure*. Pustejovsky (1991) describes the qualia structure of a lexical item as consisting of the following four roles:

> **Constitutive role:** The relation between an object and its constituents or proper parts.
> **Formal role:** That which distinguishes the object within a larger domain.
> **Telic role:** Purpose and function of the object.
> **Agentive role:** Factors involved in the origin or "bringing about" of an object.

Pustejovsky argues that, rather than assuming that nominals just behave as passive objects when they combine with verbs, we should treat them as being as active in the semantics as the verb itself is. He refers to this behavior as *cocompositionality*. The cocompositional behavior of a noun is determined by its qualia structure.

For example, many verbs such as *enjoy* which can take a VP complement, can be described as selecting semantically for an event.

(1)   Mary enjoys playing the guitar.

However *enjoy* can also take an NP complement, and in sentences such as (2) the complement *the book* apparently denotes an object.

(2)   Mary enjoyed the book.

Traditionally the only way to handle this is to assume two lexical entries for *enjoy* and to relate the different senses by meaning postulates. However this is unsatisfactory since it leads to a proliferation of senses in the lexicon and it does not generalize to other cases where a noun phrase is interpreted as an event, such as (3).

(3)   After three glasses of champagne, John felt much happier.

Furthermore, examples such as (4) seem perfectly acceptable:

(4)   Mary enjoys books, television and playing the guitar.

However, under quite generally accepted assumptions about the nature of coordination and lexical ambiguity (e.g., Zwicky and Sadock, 1975; Cruse, 1986), only one sense of *enjoy* can be involved in (4).

Pustejovsky proposes that examples such as (2) be treated as involving *logical metonymy*. The sentence is interpreted as:

(5)   Mary enjoyed some event associated with the book.

The qualia structure for nouns specifies possible associated events. In this case, for example, the Telic (purpose) role of the qualia structure for *book* has a value equivalent to *reading*. When combined with *enjoy*, type coercion occurs, because *enjoy* selects for an event rather than an object, and the particular sort of event which is likely to be involved can be determined from the qualia structure, which results in a default interpretation for (2) equivalent to:

(6)   Mary enjoyed reading the book.

In a marked context the default interpretation might be overridden or blocked. For example, if Mary was the name of a goat, it might be inferred that she enjoyed eating the book rather than reading it; this is assumed to be part of pragmatics rather than lexical semantics. In such cases the type coercion to an event still occurs but the nature of the event is overridden. In cases where the lexical semantics of the noun would not specify a Telic role, or where the event specified would not be of an appropriate type, the corresponding sentences are odd:

(7)   ? John enjoyed the rock.

Since *rock* is not regarded as having a specified Telic role, the type of event which results from the metonymic coercion process is unknown, and the sentence seems bad.

For details of the way in which qualia structure and logical metonymy can be formally represented using a computationally tractable language, see Briscoe et al. (1990) and Copestake and Briscoe (1992). In the remainder of this chapter, we will describe our current lexical representation language, and illustrate how we can use this to represent group nouns, in a way which integrates with the earlier accounts. As in the earlier chapters, we concentrate on the issues of how the lexicon may be structured, in order to provide an efficient representation of lexical semantic information in the paradigmatic plane, and on how the description of lexical semantic structure may be integrated with a compositional semantic account. We conclude by describing how lexical information about group nouns may be extracted automatically from dictionary definitions.

10.2   The lexical representation language

Our lexical representation language (LRL) is unification-based, allowing complex interconnections between syntactic and semantic information to be defined, and making a tight interface possible between the lexicon and other components of NLP systems, e.g., the parser/interpreter, the generator and even the transfer component in a machine translation system. In fact LRL is a slight misnomer, since grammar rules can also be written in the language and a parser is incorporated in the LKB system in order to test lexical entries. In designing the language we adopted a similar philosophy to that behind PATR-II (Shieber, 1986), in that the LRL is intended to be sufficiently general to encode a range of possible approaches to linguistic representation. Like PATR-II, the LRL is based on the use of feature structures. However, in contrast to PATR-II, feature structures are typed in a manner similar to that proposed by Carpenter (1990, 1992). Feature structures must be well formed with respect to types and particular features will only be appropriate to specified types and their subtypes. The type system allows only non-default inheritance; we augment this with a restricted concept of default inheritance from feature structures, referred to as *psorts* in this context. Default inheritance is formalized in terms of default unification and is constrained by the type system. The LRL itself is a relatively 'theory neutral' language – a type system has to be developed to instantiate it in order to use it for representation based on a particular linguistic theory. The LRL is described in detail in various papers in Briscoe et al. (1993) and also in Copestake (1992). Here we will not attempt a formal description of the LRL but will give an informal overview, illustrated with relevant examples.[2] We will start by giving an example, which is intended to give an intuitive idea of the representation language and type system, and then consider the LRL in slightly more detail.

The following is a description of feature structure which corresponds to a lexical entry for *musician:*

```
musician L_0_1
    < >  < lex-individual < >
    < QUALIA >  < person_L_0_1 < QUALIA >
    < QUALIA : TELIC >  <= perform_L_0_2 < SEM > .
```

The identifier, L_0_1, indicates that the entry is intended to (roughly) correspond to the LDOCE sense *musician 1:*

> **musician 1** a person who performs on a musical instrument . . .

The feature structure into which this description expands is shown as an attribute-value matrix (AVM) in Figure 10.1. The expansion is due to the combination of the type system, which defines the underlying 'templates' for all feature structures, and to (default) inheritance from psorts. Lowercase bold font indicates types (e.g., **human**), uppercase is used for features (e.g., QUALIA), in AVM diagrams, descriptions and text. Lowercase typewriter font is used for psorts in descriptions and text (e.g., person_L_0_1, lex-individual). Reentrancy is indicated by a boxed integer in the AVM diagrams. Some parts of the entry are not shown fully expanded in this figure – this is indicated by a box round the type name. The description specified states that musician_L_0_1 is to default inherit from the entire psort lex-individual, that its qualia structure is default inherited from the qualia structure of person_L_0_1 and that the Telic role is non-default inherited from the semantics of perform_L_0_2.

The lexical entry consists of four main components. The value for ORTH is a simple string representing the orthography. The syntactic component is indicated by the feature CAT, but is shown unexpanded here. We adopt a categorial approach to syntax, for details of which see Sanfilippo (1993). SEM introduces the formal semantic structure, which is encoded in a way which is basically equivalent to the lambda calculus expression $\lambda x[\textbf{musician\_L\_0\_1}(x)]$. Agreement is specified on the indices, following Pollard and Sag (1994).

The feature QUALIA introduces the lexical semantic structure. The lexical semantic type of the entry is **human** (see Figure 10.3). The Telic role is shown in

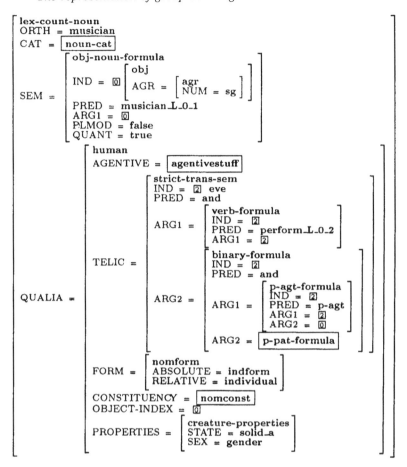

Figure 10.1. Lexical entry for *musician*.

detail (although it is not completely expanded); it has been instantiated with the semantics for the lexical entry for *perform*. Verb semantics are expressed in the type system as a whole in a neo-Davidsonian representation making use of thematic roles (see Sanfilippo, 1993). The formula given for the Telic role is equivalent to $\lambda e[\mathbf{perform\_L\_0\_2}(e) \wedge agent(e,x)]$ where x is bound in the expression of the semantics of the lexical entry as a whole so that $\mathbf{musician\_L\_0\_1}(x)$.

10.2.1 *The type system*

The type system is the basis for setting up linguistic representations in the LRL. The type hierarchy defines a partial ordering on the types and specifies which types are *consistent*. Only feature structures with mutually consistent types can be unified – two types which are unordered in the hierarchy are assumed to be incon-

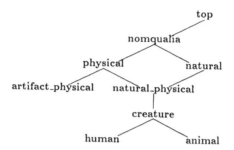

Figure 10.2. A fragment of the lexical semantic type hierarchy.

sistent unless the user explicitly specifies a common subtype. Every *consistent* set of types has a unique greatest lower bound or meet; when two feature structures are successfully unified the type of the resulting feature structure will be the meet of their types. Thus, in the fragment of a type hierarchy shown in Figure 10.2, **natural** and **physical** are consistent; unifying a feature structure of type **natural** with one of type **physical** will result in a feature structure of type **natural_physical**.

Our formalism differs somewhat from that described by Carpenter in that we adopt a different notion of *well-formedness* of typed feature structures (i.e. consistency of feature structures with the type system). In the LRL, every type must have exactly one associated feature structure which acts as a constraint on all feature structures of that type; by subsuming all well-formed feature structures of that type. The constraint also defines which features are *appropriate* for a particular type – a well-formed feature structure may only contain appropriate features. Constraints are inherited by all subtypes of a type, but a subtype may introduce new features (which will be inherited as appropriate features by all its subtypes). A constraint on a type is a well-formed feature structure of that type; all constraints must therefore be mutually consistent. The constraint on the type **human** is shown in Figure 10.3: in effect the information expressed in this is inherited non-defeasibly by the qualia structure of lexical entries such as that for *musician*. The type system has to be completely specified before any lexical entries can be expanded; this allows the well-formedness of lexical entries to be checked but is too inflexible to be the sole means of inheritance.

10.2.2   *Psort inheritance*

To allow default inheritance and more flexible non-default inheritance, we introduce the concept of a *psort*; a feature structure from which another feature structure inherits information, normally by default. The hierarchical ordering on psorts (which must be consistent with the type hierarchy) provides an order on defaults. Default inheritance is implemented by a version of default unification (e.g. Car-

$$
\begin{bmatrix}
\text{human} \\
\text{AGENTIVE} = \boxed{\text{agentivestuff}} \\
\text{TELIC} = \boxed{\text{verb-sem}} \\
\text{FORM} = \begin{bmatrix} \text{nomform} \\ \text{ABSOLUTE} = \text{indform} \\ \text{RELATIVE} = \text{(individual plural group)} \end{bmatrix} \\
\text{CONSTITUENCY} = \boxed{\text{nomconst}} \\
\text{OBJECT-INDEX} = \text{entity} \\
\text{PROPERTIES} = \begin{bmatrix} \text{creature-properties} \\ \text{STATE} = \text{solid\_a} \\ \text{SEX} = \text{gender} \end{bmatrix}
\end{bmatrix}
$$

Figure 10.3. Constraint on the lexical semantic type **human.**

penter, 1993). Multiple inheritance is restricted to the case where information inherited from different sources is consistent. Non-default inheritance from psorts is also allowed; this is simply implemented using ordinary unification. Default inheritance from a psort is indicated in the description language by <, non-default inheritance by <=.

Psorts may correspond to lexical entries or be specially defined in order to conveniently group some information. In the previous description for *musician* lex-individual, person_L_0_1 and perform_L_0_2 are all psorts. The first is specially defined; the latter two are lexical entries. Because of the condition that the type hierarchy and the default inheritance hierarchy must be consistent, the default inheritance specification also determines the type of the qualia structure for *musician* to be **human**, non-defeasibly. The non-default inheritance from perform_L_0_2 allows the appropriate semantic structure to be copied to fill the Telic role. (Details of these psorts are shown in the appendix.) Other lexical entries, for example that for *minstrel*, will themselves inherit information taxonomically from the psort musician_L_0_1 which is set up by the lexical entry. In the remainder of this chapter, we will consider how group nouns may be represented in the LRL in a manner which is consistent with the rest of the type system.

10.3 Group nouns

Group nouns, such as *band, crowd, quartet, flock, management* and *group* itself, are distinctive in English in that, when morphologically singular, they behave in some respects like singular nouns and in others like plurals. This manifests itself in several ways:

1. Singular or plural pronouns can be used:

    (8) The band played well tonight. Its/their tour has sold out.

2. Either singular or plural agreement with the verb is possible (plural agreement with group nouns is, in general, less common in American English):

    (9) That band play/plays well.

In the case of group nouns which denote groups of humans, a relative clause is introduced by *who* if plural agreement is used, and by *which* if it is not:

(10) The band who get/*gets top billing at the festival receive/
*receives £20,000.
The band which gets/*get top billing at the festival receives/
*receive £20,000.

3. Individual members can be referred to by using *one of* etc.

(11) One of the band smashed her guitar.

The final criterion distinguishes between group nouns and those such as *barracks* and *gallows* which can take either singular or plural agreement (when referring to the same entity). Note also that unpluralized group nouns always take a singular determiner, even if verbal agreement is plural.

(12)   This barracks is/*are new.
These barracks are/*is new.
That band has/have been playing well.

However, there are other nouns which do not meet these criteria, even though they refer to entities which can be regarded as being made up of several discrete individuals. For example, consider the LDOCE definition of *dolmen*:

> **dolmen** a group of upright stones supporting a large flat piece of stone, built in ancient times in Britain and France

Despite the fact that a *dolmen* can evidently be regarded as a group of entities, it does not behave as a group noun; the following are all unacceptable:

(13)   a   The dolmen is on a mountain. *They're very eroded.
b   *The dolmen have fallen down.
c   *One of the dolmen fell down.

There is clearly a semantic distinction between group and non-group nouns; when a group noun is used the individual components of the entity denoted are sufficiently obvious that it can be referred to as though it were a plural term. Collectives such as *terrace* and *range*, which denote groups of entities of a particular type and which usually appear with *of* phrases (*terrace of houses, range of mountains*), do share some of the behavior of group nouns, however. These nouns always take singular agreement when morphologically singular (at least when the *of* phrase is absent), and thus are not group nouns by the first two tests, but they can meet the third, although only in contexts where the individual members are explicitly mentioned.

(14)   a   The house was one of a terrace.
b   * One of the terrace had a green front door.

Example (14a) is taken from the Lancaster-Oslo/Bergen (LOB) corpus; when checking for *one of*, followed by a morphologically singular noun phrase, this was the only example where the head of the NP was not a group noun by the agreement tests. There is a contrast between *terrace* and *group*, as the latter is not at all limited in the semantic type of its *of* complement (e.g., *group of houses, group of statistics, group of actions*), but which refers to people when used without the *of* phrase in an unmarked context.

The singular/plural dual behavior of true group nouns to some extent corresponds to whether the predicate is seen as applying to the group as a whole or to its individual members.

(15)   The band was formed in 1977.
       The team were killed in a plane crash.

There is a tendency for singular agreement to be used when the group as an entity is referred to, and for plural agreement to be used when the individuals are concerned. The previous examples are odd when the agreement is changed:

(16)   ? The band were formed in 1977.
       ? The team was killed in a plane crash.

Sometimes differences in agreement alone suggest a semantic distinction. In (17a) the implication is that the committee as an entity gets the money, (17b) suggests that it goes to the individual members and there is a possible distributive reading, forced in (17c). Note that (17d) is bad.

(17)   a   The committee gets £20,000 per annum.
       b   The committee get £20,000 per annum.
       c   The committee get £20,000 per annum each.
       d   ? The committee gets £20,000 per annum each.

However, plural agreement with verb phrases which apparently refer to the group as a single entity is quite normal in some contexts, such as when referring to sports teams or clubs.

(18)   a   Forfar are a good side. (LOB corpus)
       b   But there was to be no bargaining [on players' contracts] as far as the club were concerned. (*The Guardian*)

It is useful to distinguish between ordinary group nouns and those which refer generically, since the latter class involve some different problems which we will not discuss here. Ordinary group nouns form plurals in the normal way, (e.g., *bands, crowds, quartets, flocks*), but others do not normally form plurals because they refer generically (e.g., *aristocracy, clergy*), or to an entity usually regarded as unique (e.g., *admiralty*), although plurals are possible in phrases such as *the admiralties of England and France*. The generic group nouns have dual group-entity/plural behavior, but their plural behavior parallels that of bare plural noun phrases in 'universal' position, in contrast to normal group nouns. For example (19a) implies (19b) but (19c) does not imply (19d), but only (19e).

(19)   a   The clergy are badly paid.
       b   Clergymen are badly paid.

    c The committee are badly paid.
    d Committeemen are badly paid.
    e The committeemen are badly paid.

In what follows we will make the simplest assumption about the nature of the plural reading of ordinary group nouns, which is that it is equivalent to a normal plural. The plural reading corresponds to an entity which can be regarded as the sum of the members of the group, and has a qualia structure appropriate for a normal plural entity.[3] This straightforwardly accounts for the verbal and pronominal agreement, and for the use of partitives with the plural interpretation. On this assumption, we should get both distributive and collective plural readings. Distinguishing the group reading and the collective plural reading is not easy but there are examples such as (20a) which should probably be treated as a collective plural, since the predicate refers to individual members rather than the group entity. Similarly (20b) has a cumulative reading (Scha, 1983), where the committee members are distributed in some unspecified way between the cars.

(20)   a The committee are arriving in a car.
       b The committee are arriving in three cars.

We then have to address the question of relating the group and the plural readings. We will assume that a group and the plural sum of its members are distinct entities, and that the plural reading is produced from the group reading by a process of logical metonymy, similar to that discussed in Section 10.1. In this case, the instantiation involves the composition of the entity rather than its purpose. The metonymic account allows for the examples of group nouns such as *club*, *committee* and *company*, where the entity denoted seems to have an existence independent of its members, even when a purely extensional viewpoint is taken. One can imagine a club, for example, which currently has no members but nonetheless still exists as a legal entity. This is problematic for theories which make the representation the group entity dependent on its members, but does not pose any problems for the metonymic account.[4]

So this suggests that in order to provide an adequate lexical semantics for group nouns, information about their membership must be represented, in order to allow appropriate semantic information to be associated with phrases such as *one of the band*. We associate this information with the CONSTITUENCY role of the qualia structure.

It appears that group nouns in English always refer to entities whose individual members are seen as capable of independent, agentive action, usually humans or other 'higher' animals. We have tested this assumption in a preliminary way using LDOCE; group nouns can, in theory, be retrieved as a class quite simply, since they are marked in the dictionary by the grammar codes GC (group countable, e.g., *committee*) or GU (group uncountable, e.g., *Admiralty*). Unfortunately the LDOCE coding is far from comprehensive in this case (*army*, *assembly*, *band*, *coven* have no senses marked as being group nouns, for example) and the GU code has been given to a considerable number of entries which would not be characterized as group nouns by the tests just mentioned, especially plural forms such as *letters* and *tactics*. We thus considered only nouns with grammar code GC, and excluded the morphologically plural forms *games*, *Olympic Games* and *vibes*, which also do not meet all the tests. The remaining senses all refer to collections of humans or human organizations, or (less frequently) animals, with the exceptions *fleet* and *convoy*, where the individual entities are ships.[5] There are some group nouns which can refer to collections of people or organizations which may themselves be groups;

> **league**[2]3 a group of sports clubs or players . . .

Thus grouping is not restricted to a single level.

It thus seems that lexicalization of a concept of a collection of entities as a group noun is restricted to a small semantic class of entities, which we will provisionally limit to humans, organizations and animals, ignoring the ship examples for the time being, since further work is necessary to more precisely delimit the class.

10.3.1 *Representing group denoting nouns in the LRL*

We can describe entries for group denoting nouns in the LRL, which allow us to formalize most of the aspects of their behavior discussed earlier. An entry for *band*, in the sense meaning a group of musicians is shown in Figure 10.4. This feature structure corresponds to the group entity reading for *band*. Here we have assumed that number agreement is tightly linked to the group/plural distinction, and thus agreement is specified as **sg**. Alternatively it could be underspecified as **num** to allow for examples, such as those given earlier, where plural agreement is used in sentences which seem on semantic grounds to involve an uncoerced group entity.[6]

The lexical semantic type of the entry is **human**, but the values for the features CONSTITUENCY and FORM : RELATIVE are specific to group denoting nouns. The representation for the lexical semantics of group denoting nouns has to be compatible with the rest of the type system. Given the results mentioned, which suggest that there are only restricted semantic classes of group nouns, it clearly would be inappropriate to parallel the entire existing lexical semantic type hierarchy with a group type hierarchy. Furthermore much of the information about group nouns will be comparable with that about their individual members. We therefore allow types such as **human** to apply to both individuals and groups, and distinguish between the two by specifying that the CONSTITUENCY feature either takes type **nongroupconst** or **groupconst**. Only the latter has ELEMENTS as an appropriate feature. The lexical semantics of the plural sum of the individuals making up a group noun is specified as the value of the ELEMENTS feature. In the case of *band* the individuals involved are *musicians*, thus the ELEMENTS slot is instantiated with the qualia structure corresponding to the pluralized form of musician_L_0_1. (In Figure 10.4 this is shown unexpanded so only the type, **human**, is apparent.) The value of FORM : RELATIVE is also specific to group denoting nouns. In general

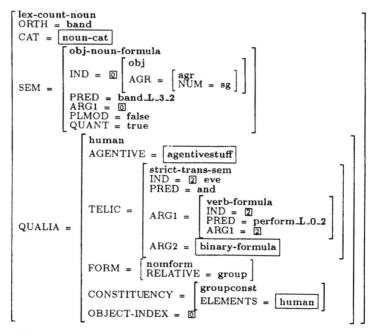

Figure 10.4. Lexical entry for *band*.

FORM : RELATIVE specifies individuation relative to a predicate – other possible values include **individual, plural** and **mass**.

The lexical entry just given does not directly account for the plural reading of group nouns. Our treatment of the group/members logical metonymy is very similar to that of the entity/event coercion, but in this case type coercion will occur in contexts where a plural entity is required. We implement this in the LRL with a unary rule, group-to-plural, which applies to a group denoting noun phrase. Rules in the LRL are themselves feature structures, which can be taken as describing the relationship between an input structure and an output structure. The rule group-to-plural is actually quite complex, since it has to apply to type-raised noun phrases. It is given in full in the appendix – here we will summarize its effects on the various parts of the sign:

- The orthography is unchanged.
- The categorial syntactic structure remains of type **raised-np-cat**, but is changed so that it integrates appropriately with the new semantics and qualia structure.
- The formal semantics is set up so that it is essentially equivalent to 'the members of [input NP]' (e.g., *the members of the band*). The operator **membership** applies to the group entity, to give the plural entity.

- The output sign has plural agreement.
- The qualia structure for the output sign is equal to the value of
  < QUALIA : CONSTITUENCY : ELEMENTS > in the input sign. This
  will have the FORM appropriate for a plural entity.

The sign which would result from the application of group-to-plural to *the band* is shown in Figure 10.5. This sign has obligatory plural agreement and denotes the plural entity which consists of the members of the band. The unary rule application is forced in contexts where a formally plural entity is required, for example, a partitive construction, such as *one of*. When this is used with a group noun (e.g., *one of the band*) the unary rule is applied to the group to give a plural entity, and the appropriate specification of the individuals involved is then produced in much the same way as for the ordinary plural (e.g., *one of the members of the band*).

The representation of lexical semantic information about the individuals which comprise the group thus allows the plural-like aspects of the behavior of group nouns to be accounted for. The group-to-plural rule specifies the qualia structure of the resulting plural entity according to the composition described in the CONSTITUENCY feature and the effect on the lexical semantics thus parallels the effect on the logical representation.

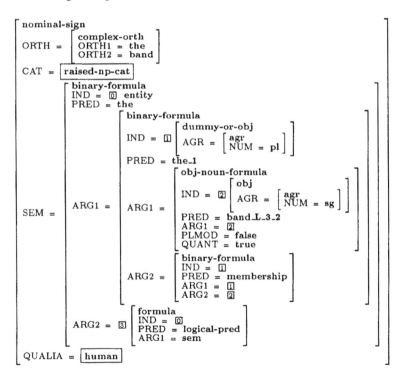

Figure 10.5. Coerced form of *the band*.

10.4   The use of MRDs

To some extent, lexical entries such as those shown in this chapter can be acquired semi-automatically from LDOCE. To do this we make use of a combination of information from the definition and from the LDOCE grammar codes. For example, consider again the definition of *musician* and the corresponding LRL entry:

> **musician 1** a person who performs on a musical instrument . . .

```
musician L_0_1
    < > < lex-individual < >
    < QUALIA > < person_L_0_1 < QUALIA >
    < QUALIA : TELIC > <= perform_L_0_2 < SEM > .
```

Syntactic information can be derived from LDOCE's grammar codes; in this case *musician* corresponds to an ordinary count noun, which results in the inheritance from lex-individual. We will not discuss extraction of information from grammar codes in detail here.

Noun definitions can be split into a *genus* and *differentia*; the genus can usually be taken to be the syntactic head of the definition. Here the genus term is taken to be (a particular sense of) *person*. The basis for our use of noun dictionary definitions as a source of lexical semantic information is that, in general, we can specify that entries inherit lexical semantic information by default from the entry corresponding to their genus term. The differentia may augment or override the information inherited from the genus term.

We can automatically extract genus terms reliably from noun definitions such as that above (Vossen, 1990) and lexically disambiguate them (semi-)automatically (Copestake, 1990).[7] Extracting information from the differentia is more difficult. It is possible, once the semantic type of a sense is known, to use the type as a template to guide analysis of the definitions, but a considerable amount of work is required to achieve this, and in ACQUILEX so far this has been only attempted on limited classes of definitions (see, for example, Ageno et al., 1992; Vossen, 1992). Thus the Telic role for the previous entry was manually specified. In general, associating information manually with lexical entries which are frequently used as psorts is an effective way of acquiring information, since inheritance will result in a large number of other entries being instantiated. However there are many special cases where definitions do not straightforwardly yield genus terms which can be interpreted as psorts. This is extensively discussed in Vossen and Copestake (1993); here I will concentrate on the particular case of group nouns.

10.4.1   *Dictionary definitions of group nouns*

It is usually assumed that dictionary definitions should, in general, be substitutable, in context, for the word being defined (e.g., Landau, 1984). Because of this principle of substitutability, definitions of group nouns in dictionaries such as LDOCE will normally be group denoting noun phrases. In some cases the genus term will be a relatively specific group noun, for example:

crew [1]**3** a rowing team

Such definitions can be treated as illustrated: the entire qualia structure is default inherited from the entry for the genus sense, *team 2:*

```
crew L_1_3
    < > < lex-group < >
    < QUALIA > < team_L_0_2 < QUALIA >.
```

However there is another class of definitions where the genus phrase is of the form 'DET *group of* N ' and the noun is principally being defined in terms of its members, for example:

band[3]**2** a group of musicians . . .

Such cases pose more problems, since there is very little semantic information that can be inherited from *group.* As illustrated with the example of *dolmen,* given earlier, the use of *group of* does not necessarily indicate a noun which is group denoting in the technical sense. In other cases, a group noun may be defined using a plural genus term, for example:

audience 1 the people listening to or watching a performance, speech, television show, etc.

In this case, the definition cannot be substituted for *audience* in contexts where it is used with singular agreement or refers to the group as a whole.

(22)   The audience were very noisy tonight.
         The people listening to the performance were very noisy tonight.
         The audience was very noisy tonight.
         *The people listening to the performance was very noisy tonight.
         The audience was tiny.
         *The people listening to the performance was tiny.

(Presumably the lexicographer felt that it was better to use *people* than *group of people*, for example, which perhaps suggests a greater cohesion between the individuals than is appropriate here.) For such examples, a representation has to be built based on information about the individual members, rather than about the group as a whole.

Clearly, given the type system outlined earlier, information about the type of a group's members makes it possible to infer the type of the group noun. If the members are of type **human** then the group as a whole will be of type **human**, and so on. Furthermore the CONSTITUENCY role can be instantiated with the qualia structure for the members. So the following entry could be produced for *band,*[3]*2:*

```
band L_3_2
    < > < lex-group < >
    < QUALIA > = human
    < QUALIA : CONSITUENCY : ELEMENTS >
             < ( musician_L_0_1 + plural ) < QUALIA >.
```

Here (`musician_L_0_1` + `plural`) indicates that the rule for plural formation is applied to the psort `musician_L_0_1` before inheritance of the qualia structure takes place (see appendix).

However this leaves some information unspecified, in particular the Telic role. We assume that this can be inherited from the Telic role of the members, so the Telic role of *band*,[3]2 is inherited from *musician,* for example,

```
< QUALIA : TELIC >
        < musician_L_0_1 < QUALIA : TELIC >.
```

Adding this to this description we get a specification which will expand out into the feature structure shown in Figure 10.4.

The inheritance of the Telic role needs some justification, since in general usage it is not possible to assume that a group as a whole has a property even if all its members have that property, and the property is one which could hold of the group as a whole. For example:

All the members of the committee are against the poll tax.

does not entail that:

The committee is against the poll tax.

Inheritance of the Telic role might also be problematic. There could be a group of musicians who got together to play football, for example, so:

The King's Road football team is a group of musicians.

could be true, in which case the purpose of the group described would not be equivalent to that lexically specified by *musician.* However such examples are exceptional, and in the special case of dictionary definitions, if a group is defined in terms of its members, it can be taken to inherit appropriate properties from them; we have not found any counter-examples to this in LDOCE so far. Intuitively, it seems unlikely that a dictionary would define a group in terms of its members, if they had a purpose or function which was distinct from that of the group. Even if a concept such as the musicians' football team were lexicalized, the lexicographer would have to specify the function of the group explicitly to avoid being misleading, and thus the default inheritance from its members' Telic role would be overridden.

Thus, on the assumption that we can recognize the class of group nouns, and distinguish their members in the definitions, we can (semi-)automatically extract reasonably adequate entries, such as that shown for *band.* This is quite straightforward for nouns which are specified as GC in the LDOCE grammar coding scheme and which have entries of the form, 'DET *group of* N'. However there are problems in recognizing the class of group nouns. As we mentioned earlier, the grammar coding scheme has not been applied consistently to group nouns. There are a variety of ways in which group nouns can be defined, and some of these patterns of definitions can also be used for non-group nouns. Although we can use a range of heuristics to identify candidate group nouns, these rely on certain assumptions, for example that any noun which denotes more than one person, but which is not marked as plural, is likely to be a group noun. Clearly, we need other sources of information in order to attempt comprehensive extraction.

Other MRDs could be used to enhance our existing data, but since sense-to-sense mapping on independent dictionary sources is a hard problem, which itself requires some form of LKB, we could at best determine that a headword has some sense which is marked as being a group noun, and use this as an additional heuristic. Corpora could also be used, but a massive amount of data is needed to have a significant chance of finding the less frequent group nouns used in a context where their distinctive behavior is apparent. There are about 30 occurrences of *crowd* as a singular noun in the approximately 1.2 million word LOB corpus, and only one of these is in a context where singular/plural agreement can be distinguished. Checking a range of nouns manually for dual agreement on corpora of sufficient size would be an extremely labor-intensive task without tools to partially parse selected sentences. Even then, the problem of sense distinction still remains – the skills of the professional lexicographer are really needed here. We believe that the way forward for computational lexicology and lexicography is collaboration with lexicographers and dictionary publishers, giving them the tools with which to instantiate LKBs, which could then be used for linguistic research, for NLP, and for the production of conventional dictionaries.

10.5   Conclusion

We have used the example of group nouns in this chapter to illustrate the way in which we attempt to combine ideas and techniques from lexical semantics, lexicography and knowledge representation. Although the fragment shown here is integrated into a system which treats other complex aspects of lexical semantics, such as logical metonymy and sense extension, much more work is clearly needed to produce a comprehensive treatment of noun semantics which would properly test our approach. Furthermore there are some issues which appear to require modifications to the LRL, in particular with respect to the treatment of defaults. We are currently investigating richer representational frameworks, which should, for example, allow a better treatment of agreement than that shown here. Briscoe et al. (this volume) discusses one way in which a more general notion of defaults can be combined with a feature structure-based representation language.

Appendix

In this appendix we give more detailed descriptions of the structures used in the examples given in the chapter.

Types, psorts and lexical entries

The following structure shows the type, **lex-count-noun**, which is the type of all the lexical entries described:

$$
\begin{bmatrix}
\text{lex-count-noun} \\
\text{ORTH} = \text{orth} \\
\text{CAT} = \boxed{\text{noun-cat}} \\
\text{SEM} = \begin{bmatrix}
\text{obj-noun-formula} \\
\text{IND} = \boxed{0}\begin{bmatrix}
\text{obj} \\
\text{AGR} = \begin{bmatrix} \text{agr} \\ \text{NUM} = \text{number} \end{bmatrix}
\end{bmatrix} \\
\text{PRED} = \boxed{1}\ \text{logical-pred} \\
\text{ARG1} = \boxed{0} \\
\text{PLMOD} = \text{boolean} \\
\text{QUANT} = \text{boolean}
\end{bmatrix} \\
\text{QUALIA} = \begin{bmatrix}
\text{nomqualia} \\
\text{AGENTIVE} = \text{nomagent} \\
\text{TELIC} = \boxed{\text{verb-sem}} \\
\text{FORM} = \begin{bmatrix}
\text{nomform} \\
\text{ABSOLUTE} = \text{real-form} \\
\text{RELATIVE} = \text{countable}
\end{bmatrix} \\
\text{CONSTITUENCY} = \boxed{\text{nomconst}} \\
\text{OBJECT-INDEX} = \boxed{0}
\end{bmatrix}
\end{bmatrix}
$$

For current purposes the important points about this type are:

1. A value of **true** for the feature PLMOD in the semantics is intended to be interpreted as equivalent to modifying the predicate by the closure operator *. The value **false** indicates that the predicate is not so modified.

2. The feature QUANT encodes the cumulative/quantized distinction (see Krifka, 1987).

3. The type **countable** given as the value of the relative form in the qualia structure has several subtypes – those relevant here are **individual**, **plural** and **group**.

All noun lexical entries are specified as inheriting from one of a range of psorts which specify their mode of individuation. Those relevant here are `lex-individual`, `lex-plural` and `lex-group`:

```
lex-individual
    < > = lex-count-noun
    < QUALIA : FORM : RELATIVE > = individual
    < SEM : IND : AGR : NUM > = sg
    < SEM : PLMOD > = false
    < SEM : QUANT > = true .
lex-plural
    < > = lex-count-noun
    < QUALIA : FORM : RELATIVE > = plural
    < SEM : QUANT > = false
    < SEM : IND : AGR : NUM > = pl.
```

```
lex-group
    < > < lex-individual < >
    < QUALIA : FORM : RELATIVE > = group
    < QUALIA : CONSTITUENCY > = groupconst.
```

Since these are psorts, values may be overridden. This allows for nouns like *barracks* or *gallows* which are treated as basically individual denoting, although they may take plural agreement.

The relevant parts of the lexical entries for *person* and *perform* from which the entry for *musician* inherits are as follows.

$$
\begin{bmatrix}
\text{lex-count-noun} \\
\text{ORTH} = \text{person} \\
\text{CAT} = \boxed{\text{noun-cat}} \\
\text{SEM} = \boxed{\text{obj-noun-formula}} \\
\text{QUALIA} = \begin{bmatrix}
\text{human} \\
\text{AGENTIVE} = \begin{bmatrix} \text{agentivestuff} \\ \text{ORIGIN} = \text{basic} \end{bmatrix} \\
\text{TELIC} = \boxed{\text{verb-sem}} \\
\text{FORM} = \begin{bmatrix} \text{nomform} \\ \text{ABSOLUTE} = \text{real-form} \\ \text{RELATIVE} = \text{individual} \end{bmatrix} \\
\text{CONSTITUENCY} = \boxed{\text{nomconst}} \\
\text{OBJECT-INDEX} = \boxed{1} \begin{bmatrix} \text{obj} \\ \text{AGR} = \begin{bmatrix} \text{agr} \\ \text{NUM} = \text{sg} \end{bmatrix} \end{bmatrix} \\
\text{PROPERTIES} = \begin{bmatrix} \text{creature-properties} \\ \text{STATE} = \text{solid\_a} \\ \text{SEX} = \text{gender} \end{bmatrix}
\end{bmatrix}
\end{bmatrix}
$$

$$
\begin{bmatrix}
\text{strict-trans-sign} \\
\text{ORTH} = \text{perform} \\
\text{CAT} = \boxed{\text{strict-trans-cat}} \\
\text{SEM} = \begin{bmatrix}
\text{strict-trans-sem} \\
\text{IND} = \boxed{0} \text{ eve} \\
\text{PRED} = \text{and} \\
\text{ARG1} = \begin{bmatrix} \text{verb-formula} \\ \text{IND} = \boxed{0} \\ \text{PRED} = \boxed{1} \text{ perform\_L\_0\_2} \\ \text{ARG1} = \boxed{0} \end{bmatrix} \\
\text{ARG2} = \begin{bmatrix}
\text{binary-formula} \\
\text{IND} = \boxed{0} \\
\text{PRED} = \text{and} \\
\text{ARG1} = \boxed{2} \begin{bmatrix} \text{p-agt-formula} \\ \text{IND} = \boxed{0} \\ \text{PRED} = \text{p-agt} \\ \text{ARG1} = \boxed{0} \\ \text{ARG2} = \begin{bmatrix} \text{obj} \\ \text{AGR} = \begin{bmatrix} \text{agr} \\ \text{NUM} = \text{number} \end{bmatrix} \end{bmatrix} \end{bmatrix} \\
\text{ARG2} = \boxed{3} \begin{bmatrix} \text{p-pat-formula} \\ \text{IND} = \boxed{0} \\ \text{PRED} = \text{p-pat} \\ \text{ARG1} = \boxed{0} \\ \text{ARG2} = \begin{bmatrix} \text{obj} \\ \text{AGR} = \begin{bmatrix} \text{agr} \\ \text{NUM} = \text{number} \end{bmatrix} \end{bmatrix} \end{bmatrix}
\end{bmatrix}
\end{bmatrix}
\end{bmatrix}
$$

Unary rules

The examples in the chapter use two unary rules, `group-to-plural` and `plural`. Unary rules in the LRL are feature structures of type **unary-rule**. This has two features 1 and 0 which indicate the input and output of the rule respectively. Unary rules are used to encode type shifting, morphological rules and sense extensions – the only distinction between these types of rule is that morphological rules are the only ones which involve orthographic changes and that type shifting rules may involve phrasal signs, whereas morphological and sense extension rules are limited to lexical signs. Thus `group-to-plural` is a type shifting rule which takes a phrasal sign as input (in this case an NP) but `plural` is a morphological rule. The sign for the unshifted NP, *the band*, is shown in Figure 10.6. It can be seen that this will unify with the the input section of the unary rule `group-to-plural` which is shown in Figure 10.7, giving the feature structure shown in Figure 10.5 as output.

The plural rule which was referred to in Section 10.4 is shown in Figure 10.8 for completeness.

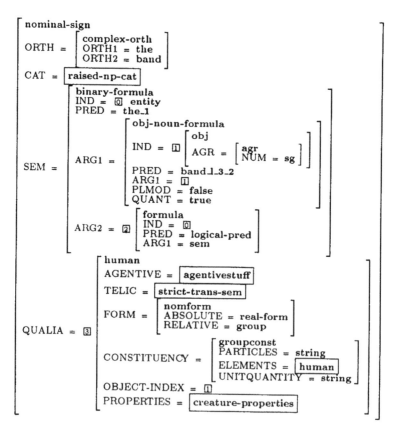

Figure 10.6. AVM diagram for the phrasal sign *the band*.

$$
0 = \begin{bmatrix}
\text{unary-rule} \\[4pt]
\begin{bmatrix}
\text{nominal-sign} \\
\text{ORTH} = \boxed{0}\ \text{orth} \\[4pt]
\text{CAT} = \begin{bmatrix}
\text{raised-np-cat} \\
\text{RESULT} = \boxed{1}\ \boxed{\text{sign}} \\
\text{DIRECTION} = \boxed{2}\ \text{direction} \\[4pt]
\text{ACTIVE} = \begin{bmatrix}
\text{sign} \\
\text{ORTH} = \text{orth} \\[4pt]
\text{CAT} = \begin{bmatrix}
\text{complex-cat} \\
\text{RESULT} = \boxed{1} \\
\text{DIRECTION} = \boxed{2} \\
\text{ACTIVE} = \boxed{\text{nominal-sign}}
\end{bmatrix} \\[4pt]
\text{SEM} = \boxed{3}\ \boxed{\text{formula}}
\end{bmatrix}
\end{bmatrix} \\[6pt]
\text{SEM} = \begin{bmatrix}
\text{binary-formula} \\
\text{IND} = \boxed{4}\ \text{entity} \\
\text{PRED} = \text{the} \\[4pt]
\text{ARG1} = \boxed{5}\begin{bmatrix}
\text{binary-formula} \\
\text{IND} = \boxed{6}\begin{bmatrix}\text{dummy-or-obj}\\ \text{AGR} = \begin{bmatrix}\text{agr}\\ \text{NUM} = \text{pl}\end{bmatrix}\end{bmatrix} \\
\text{PRED} = \text{logical-pred} \\
\text{ARG1} = \boxed{\text{formula}} \\
\text{ARG2} = \begin{bmatrix}
\text{binary-formula}\\ \text{IND} = \text{entity}\\ \text{PRED} = \text{membership}\\ \text{ARG1} = \boxed{6}\\ \text{ARG2} = \boxed{7}\ \text{entity}
\end{bmatrix}
\end{bmatrix} \\[4pt]
\text{ARG2} = \boxed{3}
\end{bmatrix} \\[6pt]
\text{QUALIA} = \boxed{8}\begin{bmatrix}
\text{nomqualia} \\
\text{AGENTIVE} = \text{nomagent} \\
\text{TELIC} = \boxed{\text{verb-sem}} \\[4pt]
\text{FORM} = \begin{bmatrix}\text{nomform}\\ \text{ABSOLUTE} = \text{real-form}\\ \text{RELATIVE} = \text{plural}\end{bmatrix} \\[4pt]
\text{CONSTITUENCY} = \boxed{\text{nomconst}} \\
\text{OBJECT-INDEX} = \text{entity}
\end{bmatrix}
\end{bmatrix}
\end{bmatrix}
$$

$$
1 = \begin{bmatrix}
\text{nominal-sign} \\
\text{ORTH} = \boxed{0} \\
\text{CAT} = \boxed{\text{raised-np-cat}} \\
\text{SEM} = \boxed{5} \\[6pt]
\text{QUALIA} = \begin{bmatrix}
\text{nomqualia} \\
\text{AGENTIVE} = \text{nomagent} \\
\text{TELIC} = \boxed{\text{verb-sem}} \\[4pt]
\text{FORM} = \begin{bmatrix}\text{nomform}\\ \text{ABSOLUTE} = \text{real-form}\\ \text{RELATIVE} = \text{group}\end{bmatrix} \\[4pt]
\text{CONSTITUENCY} = \begin{bmatrix}\text{groupconst}\\ \text{PARTICLES} = \text{string}\\ \text{ELEMENTS} = \boxed{8}\\ \text{UNITQUANTITY} = \text{string}\end{bmatrix} \\[4pt]
\text{OBJECT-INDEX} = \text{entity}
\end{bmatrix}
\end{bmatrix}
$$

Figure 10.7. The group-to-plural type-shifting rule.

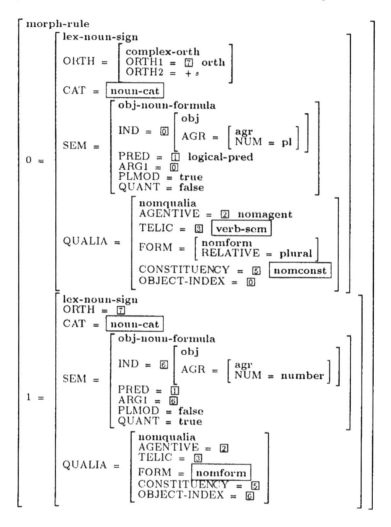

Figure 10.8. Rule for plural formation.

Notes

1. ACQUILEX: 'The Acquisition of Lexical Knowledge for Natural Language Process-
    ing Systems': Esprit BRA-3030. For an overview of ACQUILEX as a whole see
    Briscoe (1991).
2. The type system described in this chapter was developed following on from that used
    on the ACQUILEX project as a whole, which was described in Copestake (1992),
    for example. The new system is somewhat simpler, it is less directly related to dic-
    tionary definitions and the treatment of some aspects of noun semantics has been
    improved.

3. In the formal semantics we treat the domain of individuals as having a lattice structure (Link, 1983). The semantics assumed are based on work by Krifka (1987). Plural individuals consist of a sum of ordinary individuals, but there is no distinction in formal semantic type between an ordinary individual and a plural one. Ordinary singular count predicates, such as **musician'**, denote sets of non-plural individuals. Plural predicates are formed by taking the closure of the denotation of the singular predicate, e.g. ***musician'**.

4. The metonymic treatment is less plausible with group nouns such as *crowd* which cannot exist without members, and thus where the distinction between the group and its members has less justification on a purely extensional treatment. Landman (1989) has an extensive discussion of groups in the context of the treatment of plurality. For example, Landman treats the collective reading of sentences such as (21) as involving a group, rather than the plural sum.

(21)   John and Mary lifted a piano.

Landman makes a type distinction between a group and the plural sum of its members. However, since group formation can iterate indefinitely, this leads to a proliferation of types. Since we do not think that Landman's treatment adequately accounts for the properties of group nouns such as *club*, we have not adopted it here.

5. There may be a connection here with the use of feminine gender personal pronouns when referring to ships, given that group nouns are normally associated with humans and higher animals.

6. Neither of these options is completely satisfactory, of course. We would like to say that, by default, agreement is determined by the group/plural distinction, but that this default may be overridden. This is not possible in the current LRL, since defaults are part of the description language and thus operate only on the paradigmatic plane and do not affect syntagmatic combination.

7. The disambiguation procedure is semi-automatic in that a series of heuristics are used to determine the sense of the genus term, and the user is asked to confirm the choice made by the heuristics in some cases, to avoid large numbers of lexical entries inheriting information incorrectly. When creating hierarchies of concrete nouns from LDOCE, the user checks about 5% of the entries.

References

Ageno, A., I. Castellon, G. Rigau, H. Rodriguez, M. F. Verdejo, M. A. Marti, M. Taule. (1992). 'SEISD: an environment for extraction of semantic information from on-Line dictionaries', *Proceedings of the 3rd Conference on Applied Natural Language Processing (ANLP-92),* Trento, Italy, pp. 253–255.

Briscoe, E. J. (1991). 'Lexical issues in natural language processing' in E. Klein and F. Veltman (ed.), Natural language and speech, Springer-Verlag, pp. 39–68.

Briscoe, E. J., A. Copestake and B. Boguraev (1990) 'Enjoy the paper: lexical semantics via lexicology', *Proceedings of the 13th International Conference on Computational Linguistics (COLING-90),* Helsinki, pp. 42–47.

Briscoe, E. J., A. Copestake and V. de Paiva (eds.) (1993) *Inheritance, defaults and the lexicon,* Cambridge University Press.

Carpenter, R. (1990) 'Typed feature structures: inheritance, (in)equality and extensionality', *Proceedings of the First International Workshop on Inheritance in Natural Language Processing,* Tilburg, The Netherlands, pp. 9–18.

Carpenter, R. (1992) *The logic of typed feature structures,* Cambridge University Press.

Carpenter, R. (1993) 'Skeptical and credulous default unification with applications to templates and inheritance', in E. J. Briscoe, A. Copestake and V. de Paiva (eds.), *Inheritance, defaults and the lexicon,* Cambridge University Press.

Copestake, A. (1990) 'An approach to building the hierarchical element of a lexical knowledge base from a machine readable dictionary', *Proceedings of the First International Workshop on Inheritance in Natural Language Processing,* Tilburg, The Netherlands, pp. 19–29.

Copestake, A. (1992) 'The ACQUILEX LKB: representation issues in semi-automatic acquisition of large lexicons', *Proceedings of the 3rd Conference on Applied Natural Language Processing (ANLP-92),* Trento, Italy, pp. 88–96.

Copestake, A. and E. J. Briscoe (1992) 'Lexical operations in a unification based framework', in J. Pustejovsky and S. Bergler (eds.), *Lexical Semantics and Knowledge Representation. Proceedings of the first SIGLEX Workshop, Berkeley, CA,* Springer-Verlag, Berlin, pp. 101–119.

Cruse, D. A. (1986) *Lexical semantics,* Cambridge University Press, Cambridge, England.

Krifka, M. (1987) 'Nominal reference and temporal constitution: towards a semantics of quantity', *Proceedings of the 6th Amsterdam Colloquium, University of Amsterdam,* pp. 153–173.

Landau, S. I. (1984) *Dictionaries: the art and craft of lexicography,* Scribner, New York.

Landman, F. (1989) 'Groups I + II', *Linguistics and Philosophy,* **12 (5,6),** 559–606, 723–744.

Link, G. (1983) 'The logical analysis of plurals and mass terms: a lattice-theoretical approach', in Bäuerle, Schwarze and von Stechow (eds.), *Meaning, use and interpretation of language,* de Gruyter, Berlin, pp. 302–323.

Pollard, C. and I. A. Sag (1994) *Head-Driven Phrase Structure Grammar,* University of Chicago Press, Chicago.

Procter, P. (editor) (1978) *Longman Dictionary of Contemporary English,* Longman, England.

Pustejovsky, J. (1991) 'The generative lexicon', *Computational Linguistics,* **17(4),** 409–441.

Sanfilippo, A. (1993) 'LKB encoding of lexical knowledge from machine-readable dictionaries', in E. J. Briscoe, A. Copestake and V. de Paiva (eds.), *Inheritance, defaults and the lexicon,* Cambridge University Press.

Scha, R. J. H. (1983) 'Logical foundations for question answering', PhD thesis. Rijksuniversiteit, Groningen.

Shieber, S. M. (1986) *An introduction to unification-based approaches to grammar,* CSLI Lecture Notes 4, Stanford, CA.

Vossen, P. (1990) 'A parser-grammar for the meaning descriptions of LDOCE', Links Project Technical Report 300–169–007, Amsterdam University.

Vossen, P. (1992) 'An empirical approach to automatically construct a knowledge base from dictionaries', *Proceedings of the 5th EURALEX,* Tampere, Finland.

Vossen, P. and A. Copestake (1993) 'Untangling definition structure into knowledge representation', in E. J. Briscoe, A. Copestake and V. de Paiva (eds.), *Inheritance, defaults and the lexicon,* Cambridge University Press.

Zwicky, A. M. and J. M. Sadock (1975) 'Ambiguity tests and how to fail them', in J. P. Kimball (ed.), *Syntax and Semantics IV,* Academic Press, New York, pp. 1–36.

11   A preliminary lexical and conceptual analysis of BREAK: A computational perspective

MARTHA PALMER AND
ALAIN POLGUÈRE

"We want the ring. Without the ring there can be no wedding. May we break the finger?"

"Old age," said Sir Benjamin, breathing deeply and slowly, "is a time when deafness brings its blessings. I didn't hear what you said then. You have another chance."

"May we break the finger?" asked Ambrose again. "We could do it with a hammer."

"I thought, sir," said Sir Benjamin, "that those were the words. The world is all before you. By God, my hiccoughs have gone, and no wonder. As for 'break', 'break' is a trull of a word, it will take in everything. Waves, dawns, news, wind, hearts, banks, maidenheads. But never dream of tucking into the same predicate my statues as object and that loose-favoured verb. That would be a most reprehensible solecism."

The Eve of Saint Venus, Anthony Burgess[1]

11.1   Introduction

We are interested in how a verb's description changes as it evolves into different usages. In order to examine this issue we are attempting to combine a LEXICAL ANALYSIS of a particular verb with a CONCEPTUAL ANALYSIS. LEXICAL ANALYSIS is aimed at producing a LEXICAL **DEFINITION** which functions as a linguistic paraphrase. This should ideally be a lexical decomposition composed of terms with simpler, "more primitive" meanings than the term being defined (Mel'čuk 1988; Wierzbicka 1984). In contrast, a conceptual analysis produces a CONCEPTUAL **DESCRIPTION** of the lexical item.

Criteria for building a conceptual description are linked to arguments borrowed from "real-world" considerations or expressed in terms of denotations. What are the necessary conditions in the environment that allow the situation/event denoted by the verb to take place, and what are the effects on the environment that are produced by this situation/event? It is our ultimate goal that the conceptual descriptions will be able to perform as procedures for verb analysis within a natural language processing system.

As preliminary as this work is, it would be even more preliminary if it had not benefited from insights and comments contributed by Beth Levin, Igor Mel'čuk, K. P. Mohanan, Tara Mohanan, Ong Chih Hao and Háj Ross. Our grateful thanks to all of them

231

According to our definition of both lexical definition and conceptual description, the following criteria are sufficient for us to characterize a lexical study as aiming at conceptual descriptions:

- semantic components are sought, which are to be associated with lexical units;
- these components are not linguistic meanings (associated with other lexical units of the language), but are technical concepts whose interpretation functions outside natural language itself;
- more specifically, the interpretation of these components is based on real-world/denotational criteria.

It is clear that such a semantic component as "external controller", which we will be using later when working on our conceptual descriptions, belongs to the second type of criterion as it is based on a denotational interpretation; cf.:

Smith characterizes the difference between those intransitive verbs which do and do not have transitive causative uses by means of the notion of "control", which we adopt. Verbs like *break*, Smith proposes, denote eventualities that are under the control of some external cause which typically brings such an eventuality about. We refer to this cause as the "external controller" of the eventuality. (Levin and Rappaport Hovav, 1994)

Notice that the intuitive perception, by the native speaker, of a paraphrastic relation between a lexeme and its definition is not considered by us as an "extralinguistic" criterion. This criterion functions exactly like the judgment of grammaticality/ungrammaticality, which is so commonly used in linguistic studies.

By carefully classifying the different usages of a verb, and by specifying the conceptual description of each usage, we should be able to point clearly to the component of the underlying conceptual representation that reflects the difference in meaning between each usage. We do not expect to capture precisely the entire meaning of any one usage, but our goal is to capture enough of the meaning to allow a natural language processing system to distinguish between each different usage. We have chosen the verb BREAK for our analysis, and at this point have attempted to categorize approximately one third of the examples of the use of BREAK from the Brown Corpus. We chose BREAK because its basic meaning – separation into pieces of a rigid object – is concrete and can be clearly described conceptually, and yet extends in a multitude of different directions. In addition, it is a verb which has already received a fair amount of attention, thus providing us with comparison points for our analysis.

The original motivation for this investigation came from experience with a text analysis system called KERNEL (previously known as PUNDIT) [Palmer et al., 1993]. This system provides an automated analysis facility for short, telegraphic messages about specialized topics. It handles a small fraction of the message traffic for several different specialized topics, i.e., domains with their corresponding sublanguages: messages from field engineers reporting on computer repairs (MAINTENANCE REPORTS); messages about repairing starting air compressors on ships (CASREPS); messages about repairing computer systems on submarines (TRIDENT); and messages about naval sightings of enemy vessels (OPREPS). The verb representations in KERNEL, which play a major role in driving the semantic interpretation process, are called Lexical Conceptual Clauses, and are derived from Jackendoff's Lexical Conceptual Structures – with a similar emphasis placed on thematic relations as an important element of conceptual structure (Jackendoff, 1972, 1990; Palmer, 1981, 1990).

A major task in the development of KERNEL has been porting it to new domains, i.e., adding all of the necessary domain-dependent information that is relevant to a new specialized topic. Adding the verb descriptions is especially critical, since they provide the bridge between the lexical items and the domain model. At the moment, new domain-dependent information, including the verb descriptions, must be added by a trained linguist. In spite of the very restricted nature of the domains involved, the same verb descriptions often need to be rewritten for application to a new domain, even when the verb usage is quite similar (Palmer, 1990). The following examples of BREAK all came from KERNEL domains: *broken wire, broken insulation, the lamp contact was broken off, broken engagement (between ships)*. The necessity of rewriting verb descriptions has motivated a search for more general definitions/descriptions which can be easily tailored to new usages, with the aim of eventually automating the tailoring process.

What we present here is far from a definitive, exhaustive analysis of BREAK. Looking for consistencies between the lexical analysis and the conceptual analysis has actually made our task much more difficult, since there are often conflicts between the two styles of analysis. There is no defined methodology for correlating them. As we work through the sections of this chapter, we will raise many questions that we cannot yet provide answers for. We have, however, found that there are instances where the conceptual analysis and the lexical analysis are in agreement, and this has led us to some surprising conclusions with respect to the use of an intentional INSTRUMENT in this context. The presence or absence of such an INSTRUMENT has proven to be a valuable determining factor in the resolution of more than one conflict.

11.2 Choosing a methodology

One of the most difficult tasks we have been faced with is establishing a methodology for performing a conceptual analysis and relating it to the lexical analysis. There is no consensus on how closely lexical and conceptual analyses should be correlated, or on how they should be distinguished. Are there in fact any benefits to be had from considering them in parallel? Intuitively, one would hope that there is a relationship between a word's meaning and how it can be used in a given context of communication, but the evidence for this sometimes seems a bit scarce. As a methodology for our lexical analysis, we have chosen the Explanatory Combinatorial Dictionary as defined by Mel'čuk (1988). For our conceptual analysis, we have turned to Fillmore (1970), Levin and Rappaport Hovav (1994), Jackendoff (1990), and Dowty (1991).

11.2.1 *Making lexical distinctions*

One of the first of many contentious issues that arises, even with the primary, concrete meaning of BREAK, is the question: *What constitutes a lexical unit and is there a corresponding conceptual unit?*

In his seminal paper on *The Grammar of Breaking and Hitting* (Fillmore, 1970), Fillmore postulates that cases (or semantic roles, or thematic roles) such as AGENT and INSTRUMENT should play a fundamental role in the semantic description. This allows three different syntactic realizations to be produced from a single lexical entry for the primary, or established, sense of BREAK – for a definition of *established sense,* see Cruse (1986:68):

(1)   a. *The stick broke.*
        b. *The rock broke the stick.*
        c. *John broke the stick with a rock.*

According to Fillmore, (1a) indicates that some object P,[2] in this case the stick, was broken. (1b) indicates that another object, the rock, in the role of an INSTRUMENT, broke P, the stick. (1c) describes the entire event, in which an animate AGENT, John, intentionally used a rock as an INSTRUMENT to break P, the stick. Since Fillmore sees the objects, stick, rock, and John, as playing consistent semantic roles in all three sentences, he assigns them the P, INSTRUMENT and AGENT cases respectively. He is then able to give the following formula as a single, underlying semantic representation for all three sentences:

  (*agent*) (*instrument*) P

The parentheses indicate that BREAK requires a P (the stick) and permits either an AGENT or an INSTRUMENT or both. For Fillmore, the basic form of BREAK is the intransitive form, *the stick broke.*

Using our chosen methodology for lexical analysis, do we agree with Fillmore that (1a–c) correspond to a single lexical unit? We have to apply specific linguistic tests to the sentences: identity of semantic decomposition, identical number of actants, etc. Since the verb in each of these examples has a different number of actants we consider that these realizations correspond to three separate lexemes of the same vocable BREAK.[3] However, we can agree that (1c) includes an assertion of **intentional causation** absent from the other two sentences, and that there is a semantic bridge between the three lexemes BREAK in (1a-c) involving something like a **separation of a whole into pieces.** A corresponding Brown Corpus example (marked by its section derivation, ce10) is:

(2)   ce10 (1):   *You can unscrew this tube and replace it with a smooth-*
                      bore insert for use with shotshells -- to break the little
                      Targo clay targets.

11.2.2   *Making conceptual distinctions*

Should our conceptual analysis consider these three lexical units as mapping onto a single conceptual unit or onto three separate ones? This gives rise to our second major issue: *Assuming three separate lexemes, are there valid conceptual distinctions that are reflected in the changing argument structure from one sentence to the next?*

The significance of the AGENT

Following Fillmore, it would seem that the difference between (1b) and (1c) is the presence or absence of the AGENT. It is possible, given the right context and an implied AGENT, John, that *rock* in (1b) can be understood as an INSTRUMENT. This follows from the notion of indirect causation (for an explanation of indirect causation, see Comrie, (1981:172), that if John threw the rock at the stick, and the rock hit the stick, and the stick broke, it could be said that the rock broke the stick. However, we claim that the standard, context-free, interpretation of the *rock* in this sentence, without reference to knowledge of John throwing the rock, must be quite different. To understand, out of context,

(3)   *The hammer broke the window.*

it is necessary to either attribute intention and voluntary action to the hammer, as in Thor's hammer, or to assume that a natural force, such as gravity or a magnetic field, was involved. The first argument of the transitive verb must in some sense indicate an agent of the event. The agent must itself be capable of some form of independent action. Rocks and hammers in isolation are inert objects that are incapable of independent action and cannot exert force. In fact, we find these particular examples somewhat odd out of context, and prefer examples such as

(4)   a.   *The sudden gust of wind broke all of the windows.*
         b.   *The hailstones broke the greenhouse roof.*

where a natural force is being referred to which can in fact apply force autonomously. Then the distinction between (1b) and (1c) is whether or not the source of the force being exerted is an animate AGENT with whom intentionality can also be associated. Other possible exerters of force are natural forces or events such as shocks or falls with whom intentionality cannot be associated. We are not ignoring sentences in which animate subjects unknowingly perpetrate events, as in

(5)   *John broke the heads off of all of the peonies when the dog rolled him through the flower beds. He was horrified when he saw what had happened.*

However, the very fact that the sentence sounds more natural when *accidentally* is inserted,

(6)   *John accidentally broke the heads off of all of the peonies when the dog rolled him through the flower beds.*

confirms the strong assumption of intentionality that is associated with an animate AGENT in this context, and which is overridden explicitly in (6).

According to Dowty's recent definition of a PROTO-AGENT role (cf. Dowty, 1991), both natural forces and animate beings qualify as AGENTS in this context, since causation is a sufficient criterion for AGENT-hood whether or not intentionality is involved. His four contributing properties for the AGENT Proto-Role are:

1. volitional involvement in the event or state,
2. being sentient (and/or having perceptions),
3. causing an event or change of state in another participant,
4. movement relative to the position of another participant;

any one of which is deemed sufficient for conveying status as an AGENT. Simply labeling both natural forces and animate beings as AGENTS loses the distinction between them which we have just labored so hard to make, namely, that an animate being involved in a *breaking* event includes an additional intentional or volitional entailment. It may be useful to class them together for purposes of argument selection, but it is important to continue to distinguish between them from a conceptual point of view, as illustrated in the following section.

The significance of the INSTRUMENT

Is it true that (1b) and (1c) can both occur with INSTRUMENTAL *with*-phrases? If this were so, then it would blur the lexical distinction between (1b) and (1c). The easiest way to resolve this is to assume that INSTRUMENTS must be wielded intentionally, which rules out natural forces. (Although natural forces can be anthropomorphized in fairy tales, this is not the standard interpretation.) The following sentence,

(7)   *The fierce hail storm broke several roofs with its unusually large hailstones.*

strongly prefers a manner reading over an instrumental reading. Intentionality associated with an animate AGENT also allows us to maintain a distinction between (8a) and (8b),

(8)   a. *John broke the window.*
        b. *The wind broke the window.*

where neither sentence has a *with*-PP. We are left with a clear conceptual distinction between the two sentences (1b) and (1c) that is reflected in the syntactic realizations.

A formalization of the conceptual description

We can distinguish conceptually between our three lexical units. Q breaks P (with an INSTRUMENT),[4] where Q is animate, includes a conceptual notion of intentionality that is absent from Q breaks P where Q is not expected to be animate. Both of these indicate events in which Q as an actant causes P to become broken by exerting sufficient force to cause P to separate into pieces. P must be a rigid solid object such as a window or a vase that is BRITTLE,[5] and which will no longer be considered intact if it is in pieces. We will represent the basic conceptual predicate underlying the break-event, using predicate logic notation,[6] as a binary **exert_Sforce(Q,P)** predicate, where it is understood that a **sufficient force** must have been exerted by Q. The addition of intentional causation will be indicated by a ternary **causeI(Q, Event, Instrument)** predicate where **Event** is instantiated with **exert_Sforce(Q,P)** and **Instrument** is optional. After the event has occurred, a change of state has taken place, and P is in a new state of being broken. The semantic predicate associated with this change of state will be a unary **separated_in to_pieces(P)** predicate. Our remaining lexical unit, P breaks, refers simply to the change of state. This change of state has been triggered by an implicit **exert_Sforce(unknown,P)** event, which can be made explicit if needed.

The conceptual descriptions are expressed as logical inference rules, which are compatible with the verb representations in the KERNEL text processing systems. (For more details on the formalism used here and in KERNEL, see Palmer, 1990.)

11.2.3 *The controversy surrounding the choice of the basic BREAK*

We have three conceptual representations corresponding to the three lexical units. The only remaining unresolved issue is which unit is the basic unit. There are some verbs, such as *laugh* and *sleep,* where the basic unit is clearly the intransitive verb – there are no transitivized forms for these verbs. There are other verbs such as *drive* (as in *he drives the car* vs. *this car still drives*) where the transitive form is unarguably the basic form. Unfortunately, the basic form of BREAK is not as easily determined. At this stage of our research, we are not able to present a final solution to this problematic issue, and will simply present arguments for both sides. Furthermore, it is possible that the basic conceptual unit is not the same as the basic lexical unit.

Support for a transitive basic unit

As reported in the previous version of this chapter (Palmer and Polguère, 1992), we see strong arguments in favor of the binary predicate, *Q broke P* as the basic conceptual form. Commonsense knowledge tells us that, for the "connectedness" or "intactness" of a concrete object to be violated, a certain amount of force must be exerted by an animate agent or a natural force, against that object, preferably, but not necessarily, in one quick, sudden motion. (This does not entail that the object must be struck by another solid object. The force could consist of sound waves or air currents, or some other form of invisible pressure.) Therefore, we see the intransitive *P broke* as reporting on a change of state that has occurred as the result of a break-event in which force was exerted. The break-event is a necessary and sufficient condition for the occurrence of the *broken* state, so the transitive *Q broke P* is our basic form for conceptual purposes.

This approach is in accordance with a current view in linguistics that includes BREAK in a class of inherently transitive verbs (Levin and Rappaport Hovav, 1994). In their analysis of verbs with both transitive and intransitive alternations, Levin and Rappaport Hovav distinguish between several different verb classes, a full exposition of which is beyond the scope of this chapter. However, an important element in their characterization is the notion of external and internal control originating with Carlota Smith, (Smith, 1970:107). A verb that is internally controlled such as *laugh* or *sleep* reports an activity that is "controlled only by the person engaged in it"; that is, control "cannot be relinquished." Externally controlled verbs have outside controllers with immediate control over the event: an agent, natural force, or circumstance. There are verbs of a particular class, typified as emission verbs – e.g., *buzz, ring, rustle, beam*, etc., which are internally controlled, and are monadic with a basic intransitive form. These verbs can be causativized to make the transitive form. Another class, including *break, pierce, close, open, hang*, etc., is externally controlled, and is thus inherently dyadic. These verbs naturally appear as transitive verbs and can be (de)causativized to form intransitive ones. In our conceptual analysis, the agent or natural force involved in the exerting force event corresponds to Levin and Rappaport Hovav's external controller.

Support for an intransitive basic unit

However, the traditional view of BREAK is that the intransitive form is the basic form, and this agrees with arguments stemming from a methodology for lexical analysis. The most primitive meaning involved in BREAK is the meaning of the intransitive verb, where an entity becomes separated into pieces. The most straightforward presentation is one in which we decompose the intransitive *X breaks* into 'X undergoes a separation into pieces'. This decomposition becomes our basic building block, and we then define the more complex usages in terms of it. This is the approach we choose for the following presentation of our lexical analysis.[7]

We are not attempting to resolve this conflict here. Close examination of the analysis presented in the next section will show that the conceptual description of the intransitive verb is in fact derived from the conceptual description of the simple transitive one, whereas the lexical definition of the intransitive verb is embedded in the definition of the transitive verb.

11.2.4   *A preliminary analysis of the primary sense of BREAK*

We present here the definitions of the three primary lexical units of the vocable BREAK, with their corresponding conceptual descriptions, beginning with the basic lexical unit: the intransitive BREAK. The complete, hierarchical analysis is illustrated by the graph in Figure 11.1. Each lexeme is related in a specific way to the basic lexical unit; cf. the links in the graph and the shared semantic components in the definitions. For each lexeme we give a definition, some examples

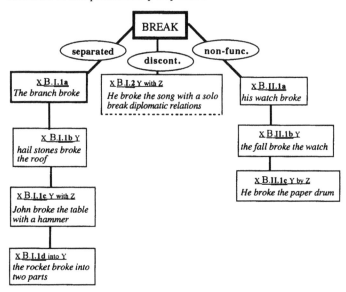

Figure 11.1. Structure of the vocable BREAK.

and a conceptual description in predicate-argument form. The lexical definitions follow the format of the Explanatory Combinatorial Dictionary (for a French ECD, see Mel'čuk et al., 1984, 1988, and 1992). X, Y, and Z represent the actants of the verb. X is the first actant for each lexeme, which is usually realized as the grammatical subject of the verb in active constructions. The conceptual descriptions we give here should all be seen as guidelines that indicate conceptual preferences, some of them stronger than others, that can be explicitly overridden.

BREAK, verb

*X breaks***I.1a** = X undergoes a change such that it separates into two or more pieces with the result that X is no longer intact

Ex.: *The attic was a pretty comfortable place, until the roof beam broke.*
The branch broke during the ice storm.

[As implied by the use of the 'separates into pieces' semantic component, B.**I.1a** can apply only to solid, fairly rigid objects. Body parts would seem to be an exception to this, as in broken leg or broken hand, but metonymy applies here, and it is actually the bone of the leg that is broken, or the bones of the hand. Bones are unquestionably solid, rigid objects whose intactness is violated by being broken. It may be necessary to postulate a distinct lexeme for the breaking of body parts (cf. our motto for this article, where A. Burgess plays wittily with the ambiguity of *to break a finger*).]

[exert_Sforce(unknown,X) ->] become(separated_into_pieces(X))

*X breaks***I.1b** *Y* = X_1, which is involved in the situation X_2, exerts a force on Y that causes Y to break**I.1a**.

Ex.:   *The falling hail stones broke the greenhouse roof.*
        All these books are too heavy; they will break the shelf sooner or later.

[This lexeme is taken as being built on the more basic mono-actancial one B.**I.1a**. The split of the first actant into two separate participants, X_1 for the object in contact and X_2 for the situation itself, accounts for the possibility of either one to be realized as the first deep-syntactic actant (and therefore, the grammatical subject).]

$$\text{exert\_Sforce}(X,Y) \rightarrow \text{become(separated\_into\_pieces}(Y))$$

*X breaks***I.1c** *Y with Z* = X uses Z to cause Z to break**I.1b** Y.

Ex.:   *John broke the stick with a rock.*
        ca10 (1):   *You can unscrew this tube and replace it with a smooth-*
                     bore insert for use with shotshells -- to break the little
                     Targo clay targets.
        ca10 (2):   *They'll travel 50 feet or more when thrown from the*
                     spring trap but it's almost impossible to break one after it
                     passes the 35-foot mark.

[X must be animate and the action must be intentional, which is implied by the semantic component 'use'. If no Z is mentioned explicitly, it is possible that X has used his/her hands or any part of his/her body as an instrument.]

causeI(X, exert_Sforce(X,Y), Z) -> become(separated_into_pieces(Y))

11.3   Extended meanings of BREAK

In this section we discuss three separate extended meanings of BREAK. Conceptually these are divided into functioning objects becoming dysfunctional, objects PURPOSELY separating into pieces, and continuities becoming discontinuous. We find once again that the co-occurrence of intentionality and of the use of an INSTRUMENT serves to clarify the distinctions between lexical units. We also see an illustration of the coercion of an object's definition into a semantic class that fits the application of a particular conceptualization of BREAK.

This is not by any means an exhaustive survey of BREAK. It is a semantically complicated verb, and it contains a wide range of meanings that are far beyond the scope of this chapter. We are not addressing verb particle constructions such as *break off, break in, break out, break down,* and *break up.* Lexically we would automatically distinguish between each verb-particle construction (many of which comprise more than one lexeme). Conceptually, the distinctions are not so clear, since some verb-particle constructions seem quite similar to usages without particles. We are also not discussing "broken contracts", as in *break the treaty, break parole, break the law* or a "release from containment" as in *break out of jail, break the code* and *the news broke* (Palmer, 1990). Some of these are specialized usages which are not productive and might perhaps be best handled by LEXICAL FUNCTIONS as cases of RESTRICTED LEXICAL CO-OCCUR-RENCES (idiomatic expressions) – on these two linguistic concepts, see Mel'čuk and Polguère (1987). Finally, we have not addressed metaphorical usages that include the following example and usages such as *break the will of the people* and *break his heart*.

Ex.: ca36: *In this manner, every scheme for direct control broke to pieces on the great protective rock of the anti-trust laws.*

11.3.1 *Non-functionality*

A plausible inference when something is no longer intact is that it no longer functions properly. It can probably be inferred of broken vases, broken windows, and broken latches that they are incapable of performing their normal functions when they have been separated into pieces. One of the most logical extensions of the primary conceptual representation of BREAK is to go past the separation into pieces stage, and straight to the non-functioning, or damaged, stage. This usage applies primarily to the set of objects which can be described as **functioning**, and hence can **cease to function**. The clearest examples of these types of objects are **mechanical devices**, such as watches, printers, monitors, dishwashers, starting air compressors, and so on. It is possible that the cause of the non-functioning is a broken part but it is not necessary. The mechanical failure could be due to other specific problems such as faulty wiring or clogged filters, and the mechanical device is still described as broken. There may or may not have been a force exerted. The damage could be due to erosion or mildew or other factors, any one of which could be seen as an external controller.

The significance of the INSTRUMENT

The INSTRUMENT is once more a determining factor in our specification of the conceptual description. We conclude that the INSTRUMENT is not a participant in the non-functioning situation, since a *with*-INSTRUMENT phrase cannot be associated with this type of break-event. The introduction of the INSTRU-MENT in

(9) *John broke his watch with a hammer.*

forces the **separated_into_pieces** reading.

   A solid object functioning as an intentionally wielded INSTRUMENT in this context selects for **exert_Sforce** *and* **separated_into_pieces**.

   We find that intentionality has a different place in this conceptualization as well. It is still possible to associate intentionality with a non-functional break-event, but this has to be done more overtly, as in

(10) *He broke the paper drum by purposely using the wrong voltage.*

It is no longer necessary to use *accidentally* to override an assumption of intentionality. It is our conclusion that this predicate is neutral (vague) regarding intentionality. In addition to mechanical devices which can become non-functional, there are other, more abstract objects such as computer programs which can also become non-functional, and hence *broken* (see the upcoming section on idealizing objects). The general conceptual class associated with this usage is **mechanical devices**.

A preliminary analysis of the secondary sense of BREAK

With the general, non-functional usage, we have an intransitive BREAK**II.1a**, and a transitive BREAK**II.1b** with a situation or natural force or animate acting as an external controller. This usage is distinguished conceptually by the nature of the change of state that takes place, **non-functional** rather than **separated_into_pieces,** and because it is not necessary for a force to have been exerted, obviating the need for an INSTRUMENT. We represent conceptually the transitive verb by means of the binary predicate **act_upon** which leaves unspecified the exact nature of the action. This usage is distinguished lexically from the primary sense (see Section 11.2.4), because the ternary predicate cannot occur with an INSTRU-MENTAL *with*-phrase. The ternary predicate can occur with a *by*-phrase which is not an INSTRUMENT but serves a similar purpose (still leaving intentionality unspecified), an interesting phenomenon that requires further study.

X breaksII.1a = X undergoes a change such that it no longer functions.

Ex.:   *His watch broke.*

[Note that '(X) no longer functions' entails that X must be a "functioning entity" (such as a mechanical device).]

    become(non-functional(Y))

X breaksII.1b Y = X_1, which is involved in the situation X_2, acts upon Y in such a way that Y *breaksII.1a*

Ex.:   *The shock broke my watch*
         He broke the paper drum.

    act_upon(X, Y) -> become(non-functional(Y))

X breaksII.1c Y *by Z-ing* = X, doing Z, causes that Z *breaks II.1b* Y.

Ex.:   *He broke the paper drum by using the wrong voltage.*

    do(X,Z) AND act_upon(Z, Y) -> become(non-functional(Y))

Idealizing objects as mechanical devices

Does the non-functional meaning apply only to mechanical devices, or can it be extended to other types of objects? In certain communities it is acceptable to refer to broken software, as in *he broke lexical lookup yesterday by adding two new variable names,* as well as broken hardware. This is because to a programmer, a program, when it is running, can be idealized as a functioning device that consists of several parts (i.e., subprograms) that play distinct functional roles. It seems likely that any object that can be idealized as a mechanical device, i.e., a functioning system with distinct functioning subparts, can be said to be *broken* with the non-functional reading. We consider this an instance of coercion.

Intensifiers

Since there are many solid, rigid objects which also function, there is sometimes an ambiguity as to what exactly is meant by stating that they have broken. Can a broken wheelbarrow be used to cart rocks? Can a broken screwdriver be used for repair tasks? Can a broken TV display TV programs? There are contexts in which all of these questions can be answered affirmatively. Many solid objects can be slightly separated *into pieces* and still be capable of functioning. One method that is often used to avoid this potential ambiguity is the inclusion of an optional into pieces phrase which refers somewhat redundantly to the newly separated into pieces state. We see this as having the effect of an intensifier,[8] as in

(11)   *Anna's 6-yr-old son broke her Waterford vase into pieces, when he accidentally knocked it off the living room table.*

A separate, distinct use of an optional *into pieces* phrase, which does not correspond to a typical intensifier for B.**I.1a-c**, is as an elaboration on the new state of the broken object, as in

(12)   *The fall to the floor broke the vase into three separate pieces that could easily be glued back together. It could still be used as a vase, and even be as pleasing to the eye when viewed from the right angle, but its financial value was sadly diminished.*

11.3.2   *Internal control and Y breaks into Z*

There is another distinct extended usage of BREAK, the intransitive *break (into)*, soon to be defined, which has a very specialized meaning where we do consider the *into*-PP as the realization of a necessary internal argument. This usage occurs only as an intransitive verb and is not to be confused with the more common transitive use of *break into*, as in *I broke the cookie into three pieces*. There is a restricted set of objects that intransitive *break into* can apply to, since, in this usage, it is part of the object's fundamental nature that it can "purposely" separate into segments. This can be true of a river, as in

(13)   *The river breaks into a number of channels.*

or a rocket, as in

(14)   *When it reached 10,000 meters, the rocket broke into two parts.*

or even a convoy, as in

(15)   *The convoy will break into five sections before reaching the city.*

The necessity of the *into*-phrase is demonstrated by its removal:

(16)   *The convoy will break before reaching the city.*

has a very different reading in which it is implied that the convoy will fall apart against its will with serious negative connotations probably including dispersal. In all of the *break into* examples, there is a meaning component in which the object is voluntarily being separated into parts – in other words, in which the object is the internal controller of the *breaking into* event. In French, for instance, this usage cannot be expressed by means of the standard reflexive verb corresponding to the intransitive BREAK, SE CASSER, but only by means of a related verb, SE SEPARER (roughly, 'to separate oneself').

We claim that this meaning can occur only in the intransitive form. It is a property of internally controlled events that they causativize only when it is possible to relinquish control to a certain extent, as in *The nurse burped the baby* (Levin and Rappaport Hovav, 1994). There are no causatives for *laugh* or *sleep,* where internal control presumably cannot be relinquished. There is an even stronger case here against a possible causative, since, similar to the French, the English usage seems to be basically an implicit reflexive,

(17)   *The rocket broke itself into 2 parts.*

The sentence

(18)   *NASA broke the rocket into 2 parts when it reached 10,000 meters.*

does not have the desired meaning of an object separating into predetermined sections as part of its normal functioning. The more likely interpretation is that *NASA damaged the rocket.* With this usage, if the internal controller relinquishes control, the meaning changes back to the primary sense which already has a causative. We cannot use intentional causation for the following conceptual description since we do not have animate agents, so we choose the more neutral **act_upon.**

*X breaks***I.1d** *into Y* = X undergoes a change, in the course of its normal functioning, such that X is in Y parts, as if X were breaking**I.1a.**

Ex.:   *The convoy will break into five sections before reaching the city.*

[The component 'in Y parts' controls some restrictions on X, such that X cannot be a liquid, a gas, etc.]

$$\text{act\_upon}(X,X) \rightarrow \text{become}(\text{separated}(X,\text{Parts}))$$

11.3.3   *Discontinuities*

If a concrete or abstract entity such as the horizon, a journey or a song or an act of communication can be described as being continuous, then it is possible to create a discontinuity, i.e., a separation into parts of a continuum and thus "break" it, as in *break the journey with an overnight stop, break the song with a drum solo, break his winning streak,* etc. This comprises one of the Brown Corpus's most popular categories for BREAK, all of which can be expressed only as a ternary predicate – in the transitive form with an animate agent. We do not present this as a completed lexical analysis, because we feel that there are valid distinctions which can still be made within this conceptual category which we will leave for future work. In other words, our **B.I.2** stands in fact for a family of lexemes which needs further analysis.

*X breaks**I.2** Y with Z* = X makes the event Y look discontinuous in space or in time, as if X were breaking**I.1c** Y with Z.

Ex.:   *He should break the song after the second verse with a drum solo.*

        cb02(2):   *Grasslands would extend, unfenced, unplowed, unbroken by silo or barn as the first settlers saw them.*

        cb25:   *He may break with China (which would be infernally difficult and perhaps disastrous), or he may succeed, by all kinds of dangerous concessions, in persuading China to be patient.*

        cb01:   *Last year, after Trujillo had been cited for numerous aggressions in the Caribbean, the U.S. and many other members of the OAS broke diplomatic relations with him.*

        ca11(1):   *If the Orioles are to break their losing streak within the next two days,*

causeI(X, become(discontinuous(Y)), Z)

In all of these usages, there is the assumption that the continuous activity involved can be resumed after the occurrence of the discontinuity. There is another set of examples, all involving forms of communication between animate agents where this assumption no longer holds: where it is more likely that there will be no resumption of the communication. We have not yet been able to distinguish this set lexically from the previous set, so at this point we will assume that they share the same usage, and the difference in the possibility of resumption stems from the inherent conceptual content of the objects involved rather than something implied by the verb. We have included two *break up* examples in this set, since they seem conceptually identical to the other examples. This is also the category where we place *broken engagement (between ships)*.

        ca20:   *Just how many secrets were being handed over when the ring, watched for 6 months, was broken, remained untold.*

        cc11:   *Only a plea from the house manager, J. C., finally broke up the party.*

        ca11(2):   *He hopes to melt off an additional 8 pounds before the Flock breaks camp three weeks hence.*

        cb25:   *The maneuvers were held "in secret" after a regional seminar for the Minutemen, held in nearby Shiloh, Ill., had been broken up the previous day by deputy sheriffs, who had arrested regional leader R. L. of Collinsville, Ill., and (. . .)*

To conclude this section, Figure 11.1 describes the partial lexical analysis of the vocable BREAK that we have discussed in this chapter.

11.4   Related Literature

11.4.1   *Comparison to Jackendoff's Lexical Conceptual Structure*

This is an appropriate point to compare our representations with the Lexical Conceptual Structure for BREAK proposed by Jackendoff (1990:121). As previously mentioned, our style of conceptual description is in general modeled after Jackendoff's Lexical Conceptual Structures. However, we find a certain divergence of opinion with respect to BREAK. He classifies BREAK as a verb of Material Composition, along with *split, crack, splinter, crumble, divide, grind, pulverize, chop, disassembled.* These are in the same major class as *form, build, construct, erect, manufacture, create,* although they contrast with the latter in that they basically refer to the act of **decomposition** rather than **composition**. In all of Jackendoff's lexical conceptual structures he makes use of a small set of primitive predicates that include CAUSE, GO, INCH(oative), TO, FROM and AT, as well as others. These predicates are all precisely defined and used consistently in his many verb definitions. The representation he gives for BREAK is:

$$[\text{CAUSE ([AGENT], [GO}_{comp+} \text{ ([SOURCE], [TO [GOAL]])])}]$$

where some AGENT CAUSES an event in which in the resulting state the SOURCE (the object itself) has been DECOMPOSED, $(\text{GO}_{comp+)}$, into the form given by the GOAL. The sentence

(19)   *Sam broke the bowl into pieces.*

is represented by Jackendoff as:

$$[\text{CAUSE ([SAM], [GO}_{comp+} \text{ ([BOWL], [TO [PIECES]])])}]$$

In previous treatments by Jackendoff, the inchoative reading was implicit in the GO predicate (Jackendoff, 1983). In this volume Jackendoff introduces a separate INCH predicate for the inchoative and reserves GO for motion verbs that appear with a range of Path prepositions (Jackendoff, 1990:92–95). In spite of this, he ends up choosing GO instead of INCH to represent verbs of composition/decomposition, because he allows TO and FROM as types of arguments of GO, whereas with INCH he has restricted himself to AT. He admits that this is somewhat problematic, and leaves unresolved the issue of BREAK's inchoative nature. This confusion between the inchoative and the change in location reading gives rise to the main point of difference between our representation and Jackendoff's, which is his inclusion of the TO[GOAL] to indicate an internal verb argument.

Our conceptual analysis includes Jackendoff's notion of **causation**, and we also see the fundamental meaning as the transitive form of the verb. We agree that the new separated-into-pieces state is an essential part of the representation, but we do not see it as a separate internal verb argument. Also, as explained in Section 11.3.1, we see the occasional use of an *into* (*pieces*) phrase with the primary sense of BREAK as an optional adjunct that can act as an intensifier, or as further elaboration on the break-event to disambiguate between the separate into pieces reading and the non-functional reading, but not as an obligatory internal verb argument. The new state of the object, the broken state, is the necessary result of the break-event occurring.

11.4.2 *Comparison to Ney's description*

We should also mention a fairly comprehensive analysis of BREAK given by J. Ney (1990), which he based on the OED entry and a paper by Ruhl (1979). He is interested primarily in classifying the types of subjects and objects that can occur with each different usage, and selecting an appropriate "synonym" – related verb – to reflect the unique characteristics of each lexeme. He is in agreement with our analysis of the basic lexical unit of BREAK as the 'separate into pieces' predicate, which he calls the primary meaning, and also recognizes that other secondary and tertiary meanings, i.e., lexemes, can be realized with different argument structures. He gives three distinct synonyms, *shatter, snap* and *burst,* as corresponding to his three primary meanings or lexemes, all of which are ternary predicates. In his analysis, these synonyms are chosen because they preserve both the semantic and syntactic patterning of a particular usage. *Break a twig* is synonymous with *snap a twig, break a glass* with *shatter a glass,* and *break a balloon* with *burst a balloon.*

Most of the Brown Corpus examples fell into his secondary and tertiary categories, and we also classified them in secondary or tertiary levels of our hierarchy. Without quibbling over particular examples and whether they can or cannot be three place predicates, and leaving aside verb-particle constructions that we have not yet addressed, our main contention would be that we would classify his *destroy, abrogate, cause to be inoperable,* and *loosen* as examples of the **non-functional** category, while *start* and *change* introduce **discontinuities** (Palmer and Polguère, 1992)**.**

We have a more serious disagreement with his three primary lexemes since we consider them to be identical with the single primary **separated_into_pieces** sense that we have been concerned with here. The distinctions he makes have to do with the type of object that is being broken, and how its physical makeup responds to being involved in a break-event. Twigs, sticks, wires, glass tubes, flagpoles, chains, etc., are all solid, fairly rigid objects with roughly two-dimensional shapes that tend to separate into pieces at their weakest point when force is exerted. Ceramics, gold and silver hollowware, statues, walls, etc., are solid, fairly rigid objects with roughly three-dimensional shapes that separate in a much more random fashion when force is exerted. Is the way these objects break an intrinsic semantic property of the verb or of the objects themselves? Or is it part of our commonsense knowledge of objects breaking and has no place at all in a linguistic analysis?

11.5 Conclusion

We have presented a preliminary lexical and conceptual analysis for BREAK. We have assumed that distinct lexical units should have corresponding distinct conceptual representations, and for the lexemes we have presented this has been the case. Whenever the lexical argument structure has changed, we have found corresponding differences in the underlying conceptual description. In particular, the use of an INSTRUMENT *with*-phrase seems to correlate with the intentional exertion of force. Where the verb's conceptualization does not require intentionality or the exertion of force, as in the **non-functional** BREAK, the INSTRUMENTAL *with*-phrase is absent.

However, as we promised in the introduction, we have also raised many more questions than we have answered. How can the basic form be determined? What constitutes a lexical unit and is there a corresponding conceptual unit? Is the way in which objects break an intrinsic semantic property of the verb or of the objects themselves? More than anything else, the questions that have arisen in this chapter point out the need for a rigorous methodology for distinguishing conceptually between different lexemes. They also illustrate the amount of complexity involved in the underlying conceptual descriptions. Fillmore proffers sage advice in his break paper, cautioning against "seek[ing] critical [conceptual] differences between *break, smash, shatter*" (Fillmore, 1970:129). Would that we had followed it, rather than rushing in where the angels have been far too clever to go.

Notes

1. Many thanks to Igor Mel'cuk for signaling this more than appropriate quotation to us.
2. Fillmore uses X instead of P. But since we use X later on, we have changed his notation to avoid any possible confusion of symbols.
3. In this chapter, we make use of some terminology for lexicographic description which has been precisely defined within the linguistic approach known as Meaning-Text theory – see Mel'cuk (1981) for a general presentation of Meaning-Text theory and Mel'cuk (1988) for the definition of the basic concepts of lexicographic description. More specifically, two technical terms are very useful here, **lexeme** and **vocable**:

    • A lexeme is a unit of lexicographic description, i.e., roughly, a word associated with a well-specified meaning and grammatical behavior. We write lexemes in uppercase letters with distinctive numbers (when needed): e.g., BREAKI.1a, BREAKI.1b, etc.
    • A vocable is a set of lexemes which have the same surface realizations and are semantically related. Vocables are written in uppercase letters: e.g., the BREAK vocable, BREAK AWAY, etc.

    Vocables correspond, in traditional dictionaries, to the so-called headwords, while the lexemes correspond to the entries found under the headword.
4. The parentheses indicate optionality.
5. The occurrence of the label BRITTLE does not mean that we define BREAK by means of BRITTLE, i.e. BREAKABLE – which would be redundant. This is an abstract label which simply selects objects from the domain model which have been typed as brittle. From a linguistic point of view, BRITTLE has to be defined in terms of BREAK.

6. We will follow the Prolog conventions of indicating variables with uppercase, and constants with lowercase.

7. In Meaning-Text lexicography, the choice of a basic lexical unit for a vocable is based on strictly SYNCHRONIC LINGUISTIC principles. By choosing the intransitive BREAK as the basic lexical unit, we do not pretend that it must have appeared in English before the transitive one. Moreover, we do not pretend to capture any psychological or pragmatic fact: which BREAK is more "active" in the brain of the native speakers, which one is more frequently used, etc.

8. In the Explanatory Combinatorial Dictionary terminology, such a construction is described as a **Magn** (from Lat. *magnus* 'big') for B.**I.1a-c**, a particular type of lexical function.

References

Comrie, B. 1981. *Language Universals and Linguistic Typology,* Basil Blackwell, Oxford.

Cruse, D. A. 1986. *Lexical Semantics,* Cambridge University Press, Cambridge.

Dowty, D. 1991. Thematic, Proto-Roles and Argument Selection, *Language,* CXVII, 547–619.

Fillmore, C. J. 1970. The Grammar of Hitting and Breaking, *Readings in English Transformational Grammar,* Eds. Jacobs, R. A., and Rosenbaum, P. S., Ginn and Company, Waltham, Mass, 120–133.

Jackendoff, R.S. 1972. *Semantic Interpretation in Generative Grammar,* MIT Press, Cambridge, Mass.

Jackendoff, R.S. 1983. *Semantics and Cognition,* MIT Press, Cambridge, Mass.

Jackendoff, R.S. 1990. *Semantic Structures,* MIT Press, Cambridge, Mass.

Levin, B. and M. Rappaport Hovav. 1994. A Preliminary Analysis of (De) Causative Verbs in English, *Lingua* 92, 35–77.

Mel'cuk, I. A. 1981. Meaning-Text Models: A Recent Trend in Soviet Linguistics, *Annual Review of Anthropology,* X, 27–62.

Mel'cuk, I. A. 1988. Semantic Description of Lexical Units in an Explanatory Combinatorial Dictionary: Basic Principles and Heuristic Criteria, *International Journal of Lexicography,* I:3, 165–188.

Mel'cuk, I. A., N. Arbatchewsky-Jumarie, L. Elnitsky, L. Iordanskaja et A. Lessard. 1984. *Dictionnaire explicatif et combinatoire du français contemporain – Recherches lexico-sémantiques I,* Presses de l'Université de Montréal, Montréal. Mel'cuk, I. A., A. Arbatchewsky-Jumarie, L. Dagenais, L. Elnitsky, L. Iordanskaja, M.-N. Lefebvre and S. Mantha. 1988. *Dictionnaire explicatif et combinatoire du français contemporain – Recherches lexico-sémantiques II,* Presses de l'Université de Montréal, Montréal.

Mel'cuk, I. A., A. Arbatchewsky-Jumarie, L. Iordanskaja and S. Mantha. 1992. *Dictionnaire explicatif et combinatoire du français contemporain – Recherches lexico-sémantiques III,* Presses de l'Université de Montréal, Montréal.

Mel'cuk, I. A. and A. Polguère. 1987. A Formal Lexicon in the Meaning-Text Theory (or How to Do Lexica with Words), *Computational Linguistics,* XIII:3–4, 261–275.

Ney, J. 1990. Polysemy and syntactic variability in the surface verb 'break', *Proceedings of the 17th LACUS Forum,* Ed. Volpe, A.D., published by the Linguistic Association of Canada and the United States, Lake Bluff, Ill., 264–278.

Palmer, M. 1981. A Case for Rule-Driven Semantic Analysis, *Proceedings of the 19th Annual Meeting of the Association for Computational Linguistics,* Stanford, CA.

Palmer, M. 1990. Customizing Verb Definitions for Specific Semantic Domains, *Machine Translation Journal 5,* Kluwer Academic Publishers, 5–30.

Palmer, M. and A. Polguère. 1992. A Computational Perspective on the Lexical Analysis of Break, *Proceedings of the Workshop on Computational Lexical Semantics,* Toulouse, 145–156.

Palmer, M., R. Passonneau, C. Weir and T. Finin. 1993. The Kernel Text Understanding System, special issue of *AI Journal,* October.

Ruhl, C. 1979. The Semantic Field of Break, Cut and Tear. In William C. McCormack and Herbert J. Izzo (Eds.), *The Sixth LACUS Forum.* Hornbeam Press, Columbia, SC, 200–214.

Smith, C. S. 1970. Jespersen's 'Move and Change' Class and Causative Verbs in English. In: M. A. Jazayery, E. C. Palome and W. Winter (Eds.), *Linguistic and Literary Studies in Honor of Archibald A. Hill, Vol. 2, Descriptive Linguistics,* Mouton, The Hague, 101–109.

Wierzbicka, A. 1984. Cups and Mugs: Lexicography and Conceptual Analysis, *Australian Journal of Linguistics,* IV:2, 205–255.

12 Large neural networks for the resolution of lexical ambiguity

JEAN VÉRONIS AND NANCY IDE

12.1 Introduction

Many words have two or more very distinct meanings. For example, the word *pen* can refer to a writing implement or to an enclosure. Many natural language applications, including information retrieval, content analysis and automatic abstracting, and machine translation, require the resolution of lexical ambiguity for words in an input text, or are significantly improved when this can be accomplished.[1] That is, the preferred input to these applications is a text in which each word is "tagged" with the sense of that word intended in the particular context. However, at present there is no reliable way to automatically identify the correct sense of a word in running text. This task, called *word sense disambiguation,* is especially difficult for texts from unconstrained domains because the number of ambiguous words is potentially very large. The magnitude of the problem can be reduced by considering only very gross sense distinctions (e.g., between the pen-as-implement and pen-as-enclosure senses of *pen,* rather than between finer sense distinctions within, say, the category of pen-as-enclosure – i.e., enclosure for animals, enclosure for submarines, etc.), which is sufficient for many applications. But even so, substantial ambiguity remains: for example, even the relatively small lexicon (20,000 entries) of the TRUMP system, which includes only gross sense distinctions, finds an average of about four senses for each word in sentences from the *Wall Street Journal* (McRoy, 1992). The resulting combinatoric explosion demonstrates the magnitude of the lexical ambiguity problem.

Several different kinds of information can contribute to the resolution of lexical ambiguity. These include word-specific information such as morphological information, part of speech (the syntactic category of the word), relative sense frequency (preferred sense, either generally or for the determined domain), semantic features (the semantic components, often drawn from a potentially large set of primitives, that contribute to meaning); as well as contextual information such as syntactic role (e.g., a particular sense may be the only one allowed as the object

The present research has been partially funded by the GRECO-PRC Communication Homme-Machine of the French Ministry of Research and Technology, U.S.-French NSF/CNRS grant INT-9016554 for collaborative research, and U.S. NSF RUI grant IRI-9108363. The authors would like to thank Collins Publishers for making their data available for research within the project. The authors would also like to acknowledge the contribution of Stéphane Harié for his pre-processing of the *CED*.

of a given preposition), role-related preferences (selectional restrictions defining relations between a noun and verb), semantic relations (most usually, senses of or associations with surrounding words), etc. It has recently been suggested that an effective word sense disambiguation procedure will require information of most or all these types (McRoy, 1992). However, most methods utilize only one or two of the potential information sources just mentioned. One common approach follows in the case-based tradition of Fillmore (1968) and Schank (1975), and involves matching role restriction specifications with semantic features in order to choose the appropriate senses for other words in the sentence (for example, the agent role for a given verb must have the feature animate) (see, for example, Wilks and Fass, 1990; Fass, 1988). Another approach to word sense disambiguation uses semantic context as an indicator of sense, and involves the traversal of semantic networks that indicate word and/or concept associations, typically utilizing marker-passing techniques (Charniak, 1983; Hirst, 1987; Norvig, 1989). A similar approach implements connectionist models of human meaning representation based on semantic features, using a spreading activation strategy (Cottrell and Small, 1983; Waltz and Pollack, 1985).

All of these techniques require the prior creation of a potentially complex lexical and/or semantic knowledge base, which poses theoretical and practical problems. Designing role-related systems and identifying appropriate feature sets for unrestricted language is not straightforward in the state of the art. In any case, it is often impractical to manually encode this information for a lexicon of substantial size.[2] As a result, several studies have attempted to use ready-made information sources such as machine-readable versions of everyday dictionaries (Lesk, 1986; Wilks et al., 1990) and word-aligned bi-lingual corpora (Gale, Church, and Yarowsky, 1983) for word sense disambiguation, in order to avoid the high costs of creating large lexical and semantic knowledge bases.

We describe here a method for word sense disambiguation that builds upon both connectionnist models and the work of Lesk and Wilks. We automatically construct very large neural networks from definition texts in machine-readable dictionaries, and therefore no hand coding of large-scale resources is required. Further, the knowledge contained in the network therefore potentially covers all of English (90,000 words), and as a result, this information can potentially be used to help disambiguate unrestricted text. Creation of the networks requires only minimal pre-processing of definition texts, involving the elimination of non-content words and lemmatization. There are nodes in the network for the root forms of all words appearing in the dictionary, linked to concept nodes corresponding to their senses. Concept nodes are in turn linked to the root forms of words appearing in their definitions. The fundamental assumption underlying the semantic knowledge represented in these networks is that there are significant semantic relations between a word and the words used to define it. The connections in the network reflect these relations. There is no indication within the network of the *nature* of the relationships, although the presence of words with important and relatively fixed semantic relations to their headwords in dictionary definitions is well known, and much work has been applied to identifying and extracting this information (see, for instance, Amsler, 1980; Calzolari, 1984; Chodorow, Byrd and Heidorn, 1985; Markowitz, Ahlswede and Evens, 1986; Byrd et al., 1987; Véronis and Ide, 1991; Nakamura and Nagao, 1988; Klavans, Chodorow, and Wacholder, 1990; Wilks et al., 1990). Such information is not systematic or even complete, and its extraction from machine-readable dictionaries is not always straightforward. However, it has been shown that in its base form, information from machine-readable dictionaries can be used, for example, to find subject domains in texts (Walker and Amsler, 1986). More important, it is not clear that knowing the nature of the relationships would significantly enhance the word sense disambiguation process.

Input to the network consists of words from running text. There is no requirement for complex processing of the input text, which means that the method can be applied to unrestricted text. This is in contrast to the role-related approach, which demands the a priori identification of syntactic elements, a costly process which in the current state of the art is almost impossible for unrestricted text. We apply a spreading activation strategy which ultimately identifies the sense of each input word that shares the most relations with other input (context) words. As such, our work, like the semantic network and connectionnist approaches already mentioned, relies on semantic context for disambiguation, and thus follows from work in lexical cohesion which shows that in order to create text unity, people repeat words in a given conceptual category or which are semantically associated (Halliday and Hasen, 1976; Morris and Hirst, 1991). Output from the network is the text with each word tagged with its appropriate sense (as identified in the dictionary used to construct the network), which can in turn serve as input to other processes.

This work has been carried out in the context of a joint project of Vassar College and the Groupe Représentation et Traitement des Connaissances of the Centre National de la Recherche Scientifique (CNRS), which is concerned with the construction and exploitation of a large lexical database of English and French.

12.2   Previous work

12.2.1   *Machine-readable dictionaries for disambiguation*

The most general and well-known attempt to utilize information in machine-readable dictionaries for word sense disambiguation is that of Lesk (1986), which computes the degree of overlap – that is, number of shared words – in definition texts of words that appear in a ten-word window of context. The sense of a word with the greatest number of overlaps with senses of other words in the window is chosen as the correct one. For example, consider the definitions of *pen* and *sheep* from the *Collins English Dictionary* (*CED*), the dictionary used in our experiments, in Figure 12.1.

pen[1] *n.* **1.** an implement for writing or drawing using ink, formerly consisting of a sharpened and split quill, and now of a metal nib attached to a holder. **2.** the writing end of such an implement; nib. **3.** style of writing. **4. the pen. a.** writing as an occupation. **b.** the written word. **5.** the long horny internal shell of a squid. *~vb.* **6.** *(tr.)* to write or compose.

pen[2] *n.* **1.** an enclosure in which domestic animals are kept. **2.** any place of confinement. **3.** a dock for servicing submarines. *~vb.* **4.** *(tr.)* to enclose or keep in a pen.

pen[3] *n.* short for **penitentiary.**

pen[4] *n.* a female swan.

sheep *n.* **1.** any of various bovid mammals of the genus *Ovis* and related genera, esp. *O. aries* (**domestic sheep**) having transversely ribbed horns and a narrow face. There are many breeds of domestic sheep, raised for their wool and for meat. **2. Barbary sheep.** another name for **aoudad. 3.** a meek or timid person, esp. one without initiative. **4. separate the sheep from the goats.** to pick out the members of any group who are superior in some respects.

goat *n.* **1.** any sure-footed agile bovid mammal of the genus *Capra,* naturally inhabiting rough stony ground in Europe, Asia, and N Africa, typically having a brown-grey colouring and a beard. Domesticated varieties (*C. hircus*) are reared for milk, meat, and wool. **2.** short for **Rocky Mountain goat 3.** *Informal.* a lecherous man. **4.** a bad or inferior member of any group (esp. in the phrase **separate the sheep from the goats**). **5.** short for **scapegoat. 6. act** (or **play**) **the** (**giddy**) **goat.** to fool around. **7. get** (**someone's**) **goat.** *Slang.* to cause annoyance to (someone)

page[1] *n.* **1.** one side of one of the leaves of a book, newspaper, letter, etc. or the written or printed matter it bears. **2.** such a leaf considered as a unit **3.** an episode, phase, or period **4.** *Printing.* the type as set up for printing a page. *~vb.* **5.** another word for *paginate.* **6.** *(intr.;* foll. by *through)* to look through (a book, report, etc.); leaf through.

page[2] *n.* **1.** a boy employed to run errands, carry messages, etc., for the guests in a hotel, club, etc. **2.** a youth in attendance at official functions or ceremonies. **3.** *Medevial history.* **a.** a boy in training for knighthood in personal attendance on a knight. **b.** a youth in the personal service of a person of rank. **4.** (in the U.S.) an attendant at Congress or other legislative body. **5.** *Canadian.* a boy or girl employed in the debating chamber of the house of Commons, the Senate, or a legislative assembly to carry messages for members. *~vb.* *(tr.)* **6.** to call out the name of (a person). **7.** to call (a person) by an electronic device, such as a bleep. **8.** to act as a page to or attend as a page.

Figure 12.1. Definitions of *pen, sheep, goat* and *page* in the *CED.*

If these two words appear together in context, the appropriate senses of *pen* (2.1: *enclosure*) and sheep (1: *mammal*) will be chosen because the definitions of these two senses have the word *domestic* in common. However, with one word as a basis, the relation is tenuous and wholly dependent upon a particular dictionary's wording. The method also fails to take into account less immediate relationships between words. As a result, it will not determine the correct sense of *pen* in the context of *goat.* The correct sense of *pen* (2.1: *enclosure*) and the correct sense of *goat* (1: *mammal*) do not share any words in common in their definitions in the *Collins English Dictionary;* however, a strategy which takes into account a longer path through definitions will find that *animal* is in the definition of *pen* 2.1, each of *mammal* and *animal* appear in the definition of the other, and *mammal* is in the definition of *goat* 1.

Similarly, Lesk's method would also be unable to determine the correct sense of *pen* (1.1: *writing utensil*) in the context of *page*, because seven of the thirteen senses of *pen* have the same number of overlaps with senses of *page*. Six of the senses of *pen* share only the word *write* with the correct sense of *page* (1.1: *leaf of a book*). However, *pen* 1.1 also contains words such as *draw* and *ink*, and *page* 1.1 contains *book, newspaper, letter,* and *print*. These other words are heavily interconnected in a complex network which cannot be discovered by simply counting overlaps. Wilks et al. (forthcoming) build on Lesk's method by computing the degree of overlap for related word-sets constructed using co-occurrence data from definition texts, but their method suffers from the same problems, in addition to combinatorial problems that prevent disambiguating more than one word at a time.

12.2.2 *Connectionnist approaches*

Previously suggested connectionnist models proposed by Cottrell and Small (1983) and Waltz and Pollack (1985) use a local representation of word meaning. In such representations, each node (or "neuron") represents one word or one concept. Activatory links connect words and the concepts to which they are semantically related, and lateral inhibitory links connect competing concept nodes corresponding to the various senses of a given word.[3] For example, the word *pen* is represented by a word node connected by activatory links to (at least) two concept nodes, PEN-AS-WRITING-IMPLEMENT and PEN-AS-ENCLOSURE, which are in turn connected to each other by inhibitory links. The connections in these networks and their weights are constructed manually; it is not within the scope of these studies to consider how such configurations might be learned.

These models use recurrent networks over which a relaxation process is run through a number of cycles, after the spreading activation and lateral inhibition strategy introduced by McClelland and Rumelhart (1981). Initially, the nodes corresponding to the words in the sentence to be analyzed are activated. These words activate their concept node neighbors in the next cycle, and, in turn, the neighbors activate their immediate neighbors, and so on. Concept nodes that correspond to different senses of the same word inhibit each other. These nodes can be considered to be "in competition", since the more active one sense node becomes, the more it will tend to decrease its neighbors' activation levels. The total amount of activation received by any node at any cycle is the sum of the activation and inhibition received from all of its neighbors. As the cycles progress, activation and inhibition cooperate in a "winner-take-all" strategy to activate increasingly related word and sense nodes and deactivate the unrelated or weakly related nodes. Eventually, after a few dozen cycles, the network stabilizes in a configuration where the only nodes activated in the output layer are the sense nodes with the strongest relations to other nodes in the network. Because of the "winner-take-all" strategy, at most one sense node per word is ultimately activated.

Earlier experiments with neural network approaches to word sense disambiguation have demonstrated the promise of the approach. However, the models described suffer several drawbacks. First, the networks used so far are handcoded and thus necessarily very small (at most, a few dozen words and concepts). Due to a lack of real-size data, it is not clear that the same neural net models will scale up for realistic application. A second problem concerns the way context is handled. Early approaches rely on priming "context-setting" concept nodes to force the correct interpretation of the input words. For example, the concept node WRITING must be primed to help select the corresponding sense of *pen*. However, context-setting nodes must be artificially primed by the experimenter, and it is not clear how they could be automatically activated in a text processing system. As Waltz and Pollack (1985) point out, the word immediately corresponding to a contextually important concept (e.g., the word *writing*) may not be explicitly present in the text under analysis, although the concept can usually be inferred from other words in the text (e.g., *page, book, ink,* etc.).

To solve this problem, Waltz and Pollack (1985) and Bookman (1987) include sets of semantic "microfeatures," corresponding to fundamental semantic distinctions (animate, edible/inedible, threatening/safe, etc.), characteristic duration of events (second, minute, hour, day, etc.), locations (city, country, continent, etc.), and other similar distinctions, in their networks. To be comprehensive, the authors suggest that these features must number in the thousands. Each concept node in the network is linked, via bi-directional activatory or inhibitory links, to a subset of the microfeatures. Collections of closely related concepts share many common microfeatures, and therefore provide a representation of context that influences the interpretation of ambiguous words in the text. In Waltz and Pollack (1985), sets of microfeatures have to be manually primed by a user, but Bookman (1987) describes a dynamic process in which the microfeatures are automatically activated by the preceding text, thus acting as a short-term context memory.

Microfeature-based schemes are problematic due to the difficulties of designing an appropriate set. Despite several efforts (see Smith and Medin, 1981), we are still very far from identifying a universally accepted list of semantic features. This becomes clear when one examines the sample microfeatures given by Waltz and Pollack: they specify microfeatures such as CASINO and CANYON, but it is obviously questionable whether such concepts constitute fundamental semantic distinctions. On a more practical level, it is simply difficult to imagine how vectors of several thousands of microfeatures for each one of the tens of thousands of words and hundreds of thousands of senses can be realistically encoded by hand.

We demonstrate that semantic microfeatures are not required in order to automatically set context from words in the preceding text. We believe that what microfeatures achieve in the models proposed by Waltz and Pollack (1985) and

Bookman (1987) is a high degree of connection among concepts. We show that context can be handled automatically with a network consisting of only word and concept nodes (and no microfeatures), provided the network is large enough and very densely connected. This results in a substantially more economical model.

12.3 Network architecture and construction

12.3.1 *Creating networks from dictionaries*

Everyday dictionaries represent ready-made, highly connected networks of words and concepts. For example, in the *CED*, the definition of *pen* (as a writing implement) contains words such as *write, draw,* and *ink.* The definition of *page* contains *book, newspaper, letter, write, print.* The definition of *ink* contains *print, write,* and *draw.* The definition of *draw* contains *pencil* and *pen.* The definition of *book* contains *print, write, page, paper.* The definition of *paper* contains *write* and *print;* and so on. All of these connections obviously form a dense cluster of semantically related words.

Because several dictionaries are available in machine-readable form, we have used them to build large networks of words and concepts. We exploit the existing structure of dictionaries, in which each word is connected to one or more senses (roughly equivalent to concepts), and each sense is in turn connected to the words in its definition. If the words *pen* and *page* are fed to such a network containing all the connections in the CED, we can expect that the appropriate senses of both *pen* and *page* will be triggered because of the activation they receive through their mutual, direct connections to the word *write,* as well as numerous other indirect paths (through *ink, paper,* etc.). Conversely, the sense of *pen* as enclosure, which contains words like *enclosure, domestic,* and *animal,* should receive no reinforcement and eventually die off because of the inhibition sent from the more activated sense of *pen.* The sheer density of the connections between the two related senses of *pen* and *page* should override other spurious connections (e.g., *page* → (to)*bear* →*animal* →*pen*) between other senses of the two words.

The network is constructed by a straightforward automatic procedure that does not require hand coding or sophisticated analysis of definitions. Definition texts from the *CED* are simply pre-processed to remove function words and frequent words, and all remaining words are morphologically normalized (see Figures 12.1 and 12.2). A simple program then scans the pre-processed definition texts, creates the appropriate nodes and links, and assigns weights.

Ideally, the network we build would include the entire dictionary. However, the resulting network for the *CED* would be enormous, and so for practical reasons we currently limit the size of the network to a few thousand nodes and 10- to 40,000 non-null weighted links. We do this by building only the portion of the network that represents the input words, the words in their definitions, and the words in these words' definitions in turn (as well as the intervening sense nodes). Thus for each set of input words, a potentially different network is constructed.

pen1.1	implement write draw ink sharp split quill metal nib attach holder.
pen1.2	write end implement nib.
pen1.3	style write.
pen1.4	write occupation write word.
pen1.5	long horn internal shell squid.
pen1.6	write compose.
pen2.1	enclosure domestic animal keep.
pen2.2	place confinement.
pen2.3	dock service submarine.
pen2.4	enclose keep pen.
pen3	penitentiary.
pen4	female swan.

Figure 12.2. Pre-processed definition for the word *pen*.

12.3.2 *Network architecture*

Our network consists of two layers: the input layer, consisting of *word nodes,* and an output layer consisting of *sense nodes* (Figure 12.3). Each word defined in the *CED* is represented by a word node in the input layer. For each word node a number of sense nodes in the output layer represent the different senses (definitions) of this word in the CED. Thus, for the lexical entry *pen,* 12 sense nodes exist, one corresponding to each of the 12 senses of *pen* given in the *CED* (Figure 12.1). The two layers are fully interconnected: there are *feedforward* links from the input layer to the output layer, and *feedback* links from the output to the input layer (the weight on a link might be null) as well as between nodes of the output layer as lateral inhibition. This network is therefore a recurrent network (as opposed to a multilayer, feedforward network), as in McClelland and Rumelhart (1981) and Hopfield (1982, 1984). Its two-layer architecture bears some similarity to the ART network proposed by Grossberg and Carpenter (1988), in which the continually modified input vector is passed forward and backward (resonated) between the layers in a cyclic process.

When entries are scanned in creating the network, positive weights are assigned to links between the word node for the headword and its sense nodes, thus creating *excitatory* links. Positive weights are also assigned to links between a sense node and the nodes corresponding to the words that appear in its definition. Lateral *inhibitory* links between sense nodes of the same word node are assigned negative weights. Finally, for each connection from a node i to a node j, the same weight is assigned to the reciprocal connection from node j to node i, thus creating a symmetrically weighted network.

In early experiments, weights were the same for all excitatory links, but we discovered that "gang effects" appear due to extreme imbalance among words

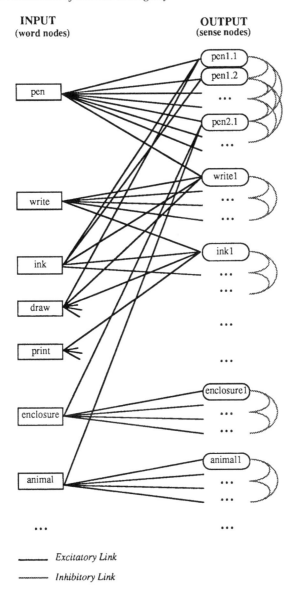

Figure 12.3. Topology of the network.

having few senses and hence few connections, and words containing up to 80 senses and several hundred connections, and that therefore dampening is required. In our current experiments, connection weights are normalized by a simple decreasing function of the number of outgoing connections from a given node.

12.3.3   *The activation strategy*

We can describe the activation strategy in mathematical terms as follows. At any instant t, a node i in the network has an activation level $a_i(t)$ with a real value. If a node has a positive activation level, it is said to be active. If the node receives no input from its neighbors, it tends to return to a *resting level* r_i, more or less quickly depending on decay rate θ_i. The active neighbors of a node affect its activation level either by excitation or inhibition, depending on the nature of the link. Each connection toward a given node i from a node j has a weight w_{ji}, which has a positive value for excitatory links and a negative value for inhibitory links (note that for each link to node i from a node j there is a reciprocal link in the network from i to j, and $w_{ij} = w_{ji}$). At any cycle, the total input $n_i(t)$ of input from its neighbors on node i is the inner product of the vector of the neighbors' activation levels by the connection weight vector:

$$n_i(t) = \sum_j w_j a_j(t)$$

This input is constrained by a "squashing function" s which prevents the activation level from going beyond a defined minimum and maximum: a node becomes increasingly difficult to activate as its level approaches the maximum, and increasingly difficult to inhibit as it approaches the minimum. In mathematical terms, the new activation level of a node i at time $t + \Delta t$ corresponds to the activation of this node at time t, modified by its neighbors' effect and diminished by the decay $\theta_i(a_i(t) - r_i)$:

$$a_i(t + \Delta t) = a_i(t) + \sigma(n_i(t)) - \theta_i(a_i(t) - r_i).$$

Finally, each node is affected by a threshold value τ_i, below which it remains inactive.

12.4   Experiment

12.4.1   *Method*

Ultimately, the input to the network would be taken from a window of unanalyzed, raw text, subjected to minimal processing to remove grammatical function words and to identify root forms; or it may consist of syntactically related words (e.g., the verb and the noun-head of PP) from a partially analyzed text. However, in order to test the network, we have used a simplified case in which the input is restricted to two words only: a "context word" and a second ambiguous word. Using only two words as input enables us to better understand the behavior of the network, although with only one word of context, the disambiguation task may be more difficult. After the spreading activation algorithm is run, only one output sense node attached to each input word node is active in the network. This node should identify the *CED* sense that is intended in the given context.

We tested this strategy with 23 clearly ambiguous words, such as *ash, bay, cape*, etc., in different contexts (Figure 12.4). For each of these words, at least

WORD	CONTEXT 1	CONTEXT 2	CONTEXT 3
ash_1	*residue*	*fire*	*tobacco*
ash_2	*tree*	*branch*	*lawn*
bay_1	*peninsula*	*cape*	*sail*
bay_2	*wall*	*window*	*house*

Figure 12.4. A sample of the corpus.

two homographs (with unrelated etymologies – for example, ash_1 as residue and ash_2 as tree) exist in the *CED*. In turn, each homograph may have several different senses (ash_2, for instance, has a sense defining the ash tree itself and another defining the wood of that tree). On average, each word in our list has 2.9 homographs and 6.7 senses.

For each of the 23 words, we constructed 2 groups of 3 context words, using examples from the *Brown Corpus of American English* (Kucera and Francis, 1967) whenever possible. Each of the two groups is semantically related to one homograph. Therefore, the final experimental corpus consists of 138 word pairs.

In these experiments, we were concerned with identifying the correct homograph, rather than the correct sense within a homograph. Sense distinctions within a homograph are very often too subtle to be differentiated by the network in experiments with only one word of context, and may even be impossible for humans to distinguish. For example, the *CED* gives three senses for the second homograph of *ash:* (1) the tree, (2) the wood of that tree, and (3) any of several trees resembling the ash. In the context of the word *tree* alone, it is not clear, even for a human, which sense of *ash* is intended. Furthermore, most language processing applications would not require this level of fine semantic distinction. Because we were not interested in the exact sense selected with a homograph, we created a bias that favors the senses which appear first within each homograph (these senses are typically the most basic or common; other senses are often qualifications of the first, or metonymic uses, synecdoches, etc. – e.g., "the pen" as a style of writing). This bias is achieved with a decreasing function applied to the weights of the links between a word and its sense nodes within each homograph.

12.4.2 *Quantitative results*

The network can settle in two possible states: it can identify a disambiguated sense for the input word, or all sense nodes can "die off" after a number of cycles, thus giving no answer. We therefore need to evaluate both the *efficiency* of the method (the ratio of correct answers to the total number of word pairs) and its *reliability* (the percentage of correct answers to the total number of actual answers). We do not expect 100% efficiency, and this method will probably have to be combined with other sources to achieve perfect results.[4] However, combining sources is possible only if each is very reliable. Therefore, it is obviously better for the network to give a "don't know" answer than to give an erroneous result.

The behavior of the network was very sensitive to parameter tuning (e.g., threshold values, decay rate, etc.). In the experiments with the best results, the correct homograph was indentified in 85% of the cases (118 word pairs), which is much better than chance (39%).[5]

In 12% of the cases (16 word pairs), the network failed to identify any homograph as the correct one, because the appropriate links between words were not found. Because the purpose of dictionaries is to define individual lexical entries, much broad contextual or world knowledge is not represented in dictionary definition texts. For instance, it is interesting to note that there is no direct path between *lawn* and *house* in the *Collins English Dictionary*, although it is clear that the connection is part of human experience.

In 3% of the cases (4 word pairs) a wrong result was given because good connections exist between the wrong sense pairs. For example, the network identified the wrong sense of *ash* when given the pair *ash-tobacco*, because the connections between the "tree" sense of *ash* and *tobacco* are more direct (both are plants) than those between the "residue" sense of *ash* and *tobacco*. On logical grounds, the connection between the "tree" sense of ash and tobacco is not "wrong"; it is simply that world knowledge based on the experience of most human beings provides a stronger connection to the "residue" sense of ash. As in the case of *lawn-house*, this piece of knowledge is not directly represented in the dictionary.

12.4.3 Detailed example

Figures 12.5 and 12.6 show the state of the network after being run with *pen* and *goat*, and *pen* and *page*, respectively. The figures represent only the most activated part of each network after 100 cycles. Over the course of the run, the network reinforces only a small cluster of the most semantically relevant words and senses, and filters out the rest of the thousands of nodes. The correct sense for each word in each context (*pen* 2.1 with *goat* 1, and *pen* 1.1 with *page* 1.1) is the only one activated at the end of the run.

Sense 1.1 of *pen* would also be activated if it appeared in the context of a large number of other words – e.g., *book, ink, inkwell, pencil, paper, write, draw, sketch*, etc. – which have a similar semantic relationship to *pen*. For example, Figure 12.7 shows the state of the network after being run with *pen* and *book*. It is apparent that the subset of nodes activated is similar to those which were activated by *page*.

12.4.4 Discussion

Although our model is only preliminary, the results are promising. The network's efficiency is good (85%, or 118 correct answers out of 138 cases); its reliability is also very good (97%, or 118 correct answers out of 122 actual answers).

Our results are particularly encouraging because we can see that further improvements to the network are possible without the need for substantial processing or manual encoding. We can, for instance, further analyze definition texts

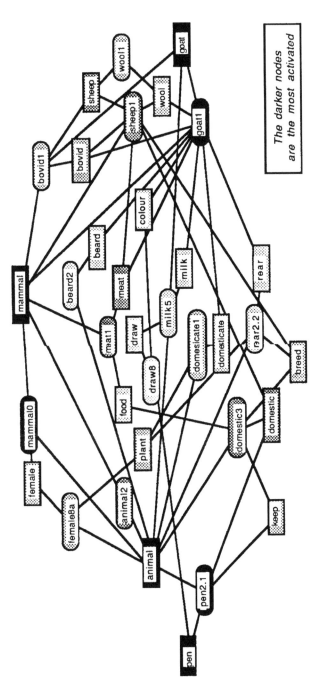

The darker nodes
are the most activated

Figure 12.5. State of the network after being run with *pen* and *goat*.

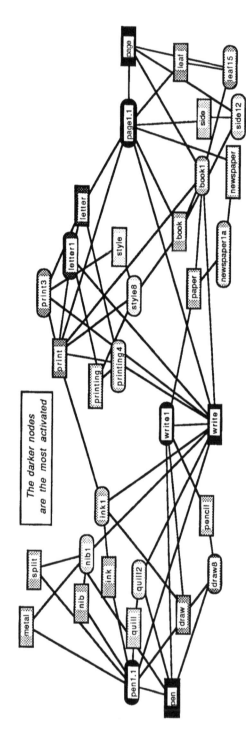

The darker nodes
are the most activated

Figure 12.6. State of the network after being run with *pen* and *page*.

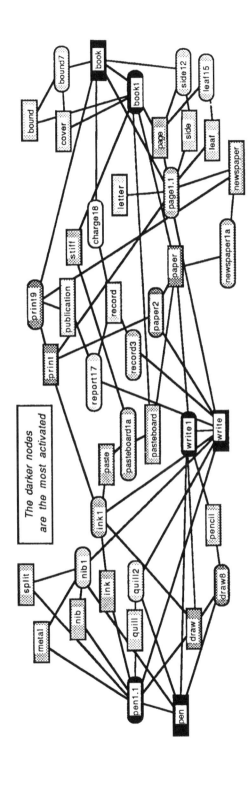

The darker nodes
are the most activated

Figure 12.7. State of the network after being run with *pen* and *book*.

to identify part of speech for each word using straightforward procedures with good efficiency (see, for example, Church, 1988; DeRose, 1988). Syntactic tags are often all the information that is needed for sense discrimination, since many words which can be used in two or more syntactic categories are unambiguous within any one category. For example, the word *bear* is ambiguous only without part of speech information; distinguishing the noun *bear* and the verb *bear* eliminates the ambiguity. The identification of syntactic categories within the network would remove many spurious connections, such as the connection mentioned earlier between *page* and *pen* through the word *bear.*

Other kinds of information could be added to the network with low processing cost. For example, the network could be augmented to provide information about genus relations, which several studies have shown to be of special importance for language understanding and disambiguation (Fass, 1988; Wilks and Fass, 1990; Iverson and Helmreich, 1992; McRoy, 1992). In our network, links between a sense and a genus word appearing in its definition could be more heavily weighted, in order to make them bear more importance in the process of sense identification. Unlike other semantic relations, genus terms can be extracted from dictionary definitions with good accuracy using a straightforward procedure requiring no sophisticated parsing (Chodorow, Byrd, and Heidorn, 1985). Similarly, links could be created between senses of words that appear together in collocations on the basis of data extracted from corpora.

It is also possible to add weight to links between a word and its preferred sense or senses, by exploiting a source such as the *COBUILD Dictionary* (which exists in machine-readable form as a part of the Vassar/CNRS database). This dictionary, constructed on the basis of word use in a 20 million word corpus of British English, lists all word senses in order of decreasing frequency of use. Domain-specific senses could also be identified using information about domain relevance such as that contained in the *Longman's Dictionary of Contemporary English* (also part of the Vassar/CNRS database). This would require the addition to the network of "domain" nodes, and/or the creation of links between word senses sharing a common domain.

Apart from adding information to the network, increasing its size can also improve its performance, since many of the failures in these experiments result from too-remote relations between the input words. As already noted, in our current implementation, the content of the network is limited to the input words, the words in their definitions, the words in the definition of these words, and the intervening sense nodes. The results may be improved with additional iterations or, ideally, with a single network covering the entire dictionary. For example, in the case of *lawn-house, garden* is not included in the network. However, since the definition of *garden* contains *house,* and at the same time shares the words *grass* and *area* with the definition of *lawn,* there would be a straightforward path between *lawn* and *house* if the entire dictionary were used. We are currently working on a large-scale implementation which would enable us to experiment with the use of a network built from an entire dictionary.

In general, our results show that a connectionnist model embodying information about word associations can contribute significantly to the process of automatic word sense disambiguation. Our model and method seem to at least partially overcome many of the shortcomings of the word association/semantic context approach, often criticized for revealing too many false paths between words or concepts, because of the "winner-take-all" strategy and the ability to adjust link weights and network parameters. Nonetheless, we realize that the approach has its limitations, and with McRoy, we believe that the best strategy will ultimately prove to be one that utilizes multiple knowledge sources. However, we are more optimistic than McRoy about the possibilities for automatic word sense disambiguation without the cost of creating massive semantic knowledge bases. McRoy herself states that their studies show the most important sources of information for word sense disambiguation are syntactic tags, morphology, collocations, and word associations. Our network currently includes two of these four sources of information (morphology and word associations), and could be augmented to include syntactic tags with little processing cost. We expect that the network with some augmentation of this kind could perform significantly better.

12.5   Conclusion

We construct networks of words and concepts from machine-readable dictionaries in order to achieve word sense disambiguation. This enables real-size experiments with models proposed previously (Cottrell and Small, 1983; Waltz and Pollack, 1985; Bookman, 1987). The good success rate in our results demonstrates the validity of the approach, and suggests that used in conjunction with other knowledge sources, it can be used effectively to disambiguate words in unrestricted text. We also show that there is no need for an additional layer of microfeatures to provide contextual information, as proposed in Waltz and Pollack (1985) and Bookman (1987). The high density of connections in a network built from dictionaries can provide adequate contextual information, especially if the entire dictionary were to be represented in the network.

Notes

1. For example, preliminary evidence shows that sense tagging of words in the input text significantly improves the performance of information retrieval systems (Krovetz, 1989).
2. This partially explains why a recent survey of existing language processing systems (excluding large machine translation systems) revealed that the average size of their lexicons is only 30 or 40 words (Boguraev and Briscoe, 1989).
3. These models integrate syntactic and semantic information in the network. Here, we are concerned only with the semantic component.

4. The use of multiple knowledge sources for word sense disambiguation is increasingly recognized as a promising strategy (McRoy, 1992).
5. Note that these results are better than those given in Ide and Véronis (1990), due to the discovery of better parameter values in later experiments.

References

Amsler, R. A. (1980). *The Structure of the Merriam-Webster Pocket Dictionary.* Ph. D. Dissertation, University of Texas at Austin.
Boguraev, B., Briscoe, T. (1989). *Computational Lexicography for Natural Language Processing.* London and New York: Longman.
Bookman, L. A. (1987). A Microfeature Based Scheme for Modelling Semantics. *Proceedings of the 10th International Joint Conference on Artificial Intelligence, IJCAI'87,* Milan, Italy, 611–614.
Byrd, R. J., Calzolari, N., Chodorov, M. S., Klavans, J. L., Neff, M. S., Rizk, O. (1987). Tools and methods for computational linguistics. *Computational Linguistics,* 13, 3/4, 219-240.
Calzolari, N.(1984). Detecting patterns in a lexical data base. *COLING'84,* 170–173.
Charniak, E. (1983). Passing markers: A theory of contextual influence in language comprehension. *Cognitive Science,* 7, 3, 171–90.
Chodorow, M. S., Byrd., R. J., Heidorn, G. E. (1985). Extracting semantic hierarchies from a large on-line dictionary. *ACL Conference Proceedings,* 299–304.
Church, K. W. (1988). A stochastic parts program and noun phrase parser for unrestricted texts. In *Proceedings of the Second Conference on Applied Natural Language Processing.* Austin, Texas, 136–143.
Cottrell, G. W., Small, S. L. (1983). A connectionist scheme for modelling word sense disambiguation. *Cognition and Brain Theory,* 6, 89–120.
DeRose, S. J. (1988) Grammatical category disambiguation by statistical optimization. *Computational Linguistics,* 14, 1, 31–39.
Fass, D. (1988). Collative semantics: A semantics for natural language processing. MCCS-88-118, Computing Research Laboratory, New Mexico State University, Las Cruces, NM.
Fillmore, C. (1968). The case for case. In Bach and Harms (Eds.), *Universals in Linguistic Theory,* Holt, Chicago, IL.
Gale, W., Church, K., Yarowsky, D. (1993). A method for disambiguating word senses in a large corpus. *Computers and the Humanities,* Special issue on Common Methodologies in Computational Linguistics and Humanities Computing, N. Ide and D. Walker, eds.
Grossberg and Carpenter (1988). The ART of Adaptive Pattern Recognition. *IEEE Computer,* 21, 3.
Halliday, M., Hasan, R. (1976). *Cohesion in English.* Longman, London.
Hirst, G. (1987). *Semantic Interpretation and the Resolution of Ambiguity.* Cambridge University Press, Cambridge.
Hopfield, J. J. (1982). Neural networks and physical systems with emergent collective computational abilities. *Proceedings of the National Academy of Sciences,* U.S.A., 79, 2554–2558.
Hopfield, J. J. (1984). Neurons with graded response have collective computational properties like those of two-state neurons. *Proceedings of the National Academy of Sciences,* U.S.A., 81, 3088–3092.
Ide, N.M., Véronis, J. (1990). Very large neural networks for word sense disambiguation. *Proceedings of the 9th European Conference on Artificial Intelligence, ECAI'90,* Stockholm, 366–368.

Iverson, E., Helmreich, S. (1992). Metallel: An integrated approach to non-literal phrase interpretation. *Computational Intelligence*, 8, 1, 477–93.

Klavans, J., Chodorow, M., Wacholder, N (1990). From dictionary to knowledge base via taxonomy. *Proceedings of the 6th Conference of the UW Centre for the New OED*, Waterloo, 110–132.

Krovetz, R. (1989). Lexical acquisition and information retrieval. *First International Lexical Acquisition Workshop*, Uri Zernick, ed.

Kucera, H., Nelson, F. W. (1967). *Computational Analysis of Present-Day American English*. Brown University Press, Providence, RI.

Lesk, M. (1986). Automated Sense Disambiguation Using Machine-readable Dictionaries: How to Tell a Pine Cone from an Ice Cream Cone. *Proceedings of the 1986 SIGDOC Conference*.

McClelland, J. L., Rumelhart, D. E. (1981). An interactive activation model of context effects in letter perception: Part I. An account of basic findings. *Psychological Review*, 88, 375–407.

McRoy, S. W. (1992). Using multiple knowledge sources for word sense discrimination. *Computational Linguistics*, 18, 1, 1–30.

Markowitz, J., Ahlswede, T., Evens, M. (1986). Semantically significant patterns in dictionary definitions. *ACL Conference Proceedings*, 112–119.

Morris, J., Hirst, G. (1991). Lexical cohesion computed by thesaural relations as an indicator of the structure of text. *Computational Linguistics*, 17, 1, 21–48.

Nakamura, J., Nagao, M. (1988). Extraction of semantic information from an ordinary English dictionary and its evaluation. *COLING'88*, 459–464.

Norvig, P. (1989). Marker passing as a weak method for text inferencing. *Cognitive Science*, 13, 4, 569–620.

Schank, R. C. (1975). *Conceptual Information Processing*. North Holland, Amsterdam.

Smith, E. E., Medin, D. L. (1981). *Categories and Concepts*. Harvard University Press, Cambridge, MA.

Véronis, J., Ide, N.M. (1991). An assessment of information automatically extracted from machine readable dictionaries, *Proceedings of the Fifth Conference of the European Chapter of the Association for Computational Linguistics*, Berlin, Germany, 227–232.

Walker, D.E., Amsler, R.A. (1986). The use of machine-readable dictionaries in sublanguage analysis. In R. Grishman and R. Kittedge (Eds.), *Analysing Language in Restricted Domains*, Lawrence Erlbaum, Hillsdale, NJ.

Waltz, D. L., Pollack, J. B. (1985). Massively parallel parsing: A strongly interactive model of natural language interpretation. *Cognitive Science*, 9, 51–74.

Wilks, Y., D. Fass (1990). Preference semantics: A family history. MCCS-90-194, Computing Research Laboratory, New Mexico State University, Las Cruces, NM.

Wilks, Y., D. Fass, C. Guo, J. MacDonald, T. Plate, B. Slator (1990). Providing machine tractable dictionary tools. In J. Pusteovsky (Ed.), *Semantics and the Lexicon*. MIT Press, Cambridge, MA.

PART IV

Lexical semantics and artificial intelligence

Lexical semantics knowledge often requires various kinds of inferences to be made in order to make more precise and more explicit the meaning of a word with respect to the context in which it is uttered. The treatment of inheritance is particularly crucial from this point of view since linguistic as well as conceptual hierarchies allow us to relate a word with more generic terms that contribute, in a certain sense, to the definition of the meaning of that word. Because hierarchies are complex, inheritance often involves non-monotonic forms of reasoning. Another relation with artificial intelligence is the development of models and techniques for the automatic acquisition of linguistic knowledge.

In "Blocking", Ted Briscoe et al. elaborate on the introduction of default inheritance mechanisms into theories of lexical organization. Blocking is a kind of inference rule that realizes a choice when two kinds of inheritances can be drawn from resources occurring at different levels in the lexical organization. For example, a general morphological rule adds -ed at the end of verbs for the past construction. A subclass of verbs consists of irregular verbs, which receive a particular mark for the past. A default rule states that the exceptional mark is preferred to the general case. However there exist verbs such as dream, which accept both flections (dreamt, dreamed). Then the default rule is no longer adequate and a more flexible solution is required. In this chapter, a framework based on a non-monotonic logic that incorporates more powerful mechanisms for resolving conflicts of various kinds is introduced. By representing conflict among feature-value pairs as default statements, this framework can support inferences that underlie blocking without making it an absolute principle of lexical organization. Furthermore, this framework provides a basis for characterizing interactions between lexical and other interpretative principles.

The idea of generativity in a lexicon is addressed within an artificial intelligence perspective in the next chapter, "A non-monotonic approach to lexical semantics", by Daniel Kayser and Hocine Abir. The basic idea is that a lexicon must contain for each word all the information that is necessary and sufficient to allow for the elaboration, by means of various inferential forms, of an adequate and sufficiently accurate meaning. Parameters for general rules of lexical adaptation and for the treatment of exceptions are introduced and several inferential forms are defined within a non-monotonic logical system.

The notion of regular polysemy is addressed in the next text, "Inheriting poly-semy", by Adam Kilgarriff. This notion is examined and defined more precisely than it was in the previous literature. A number of generalizations to capture the notions introduced by domain-dependencies make that approach more compact and productive. Finally, polysemy is contrasted with the notion of metonymy, with which it strongly overlaps.

Finally, in "Lexical semantics: Dictionary or encyclopedia?" Marc Cavazza and Pierre Zweigenbaum address the problem of the nature of lexical information and, consequently, of the types of information that should or could be included in a semantic lexicon. Preliminary results attempt to establish a link between general purpose and domain knowledge representations and linguistic data.

13 Blocking

TED BRISCOE, ANN COPESTAKE, AND
ALEX LASCARIDES

13.1 Introduction

A major motivation for the introduction of default inheritance mechanisms into
theories of lexical organization has been to account for the prevalence of the family of phenomena variously described as blocking (Aronoff, 1976:43), the elsewhere condition (Kiparsky, 1973), or preemption by synonymy (Clark & Clark,
1979:798). In Copestake and Briscoe (1991) we argued that productive processes
of sense extension also undergo the same process, suggesting that an integrated
account of lexical semantic and morphological processes must allow for blocking.
In this chapter, we review extant accounts which follow from theories of lexical
organization based on default inheritance, such as Paradigmatic Morphology
(Calder, 1989), DATR (Evans & Gazdar, 1989), ELU (Russell et al., 1991, in press),
Word Grammar (Hudson, 1990; Fraser & Hudson, 1992), or the LKB (Copestake
1992; this volume; Copestake et al., in press). We argue that these theories fail to
capture the full complexity of even the simplest cases of blocking and sketch a
more adequate framework, based on a non-monotonic logic that incorporates
more powerful mechanisms for resolving conflict among defeasible knowledge
resources (Common-sense Entailment, Asher & Morreau, 1991). Finally, we
explore the similarities and differences between various phenomena which have
been intuitively felt to be cases of blocking within this formal framework, and
discuss the manner in which such processes might interact with more general
interpretative strategies during language comprehension. Our presentation is necessarily brief and rather informal; we are primarily concerned to point out the
potential advantages using a more expressive default logic for remedying some of
the inadequacies of current theories of lexical description.

13.2 Data

The type of phenomenon which is typically discussed under the rubric of blocking
involves inflectional morphological irregularities; for example, the past participle
of *walk* is *walked* and we can describe this regular morphological operation
(roughly) in terms of a rule of concatenation <stem>+*ed*.[1] However, this rule
should not be applied either to non-verbal stems (e.g., *beast, *beasted*) or to the
subset of verbal stems which exhibit irregular behavior (e.g., *sink, sunk, *sinked;
bring, brought, *bringed; make, made, *maked*). These observations are captured
in default inheritance based approaches to the lexicon by specifying that the rule
in question applies to the subclass of verb stems, but allowing subclasses of this

class to override its application (where in the limit a subclass may consist of a specific word). Thus, the rule is interpreted as a default within a class and more specific subclasses can prevent its application via stipulative statements. In the case where a rule does not apply to a subclass or single member of the class over which it is defined the rule is said to be blocked. There are cases though, where both a morphologically irregular and regular form coexist, so that blocking cannot be treated as an absolute property of lexical organization (e.g. *dream, dreamt, dreamed; burn, burnt, burned*). Proposals for accounting for such exceptions to blocking have not treated blocking itself as a default, but have either, in effect, denied that any such general principle is at work in the lexicon by stipulating its effect on a word-by-word basis (Fraser & Hudson, 1992) or treated those verbs which allow both irregular and irregular forms as a further subclass of 'dual-class' verbs which specify an irregular variant but also inherit the regular pattern (Russell et al., 1991). Even in the clear cases of blocking the productive forms surface as common errors in the language of first and second language learners and, though we may not be happy to accept *sleeped* as a word of English, we are able to interpret utterances such as *I sleeped well* with considerably more ease than many other forms of putative ungrammaticality.

Blocking is not restricted to inflectional morphology, but appears to be pervasive throughout the lexicon: we can see its effects in derivational morphology, conversion and metonymic processes of sense extension. It appears to account for some of the semi-productivity of most synchronic, generative lexical rules (see Bauer, 1983:84f, for a discussion of other factors restricting productivity). However, blocking rarely if ever appears to be an absolute constraint on word (sense) formation. For example, there is a derivational rule of noun formation from adjectives by suffixation of +*ity* (e.g., *curious, curiosity; grammatical, grammaticality*). This rule is generally blocked by the existence of a non-derived synonymous noun (e.g., *glorious, glory, *gloriousity; tropical, tropic(s), *tropicality*). The similar rule of noun formation from adjectives by suffixation of +*ness* is apparently not blocked or not blocked to the same extent under these circumstances (e.g., *?curiousness, ?grammaticalness, ?gloriousness, ?tropicalness*). Nevertheless, there is a sense of markedness or awkwardness about such examples which is not present with forms which do not undergo noun formation with +*ity* or compete with a non-derived synonymous form (e.g., *awkwardness, markedness, weakness, kindness*). Aronoff (1976) argues that noun formation with +*ness*, in contrast to +*ity*, is fully productive, hence the lack of blocking with +*ness* forms. This account does not address the difference in acceptability between those +*ness* forms which are preempted by a synonymous underived form or one formed with +*ity*.

In general, even clearly productive derivational rules can be, at least partially, blocked. Rappaport and Levin (1990) argue convincingly that noun formation via suffixation with +*er* on verbs is highly productive and creates a meaning change where the derived noun denotes the class of objects which can serve as the verb's subject (or external argument in their terminology). Thus *teacher* denotes the agent of *teach*, whilst *opener* can denote the agent or more usually instrument of *open*. Bolinger (1975:109) cites *stealer* as an example of a form blocked by *thief*. In fact, *stealer* is fairly clearly blocked in contexts where its meaning is synonymous with *thief*, but may be used in contexts where its productively derived meaning has been specialized or modified; for example, Bauer (1983:87–8) points out that *stealer* can be used metonymically as in Shakespeare's *the ten stealers* (fingers) or when the denotation is restricted via mention of the object (e.g., *stealer of hearts/fast sports cars*).

Nominalization with +*er* also illustrates another apparent type of blocking which cannot be described as preemption by synonymy but which can be characterized as preemption by equality at some level of representation. Rappaport and Levin (1990) point out that the class of words which allow middle formation (e.g., *John stuck the poster (to the wall), The poster stuck easily (to the wall)*) tend to form nominalizations with +*er* which denote stereotypical objects, rather than subjects (e.g., *sticker, broiler, bestseller*).[2] It is difficult for these nominalizations to also denote subjects and, where this can be forced, the meaning is inherently specialized; for example, *sticker* can be used to refer to a person who is determined, as in *He is a sticker when it comes to crosswords*, but is very odd in *?He works as a sticker of posters*. Productive nominalization with +*er* can also be blocked by the existence of a non-productive sense of the derived form; for example, *stationer* means a person who sells stationery and not a person who stations, say, troops, and *banker (at Barclays)* refers to a person who works in a (senior) position in a bank, and not to one who banks his money there. In these cases, what is blocked is generation of an orthographically or phonologically identical word form with the productive meaning associated with the relevant derivational rule.

In addition to rules of derivation there are similarly productive processes of conversion and sense extension which also appear to be subject to blocking. In Briscoe and Copestake (1991) and Copestake and Briscoe (1991) we argued in detail that derivation, coercion and sense extension should be treated within the same general framework. Conversion processes are often highly productive as the host of noun-verb conversions such as *hoover* illustrate. However, derived forms such as *arrival* do not undergo this process because of the existence of *arrive*. Briscoe and Copestake (1991), Copestake and Briscoe (1991) and Ostler and Atkins (1991) argue that metonymic and metaphorical processes of sense extension must be treated as lexical rules which can undergo blocking; for example, the productive sense extension of 'grinding' (see e.g., Pelletier & Schubert, 1986), whereby a count noun denoting an individuated object becomes a mass noun denoting a substance derived from that object, when applied to animals typically denotes the meat or edible flesh of that animal (e.g., *lamb, haddock, rabbit*). However, this process is blocked by the existence of a synonymous form (e.g., *pork, pig; beef, cow*). In these cases, blocking does not prevent the more general process of grinding but makes the typical interpretation highly marked.

It seems that blocking is pervasive, or at least that use of the term in the literature is pervasive. However, all the cases we have considered appear to share some properties: blocking itself is rarely if ever absolute, and blocking is preemption of rule application by equality at some level of lexical representation. In what follows, we explore the hypothesis that a uniform account of blocking can be provided which subsumes both the morphological and lexical semantic cases.

13.3   Inadequacies of current approaches

Extant accounts of blocking in recent theories of lexical organization based on default inheritance have mostly treated blocking as an absolute principle of lexical organization. That is, if some derivational behavior is given for a class, specifying some distinct behavior for a subclass *always* has the effect of preventing the more general behavior from applying. The sole exception that we are aware of is the theory of Word Grammar (Hudson, 1990; Fraser & Hudson, 1992), which treats blocking as the exception rather than the rule. Thus, in Word Grammar, by default, the lexical rules specified for a class apply to all subclasses, even those that have been stated to have exceptional behavior – the more specific information augments, rather than overrides, the more general information. This approach would be natural if it were the case that the lexicon appeared to tolerate the rule-governed production of synonymous or homophonous words, but the cases considered in Section 13.2 suggest that this is not so. As a result, it is necessary to stipulate that blocking does occur with forms such as *sleeped*, whilst cases like *dreamed* or *curiousness* are predicted to be the norm rather than the exception. At the very least, this obliges the lexicographer to include many idiosyncratic exception statements in a lexical description (e.g., Cahill, 1992). In addition, there are theoretical reasons for believing blocking to be a general principle of lexical organization: a lexicon which did not impose some such constraint would be in danger of becoming dysfunctional with language change and development, resulting in too many distinct word forms conveying the same meaning or too many distinct meanings associated with homophonous forms.

All other theories of lexical organization which account for blocking impose it as an absolute principle. We will illustrate some approaches to blocking within default inheritance based accounts by discussing how inflectional morphology may be described within the LKB system and compare this to some other formalisms, concentrating on those which are similar to the LKB, in that lexical information is represented as feature structures (FSs). The LKB, in effect, incorporates two inheritance mechanisms – the type system, based on Carpenter (1992), enforces constraints on FSs which cannot be overridden, and psorts provide a default inheritance mechanism. Psorts are named FSs which are used in the LKB description language in a manner similar to the use of templates in PATR-II. Psorts may be specifically defined, or be ordinary lexical entries or rules, since these are also represented as FSs. In the LKB, psorts may be combined using either ordinary unification or default unification, the latter giving default inheritance (Copestake et al., in press). In this case the FS description may specify information which conflicts with that of the psort and which will override it.

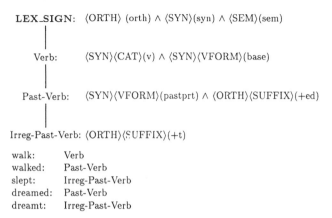

LEX_SIGN: ⟨ORTH⟩ (orth) ∧ ⟨SYN⟩(syn) ∧ ⟨SEM⟩(sem)

Verb: ⟨SYN⟩⟨CAT⟩(v) ∧ ⟨SYN⟩⟨VFORM⟩(base)

Past-Verb: ⟨SYN⟩⟨VFORM⟩(pastprt) ∧ ⟨ORTH⟩⟨SUFFIX⟩(+ed)

Irreg-Past-Verb: ⟨ORTH⟩⟨SUFFIX⟩(+t)

walk:	Verb
walked:	Past-Verb
slept:	Irreg-Past-Verb
dreamed:	Past-Verb
dreamt:	Irreg-Past-Verb

Figure 13.1. LKB psort hierarchy and lexical entries.

For ease of comparison with other untyped systems, the examples which follow are based on the use of inheritance via the psort mechanism, rather than the type mechanism. We will simply assume a most general type **lex-sign** which will constrain all the FSs representing lexical signs to have the three features ORTH, SYN and SEM. Thus, if we specify the hierarchy of psorts illustrated in Figure 13.1, Past-Verb and Irreg-Past-Verb introduce incompatible values for the feature SUFFIX so that FSs for verbs in the latter class will not be subsumed by those for Past-Verb.[3]

There are clearly some infelicities in this approach, since we are forced to associate one and only one type of FS with each type or psort and therefore cannot capture the morphological relationships between inflectional variants of a verb. For this reason, the LKB includes a notion of lexical rule which can encode essentially arbitrary mappings between FSs, and it would be more natural to treat past participle formation as a rule of this type. One possible treatment is shown in Figure 13.2. Here the inflectional variants are generated by rule application but we need to introduce a new feature MORPH on lexical signs, in order to specify the appropriate irregular forms. We also must ensure that only the correct rules apply and this is done by typing the stem values as either **regular** or **irregular**. Verb, by default, specifies that the value of <ORTH> <STEM> has to be a subtype of **regular**, but this is overridden by the psort Irregbase.

A lexical rule of past participle formation, shown in Figure 13.2, maps regular base verbs to regular past participle forms. In the LKB, lexical rules are themselves FSs, and thus can be treated as psorts and inherit information from each other, thus the lexical rule for irregular suffixation default inherits from the standard rule. A lexical rule is applicable to a FS if its input half, that is, the section of the lexical rule found by following the path <1>, is unifiable with that FS. The result of lexical rule application is indicated by the path <0>. In Figure 13.2, we assume that

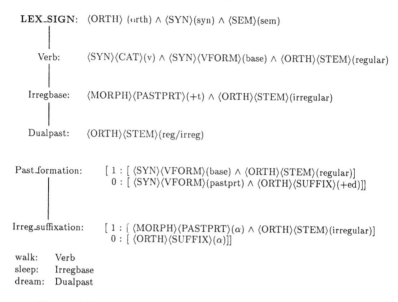

Figure 13.2. LKB lexical rules (α is a variable indicating re-entrancy).

unspecified parts of the FS are the same in the input and output. Thus the effect of the rule Past_formation is to add the suffix *ed* and to change the value of <SYN> <VFORM>. The lexical entry for *walk* simply inherits from Verb and *sleep* inherits from Irregbase. The regular lexical rule applies to *walk* but the irregular one does not, because the types **regular** and **irregular** are disjoint. Note that we have to explicitly specify the stem of *walk* as **regular** to avoid the incorrect lexical rule applying. In order to allow the regular past participle form of *dream* to be produced, we have to ensure that both lexical rules can apply, and we do this by specifying that the value for < ORTH> <STEM> for the psort Dualpast is the type **reg/irreg** which subsumes both **regular** and **irreg**. Thus *dream* has both an irregular suffix and a regular one.[4]

Although this approach is better than the first, it is still far from perfect. The lexical rule is not directly blocked by the existence of a 'competing' form, instead we have associated the existence of the irregular form with a class which also specifies that the stem is irregular, and it is this specification that blocks the application of the lexical rule. This, in turn, is overridden for dual class verbs such as *dream*. Thus we have made blocking non-absolute at the cost of increasing the complexity of the representation. A third option is to give the suffixes themselves lexical entries which are combined with the base forms in more or less the same way as word forms are combined in the grammar. This approach however suffers from much the same problem with respect to blocking.

In contrast to the LKB, ELU and DATR represent inflectional paradigms by inheritance, without introducing the concept of a lexical rule. ELU makes use of a variant set mechanism which causes a verbal class or paradigm to generate separate

Verb: $\langle$SYN$\rangle\langle$CAT$\rangle$(v) $\wedge$ $\langle$MORPH$\rangle\langle$PASTPRT$\rangle$(+ed)

$|$

$\langle$VFORM$\rangle$(base)

$|$

$\langle$VFORM$\rangle$(pastprt) $\wedge$ $\langle$ORTH$\rangle\langle$SUFFIX$\rangle(\alpha)$ $\wedge$ $\langle$MORPH$\rangle\langle$PASTPRT$\rangle(\alpha)$

Dual-past: $|$

$\langle$VFORM$\rangle$(pastprt) $\wedge$ $\langle$ORTH$\rangle\langle$SUFFIX$\rangle$(+t)

$|$

walk: Verb

sleep: Verb
$\langle$MORPH$\rangle\langle$PASTPRT$\rangle$(+t)

dream: Dual-past Verb

Figure 13.3. ELU-like fragment.

FSs for each inflectional variant. Constraints on FSs are specified as path equations and hierarchical class membership is used to enforce default inheritance so that blocking is absolute whenever a subclass introduces a constraint which clashes with that introduced by a superclass. Therefore, Russell et al. (1991) introduce a separate class of dual past verbs and treat *dream* as a member of both this and the regular class. A slight variant of their analysis is reproduced in Figure 13.3.[5] Vertical bars separating constraints indicate ELU variant sets, that is, disjunctive constraints on (distinct) FSs. The empty variant set in Dual-past allows dream to inherit all the information from Verb as well as the variant specified by Dual-past. The order of inheritance in this example is dependent on textual order – that is, dream inherits first from Dual-past and then from Verb. An equivalent approach would be to make Dual-past inherit from Verb. This would be slightly more elegant, because it would remove the need to specify that the lexical entries inherited from two classes, and avoid the dependency on textual order. However, in both cases the same form of redundancy is present in the analysis as in the LKB description already considered: the irregular past specification has been made in several parts of the lexical description in order to circumvent the absolute effects of blocking.

DATR (Evans & Gazdar, 1989) also employs a notion of hierarchical class membership to specify lexical entries and to control default inheritance. However, unlike the LKB and ELU, DATR is a language which is intended to be specific to lexical representation and to be usable by any grammar which can be encoded in terms of attributes and values. DATR does not specify or manipulate FSs directly – DATR queries result in the values of paths at particular nodes being returned. There are essentially two components – a monotonic component which explicitly specified values for paths and a non-monotonic operation of path closure which can intuitively be thought of as 'filling in the gaps' to give values for all node/path pairs not defined in the theory. However, despite the differences between DATR and the other theories, similar redundancy arises as in the analyses sketched here when we attempt to account in a straightforward way for alternative forms such as *dreamed* and *dreamt*, since the specification of a value for a node blocks any alternative inherited value.

To summarize, the inelegancy and redundancy in these descriptions arises from the fact that each is forced to treat blocking as an absolute constraint enforced via default inheritance. The undesirable effects of this are circumvented by introducing additional classes which are otherwise unmotivated. Less restricted approaches such as those of Daelemans (1987) or de Smedt (1984) might, in principle, be able to use additional object-oriented techniques to achieve a less redundant lexical description, by allowing the option of accumulating rather than overriding inherited information, for example. However, this is difficult to evaluate in view of the open-ended nature of these techniques. Furthermore, it is far from clear that any inheritance based treatment of blocking can allow for the examples discussed in the previous section where the lexical item responsible for the blocking of the productive process is morphologically unrelated (e.g., *stealer/thief, pig/pork*). This would imply that we would have to structure the lexicon so that, for example, *thief* was related to *steal* by some form of the process of *+er* nominalization. Clearly there is some semantic relationship, but requiring that a relationship between the lexical items as a whole be specified directly as though it were a variant of the productive process is very unappealing.

13.4   A new framework

In this section, we outline a novel approach to lexical description in which we utilize a default logic as a constraint language on possible lexical entries specified as FSs. (For a detailed description of constraint-based languages in linguistic description, see Shieber, 1992.) Within this framework we believe that it is possible to characterize blocking more satisfactorily. The default logic that we utilize is the propositional variant of Commonsense Entailment (CE, Asher & Morreau, 1991). This logic is appropriate because we can encode FSs using nominal modal propositional logic (Blackburn, 1992a,b); CE supports the patterns of default reasoning required to characterize blocking; and the propositional variant is decidable which is one crucial (and minimal) requirement for a theory of lexical description.

13.4.1   *A language for describing FSs*

Blackburn (1992a,b) demonstrates that attribute value structures expressed as directed graphs are, in effect, languages of propositional modal logic in which attributes are modal operators and values are propositional variables. Furthermore, he proves that the subset of attribute value structures that can be expressed as directed acyclic graphs (DAGs) incorporating re-entrancy are characterized by the nominal propositional modal logic (NPL). This is a modal logic augmented with an atomic propositional variable sort called *nominals*, where a nominal is

$$
\begin{bmatrix}
\text{ORTH} = \begin{bmatrix} \text{STEM} = \textbf{sleep} \end{bmatrix} \\
\text{SYN} = \begin{bmatrix}
\text{CAT} = \textbf{verb} \\
\text{SUBJ} = \begin{bmatrix} \text{SYN} = \begin{bmatrix} \text{CAT} = \textbf{np} \end{bmatrix} \\ \text{SEM} = \boxed{1}\ \textbf{obj} \end{bmatrix} \\
\text{VFORM} = \textbf{base}
\end{bmatrix} \\
\text{SEM} = \begin{bmatrix} \text{PRED} = \textbf{sleep} \\ \text{ARG1} = \boxed{1} \end{bmatrix}
\end{bmatrix}
$$

Figure 13.4. FS for *sleep*.

constrained to be true on a unique node. Blackburn (1992b) discusses why modal logics are particularly natural ways of describing FSs. In effect, the standard notations for describing FSs, such as AVMs, assume an internal view: that describing what happens at arbitrary nodes, the graph structure is described in terms of transitions from some particular node. Thus these notations are equivalent to a language where all quantifiers are bounded and the richness of the variable binding machinery of the first order languages is unnecessary. Modal operators and AVMs both precisely capture this restriction. Blackburn's results extend those of Kaspar and Rounds (1990) and others concerning the logical characterization of unification-based formalisms utilizing DAGs (e.g. Shieber, 1986).

In what follows, we develop a theory in which lexical signs are encoded as FSs; that is, DAGs incorporating re-entrancy. And we utilize a notational variant of NPL to describe FSs. An example of a lexical entry represented as a FS in AVM notation is given in Figure 13.4. We will mostly refer to such FSs as lexical signs and assume that all such signs are minimally specified for ORTH, SYN and SEM (e.g., Pollard & Sag, 1987).

Descriptions in NPL can be partial in the sense that more than one FS may satisfy a set of NPL formulas; we will use a sorted version of NPL, in order to achieve the required fine-grainedness of descriptions, in which a partial specificity ordering induces a lattice over propositional variables from which we can derive a subsumption relation (Mellish, 1988). The minimal model which satisfies a lexical description will correspond to the set of well-formed FSs or lexical signs according to that description. The sortal axioms in (1) define some useful sorts and values for verbal features.

(1) a *vform $\equiv$ base $\sqcup$ finite $\sqcup$ infinite $\sqcup$ pastprt $\sqcup$ pass $\sqcup$ presprt*

     b *suffix $\equiv$ +ed $\sqcup$ +t $\sqcup$ ...*

     c *stem $\equiv$ vstem $\sqcup$ nstem $\sqcup$ ...*

     d *vstem $\equiv$ walk $\sqcup$ dream $\sqcup$ sleep $\sqcup$ ...*

     e *irregvstem $\equiv$ dream $\sqcup$ sleep $\sqcup$ ...*

     f *dualvstem $\equiv$ dream $\sqcup$ ...*

     g *cat $\equiv$ verb $\sqcup$ noun $\sqcup$ ...*

A partial description of the class of FSs that we have been assuming for verbs is given in (2).

(2)   <SYN>(<CAT>(verb) ∧ <VFORM>(vform)) ∧ <ORTH><STEM>(vstem)

Modal operators representing attributes are written in uppercase between angle
brackets, propositional variables are lowercase, and round brackets, delimiting the
scope of operators, are mostly suppressed where this is unambiguous. This
description is satisfied by any of the FSs containing values for CAT, VFORM and
STEM subsumed by the propositional variables 'verb', 'vform' and 'vstem', such
as that in Figure 13.4. We can define the closure of a lexical description as the set
of FSs which satisfy all theorems of that description. An algorithm for computing
(membership of) this set can be defined in terms of substitutions of atomic propositional variables (such as 'verb' in the sort system defined in (1)) guided by the
subsumption relation. Whether the closure of a lexical description remains finite
will depend, first, on the finiteness of the sort system and, second, on the manner
in which we restrict the inference mechanisms available via the constraint language.

   In general, to properly constrain the set of lexical signs compatible with a
description, it will be necessary to specify re-entrancy or structure sharing within
and between lexical signs. Blackburn (1992a) uses nominals, denoted by alpha-
betical indices, to describe re-entrant FSs. Thus, the FS in Figure 13.4 specifies
that ARG1 of the predicate 'sleep' is the same as the value of SEM under SUBJ. A
constraint enforcing this equivalence is given in (3).

(3)   <SEM> <ARG1> (i) ∧ <SYN> <SUBJ> < SEM> (i)

   We will use NPL to model the lexicon as a whole, including the relationships
between individual lexical signs. We will employ a notion of lexical rule similar
to that presented in Pollard and Sag (1987:209f) in which such rules are treated
as conditional assertions relating one (basic) lexical sign to another (derived) lexical sign. (This notion of lexical rule is essentially equivalent in expressive power
to that utilized in the LKB, allowing arbitrary relationships between FSs to be specified.) We represent this in terms of a structure where derived signs 'fan out' from
the basic signs, using a conventionally named set of modal operators, LR1, LR2
. . . LRn, in order to denote the transitions described by the different lexical rules.
In NPL, we can express the fact that conjunctive constraints must hold for a single
lexical sign by naming the superordinate node in the DAG corresponding to the
appropriate FS. For example, (4) illustrates a simple lexical rule for past participle
formation expressed in NPL: here i, j and k are metavariables ranging over nominals. Models corresponding to descriptions which include lexical rules may
include more than one FS to which the rule has been applied.

(4) $(i \rightarrow$ (<SEM> (j) ∧ <ORTH> <STEM> (k) ∧ <SYN> <VFORM> $(base)))$
           $\rightarrow$
           $(i \rightarrow$
           (<LR1> (<SYN> <VFORM> (pastprt) ∧ <SEM> (j)
                        ∧ <ORTH> (<STEM>(k) ∧ <SUFFIX> (+$ed)))))$

In this framework, we are treating lexical rules as constraints on connected FSs containing one basic and further derived lexical entries connected by a distinguished attribute naming the relevant rule. This notation is verbose, so we will represent lexical rules using more familiar AVM notation in which boxed values translate as nominals and standard AVM formating conventions are used to indicate the scope of modal operators, conjunction, and so forth (Blackburn, 1992a). Rather than explicitly indicating the conventional modal operators, LR1 etc., we will use the syntax $\rightarrow_{LR1}$ etc. to indicate that the implied feature structure is connected by an LR operator. We will also omit the explicit specification of the outermost nominal (i) in the AVM diagrams; thus (4) will become (5).

(5)
$$
\begin{bmatrix}
\text{ORTH} = \begin{bmatrix} \text{STEM} = \boxed{k} \end{bmatrix} \\
\text{SYN} = \begin{bmatrix} \text{CAT} = verb \\ \text{VFORM} = base \end{bmatrix} \\
\text{SEM} = \boxed{j}
\end{bmatrix}
\rightarrow_{LR1}
\begin{bmatrix}
\text{ORTH} = \begin{bmatrix} \text{STEM} = \boxed{k} \\ \text{SUFFIX} = +ed \end{bmatrix} \\
\text{SYN} = \begin{bmatrix} \text{CAT} = verb \\ \text{VFORM} = pastprt \end{bmatrix} \\
\text{SEM} = \boxed{j}
\end{bmatrix}
$$

13.4.2 *Default logic as a constraint language*

The lexical rule of past participle formation in (5) is far too strong since it does not hold of all (English) verbs and would therefore produce many linguistically unmotivated FSs. The approach taken in theories of lexical description based on default inheritance is, first, to restrict the domain of application of such a constraint to a subclass of verbs and, second, to allow the constraint to be overridden on stipulated further sub-classes or cases. We can restrict the application of a rule such as (5) to an appropriate subclass via the sort system and we can express its default nature by relaxing $\rightarrow$ to default implication (>), as in (6) ($\varphi > \psi$ is to be read as *If φ then by default, ψ*).

(6)
$$
\begin{bmatrix}
\text{ORTH} = \begin{bmatrix} \text{STEM} = \boxed{k} \end{bmatrix} \\
\text{SYN} = \begin{bmatrix} \text{CAT} = verb \\ \text{VFORM} = base \end{bmatrix} \\
\text{SEM} = \boxed{j}
\end{bmatrix}
>_{LR1}
\begin{bmatrix}
\text{ORTH} = \begin{bmatrix} \text{STEM} = \boxed{k} \\ \text{SUFFIX} = +ed \end{bmatrix} \\
\text{SYN} = \begin{bmatrix} \text{CAT} = verb \\ \text{VFORM} = pastprt \end{bmatrix} \\
\text{SEM} = \boxed{j}
\end{bmatrix}
$$

Default logics incorporate a rule of defeasible modus ponens (DMP: $\varphi > \psi$, $\varphi \models \psi$, where $\models$ stands for non-monotonic validity) which ensures that within the class of verbs *vstem*, (6) will apply unless the result is inconsistent with the premises. We cannot, though, prevent the application of (6) to irregular verbs merely by adding the more specific rule in (7).

(7)
$$
\begin{bmatrix}
\text{ORTH} = \begin{bmatrix} \text{STEM} = {}_{irregvstem} \wedge \boxed{k} \end{bmatrix} \\
\text{SYN} = \begin{bmatrix} \text{CAT} = {}_{verb} \\ \text{VFORM} = {}_{base} \end{bmatrix} \\
\text{SEM} = \boxed{j}
\end{bmatrix}
>_{LR2}
\begin{bmatrix}
\text{ORTH} = \begin{bmatrix} \text{STEM} = \boxed{k} \\ \text{SUFFIX} = {}_{+t} \end{bmatrix} \\
\text{SYN} = \begin{bmatrix} \text{CAT} = {}_{verb} \\ \text{VFORM} = {}_{pastprt} \end{bmatrix} \\
\text{SEM} = \boxed{j}
\end{bmatrix}
$$

This is because as things stand, there is no statement in the premises asserting that the consequents of (6) and (7) don't usually both hold in any given knowledge base (KB). So no inconsistency arises through the application of DMP to both (6) and (7) (which we can represent schematically as $\varphi > \psi$, $\chi > \zeta$, φ, $\chi \vDash \psi$, ζ). Therefore, as the system stands we do not incorporate blocking. And, in fact, this is the result that we want because, although we intuitively understand these values for SUFFIX to be in conflict, the existence of forms such as *dreamed* and *dreamt* tells us that we do not want this conflict to be as strong as logical inconsistency. In order to create a conflict, we can include a further constraint (8), which represents the effect of blocking in irregular past participle formation.

(8)   < LR2>(<ORTH>(<STEM>(irregvstem)   ∧   <SUFFIX>(+t)))   >
         ¬<LR1>(<ORTH>(<STEM>(irregvstem) ∧ <SUFFIX>(+ed)))

(8) captures the intuition that the SUFFIXs +t and +ed are usually, but not always, in conflict. The motivation for including (8) is to override the default application of (6) in appropriate circumstances. In fact, this is an inference that will not follow in all theories of default logic. However, we postpone detailed discussion of the precise theory of non-monotonic reasoning required to validate the desired patterns of reasoning until Section 13.4.4. In addition, we want irregular past participle formation to continue to apply. The (minimal) pattern of reasoning required is thus schematized in (9).

(9)   a $\varphi_{ls} > \psi_{ss} \wedge \psi_o$
         b $\chi_{ls} > \zeta_{ss} \wedge \zeta_o$
         c $\zeta_o > \neg \psi_o$
         d $\varphi_{ls} \sqsupset \chi_{ls}$
         e χ_{ls}
         f $\vDash \zeta_{ls}$
             $\nvDash \psi_{ls}$

Lowercase Greek symbols range over lexical signs and subscripts are used to refer to the values of paths, SYN and SEM (φ_{ss}) and ORTH (φ_o) within a derived lexical sign (φ_{ls}). In this case, (9a, b) represent the rules of regular and irregular past participle formation respectively. (9d, e) follow from the sort system, and (9c) represents the blocking constraint for past participle formation, that is, the default rule (8). However, note that $>_{LR1}$ is a special case of > so that the schema can be thought of as generalizing over all lexical rules (and other defeasible conditionals) in the description language. When we have an irregular verb (χ) we wish to conclude that we have an irregular derived past participle (ζ) and to prevent the derivation of a regular past participle (ψ); that is, not infer ψ and optionally infer $\neg\psi$. (9c) is a specific default rule relevant to the blocking of regular past formation by irregular past participle formation. In Section 13.5 we argue that this and many other blocking rules can be derived from an indefeasible principle of blocking, so it is not necessary to stipulate all the specific rules required to implement every individual case of blocking.

13.4.3 *Unblocking*

The fact that specific blocking rules, such as (8), are defaults can be exploited to develop a more elegant and conceptually clearer account of 'unblocking', where 'competing' rules do both fire. In the case of dual past verbs, such as *dream*, given the sort system defined in (5) the dual past class of verbs are subsumed by the class of irregular verbs. Therefore, these verbs will be treated like *sleep* with respect to past participle formation. In order to unblock regular past participle formation for these verbs we can override the blocking default by explicitly adding the assertion that dual past verbs are exceptional in that they tolerate both regular and irregular past participle forms. This information is represented in (10).

(10)   <LR2> (<ORTH> (<STEM>(dualvstem) $\wedge$ <SUFFIX>(+t))) $\rightarrow$
        <LR1> (<ORTH> (<SUFFIX> (+ed))))

By adding (10), we introduce an indefeasible assertion concerning dual class verbs' orthographic forms which will override the blocking default rule of (8), since indefeasible information always has priority over defeasible information (that is, supported in all non-monotonic logics). The schematic pattern of inference involves the addition of the subsumption relation and (XXX) to the pattern given in (9), as (11) illustrates.

(11)   a $\varphi_{ls} > \psi_{ss} \wedge \psi_o$
        b $\chi_{ls} > \zeta_{ss} \wedge \zeta_o$
        c $\zeta_o > \neg\psi_o$
        d $\delta_o \wedge \psi_o$
        e $\varphi_{ls} \sqsupset \chi_{ls}$
        f $\chi_{ls} \sqsupset \delta_{ls}$
        g δ_{ls}
        h $\vDash \zeta_{ls}, \psi_{ls}$

The unblocking constraint is represented in (11d) and will prevent application of the blocking default in (11c), thus both (11a) and (11d) will apply to dual class verbs. So far, we have developed an account in which dual past verbs can be represented as a subclass of irregular verbs and the regular and irregular rules of past participle formation need only be stated once.

13.4.4   *Choosing a suitable logic*

We have proposed that to account for blocking, the statements about conflict among feature values must be defeasible. This had ramifications on the inferences we need to validate, and hence on the kind of logic that will be suitable. In this section, we introduce a logic for defeasible reasoning called commonsense entailment (or CE) (Asher and Morreau, 1991), and argue that for our purposes it has certain features that make it more attractive than other candidate logics. In particular, we'll suggest that CE's logical consequence relation supports the patterns of inference (9) and (11) in a straightforward and more elegant way than the other candidate logics.

The default constraint language that we use is a sorted version of NPL, augmented with a non-monotonic conditional operator >; CE supplies a modal semantics for such default formulas. Intuitively, $\varphi > \psi$ is read as *If φ then normally ψ*. The constraint language incorporates two logical consequence relations. The first relation is represented as $\models$; it is monotonic and supra-classical. It applies to the truth conditional component of the logic, and supports intuitively compelling monotonic patterns of inference involving defeasible statements, such as Facticity.

- Facticity: $\models \varphi > \varphi$

In words, Facticity validates *If φ then normally φ*.

The second logical consequence relation is non-monotonic and written as $\approx$. It underlies a partial dynamic theory of belief, which is defined on top of the truth conditional semantics for defeasible statements. It supports intuitively compelling patterns of defeasible inference, such as the following:

- Defeasible Modus Ponens: $\varphi > \psi, \varphi \approx \psi$
  (e.g., birds normally fly, Tweety is a bird $\approx$ Tweety flies)
- The Penguin Principle: $\varphi > \psi, \chi > \neg\psi, \chi \rightarrow \varphi, \chi \approx \neg\psi$
  (e.g., birds fly, penguins don't fly, penguins are birds, Tweety is a penguin $\approx$ Tweety doesn't fly.)
- The Nixon Diamond: $\varphi > \psi, \chi > \neg\psi, \varphi, \chi \not\approx \psi$ (and $\not\approx \neg\psi$)
  (e.g., Quakers are pacificists, Republicans are non-pacifists, Nixon is a Quaker and Republican $\not\approx$ Nixon is a pacifist, and $\not\approx$ Nixon is a non-pacifist.)

Defeasible Modus Ponens captures the intuition that one can infer the consequent of a default rule if it is consistent with what is already known. The Penguin Principle contains two conflicting default rules in the premises, in that the consequents of both laws cannot hold in a consistent knowledge base (KB). The antecedents of these rules are logically related because χ entails φ; in this sense $\chi > \neg\psi$ is more specific than $\varphi > \psi$. The Penguin Principle therefore captures the intuition that one prefers specific defaults to general ones when they conflict. The Nixon Diamond is like the Penguin Principle in that two conflicting default laws apply. However it differs in that these default laws do not stand in a relation of specificity to each other. CE is a logic where no conclusion is drawn under these circumstances without further information. In other words, it supports the intuition that conflict among default laws is irresolvable when they're unrelated.

The way CE is set up gives at least two advantages over other logics for defeasible reasoning. First, it splits the monotonic component of the theory from the non-monotonic component, and this can, on occasion, prove conceptually useful when the premises form complex logical structures. Second, unlike Hierarchical Autoepistemic Logic (Konolige, 1988) and Prioritized Circumscription (McCarthy, 1980; Lifschitz, 1984), it captures the Penguin Principle without the intervention of a device which is extraneous to the semantic machinery. We find this latter property of CE attractive, since intuitively, whatever kind of reasoning default reasoning is, that more specific information takes precedence is intrinsic to it and so should be captured in the semantics of defaults.

We will shortly give a brief description of the way the dynamic partial theory of belief supports non-monotonic patterns of inference, and in particular how it supports the inferences (9) and (11). But first, we consider the truth conditional component of the theory. The semantics of defeasible statements are defined in terms of a function *from worlds and propositions to propositions. This function forms part of the model. And intuitively, $*(w,p)$ is the set of worlds where the proposition p holds together with everything else which, in world w, is normally the case when p holds. So *encodes assumptions about normality. The truth conditions of defeasible statements are defined as follows:

- $M,w \vDash \varphi > \psi$ if and only if $*(w, [\![\varphi]\!]) \subseteq [\![\psi]\!]$

In words, this says that *If φ then normally ψ* is true with respect to a model M at a possible world w if the set of worlds that defines what is normally the case when φ is true in w all contain the information that ψ is also true. Thus CE is a conditional logic in the Acqvist (1972) tradition; it differs from previous conditional logics in the constraints it puts on *.

There are two constraints: the first is Facticity, which intuitively states that however few propositions normally hold when p is the case, one of them is p.

- Facticity: $*(w,p) \subseteq p$

This constraint enables the monotonic inference Facticity stated previously to be verified. The second constraint is Specificity: it is essential for capturing the Penguin Principle as we will see shortly. It expresses the intuition that penguins aren't normal birds, because penguins don't have the flying property associated with normal birds. To see this, think of p as *Tweety is a penguin*, and q as *Tweety is a bird*; so $*(w,p)$ is *Tweety is a normal penguin* and $*(w,q)$ is *Tweety is a normal bird*.

- Specificity: If $p \subseteq q$ and $*(w,p) \cap *(w,q) = \emptyset$, then $*(w,q) \cap p = \emptyset$

The dynamic semantics of information states is set up so that intuitively, Defeasible Modus Ponens goes as follows: first, one assumes the premises φ>ψ and φ and no more than this. Second, one assumes that φ is as normal as is consistent with these premises. Finally, from these two assumptions, one concludes that ψ. The theory makes precise the notion of assuming no more than the premises of an argument (in terms of an update function), and assuming everything is as normal as is consistent with those premises (in terms of a normalization function). Information states are considered to be sets of possible worlds. The update function + is defined on an information state s and a set of WFFS Γ, and it outputs a new information state that supports everything in the old information state as well as supporting Γ.

- Update Function: $s + \Gamma = \{w \in s : w \vDash \Gamma\}$

The normalization function N uses a definition of $*$ on information states (as opposed to possible worlds):

- Definition of $*$ on information states: $*(s,p) = \cup_{\omega \in \sigma} *(w,p)$

N takes an information state s and a WFF φ as input, and it outputs a new information state s'. Intuitively, s' isolates those worlds in s where either φ isn't true at all, or it's true but normal, if there are any worlds where φ is normal; otherwise it 'gives up' and simply returns the original state s.

- The Normalization function:
  $N(s,\varphi) = \{w \in s : w \notin \in [\![\varphi]\!] \setminus *(s,[\![\varphi]\!])\}$ if $*(s,[\![\varphi]\!]) \cap s \neq \emptyset$
  $= s$ otherwise

Or to put it another way, if it is consistent in s to assume that φ is normal (and therefore by Facticity it is also consistent to assume φ is true), then $N(s,\varphi)$ eliminates all those worlds from s where φ is true but abnormal. So normalization is the process where one revises the information state to include the assumption that φ is as normal as possible, given what is already known. Pictorially, we can represent the effect of normalization as in Figure 13.5, where the shaded areas define the value of $N(s,\varphi)$.

Suppose one knows the premises Γ. Then from the normalization function, one can build a normalization *chain* for Γ. First, one orders the antecedents of the default rules in Γ into a sequence μ. One then builds the normalization chain by repeated applications of N: one applies N to the current information state and the first element in μ; then one applies N to the result of this first application of N, and the *second* element in μ; and so on until one reaches a fixed point (such a point will be reached since N is non-increasing). In order to see what non-monotonically follows from the premises Γ, one starts with the information state ☺+Γ, where ☺ is the information state containing nothing but the laws of logic, and one sees what holds in all the fixed points of all the normalization chains for all possible enumerations μ.[6] In propositional CE, $\vDash$ and $\vDash$ are both sound, complete and decidable (see Lascarides and Asher, in press).

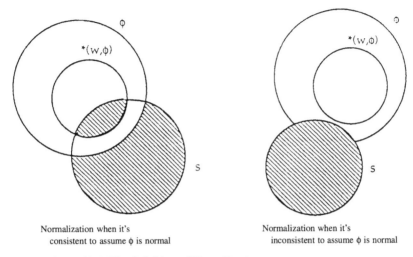

Figure 13.5. The definition of Normalization.

To clarify this, let's see informally how ∗, + and N interact to ensure that ⊨ supports The Penguin Principle. Let $\Gamma = \{\varphi{>}\psi, \chi{>}\neg\psi, \chi \rightarrow \varphi, \chi\}$ (i.e., the premises of a Penguin Principle). Then there are essentially two possible enumerations μ_1 and μ_2, where in the former we normalize on χ first and then on φ, and in the latter we normalize on φ first and then χ. Consider the normalization chain for μ_1. We must first calculate the value of the function $N(\ominus +\Gamma,\chi)$. Note that $\ominus$ +Γ contains worlds where χ is normal, and so the first clause in the definition of N applies. Thus, given the truth definition of $\chi{>}\neg\psi$, $N(\ominus +\Gamma,\chi) = s$ for some information state s that is contained in $[\![\,\neg\psi\,]\!]$. Pictorially, s corresponds to the shaded areas in the diagram in Figure 13.6.

Now we must work out the value s' of $N(s,\varphi)$. Since $s \subseteq [\![\,\neg\psi\,]\!]$, and by the definition of $\varphi > \psi$ ∗$(w,[\![\,\varphi\,]\!]) \subseteq [\![\,\psi\,]\!]$, there are no worlds in s where φ is normal. This situation is depicted in Figure 13.7: the second clause in the definition of N applies. Therefore $s' = s$, and so it also supports $\neg\psi$. Since N is non-increasing, it should be clear that $\neg\psi$ will be in the fixed point of this normalization chain.

Now consider the enumeration μ_2. We must first work out the value of $N(\ominus +\Gamma,\varphi)$. By the truth conditions of $\varphi\psi$ and $\chi > \neg\psi$, ∗$(w,[\![\,\varphi\,]\!]) \cap ∗(w,[\![\,\chi\,]\!]) = \emptyset$. And $\chi \rightarrow \varphi$ means that $[\![\,\chi\,]\!] \subseteq [\![\,\varphi\,]\!]$. So the Specificity Constraint on ∗ applies here; for all worlds w in $\ominus+\Gamma$, ∗$(w,[\![\,\varphi\,]\!]) \cap [\![\,\chi\,]\!] = \emptyset$. But $\ominus+\Gamma \subseteq [\![\,\chi\,]\!]$. So there are no worlds in $\ominus+\Gamma$ where φ is normal. Therefore $N(\ominus+\Gamma,\varphi) = \ominus+\Gamma$. Now we calculate the value of $N(\ominus+\Gamma,\chi)$, and as before, $N(\ominus+\Gamma,\chi) \subseteq [\![\,\neg\psi\,]\!]$. So this normalization chain also supports $\neg\psi$ in its fixed point. From this brief sketch, one can intuitively see that ⊨ supports the Penguin Principle, since $\neg\psi$ holds in all fixed points of all normalization chains. What's more, it has done so without having to assume a particular order of application of the default rules. This is in sharp

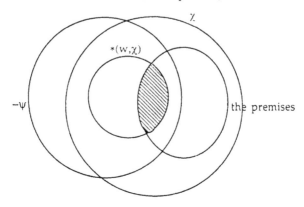

Figure 13.6. The Penguin Principle: application of N to χ with respect to sequence μ_1.

contrast to HAEL and Prioritized Circumscription. In these logics, one must constrain the reasoning process so that one applies the more specific default rule first, which then blocks applying the second more general rule.

The advantages of having specificity baked into the semantics of default statements really come into their own when one considers the pattern of inference in (12), which we claim underlies blocking.

(12)   a $\varphi_{ls} > \psi_{ss} \wedge \psi_o$
         b $\chi_{ls} > \zeta_{ss} \wedge \zeta_o$
         c $\zeta_o > \neg\psi_o$
         d $\varphi_{ls} \sqsupset \chi_{ls}$
         e χ_{ls}
         f $\models \zeta_{ls}$
            $\not\models \psi_{ls}$

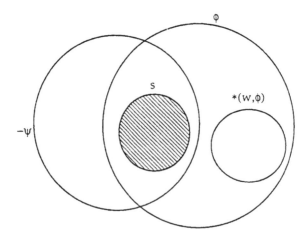

Figure 13.7. The Penguin Principle: application of N to φ with respect to sequence μ_1.

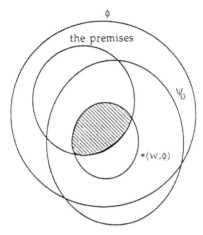

Figure 13.8. Blocking: Normalizing on the general default first.

To see this, we will indicate how CE supports (12), and then briefly consider how HAEL and prioritized circumscription would deal with it. Let the premises in (12) be Γ. There are three default rules in Γ, making six possible enumerations. First consider the enumeration μ_1 where we normalize in the order: $\varphi_{ls}, \chi_{ls}, \zeta_o$. The Specificity Constraint doesn't apply here, since even though the premises entail $[\![\, \chi_{ls} \,]\!] \subseteq [\![\, \varphi_{ls} \,]\!]$, they don't allow us to assume $*(w,[\![\, \varphi_{ls} \,]\!]) \cap *(w,[\![\, \chi_{ls} \,]\!]) = \emptyset$. So we cannot assume $*(w,[\![\, \varphi_{ls} \,]\!]) \cap [\![\, \chi_{ls} \,]\!] = \emptyset$. Therefore, the first clause in the definition of N applies when calculating $N(\ominus+\Gamma,\varphi_{ls})$, for there are worlds in $\ominus+\Gamma$ where φ_{ls} is normal. So $N(\ominus+\Gamma,\varphi_{ls}) = s$ where $s \subseteq [\![\, \psi_{ss} \wedge \psi_o \,]\!]$. This normalization is depicted in Figure 13.8, where s is characterized by the shaded areas.

Now s must contain worlds where χ_{ls} is normal, since this is consistent with what is known, and therefore $N(s,\chi_{ls}) = s'$, where $s' \subseteq [\![\, \zeta_{ss} \wedge \zeta_o \,]\!]$. Normalization on the specific default is given in Figure 13.9: s' is the shaded area.

Furthermore N is non-increasing, and so $s' \subseteq s \subseteq [\![\, \psi_o \,]\!]$. By the truth conditions of (12c), $*(w,[\![\, \zeta_o \,]\!]) \cap [\![\, \psi_o \,]\!] = \emptyset$. So there are no worlds in s' where ζ_o is normal. Therefore $N(s',\zeta_o) = s'$. Thus the final link in the normalization chain is depicted in Figure 13.10. In fact, the fixed point of this normalization chain μ_1 contains $[\![\, \zeta_{ls} \,]\!]$ and $[\![\, \psi_{ls} \,]\!]$.

Now consider the enumeration μ_2, where we normalize in the order: $\chi_{ls}, \zeta_o, \varphi_{ls}$. $N(\ominus+\Gamma,\chi_{ls}) = s$, where $s \subseteq [\![\, \zeta_{ss} \wedge \zeta_o \,]\!]$. And $N(s,\zeta_o) = s'$, where $s' \subseteq [\![\, \neg\psi_o \,]\!]$. By the truth definition of (12a), $*(w,\varphi_{ls}) \cap [\![\, \neg\psi_{ls} \,]\!] = \emptyset$. So s' doesn't contain any worlds where φ_{ls} is normal (because $s' \subseteq [\![\, \neg\psi_o \,]\!] \subseteq [\![\, \neg\psi_{ls} \,]\!]$). So $N(s',\varphi_{ls}) = s'$. In fact, the fixed point of this normalization chain μ_2 contains $[\![\, \zeta_{ls} \,]\!]$ and $[\![\, \neg\psi_{ls} \,]\!]$.

These normalization chains show that the following holds, as we required in (12):

- $\Gamma \not\vdash \psi_{ls}$
  $\Gamma \not\vdash \neg\psi_{ls}$

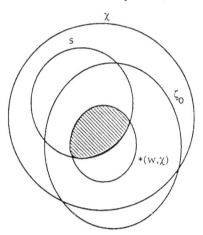

Figure 13.9. Blocking: Normalizing on the specific default second.

In fact, using a similar line of reasoning, the other four normalization chains lead to fixed points that all support ζ_{ls} (the details are omitted for reasons of space). So the following also holds, as we require:

- $\Gamma \models \zeta_{ls}$

Hence the pattern of inference (12), which underlies lexical blocking, is supported in CE. So CE provides a suitable default logic with which to formalize the constraint language.

There are other candidate logics for defeasible reasoning, so why choose CE? Let's assess how the other logics deal with (12). A few comments about the log-

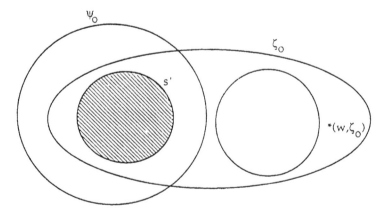

Figure 13.10. Blocking: Normalizing on the blocking default last.

ical structure of (12) will help clarify the discussion. The default rule (12a) is more specific than (12b) because of (12d). Furthermore, because of (12c), the consequents of these rules *conflict by default*. The inference in (12) resolves this conflict in favor of the more specific rule. So a logic will be adequate for our purposes only if it has the means to resolve conflict. Not all logics for defeasible reasoning have this facility; for example, Reiter's (1980) default logic, autoepistemic logic (Moore, 1984) and circumscription (McCarthy, 1980). There are at least two logics apart from CE that have the facility to resolve conflict among defeasible rules: HAEL, and prioritized circumscription. As we've mentioned, these logics resolve the conflict by constraining the reasoning processes with machinery that is extraneous to the semantics of default statements.

HAEL is an extension of autoepistemic logic motivated in part by the need to validate the Penguin Principle. An autoepistemic logic is a theory of KB extension: if the consequent of a default law is consistent with the rest of the contents of the KB, then it is added to that KB. In HAEL, certain KB expansions are preferred on the basis that the defaults used in them have a higher priority in some well-defined sense than the ones used in the alternative expansions. Informally, the contents of a KB are structured into a hierarchy. The information at each level in the hierarchy represents different sources of information available to an agent, while the hierarchy expresses the way in which this information is combined. Facts and indefeasible laws are placed at the first level, and more specific default laws are placed at a lower level in the hierarchy than less specific default laws; the way the logic works ensures that information at level n has priority over information at level m where $n < m$; in other words the effects of default laws at lower levels in the hierarchy can block the action of more general defaults, placed higher in the hierarchy. The only constraint on the hierarchy is that more specific defaults must be at a lower level. Since (12b) and (12c) have unrelated antecedents, they can appear in any relative order in the hierarchy, even though they conflict. This proves problematic, if we wish to support (12) in HAEL. For suppose we put (12b) at a lower level in the hierarchy than (12c). This means that in the KB extension, (12b) will have priority over (12c). Hence ψ_{ls} will follow from the premises (12a–e), contrary to our requirements. To avoid this undesirable result, we would have to constrain the way we construct the hierarchy, in order to ensure that (12c) is always placed at a lower level than (12b) (if they're at the same level, we would in fact still infer ψ_{ls}). But this has serious ramifications on the translation process of default statements into the object language. We would be committed to constraining the hierarchy in this case so that two defaults with logically unrelated antecedents appear in a particular order. But it is not always the case that we wish to constrain the order of two such defaults (cf. the premises of a Nixon Diamond). So we have sacrificed the means to translate default statements into the logic in a uniform way.

A similar problem arises in prioritized circumscription, where the abnormality predicates are ordered into a hierarchy, and one prefers models that satisfy the premises and which minimize on abnormality predicates higher in the hierarchy than those lower down. Again, we would have to be careful about the order in which we place the abnormality predicates associated with the default rules (12b) and (12c), if the logic is to capture the pattern of inference we need to do blocking. Again, we would fail to supply a uniform translation of default statements into the formal language. By contrast, our formalization of blocking in CE captures the pattern of inference we need, while at the same time maintaining a uniform translation of default statements into the object language. This is desirable because it allows for a more direct, perspicuous and elegant encoding of lexical rules and other constraints without the need to impose any external, linguistically unmotivated ordering.

13.5   Blocking – A unified phenomenon?

The account we have developed would be unsatisfactory if we were unable to derive any general principle of blocking, since intuitively the same principle is involved in many other examples including those cited in Section 13.2. We argue that specific blocking defaults, such as that for irregular past verbs, follow from an indefeasible rule which can express a version of 'preemption by synonymy' restricted via the subsumption relation. This rule enforces the principle that, if there are two lexical rules which validate derived signs with equivalent SYN and SEM components but distinct ORTH components, and the antecedents of these rules stand in a subsumption relation, then a blocking default is validated negating the derived orthography of the more general rule. We express the first version of the blocking principle as a deductive propositional schema; that is, as a 'metalevel' indefeasible implication over lexical descriptions, in (13).[7]

$$
\begin{aligned}
(13) \quad & \text{a)} \ (\varphi_{ls} > \psi_{ls}) \wedge (\chi_{ls} > \zeta_{ls}) \wedge \\
& \text{b)} \ (\chi_{ls} \to \varphi_{ls}) \wedge \neg(\varphi_{ls} \to \chi_{ls}) \wedge \\
& \text{c)} \ \psi_{ss} \leftrightarrow \zeta_{ss} \wedge \neg(\psi_o \leftrightarrow \zeta_o)) \\
& \to (\zeta_o > \neg\psi_o)
\end{aligned}
$$

The schema in (13a) represents any two lexical rules, and (13b) states that there must be an (indirect) unidirectional subsumption relation between the antecedents of these rules (inferrable from the sort system). (13c) states that these rules must result in derived lexical signs with equivalent values for SYN and SEM and distinct values for ORTH. If the conditions expressed in the antecedent of (13) are met the principle validates the deduction of a specific blocking default negating the orthography of the more general derived rule. This deduction takes place in the monotonic component of the constraint language (since it is an indefeasible implication). Hence if (12a,b,d) are verified, the default statement (12c) of conflict is inferred *before* normalization starts. And as we saw in Section 13.4.4, the non-monotonic component can use this default statement of conflict to achieve the desired effect of blocking. Moreover, it's important to stress that the statement of conflict is a default; so even if its antecedent is verified by the KB, its effects can be overridden by indefeasible unblocking assertions of the form $\psi_o \wedge \zeta_o$ (as in the case of the dual class verbs in Section 13.4.3).

The blocking principle in (13) is adequate to generate the blocking default required to prevent *sleeped* discussed in Section 13.4.2 and many others. The case of +*ness* and +*ity*, introduced in Section 13.2, can be treated in a manner analogous to past participle formation, since we have two lexical rules which clearly stand in a subsumption relation and generate differing forms with the same syntax (and meaning). However, an account of the *curious, curiosity; glorious, glory, *gloriousity* case cannot be obtained for the blocking principle as stated in (13) because we require the blocking of a (derivational) morphological rule in the presence of an underived synonymous but orthographically distinct lexical sign. A similar situation obtains with the rule of 'animal grinding' sense extension or conversion which produces the meat reading of *lamb*, and so forth, but is blocked in the case of *pig* by *pork*. In these cases, it appears that we must state that 'preemption by synonymy' also occurs when a non–rule-generated synonymous word exists. We will concentrate on developing an account of the blocking of animal grinding, since this putative lexical rule has motivated much of our interest in blocking (Copestake & Briscoe, 1991). We can recast the rules of grinding and animal grinding as lexical rules, as in (14a,b).

$$
a \begin{bmatrix} \text{ORTH} = \boxed{i} \\ \text{SYN} = \begin{bmatrix} \text{CAT} = noun \\ \text{CNT} = + \end{bmatrix} \\ \text{SEM} = \begin{bmatrix} \text{REF} = ind\_obj \wedge \boxed{k} \end{bmatrix} \end{bmatrix} \rightarrow_{LR3} \begin{bmatrix} \text{ORTH} = \boxed{i} \\ \text{SYN} = \begin{bmatrix} \text{CAT} = noun \\ \text{CNT} = - \end{bmatrix} \\ \text{SEM} = \begin{bmatrix} \text{REF} = substance \\ \text{ORIGIN} = \boxed{k} \end{bmatrix} \end{bmatrix}
$$

$$
b \begin{bmatrix} \text{ORTH} = \boxed{i} \\ \text{SYN} = \begin{bmatrix} \text{CAT} = noun \\ \text{CNT} = + \end{bmatrix} \\ \text{SEM} = \begin{bmatrix} \text{REF} = animal \wedge \boxed{k} \end{bmatrix} \end{bmatrix} >_{LR4} \begin{bmatrix} \text{ORTH} = \boxed{i} \\ \text{SYN} = \begin{bmatrix} \text{CAT} = noun \\ \text{CNT} = - \end{bmatrix} \\ \text{SEM} = \begin{bmatrix} \text{REF} = nat\_food\_subst \\ \text{ORIGIN} = \boxed{k} \end{bmatrix} \end{bmatrix}
$$

We assume that the class of 'animals' is subsumed by the class of 'ind(ividuated)_obj(ects)', that (14a) is an indefeasible rule, and that (14b) applies by default to further specify the interpretation of grinding applied to animals (see Copestake & Briscoe, 1991, for a more detailed justification of this analysis, explication of ORIGIN, and so forth). In order to not generate this more specified meaning for *pig*, by default, we must express the manner in which *pork* takes precedence over *pig*. As it stands the blocking principle apparently states that blocking applies when two lexical rules are involved, but in this case blocking is caused by the presence of an underived lexical sign (standing in the same general relationship to the derived sign). But the underived sign does not stand in a subsumption relation to either sign in the lexical rule. Intuitively, though the underived sign is more 'reliable' than the derived one because it represents a fact, rather than a (non-monotonic) inference. We can incorporate this intuition into the blocking principle without modification, given that we use CE, because the axioms of CE in (15a,b) allow us to make this pattern of inference parallel to the earlier case.

(15)   a $\models\ \rightarrow\psi$
        b $\models (\psi \rightarrow \varphi) \rightarrow (\psi{>}\varphi)$

In (16) χ_{ls} represents a basic lexical sign such as *pork* and we use the axioms in (15a,b) to obtain the formula in (16b) and (15a) to obtain (16c).

(16)   a $\varphi_{ls}{>}\psi_{ls}$
        b $\perp {>}\chi_{ls}$
        c $\perp \rightarrow \varphi_{ls} \wedge \neg(\varphi_{ls} \rightarrow \perp)$
        d $\psi_{ss} \leftrightarrow \chi_{ss} \wedge \neg(\psi_o \leftrightarrow \chi_o))$

If (16a) represents animal grinding then application of this rule to *pig* will produce a lexical sign which stands in the relation to *pork* (i.e., χ_{ls}) defined by (16d), and the formulas of (16) together will instantiate the blocking principle given in (13). Therefore, we will derive the specific blocking default that we require to prevent animal grinding validating *pig*, meaning meat; schematically, $\chi_o{>}\neg\psi_o$; and the application of animal grinding in this case will be blocked because the premises will be analogous to the case of irregular past participle formation in Section 13.4.2. Thus, these axioms allow us to formalize the similarity between these two examples of blocking without stating that *pork* is subsumed by *pig* (meat), as we would have been forced to do in a purely inheritance based account.

The type of blocking which is occurring in the case of words such as *sticker* or *banker* is apparently rather different to 'preemption by synonymy'. In these cases, a different meaning for an orthographically identical form is blocked. Ostler and Atkins (1991) refer to this as 'lexical preemption'. Nevertheless, the pattern of inference required to block the derived, productive sign resulting from +*er* nominalization is very similar to the cases of semantic preemption we have considered. We assume that the non-productive meaning of forms such as *sticker* means that underived lexical signs are present expressing such senses. Application of +*er* nominalization will be blocked by a specific blocking default which asserts that the 'more reliable' monotonically derivable semantics of the basic sign for *sticker* negates the productive default semantics produced by the rule. In (17) we give a (simplified) rule of +*er* nominalization.

$$
\begin{bmatrix}
\text{ORTH} = \begin{bmatrix} \text{STEM} = \boxed{j} \wedge vstem \end{bmatrix} \\[4pt]
\text{SYN} = \begin{bmatrix}
\text{CAT} = verb \\
\text{SUBJ} = \begin{bmatrix} \text{SYN} = \begin{bmatrix} \text{CAT} = np \end{bmatrix} \\ \text{SEM} = \begin{bmatrix} \text{REF} = \boxed{k} \end{bmatrix} \end{bmatrix} \\
\text{VFORM} = base
\end{bmatrix} \\[4pt]
\text{SEM} = \begin{bmatrix} \text{PRED} = pred \\ \text{ARG1} = \boxed{k} \wedge anim\_obj \end{bmatrix} \\[4pt]
\begin{bmatrix}
\text{ORTH} = \begin{bmatrix} \text{STEM} = \boxed{j} \\ \text{SUFFIX} = +er \end{bmatrix} \\
\text{SYN} = \begin{bmatrix} \text{CAT} = noun \end{bmatrix} \\
\text{SEM} = \begin{bmatrix} \text{REF} = \boxed{k} \end{bmatrix}
\end{bmatrix}
\end{bmatrix} > LR5
$$

This rule will produce a meaning for *sticker* which can be glossed as 'person who sticks (things)'. We represent the pattern of inference required to block derivation of this sign in (18).

(18) a $\varphi_{ls} > \psi_{se} \wedge \psi_{sy} \wedge \psi_{o}$
     b $\chi_{se} > \neg\psi_{se}$
     c φ_{ls}
     d χ_{ls}
     e $\nvdash \psi_{ls}$

This pattern results in ψ_{ls} being blocked, because there is irresolvable conflict between the default rules (18a) and (18b). In order to derive the blocking default in (18b) we need to introduce a second related blocking condition which introduces semantic blocking defaults when the conditions for 'lexical preemption' are satisfied. We give this version of the blocking principle in (19).

(19) a) $(\varphi_{ls} > \psi_{ls}) \wedge (\chi_{ls} > \zeta_{ls}) \wedge$
     b) $(\chi_{ls} \rightarrow \varphi_{ls}) \wedge \neg(\varphi_{ls} \rightarrow \chi_{ls}) \wedge$
     c) $\psi_{os} \leftrightarrow \zeta_{os} \wedge \neg(\psi_{se} \leftrightarrow \zeta_{se}))$
     $\rightarrow (\zeta_{se} > \neg\psi_{se})$

This second principle is symmetric with the first in (13), but reverses the conditions for preemption. ψ_{os} abbreviates values for ORTH and SYN on a lexical sign and ψ_{se} those for SEM. As before, (19) will generate the required blocking default when an underived lexical sign bears the relation defined in (19c) to a lexical sign derived by default. So in particular, (19) will generate (18b).

It might be thought that the availability of the axioms in (17) makes the blocking principles too unconstrained. For example, what is there to stop us blocking one sense of a homonymous form such as *bank* by applying the axioms of (17) to two basic signs which satisfy the conditions of the second principle in (19)? In fact, condition b) in the antecedent of the blocking principles prevents two underived forms satisfying them, despite the availability of axioms which allow any underived sign to be expressed as the consequent of a default implication. Condition b) fails to be satisfied in such a situation because $\neg(\bot \to \bot)$ can never be true in any model.

The symmetry between the two versions of the blocking principle, encoding the conditions of semantic and lexical pre-emption mean that it is possible to merge the two principles into one schematic blocking principle, which illustrates more clearly the similarities between the two subcases. (20) is the final version of the blocking principle and replaces both previous versions.

(20)   a) $(\psi_{ls} > \varphi_{ls}) \wedge (\chi_{ls} > \zeta_{ls}) \wedge$
        b) $(\chi_{ls} \to \psi_{ls}) \wedge \neg(\psi_{ls} \to \chi_{ls}) \wedge$
        c) $\varphi_{syn} \leftrightarrow \zeta_{syn} \wedge$
        d) $\varphi_x \leftrightarrow \zeta_x \wedge$
        e) $(\neg(\varphi_y \leftrightarrow \zeta_y))$
        $\to (\zeta_y > \neg\varphi_y)$

Clauses c) – e) express two subcases: for preemption, syntactic identity is always required, x and y are variables ranging over SEM and ORTH. If x is instantiated to SEM and y to ORTH, we have semantic preemption, otherwise we have lexical preemption.

We've seen how a general blocking principle can be encoded in our constraint language. It is interesting to note that such a principle wouldn't have the desired effect in HAEL. This is because in HAEL, the default information is 'drip-fed' into the reasoning process as one climbs the hierarchy. (20) will be known from the start (i.e., at level 0) since it is indefeasible knowledge, but its antecedent won't be verified until the reasoning process reaches the level where the general default $\psi_{ls} > \varphi_{ls}$ is introduced. Therefore, given the way HAEL works, the consequents of both (20) and this general default will be inferred at the next level in the hierarchy. Consequently, the blocking default is eventually inferred, but it is too late, because φ_{ls} has also been inferred: the blocking principle has failed to block it. Here, we see another advantage in the way CE is set up. In contrast to HAEL, *all* the defeasible information is known from the start of the reasoning process, and all monotonic inferences are carried out before the non-monotonic ones.

13.6   (Un)blocking and interactions with interpretation

A major motivation for developing a default account of blocking was to provide an account of interactions during interpretation, which would allow, say, *pig* to have the meaning of meat in an appropriate context; for example, *I ate pig last night in this awful restaurant*. In the extant theories of lexical organization which we have considered in Section 13.3, there is no way of blocking the application of animal grinding to a form such as *pig* deriving a meaning synonymous with *pork*. In addition, in those theories, if it were possible to block *pig* meaning meat via the existence of the underived form *pork*, then there would be no way of unblocking it; just as in those theories there is no way of unblocking *dreamed* in a manner which also captures the intuition that *dreamed* is a subclass of the irregular past participle formation verbs.

A full account of the unblocking of animal grinding is beyond the scope of this chapter. However, we can illustrate the approach that might be taken within this framework with respect to the blocked form **sleeped*. In a context where a (first or second) language learner utters, say, *I sleeped well*, it seems plausible that listeners infer an unblocking default 'on-line'. The problem is: why do we interpret *sleeped* as the past participle of *sleep* in this case? Intuitively, one recognizes that the more general default for constructing past participle verb forms applies. One can express this intuition declaratively in CE plus NPL. Let Γ be (21a–e); i.e., the premises of the inference that enables us to infer that the past participle form of *sleep* is *slept*.

(21)   a $\varphi_{ls} > \psi_{ss} \wedge \psi_o$ where $\psi_o = i \rightarrow LRn$ <ORTH> (α_o)

       b $\chi_{ls} > \zeta_{ss} \wedge \zeta_o$

       c $\zeta_o > \neg\psi_o$

       d $\varphi_{ls} \sqsupset \chi_{ls}$

       e χ_{ls}

       f $\models \zeta_{ls}$

         $\not\models \psi_{ls}$

We formalize the effect of the utterance of *sleeped* as adding $\Diamond\alpha_o$ to these premises. The possibility operator has the effect that we are asserting that α_o (i.e., the orthography "sleeped") is true at some node in the feature structure, since $\Diamond\alpha_o$ means that α_o is true at some node, but not necessarily the current one. Then the embedded default in (22) captures the intuition that, upon learning that α_o must hold at some node (through the utterance of *sleeped*), one assumes that by default, the consequent of the more general default rule holds and thus α_o is true as the value of the orthography for ψ_{ls}.

(22) $(\Gamma \wedge \Diamond\alpha_o) > \psi_{ls}$

So, suppose the KB verifies Γ and $\Diamond\alpha_o$. Then (22) is the most specific default that applies. So by the Penguin Principle its consequent is inferred. This means that in the case of hearing *sleeped*, one infers that it is to be interpreted as the past participle form of *sleep*.

Our use of a default logic incorporating a dynamic theory of belief guarantees us intertranslatibility between the constraint language we use to describe the lexicon and the logic in which we characterize processes of interpretation (e.g. Lascarides & Asher, in press). This enables us to elegantly capture such interactions by seemlessly extending the lexical KB into the more general modular, but interacting KB underlying language interpretation. In addition, the fact that we model the inference underlying the interpretation of *sleeped* using an embedded default has ramifications on the kind of logic that can account for these phenomena. Embedded defaults are syntactically ill formed in HAEL and default logic, but well formed in circumscription and CE.

13.7   Conclusion

In this chapter, we have shown that it is possible to derive a default account of blocking. This account is more compatible with linguistic facts. By representing conflict among feature values as default statements, we were able to support inferences that underlie blocking without making blocking an absolute principle of lexical organization. This paves the way for more insightful accounts of the status of words, such as *pig* meaning meat, *?curiousness*, and so forth. In this chapter, we have sketched preliminary accounts of a few of these cases in the logic CE, and argued that this is more appropriate for this application. In addition we have argued that our approach provides a basis for characterizing interactions between lexical and wider interpretative principles.

Much work remains to be done: we think that the approach could be improved by being recast within a typed framework (Carpenter, 1992) which would disallow arbitrary extensions of feature structures. Within such a treatment the notion of lexical rule could be constrained: here we have assumed an arbitrary mapping between feature structures is possible, but we would like to limit this to monotonic operations plus restricted mappings between particular types in the hierarchy. In general the computational complexity and consequent tractability of this approach needs to be investigated. We intend to explore the applicability of this approach to other examples of blocking and to examine interactions between lexical blocking and other knowledge resources used in interpretation.

Notes

1. Throughout this chapter we will ignore complications of morphographemics and morphophonemics. For proposals on how such complications can be dealt with within the accounts of the lexicon we consider see, e.g., Calder (1989), Cahill (1990), Russell et al. (1991) or Bird (1992).
2. Whether these cases can be subsumed under a general rule based on subject/external argument nominalization is controversial, but it seems clear that this (sub-)pattern is less productive in terms of the restrictions imposed on the denotation of the derived nominal.
3. For consistency we use a notation based on Blackburn (1992a,b) to encode constraints on FSs. We discuss this further in Section 13.3.
4. The value of < ORTH> <STEM> has actually to be constrained to be equal to **reg/irreg** rather than just subsumed by it, in order that Dualpast can inherit from Irregstem, without < ORTH> <STEM> being specified to be **irreg**. The LKB incorporates a notion of an equality or mutual subsumption specification as well as ordinary value specification, which allows this to work.
5. We have modified their notation and analysis to make it more consistent with Blackburn (1992a,b) and the LKB descriptions above.

6. ☉ is defined to be the set of worlds in the canonical model, that's used to prove completeness of ⊨ . Since this corresponds to knowing nothing but the laws of logic, ☉+Γ corresponds to knowing nothing but Γ and the laws of logic.

7. It's important to stress that (13) is a metalevel rule only in the sense that it is a schema; its desired effects are captured in the logic without have to assume metalevels of reasoning.

References

Aqvist, L. (1972) 'Logic of Conditionals', *Journal of Philosophical Logic, Vol. 1.*

Aronoff, M. (1976). *Word Formation in Generative Grammar,* Linguistic Inquiry Monograph 1. MIT Press, Cambridge, Mass.

Asher, N. and M. Morreau (1991) 'Commonsense Entailment: A Modal Theory of Non-monotonic Reasoning', *Proceedings to the 12th International Joint Conference on Artificial Intelligence,* Sydney, Australia, pp. 387–392.

Bauer, L. (1983) *English Word-formation,* Cambridge University Press, Cambridge, England.

Bird, S. (1992) 'Finite-state phonology in HPSG', *Proceedings of the 15th International Conference on Computational Linguistics (COLING-92),* Nantes, France, pp. 74–80.

Blackburn, P. (1992a) 'Modal Logic and Attribute Value Structures', in M. de Rijke (eds.), *Diamonds and Defaults,* Studies in Logic, Language and Information. Kluwer, Dordrecht, Holland (available as University of Amsterdam, ITLI, LP-92-02).

Blackburn, P. (1992b) *Structures, Languages and Translations: The Structural Approach to Feature Logic,* Research Paper HCRC/RP-33. HCRC Publications, University of Edinburgh.

Bolinger, D. L. (1975) *Aspects of Language,* Harcourt, Brace and Jovanovich: New York.

Briscoe, E. J., and A. Copestake (1991) 'Sense Extensions as Lexical Rules', *Proceedings of the IJCAI Workshop on Computational Approaches to Non-Literal Language,* Sydney, Australia, pp. 12–20.

Cahill, L. (1990) 'Syllable Based Morphology', *Proceedings of the 13th Coling,* Helsinki, pp. 48–54.

Cahill, L. (1992) "Review of 'English Word Grammar'", *Computational Linguistics, vol. 18 (1),* 92–94.

Calder, J. (1989) 'Paradigmatic Morphology', *Proceedings of the 4th Conference of the European Chapter of the Association for Computational Linguistics (EACL-89),* Manchester, England, pp. 58–65.

Carpenter, R. (1992) *The Logic of Typed Feature Structures* (Tracts in Theoretical Computer Science), Cambridge University Press, Cambridge, England.

Clark, E. V. and H. H. Clark (1979) 'When Nouns Surface as Verbs', *Language, vol. 55,* 767–811.

Copestake, A. (1992) 'The ACQUILEX LKB: Representation Issues in Semi-automatic Acquisition of Large Lexicons', *Proceedings of the 3rd Conference on Applied Natural Language Processing (ANLP-92),* Trento, Italy, pp. 88–96.

Copestake, A., A. Sanfilippo, E. J. Briscoe and V. de Paiva (in press) 'The ACQUILEX LKB: An Introduction Defaults, Inheritance and the Lexicon', in E. J. Briscoe, A. Copestake and V. de Paiva (eds.), *Defaults, Inheritance and the Lexicon,* Cambridge University Press, Cambridge, England.

Copestake, A. and E. J. Briscoe (1991) 'Lexical Operations in a Unification Based Framework', *Proceedings of the ACL SIGLEX Workshop on Lexical Semantics and Knowledge Representation,* Berkeley, California, pp. 88–101.

Daelemans, W. (1987) 'Inheritance in Object-Oriented Natural Language Processing', *Proceedings of the 3rd Conference of the European Chapter of the Association for Computational Linguistics (EACL-1987)*, Copenhagen, Denmark, pp. 70–74

Evans, R. and G. Gazdar (1989) 'Inference in DATR', *Proceedings of the 4th Conference of the European Chapter of the Association for Computational Linguistics (EACL-1989)*, Manchester, England, pp. 66–71.

Fraser, N. M. and R. A. Hudson (1992) 'Inheritance in Word Grammar', *Computational Linguistics, vol. 18 (2)* 133–158.

Hudson, R. A. (1990) *Word Grammar,* Blackwell, Oxford.

Kasper, R. T. and W. C. Rounds (1990) 'The logic of unification in grammar', *Linguistics and Philosophy, vol. 13 (1)* 35–58.

Kiparsky, P. (1973) 'Elswhere in Phonology', in S. R. Anderson and P. Kiparsky (eds.), *A Festschrift for Nomis Halle,* Holt, Rinehart and Winston.

Konolige, K. (1988) *Hierarchic Autoepistemic Theories for Nonmonotonic Reasoning: Preliminary Report*, Technical Note No. 446, SRI International.

Lascarides, A. and Asher, N. (in press) 'Temporal Interpretation, Discourse Relations and Commonse Sense Entailment', *Linguistics and Philosophy, vol. 176, no. 5.*

Lifschitz, V. (1984) 'Some Results on Circumscription', *Proceedings of the Nonmonotonic Reasoning Workshop*, AAAI, New York, pp. 151–164.

McCarthy, J. (1980) 'Circumscription: A Form of Nonmonotonic Reasoning', *Artificial Intelligence, vol. 13*, 27–39

Mellish, C. M. (1988) 'Implementing systemic classification by unification', *Computational Linguistics, vol. 14(1)* 40–51.

Moore, R. C. (1984) *A Formal Theory of Knowledge and Action*, Technical Note, SRI International Number 320.

Ostler, N. and B. T. S. Atkins (1991) 'Predictable Meaning Shift: Some Linguistic Properties of Lexical Implication Rules', *Proceedings of the ACL SIGLEX Workshop on Lexical Semantics and Knowledge Representation*, Berkeley, California, pp. 76–87.

Pelletier, F. J., and Schubert, L. K. (1986) 'Mass Expressions.' in Gabbay and Guenthner (eds.), *Handbook of Philosophical Logic, Vol 4*, Reidel, Dordrecht.

Pollard, C. and I. Sag (1987) *An Information-based Approach to Syntax and Semantics: Volume 1 Fundamentals*, CSLI Lecture Notes 13, Stanford CA.

Rappaport, M. and B. Levin (1990) '-*er* Nominals: Implications for the Theory of Argument Structure' in E. Wehrli and T. Stowell (eds.), *Syntax and the Lexicon,* Syntax and Semantics 26, Academic Press, New York.

Reiter, R. (1980) 'A Logic for Default Reasoning', *Artificial Intelligence, vol. 13*, 81–132.

Russell, G., J. Carroll and S. Warwick (1991) 'Multiple Default Inheritance in a Unification-based Lexicon', *Proceedings of the 29th Annual Meeting of the Association for Computational Linguistics (ACL-91),* Berkeley, California, pp. 215–221.

Russell, G., A. Ballim, J. Carroll and S. Warwick-Armstrong (in press) 'Practical Multiple Default Inheritance Defaults, Inheritance and the Lexicon', in E. J. Briscoe, A. Copestake and V. de Paiva (eds.), *Defaults, Inheritance and the Lexicon,* Cambridge University Press, Cambridge, England.

Shieber, S. M. (1986) *An Introduction to Unification-based Approaches to Grammar,* CSLI Lecture Notes 4, Stanford, CA.

Shieber, S. M. (1992) *Constraint-based Grammar Formalisms*, MIT Press, Cambridge, Mass.

de Smedt, K. (1984) 'Using Object-oriented Knowledge-representation Techniques in Morphology and Syntax Programming', *Proceedings of the ECAI-84*, Pisa, pp. 181–184.

14 A non-monotonic approach to lexical semantics

DANIEL KAYSER AND HOCINE ABIR

14.1 Introduction

The work described in this chapter starts from the observation that a word in a text has a semantic *value* which is seldom identical with any of the definitions found in a dictionary. This fact was of little importance as long as dictionaries were primarily intended for human beings, since the process used to convert the lexical meaning into the semantic value seems well mastered by humans – at least by the potential users of dictionaries – but it becomes of prominent importance now that we need computer-oriented dictionaries.

As a matter of fact, the computation of the semantic value for a given word requires lexical information about that word, about the other words of the text, about syntax, and about the world. The set of the possible *values* for a given word **X** is open-ended, i.e., a list of values being given, it is always possible to build some context where **X** takes a value not present in the list. As a consequence, no dictionary – as thick as it could be – may contain all of them. Therefore, in any case, it is necessary to implement a mechanism which constructs the value from information taken in the dictionary, as well as from knowledge of the grammar and of the world.

In artificial intelligence (henceforth A.I.), the main objective is not to find the "correct" meaning of each word or phrase, but to get the set of *consequences* which can be drawn from a text; if the same set is obtained from "different" interpretations (i.e., interpretations using different values for some word), then the difference is irrelevant. Therefore, we may stay rather vague about the "proper" definition of what we call semantic *values:* these values should only be seen as **inference triggers**.

As we have stated, the semantic values chosen for the other words of the text and the syntactic construction which organizes them may influence the choice of the value for every word. This seems to yield circularity. As a matter of fact, we believe the semantic interpretation to be the result of a kind of fixpoint equation; several fixpoints may exist, and this is fortunate when several readings of the text are possible. As this kind of construction is to be found in most **non-monotonic logics**, we thus attempt to give an account of understanding in terms of non-monotonic inferences.

We present in Section 14.2 the general framework implied by our approach and, in Section 14.3, we develop the formal language in which we express it; Sec-

303

tion 14.4 discusses several examples of the problems encountered. The examples are in French, for lack of a sufficient competence of the authors concerning the shades of meaning in English. Section 14.5 relates our work with some systems which attempt to deal with shifts in meaning.

14.2   General framework

Our proposal consists of four components:

(i)   a **lexicon** which provides for each lexeme one basic meaning as well as several "lexicalized" derived meanings;

(ii) **encyclopedic** (world) knowledge, as in most A.I. systems;

(iii) **rules** for constructing new derived meanings; these rules will be henceforth called rules (iii);

(iv) **rules** for establishing the semantic values for each part of the text; these rules will be henceforth called rules (iv).

We explain more precisely in this section the content of each component.

Component (i) raises the issue of what information should be present in the dictionary for a given entry. Let us first remark that, if the mechanism described by rules (iii) is versatile enough, the same results will be obtained even if the starting point (i.e., the definition of a word) varies within reasonable limits. We may therefore remain more or less neutral on questions such as the existence of "literal" meanings (Gibbs, 1989). We consider however that a lexeme has only one starting point: if there is no obvious choice between two possible values (which being taken as literal, and which taken as derived), we prefer to view the word as having two homographs, each one with a single starting point. This choice favoring a single starting point is however not very critical and we could modify it without modifying other parts of the system.

Lexicalized derived values are semantic values which various factors, mainly historical, have conferred to a word. They differ:

• from starting points in that they are not the preferred interpretation in a zero context, and

• from constructed semantic values in that no rule (iii) is able either to yield them at all, or to yield them with their correct priority.

The current, human-oriented lexicons are the best sources for both starting points and lexicalized derived values. They include sometimes, however, derived values which are easily recoverable with rules (iii), and do so in a fairly irregular way (Kayser, 1992); therefore, these values are better pruned off from computerized lexicons.

The world knowledge (**component ii**) necessary to understand a text cannot be a priori bounded. We try to represent only the most obviously needed information, such as selectional restrictions à la Katz and Fodor (1963), under a relational format. Relations will be expressed as general case frames. They link together groups of semantic values by means of a set of predefined relational constants (which act as semantic primitives). They will be used in premises of rules, in order to constrain the derivation of new values as well as the process of semantic interpretation.

The most important parts for our study are **(iii) and (iv)**. First of all, it should be clear that rules (iii) yield <u>potential</u> values, while rules (iv) are supposed to provide the <u>actual</u> ones in a given context. The discussion in the introduction shows that rules (iii) can in principle build infinite sets and that rules (iv) should be non-monotonic. We will use for both the same logical language, namely, a slightly modified version of Default Logic (Reiter, 1980). The details are given in Kayser and Abir (1991). The "defaults" will concern only part (iv). This part will thus contain, as defaults, rules mapping syntactic constructions into semantic formulas. In other words, we consider compositionality (i.e., the ability to get the value of the whole from the values of the parts) as a default characteristic of natural languages, and not as a hard constraint.

Concerning **rules (iii)**, there is no obvious source where to draw. Linguists have studied various forms of metonymy (see e.g., Bonhomme, 1987) but, as far as we know, no general framework has been proposed to cope with all shifts in meaning. We have found however a very fruitful inspiration in a work actually devoted to (diachronical) changes in meaning (Stern, 1931), but the main lines of which apply equally well to (synchronic) shifts. The philosophy underlying this study is illustrated by the following excerpt (p. 119):

A sense-change may be said to occur at the moment when the word arises in mind and is connected, as its symbol, with a sufficiently determined item of mental content, with which it has not previously been connected (. . .). The variations of mental content that we wish to express are infinite, and the limited – even if very large – number of words and habitual meanings is not sufficient to meet the demands we are constantly making for adequate expression. In such situation the extreme variability of the mental processes preceding speech, and the infinite possibility of combinations of words and meanings, provide us with the means of adapting speech to our needs and purposes in each single case: we are able to make the words express mental content that they have never expressed before.

According to this idea, Stern defines seven "classes of sense-change" (ibid., pp. 166 sqq.), namely:

- "substitution" ("sense-changes due to external, non-linguistic causes"),
- "analogy" ("The English adjective <u>fast</u> has two meanings that are almost contradictory, 'firm, immovable' and 'quick' [with] no intermediate senses (. . .). The adverb <u>fast</u> (. . .) shows a continuous development from the early sense 'firmly, immovably' to the later sense 'quickly'. (. . .) When the adverb had acquired the new sense, it was, by analogy, extended also to the adjective"),
- "shortening" ("<u>private</u> is a shortening of <u>private soldier</u>"),
- "nomination" ("Nominations are transfers in which a name is intentionally transferred from one referent to another. The distinction between intentional and unintentional is often vague"),

- "(regular) transfer" ("unintentional transfers, based on some similarity between the original (primary) referent of the word and the new (secondary) referent"),
- "permutation" ("In the phrase <u>he is counting his beads</u>, the last word originally meant 'prayers'. In the middle ages (. . .) to count one's prayers and to count the balls of one's rosary was almost the same thing as regards the purpose of the action"), and finally
- "adequation" ("adaptation of the meaning to the actual characteristics of the referents which the word is employed to denote, but in contradistinction to substitution, the cause of the shift lies in the subjective apprehension of the speakers").

Some of these classes are subdivided into refined categories which prove very helpful in order to create potential semantic values. Another interesting source that we have not yet taken advantage of is Nunberg, (1978).

Rules (iv) must cope with a variety of phenomena: grammatical norms as to how syntax usually yields semantic interpretations, physical facts and cultural norms concerning the properties that objects actually have or are said to have in different contexts. They have also access to the results of rules (iii), i.e., to lexical norms which tell how a word is likely to be understood. All these norms are likely to conflict with each other, and rules (iv) must hence handle priorities between them. Several schemes are here possible.

- Either priorities are numbers, and there are well-known mechanisms to combine them (MYCIN-like certainty factors, "possibility theory", plausibilities of various kinds), but in any case, there are two hard problems: how to give the initial numbers, and, since numbers are totally ordered, how to cope with unrelated phenomena.
- The alternative is to give qualitative strengths to norms: it amounts to putting **labels** on the semantic values, but the problem is then how to combine them when trade-offs between norms seem advisable.

We wish to leave open both possibilities, and will therefore treat priorities as an extra-argument in the relevant predicates; this argument can be passed to an as-yet-unspecified combination rule.

14.3   Formal description

14.3.1   *The predicates*

We list here the main predicates which we need, and explain what they are supposed to represent. Their actual role is however better described by the rules in which they appear, which will be described in Section 14.3.2.

Lex is a two-place predicate corresponding to a morphological analysis; Lex(X', X) holds whenever X' is an occurrence in the text and X the lexical entry under which X′ should be sought for in the lexicon. Recall that, in principle, one lexical entry corresponds to one semantical entry point; therefore, several words are homographs and Lex is not injective.

Sem reflects the knowledge contained in the lexicon, i.e., what we called part (i) in the previous section. It is a three-place predicate relating an entry of the lexicon and a "concept" (i.e., an inference trigger); the third argument describes the nature of the relationship between the word and the concept. If it is *nil*, the concept is taken to be the literal interpretation of the word. A partial order on the values of the third argument is reflected by the two-place predicate **stronger.**

Relation expresses that part of the world knowledge – or, more accurately, of the public beliefs shared by the users of language – which is required to understand some given kinds of texts, i.e., what we call part (ii) in the previous section. It is a three-place predicate; the third argument acts as a binary relation between the first two; it takes its value in a list of tentative semantic primitives, chosen in close relationship with a case frame approach. Its role is twofold:

- it appears in premises of rules for constructing new semantic values of a given lexical item;
- it provides constraints between the possible role fillers of the actants in the interpretation of a text; with this point of view, it plays a role similar to selectional restrictions in a classical semantic theory. **Compatible** is the reflexive and transitive closure of Relation through the taxonomy, i.e., if Relation(A,B,r) is known, everything more specific than A is compatible with B (and symmetrically, everything more specific than B is compatible with A) relative to r.

Symblog is a two-place predicate relating an "internal entity" with a substring of the text. Symblog(y,X′) is intended to mean that y is the interpretation of X′. The fact that normally a word gets its literal interpretation would thus be represented by the (iv) default rule: Lex(X′,X) ∧ Symblog(y,X′) ∧ Sem(X,A,*nil*): Element-of(y,A).[1]

Instead of reasoning at the level of instances, we prefer to stay as much as possible at the level of classes. **Interp**(X′,A) will thus represent the fact that the interpretation of X′ is some element of class A (formally (∃ y)(Symblog(y,X′) ∧ Element-of(y,A)) ≡ Interp (X′A)). The important point here is that Sem reflects potential meanings of a lexical entry, obtained through rules (iii), while Interp represents the (unique in one extension) interpretation of an occurrence, obtained through rules (iv).

Semrole is a predicate built during the construction of meaning, and denotes the ascription of semantic roles to the various symblogs appearing in the sentence. Semrole (x,y,r) means that symbol x plays role r with regard to symbol y. The Relation predicate imposes constraints as to how symbols can be arranged in semantic roles.

14.3.2   *The rules*

We describe the main rules, and illustrate them with the shift in meaning which makes possible that a word primarily denoting an action may also denote the object of that action. The prototypical example of such a shift is the (French) word *achat* (*purchase*) which means the act of purchasing as well as the thing purchased. We thus have:

> Sem (achat,A,*nil*)
> Relation (A,action,is-a)

In the absence of any context, the rule (iv) of construction of the interpretation:

(1) $Lex(X',X) \wedge Sem\ (X,A,s): Interp(X',A)\ [R_1\ (X',A)]^2$

yields the intended result. When several meanings are provided by the lexicon, the rule:

(2) $Lex(X',X) \wedge Sem\ (X,A,s) \wedge Sem\ (X,B,s') \wedge stronger(s,s'): \neg R_1(X',B)$
                                    $[Interp(X'A)]$

is, as it were, the definition of "stronger": it blocks the weaker interpretation as long as the stronger one is consistent. The rule:

(3) $stronger(nil,s)$

for any $s \neq nil$ implements the policy according to which literal meanings should be preferred when it is consistent to do so.

Let us check that (1) – (3) work as expected:

If we know that $W = \{Lex(X',X),\ Sem(X,A,nil),\ Sem(X,B,s),\ s \neq nil\}$, we get a unique extension $Th^3(W \cup [stronger\ (nil,s),\ Interp(X',A),\ \neg R_1(X',B)])$ because there is no way to block default (2), the application of which blocks one of the possible application of default (1) (namely, the one which would have yielded $Interp(X',B)$).

If we learn that $\neg Interp(X',A)$ (e.g., because of selectional restrictions due to the environment, there is no way to interpret X' as being an element of class A), $W' = W \cup (\neg Interp(X',A)\}$ has also a unique extension, $Th(W' \cup \{Interp(X',B)\})$ because default (2) is now blocked, which releases the application of default (1) concerning B, while its application concerning A is blocked on the grounds of having the negation of its conclusion.

This shows that in the absence of specific information, only the literal meaning yields an extension, but as soon as this meaning is ruled out, the next strongest meaning(s) is(are) selected.

The next step is to derive other Sems when needed, and to have rules that block the stronger interpretations when they cannot be the meaning intended by the author. Concerning the first problem, let us consider some further details of one of Stern's categories, viz., his class VI, "permutation" (p. 362 sqq.), and more precisely what he says concerning nouns:

```
13.21--> Object's names
13.211--> Material for object made of it
13.212--> Receptacle for content
13.213--> Part or constituent detail for the whole and vice versa
13.214--> Symbol for thing symbolized
13.215--> Instrument for action
13.216--> Instrument for production
13.217--> Organ for capability of perception and intellection,
Object for perception
13.218--> Articles of dress or equipment for a person
13.219--> Name for concomitant circumstances
13.22--> Nomina actionis
13.221--> Action for product, result or object: a very common type
13.222--> Action for instrument or means of action
13.223--> Action for agent
13.224--> Action for place of action: very common
13.23--> Names of qualities in various uses
13.24--> Names of persons for products, etc.
13.25
13.251--> Place-name for action or event
13.252--> Place-name for inhabitants or frequenters
13.26--> Mental states for objects or person causing it: very common
```

Most of the cases that we previously considered (such as in Kayser & Abir, 1991) are mentioned in this list, and the category we shall focus on here is described under the number 13.221. The rule (iii) which captures this shift is:

(4)   Relation (A,B,object) $\wedge$ Sem(X,B,s) $\supset$ Sem(X,A,f(s,act->obj))

This rule says that if the (literal or otherwise) meaning of lexeme X is B, and if A is known to be the object of action B, then A is a possible meaning for X. The label of this meaning is computed by some function f which operates on two arguments: the prior label and the label of the shift. As explained earlier, we do not want to choose yet whether f will merely be a numerical composition, in which case *nil*, act->obj, etc. would just be names for constants, or more ambitiously, if f will be a qualitative composition. In both cases, we expect f to satisfy:

$f(nil,s) = s$ for any s
stronger(s,f(s,s')) and stronger(s,f(s',s)) for any s, and for any $s' \neq nil$

N.B.: these requirements include (3) as a special case.

The next step is to grow the interpretation from the lexical level to the sentence level, and this is captured by rules (6) to (8), which operate on the predicates Interp provided by (1) and (2). Four new predicates appear: semrole(X',Y',r) expresses that syntagm X' plays the semantic role r with regard to syntagm Y'; Head denotes the usual linguistic property (e.g., the noun is the "head category" of a noun group), Union operates as the concatenation of contiguous syntagms (but may be used on discontinuous syntagms too); finally, Compatible generalizes Relation to the case of subcategories; more precisely, it ensures that if A and B are compatible relative to the relation r, every subcategory C of A will be compatible relative to r with every subcategory D of B under closed word assumption, i.e.:

(5.1) $Relation(A,B,r) \supset Compatible(A,B,r)$

(5.2) $Relation(A,B,is\text{-}a) \wedge Compatible(B,C,r) \supset Compatible(A,C,r)$

(5.3) $Relation(A,C,is\text{-}a) \wedge Compatible(B,C,r) \supset Compatible(B,A,r)$

(5.4) $: \neg Compatible(A,B,r)$

In order to stay at the level of the classes, we abridge the formula: symblog $(x,X') \wedge symblog(y,Y') \wedge semrole(x,y,r)$ into $SEMROLE(X',Y',r)$.

(6) $Interp(X',A) \wedge Interp(Y',B) \wedge Compatible(A,B,r)$
                    $: SEMROLE(X',Y',r)$

(7) $Interp(X',A) \wedge Interp(Y',B) \wedge \neg Compatible(A,B,r)$
                    $\supset \neg SEMROLE(X',Y',r)$

(compatibility is a default argument for semantic role, but incompatibility is a valid argument against it)

Semantic binding is then achieved through:

(8.1) $Interp(X',A) \wedge Interp(Y',B) \wedge SEMROLE(X',Y',r) \wedge Union(X',Y',Z')$
                    $\wedge Head(X',Z') \supset Interp(Z',A)$

(8.2) $Interp(X',A) \wedge Interp(Y',B) \wedge SEMROLE(X',Y',r) \wedge Union(X',Y',Z')$
                    $\wedge Head(Y',Z') \supset Interp(Z',B)$

The semroles are default consequences of the syntactic analysis: as a matter of fact, the compositional rules have the form of a correspondence between syntactic cases and semantic roles. More precisely, if we suppose that a standard parser has built a tree, (which we translate into logical formulas, like: **sentence** (X1); **subject** (X2,X1); **VP** (X3,X1); **verb** (X4,X3); **object** (X5,X3); etc.), we write our rules as:

(9)   **subject**$(X,Y) : SEMROLE(X,Y,agent)$

(10)   **object**$(X,Y) : SEMROLE(X,Y,object)$

As these rules are defaults, whenever the choice of a literal meaning yields a contradiction, we typically get two extensions: one in which we keep the correspondence between syntax and semantics, and select another meaning through rules (1) – (4), and the other in which we stick to literal meaning but derive through (7) statements such as $\neg semrole(x,y,r)$, which block defaults (9) – (10). This is as it should be . . . as long as both extensions correspond to possible readings of the text, i.e., if there exist a consistent derived meaning and another semrole. This notion is mirrored by the fact that every symbol corresponding to a syntagm must be interpreted in a category. This requirement cannot be expressed in the logic itself, and we must spell it out as a separate principle:

(11)   For every syntagm X′ there must exist a concept A such that
         Interp(X′,A)

Any extension which does not satisfy (11) will be considered ill-formed.

14.4   Discussion

14.4.1   *The rules (iii)*

We have written, in the previous section, a rule, (4), which states that a word denoting an action may denote also its object. This rule expresses an important phenomenon (Stern says this shift is "a very common type"), but neglects an equally important aspect, namely, that many words denoting actions do not shift, or at least shift very poorly, toward the object. Two possibilities are thus open:

- list all the words that satisfy the pattern and add in the lexicon a specially derived meaning;
- find regularities and express them as additional premises in rule (4).

A very crude study on (French) words gives the following list of words shifting easily from action to object:

achat, acquisition, assemblage, chasse, composition, confection, construction, création, cueillette, don, emprunt, fabrication, gain, lecture, livraison, montage, parcours, pêche, peinture, préparation, prêt, production, rapport, rassemblement, réalisation, récolte, rejet,
. . .
N.B: The presence of some items in the list is justified only for some uses of the notion of object. This can easily be seen in the case of *peinture* (it denotes the act of painting and its object in constructions such as *il peint un tableau*, but the shift is much harder in *il peint une rue de Paris*). Similarly, *gain* , *prêt* and *rapport* shift only when they denote money.

Is it possible to find regularities in this list? Some of these words seem to arrange into fairly homogeneous sets; the most striking ones are:

- E1 = {*assemblage, composition, confection, construction, création, fabrication, montage, peinture, préparation, production, réalisation*} built around the idea of making something,
- E2 = {*chasse, cueillette, pêche, récolte, rassemblement*} where something is gathered,
- E3 = {*achat, acquisition, don, emprunt, gain, prêt, rapport*} where something is traded.

But in each case, the common factor is only vaguely defined, and, worse, several words representing actions described by E1, E2, or E3 do not exhibit the shifting behavior. This is the case of *exécution, génération* for E1, *ramassage* for E2, *vente* for E3, . . .

It is therefore possible either to give more accurate premises to rule (4) and to list exceptions, or to have only lexicalized derived meanings for this category. The first case implies that we have a good taxonomy of the words of action; in this case, (4) should be rewritten into:

(4.1)   Relation (A,B,object) $\wedge$ Relation (B,producing,is-a) $\wedge$ Sem(X,B,s) $\supset$
                    Sem(X,A,f(s,easy act->obj))
(4.2)   Relation (A,B,object) $\wedge$ Relation (B,gathering,is-a) $\wedge$ Sem(X,B,s) $\supset$
                    Sem(X,A,f(s,easy act->obj))
(4.3)   Relation (A,B,object) $\wedge$ Relation (B,trading,is-a) $\wedge$ Sem(X,B,s) $\supset$
                    Sem(X,A,f(s,easy act->obj))

In both cases, (4) should remain as a residual hypothesis, with the label "hard act->obj", because even if it is not common, most words denoting an action can, in peculiar contexts, shift toward their object (*il m'a montré son ramassage* will be judged as bizarre but still interpreted by most French native speakers as "*he showed me what he picked up*"; similarly, *il livre ses ventes* will be understood as "*he delivers the objects he sells*").

14.4.2   *The rules (iv)*

The set of rules (iii) provides for each word an open-ended set of possible semantic values (through iteration on the rules). Now, in a given context, we must avoid generating each of them; we thus need a strategy which forges only those values which might play a role in the interpretation. Ideally, a strategy should be complete, in the sense that it should provide exactly the extensions of a default theory. Although default logic is inherently indecidable, there exist special cases where the extensions can be effectively computed (Bonté & Lévy, 1989), and we might well be in such a case.

Anyhow, we can design strategies more motivated by (psycho-)linguistic factors, even if they are not proven complete; one such strategy consists in giving first its literal meaning to the main verb v and to try and find interpretations of all the other components in a way which satisfies the case-frame relationships of this meaning of v. What we need, then, is a module able to produce the strongest Sems for a given occurrence C' that satisfies a set of conditions. If S is the whole sentence, we get then for some A and some s: Sem(S,A,s); if s is stronger than any other possible interpretation of v, we are done; if it is weaker than some interpretation of v, we must iterate the process with these interpretations. Every time that we get incomparable strengths, several readings of the sentence are considered, that is, technically, several extensions are computed.

So far, this strategy relies on the fact that the syntactic cases are strictly translated into semantic roles, and this is certainly not correct. Well-known examples (e.g., in Fillmore, 1968) show that syntactic subjects may not only be semantic agents, but also objects, instruments. Therefore, we should supply the system with rules like (9) – (10) but having a strict conclusion on a predicate like "possible-semrole" with a given strength, the actual semrole being the result of a trade-off between that strength and the strengths of the shifts required to satisfy the case-frame relations.

In order to design properly these rules, more should be known about the very notion of strength. To this aim, experiments must be designed in order to see whether people tend to have consistent preferences between the various constraints given by the "normal" readings of the words and the "normal" semantic interpretation of syntax when they provide conflictual hints.

14.4.3   *The relations*

The semantic relations are traditionally defined by constraints that hold between an operator and its arguments. This approach is well suited to the framework provided for Semantics since generative grammar. Within this framework, the arguments are described as semantic features, such as human, concrete, etc. However, this view of language processing has unfortunate consequences:

- in order to cope for every possible situation, the conditions bearing on each operator are very general; therefore, several operators get the same conditions on their arguments, while the actual constraints on them are rather different.
- This approach has put more emphasis on the operator, and the semantic nature of the arguments is thus neglected. Participants thus seem to appear as ambiguous entities.

In contrast with this traditional approach, the relational framework we suggest is developed in response to cognitive demands for a linguistically adequate description of word behavior. This framework is based on the assumption that some relations between the semantic values must be considered by language users in order to construct the model of the sentence. These relations differ from semantic values in that they form a closed class – intended as a means for organizing knowledge – whereas we insisted on the fact that semantic values form an open class.

The relations which must be represented for each semantic value are often an adaptation of the definition of the corresponding sense of the word, given in a dictionary. But adaptation does not mean mere translation.

Consider for instance the word *marché* (market) with the following dictionary definition:

lieu public où se tiennent des marchands pour exposer et vendre des objets

("*public place where stall-keepers display and sell objects*"). The corresponding semantic value, say "M", is taken as the literal meaning of the word *marché*, i.e., we have Sem (*marché*,M).

We might translate, literally as it were, this definition by the following relations:

[1]   Relation(M, location, is-a)
[2]   Relation(public, M, qualify)
[3]   Relation(stall-keepers, M, stand)
[4]   Relation(stall-keepers, objects, display)
[5]   Relation(stall-keepers, objects, sell)

314 D. Kayser and H. Abir

but this would be of little help: it is difficult to conceive a rule either for constructing derived meaning (rule iii) or to get a semantic value (rule iv) having a premise
like [2]. (Is there any linguistic phenomenon which applies, say, to public entities
but not to private ones?) Moreover, words such as "stand", "display", "sell" are
not good candidates to belong to that closed class of relation names which we
want to manage.

It seems therefore much more interesting to select among these relations those
which seem relevant for potential rules, and to modify freely the terms in order
to better answer our expectations. Here, we would like to mention:

- that *marché* is primarily a location,
- that it is the situation (or mediation) of the action of trading.

We may thus keep [1] as rendering correctly the first point, and suggest:

   [6]   Relation(M, trading, situation)

for the second one. As a matter of fact, let us accept, at least as a working hypothesis, "situation" as one item of our closed class expressing a rather loose connection, i.e., Relation(A,B,situation) holds iff B is an action which is normally situated in A. As trading is also normal in stores, shops, and other places which are
not markets in the sense M, we may expect to have in our world knowledge statements like Relation(store, trading,situation), Relation(shops,trading,situation); the
closed-world assumption (5.4) will circumscribe the "normal places" where trading takes place to these three entities and their known sub-entities.

Closed-world assumption might seem a bit too strong, especially if the Relation
predicate is not handled consistently throughout the constitution of part (ii). But
it is the price that must be paid in order to derive negative statements through (7),
thus avoiding always the preference to literal meanings.

14.5   Related works

In this section, we review some knowledge representation systems and their treatment of shift in meaning.

14.5.1 *Hobbs et al.*

Hobbs et al. (1987, 1988) are concerned with the interpretation of expressions
such as: "*Disengaged compressor after lube-oil alarm*", where the literal meanings of the words are not compatible with the semantic constraints associated with
the structure of the expression. This problem is obviously similar to our "shifts in
meaning".

Hobbs uses a first-order language to represent the semantic constraints and
adds "coercion" rules in order to find the proper interpretation. For example,
understanding the noun phrase "*after lube-oil alarm*" (after requires an event or
condition) requires finding two entities o and a. The entity " o " must be lube-oil
and " a " must be an alarm and there must be some <u>implicit relation</u> between

them. He calls that implicit relation nn. Then the expression (provided by the syntactic and semantic analysis) that must be proved is:

$$(\exists \; o,a,nn) \; (\text{lube-oil}(o) \wedge \text{alarm}(a) \wedge nn \; (o,a))$$

Treating nn as a predicate variable in this way leads to second-order logic. In a first order simulation:

- the symbol nn is treated as a predicate constant, and
- the most common relations are encoded in axioms. In "*lube-oil alarm*", the appropriate coercion rule is:

$$(\forall x,y) \; \text{for}(y,x) \supset nn(x,y)$$

This analysis is similar to ours in the fact that we also have at our disposal rules (iii) to allow for implicit relations. Another feature in Hobbs' work is the use of an "assumability cost": axioms are stated under the form:

$$P \; w \wedge P' \; w' \supset Q$$

i.e., P and P' imply Q, and if the cost of assuming Q is c , then the cost of assuming P (respectively P') is wc (respectively w'c), where the weights are assigned according to the semantic contribution of each conjunct. To solve roughly the same problem, we have introduced a partial order reflected by our **stronger** predicate, but admittedly neither Hobbs' nor our solution has yet been validated. Our non-monotonic framework enables us to consider as defeasible the conclusions of the semantic attachment as well as the interpretation of the syntactic constraints (e.g., in *the hammer breaks the window*, the syntactic subject is not the agent, but the instrument); similarly, Hobbs integrates syntax, semantics and pragmatics (section 4.3. of Hobbs et al., 1988) and the computation of the costs enables him to blend the respective strengths of the syntactic constraints and the coercion rules.

Still one difference is worth noticing: there is no mention in Hobbs' system of a possible iteration over the shifts. Now, for a sentence such as "*John heard lube-oil alarm*", Hobbs would need to prove:

$$\ldots \wedge \text{hear}(J,s) \wedge \text{sound}(s) \wedge \text{rel}(s,a) \wedge \text{alarm}(a) \wedge \; \ldots$$

but his rules are unable to prove rel(s,a) since this would require an intermediate step: a being the device, we need a b to represent the action of this device, and only that b might lead to s, the product of that action, namely, the sound. What would be required is a rule such as:

$$(\forall k,y,x) \; \text{rel}(k,x) \wedge \text{rel}(x,y)$$
$$[\wedge \text{ possibly some further constraint on } x] \supset \text{rel}(k,y)$$

14.5.2 *Pustejovsky et al.*

Pustejovsky (see Boguraev & Pustejovsky, 1990; Briscoe et al., 1990) develops a lexical semantics theory, which structures the knowledge into four components:

- Argument Structure
- Event Structure (to identify the particular event type for a verb or a phrase)
- Qualia Structure: it is a system of relations that characterizes the semantics of nominals. It defines the essential attributes of an object associated with a lexical item, i.e., the qualia structure of a noun determines its meaning the same way as the list of arguments determines a verb meaning. The elements that make up a qualia structure are also divided into four categories:

  [1] Constitutive Role: «the relation between an object and its constituent parts»
  [2] Formal Role: «that which distinguishes it within a larger domain»
  [3] Telic Role: «its purpose and function, the activity being performed»
  [4] Agentive Role: «factors involved in its origin or "bringing it about"»

- Lexical Inheritance Structure (to determine the way(s) in which a word is related to other concepts in the lexicon)

As an example, the adjective *fast* has the following lexical constraints:

$$\text{fast } (*x*) \Rightarrow (\text{Telic: } \lambda \text{ P } \exists \text{E } [\text{fast(E)} \wedge P(E,*x*)]$$

that is, *fast* modifies the telic role of the noun. If it occurs in a noun phrase such as *fast car*, where *car* is defined as:

$$\text{car}(*x*) \quad \begin{array}{l} [\text{ Const: } \dots] \\ [\text{ Form: } \dots] \\ [\text{ Telic: } \text{move(P,*x*) , drive(P,y,*x*)}] \\ [\text{ Agent: } \dots] \end{array}$$

it is supposed to provide two interpretations: a car that is inherently fast, a car driven quickly.

An interesting idea in Pustejovsky's model is the inclusion of nouns as relational terms. But its most important feature is the structure of the constraints; although it obviously efficiently guides the search for the correct meaning, and therefore reduces the risk of combinatorial explosion, some lexical constraints fall into several of the four categories, therefore requires a copy of the structures (as explained in Briscoe et al., 1990, *long* can modify the telic as well as the formal role; if a great deal of words display a similar behavior, the benefit of the strategy is lost).

14.5.3 *Fauconnier and Dinsmore*

The theory of discourse analysis proposed by Fauconnier (1984) analyzes discourse interpretation into two components: mental spaces and connectors.

Mental spaces are domains for consolidating certain kinds of information. Within spaces, objects may be represented as existing and relations may be represented as holding between those objects. A *connector* relates objects in different spaces: if two objects a and b are related by a connector, then a description of a can be used in referring to b.

Although not directly aimed at shifts in meaning, this theory provides interesting insights into the phenomenon. Unfortunately, it is not spelled out with sufficient detail and rigor to be used as a basis for designing a computer model.

Dinsmore's system (1987, 1991) is a direct outgrowth of the work of Fauconnier. Knowledge is partitioned into spaces. Spaces are fixed structural components within which normal rules of inference are observed. A special space, called "base" represents reality. The semantic of a sentence in "base" correponds to that of standard logic. Inferences performed locally within a single space are called parochial. The definitions of spaces and their organization reflect the author's concern for presupposition and temporal expression representations. None of these tools, however, seems able to take directly into account the creative aspect of words, i.e., the ability to derive new meanings for words.

14.6   Conclusion

We have described an approach to Natural Language Understanding with four components: a lexicon (i), an encyclopedia (ii), rules for shifts in meaning (iii), and rules for constructing an interpretation (iv). These four components share a common logical language, the non-monotonic part of which is exclusively located in part (iv). Some principles, e.g., (11) remain outside of the Logic.

Admittedly, this approach is far from having reached maturity, but the ideas on which it rests seem both different from the generally accepted views in Semantics, and promising. The original feature – at least in our opinion! – consists in having a formal framework, while denying a central role to the notion of truth, contrary to most contemporary treatments of formal Semantics (e.g., Chierchia & McConnell-Ginet, 1990). We believe this to be much more suitable to Natural Language. Of course, our approach can be described using a notion of truth, but it is neither an intrinsic truth (imposed by the nature of the real-world objects referred to), nor a linguistic truth (imposed by the existence of meaning postulates), but a truth <u>derived</u> from the existence of a model of the speaker's standpoint. As a matter of fact, by the mere fact of uttering a sentence, the speaker announces that she/he is building a model. If he/she intends the sentence to be correctly understood, the model should satisfy as much as possible the formulas representing the "public knowledge" universally accepted (in a given community). Predicates like Sem and Relation reflect this public knowledge, which is supposed to remain invariant from speaker to speaker.

The main problem that we have to face now is a correct management of the "stronger" relation in order to keep all the possible readings while eliminating all the spurious ones.

Notes

1. For simplicity, we note A: B the normal default $\dfrac{A:M\ B}{B}$ in Reiter's notation.

2. For simplicity, we note A: B [C] the semi-normal default $\dfrac{A:M\ (B \wedge C)}{B}$ in Reiter's notation.

3. As usual, Th stands for first-order deductibility.

References

Branimir Boguraev and James Pustejovsky. (1990). *Lexical Ambiguity and the Role of Knowledge Representation in Lexicon Design* in Proc. Coling 1990, vol. 2 pp. 36-41.

Marc Bonhomme. (1987). *Linguistique de la métonymie*. Sciences pour la communication, Editions Peter Lang.

Éric Bonté and François Lévy. (1989). *Une procédure complète de calcul des extensions pour les théories de défauts en réseau*. 7ème Congrès A.F.C.E.T.-R.F.I.A., Paris (F), Proc. pp. 1315-1325.

Ted Briscoe, Ann Copestake, and Bran Boguraev. (1990). *Enjoy the Paper: Lexical Semantics via Lexicology*, Coling 90, vol. 2 pp. 42–47.

Gennaro Chierchia and Sally McConnell-Ginet. (1990). *Meaning and Grammar. An Introduction to Semantics*, M.I.T. Press.

John Dinsmore. (1987). *Mental Spaces from a Functional Perspective*. Cognitive Science 11, pp. 1–21.

John Dinsmore. (1991). Logic-Based Processing of Semantically Complex Natural Language Discourse. *New Generation Computing*, vol. 9 pp. 39–68

Gilles Fauconnier. (1984). *Espaces Mentaux*. Les Editions de Minuit, Paris.

Charles J. Fillmore. (1968). The Case for Case in *Universals in Linguistic Theory* (E. Bach & C. T. Harms, eds.), pp. 1–90, Holt, Rinehart & Winston, New York.

Raymond W. Gibbs, Jr. (1989). Understanding and Literal Meaning. *Cognitive Science*, vol.13, pp. 243–251.

Jerry R. Hobbs, William Croft, Todd Davies, Douglas Edwards, and Kenneth Laws. (1987). Commonsense Metaphysics and Lexical Semantics, *Computational Linguistics*, vol. 13, 3–4

Jerry R. Hobbs , Mark Stickel, Paul Martin, and Douglas Edwards. (1988). *Interpretation as Abduction*, Proc. of the ACL, pp. 95–103, Buffalo, N.Y.

Jerry R. Hobbs and Megumi Kameyama. (1990). *Translation by Abduction* , Proc. Coling 1990, vol. 3, pp. 1555–1561.

Jerrold J. Katz and Jerry A. Fodor. (1963). The Structure of a Semantic Theory, *Language*, vol. 39, pp. 170–210.

Daniel Kayser. (1992). *Sur les glissements de sens lexicaux*. In Lexique et Inférences (J. E. Tyvaert, Ed.) *Recherches Linguistiques XVIII*, pp. 231–246.

Daniel Kayser and Hocine Abir. (1991). *Lexical Semantics and Shifts in Meaning*. Actes du Premier Séminaire de Sémantique Lexicale du PRC-GDR Communication Homme-Machine, pp. 89–99, Toulouse.

Geoffrey D. Nunberg. (1978). *The Pragmatics of Reference*. Indiana University Linguistics Club, Bloomington (Indiana).

Raymond Reiter. A Logic for Default Reasoning. *A.I. Journal*, vol. 13, 1–2, pp. 81–132.

Gustaf Stern. (1931). *Meaning and Change of Meaning with Special Reference to the English Language*, Indiana University Press, 1964.

15 Inheriting polysemy

ADAM KILGARRIFF

15.1 Introduction

This chapter builds on the title and theme of Apresjan's 1974 paper, *Regular Polysemy*. Apresjan was concerned merely to define the phenomenon and identify where it occurred. Here, we shall explore how it can be exploited.

Regular polysemy occurs where two or more words each have two senses, and all the words exhibit the same relationship between the two senses. The phenomenon is also called 'sense extension' (Copestake & Briscoe, 1991), 'semantic transfer rules' (Leech, 1981), 'lexical implication rules' (Ostler & Atkins, 1991), or simply 'lexical rules'. An example, taken direct from a dictionary (Longman Dictionary of Contemporary English, hereafter LDOCE) is:

> **gin** (a glass of) a colourless strong alcoholic drink . . .
> **martini** (a glass of) an alcoholic drink . . . [1]

In each case, two senses are referred to, one with the 'bracketed optional part' included in the definition and the other with it omitted; the relation between the two is the same in both cases.

Recent work on lexical description has stressed the need for the structure of a lexical knowledge base (LKB) to reflect the structure of the lexicon (Atkins & Levin, 1991) and for the LKB to incorporate productive rules, so the rulebound ways in which words may be used are captured without the lexicon needing to list all options for all words (Boguraev & Levin, 1990). These arguments suggest that generalizations regarding regular polysemy should be expressed in the LKB, and that the formalism in which the LKB is written should be such that, once the generalization is stated, the specific cases follow as consequences of the inference rules of the formalism.

As 'lexicalism' – the doctrine that the bulk of the information about the behavior of words should be located in the lexicon – has become popular in theoretical linguistics, so formalisms for expressing lexical information have been developed. The syntax, semantics and morphology of most words are shared with that of many others, so the first desideratum for any such formalism is to provide a

The author would like to thank Gerald Gazdar, Roger Evans, Ann Copestake and Lionel Moser for their valuable comments; Lynne Cahill and Roger Evans for the 'Overview of DATR', section 1.3 (from Cahill and Evans 1990); and the SERC for the grant supporting him while the work was undertaken.

319

mechanism for stating information just once, in such a way that it is defined for large numbers of words. Inheritance networks serve this purpose. If words are arranged into a taxonomy or some other form of network, then a fact which applies to a class of words can be stated at a nonterminal node in the network and inherited by the words to which it applies. Inheritance can be from a parent or from a parent's parent (and so on). Work in knowledge representation has addressed questions of different kinds of network, and the kinds of machinery needed to retrieve inherited information, in detail (see, e.g., introduction and various papers in Brachman & Levesque, 1985).

The next requirement is that exceptions and subregularities can be expressed. It must be possible to describe concisely the situation where a word or class of words are members of some superclass, and share the regular characteristics of the superclass in most respects, but have different values for some feature or cluster of features. Several lexical representation formalisms addressing these desiderata have been proposed (DATR: Evans & Gazdar, 1989a, 1989b, 1990; Russell et al., 1991; Copestake 1991). While the generalizations to be formalized are better understood for morphology and syntax, the theoretical gains, of capturing generalizations and eliminating redundancy, and the practical benefits, in terms of lexicon acquisition and maintenance, apply also to regular polysemy. The work described here will take the DATR formalism and use it to represent a collection of facts and generalizations regarding polysemy.

Patterns of regular polysemy will be called 'alternations' or 'sense alternations', and the sense that results from excluding the bracketed part, or which is listed first in the dictionary, or which is the only one listed, will be deemed the 'primary' sense, with others 'secondary'. Words have various 'senses', of which only the more frequently occurring and less predictable ones are likely to be specified in dictionaries.

In the following fragment, information about both the word and its denotation is accessed through a node in an inheritance network associated with the word. Thus a query regarding the syntax of the word *ash*, and a query asking what type of thing an ash tree is, will both be made at the same node. It might be argued that this is to confuse two different kinds of information. However, there are many kinds of information about denotations which have consequences for words, for example, that the kind of thing a word denotes determines (at least in the default case) the alternations it participates in, so there is much to be gained from holding the two types of information together. The matter receives a fuller discussion in Kilgarriff (1992). Here, we proceed on the basis that linguistic and encyclopedic information should inhabit the same representation scheme.

After some brief comments on related work and on the approach adopted toward dictionaries, DATR will be described. This chapter uses DATR but neither presupposes a knowledge of it, nor gives a formal description. Then evidence regarding regular polysemy will be introduced, in stages, with the proposed DATR account of the evidence worked through at each stage.

15.1.1 *Related work*

Polysemy has been the subject of remarkably little research. Linguists have found it insufficiently regular to succumb to their theoretical accounts, lexicographers have been concerned with instances rather than theory, and NLP has, until recently, overlooked the homonymy/polysemy distinction and ignored the relations between polysemous senses. A full literature review is to be found in Kilgarriff (1992).

Recent work which does aim to formalize phenomena closely related to regular polysemy includes Pustejovsky (1991), Briscoe, Copestake, & Boguraev (1990), Copestake & Briscoe (1991) and Kilgarriff & Gazdar (forthcoming). The first three papers are concerned with metonymy rather than polysemy, but the overlap is considerable. Crystal (1987) defines metonymy as "The use of an attribute in place of the whole, e.g. *the stage* (the theatrical profession), *the bench* (the judiciary)" (p. 70); from a lexicographic perspective, both examples are straightforward cases of polysemy. The first two papers focus on the mechanisms for parsing and semantic composition rather than inheritance. The more recent work by Copestake concentrates on inheritance, and is also concerned with metonymies more closely related to the alternations described here. The work is a similar enterprise in a different formalism. The last is a companion paper to this, exploring similar regularities in another domain and exploring the implications for linguistics.

15.1.2 *Dictionary and LKB*

At the most general level, a monolingual dictionary and an LKB share the same goal: to describe the lexical resources of the language. If a fact is in the dictionary, the lexicographers have considered it worth stating there, and that is a prima facie reason for it also needing to be in the LKB. Work which pursues the goal of automatically extracting information from dictionaries for 'populating' LKBs is reported in Byrd et al. (1987) and Boguraev & Briscoe (1989) amongst other places. A further matter of interest is the manner of representation of the facts in the dictionary. It too can be used as a clue to how the facts might fit into the LKB. The alternations studied are all represented in LDOCE using the 'bracketed optional part' mechanism, and this device indicates a regular or predictable relationship between the two types of use of a word (Kilgarriff, 1990). Working from a dictionary provides not only a supply of facts to be formalized, but also some indications, from the way they are presented, of what types of facts they are and what place they have in the overall lexical description (see also Neff & Boguraev, 1989). The dictionary is not, of course, without inconsistencies. Although liquid/glass-of alternations are generally indicated using the 'bracketed optional part', the glass-of sense of whisky is, for no apparent reason, presented as a distinct, numbered sense of the word. While a formalization may be based on a dictionary, care must be taken not to reproduce its inconsistencies.

More interesting than its inconsistencies are its systematic omissions. LDOCE does not note both options for all drinks. For *bourbon*, for example, no glass-of sense is noted. Types of usage of words are systematically omitted where they are predictable, and where they occur only rarely. For a combination of the two reasons the *bourbon* sense is omitted. Here we see a contrast between LKB and dictionary. Human dictionary-users (with the level of competence in English assumed by the LDOCE lexicographers) know enough about the regular patterns of English not to need to have the glass-of sense always specified. They can infer its availability from the facts that bourbon is a drink, and that other, more familiar drink-words display both 'liquid' and glass-of senses. They have at their disposal a general principle to the effect that words from the same semantic field that have been found to behave alike to date, will in all likelihood behave alike in novel situations. For an LKB all such generalizations and principles need to be built into the system in such a way that it follows as an inference that the alternation applies to *bourbon* and (possibly) to all drinks words, no matter how rare the glass-of sense may be. In the dictionary the glass-of sense of *bourbon* is not stated because it is predictable (and of low frequency). In the LKB it will not be explicitly stated, again, because it is predictable – but it will be there, by inference, just as it is there amongst the lexical resources of the language.

15.2   Overview of DATR

Evans & Gazdar (1989a, 1989b) presented the basic features of DATR.[2] Here we briefly review those features: more detailed discussion accompanies the formalization developed below. DATR is a declarative network representation language with two principal mechanisms: orthogonal multiple inheritance and nonmonotonic definition by default. The primary unit of a DATR network description is called a **node** and consists of a set of *path/definition* pairs where *path* is an ordered sequence of arbitrary atoms (enclosed in angle brackets), and *definition* is either a value, an inheritance specification or a sequence of definitions. **Nodes** are syntactically distinct from other atoms: they start with a capital letter. The primary operation on a DATR description is the evaluation of a query, namely the determination of a value associated with a given *path* at a given **node**. Such a value is either (a) defined directly for *path* at **node** or (b) obtained via an inheritance specification for *path* at **node** or (c) determined from the definition for the longest leading subpath of *path* defined at **node**, when *path* itself is not defined at **node**.

Inheritance specifications provide a new node, new path or both to seek a value from. The simplest form of inheritance, called 'local' inheritance, just changes the node and/or path specification in the current context. To specify that <path1> at Node1 inherits locally, we use one of the following.

        Node1:<path1> == Node2.

specifies that we inherit the value from <path1> at Node2.

        Node1:<path1> == <path2>.

specifies that we inherit the value from `<path2>` at `Node1`.

```
Node1:<path1> == Node2:<path2>.
```

specifies that we inherit the value from `<path2>` at `Node2`.

When a requested path is not defined at a node, the longest subpath (starting from the left) is used to provide a definition, with all the paths (if any) in the definition specification extended by the extra requested atoms. Thus if paths `<a b c>` and `<a b c d>` are not defined at `Node1`, a definition such as:

```
Node1:<a b> == Node2: <x>.
```

implicitly defines both the following:

```
Node1:<a b c> == Node2:<x c>.
Node1:<a b c d> == Node2:<x c d>.
```

This 'definition by default' (in the absence of any more specific path definition) gives DATR its nonmonotonic character: add a definition to a node and some of the theorems which were previously valid, but derived by this default mechanism, may cease to hold. The most common form of definition in the following DATR can now be explained:

```
Node1:<> == Node2.
```

This specifies that `Node1` inherits from `Node2` for all paths where a leading subpath of the query is not matched at `Node1`, and thus equates to the only kind of inheritance there is in a simple inheritance network.

DATR has certain desirable formal and computational properties. It is a formal language with a declarative semantics. Retrieving values for queries involves no search. The problems of clashing inheritance often associated with nonmonotonic multiple inheritance are avoided, yet the kinds of generalization most often associated with the lexicon can be simply stated. For fuller details, see references.

DATR has to date been used as a formalism for expressing syntactic, morphological, phonological and a limited amount of semantic lexical information (Evans & Gazdar, 1990; Cahill, 1990; Cahill & Evans, 1990; Gibbon, 1990). Polysemy has been addressed only briefly, in Cahill & Evans (1990), and that account makes no mention of the generalizations to be made regarding polysemy.

15.3   Trees, wood, fruit: A DATR fragment

The data we shall consider will concern trees, wood and fruit. First, consider the following definitions, from LDOCE.

> **ash** (the hard wood of) a forest tree . . .
> **beech** (the wood of) a large forest tree . . .

The bracketed optional part mechanism, combined with the near-identical form of words within the brackets, suggests an alternation, and indeed the tree/wood alternation applies to most if not all trees. In the basic taxonomy of the domain `Ash` and `Beech` inherit from `TREE`, which in turn inherits from `Plant` which, in the fragment offered here, inherits directly from `Entity`.

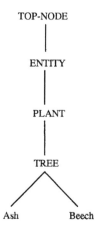

Figure 15.1. A simple taxonomy.

```
PLANT: <> ══ ENTITY.
TREE: <>   ══ PLANT.
Ash: <>    ══ TREE.
Beech: <> ══ TREE.
```

This is shown as a taxonomy in Fig. 15.1. The motivation for the higher levels of the taxonomy is theory-internal: what structure permits the most elegant treatment of the generalizations in the domain? At the lower levels, this consideration applies alongside dictionary genus terms and folk taxonomy (see papers by Rosch and Berlin in Rosch & Lloyd (1978).

To that basic structure, we wish to add a generalization about 'wood' senses. Once we have established that *ash* is being used in its wood sense, we wish to treat the word as we would *teak* and *mahogany*. We need to distinguish secondary senses from primary ones in such a way that the paths for accessing information about them are different. We do this by prefixing the path with alt (for alternation). There might be several alternations, so we identify the alternation by the path element following alt, the 'label', for which we shall use the genus term of the alternate sense, here wood. Let us also add some flesh to the bare bones of the taxonomy, and state some genus terms, word values (i.e., the word associated with the node), and collocates, words commonly found as neighbors or near neighbors of the target word (Church & Hanks, 1989), at various low-level nodes. The next version of the theory, all the details of which will be explained in due course, is presented and illustrated in Figure 15.2.[3]

```
TOP-NODE: <collocates>      ══ .
ENTITY: <>                  ══ TOP-NODE.
PLANT: <>                   ══ ENTITY.
TREE: <>                    ══ PLANT
```

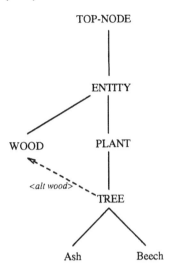

Figure 15.2. Taxonomy with tree/wood alternation.

```
        <collocates>              == plant grow chop-down PLANT
        <genus>                   == tree
        <alt wood>                == WOOD:<>.
Ash: <>                           == TREE
    <word>                        == ash
    <alt wood collocates>         == black TREE.
Beech: <>                         == TREE
        <word>                    == beech.

WOOD:<>                           == ENTITY
        <collocates>              == burn saw plane ENTITY
        <genus> == wood.
```

Now, if we query the system to obtain a value for

    Ash:<genus>

the value is tree, whereas for

    Ash:<alt wood genus>

the alt wood path prefix diverts the inheritance to WOOD. The effect of the empty path on the right hand side of the equation

    TREE: <alt wood>   == WOOD:<>.

is to direct the inheritance to the WOOD node with the path prefix replaced by the null path. In this case, that leaves the path <genus>, which is evaluated at WOOD to give wood. This 'prefix-stripping' action gives the desired behavior in that, once we have specified that we have the 'wood' sense of a word, it behaves as if its primary sense were a 'wood' sense.

Many collocates apply to all words in a given class. For example *grow* applies
to all plant-words. The theory has been written so these are stated once at a non-
terminal node in the taxonomy rather than at every relevant node, so listing all
the collocates for a word is a matter of working up through the taxonomy, gathering all collocates along the way. The relevant axioms use DATR's sequence facility. The rule for evaluating sequences is that each sequence member is treated as
if it were alone on the right-hand side of the equation, is evaluated, and the value
is placed back in the sequence. If we wish to find the collocates of the 'wood'
sense of *ash*, we need to evaluate

```
Ash:<alt wood collocates>.
```

At the Ash node, we find an equation for which the left-hand side matches, and
the right-hand side is a sequence. The first element of the sequence is an atom,
black, so that becomes the first element of the sequence that is returned. The second element is not an atom, but a node, so for the remainder of the sequence we
need to evaluate

```
TREE:<alt wood collocates>.
```

The prefix is stripped and the query diverted to WOOD, as we have seen, so we next
need to evaluate

```
WOOD:<collocates>
```

which is again specified as a sequence. The first three elements are atoms so they
are returned unchanged. The last element is a node, ENTITY. We pass straight
through ENTITY to TOP-NODE, and find that there <collocates> is defined as the
null sequence. We now have all the members of the sequence that forms the value
for the original query. The empty sequence disappears and the value returned is

```
black burn saw plane
```

as desired.

There is also a syntactic distinction to be noted. The 'tree' senses are count
nouns whereas the 'wood' senses are mass nouns. So let us add a little syntactic
information to the fragment.

```
ENTITY: <syntax>          == NOUN:<>.
WOOD: <syntax>            == MASS-NOUN:<>.
NOUN: <cat>              == noun
<concrete>               == yes
<count>                  == yes.
MASS-NOUN:<>            == NOUN
<count>                  == no.
```

We use syntax as a path prefix for syntactic information, which is stripped off
when we pass from general-purpose nodes to ones which are specific to syntactic
information. Entity-words are nouns unless there is a stipulation to the contrary,
and nouns by default are concrete, count nouns so these values are stated at NOUN,
the highest node in the hierarchy for nouns. Mass nouns differ from this paradigm

in various ways, which we shall gesture toward in this fragment simply by specifying a no value for the count feature. In other respects they are regular nouns, so MASS-NOUN otherwise inherits from NOUN.

The 'bracketed optional parts' indicating the 'wood' senses for *ash* and for *beech* were not identical. For *ash*, there was a further specification that the wood was "hard". Regular polysemy is often not entirely regular, and in general it will often be necessary to overrule inherited values, or to add specifications that are not inherited to an inherited sense. This is easily done in DATR. Dictionary definitions comprise genus and differentiae (which might be numbered), and the hardness of ash wood is one of the differentiae, so the addition to the theory is:

```
Ash: <alt wood differentia-1>      == hard.
```

In general, any number of further specifications may be added to an inherited sense in this way.

In LDOCE we have

> **teak** (a large tree from India, Malaysia and Burma that gives) a very hard yellowish brown wood . . .

and this illustrates there is a wood/tree as well as a tree/wood alternation. Lexicographers have not used the same formula for *teak* as for *ash* and *beech*, and this corresponds to the fact that the 'wood' sense is the more salient for the former, the 'tree' sense for the latter. To represent the two patterns as the same would be to throw away a principled distinction made by the lexicographer.[4]

In this fragment, all alternations are represented as directional links and the relation between the two alternations is not expressed. The following code adds *teak*, and the wood/tree alternation, to the fragment.

```
WOOD:<>                      == ENTITY
     <genus>                 == wood
     <collocates>            == table desk ENTITY
     <alt tree>              == TREE:<>.

Teak:<>                      == WOOD
     <word>                  == teak.
```

15.3.1 *Transitive alternations*

> **cherry 1** a small soft fleshy red, yellow or black round fruit . . . **2** (the wood of) the tree on which this fruit grows

The definition displays two alternations involving three senses. The primary sense is the fruit. Then there is the tree on which it grows, and then the tree/wood alternation applies to the secondary, 'tree' sense giving the 'wood' sense. The definition might have used nested bracketed-optional-parts, thus:

> **cherry** ((the wood of) a tree that produces) a small soft fleshy red, yellow or black round fruit . . .

but for the fact that user-friendliness is an overrriding concern of lexicographers, and a recursive metalanguage falls fatally at that hurdle.

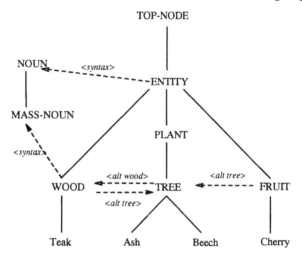

Figure 15.3. Taxonomy showing transitive alternations.

The pattern is productive. The 'wood' senses of *pear*, *orange* or *mango* are, like the glass-of sense of *bourbon*, too predictable and rare to be mentioned in LDOCE, yet, in the appropriate, carpenter's yard context, the use of the words to denote kinds of wood will be unexceptional. In DATR, we have

```
FRUIT:<>                        == ENTITY
    <word>                      == fruit
    <collocates>                == eat pick rot
    <genus>                     == fruit
    <alt tree>                  == TREE:<>
    <alt tree collocates>       == blossom TREE:<collocates>.

Cherry:<>                       == FRUIT
    <collocates>                == morello FRUIT
    <word> == cherry.
```

as shown in Figure 15.3.

The basic mechanism for 'transitive' alternations is to use as many <alt x> prefixes (where x is the identifier for the alternation) as required. Thus

```
Cherry:<alt tree alt wood genus>       = wood.
Cherry:<alt tree syntax count>         = yes.
Cherry:<alt tree alt wood syntax count> = no.
```

There may be any number of <alt x> prefixes, and a query may be redirected any number of times. In a larger DATR lexicon, there would often be several alternations specified at nodes, each time redirecting inheritance to another node and stripping off a prefix. Thus, as the number of <alt x> prefixes grows, so the number of potential usage-types which the theory is describing for the word increases exponentially. A search space of possible uses fans out. All the alternations directly available to the primary sense of the word form a set of possibilities at depth 1. For some of the nodes which the query has been redirected to, further 'one-step' alternations are defined, as the alternation to WOOD is defined from TREE for *cherry*, and they form the possibilities at depth 2, and so on recursively.

This kind of behavior is an outcome of the productivity of alternations, combined with the fact that alternations can apply to secondary usage-types as well as to primary ones. In modeling alternations in this way, we are adopting a position similar to that argued in Nunberg (1978) and implying that words have an indefinite number of potential senses.

15.3.2 *Trees and plants, cherries and strawberries*

We now have an axiom for which the first-pass interpretation is that fruit grows on trees – but not all fruit does. Correspondingly, we have some unwanted theorems. Also, we do not yet have at our disposal the machinery to express relationships between alternations.

Consider the following definition.

> **strawberry 1** (a plant that grows near the ground and has) a soft red juicy fruit

Here we have a fruit/plant alternation, a more general variant of the fruit/tree pattern. If a Strawberry node which inherits by default from FRUIT is added to the theory, then, if we query the node with a path commencing <alt tree> or <alt tree alt wood>, the inheritance follows exactly the same course as for Cherry. If there are values for syntax, collocations or anything else which Cherry will pick up from higher up the TREE or WOOD parts of the taxonomy, then Strawberry will also pick them up. The theory just mentioned when supplemented with

```
Strawberry:<>  ==  FRUIT
<word>         ==  strawberry.
```

has theorems

```
Strawberry:<alt tree genus>                  = tree.
Strawberry:<alt tree syntax count>           = yes.
Strawberry:<alt tree alt wood genus>         = wood.
Strawberry:<alt tree alt wood syntax count>  = no.
```

The direct approach to this problem would be to insert a TREE-FRUIT node between nodes for tree-growing fruit and FRUIT, and for that to be the point at which paths starting <alt tree> were redirected to TREE. However, the motivation for such a node is weak. 'Tree-growing fruit' is not used in the dictionary as a genus term, so the node is not sanctioned by the taxonomy described by the LDOCE lexicographers. Also, there seems no reason for introducing a node for tree-growing fruit that does not also apply to distinctively-colored fruit (and potentially other subsets of fruit), since both give rise to alternations. But then if there were two more intermediate nodes on the default inheritance path for Cherry (and other tree-growing, distinctively-colored, fruit) they would have to be ordered. Either ordering would be unsatisfactory, since tree-growing fruit are not a subset of distinctively-colored fruit and distinctively-colored fruit are not a subset of tree-growing fruit.

The strategy adopted here accepts that `Strawberry:<alt tree>` will give unwanted results, but also asserts that only some `<alt x>` prefixes at a node receive interpretations, and are thus interesting to query. DATR's default inference ensures that any interesting theory has an infinite number of 'uninteresting' theorems following from it, since, if `<path>` at `Node` evaluates to `val`, then so do `Node:<path foo>`, `Node:<path baz>`,[5] and all other paths starting with `path` which are not otherwise defined. There is therefore nothing novel in stating that classes of node-path pairs are uninteresting.

15.3.3 *Altlists: Identifying interesting paths*

The mechanism for distinguishing interesting and uninteresting paths at a node is this. For each node associated with a word, a path called `<altlist>` is defined, and the value for this path is a list of all the alternation-labels for one-step alternations from the node. We add to the theory

```
TOP-NODE:<altlist>            == .
TREE:<altlist>                == wood PLANT.
FRUIT:<altlist>               == "<grows-on>" ENTITY.
WOOD:<altlist>                == tree WOOD.
FRUIT :<grows-on>             == plant.
Cherry:<grows-on>             == tree.
Strawberry:<>                 == FRUIT.
```

The mechanism employed is as for collecting up lists of collocates. The value is defined as a sequence with two parts, locally specified items and items specified by inheritance. Where there are no locally specified items, no equations need adding to the code as the inheritance goes through by default. The double-quotes around `<grows-on>` denote DATR's global inheritance. For each DATR query, a 'global' context comprising a node and a path is initialized to the node and path of the original query, and then stored. When a quoted path is encountered, as here, the value is inherited from the stated path at the global-context node (and the global-context path is changed to the one quoted). So, in evaluating `Cherry:<altlist>`, we inherit a sequence at `FRUIT`, the first element of which is `"<grows-on>"`, which is evaluated at the query node, `Cherry`, where `Cherry: <grows-on>` `== tree.`, so the first element of the sequence is `tree`.

The approach enables us to capture, in a limited way, the relation between the 'plant' sense of *strawberry* and the 'tree' sense of *cherry*, and to do this by referring to the facts about cherries and strawberries which will be needed in a full lexical entry independently of considerations relating to alternations. The encyclopedic information is simply stated as the value of the `<grows-on>` path. By default (specified for all fruit at `FRUIT`) fruit grows on plants, and in the case of *cherry* this is overridden locally.[6] The relation between the two alternations comes in in the definition of `<altlist>` at `FRUIT`. The first element of the sequence is `"<grows-on>"`. For `Cherry`, it evaluates to `tree`, for `Strawberry`, to `plant`, so the two alternations fill the same spot in their respective `altlists` and the fact that the two alternations are in a sense the same has been captured.

A method of access that the dictionary permits, but which has not yet been provided for the DATR fragment, is 'blind listing'. If we look up a word in the dictionary without any further knowledge about its possible primary or other senses, we access a list of all the dictionary senses. As yet, to access information in the DATR theory about any senses but the primary one, we must already know the alternation identifiers. The `altlist` path makes blind listing possible. Blind breadth-first or depth-first search will then generate all the alternations for a word. All the labels for alternations at depth 1 in the search space are listed with *Word:* `<altlist>`. The labels for depth 2 are listed with *Word:*`<alt mem1 altlist>` where *mem1* takes any of the values from depth 1. The labels for depth 3 are listed with *Word:*`<alt mem1 alt mem2 altlist>`, where, for each value of *mem1*, *mem2* takes in turn each value of the `altlist` generated with that value for *mem1*, and so on.

A complete listing will be impossible unless loops are excluded, and impractical even without loops in a substantial lexicon where multiple alternations are defined at a large number of nodes. This is to say no more than that there would be little point in listing all the plausible ways a word might be used, as this is a large set. A listing of all alternations of depth less than some fixed number is more likely to be practical.

The issue of loops is already present in the fragment. The following formulas

```
Ash:<alt wood>
Ash:<alt wood alt tree alt wood>
Ash:<alt wood alt tree alt wood alt tree alt wood>
```

all take us to the same location in the inheritance network. It cannot be assumed that the 'looping' path will never be used. A recent innovation of the fish-marketing industry is to reconstitute the flesh of the fish into fish-shapes (and coat it in breadcrumbs for a quick-fried family meal). When the parent asks the child "how many fish do you want?" there is clearly one alternation from animal to food in evidence, and another which re-converts the mass, 'food' sense into a countable, 'fish' sense, yet the characteristics of the bread-crumbed version accessed through `Fish:<alt food alt fish>` are clearly not all the same as those of the original, and we might expect to find specifications such as

```
Fish: <alt food alt fish manufacturer> == bird's eye.
```

even though `<alt food alt fish>` might describe a loop in the hierarchy. So looping paths may occasionally give rise to interesting theorems, though usually they will not.[7]

15.4 Polysemy and homonymy in DATR

'Homonymy' and 'polysemy' are both useful concepts for the description of the lexicon of a language, although it is impossible to cleanly distinguish them (Lyons, 1977). How might this state of affairs be modeled in DATR? The natural

DATR treatment for homonymy is to carry information, and make queries, about different words at different nodes. But if polysemy often cannot be distinguished from homonymy, should polysemy not be treated similarly, with distinct polysemous senses each having its own DATR node?

The idea has some appeal, but it would mean that information about a word sense was never defined in the theory unless a node for the sense had explicitly been added. The fragment presented has said nothing explicitly about the 'tree' or 'wood' senses of *cherry* yet it represents facts about their syntax, genus terms and collocations. The senses are predictable and follow from generalizations and should not need explicit mention. It seems likely DATR theories will need to continue working with the homonymy/polysemy distinction, with homonyms treated as distinct nodes, and polysemous senses as sets of node-path pairs with a distinct path prefix. This offers the kind of flexibility required. To turn a sense treated as polysemous into one treated as homonymous is trivial. If we add

```
Cherry2: <>        == Cherry:<alt tree>
        <word>     == cherry.
```

to the theory, we now retrieve the same values for theorems of the form

```
Cherry2: <PATH>
```

as for ones of the form

```
Cherry: <alt tree PATH>.
```

All the polysemous senses described in the previous fragment can be treated as homonyms, each with a distinct node, in this way.

If distinct nodes were wanted for a pre-defined range of regularly polysemous or homonymous senses, they could be generated automatically. (The node names would then be automatically generated so we might expect them to take a form Word1, Word2 etc. rather than the mnemonic Cherry2. Since node names are only ever mnemonic, and never appear as values in DATR theorems, this is not an issue.) We may even say that these anonymous node-definitions would be part of the DATR theory, although they need never actually be typed in. A practical application of the theory may then generate and query anonymous nodes as and when they are needed in the course of language processing. Evans and Gazdar use this technique widely in The DATR Papers. The catch, of course, lies in 'pre-defining' the range of words and <alt *x*> prefixes that the automatic-generation process should apply to.

In general, the cases where there are generalizations to be made regarding polysemy are not the cases which are indeterminate between polysemy and homonymy. So regular polysemy will be treated with path prefixes, unequivocal homonymy with distinct nodes, and for indeterminate cases we may readily switch between the two kinds of treatment.

15.5 Polysemy and metonymy in DATR

As between polysemy and homonymy, so between polysemy and metonymy. Nunberg's arguments show that the two phenomena have a large overlap, and that there is nothing to be gained from treating them as different in kind. The DATR theory does not draw a distinction. There is a population of words, and a population of alternations (in DATR, ⟨alt *x*⟩ prefixes) and an alternation applied to one word will give a polysemous sense, while applied to another word it might describe a much lower-frequency usage-type which would usually be considered metonymy. The criterion according to which we call one and not the other polysemous will not be based on any difference of kind. The possibilities for how a word may be used will fan out far beyond the lexicographer's finite lists.

The previously described altlist mechanism, combined with a ceiling for depth of search, is one device for specifying regions of the search space which are more salient than others. We are relatively likely to encounter a word in a usage-type as described on the altlist of, say, depth 2. The altlist mechanism is essentially negative: an alternation not appearing on it for a given word will not apply to that word. But to distinguish those word-alternation pairs which occur significantly often from those of negligible frequency, a positive mechanism is wanted. While the 'wood' sense of *mango*, to be queried as

```
Mango: <alt tree alt wood>
```

is perfectly usable and understandable (in the right context), this is a separate kind of fact to the bald, statistical one that (in England) it almost never occurs. Among all the possibilities defined in the search space, there are many that are never used, many that are very rarely used, and a few that are commonly used. Setting aside the serious questions of what 'almost never' and 'commonly' mean, the minimal distinction between those word senses which are attested and those which are not may be expressed in DATR as follows. If only the 'wood' sense of *ash* and the 'tree' sense of cherry are attested, we add the following statements to the theory:

```
Ash: <alt wood known>        == yes.
Cherry: <alt tree known>     == yes.
TOP-NODE: <known>            == no.
```

The default value for the question, "Is there any empirical evidence for any given alternation having ever occurred in the language?" is "no". The information is stated at Top-node. Then for every sense for which there is evidence of its occurrence, a statement overriding the default and stating that the alternation is known is added. If a DATR lexicon were being used in an NLP application, such statements could be added wherever the system concluded that a word was being used in a previously unfamiliar sense, so the theory would develop as it 'learnt' from its input.

15.6 Conclusion

A lexical knowledge base needs inference mechanisms, particularly for inheritance, and a structure which reflects the structure of the lexical knowledge it conveys. DATR is a default inheritance formalism, the inference mechanisms being specially chosen for lexical representation. Regular polysemy is one level of structure in the lexicon of English, about which a desk dictionary provides an ample supply of facts. In this chapter we have examined and formalized the regular polysemy of a very small fragment of English. We have been able to exploit a number of generalizations about the domain to make the theory compact and productive. The formalization both presents a theory of the operation of regular polysemy in one corner of the domain of trees and fruit, and is a study for how regular polysemy may be used to structure the dictionaries and lexical knowledge bases of the future.

Notes

1. As the LDOCE entry for *glass* notes, a receptacle need not be made of glass to be a glass.
2. This section borrows heavily from Cahill & Evans (1990).
3. In accounts of DATR published to date, sequences are enclosed in round brackets. However the brackets are redundant in that they can be omitted without ambiguity, and future definitions of the language will not include them, so they have not been included here.
4. We do not address the vexed question of how to determine which is a more salient, or primary, sense. As far as possible we do as the dictionary suggests.
5. Assuming foo and baz do not otherwise occur in relevant axioms.
6. It is arguable that most fruit grows on trees so it would be more concise to set the default to tree than to plant. However, setting the default to plant serves a further function. Since anything that grows on a tree grows on a plant, the resulting theorems will be true for tree-growing fruit even where the lexical entry omits to mention what the fruit grows on.
7. They will remain more 'visible' than other uninteresting theorems, since any simple mechanism for listing all alternations will include them in its listing.

References

Atkins, B. T. S., & Levin, B. (1991). "Admitting Impediments " In Zernik, U. (Ed.), *Lexical Acquisition: Exploiting On-Line Resources to Build a Lexicon*, pp. 233–262. Lawrence Erlbaum, Hillsdale, New Jersey.

Boguraev, B. K., & Briscoe, E. J. (1989). *Computational Lexicography for Natural Language Processing*. Longman, Harlow.

Boguraev, B. K., & Levin, B. (1990). Models for lexical knowledge bases. In *Electronic Text Research: Proc. Sixth Ann. Conf. of the UW Centre for the New OED*, pp. 65–78. Waterloo, Canada.

Brachman, R. J., & Levesque, H. J. (1985). *Readings in Knowledge Representation*. Morgan Kaufmann, Los Altos, California.

Briscoe, E. J., Copestake, A. A., & Boguraev, B. K. (1990). Enjoy the paper: Lexical semantics via lexicology. In *COLING 90*, Vol. 2, pp. 42–47. Helsinki.

Byrd, R. J., Calzolari, N., Chodorow, M. S., Klavans, J. L., Neff, M. S., & Rizk, O. A. (1987). Tools and methods for computational lexicology. *Computational Linguistics*, *13*, 219–240.

Cahill, L. J. (1990). Syllable-based morphology. In *COLING 90,* Vol. 3, pp. 48–53. Helsinki.

Cahill, L. J., & Evans, R. (1990). An application of DATR : The TIC lexicon. In *Proc. ECAI-90,* pp. 120–125.

Church, K., & Hanks, P. (1989). Word association norms, mutual information and lexicography. In *ACL Proceedings, 27th Annual Meeting,* pp. 76–83. Vancouver.

Copestake, A. A. (1991). Defaults in the LRL. In Briscoe, E. J., Copestake, A. A., & de Paiva, V., (Eds.), *Proc. ACQUILEX Workshop on Default Inheritance in the Lexicon.* Tech. report 238, University of Cambridge Computer Laboratory.

Copestake, A. A., & Briscoe, E. J. (1991). Lexical operations in a unification-based framework. In Pustejovsky, J., & Bergler, S. (Eds.), *Lexical Semantics and Knowledge Representation: ACL SIGLEX Workshop.* Berkeley, California.

Crystal, D. (1987). *The Cambridge Encyclopedia of Language.* Cambridge University Press, Cambridge, England.

Evans, R., & Gazdar, G. (1989a). Inference in DATR. In *ACL Proceedings, 4th European Conference,* pp. 1–9. Manchester.

Evans, R., & Gazdar, G. (1989b). The semantics of DATR. In Cohn, A. G. (Ed.), *Proc. Seventh Conference of the AISB,* pp. 79–87. Falmer, Sussex.

Evans, R., & Gazdar, G. (1990). The DATR Papers. Tech rep. CSRP 139, School of Cognitive and Computing Sciences, University of Sussex, Falmer, Sussex.

Gibbon, D. (1990). Prosodic association by template inheritance. In *Proc. Workshop on Inheritance in Natural Language Processing,* pp. 65–81 Tilburg. ITK .

Kilgarriff, A. (1990). An analysis of distinctions between dictionary word senses. Tech rep. CSRP 184, School of Cognitive and Computing Sciences, University of Sussex.

Kilgarriff, A. (1992). *Polysemy.* Ph.D. thesis, University of Sussex, CSRP 261, School of Cognitive and Computing Sciences.

Kilgarriff, A., & Gazdar, G. (1993, forthcoming). Polysemous relations. In Palmer, F. R. (Ed.), *Festschrift for Sir John Lyons.* Cambridge University Press, Cambridge, England.

LDOCE. (1987). *Longman Dictionary of Contemporary English, New Edition.* Edited by Della Summers et al. Harlow.

Leech, G. (1981). *Semantics.* Cambridge University Press, Cambridge, England.

Lyons, J. (1977). *Semantics.* Cambridge University Press, Cambridge, England.

Neff, M. S., & Boguraev, B. K. (1989). Dictionaries, dictionary grammars and dictionary entry parsing. In *ACL Proceedings, 27th Annual Meeting,* pp. 91–101. Vancouver.

Nunberg, G. (1978). *The Pragmatics of Reference.* University of Indiana Linguistics Club, Bloomington, Indiana.

Ostler, N., & Atkins, B. T. S. (1991). Predictable meaning shift: Some linguistic properties of lexical implication rules. In Pustejovsky, J., & Bergler, S. (Eds.), *Lexical semantics and knowledge representation: ACL SIGLEX Workshop,* Berkeley, California.

Pustejovsky, J. (1991). The generative lexicon. *Computational Linguistics, 17*(4), 409–441.

Rosch, E., & Lloyd, B. B. (1978). *Cognition and Categorization.* Lawrence Erlbaum, New Jersey.

Russell, G., Ballim, A., Carroll, J., & Armstrong-Warwick, S. (1991). A Practical Approach to Multiple Default Inheritance for Unification-Based Lexicons. In Briscoe, E. J., Copestake, A. A., & de Paiva, V. (Eds.), *Proc. ACQUILEX Workshop On Default Inheritance in the Lexicon,* Tech. report 238, University of Cambridge Computer Laboratory.

16 Lexical semantics: Dictionary or encyclopedia?

MARC CAVAZZA AND PIERRE ZWEIGENBAUM

16.1 The issue of lexical content for NLU

The basic elements of most recent Natural Language Understanding (NLU) systems are a syntactic parser which is used to determine sentence structure, and a semantic lexicon whose purpose is to access the system's factual knowledge from the natural language input. In this regard, the semantic lexicon plays the key role of relating words to world knowledge. But the semantic lexicon is also used in solving some specifically linguistic issues when recovering sentence structure, and should contain linguistic knowledge. In this chapter we discuss the issue of lexical content in terms of linguistic and world knowledge, through the so-called dictionary–encyclopedia controversy. To illustrate the discussion we will describe the lexical semantics approach adopted in our NLU program processing sentences from medical records (Zweigenbaum and Cavazza, 1990). This program is a small-scale but fully implemented prototype adopting a broad view to NLU, from syntactic analysis to complex domain inferences through model-based reasoning (Grishman and Ksiezyk, 1990). The dictionary–encyclopedia controversy opposes two extreme conceptions of word definitions: according to the dictionary approach a word is described in terms of linguistic elements only, without recourse to world knowledge, whereas an encyclopedic definition includes

an indication of the different species or different stages of the object or process denoted by the word, the main types of behavior of this object or process, . . . (Mel'cuk and Zholkovsky, 1988).

This point has been discussed by many authors including Katz and Fodor (1963), Eco (1984), Wierzbicka (1985) and Taylor (1989). Although most of the philosophical debate seems to arise from a confusion on whether the definition concerns the *word* (hence from a linguistic standpoint) or a putative corresponding *concept,* it still retains heuristic value in the framework of NLU. However in the NLU setting the question adopts a different presentation: "how much world knowledge should be embedded in the lexicon?" According to the dictionary approach, a word is defined through *linguistic* knowledge, for instance with the help of relations to other words like synonymy-antonymy, or hyperonymy-

François Rastier is thanked for many discussions and advice. However the authors have sole responsibility for any misinterpretations. This work was partly supported by PRC-GDR Communication Homme-Machine through grants to one of the authors (MC).

hyponymy (an illustration can be found in the analysis of "respect" in Décary & Lapalme, 1990). A typical dictionary definition would be:

> Antibody: defensive substance produced by the body when challenged with an *antigen.*

The dictionary definition provides linguistic information that is useful in performing word meaning composition but since it does not embed world knowledge it provides a limited basis for inference.

In the framework of cognitive linguistics and artificial intelligence (AI) much research has been concerned with prototype theory. Prototypes gather default world knowledge associated to a given word and this knowledge naturally leads to an encyclopedic approach to word definition. An encyclopedic definition for the previous example would be:

> Antibody: an Immunoglobulin produced by B lymphocytes in the course of a humoral immune response. An antibody specifically recognizes a fragment of the antigen (epitope) through its active site (paratope). Antibody binding initiates several reactions: complement binding and cell lysis, Antibody Dependent Cell-mediated Cytotoxicity . . .

Such an encyclopedic definition relates a lexical entry to schemata in memory, notably those who describe object behavior (Mel'čuk and Zholkovsky, 1988). While the former definition could explain the use of the word "antibody" in some corpus occurrences, only the latter enables a real understanding of sentences using it, thanks to domain inferences. Many AI systems hence tend to adopt an encyclopedic lexicon because inference is a major concern. Yet a constant problem with the encyclopedic approach stands in the amount of world knowledge that should be incorporated in the lexical entry, and how it is to be connected to other knowledge sources. Another problem with encyclopedic lexicons is that they force into a priori knowledge description and representation, a process which may threaten knowledge declarativity and modularity. Finally, it is difficult to characterize the boundaries of a word "meaning", i.e., which concepts should be associated to a given lexical entry. As a result, the building of large, multi-purpose, encyclopedic lexicons for NLU seems an intractable task.

In the context of computational linguistics, we think that the nature of the semantic lexicon should be discussed from a technical rather than from a cognitive or philosophical standpoint. Since there are multiple strategies for NLU, the nature of the semantic lexicon will depend on some fundamental choices made during system design concerning the use of linguistic and world knowledge throughout processing. The lexicon description can nonetheless be firmly grounded in linguistics, which then acts as a descriptive science, helping in the identification of relevant issues appearing inside a representative corpus. It is this hypothesis that we will develop in this chapter, namely that in a NLU system, *the nature of the semantic lexicon depends on the overall processing architecture.* More precisely, separating a linguistic step from a conceptual step enables us to consider the semantic lexicon from a dictionary perspective, i.e., building it from linguistic data only.

16.2   A two-step processing strategy

Our NLU system is a fully implemented prototype processing sentences from
actual medical texts, though in a toy domain: thyroid cancer care. The relevant
linguistic problems were identified during a preliminary corpus study which
examined 2,000 sentences from 80 medical records. These sentences are real-
world descriptions with a high implicit content that can be recovered through the
use of domain knowledge. From a linguistic viewpoint the most relevant issues
are noun phrase descriptions, implicit semantic relations and, to some extent,
metonymy. Lexical ambiguity is not encountered in such a restricted domain,
even considering non-technical vocabulary (although artificial examples can, of
course, be constructed, no one appears in our corpus). Since these sentences are
real-world descriptions, a possibility for interpreting them consists in building a
model of the corresponding state of affairs (Waltz, 1981), featuring domain
objects and simulating their behavior. Model-based simulation supports domain
inferences, which enables recovering implicit information conveyed by the sentence (Cavazza and Zweigenbaum, 1994). The program operates in a two-step
fashion (see Figure 16.1):

- The first step builds a semantic representation from the syntactic structure – provided by a Lexical-Functional Grammar (LFG) (Kaplan and
  Bresnan, 1982) parser – by accessing the semantic lexicon and solving specific linguistic problems (reference, negation, quantification)
  with heuristic rules. It is dedicated to the solution of linguistic presentation problems.
- From this semantic representation, a situational model is assembled.
  The semantic representation activates knowledge on domain objects
  and actions; as a result, objects are introduced in the model and the
  effects of specific actions are simulated. Finally, common sense and
  domain knowledge are injected into the model and result in further
  inferences.

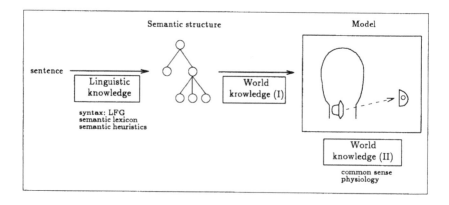

Figure 16.1. Overall strategy of the program.

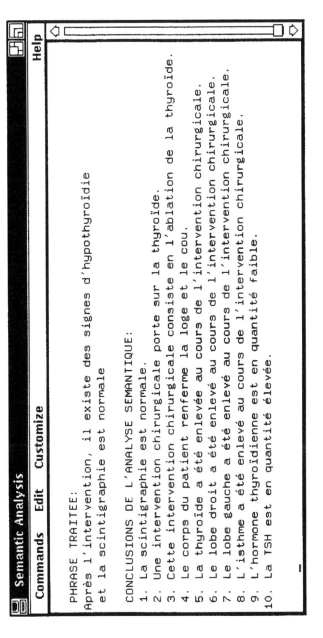

Figure 16.2. Sample session.

A sample output is presented on Figure 16.2; as a result of sentence analysis and model building the program outputs its conclusions through a natural language generator. For more detail on the model building process, the reader is referred to Cavazza (1991) and Cavazza and Zweigenbaum (1994).

16.3   A dictionary approach to the semantic lexicon

From the strategy we have just outlined, it appears that the first step of processing is essentially dedicated to the construction of a conceptual representation of the sentence, through the use of linguistic knowledge. The knowledge sources will be an LFG grammar, a semantic lexicon and a set of heuristic rules to treat the simple reference issues encountered in our corpus. In this chapter, we will be concerned with the semantic lexicon only. What is sought for the semantic lexicon is a means of describing relevant linguistic information associated to a given word.

Figure 16.3 summarizes various approaches to lexical information acquisition. Introspection is of course criticizable as it does not rely on attested linguistic evidence (except perhaps if the user is him/herself an experienced lexicographer). Extraction from existing dictionaries is limited by the confidence one has in the original dictionary but one considerable advantage is that automated methods are being developed for this task (Boguraev et al., 1989; Véronis et al., 1989). A possible solution to issues of reliability is to merge data from several dictionaries (Véronis and Ide, 1991). Some dictionaries such as the *Longman Dictionary of Contemporary English* (Proctor, 1979) make use of a restricted number of "primitive" words (perhaps not exactly in Wilks' sense, Wilks, 1977) and are good candidates to support automated extraction (Boguraev and Briscoe, 1989). This kind of approach could also reduce difficulties posed by the circularity of definitions (Décary and Lapalme, 1990).

Yet the ideal way to acquire word linguistic content would be through corpora studies of real lexical occurrences. Recently this approach has been automated (Velardi et al., 1991) and although it concerns mainly syncategorematic aspects of lexical relations and few paradigmatic ones, this study and other related ones (Jacobs and Zernik, 1988) could lead to a breakthrough in lexical semantics.

The method we will introduce is a linguistic, manual method for acquiring lexical content from corpus study; what is needed in this perspective is a linguistic theory to describe the linguistic problems encountered. We thus subscribe to the view that future NLU systems may benefit more from a good descriptive linguistic theory rather than from a new formal one (Rastier, 1991).

We have placed ourselves in the framework of continental structural linguistics (Greimas, 1966; Pottier, 1987; Rastier, 1987). This theory is lexicon-centered and describes lexical content in terms of meaning components, called *semes*.[1] Several approaches have been taken with semantic components among which those of Katz and Fodor (1963) and Schank (1972) have been the most debated. Le Ny (1979) has studied components from a psychological viewpoint. However in our

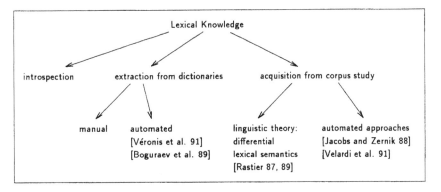

Figure 16.3. Approaches to lexical information acquisition.

framework, components have a *linguistic basis*. To emphasize this point this theory has been termed *differential* decompositional theory (Rastier, 1987b). This term refers to the differential paradigm (Eco, 1980), which states that the content of any object can be described by opposing it to other objects through structural relations. In the field of lexical semantics these relations are essentially hyponymy-hyperonymy and synonymy-antonymy.[2] Opposing related lexemes through these relations yields linguistically significant components (as we shall see). It is important to stress that semes are relative both to the natural language and the corpus studied: they have no claim of being universal and do not satisfy criteria for primitiveness (Wilks, 1977). To illustrate the difference with earlier approaches, the word "chair," which comprised more than 20 components according to Katz and Fodor, was described by Pottier with only 4 linguistically relevant components, those which distinguish the word among names of related furniture.[3] Katz and Fodor's approach can be termed *referential* as opposed to differential ones (Rastier, 1987b): this is because the components used by Katz and Fodor were in fact properties of the *referent*, hence incorporating encyclopedic knowledge into an endless description. This also explains why the dictionary–encyclopedia controversy is active in Katz and Fodor's (1963) paper. We can give some evidence that lexical decomposition into linguistically motivated components bears resemblance with a "pure" dictionary definition: as a matter of fact, dictionary definitions use structural relations such as hyperonym (i.e., arthritis is an *inflammatory* disease) and antonym relations (e.g., "somatotropic" is opposed to "gonadotropic").

But the debate over analyticity of definitions is not relevant to the linguistic approach; it appears only in referential approaches since such definitions aim at describing the referent in terms of analytical components, soon leading to meaning postulates.[4] In the next section, we introduce the linguistic methods by which semantic components for a given word are established (Cavazza, 1991).

16.4   The semantic lexicon: Linguistic knowledge acquisition

The fundamental point for seme determination is that there should be reasonable linguistic evidence for the existence of a given seme, in terms of corpus data. Linguistic content shows up in corpus occurrences (this point has also been discussed by Wierzbicka, 1985). For instance, the words "body" and "corpse" obviously differ by the component /alive/, as can be evidenced by many corpus occurrences. But it would be nonsense to discriminate "peach" from "banana" with a seme such as /has a large seed/ for which there would be no linguistic evidence (example from Hirst, 1987, p. 117). To describe linguistically relevant components, words are compared along structural relations inside *minimal meaning* sets called taxemes. A taxeme is thus a set of related words all sharing a "family resemblance", but there are currently no methods besides linguistic expertise for determining such minimal sets. As an illustration, a taxeme for surgical actions involving removal of an object is presented on Figure 16.4. Every word in a taxeme shares a common component characteristic of the taxeme itself: in the last example, the /removing/ component. Inside a taxeme each word possesses specific components; here the word "thyroïdectomie" has a specific component distinguishing it from related names of surgical operations, this component being /object = thyroid/. Taxemes are included in two kinds of more general meaning classes: *domains* and *dimensions*. Domains have a linguistic basis as indicated by their mention in dictionary definitions, e.g., *medicine, navy*. A single domain considered from a general language viewpoint (e.g., *medicine*) may in fact be partitioned into several sub-domains. Dimensions correspond to general classes like animate-inanimate, which can also have linguistic correlates (for instance pronouns). Domains and dimensions may admit cues for their existence, taxemes do not, at least on a dictionary basis.[5] Domains and dimensions determine semes which are inherited by words belonging to included taxemes. For instance the word "thyroïdectomie"[6] is defined as /action/ , /surgery/ , /removing/ , /object = thyroid/ (corresponding to dimension, domain, taxeme and specific semes).

Despite the fact that recourse to components has been said to be equivalent to semantic networks with inheritance, we resist this kind of reduction. First, because the taxemes serving to determine such components are set structures rather than hierarchies: inheritance is a phenomenon occurring inside meaning classes, which concerns only semes corresponding to the class itself (called *generic* semes[7]). Another, more technical argument is that component assembly bears more similarity with slot-filling approaches (Hirst, 1987) than with graph-network unification (Sowa, 1988). Slot-filling approaches tend to be more content-driven than graph-unification methods, and this aspect cannot be grasped if one reasons in terms of formal equivalence.

The decompositional differential theory does not address relations between linguistic and world knowledge, since it restricts itself to the description of linguistic content. While in the general case this connection resorts to various disciplines ranging from psycholinguistics to philosophy, when building NLU systems the

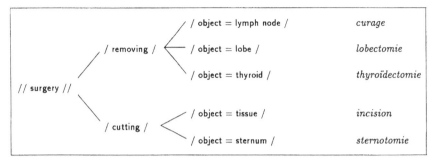

Figure 16.4. Taxemes.

connection between linguistic knowledge (lexical content) and world knowledge (domain knowledge base(s)) can be simply part of the system's architecture.

The lexical content obtained with the above-described method is relative to a given corpus. It should be used in the setting of a given processing strategy which prescribes interaction between linguistic content and world knowledge. There are, however, some direct connections between linguistic data and world knowledge: for instance a differential component between *adenoma* and a*denocarcinoma,* which is the component /malignant/, obviously has conceptual relevance. Actually most if not all semantic components can be used as knowledge representation elements, hence bridging the gap between the semantic lexicon and the elements of the knowledge base.

The elements of our knowledge base are concept prototypes with default attributes as well as procedural attachments corresponding to dynamic knowledge such as action consequence and object behavior. These concept prototypes are not activated from a single word meaning but on the contrary are activable by a given linguistic content that can be scattered through, e.g., a noun phrase. Activating a concept produces the creation of an instance which can result in model building and modification (for instance setting up a new object in the model, or altering one to simulate the effect of an action). Hence in the design of the knowledge base a bridge is built between linguistic knowledge and domain concepts, not from a word-to-concept perspective but through incorporation of individual linguistic units into conceptual descriptions.

16.5   Building a semantic structure

In this section we describe how the semantic lexicon is used to assemble a conceptual structure (Figure 16.1, first step) taking as a starting point an LFG parse tree of the sentence. The overall process is summarized on Figure 16.5: it consists in assembling semes (from various syntactically linked words) into clusters (Figure 16.5a) in order to activate a concept prototype of the knowledge base (Figure 16.5b). Like many compositional approaches,[8] it relies on a correct attribution of

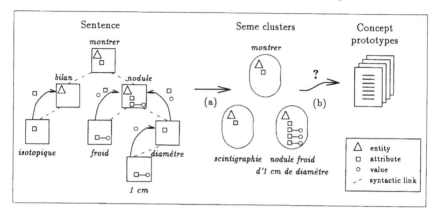

Figure 16.5. Assembling semes to substantiate prototypes.

syntactic links; this is, of course, a strong hypothesis since, because of attachment ambiguities, our LFG analyzer currently achieves only 80% correct parses, the erroneous attachments being solved through user intervention (in a further version disambiguation should be automated through access to lexical content).

The overall strategy for assembling a conceptual structure is the following (Cavazza, 1991):

- Each lexeme in the parse tree is replaced with a list of semantic components. Since the global strategy for assembly consists in collecting compatible components into clusters there is no need for structuring the lexical content, as in the systems based on lexical graphs unification. In this first implementation, we have given semes one of the following types: *entity, attribute* and *value* to ease the assembling process.[9]
- In the second step, semes migrate along syntactic links to form clusters of related semes according to their type in such a way as to assemble compatible semes from a same NP or VP. The assembling process is driven by seme type and by syntactic links existing between words, potential ambiguities being solved on a nearest-neighbor basis. As a result, semes of type *entity*[10] are associated with many *attribute* and *values* semes, constituting a seme cluster.
- These clusters are then compared to the prototypes of the knowledge base, through a set of heuristic rules; whenever comparison is successful an instance of the prototype is created (Figure 16.5b). Conceptual relations between prototypes can be drawn on the basis of syntactic links and prototype content (Cavazza, 1991).

This assembly mechanism enables us to treat some linguistic phenomena occurring in our corpus, mainly noun phrase descriptions, semantic relations and a few metonymic expressions. Let us take the following example:

> une formation arrondie suspecte . . .
> an anomalous round-shaped object . . .

The assembly of components scattered through the NP, in this case /object/, /shape=round/ and /pathological/ is sufficient to activate a prototype of *initial-tumor* on a linguistic basis. The minimal content for lexemes we have adopted thus enables us to treat various paraphrastic presentations. This is more a matter of recognizing the distribution of lexical content on a corpus basis rather than having very abstract and general primitives like those of Schank which tend to represent similarly with the INGEST primitive such different entries as "to smoke", "to nibble at", "to inject", etc. . . . (Waltz, 1989).

16.6 Conclusion

We have suggested that under certain design assumptions it is possible to keep the semantic lexicon reduced to linguistic elements only. The major advantage – from a technical standpoint – is that of having modular knowledge bases (a linguistic, a commonsense and a domain knowledge base) which can interact during processing but are not compiled into the semantic lexicon. A drawback is that feedback to the syntactic parser (Hirst, 1987) can be provided by linguistic knowledge only. Whether this is sufficient in most cases is yet to be determined.

The main issue for computational lexical semantics stands in the acquisition of linguistic knowledge from a reference corpus for which we have proposed a possible method (Cavazza, 1991) derived from a modern linguistic theory (Rastier, 1987). Throughout this chapter we have been concerned more with lexical content than with lexical structure and formalisms, chiefly because we claim that formalisms are related to the overall strategy and architecture of a NLU system. However it is not obvious that any formalism will be adequate in handling the kind of linguistic content we have introduced. We would like to suggest as a basis for further work that slot-filling methods (Hirst, 1987) and non-standard logics (including constraints-propagating logics) would perhaps cope better than predicate logic or formal graph-unification methods (Sowa, 1988) with the fact that not any combination of semes is relevant.

Notes

1. Issues like semantic relations, metonymy (Eco, 1984) and paraphrases (Waltz, 1989) can be conveniently treated through semantic components.
2. These structural relations which have a methodological role in establishing lexical content should not be confused with semantic relations between words discussed in Cruse (1991) and Chaffin & Herrman (1988).

3. Though this example does not seem convincing to Lyons (1977).
4. Berwick (1989) used the classical refutation of meaning postulates to explain the inadequacy of any definition. But this criticism applies only to word-concept definition from a referential perspective. A further point states that definitions are adequate for technical terms only: there is wide evidence that the medical language we study is more than a simple terminology, displaying many features of general language.
5. It is not clear whether some thesaurus entries can be helpful in setting up taxemes. The textual foundation of taxemes is introduced in Rastier (1989).
6. It should be noted that the morpheme rather than the word is a basis for decomposition (Rastier, 1987).
7. Differential semantics admits two kind of semes: *generic* semes are associated to meaning sets while *specific* semes characterize words inside sets. Referential semantics admitted a similar distinction between *markers* and *distinguishers* (Katz and Postal, 1964).
8. We have assumed compositionality much more from a technical standpoint than from a fundamental one. There exists abundant evidence that compositionality is not a general rule in natural language.
9. Yet we insist that in the original theory assembly is content-driven; this is an advantage that we could not keep, since it poses many implementation difficulties.
10. Examples of *entity* semes are: /action/ /object/ /person/, corresponding to basic categories (these arise from *dimensions*).

References

Berwick, R. C., 1989. Learning Word Meanings From Examples. In: Waltz, D. (ed.), *Semantic Structures*. Hillsdale: Lawrence Erlbaum Associates.

Boguraev, B. and Briscoe, E., 1989. *Computational Lexicography for Natural Language Processing*. New York: Wiley.

Boguraev, B., Byrd, R., Klavans, J. and Neff, M. 1989. From Machine Readable Dictionaries to Lexical Databases. *First Lexical Acquisition Workshop,* Detroit.

Cavazza, M., 1991. Analyse Sémantique du Langage Naturel par Construction de Modèles. *Unpublished Ph.D. dissertation. Université Paris 7.*

Cavazza, M. and Zweigenbaum, P., 1994. A Semantic Analyzer for Natural Language Understanding in an Expert Domain. *Applied Artificial Intelligence,* 8(3), 425–453.

Chaffin, R. and Herrman, D. J. 1988. The Nature of Semantic Relations: A Comparison of Two Approaches. In: Evens, M. (ed.), *Relational Models of the Lexicon*. Cambridge: Cambridge University Press.

Cruse, A., 1991. Aspects of Lexical Relations. *First Lexical Semantics Workshop of the GDR-GRECO Communication Homme-Machine, Toulouse.*

Décary, M. and Lapalme, G., 1990. An Editor for the Explanatory and Combinatory Dictionary of Contemporary French (DECFC). *Computational Linguistics,* 16(3), 145–154.

Eco, U., 1980. *Segno*. Milano: Arnoldo Mondadori.

Eco, U., 1984. *Semiotica e filosofia del linguaggio*. Torino: Einaudi.

Greimas, A., 1966. *Sémantique structurale*. Paris: Larousse.

Grishman, R. and Ksiezyk, T., 1990. Causal and Temporal Text Analysis: The Role of the Domain Model. *Proceedings of 13th COLING Conference, Helsinki.*

Hirst, G. 1987. *Semantic Interpretation and the Resolution of Ambiguity*. Cambridge: Cambridge University Press.

Jacobs, P. and Zernik, U., 1988. Acquiring Lexical Knowledge from Text: A Case Study. *Proceedings of AAAI'88 Conference,* St Paul, 739–744.

Kaplan, R. M. and Bresnan, J., 1982. Lexical-Functional Grammar: A Formal System for Grammatical Representation. In: Bresnan, J. (ed.), *The Mental Representation of Grammatical Relations,* chapter 4, 173–281. Cambridge: MIT Press.

Katz, J. and Fodor J., 1963. The Structure of a Semantic Theory. Language 39: 170–210.

Katz, J. and Postal, P., 1964. *An Integrated Theory of Linguistic Descriptions.* Cambridge: MIT Press.

Le Ny, J.-F. 1979. *La sémantique psychologique.* Paris: Presses Universitaires de France.

Lyons, J., 1977. *Semantics.* Cambridge: Cambridge University Press.

Mel'cuk, I. and Zholkovsky, A., 1988. The Explanatory Combinatorial Dictionary. In: Evens, M.W. (ed.), *Relational Models of the Lexicon,* 41–74. Cambridge: Cambridge University Press.

Pottier, B. 1987. *Théorie et Analyse en Linguistique.* Paris: Hachette Université.

Proctor, P. 1979. *Longman Dictionary of Contemporary English.* London: Longman.

Rastier, F. 1987a. *Sémantique Interprétative.* Paris: Presses Universitaires de France.

Rastier, F. 1987b. Représentation du Contenu Lexical et Formalismes de l'Intelligence Artificielle. *Langages,* 67, 77–102.

Rastier, F. 1989. *Sens et Textualité.* Paris: Hachette Université.

Rastier, F. 1991. *Sémantique et Recherches Cognitives.* Paris: Presses Universitaires de France.

Schank, R. 1972. Conceptual Dependency: A Theory of Natural Language Understanding. *Cognitive Psychology,* 3(4):552–631.

Sowa, J. 1988. Using a Lexicon of Canonical Graphs in a Semantic Interpreter. In Evens, M.W. (ed.), *Relational Models of the Lexicon,* 113–137. Cambridge: Cambridge University Press.

Taylor, J. R., 1989. *Linguistic Categorisation.* Oxford: Clarendon Press.

Velardi, P., Fasolo, M. and Pazienza, M. T., 1991. How to Encode Semantic Knowledge: A Method for Meaning Representation and Computer-Aided Acquisition. *Computational Linguistics,* 17(2), 153–170.

Véronis, J. and Ide, N., 1991. Extraction de connaissances des dictionnaires courants: une évaluation. *First Lexical Semantics Workshop of the GDR-GRECO Communication Homme-Machine, Toulouse.*

Véronis, J., Wurbel, N. andt Ide, N. E., 1989. Extraction d'Informations Sémantiques dans les Dictionnaires Courants. Proceedings of the 7th AFCET-RFIA, 1381–1395, Paris.

Waltz, D. L., 1981. Toward a Detailed Model of Processing for Language Describing the Physical World. *Proceedings of 7th IJCAI,* 1–6.

Waltz, D.L., 1989. Preface to *Semantic Structures.* Hillsdale: Lawrence Erlbaum Associates.

Wierzbicka, A., 1985. *Lexicography and Conceptual Analysis.* Ann Arbor: Karoma.

Wilks, Y. 1977. Good and Bad Arguments about Semantic Primitives. Technical Report n. 42, Department of Artificial Intelligence, Edinburgh University.

Zweigenbaum, P. and Cavazza, M., 1990. Deep Sentence Understanding in a Restricted Domain. *Proceedings of 13th COLING Conference, Helsinki.*

PART V

Applications

Lexical semantics offers a large variety of uses in natural language processing and it obviously allows for more refined treatments. One of the main problems is to identify exactly the lexical semantic resources that one needs to solve a particular problem. Another main difficulty is to know how best to organize this knowledge in order to keep the system reasonably efficient and maintainable; this is particularly crucial for a number of large-scale applications. This volume contains two chapters that explore application of lexical semantics in the area of natural language generation and in the area of machine translation with an interlingua representation.

The first chapter of this section, "Lexical functions of the *Explanatory Combinatorial Dictionary* for lexicalization in text generation", by Margarita Alonso Ramos et al., applies Mel'čuk's framework to natural language generation. It shows that the problem of lexicalization, i.e., the relation between a concept (or a combination of concepts) and its linguistic realization, cannot really be correctly carried out without making reference to a lexicon that takes into account the diversity of the lexico-semantics relations. This approach views lexicalization both as a local process (lexicalization is solved within a restricted phrase) and a more global one, taking into account the 'contextual effects' of a certain lexicalization with respect to the others in a sentence or in a text. Paradigmatic lexical functions are shown to be well adapted to treat lexicalization in the context of a text, whereas syntagmatic ones operate at the sentence or proposition levels.

The use of lexical semantic information for the interlingua component is modeled and illustrated in depth in "A lexical-semantic solution to the divergence problem in machine translation" by Bonnie Dorr. It sheds a new light on the domain of machine translation by the introduction of a well-motivated and well-defined use of Jackendoff's lexical conceptual structure (LCS) system as an intermediate level representation between the source and the target languages of a machine translation system. This approach is validated by a study of cross-linguistic variations among a number of languages such as English, German, French and Spanish. Furthermore, this chapter shows in a number of examples the intimate relations between syntactic structures and lexical conceptual representations, which is of much interest for the realization of parsers and generators.

17 Lexical functions of the *Explanatory Combinatorial Dictionary* for lexicalization in text generation

MARGARITA ALONSO RAMOS, AGNES TUTIN, AND
GUY LAPALME

17.1 Introduction

Lexical choice cannot be processed in text generation without appealing to a lexicon which takes into account many lexico-semantic relations. The text generation system must be able to treat the immediate and the larger lexical context.

a) The **immediate lexical context** consists of the lexemes that surround the lexical item to be generated. This context must absolutely be taken into account in the case of collocational constraints, which restrict ways of expressing a precise meaning to certain lexical items, for example as in expressions like *pay attention, receive attention* or *narrow escape* (Wanner & Bateman, 1990; Iordanskaja et al., 1991; Nirenburg & Nirenburg, 1988; Heid & Raab, 1989).

b) The **larger textual context** consists of the linguistic content of previous and subsequent clauses. This context is the source for cohesive links (Halliday & Hasan, 1976) with the lexical items to be generated in the current clause, as in:

(1) Professor Elmuck *was lecturing* on lexical functions to third-year students. The *lecturer* was interesting and *the audience* was very attentive.

In the second sentence, *lecturer* is coreferential with *Professor Elmuck* and *the audience* is coreferential with *third-year students*. These semantic links are due to the lexico-semantic relations between, on the one hand, *lecturer* ("agent noun") and *lecture,* and on the other hand, between *audience* ("patient noun") and *lecture.*

In this chapter, we will show that the Lexical Functions (LFs) of the *Explanatory Combinatorial Dictionary* (hereafter ECD) (Mel'čuk et al., 1984a, 1988; Mel'čuk & Polguère, 1987; Meyer & Steele, 1990) are well suited for these tasks in text generation.

A LEXICAL FUNCTION F IS A CORRESPONDENCE WHICH ASSOCIATES A LEXICAL ITEM L, CALLED THE KEY WORD OF F, WITH A SET OF LEXICAL ITEMS F(L) – THE VALUE OF F. (Mel'čuk, 1988b)

We would like to thank Igor Mel'čuk for fruitful discussions and helpful suggestions.

We will first briefly describe the LFs, dividing them into two subsets:

- **paradigmatic LFs,** which can formalize semantic relationships such as *to lecture – lecturer* and *to lecture - audience,* and
- **syntagmatic LFs,** which formalize co-occurrence relations such as *pay attention.* We will see that each subset addresses different kinds of lexical problems.

In particular, we will show that paradigmatic LFs can solve some interesting textual problems in text generation. We will mainly examine lexical coreferential relations and the introduction of specific definite NPs.

17.2   Different kinds of lexical functions

17.2.1   *Paradigmatic LFs versus syntagmatic LFs*

There are two main kinds of LFs: paradigmatic LFs and syntagmatic LFs.

Paradigmatic LFs are used to associate with a key-word a set of lexical items that share IN THE LEXICON a non-trivial semantic component with the key-word. The value of the LF and the key word do not usually form a phrase. For example, $S_0(buy) = purchase$ (derived noun) or Gener(*cherry*) = *fruit* (generic noun) are paradigmatic LFs.

Syntagmatic LFs are used to formalize a semantic relation (possibly a null one) between two lexemes L1 and L2 which is realized IN THE TEXTUAL STRING in a non-predictable way. In other words, lexical choice for expressing a given meaning (the name of the LF) in the context of a lexical item L1 (the key-word) is not free, but this choice is restricted (this is the value L2 of the LF for the key-word L1). For example, the LF for expressing the "intensity" meaning (FL Magn) in the context of the lexeme *pluie* [rain] is not free (**grande pluie, ?pluie intense*) but the choice is restricted (*pluie torrentielle*) [heavy rain]. In the formalism of LF, we have Magn(*pluie*)= *torrentielle.*

Paradigmatic LFs

We sum up the paradigmatic LFs in Figure 17.1.

Substitutive relations. Substitutive FLs are FLs for which the FL value and the key-word are substitutable in the syntagmatic string. The Fl value and key-word belong to the same part of speech.

Syn: synonym	Syn(*calling*) = *vocation*
Anti: antonym	Anti(*small*) = *big*
Contr: contrastive	Contr(*laugh*) = *cry*
Conv$_{ijkl}$: conversive	Conv$_{3214}$(*sell*) = *buy*
Gener: generic word	Gener(*apple*) = *fruit*

Semantic derivations contain typical qualifiers, typical categories for actants, typical nouns for adverbials.

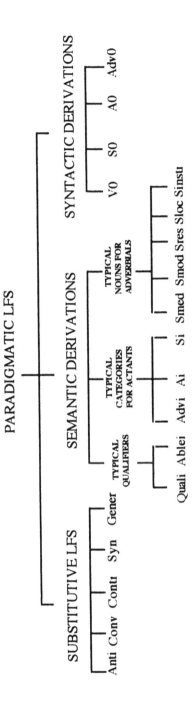

Figure 17.1. Paradigmatic LFs.

Typical categories for actants:[1]

S_i: typical noun for the i-th actant $S_1(sing) = singer$
A_i: typical qualifier for the i-th actant $A_1(love) = in\ love$
Adv_i: typical adverb for the i-th actant $Adv_1(speed) = at\ a\ speed\ of$

Typical nouns for adverbials:

S_{instr}: noun for typical instrument $S_{instr}(paint) = brush$
S_{med}: noun for typical mean $S_{med}(salt) = [to]salt$
S_{loc}: noun for typical place $S_{loc}(box) = ring$
S_{res}: noun for typical result $S_{res}(mix) = mixture$
S_{mod}: noun for typical mode $S_{mod}(write) = (hand)writing$

Typical qualifiers:

$Able_i$: adjective that qualifies what/who has the potential of being the i-th participant in the situation described by the key-word.
$Able_2(eat) = edible$
$Qual_i$: adjective that qualifies what/who has a high probability of being $Able_i$ $Qual_1(cheat) = dishonnest$

Syntactic derivations:

For syntactic derivations, key-words are synonymous with the value, but they do not belong to the same syntactic category. The key-word and the value are not necessarily linked by a morphological derivation.

S_0: derived noun $S_0(buy) = purchase$
A_0: derived adjective $A_0(sea) = maritime$
Adv_0: derived adverb $Adv_0(final) = finally$

Syntagmatic LFs

These include, roughly, the following kinds (for a complete list of LFs, see Mel'čuk & Polguère, 1987 or Mel'čuk & Zholkovsky, 1970):

Operator verbs: ($Oper_i$, $Func_i$, $Labor_{ij}$, $Real_i$, $Fact_i$, $Labreal_{ij}$, Pred):

Example:
$Oper_i$: Semantically empty verb which takes the i-th actant of the key-word as its subject and the key-word as its direct object.
$Oper_1(attention) = pay$ $Oper_2(attention) = receive$

Qualifiers expressing a particular semantic relationship (Bon, Epit, Magn, Pos_i, Ver):

Example:
Magn: intensity qualifier $Magn(escape) = narrow$

Verbs expressing a particular semantic relationship with their actant (Degrad, Nocer, Sympt, Excess, Obstr, Involv, Prox, Manif):

Example:
Degrad: degradation $Degrad(milk) = sour$

Prepositions expressing a particular semantic relationship (Propt, Instr, $Loc_{in/ad/ab}$):

> Example:
> $Loc^{in/ad/ab}$: Place in/to/from $Loc_{in}(street) = on$ [*the ~*]

Besides paradigmatic LFs and syntagmatic LFs, there are LFs which can be paradigmatic (the key-word and the value share a semantic component) and can be syntagmatic insofar as they can constitute a phrase. These are LFs like Mult: Mult(*ship*) = *fleet*, Cap: Cap(*school*) = *principal*, etc. We will call them **mixed LFs**.

In text generation, **Syntagmatic LFs** formalize collocational links that appear in the **immediate lexical context.** The importance of collocational constraints has been emphasized in the literature in text generation and machine translation, and the usefulness of LF formalism to cope with collocational constraints has been highlighted (Heid & Raab, 1989; Wanner & Bateman, 1990; Iordanskaja et al., 1991; Nirenburg & Nirenburg, 1988).

In this chapter, we will concentrate on **paradigmatic LFs** for treating **larger textual context.** We will see how they are useful to formalize some lexical textual problems: lexical coreference and introduction of specific definite NPs.

17.2.2 *Single LFs, complex LFs and composed LFs*

LFs can appear single, complex or composed. **Single LFs** appear alone to describe lexical associations like Magn(*rain*) = *heavy*.

Composed LFs are functions for which the set of values is produced through a regular combination of values of the constituent LFs. For example, S_0(Gener(*étuver*)) [steam] = *cuisson* [cooking] can be decomposed: Gener(*étuver*) = *cuire* [to cook] and S_0(*cuire*) = *cuisson* [cooking].

Complex LFs are combinations which cannot be decomposed, like Anti-Magn(*blessé*) = *légèrement* ["slightly injured"], that is, roughly LFs for which we cannot deduce the composition from the parts.

In the ECD, only the complex LFs and the single LFs are mentioned, because composed LFs can be reconstructed. Nevertheless, lexical relations that can be formalized by LF regular compositions must be studied because they appear in texts.

We will see in Section 17.3.3 how composed LFs can be exploited for creating coreferential relations.

17.3   Use of paradigmatic LFs for coreference in text generation

17.3.1 *Lexical coreference in text generation*

In text generation, textual context must absolutely be taken into account because texts like the following one are totally unacceptable:

(2)   a. Prepare the carrots, the celery and the asparagus.
         b. Cook the carrots, the celery and the asparagus in boiling water.

    c. Take the carrots, the celery and the asparagus out after 10 minutes.
    d. Cook *the vegetables* in boiling water and take them out after 10 minutes.

To avoid the unacceptable redundancy that we notice in 2b and 2c, we need to introduce anaphora, for example, *them* or *the vegetables,* as in 2d.

For us, a textual element is a **lexical coreferential anaphor** of an antecedent, a textual element previously introduced if

    a. it has the same referent as its antecedent,
    b. it belongs to an open lexical class,[2] and
    c. the anaphor and the antecedent share a semantic link.

For example, in 2d, *the vegetables* is a lexical coreferential anaphor of *the carrots, the celery and the asparagus* but *them* is not one, because it does not belong to an open lexical class. In the following example,

(3)   *Edith Cresson* arrived Monday at 9:00. At 11:00, *the Prime Minister of France* gave a press conference.

Prime Minister of France is a coreferential anaphor of *Edith Cresson,* but not a lexical one, because the coreferential link is not created by semantics but by world knowledge.

For creating lexical coreferential links in text generation, it is necessary to appeal to a large number of lexico-semantic relations. For example, let us imagine an underlying conceptual representation as a sequence of frame-like propositions, as shown in Figure 17.2. Many lexicalizations are possible for the attribute values of this representation. For example, after the first sentence:

(4a)   Professor Elmuck was lecturing on Lexical Functions to third year students.

Relying strictly on lexico-semantic and grammatical data, we could produce:

(4b)   (He/ The teacher/ Professor Elmuck/ The Professor/ The lecturer) was interesting.
(4c)   (?They/ The third year students/ The students/ The audience) was/were very attentive.

The lexical choice here depends strongly on the type of text to be generated. For example, coreferential links like *Professor Elmuck lectured . . . lecturer* are frequent in journalistic texts but rare in technical reports. We will not here discuss strategies for lexical contextual choice based on text types but we will discuss how lexical links can be created. We will try to show that LFs allow us to formalize a large number of lexico-semantic relations for lexical coreference. We will see that single LFs and composed LFs can be used for this task.

Single LFs for coreference relations

First, lexical coreferential links may appear with what is called, according to Halliday and Hasan (1976) reiteration, i.e., repetitions, synonyms, near-syn-

```
{lecture:
      agent: Elmuck_1
      destination: Students_1
      topic: Fonctions_1
}
{interesting:
      agent: Elmuck_1
}
{attentive:
      agent: Students_1
}
```

Figure 17.2. Simplified conceptual input for 4a, 4b and 4c.

onyms, superordinates. These kinds of lexico-semantic links appear in LFs, for example in:

Syn(*churchman*) = *clergyman*

(5)   Daniel confessed to *his churchman. The clergyman* blushed while listening to Daniel's sins.

Gener(*lamb*) = *meat*

(6)   Buy *New Zealand lamb. The meat* must be very fresh.

Besides these traditional coreferential relations, we can also use syntactic derivations LFs such as S_0, as in:

S_0(*buy*) = *purchase*

(7)   Mary went to St Lawrence street *to buy clothes. Her purchases* made she went back home.

Nevertheless, the use of a conversive relation does not seem to be allowed.

(8) $Conv_{3124}$(*sale*) = *purchase*
        The sale of the house has been a long process. ?* *The purchase* has been uneasy.

Until now, we have identified some types of lexical coreference between lexical items which maintain lexico-semantic relations and enable a coreferential link between the antecedent (the key-word) and the lexical anaphor (the LF value). **Direct lexical coreference** occurs between lexical items that maintain a lexical relationship directly formalizable through a LF like Syn, Gener, S0, $Conv_{ijkl}$ in some rare cases.

But, there can be coreference, not between the key-word and the LF value, but between an actant or an adverbial of the key-word and the value as we saw in (1) between *Professor Elmuck* and *lecturer* and between *third-year students* and *audience*. LFs can thus be used to formalize **indirect lexical coreference** when coreference appears between lexical items and a dependent (actantial or adverbial) if one maintains a lexical relationship directly formalizable through a LF.

In Figure 17.3, we give examples of direct and indirect coreference.

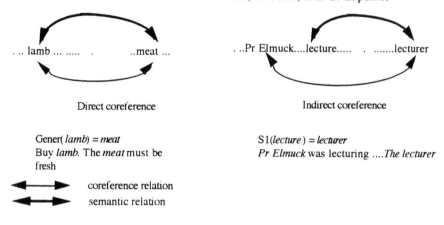

Figure 17.3. Direct and indirect conference.

In (1), *lecturer* is coreferential with *Professor Elmuck* and *third-year students* is coreferential with *audience*. Coreference can be established with the help of the actantial lexico-semantic relations. *Professor Elmuck* is the subject of *to lecture* (first actant) and as such, it can be coreferred to with the S_1 of *to lecture*, *lecturer*, and *third-year students* can be referred to as the S_2 of *lecture*, *audience*. The actant number (1,2,3,...) corresponds to the semantic actant of the lexeme. For example, the lexeme [TO] LECTURE will be described as a three actants verb: Someone (actant 1) lectures to someone else (actant 2) about something (actant 3).

In the same way, typical nouns for adverbials can be used for an indirect coreferential relation. For example, in:

(9)   Marguerite and Jean skated on the Rideau canal. This skating rink is 8 km long.

The prepositional phrase *on the Rideau canal* is dependent on the key-word *skate* in a certain semantic adverbial relation (location) and this phrase will be coreferred to by the typical adverbial, *skating rink*, of the same semantic relation (S_{loc}) of the key-word, *skate*.

The typical nouns for adverbials S_{med}, S_{loc}, S_{instr} and S_{mod} can be used for an indirect coreference relation.

Nevertheless, S_{res} (Typical result) is different. According to our analysis, the value of a S_{res} function is not a typical noun for adverbials because it cannot be coreferential with an adverbial of the key-word with which it is semantically linked. It is the typical noun denoting the result of a physical transformation. In the following example,

(10)   Mix the eggs$_i$ and the milk with the flour$_j$. Pour the mixture$_{i+j}$ in the pot.

the S_{res} of *mix*, *mixture* is coreferential with the set of *eggs*, *milk* and *flour* that has been affected by the action of mixing, i.e., with the actants II and III of *mix*. It is

Table 17.1. *LFs and compositions of LFs for direct coreference links*

LFs or composition of LFs	Key-word	Values
Gener	achat [purchase]	transaction [deal]
Gener	vente [sale]	transaction [deal]
Gener	transaction [deal]	action [action]
Gener	auto [car]	véhicule [vehicle]
Gener	voiture [car]	véhicule [vehicle]
Syn	voiture [car]	auto [car]
$Conv_{3214}$	acheter [buy]	vendre [sell]
S_0	acheter [buy]	achat [purchase]
S_0	vendre [sell]	vente [sale]
Gener o Gener	achat [purchase]	action [action]
Gener o Syn	auto [car]	véhicule [vehicle]
Gener o $Conv_{3214}$	vente [sale]	transaction [transaction]
Gener o S_0	acheter [buy]	transaction [transaction]
S0 o $Conv_{3124}$	acheter [buy]	vente [sale]
$Conv_{3214}$ o S_0	acheter [buy]	vente [sale]

not a simple case of direct coreference because, in this case, these items have been affected by a complete transformation of their characteristics.

Composed LFs for coreference relations

As we have suggested earlier, composed LFs can be profitably exploited because they also appear in coreference relations. In this section, we have only observed some of the most frequent compositions. This is just an exploratory work and we have not systematically studied what would prevent lexical coreference.

In Table 17.1, we give some examples of LF compositions. The following facts must be noted about compositions:

1. The Composition relation is not commutative. For example, $S_0(Gener(\acute{e}tuver))$ [steam] = *cuisson* [cooking] but $Gener(S_0(\acute{e}tuver))$ does not produce any value because $S_0(\acute{e}tuver)$ does not have a value.

2. Many compositions should be reduced. For example, Gener(Syn(X)) is equivalent to Gener(X) as we can see in Table 17.1. Reducible LFs should not be calculated (see Décary, 1986, and Décary & Lapalme, 1990, for an examination of reducible LFs).

Compositions involving direct coreference LFs produce direct coreference compositions:

$S_0(Gener(\acute{e}tuver))$ = *cuisson*

(11)   Faire *étuver la viande*. A la fin de *la cuisson*, ajouter les épices.
[Let the meat steam. At the end of the cooking, add the spices].

Table 17.2. *Kinds of coreferential links produced by compositions of two LFs*

LFi → LFj ↓	Type	Gener	Syn	S_0	S_i	S_{instr}	S_{med}	S_{res}	S_{loc}	S_{mod}
Gener	DC	DC	*DC	DC	IC	IC	IC	DC	IC	IC
Syn	DC	*DC	*DC	*DC	*IC	*IC	*IC	*IC	*IC	*IC
S_0	DC	DC	*DC	—	—	—	—	—	—	—
S_i	IC	IC	*IC	*IC	—	—	—	—	—	—
S_{instr}	IC	IC	*IC	*IC	—	—	—	—	—	—
S_{med}	IC	IC	*IC	*IC	—	—	—	—	—	—
S_{res}	?DC	?DC	*DC	*DC	—	—	—	—	—	—
S_{loc}	IC	IC	*IC	*IC	—	—	—	—	—	—
S_{mod}	IC	IC	*IC	*IC	—	—	—	—	—	—

Compositions involving a direct coreference LF and an indirect LF (or an indirect coreference composition) produce indirect coreference compositions. For example,

Gener(S_i(*marathon*)) [marathon] = *coureur* [runner]
S_i(*marathon*) = *marathonien* [marathonian]et Gener(*marathonien*) = *coureur*

(12)   *Jean* fait souvent le <u>marathon</u>. Le *coureur* est infatigable.
        [Jean often does the marathon. The runner is indefatigable]

In Table 17.2, we have shown compositions of two LFs that can be used in coreference relations. DC indicates that the LF can create a direct coreference relation, IC indicates that the LF can create an indirect coreference relation. The entry in the table corresponds to LF_i o LF_j. The product of the composition is indicated at the intersection. This can be:

- A DC: Ex: Gener (DC) o S_0 (DC) => DC.
- An IC: Ex: Gener (DC) o S_i (IC) => IC.
- A * before DC or IC indicates that the composition is reducible to a single function. Ex: Gener o Syn = Gener (*DC)
- No result: composition is absurd or does not produce anything.

Thus, LF formalism enables one to systematize many coreference links between open-class words in a text. These links are either direct, or indirect if the link is formed by another lexical item. Finally, coreference links can be formalized by single LFs or by compositions of LFs.

In the perspective of text generation, this formalism appears very interesting for building coreferential relations. To point back to a referent already introduced, LFs and compositions of LFs offer many possible ways for lexicalizing a given referent. For example, let us suppose that after having introduced the following sentence,

(13)   a. Laisser étuver la viande. [Let the meat steam.]

we have to refer again to the action *la viande étuve.* We could try to use a nominalization (S_0). But, as there is no nominalization for the verb *étuver,* we could use instead the nominalization of the generic term, $S_0(Gener(étuver)) = $ *cuisson.* We could thus produce the following sentence:

(13)   b. A la fin de la cuisson, ajouter les épices
             [At the end of cooking, add the spices]

Of course, we do not claim here that LFs cover all the cases of coreference. It has been noted (Hirst, 1981) that coreference often involves non-linguistic relations as we saw in example (3).

17.3.2   *Introduction of the specific definite article and lexical associations*

Choosing between the indefinite and the definite article is sometimes hard in text generation: it depends on many factors, such as extra-linguistic knowledge, situational knowledge and lexical knowledge. Following the linguistic frame defined by Hawkins (1978) for the use of the definite article, we will show in this section that the formalism of paradigmatic LFs can be usefully exploited to clarify some lexical knowledge.

Hawkins' approach to definite article

It has been noted that the specific definite article obeys many constraints, certain of which are textual. Within the frame of pragmatics, Hawkins (1978) identified four sets of shared knowledge between the speaker and the hearer that enable the introduction of a specific definite article:

- The **previous discourse set:** this includes the antecedents enabling one to make coreferential links.
- The **immediate situation set:** this enables the use of a definite deictic article. The definite NP is used to refer to something that is in the immediate environment.
- The **larger environment set:** this enables the introduction of referents whose knowledge is implicitly shared by the speaker and the hearer.
- The **association set:** this includes knowledge directly "activated" by lexical items of the previous discourse.

It seems possible and necessary to determine in a more linguistic way some of these shared sets. We will exclude from our study the immediate situation set, which is linked to the immediate environment, and the larger environment set, which contains world knowledge, because none is linguistic. Nevertheless, the previous discourse set and the association set can be described in a linguistic way.

The previous discourse set

The previous discourse set corresponds *grosso modo* to the antecedents that appear in the coreference relations. Each time a lexical coreferential anaphora is introduced, it can include a definite article. We will not go into detail here on these relations, because we have treated them in the previous section.

The association set

The definite article can be introduced in a text when it appears in a NP whose meaning is linked "paradigmatically" with one or several lexical items previously introduced.

The association set does not appear very clearly defined by Hawkins: the associations sometimes seem to be encyclopedic and they sometimes seem to be lexical. Besides, Hawkins does not detail the associations that really enable the introduction of the definite article. His perspective is based more on comprehension than on production.

We will clearly distinguish lexico-semantic relations from encyclopedic ones. We will say that there is a lexico-semantic relation between two lexical items if they share a non-trivial meaning component. For us, the prototypical aspect will be part of the encyclopedic knowledge (Lakoff, 1988; Kleiber, 1990).

As a set of associations, we will use paradigmatic LFs and we will treat only LFs whose values can be nouns.

Typical nouns for actants. When introduced in a text, typical nouns for actants are not always coreferential as in:

(14)   Le Professeur Elmuck faisait une conférence. Le sujet était intéressant et l'auditoire était attentif.[3]
        [Professor Elmuck was lecturing. The topic was interesting and the audience was attentive.]

In this example, the value of $S_3(conférence)$ [lecture] = *sujet* [topic] and the value of $S_2(\textbf{conférence})$ = *auditoire* [audience] are introduced by a specific definite article. Is this always possible for typical actants? For us, the answer is probably "yes" for the following reason: the referents which correspond to typical nouns for actants are in some way implied. As soon as the key word is uttered, the actants are "activated" because they belong to the government pattern of the word. As they are typical nouns, they fit perfectly into the semantic slots for each actant.

Typical nouns for adverbials. Since they are introduced after the key word in a text, do the typical nouns for adverbials enable the introduction of the definite article? The relationships S_{loc}, S_{instr}, S_{med} and S_{mod} maintained with the key-word are looser than those of the typical nouns for actants. Nevertheless, they seem to enable the definite article to appear, as in the following examples:

S_{instr}(peindre) = pinceau

(15)   Jean peignait ses murs. Soudain, (*la/ une) mouche s'est collée sur
       (le/ ? un) pinceau.
       [Jean was painting his walls. Suddenly, (*the/ a) fly stuck on (the/ *a)
       paintbrush.]

S_{loc}(boxeur) = ring

(16)   Le boxeur encaissait de nombreux coups. Soudain, il s'affala sur ((le
       / un*) ring / (*la / une) chaise).
       [The boxer was taking many blows. Suddenly, he collapsed on ((the /
       *a) ring/ (*the / a) chair).]

S_{med}(peindre) = peinture

(17)   Jean peignait ses murs. Soudain, ((la /?de la) peinture / (*l' / de l')
       eau) coula par terre.
       [Jean was painting his walls. Suddenly, (the/ *Ø) paint (*the/ Ø) water
       flew on the floor.]

In these examples, the indefinite article with the value of the function is used
to introduce a referent which appears to be out of the situation created by the key-
word. Thus, in (15b), *un pinceau* (a paintbrush) can not designate the paintbrush
that Jean uses in the situation (15a) but another paintbrush. In (16b), the use of
the indefinite article is not allowed because, in the situation (16a), there is only
one ring, and no other ring can be thought of.

As we saw previously, S_{res} often appears as a complex coreferential anaphor
when there is a change of state of the referents and in coreferential cases, the use
of the definite article is very natural. There are nevertheless some cases as in the
following, where a new referent is naturally introduced by a definite article, because, though the referent has not been previously introduced, it is implied by the
meaning of the key-word. For example, in:

S_{res}(photocopier) = photocopie

(18)   a. Le professeur Elmuck a photocopié les examens des étudiants.
       b. Il a fait tomber ((les / des) photocopies / (* les/ des) feuilles
          blanches) en faisant un geste brusque.
       [Professor Elmuck photocopied the student exams. He dropped ((the/
       Ø) photocopies) / (* the/ Ø) paper sheets) in making an abrupt ges-
       ture.]

les photocopies is not coreferential. It introduces a new object which did not exist
before in (18a) but which is the result of the whole process. The indefinite article
in (18b) is used to designate the photocopies which are out of the situation (18a).

Substitutive relations. Contr and Anti are the only paradigmatic functions that do
not enable introduction of coreferents. They do not seem to allow the introduction
of the definite article either. Nevertheless, they introduce coherence relations

because there is a thematic continuity in the texts, with the words belonging to the same semantic fields.

Thus, LFs formalize some of the semantic relations that allow the introduction of the definite article.

We should add the following remarks:

- Many other semantic relations can introduce a definite article. In particular, we should say that many of these semantic relations appear in the ECD within the definition of lexemes.
- Many of the associations enabling the introduction of definite article in texts are not lexico-semantic ones but encyclopedic ones (Fradin 1983).
- We should envisage LF compositions for this application.

To sum up, in texts LFs can formalize some of the introductions of the definite article, either for coferential relations (previous discourse set, in Hawkins' words) or for the association set.

17.4 Conclusion

In this chapter, we have shown the usefulness of paradigmatic LFs to treat lexico-semantic phenomena in text generation. We first divided LFs into two subsets: paradigmatic LFs and syntagmatic LFs. We showed that paradigmatic LFs are an appropriate formalism for treating lexicalization in textual context:

1. They can be exploited to systematize lexical coferential relations between a lexical anaphor and its coferential antecedent. These relations are either direct, or indirect if they are realized through a third lexeme. Coferential relations can be formalized through a single LF or composed LFs.
2. Paradigmatic FLs enable us to define in a more linguistic way the "discourse previous set" and the "association set", defined by Hawkins (1978), for explaining the introduction of the definite NP:
3. The previous discourse set contains the set of antecedents which are pointed back to by a coferential lexical anaphor introduced with the help of the definite article.
4. The association set can be partially formalized by some paradigmatic LFs. Typical nouns for actants and typical nouns for adverbials can easily be introduced with a definite article when they appear in the text immediately after their key-words, being implied by them.

Many things remain to be done:

1. We should study the question of LF compositions in depth and establish a formal grammar of LF compositions. This problem has just been touched upon here.

2. We should test LFs and LF compositions on a large corpus of texts to check whether the paradigmatic LFs are really productive for lexical cohesion.
3. We should study thoroughly strategies for implementations that use LFs because we have not addressed this problem here. Nevertheless, let us indicate that some paradigmatic functions have been implemented in Kosseim (1992) for coreferential relations in text generation. Besides, text generation systems using Meaning-Text Theory, and especially paraphrase (Mel'čuk, 1988b), necessarily make extensive use of some paradigmatic lexical functions (Iordanskaja et al. 1991, Boyer & Lapalme, 1985).

Notes

1. In the ECD, a noun like *escape* will be described as a 3 actants noun: X's (actant1) escape from Y (actant II) through Z (actant III). The number of actants (semantic and syntactic) and the way they are realized superficially (for example, with which kind of prepositions) are noted in the government pattern of the lexeme. Government pattern exists not only with verbs and predicative nouns, but also with adjectives and adverbs.
2. Lexical open classes contain the following parts of speech: nouns, verbs, adjectives and adverbs.
3. Because the meaning of the definite article can be slightly different in English and in French, we will give French examples here.

References

Boyer M. & G. Lapalme. (1985). Generating Paraphrases from Meaning-Text Semantic Networks, *Computational Linguistics.*, I, 3–4, 103–117.

Décary M. (1986). *Un éditeur spécialisé pour le Dictionnaire Explicatif et Combinatoire du Français Contemporain.*, M. Sc. Thesis, Département d'informatique et de recherche opérationnelle, Université de Montréal.

Décary M. & G. Lapalme (1990). An Editor for the Explanatory Dictionary of Contemporary French (DECFC), *Computational Linguistics*, 16, 3, 145–154.

Fradin B. (1984). Anaphorisation et stéréotypes nominaux, *Lingua*, 64, 325–369.

Halliday M. A. K & R. Hasan (1976). *Cohesion in English*, London, Longman.

Hawkins J. A. (1978). *Definiteness and Indefiniteness*, London, Croom Helm.

Heid U. & S. Raab. (1989). Collocations in Multilingual Generation, *Proceedings of EACL*, 130–136.

Hirst G. (1981). *Anaphora in Natural Language Understanding: A Survey*, Berlin, Springer-Verlag.

Iordanskaja L., R. Kittredge & A. Polguère (1991). Lexical Selection and Paraphrase in a Meaning-Text Generation Model in C. L. Paris, W. R. Swartout & W. C. Mann, eds., *Natural Language Generation in Artificial Intelligence and Computational Linguistics*, 293–312.

Kleiber G. (1990). *La sémantique des prototypes: Catégories et sens lexical*, Paris, PUF.

Kosseim L. (1992). *Génération automatique de procédés cohésifs dans les recettes de cuisine*, M.Sc. thesis, Département d'informatique et de recherche opérationnelle, Université de Montréal.

Lakoff G. (1988). Cognitive Semantics, in U. Eco, M. Santambrogio & P. Violi eds., *Meaning and Mental Representation*, Bloomington and Indianapolis, Indiana University Press, 118–154.

Mel'čuk I. & A. Polguère. (1987). A Formal Lexicon in the Meaning-Text Theory (or How to Do Lexica with Words), *Computational Linguistics*, 13, 3–4, 261–275.

Mel'čuk I. & D. Zholkovsky. (1970). Sur la synthèse sémantique, *T. A. Informations*, 2, Paris, Klincksieck, 1–85.

Mel'čuk I. et al. (1984). *Dictionnaire Explicatif et Combinatoire du Français Contemporain. Recherches Lexico-sémantiques I.* Montréal, Presses de l'Université de Montréal.

Mel'čuk I.A. et al. (1988a). *Dictionnaire Explicatif et Combinatoire du Français Contemporain. Recherches Lexico-sémantiques II.* Montréal, Presses de l'Université de Montréal.

Mel'čuk I. (1988b). Paraphrase et lexique dans la Théorie Sens-Texte, *Cahiers de Lexicologie*, LII, 5–50 et LIII, 5–53.

Meyer I. & J. Steele. (1990). Lexical Functions in the Explanatory Combinatorial Dictionary: Kinds and Definitions, in J. Steele ed., *Meaning Text Theory*, Ottawa University Press.

Nirenburg S. & I. Nirenburg. (1988). A Framework for Lexical Selection in Natural Language Generation, in *Proceedings of COLING 88*, Budapest, 471–475.

Wanner L. & J. A. Bateman. (1990). Lexical Cooccurrence Relations in Text Generation, *Proceedings of the Fifth International Workshop on Natural Language Generation*, Dawson, Pennsylvania, 31–38.

18   A lexical-semantic solution to the divergence problem in machine translation

BONNIE J. DORR

18.1   Introduction

One of the most difficult areas for research in machine translation (MT) is the representation of meanings in the lexicon. The lexicon plays a central role in any MT system, regardless of the theoretical foundations upon which the system is based. However, it is only recently that MT researchers have begun to focus more specifically on issues that concern the lexicon, e.g., cross-linguistic variations that arise during the mapping between lexical items in the source and target languages.

The traditional approach to constructing dictionaries for MT has been to massage on-line dictionaries that are primarily intended for human consumption. Given that most natural language applications have focused primarily on syntactic information that can be extracted from the lexicon, these methods have constituted a reasonable first-pass approach to the problem. However, it is now widely accepted that MT requires language-independent conceptual information in order to successfully process a wide range of phenomena in more than one language. Thus, the task of constructing lexical entries has become a much more difficult problem as researchers endeavor to extend the concept base to support more phenomena and additional languages.

This chapter describes how parameterization of the lexicon allows an MT system to account for a number of cross-linguistic variations, called *divergences*, during translation. There are many cases in which the natural translation of one language into another results in a very different form than that of the original. These divergences make the straightforward transfer from source structures into target structures impractical. The current approach adopts the view that it is possible to provide a finite cross-linguistic classification of MT divergences and to implement a systematic mapping between the internal representation of the system and the surface syntactic structure that accommodates all of the divergences in this classification. Figure 18.1 shows some of the types of divergences handled by the current approach with respect to English, Spanish, and German.

This research has been partially supported by the National Science Foundation under grant IRI-9120788, by the DARPA Basic Research Program under grant N00014–92-J-1929, and by the Army Research Office Scientific Services Program under Contract DAAL03–91-C-0034 through Batelle Corporation.

B. J. Dorr

(1)   **Thematic divergence:**
       E: I like Mary
       S. María me gusta
          (Mary (to) me pleases)
(2)   **Promotional divergence:**
       E: John usually goes home
       S: Juan suele ir a casa
          (John tends to go home)
(3)   **Demotional divergence:**
       E: I like to eat
       G: Ich esse gern
          (I eat likingly)
(4)   **Structural divergence:**
       E: John entered the hosue
       S: Juan entró en la casa
          (John entered in the house)
(5)   **Categorial divergence:**
       E: I am hungry
       G: Ich habe Hunger
          (I have hunger)
(6)   **Conflational divergence:**
       E: I stabbed John
       S: Yo le di puñaladas a Juan
          (I gave knife-wounds to John)

Figure 18.1. Divergence examples in English, Spanish, and German demonstrate the complexity of the translation problem.

Many sentences may fit into these divergence classes, not just the ones listed here. Also, a single sentence may exhibit any or all of these divergences. Throughout this chapter, the abbreviations D, E, F, G, P, and S will be used to stand for Dutch, English, French, German, Portuguese, and Spanish, respectively. (Literal translations are included for the non-English cases.)

The first divergence type is *thematic:* in (1), the theme is realized as the verbal object (*Mary*) in English but as the subject (*María*) of the main verb in Spanish. The second divergence type, *promotional*, is one of two *head switching* divergence types: in (2), the modifier (*usually*) is realized as an adverbial phrase in English but as the main verb *soler* in Spanish. The third divergence type, *demotional*, is another type of *head switching* divergence: in (3), the word *like* is realized as a main verb in English but as an adverbial modifier (*gern*) in German. The distinction between promotional and demotional divergences may not be intuitively obvious at first glance. In both (2) and (3), the translation mapping associates a main verb with an adverbial satellite, or *vice versa* (i.e., in (2), the main verb *soler* is associated with the adverbial satellite *usually*, and in (3) the main verb *like* is associated with the adverbial satellite *gern*). The distinction between these two *head switching* cases becomes more apparent when we consider the status of the participating lexical tokens more carefully. In the case of *soler-usually*, the main verb *soler* is, in some sense, the token that "triggers" the head switching operation: its presence forces the adverbial satellite *usually* to appear in English, even if we were to substitute some other event for *ir* in Spanish (e.g., *correr a la tienda, leer un libro*, etc.). By contrast, in the case of *like-gern*, the triggering element is not the main verb *like* since we are able to use *like* in other contexts that do not require *gern* (e.g., *I like the car* ⇔ *Mir gefällt der Wagen*); instead, the triggering element is the adverbial satellite *gern*: its presence forces the verb *like* to appear in English even if we were to substitute some other event in place of *essen* in German (e.g., *zum Geschäft laufen, das Buch lesen*, etc.). Additional justification for the distinction between these two cases is given in Dorr (1993).

The fourth divergence type is a *structural* divergence: in (4), the verbal object is realized as a noun phrase (*the house*) in English and as a prepositional phrase (*en la casa*) in Spanish. The fifth divergence type is *categorial*: in (5), the predicate is adjectival (*hungry*) in English but nominal (*Hunger*) in German. Finally, the sixth divergence type is *conflational*. Conflation is the incorporation of necessary participants (or arguments) of a given action. In (6), English uses the single word *stab* for the two Spanish words *dar* (*give*) and *puñaladas* (*knife-wounds*); this is because the manner argument (i.e., the *likingly* portion of the lexical token) is incorporated into the main verb in English.

UNITRAN, a machine translation system that translates English, Spanish, and German bidirectionally, has been built on the basis of this divergence classification. A central claim of this chapter is that this divergence classification covers all potential source-language/target-language distinctions based on lexical-semantic properties (i.e., properties associated with entries in the lexicon that are not based on purely syntactic information, idiomatic usage, aspectual knowledge, discourse knowledge, domain knowledge, or world knowledge).

Although most translation systems have some mechanism for processing divergent structures, they do not provide a general procedure that takes advantage of the relationship between lexical-semantic structure and syntactic structure. The current approach is more systematic in that it accounts for language-specific idiosyncrasies that distinguish two languages, while making use of lexical-semantic uniformities that tie the two languages together. The way that this is achieved is through the use of *parameters*, or switches that are set according to the characteristics of the languages involved in the translation.

The current research aims to illustrate the applicability of a lexical-based framework to the problem of MT with particular reference to this divergence classification. The MT model that is adopted is *interlingual* (i.e., an underlying lexical-semantic form of the source language is derived from which any of the target languages, Spanish, English, or German, may be produced). The interlingual approach eliminates many of the problems associated with the *direct* replacement and *transfer* approaches of previous systems. In particular, the model does not make use of direct-replacement or transfer rules that are meticulously tailored to each of the source and target languages. Instead, the current translation model is based on a parameterized lexical-semantic representation that makes it easy to change from one language to another (by setting lexical-semantic switches in the lexicon of each language) without having to write a whole new processor for each language. This is an advance over other MT systems that require at least one language-specific processing module for each source-language/target-language pair.

Perhaps the most important contribution of the research reported here is that it supports the view that it is possible to provide a finite cross-linguistic classification of MT divergences and to implement a systematic mapping between the lexical-semantic interlingua and the surface syntactic structure that accommodates these divergences. The key to being able to provide a systematic mapping is modularity: the translator is designed so that it is partitioned into two different processing levels, thus allowing for a decoupling of syntactic and lexical-semantic decisions that are made during the translation process. An advantage of this design is that lexical-semantic parameter settings may be independently specified (for each language) without having to modify the systematic mapping between the interlingua and the surface syntactic structure.

In the strictest sense, a divergence may exist even for translations in which the source- and target-language pairs do not necessarily exhibit any distinctions on the surface. In such cases, there are generally two occurrences of a *language-to-interlingua* divergence (one *from* the surface structure and one *to* the surface structure). By contrast, a *language-to-language* divergence occurs only in the context of a single language-to-interlingua divergence (or two different language-to-interlingua divergences). For the purposes of this chapter, a divergence is viewed as a consequence of the internal mapping between the surface structure and the interlingual representation (i.e., a *language-to-interlingua* divergence) rather than as an external distinction (i.e., a *language-to-language* divergence). However, it should be stressed that the MT divergences presented here are ones that any MT system must cope with, not just those that use an interlingual representation. In particular, it has been argued that such divergences must be dealt with in transfer designs as well. (See, for example, Lindop and Tsujii, 1991, and Tsujii and Fujita, 1991.) Although this chapter argues for the interlingual approach over the transfer approach, this issue is not considered to be the central point here. Rather, the focus is on the classification of translation divergences and the implementation of a systematic solution to the divergence problem based on a lexical-semantic representation.

This chapter examines each of the divergence types from Figure 18.1, showing formally how the UNITRAN system (Dorr, 1987, 1990, 1993) solves these divergences by mapping an underlying lexical-conceptual structure to a syntactic structure (and vice versa) on the basis of two general routines and their associated parametric mechanisms. The next section provides the motivation for the interlingual approach. Section 18.3 introduces the lexical-semantic representation that is used as the interlingua. Section 18.4 discusses the issue of classifying MT divergences. Section 18.5 examines each divergence type in turn, demonstrating how two general routines and their associated parametric mechanisms provide the appropriate mapping from source to target language for each type of divergence.

18.2 Motivation for the interlingual approach

MT has been a particularly difficult problem in the area of Natural Language Processing for over four decades. Early approaches to translation failed in part because interaction effects of complex phenomena made translation appear to be unmanageable. Later approaches to the problem have achieved varying degrees of success. (See Hutchins (1986), King (1987), Maxwell et al. (1988), Nirenburg (1987), Nirenburg et al. (1992), Slocum (1988), and Hutchins and Somers (1992) for cogent reviews of this area.) Only certain issues of relevance to the current approach will be discussed in this section. In particular, the motivation for the interlingual approach will be presented with specific reference to the divergence classification shown in Figure 18.1.

One might argue that several of the examples from Figure 18.1 could be translated using a *direct* approach to translation with little loss of information. For example, if we choose English to be the target language, we could translate examples (1), (2), and (3), as (7), (8), and (9), respectively:

(7)   S: María me gusta ⟹ E: Mary pleases me
(8)   S: Juan suele ir a casa ⟹ E: John tends to go home
(9)   G: Ich esse gern ⟹ E: I eat enjoyably

The problem with taking such an approach is that it is not general enough to handle a wide range of cases. For example, if we translate the word *gern* directly to the word *enjoyably* as in case (9), we will run into problems when we try to translate *gern* in other contexts. As it turns out, the adverb *gern* may be used in conjunction with *haben* to mean *like*: *Ich habe Marie gern* ('I like Mary'). The literal translation, *I have Mary enjoyably*, is not only stylistically unattractive, but it is not a valid translation for this sentence. In addition, the direct-mapping approach is not bidirectional in the general case. Thus, even if we did take (7), (8), and (9) as the desired translations, we would not be able to apply the same direct mapping in the reverse direction (i.e., translating from the more standard English version to Spanish and German) because we would still need to translate *like* and *usually* into Spanish and German. It is clear that a uniform method for bidirectional translation is required.

The direct approach to translation has been largely discounted as an alternative to the interlingual approach; however, there have been arguments for a more commonly used alternative to the interlingual approach, namely, the *transfer* approach – see, for example Arnold and Sadler (1990), Boitet (1988), and Vauquois and Boitet (1985). Paradoxically, these anti-interlingual arguments are based precisely on the same examples that have motivated the current research (e.g., those sentences that exhibit the types of divergences shown earlier). The assumption is that it would be too difficult to design an interlingual representation that includes enough information to accommodate complex divergences. This chapter argues to the contrary, i.e., that complex divergences are precisely what necessitates the use of an interlingual representation. The interlingual approach allows surface syntactic distinctions to be represented at a level that is independent from that of the underlying "meaning" of the source and target sentences. Factoring out these surface-level distinctions allows cross-linguistic generalizations to be captured at the level of lexical-semantic structure.

Some examples of the types of translations that are used to justify the use of a transfer approach are:[1]

(10)   **Demotional divergence:**
         G: Johann kußt Marie gern[2] ⇔ E: John likes to kiss Mary
         'John kisses Mary likingly'
(11)   **Promotional divergence:**
         F: Jean a failli finir le livre[3] ⇔ E: John has almost finished the book
         'John has missed to finish the book'
(12)   **Conflational divergence:**
         E: They run into the room ⇔
         F: Ils entrent dans la salle en courant[4]
         'They enter the room in running'

The implicit assumption rejected by the current approach is that it would be impossible to design an interlingual system that supports a systematic mapping between the source and target languages in cases such as (10), (11), and (12). As we will see, these types of divergences are precisely the ones that are handled by the UNITRAN system.

For the purposes of comparison, we will briefly discuss the approach taken by the MiMo system; see Arnold et al. (1988), Arnold and Sadler (1990), van Noord et al. (1989), van Noord et al. (1990), and Sadler et al. (1990) for these examples. Other systems that have attempted to deal with these (and other) divergence types are TAUM (Colmerauer et al., 1971), GETA/ARIANE (Vauquois and Boitet, 1985 and Boitet, 1987), LMT (McCord, 1989), LFG-MT (Kaplan et al., 1989), METAL (Alonso, 1990, and Thurmair, 1990), and LTAG (Abeillé et al., 1990). Specific examples of these systems are discussed in Dorr (1993).

The MiMo system developed from an effort that had its beginnings within the Eurotra framework. (For cogent descriptions of the Eurotra project, see, e.g., Arnold and des Tombe, 1987; Copeland et al., 1991; and Johnson et al., 1985.) Whereas the 'mainstream' Eurotra work stops short of describing how translation divergences are handled, the MiMo project has extended the Eurotra formalism to handle a wide range of divergence classes. MiMo is a structural transfer approach that addresses the solution to divergence cases such as (10), (11), and (12). To achieve the translation mapping in these examples, the transfer approach requires the existence of transfer entries. In particular, the verb *like* must be related to the adverb *gern* by means of a transfer entry of the form:

(13)   r!((cat = S).[mod = GERN]) ⇔ LIKE((cat = S).[r!arg1])

This rule indicates that the word *gern* would be realized as an adverbial modifier in German, whereas the English counterpart would be realized as a main verb that takes a sentential argument.

As for (11) and (12), the required transfer rules are (14) and (15), respectively:

(14) FAILLIR([1!arg1],[!arg2=r![2!arg2]]) ⇔
     r!([1!arg1],[2!arg2][mod = ALMOST])

(15) ENTRER([1!arg2],[mod = EN[!arg1=COURIR]]) ⇔
     RUN([mod=INTO[1!arg2]])

Rule (14) ensures that the French main verb *faillir* in (11) is translated as an English adverbial *almost* in English. (The r! variable is bound to *finir* in French and *finish* in English.) Rule (15) maps the compound French construction *entrer en courant* in (12) into the simple English construction *run into*.

We need not dwell on the well-known problem that such transfer entries are required for each source-language/target-language pair of the system, including pairs that exhibit less complicated divergences such as in the *like-gustar* case shown in Figure 18.1 (as well as pairs for which there is no divergence at all). Suffice it to say that specifying transfer mappings for all of the lexical items of each source-language/target-language pair is very tedious work. (See, e.g., Bennett et al., 1986, for additional discussion.) There are, however, other problems with the transfer approach that are worth mentioning here. One problem is that much of the information that is, or could be, lexically stored (e.g., the argument structure of the word *entrer*) is included in the transfer rules as well. The use of transfer rules results in a severe proliferation of redundancy on a per-language basis. For example, *faillir* is not the only verb that gives rise to the type of construction shown in (11); in fact, Arnold and Sadler (1990) present a similar verb, *venir* (which translates to the adverbial *just*) that is precisely analogous to the verb *faillir*. Thus, rules analogous to (14) must be constructed for *venir*, differing only in that *venir* is used in place of *faillir* and *just* in place of *almost*.[5] The multiplicative effect of all of these combinations wreaks havoc with the number of transfer rules that are required on a per-language basis.

Another problem with the transfer approach is that it misses a number of cross-linguistic generalizations. For example, not only do constructions such as (10), (11) and (12) arise *within* a single language, but such constructions exist *across* languages as well. The root of the problem with the MiMo approach is that it does not use a canonical representation that would factor out this redundancy. As we will see shortly, the UNITRAN system takes advantage of such a representation to map between languages in a more systematic and uniform fashion.

18.3   Lexical-semantic representation

In order to adopt an interlingual approach to MT, one must construct a language-independent representation that lends itself readily to the specification of a systematic mapping that operates uniformly across all languages. To meet this objective, one needs a clear characterization of the entire range of divergences that could possibly arise in MT. Such a characterization can emerge only from a serious cross-linguistic investigation into the adequacy of different lexical representations for natural language. Recent work (see Dorr, 1990, 1993) has provided an appropriate representation in terms of a *lexical conceptual structure* (LCS) based on work by Jackendoff (1983, 1990).[6] This representation abstracts away from syntax just far enough to enable language independent encoding, while retaining enough structure to be sensitive to the requirements for language translation and, in particular, the resolution of divergences such as those shown in Figure 18.1.

The field of MT has (almost from the beginning) been concerned with the use of a "deep semantic representation" and with looking for "universals" for translation. One of the biggest objections to the use of an interlingual representation is that it relies on defining a set of primitives (to represent the information to be translated) which allow a mapping to be defined among the languages in question. Because it is generally difficult to define such a set, many researchers have abandoned this model. (See, for example, Vauquois and Boitet, 1985.) However, recently, there has been a resurgence of interest in the area of lexical representation and organization (with special reference to verbs) that has initiated an ongoing effort to delimit the classes of lexical knowledge required to process natural language; [see, e.g., Grimshaw (1990), Hale and Keyser (1986a, 1986b, 1989), Hale and Laughren (1983), Jackendoff (1983, 1990), Levin and Rappaport (1986), Levin (1985, 1993), Pustejovsky (1988, 1989, 1991), Rappaport et al. (1987), Rappaport and Levin (1988), Olsen (1991), and Zubizarreta (1982, 1987)].

As a result of this effort, it has become increasingly more feasible to isolate the components of meaning common to verbs participating in particular classes. These components of meaning can then be used to determine the lexical representation of verbs across languages. Consequently, the representation adopted for UNITRAN (which is by no means exhaustive) is based on an adapted version of the LCS proposed by Jackendoff that takes into account recent theories of the lexicon.

The LCS approach views semantic representation as a subset of conceptual structure, i.e., the language of mental representation. Jackendoff's approach includes *types* such as Event and State, which are specialized into *primitives* such as GO, STAY, BE, GO-EXT, and ORIENT. As an example of how the primitive GO is used to represent sentence semantics, consider the following sentence:

(16)   (i) The ball rolled toward Beth.

          (ii) $[_{Event}GO\ ([_{Thing}BALL],$

                    $[_{Path}TOWARD\ ([_{Position}AT\ ([_{Thing}BALL],\ [_{Thing}BETH])])])]$

This representation illustrates one dimension (i.e., the *spatial* dimension) of Jackendoff's representation. Another dimension is the *causal* dimension, which includes the primitives CAUSE and LET. These primitives take a Thing and an Event as arguments. Thus, we could embed the structure shown in (16)(ii) within a causative construction:

(17) (i) John rolled the ball toward Beth.

(ii) [$_{\text{Event}}$CAUSE

([$_{\text{Thing}}$JOHN],

[$_{\text{Event}}$GO ([$_{\text{Thing}}$BALL],

[$_{\text{Path}}$TOWARD [$_{\text{Position}}$AT ([$_{\text{Thing}}$BALL], [$_{\text{Thing}}$BETH])])])])

Jackendoff includes a third dimension by introducing the notion of *field*. This dimension extends the semantic coverage of spatially oriented primitives to other domains such as Possessional, Temporal, Identificational, Circumstantial, and Existential.[7] For example, the primitive GO$_{\text{Poss}}$ refers to a GO event in the Possessional field as in the following sentence:

(18) (i) Beth received the doll.

(ii) [$_{\text{Event}}$GO$_{\text{Poss}}$

([$_{\text{Thing}}$DOLL],

[$_{\text{Path}}$TO$_{\text{Poss}}$ ([$_{\text{Position}}$AT$_{\text{Poss}}$ ([$_{\text{Thing}}$DOLL], [$_{\text{Thing}}$BETH])])])]

To further illustrate the notion of field, the GO primitive can be used in the Temporal and Identificational fields:

(19) (i) The meeting went from 2:00 to 4:00.

(ii) [$_{\text{Event}}$GO$_{\text{Temp}}$

([$_{\text{Thing}}$MEETING],

[$_{\text{Path}}$FROM$_{\text{Temp}}$ ([$_{\text{Position}}$AT$_{\text{Temp}}$ ([$_{\text{Thing}}$MEETING], [$_{\text{Time}}$2:00])])]

[$_{\text{Path}}$TO$_{\text{Temp}}$ ([$_{\text{Position}}$AT$_{\text{Temp}}$ ([$_{\text{Thing}}$MEETING], [$_{\text{Time}}$4:00])])])]

(20) (i) The frog turned into a prince.

(ii) [$_{\text{Event}}$GO$_{\text{Ident}}$

([$_{\text{Thing}}$FROG],

[$_{\text{Path}}$TO$_{\text{Ident}}$ ([$_{\text{Position}}$AT$_{\text{Ident}}$ ([$_{\text{Thing}}$FROG], [$_{\text{Thing}}$PRINCE])])])]

As these examples illustrate, there are also other primitives that are included in the LCS framework. In particular, the Position and Path types are used to include primitives such as AT and TO.[8] Furthermore, the Thing, Location, Time, Manner, and Property types are used. Figure 18.2 shows a subset of the types and primitives that are currently used in the LCS scheme.[9]

Figure 18.3 shows the different types of sentences that can be represented by this system of primitives and fields.[10] It should be noted that, although the LCS representation appears to be somewhat "English-like," it is only superficially so by virtue of the labels of the primitives (e.g., GO, TO, etc.) that are used in the representation. These primitives were chosen on the basis of an extensive cross-linguistic investigation, though they may be labeled and used in a fashion that appears to be modeled after a particular language.

The verb classes that are currently accommodated are shown in Figure 18.4.[11] It is expected that this verb classification scheme will need further refinement as more properties of verbs are identified.

Type	Primitives
Event	CAUSE, LET, GO, STAY
State	BE, GO-EXT, ORIENT
Position	AT, IN, ON
Path	TO, FROM, TOWARD, AWAY-FROM, VIA
Thing	BOOK, PERSON, REFERENT, KNIFE-WOUND, KNIFE, SHARP-OBJECT, WOUND, FOOT, CURRENCY, PAINT, FLUID, ROOM, SURFACE, WALL, HOUSE, BALL, DOLL, MEETING, FROG
Property	TIRED, HUNGRY, PLEASED, BROKEN, ASLEEP, DEAD, STRETCHED, HAPPY, RED, HOT, FAR, BIG, EASY, CERTAIN
Location	HERE, THERE, LEFT, RIGHT, UP, DOWN
Time	TODAY, SATURDAY, 2:00, 4:00
Manner	FORCEFULLY, LIKINGLY, WELL, QUICKLY, DANCINGLY, SEEMINGLY, HAPPILY, LOVINGLY, PLEASINGLY, GIFTINGLY, UPWARD, DOWNWARD, WITHIN, HABITUALLY

Figure 18.2. LCS primitives are divided into a handful of types. A subset of the types and primitives used by UNITRAN is shown here.

To illustrate the use of this representation in the lexicon, consider again the *like-gustar* example of Figure 18.1; the interlingua for this example looks like the following:

(21) $[_{State}BE_{Ident} ([_{Thing}I],$
             $[_{Position}AT_{Ident} ([_{Thing}I], [_{Thing}MARY])],\}$
             $[_{Manner}LIKINGLY])]$

Primitive	Primitive-Field	Example
GO	GO_{Poss}	Beth received the doll.
	GO_{Ident}	Elise became a mother.
	GO_{Temp}	The meeting went from 2:00 to 4:00.
	GO_{Loc}	We moved the statue from the park to the zoo.
	GO_{Circ}	John started shipping goods to California.
	GO_{Exist}	John built a house.
STAY	$STAY_{Poss}$	Amy kept the doll.
	$STAY_{Ident}$	The coach remained a jerk.
	$STAY_{Temp}$	We kept the meeting at noon.
	$STAY_{Loc}$	We kept the statue in the park.
	$STAY_{Circ}$	John kept shipping goods to California.
	$STAY_{Exist}$	The situation persisted.
BE	BE_{Poss}	The doll belongs to Beth.
	BE_{Ident}	Elise is a pianist.
	BE_{Temp}	The meeting is at noon.
	BE_{Loc}	The statue is in the park.
	BE_{Circ}	John is shipping goods to California.
	BE_{Exist}	Descartes exists.
GO-EXT	$GO\text{-}EXT_{Ident}$	Our clients range from psychiatrists to psychopaths.
	$GO\text{-}EXT_{Temp}$	The meeting lasted from noon to night.
	$GO\text{-}EXT_{Loc}$	The road went from Boston to Albany.
ORIENT	$ORIENT_{Loc}$	The sign points to Philadelphia.
	$ORIENT_{Circ}$	John intended to ship goods to California.

Figure 18.3. A number of different types of sentences are represented using the Event and State primitives of the LCS framework.

Class of Verb	Examples
position	be, remain, ...
change of position	fall, throw, drop, change, move, slide, float, roll, fly, bounce, move, drop, turn, rotate, shift, ...
directed motion	enter, break into, bring, carry, remove, come, go, leave, arrive, descend, ascend, put, raise, lower, ...
motion with manner	sail, walk, stroll, jog, march, gallop, jump, float, dance, run, skip, ...
exchange	buy, sell, trade, ...
physical state	be, remain, keep, leave, ...
change of physical state	open, close, melt, redden, soften, break, crack, freeze, harden, dry, whiten, grow, change, become, ...
orientation	point, aim, face, ...
existence	exist, build, grow, shape, make, whittle, spin, carve, weave, bake, fashion, create, appear, disappear, reappear, persist, ...
circumstance	be, start, stop, continue, keep, exempt, ...
range	go, last, extend, intend, aim, range, ...
change of ownership	give, take, receive, relinquish, borrow, lend, loan, steal, ...
ownership	belong, remain, keep, own, ...
ingestion	eat, drink, smoke, gobble, munch, sip, ...
psychological state	like, fear, admire, detest, despise, enjoy, esteem, hate, honor, love please, scare, amuse, astonish, bore, surprise, stun, terrify, thrill, ...
perception and communication	see, hear, smell, feel, look, watch, listen, learn, sniff, show, tell, talk, speak, shout, whisper, scream, ...
mental process	know, learn, ...
cost	cost, charge, ...
load/spray	smear, load, cram, spray, stuff, pile, stack, splash, ...
contact/effect	cut, stab, crush, smash, pierce, bite, shoot, spear, ...

Figure 18.4. A subset of the linguistic classes from Levin (1985, 1993) has been implemented using the LCS framework.

Both the Spanish and English sentences are based on this representation; the syntactic distinction is captured by means of parameterization in the lexicon:

(22)   (i) **Lexical Entry for like:**

$[_{State}BE_{Ident}$ $([_{Thing}$:EXT W],

$[_{Position}AT_{Ident}$ $([_{Thing}W], [_{Thing}$:INT Z])],

$[_{Manner}LIKINGLY])]$

(ii) **Lexical Entry for gustar:**

$[_{State}BE_{Ident}$ $([_{Thing}$:INT W],

$[_{Position}AT_{Ident}$ $([_{Thing}W], [_{Thing}$:EXT Z])],

$[_{Manner}LIKINGLY])]$

The :INT/:EXT markers are examples of lexical parameterization that will be discussed in more detail in Section 18.5. These markers allow UNITRAN to account for the subject-object reversal of the *like-gustar* example.

One could argue against this approach on the grounds that the LCS representation has been constructed a way that is biased toward the particular translation problem to be solved. That is, the choice of lexical-semantic primitives and their allowable combinations appear to rely heavily on linguistic knowledge about the nature of translation divergences. However, it is not clear that developing the interlingua on the basis of this knowledge is a drawback to the approach. It is much more worthwhile to construct a representation on the basis of a carefully studied, and finitely specified, classification system than on the basis of vague intuitions about the nature of what a word means in a particular language. Furthermore, since the divergence types addressed by this approach (i.e., the classification given in Figure 18.1) are expected to cover all potential source-language/target-language distinctions based on properties of lexical items, it is considered an advantage to use this classification as the basis for the representation. Since the range of divergence possibilities has been carefully delimited, it is feasible to use the classification to isolate components of verb meaning for the construction of an appropriate interlingua.

An additional argument for constructing the lexical-semantic representation based on a study of cross-linguistic divergences is that it is consistent with the philosophy behind well-grounded lexical-semantic theories such as *meaning-text theory* (MTT) by Mel'čuk and Polguère (1987, p. 266); that is, rather than postulating a set of semantic primitives a priori, the intention is to discover them by means of a "painstaking process of semantic decomposition applied to thousands of actual lexical items." Given that recent research has made it increasingly more feasible to isolate components of verb meaning, this approach to the construction of an interlingual representation is no longer impractical. Note that this is in direct contrast to other approaches that employ primitives that are chosen a priori such as the conceptual dependency approach by Schank (1972, 1973, 1975) and Schank and Abelson (1977), for which there has never been a cross-linguistic investigation into the applicability of the primitives. (We will return to further discussion of the conceptual dependency approach shortly.)

A final point to be made about the current interlingual representation is that it is intended to include those aspects of lexical knowledge related to argument structure, not "deeper" notions of meaning such as aspectual, contextual, domain, and world knowledge. While these "deeper" notions are indisputably necessary for a general solution to MT, previous approaches that have employed deep semantic representations say very little about how to map the representation systematically to the surface syntactic structure, especially in the context of cross-linguistic translation divergences. Alternative MT approaches that have used an interlingua based on "deeper" knowledge representations are presented by Wilks (1973), Vauquois (1975) (CETA),[12] and more recently by Carbonell and Tomita (1987) and Nirenburg et al. (1992) (KBMT), Nirenburg et al. (1987) (TRANSLATOR), Muraki (1987) (PIVOT), Uchida (1989) (ATLAS), among others. We will not survey all of the different ways that one can construct an interlingua here. However, given that the LCS representation has been commonly compared to the *conceptual dependency* (CD) representation, a brief comparison is presented here.

Early translation approaches used the CD representation as the basis for interlingual machine translation. (See, for example, Schank, 1975; Schank and Abelson, 1977; and Lytinen and Schank, 1982.) These approaches were similar to that of UNITRAN in that they relied on a compositional representation based on a small set of primitives. However, a well-known problem with the traditional CD-based approach is that it provides a target-language paraphrase of the source-language sentence rather than a target-language translation of the source-language sentence; it is now widely accepted that this approach is not adequate for machine translation. The paraphrased output is a symptom of a more serious problem, i.e., that CD-based systems lack a canonical mapping from the interlingual representation to the syntactic structure. For example, there is no uniform mechanism for handling even the simplest divergences such as the thematic reversal in the translation of *I like Mary* to Spanish (see Figure 18.1) because there is no systematic relationship between the conceptual arguments of the CD representation and the corresponding syntactic positions in which these arguments are realized. The LCS approach differs in that it provides a mapping between the underlying concept and the syntactic structure that is systematically defined in all languages. Section 18.5 describes this LCS-syntax mapping in more detail.

Traditional interlingual approaches pay a high price for incorporating too much "deeper" knowledge without preserving structurally defined lexical-semantic information. This is not to say that research should head in the direction of "shallow" interlingual representations (e.g., see Sharp, 1985). The current approach attempts to achieve a middle ground between representations that encode too much information and those that encode too little. Specifically, the current representation captures parametric information that accommodates cross-linguistic divergences without losing the systematic relation between the interlingual representation and the syntactic structure. Moreover, the representation lends itself readily to the specification of a systematic mapping that operates uniformly across all languages. This mapping will be discussed in Section 18.5. We will now turn to the issue of classifying MT divergences.

18.4   Classification of MT divergences

The divergence problem in MT has received increasingly more attention in recent literature; see, e.g., Barnett et al. (1991a, 1991b), Dorr (1990, 1993), Kameyama et al. (1991), Kinoshita et al. (1992), Lindop and Tsujii (1991), Tsujii and Fujita (1991), Beaven (1992a, 1992b), and Whitelock (1992). Related discussion can be found, for example, in work by Melby (1986) and Nirenburg and Nirenburg (1988). In particular, Barnett et al. (1991a) divide distinctions between the source language and the target language into two categories: translation *divergences*, in which the same information is conveyed in the source and target texts, but the structures of the sentences are different (as in previous work by Dorr, 1990); and translation *mismatches*, in which the information that is conveyed is different in the source and target languages (as in Kameyama et al., 1991).[13] While translation mismatches are a major problem for translation systems which must be addressed, they are outside of the scope of the model presented here. (See Barnett et al., 1991a, 1991b; Carbonell and Tomita, 1987; Meyer et al., 1990; Nirenburg et al., 1987; Nirenburg and Levin, 1989; Nirenburg and Goodman, 1990; Wilks, 1973;

among others, for descriptions of interlingual MT approaches that take into account knowledge outside of the domain of lexical semantics.)

Although researchers have only recently begun to systematically classify divergence types, the notion of translation divergences is not a new one in the MT community. For example, a number of researchers working on the Eurotra project (mentioned earlier) have sought to solve divergent source-to-target translations, although the divergences were named differently and were resolved by construction-specific transfer rules. A comprehensive survey of divergence examples is presented by Lindop and Tsujii (1991). The term used in this work is "complex transfer," but as mentioned earlier, these are a class of problems inherent in MT itself, not just in the transfer (or interlingual) approaches.

One of the claims made by Lindop and Tsujii (1991) is that the non-Eurotra literature rarely goes into great detail when discussing how divergences are handled. An additional claim is that combinations of divergences and interaction effects between divergent and non-divergent translations are not described in the literature. This chapter seeks to change this perceived state of affairs by providing a detailed description of a solution to all of the (potentially interacting) divergences shown in Figure 18.1, not just a subset of them as would typically be found in the description of most translation systems. These divergences are precisely the ones documented by Lindop and Tsujii (1991), although they are classified differently here. The classification of Lindop and Tsujii (1991) misses a variety of generalizations that could be captured if the lexical-semantic requirements of lexical items were considered. Furthermore, it relies on superficial notions such as "1-to-N lexical gaps" rather than on linguistically motivated characterizations of the divergences that are associated with the data. For comparison, a number of examples taken from the survey presented by Lindop and Tsujii (1991) are shown in Figure 18.5, reorganized according to the classification proposed in this chapter.

The survey of divergence examples by Lindop and Tsujii (1991) constitutes a valuable resource for MT researchers since it contains large numbers of complex translation examples taken from a variety of sources and also illustrates precisely the types of problems that make the construction of MT systems so difficult. However, the approach taken to resolve these divergences relies on transfer rules that miss out on important cross-linguistic generalizations that could easily be captured at the level of lexical-semantic structure. The framework assumed for the current approach makes use of a linguistically grounded classification of divergence types that may be formally defined and systematically resolved. We now turn to a detailed description of the solution to the divergence problem in UNITRAN.

18.5   Solution to the divergence problem

The translation mapping, or *linking rule*, that relates the syntactic positions of the surface structure to the positions of the LCS representation is shown in Figure 18.6.[14] In addition to this linking rule, there is another general rule associated with

Divergence Classification (Dorr)	Divergence Classification (Lindop and Tsujii)	Example
Thematic	changes in argument structure	E: I like the car G: Mir gefällt der Wagen
	changes in argument structure	E: John misses Mary F: Mary manque à John
	changes in argument structure	E: He lacks something G: Ihm fehlt etwas
Promotional	head switching	D: Hij is toevallig ziek E: He happens to be ill
	head switching	F: Il est probable que Jean viendra E: Jean will probably come
	head switching	E: The baby just fell F: Le bébé vient de tomber
	head switching	E: An attempted murder F: Une tentative de meurte
Demotional	head switching	G: Er liest gern E: He likes reading
Structural	changes in argument structure	E: He aims the gun at him G: Er zielt auf ihn mit dem Gewehr
	changes in argument structure	G: Der Student beantwortet die Frage F: L'étudiant répond à la question
	changes in argument structure	E: He seems ill D: Hij schijnt ziek tu zijn
Conflational	1-to-N lexical gaps	E: Miss P: Sentir a falta
	1-to-N lexical gaps	P: Piscina E: Swimming pool
	N-to-1 lexical gaps	E: Get up early P: madrugar
	N-to-1 lexical gaps	E: John called up Mary F: John a appelé Mary
	N-to-M lexical gaps	E: See again F: Revoir
	N-to-M lexical gaps	F: Ressortir E: Go out again
	default/exception distinctions	E: Know how F: Savoir
	default/exception distinctions	F: Aller en flottant E: Float
	default/exception distinctions	E: Commit a crime F: Commettre un crime
	interpretation	E: Walk across F: Traverser à pied
Categorial	category changes	E: Postwar (adj) G: Nach dem Krieg (pp)
	category changes	D: Hij is in Amsterdam woonachtig (adj) E: He resides in Amsterdam (verb)
	category changes	D: Het is voldoende (adj) E: It suffices (verb)
	category changes	E: Hopefully (adv) F: On espère (ip)
	category changes	E: John is fond (adj) of music F: John aime (verb) la musique
Lexical	N-to-1 lexical gaps	E: Give a cough F: Tousser
	Support verbs	E: Give a cry F: Pousser un cri

Figure 18.5. The divergence of examples of Lindop and Tsujii (1991) can be reorganized into the classification of the current framework.

Linking Rule:
Associate the positions of a syntactic structure, $[_{\text{X-MAX}}\ Q \ldots [_{\text{X-MAX}}\ W\ [_{\text{X-1}}\ [_{\text{X}}\ P]\ Z \ldots]\ ]]$, with the positions of a LCS structure, $[\ P'\ W'\ [\ Z' \ldots]\ [\ Q' \ldots]]$, as follows:

a. Syntactic head P $\Leftrightarrow$ LCS head position P'.

b. Syntactic external position W $\Leftrightarrow$ LCS subject position W'.

c. Syntactic internal positions $Z_1, \ldots, Z_n \Leftrightarrow$ LCS argument positions $Z'_1, \ldots, Z'_n$.

d. Syntactic adjunct positions $Q_1, \ldots, Q_m \Leftrightarrow$ LCS modifier positions $Q'_1, \ldots, Q'_m$.

Figure 18.6. The linking routine defines a systematic mapping between the syntactic structure of the LCS structure.

the lexical-semantic component: the *canonical syntactic representation (CSR)* rule. This rule associates an LCS type (e.g., THING) with a syntactic category (e.g., N) (see Figure 18.7).

These two rules are the only ones that are used during lexical-semantic processing (i.e., there are no transfer rules between lexical items). In order to account for lexical-semantic divergences, these rules must be parameterized. In general, translation divergences occur when there is an exception to one (or both) of these rules in one language, but not in the other. Thus, the lexical entries have been constructed to support parametric variation that accounts for such exceptions. The parameters are used in lexical entries as overrides for the linking rule and the *CSR* rule.

The advantage of this approach over the transfer approach is that the work of transfer rules is achieved by a single linking rule coupled with a small set of parameter settings. The result is that the model avoids a severe proliferation of rules – a major drawback of the transfer approach – both *across* and *within* lan-

LCS Type	Syntactic Category
EVENT	V
STATE	V
THING	N
PROPERTY	A
PATH	P
POSITION	P
LOCATION	ADV
TIME	ADV
MANNER	ADV
INTENSIFIER	ADV
PURPOSE	ADV

Figure 18.7. The Canonical Syntactic Realization (CSR) function associates an LCS type (e.g., Thing) with a syntactic category (e.g., H).

guages: the linking rule factors out the information that is common across languages, while the parameters account for information that is specific to a particular language. The reason it is possible to achieve this result is that only a small handful of parameters are needed to account for divergence phenomena. Because it is determined in advance that only certain types of lexical-semantic divergences (those of Figure 18.1) could ever arise, one need not specify a multitude of rules to cover all source-language/target-language correspondences; rather, each divergence type is accommodated through a parametric setting in the lexicon. An additional benefit of this approach is that adding a new language does not entail a modification to the translation mapping (i.e., the linking rule) or the structure of the LCS representation, but rather a provision of a new lexicon (which would be standard in *any* approach) along with a specification of parameter settings for each lexical item.

We will now examine examples of how each of the parameters is used. At the end of this section we will address the important issue of handling multiple divergence effects.

18.5.1 *:INT and :EXT parameter*

The :INT and :EXT parameters allow the linking rule to be overridden by associating a syntactic internal argument with logical subject position and a syntactic external argument with a logical argument position. These parameters accommodate cases such as the *thematic divergence* example (1) from Figure 18.1. In this case, the lexicon uses the :INT and :EXT markers in the LCS representation associated with the lexical entries for *gustar*. The English lexical entry does not contain these markers since the LCS linking rule does not need to be overridden in this case. The lexical entries and translation mapping are shown here:[15]

(23)   like: $[_{\text{State}}\text{BE}_{\text{Ident}} ([_{\text{Thing}}\text{W}], [_{\text{Position}}\text{AT}_{\text{Ident}} ([_{\text{Thing}}\text{W}], [_{\text{Thing}}\text{Z}])],$
                              $[_{\text{Manner}}\text{Q LIKINGLY}])]$

            gustar: $[_{\text{State}}\text{BE}_{\text{Ident}} ([_{\text{Thing}} \text{:INT W}], [_{\text{Position}}\text{AT}_{\text{Ident}} ([_{\text{Thing}}\text{W}], [_{\text{Thing}} \text{:EXT Z}])],$
                              $[_{\text{Manner}}\text{Q LIKINGLY}])]$

            SL: $[_{\text{I-MAX}} [_{\text{N-MAX}}\text{I}] [_{\text{V-MAX}} [_{\text{V-1}} [_{\text{V}} \text{like}] [_{\text{N-MAX}}\text{Mary}]]]] \Leftrightarrow$

            LCS: $[_{\text{State}}\text{BE}_{\text{Ident}} ([_{\text{Thing}}\text{I}], [_{\text{Position}}\text{AT}_{\text{Ident}} ([_{\text{Thing}}\text{I}], [_{\text{Thing}}\text{Mary}])],$
                           $[_{\text{Manner}}\text{LIKINGLY}])] \Leftrightarrow$

            TL: $[_{\text{I-MAX}} [_{\text{N-MAX}}\text{María}] [_{\text{V-MAX}} [_{\text{V-1}} \text{me} [_{\text{V}} \text{gusta}]] [_{\text{P-MAX}} \text{a mí}]]]]\}\}$

18.5.2 *:PROMOTE parameter*

The :PROMOTE marker also overrides the linking rule by associating a syntactic head with a logical modifier. This parameter accounts for *promotional divergence* cases such as example (2) from Figure 18.1. In this case, the lexical entry for *soler* consists of the single LCS node which contains a :PROMOTE marker. The lexical entry for *usually* does not contain this marker. Thus, this predicate is realized as the main verb in Spanish instead of as an adverbial adjunct. The lexical entries and translation mapping are shown here:

(24)   usually: [$_{\text{Manner}}$HABITUALLY]
        soler: [$_{\text{Manner}}$HABITUALLY :PROMOTE]
        SL: [$_{\text{I-MAX}}$ [$_{\text{N-MAX}}$John] [$_{\text{V-MAX}}$ [$_{\text{V-1}}$ [$_{\text{V-1}}$ usually [$_{\text{V}}$ goes]]
                                      [$_{\text{N-MAX}}$home]]]] ⇔
        LCS: [$_{\text{Event}}$GO$_{\text{Loc}}$([$_{\text{Thing}}$John],
                            [$_{\text{Path}}$TO$_{\text{Loc}}$([$_{\text{Position}}$AT$_{\text{Loc}}$([$_{\text{Thing}}$John], [$_{\text{Location}}$ Home])])],
                            [$_{\text{Manner}}$HABITUALLY])]⇔
        TL: [$_{\text{I-MA}}$X [$_{\text{N-MAX}}$Juan] [$_{\text{V-MAX}}$ [$_{\text{V-1}}$ [$_{\text{V}}$ suele] [$_{\text{V-MAX}}$ [$_{\text{V}}$ ir]
                                      [$_{\text{P-MAX}}$ a casa]]]]]

18.5.3   :DEMOTE parameter

Another parameter used during lexical-semantic processing is the :DEMOTE
marker, which allows the linking rule to be overridden by associating a logical
head with a syntactic adjunct. The difference between the :DEMOTE and the
:PROMOTE markers is that the override takes place with respect to a head and
its adjunct rather than a head and its complement. This parameter accounts for
demotional divergence cases such as example (3) from Figure 18.1. In this case,
the lexical entry for *gern* contains a :DEMOTE marker that forces the logical
head of the LCS to be mapped to a syntactic adjunct position. The lexical entry
for *like* does not contain this marker. The lexical entries and translation mapping
are shown here:

(25)   like: [$_{\text{State}}$BE$_{\text{Circ}}$ ([$_{\text{Thing}}$W], [$_{\text{Position}}$AT$_{\text{Circ}}$ ([$_{\text{Thing}}$W], [$_{\text{Event}}$Z])],
                            [$_{\text{Manner}}$Q LIKINGLY])]
        gern: [$_{\text{State}}$BE$_{\text{Circ}}$([$_{\text{Thing}}$:INT W], [$_{\text{Position}}$AT$_{\text{Circ}}$ ([$_{\text{Thing}}$W],
                                      [$_{\text{Event}}$:DEMOTE Z])],
                            [$_{\text{Manner}}$Q LIKINGLY])]
        SL: [$_{\text{I-MAX}}$ [$_{\text{N-MAX}}$I] [$_{\text{V-MAX}}$ [$_{\text{V-1}}$ [$_{\text{V}}$ like] [$_{\text{V-MAX}}$ eating]]]] ⇔
        LCS: [$_{\text{State}}$BE$_{\text{Circ}}$ ([$_{\text{Thing}}$I], [$_{\text{Position}}$AT$_{\text{Circ}}$ ([$_{\text{Thing}}$I], [$_{\text{Event}}$EAT ([$_{\text{Thing}}$I],
                                      [$_{\text{Thing}}$ food])])],
                            [$_{\text{Manner}}$LIKINGLY])]⇔
        TL: [$_{\text{I-MAX}}$ [$_{\text{N-MAX}}$Ich] [$_{\text{V-MAX}}$ [$_{\text{V-1}}$ [$_{\text{V}}$ esse] [$_{\text{ADV}}$ gern]]]]]

18.5.4   '*' parameter

The '*' parameter refers to LCS positions that are syntactically realizable in the
surface sentence. This parameter accounts for *structural divergence* cases such as
example (4) from Figure 18.1. This marker specifies the phrasal level at which an
argument will be projected: in the Spanish lexical entry for *entrar*, the marker is
associated with an LCS position that is realized at a syntactically higher phrasal
level than that of the English lexical entry for *enter*. The lexical entries and translation mapping are shown here:[16]

(26)   enter: [$_{\text{Event}}$GO$_{\text{Loc}}$ ([$_{\text{Thing}}$W], [$_{\text{Path}}$TO$_{\text{Loc}}$ [$_{\text{Position}}$IN$_{\text{Loc}}$ ([$_{\text{Thing}}$W],
                                      [$_{\text{Location}}$ *Z])])])]

entrar: $[_{Event}GO_{Loc}$ $([_{Thing}W]$, $[_{Path}*TO_{Loc}$ $([_{Position}IN_{Loc}([_{Thing}W]$,
$[_{Location}Z])])])]$

SL: $[_{I\text{-}MAX}$ $[_{N\text{-}MAX}John]$ $[_{V\text{-}MAX}$ $[_{V\text{-}1}$ $[_{V}$ entered$]$ $[_{N\text{-}MAX}$ the house$]]]]$ $\Leftrightarrow$
LCS: $[_{Event}GO_{Loc}$
$([_{Thing}John]$, $[_{Path}TO_{Loc}$ $([_{Position}IN_{Loc}([_{Thing}John]$,
$[_{Location}House])])])]$ $\Leftrightarrow$

TL: $[_{I\text{-}MAX}$ $[_{N\text{-}MAX}Juan]$ $[_{V\text{-}MAX}$ $[_{V\text{-}1}$ $[_{V}$ entró$]$ $[_{P\text{-}MAX}$ en $[_{N\text{-}MAX}$ la casa$]]]]]$

18.5.5 *:CAT parameter*

The :CAT marker provides a syntactic category for an LCS argument. Recall that the CSR function maps an LCS type to a syntactic category (see Figure 18.7). When this mapping is to be overridden by a lexical entry, the language-specific marker :CAT is used. This parameter accounts for *categorial divergence* cases such as example (5) from Figure 18.1. In this case, the :CAT(N) marker is associated with the PROPERTY argument in the German lexical entry for *haben*, thus allowing the CSR function to be overridden during realization of the word *Hunger* in this example. By contrast, the English entry for *be* does not contain this marker; thus, the default mapping provided by the *CSR* function is used for the realization of the PROPERTY argument as an adjective. The lexical entries and translation mapping are shown here:[17]

(27) be: $[_{State}BE_{Ident}$ $([_{Thing}W]$, $[_{Position}AT_{Ident}$ $([_{Thing}W]$, $[_{Property}Z])])]$
haben: $[_{State}BE_{Ident}$ $([_{Thing}W]$, $[_{Position}AT_{Ident}$ $([_{Thing}W]$,
$[_{Property}$ (:CAT N) Z$])])]$

SL: $[_{I\text{-}MAX}$ $[_{N\text{-}MAX}I]$ $[_{V\text{-}MAX}$ $[_{V\text{-}1}$ $[_{V}$ am$]$ $[_{A\text{-}MAX}$ hungry$]]]]$ $\Leftrightarrow$
LCS: $[_{State}BE_{Ident}$ $([_{Thing}I]$, $[_{Position}AT_{Ident}$ $([_{Thing}I]$, $[_{Property}HUNGRY])])]$ $\Leftrightarrow$
TL: $[_{I\text{-}MAX}$ $[_{N\text{-}MAX}Ich]$ $[_{V\text{-}MAX}$ $[_{V\text{-}1}$ $[_{V}$ habe$]$ $[_{N\text{-}MAX}Hunger]]]]$

18.5.6 *:CONFLATED parameter*

The sixth LCS parameter is the :CONFLATED marker. This marker is used to indicate that a particular argument need not be realized in the surface representation. This parameter accounts for *conflational divergence* cases such as example (6) from Figure 18.1. In this case, the argument that is incorporated in the English sentence is the KNIFE-WOUND argument since the verb *stab* does not realize this argument; by contrast, the Spanish construction *dar-puñaladas* explicitly realizes this argument as the word *puñaladas*. Thus, the :CONFLATED marker is associated with the KNIFE-WOUNDS argument in the case of *stab*, but not in the case of *dar*. The lexical entries and translation mapping are shown here:

(28) stab: $[_{Event}CAUSE$
$([_{Thing}W]$,
$[_{Event}GO_{Poss}$
$([_{Thing}Y$ KNIFE-WOUND :CONFLATED$]$,
$[_{Path}TOWARD_{Poss}$ $([_{Position}AT_{Poss}$ $([_{Thing}Y$ KNIFE-WOUND$]$,
$[_{Thing}Z])])])])]$

dar: $[_{\text{Event}}\text{CAUSE}$
        $([_{\text{Thing}}W],$
        $[_{\text{Event}}\text{GO}_{\text{Poss}}$
        $([_{\text{Thing}} *Y],$
        $[_{\text{Path}}\text{TOWARD}_{\text{Poss}} ([_{\text{Position}}\text{AT}_{\text{Poss}} ([_{\text{Thing}} *Y], [_{\text{Thing}}Z])])])])]$

SL: $[_{\text{I-MAX}} [_{\text{N-MAX}}I] [_{\text{V-MAX}} [_{\text{V-1}} [_{\text{V}} \text{stabbed}] [_{\text{N-MAX}}\text{John}]]]] \Leftrightarrow$

LCS: $[_{\text{Event}}\text{CAUSE}$
        $([_{\text{Thing}}I],$
        $[_{\text{Event}}\text{GO}_{\text{Poss}}$
        $([_{\text{Thing}}\text{KNIFE-WOUND}],$
        $[_{\text{Path}}\text{TOWARD}_{\text{Poss}} ([_{\text{Position}}\text{AT}_{\text{Poss}} ([_{\text{Thing}}\text{KNIFE-WOUND}],$
        $[_{\text{Thing}}\text{John}])])])])]$

TL: $[_{\text{I-MAX}} [_{\text{N-MAX}}\text{Yo}] [_{\text{V-MAX}} [_{\text{V-1}} [_{\text{V}} \text{le di}] [_{\text{N-MAX}} \text{puñaladas}]$
        $[_{\text{P-MAX}} \text{a Juan}]]]]$

18.5.7 *Handling multiple divergences*

We now turn to another important issue, namely, that of how this approach accounts for occurrences of multiple divergence effects. One might wonder what happens in cases where more than one parametric effect is required in order to achieve an appropriate translation mapping. This issue is one that only recently has received the attention it deserves. In particular, there have been criticisms (see, e.g., Lindop and Tsujii, 1991) of systems that perform transfer on relatively shallow analyses (e.g., early METAL and LTAG) due to the fact that such systems are not likely to be able to handle multiple divergences (although they may be able to handle each divergence type in isolation). The solution adopted in the current approach does not appeal to a shallow analysis (i.e., it does not use a set of already-coded canned "frames" with predetermined argument structure). Rather, the syntactic structures are derived *compositionally* on the basis of two pieces of information: the structure of the LCS and the parametric information associated with lexical entries. It would not be possible to handle multiple divergence types in an approach that maps directly from a set of hard-wired source-language frames to a set of hard-wired target-language frames. This is because an argument that occurs in a divergent phrasal construction might itself be a divergent phrasal construction.

Consider the following example:

(29)   **Promotional and Thematic divergence:**
        S: Leer libros le suele gustar a Juan
        'Reading books (him) tends to please (to) John'
        E: John usually likes reading books

This example exhibits a simultaneous occurrence of two types of divergences: the verb *soler* exhibits a promotional divergence with respect to its internal argument *gustar a Juan*, which itself exhibits a thematic divergence.

The LCS for example (29) is the following:

(30) $[_{\text{State}}\text{BE}_{\text{Circ}}$
               $([_{\text{Thing}}\text{JOHN}],$
               $[_{\text{Position}}\text{AT}_{\text{Circ}}$
                     $([_{\text{Thing}}\text{JOHN}], [_{\text{Event}}\text{READ} ([_{\text{Thing}}\text{JOHN}], [_{\text{Thing}}\text{BOOK}])])],$
               $[_{\text{Manner}}\text{LIKINGLY}],$
               $[_{\text{Manner}}\text{HABITUALLY}])]^{18}$

Note that there are two modifiers, LIKINGLY and HABITUALLY. The LIKINGLY component is, in a sense, an "inherent" modifier since it appears in the lexical entries of both *like* and *gustar*. In contrast, the HABITUALLY modifier is an independent constituent that corresponds to independent lexical entries for *usually* and *soler*. The lexical entries relevant to this example are the following:

(31)   usually: $[_{\text{Manner}}\text{HABITUALLY}]$
           like: $[_{\text{State}}\text{BE}_{\text{Circ}} ([_{\text{Thing}}W], [_{\text{Position}}\text{AT}_{\text{Circ}} ([_{\text{Thing}}W], [_{\text{Thing}}Z])],$
                       $[_{\text{Manner}}Q \text{ LIKINGLY}])]$
           soler: $[_{\text{Manner}}\text{HABITUALLY :PROMOTE}]$
           gustar: $[_{\text{State}}\text{BE}_{\text{Circ}} ([_{\text{Thing}} :\text{INT } W], [_{\text{Position}}\text{AT}_{\text{Circ}} ([_{\text{Thing}}W], [_{\text{Thing}} :\text{EXT } Z])],$
                       $[_{\text{Manner}}Q \text{ LIKINGLY}])]$

Suppose we were to generate the Spanish sentence for this example. When the liking rule is applied to the LCS of (30), the :PROMOTE marker in the entry for *soler* immediately triggers an exchange of the $[_{\text{Manner}}\text{HABITUALLY}]$ modifier with the $[_{\text{State}}\text{BE}_{\text{Circ}} \ldots]$. The promotional exchange crucially precedes the invocation of the thematic override exchange.[19] Thus, the $[_{\text{Manner}}\text{HABITUALLY}]$ constituent is realized as the syntactic head *soler*. This head takes an internal argument corresponding to $[_{\text{State}}\text{BE}_{\text{Circ}} \ldots]$ which is realized as the verb *gustar*.

During the promotional mapping, the structural relation between the subordinated verb and its internal argument is not changed. However, the promotional operation does not retain the relation between the subordinated verb and its external argument; rather, the argument is realized in an external position relative to the main verb. Normally, this would mean that the LCS constituent $[_{\text{Thing}}\text{JOHN}]$ would become an external argument of *soler* such as in the non-interacting case: *John suele leer libros*. In the current example, however, the attachment of the external argument is delayed until the linking routine is recursively applied to $[_{\text{State}} \text{BE}_{\text{Circ}} \ldots]$.

At this point, the :INT and :EXT markers trigger the thematic interchange, and the logical subject $[_{\text{Thing}}\text{JOHN}]$ is realized as the internal argument *a Juan*. The $[_{\text{Event}}\text{READ} \ldots]$ constituent is then taken to be the external argument of *gustar*, except that this constituent cannot be attached inside of the subordinate phrase due to the promotional divergence. Instead, the current phrase is completed and the external argument is "passed up" to the higher phrase, which then attaches it in an external position relative to the verb *soler*.

Accordingly, the English and Spanish surface structures for these two sentences are as follows:

(32)   [$_{\text{C-MAX}}$

      [$_{\text{I-MAX}}$

           [$_{\text{N-MAX}}$John]

           [$_{\text{V-MAX}}$ [$_{\text{ADV}}$ usually] [$_{\text{V-MAX}}$ [$_{\text{V}}$ likes] [$_{\text{C-MAX}}$ to read books]]]]]

(33)   [$_{\text{C-MAX}}$

      [$_{\text{I-MAX}}$

           [$_{\text{C-MAX}}$ leer libros]

           [$_{\text{V-MAX}}$ [$_{\text{V}}$ le suele] [$_{\text{V-MAX}}$ [$_{\text{V}}$ gustar] [$_{\text{P-MAX}}$ a Juan]]]]]]

The advantage to this approach is that no additional mechanisms beyond the linking routine and the parametric specifications need to be introduced to handle complicated cases such as this one.

18.6   Summary

In tackling the more global problem of MT, many researchers have addressed different pieces of the divergence problem, but no single approach has yet attempted to solve all of the divergence types presented here. Furthermore, the pieces that *have* been solved in the past are accounted for by mechanisms that are not general enough to carry over to other parts of the problem, nor do they take advantage of cross-linguistic uniformities that tie seemingly different languages together. In fairness, many of these approaches have not emphasized the handling of divergences; on the other hand, divergences constitute a major problem for translation systems which must be addressed.

The approach taken in UNITRAN borrows certain ideas from previous work (e.g., the notions of compositionality, unification, thematic role reversal, and head switching in such systems as MiMo, LFG-MT, and Eurotra). However, it attempts to provide a more uniform and systematic solution within the context of an interlingual model without recourse to language-specific transfer entries. The solution has been implemented in a bidirectional prototypical system currently operating on Spanish, English, and German, running in Common Lisp.[20]

A central claim of the current approach is that the divergence classification shown in Figure 18.1 covers all potential source-language/target-language distinctions based on lexical-semantic properties (i.e., properties associated with entries in the lexicon that are not based on purely syntactic information, idiomatic usage, aspectual knowledge, discourse knowledge, domain knowledge, or world knowledge). Although the MT approach described here is interlingual, these divergences are ones that any MT system must cope with, not just those that use an interlingual representation.

An important advantage of this translation approach is that it provides the foundation for: (1) facilitating the design and implementation of the system by clearly defining a small number of divergence categories; and (2) systematically stating the solution to the divergence problem in terms of a uniform translation mapping and a handful of simple lexical-semantic parameters. The approach tries to incorporate some of the more promising syntactic and semantic aspects of existing translation systems. Specifically, the model incorporates structural information for realization and positioning of arguments, and it also maintains the ability to select target terms on the basis of compositional properties of conceptual structure.

An area that requires further investigation is the development of a large-scale lexicon for processing within the LCS framework. Automatic lexical acquisition is becoming more critical to the success of MT because it is a tedious undertaking to construct dictionary representations by hand for each language.[21] Research is currently underway to investigate the possibility of scaling up the system through automatic means so that a wider range of phenomena and languages may be handled.

The current research would further benefit from an investigation into the applicability of the scheme to non-European languages. However, unlike the representation used in the Eurotra project, the LCS is expected to be more than just a "euroversal" representation (see Copeland et al., 1991). Several researchers have investigated the use of an LCS for languages such as Warlpiri (Hale and Laughren, 1983), Urdu (Husain, 1989), Greek (Olsen, 1991), Arabic (Shaban, 1991), and Chinese, Indo-European, and North American Indian (Talmy, 1983, 1985), among others. These investigations will be useful for future extensions of UNITRAN to handle other languages.

Notes

1. These examples are taken from Arnold et al. (1988) and Arnold and Sadler (1990). The divergence types are specified using the terminology of the present author, not that of the authors from whom these (and later) examples are taken.
2. The example given by Arnold et al. (1988) is actually a translation from the Dutch equivalent of the German sentence (i.e., *Jan kust Marie graag*), but the construction is entirely analogous.
3. This example is an adapted version of one taken from Arnold and Sadler (1990): *Jean a manqué de finir le livre.* Judgments as to the naturalness and acceptability of this sentence differ among native French speakers; the verb *manquer* does not convey the "almost" meaning for all speakers. Thus, the more acceptable version that uses *faillir* is given here. In any case, the concept of promotion is valid, regardless of which main verb is used.
4. Again, this is an adapted version of a sentence taken from Arnold and Sadler (1990); the original form of the sentence did not include the preposition *dans* which forced the sentence to have a questionable status among native French speakers. Thus, the more acceptable version that uses *dans* is given here. In any case, the concept of conflation is valid with, or without, the preposition since the lexical items of interest in this phenomenon are *entrer* and *en courant.*
5. In addition, unlike *faillir*, the verb *venir* requires the particle *de* to be inserted: *Jean vient de tomber* (John just fell).

6. Others who have studied this representation are Hale and Laughren (1983) and Hale and Keyser (1986a, 1986b, 1989). For alternative (lexical-)semantic and case representations, see, for example, Fillmore (1968), Gruber (1965), Schank (1972, 1973, 1975), and Wilks (1973).

7. As we will see shortly, the label Loc has been adopted to distinguish the spatial field from the non-spatial fields. Note that the spatial field is used to denote the primitives that fall in the spatial dimension. Jackendoff argues that spatial primitives are more fundamental than those of other domains (e.g., Possessional). Thus, spatial primitives have their own special status as an independent dimension.

8. The Position type corresponds to the Place type used by Jackendoff (1983). An extension that has been made to the Position type is that it is a two-place predicate rather than a one-place predicate. For example, in (13)(ii), the MEETING argument appears both internally and externally to the AT_{Temp} node. This is due to the observation that primitives such as AT, IN, ON, etc. are actually relations between two arguments (e.g., the representation for *the book is on the table* incorporates the relation ON(BOOK,TABLE) as part of its meaning).

9. Note that primitives have not been included for *John, Beth, I, me, it*, etc. In actuality, proper names are represented by the PERSON primitive and referring expressions (e.g., pronouns) are represented by the REFERENT primitive. For notational convenience, the examples and figures will continue to use the more informative labels in place of these primitives.

10. These examples were taken from Siskind (1989), with minor modifications.

11. This is an adapted (and extended) version of the classes presented by Levin (1985, 1993).

12. Although the CETA system has been classified as interlingual here, it should be pointed out that there have been a number of persuasive arguments against this classification due to the fact that the lexicon used in the CETA system had a bilingual transfer-like mechanism (see, e.g., Hutchins, 1986, and Nirenburg et al. 1992).

13. An example of the latter situation is the translation of the English word *fish* into Spanish: the translation is *pez* if the fish is still in its natural state, but it is *pescado* if the fish has been caught and is suitable for food. It is now widely accepted that, in such a situation, the MT system must be able to derive the required information from discourse context and a model of the domain that is being discussed.

14. The details of the syntactic representation are described by Dorr (1993). In a nutshell, each syntactic phrase of a sentence has a *maximal projection*, X-MAX, for a *head* of category X. The possibilities for the category X are: (V)erb, (N)oun, (A)djective, (P)reposition, (C)omplementizer, and (I)nflection. The Complementizer corresponds to relative pronouns such as *that* in *the man that I saw*. The Inflectional category corresponds to modals such as *would* in *I would eat cake*. In addition to the head X, a phrasal projection potentially contains *satellites* such as an external argument (e.g., the subject of a verb), internal arguments (e.g., the objects of a verb), and adjuncts (e.g., modifiers of a verb). This is a revised version of *government-binding* theory presented in Chomsky (1986).

15. In this and subsequent examples, SL stands for source language and TL stands for target language, although the translation could, in fact, be reversed. The LCS is the interlingua that mediates between the SL and TL structures.

16. The analogous French structure is handled by the * mechanism as well:
E: John entered the house ⇔ F: Jean entra dans la maison ('John entered into the house')

17. For ease of illustration, the * marker is not included in this and subsequent examples.

18. For purposes of simplicity, the READ predicate is being used as a shorthand for the following expanded representation:

[State BE Perc
   ([Thing JOHN],
   [Position AT Perc ([Thing JOHN], [Thing BOOK])],
   [Manner READINGLY])]

19. This seems to indicate that there is some notion of prioritization during the resolution of interacting divergence types. In particular, the "head swapping" cases (promotional and demotional divergences) appear to take priority over the "argument swapping" cases (thematic). Although the formal ramifications of this ordering have not yet been established, it should be noted that this prioritization fits in naturally in the current framework given that the syntactic realization process starts by realizing "outer" phrases, but then recursively realizes "inner" phrases before any attachments are made.
20. The system runs on a Symbolics 3600 series machine (with graphics) and also on a Sun Sparc Station (without graphics).
21. The lexicon has been shown to be a major bottleneck for the development of UNITRAN: it took more than one person-month to define just 150 words per language.

References

Abeillé, Anne, Yves Schabes, and Aravind K. Joshi (1990) "Using Lexicalized Tags for Machine Translation," *Proceedings of Thirteenth International Conference on Computational Linguistics*, Helsinki, Finland, 1–6.

Alonso, Juan Alberto (1990) "Transfer InterStructure: Designing an 'Interlingua' for Transfer-based MT Systems," *Proceedings of the Third International Conference on Theoretical and Methodological Issues in Machine Translation of Natural Languages*, Linguistics Research Center, The University of Texas, Austin, TX, 189–201.

Arnold, Doug and Louisa Sadler (1990) "Theoretical Basis of MiMo," *Machine Translation* 5:3, 195–222.

Arnold, Doug and Louis des Tombe (1987) "Basic Theory and Methodology in Eurotra," in *Machine Translation: Theoretical and Methodological Issues,* Sergei Nirenburg (ed.), Cambridge University Press, Cambridge, England, 114–135.

Arnold, Doug, Steven Krauwer, Louis des Tombe, and Louisa Sadler (1988) "Relaxed Compositionality in Machine Translation," *Proceedings of the Second International Conference on Theoretical and Methodological Issues in Machine Translation of Natural Languages*, Carnegie Mellon University, Pittsburgh, PA.

Barnett, Jim, Inderjeet Mani, Paul Martin, and Elaine Rich (1991a) "Reversible Machine Translation: What to Do When the Languages Don't Line Up," *Proceedings of the Workshop on Reversible Grammars in Natural Language Processing, ACL-91*, University of California, Berkeley, CA, 61–70.

Barnett, Jim, Inderjeet Mani, Elaine Rich, Chinatsu Aone, Kevin Knight, and Juan C. Martinez (1991b) "Capturing Language-Specific Semantic Distinctions in Interlingua-based MT," *Proceedings of Machine Translation Summit*, Washinton, DC, 25–32.

Beaven, John (1992a) "Lexicalist Unification-Based Machine Translation," Ph.D. University of Edinburgh Edinburgh.

Beaven, John (1992b) "Shake and Bake Machine Translation," *Proceedings of Fourteenth International Conference on Computational Linguistics*, Nantes, France, 603–609.

Bennett, P. A., R. L. Johnson, J. McNaught, J. M. Pugh, J. C. Sager, H. L. Somers (1986) *Multilingual Aspects of Information Technology,* Gower, Brookfield, VT.

Boitet, Christian (1987) "Research and Development on MT and Related Techniques at Grenoble University (GETA)," in *Machine Translation: The State of the Art,* Margaret King (ed.), Edinburgh University Press, Edinburgh, 133–153.

Boitet, Christian (1988) "Pros and Cons of the Pivot and Transfer Approaches in Multilingual Machine Translation," in *Recent Developments in Machine Translation*, Dan Maxwell, Klaus Schubert, and Toon Witkam (eds.), Foris, Dordrecht, Holland, 93–107.

Carbonell, Jaime G. and Masaru Tomita (1987) "Knowledge-based Machine Translation, the CMU Approach," in *Machine Translation: Theoretical and Methodological Issues* Sergei Nirenburg (ed.), Cambridge University Press, Cambridge, England, 68–89.

Chomsky, Noam A. (1986) *Knowledge of Language: Its Nature, Origin and Use*, MIT Press, Cambridge, MA.

Colmerauer, A. (1971) "Les systèmes-Q ou un formalisme pour analyser et synthétiser des phrases sur ordinateur," *TAUM*, 1–45.

Copeland, C., J. Durand, S. Krauwer, and B. Maegaard (1991) "The Eurotra Linguistic Specifications," in *Studies in Machine Translation and Natural Language Processing, Volume 1*, Erwin Valentini (ed.), Commission of the European Communities, Brussels.

Dorr, Bonnie J. (1987) "UNITRAN: An Interlingual Approach to Machine Translation," *Proceedings of the Sixth Conference of the American Association of Artificial Intelligence*, Seattle, Washington, 534–539.

Dorr, Bonnie J. (1990) "Solving Thematic Divergences in Machine Translation," *Proceedings of the 28th Annual Conference of the Association for Computational Linguistics*, University of Pittsburgh, Pittsburgh, PA, 127–134.

Dorr, Bonnie J. (1993) *Machine Translation: A View from the Lexicon*, MIT Press, Cambridge, MA.

Fillmore, Charles J. (1968) "The Case for Case," in *Universals in Linguistic Theory*, Bach, E., and R. T. Harms (eds.), Holt, Rinehart, and Winston, 1–88.

Grimshaw, Jane (1990) *Argument Structure*, MIT Press, Cambridge, MA.

Gruber, J. S. (1965) "Studies in Lexical Relations," Ph.D. thesis, Department of Information Science, Massachusetts Institute of Technology, Cambridge, MA.

Hale, Kenneth and S. Jay Keyser (1986a) "Some Transitivity Alternations in English," Center for Cognitive Science, Massachusetts Institute of Technology, Cambridge, MA, Lexicon Project Working Paper 7.

Hale, Kenneth and S. Jay Keyser (1986b) "A View from the Middle," Center for Cognitive Science, Massachusetts Institute of Technology, Cambridge, MA, Lexicon Project Working Paper 10.

Hale, Kenneth and S. Jay Keyser (1989) "On Some Syntactic Rules in the Lexicon," Center for Cognitive Science, Massachusetts Institute of Technology, Cambridge, MA, manuscript.

Hale, Kenneth and Mary Laughren (1983) "Warlpiri Lexicon Project: Warlpiri Dictionary Entries," Massachusetts Institute of Technology, Cambridge, MA, Warlpiri Lexicon Project.

Husain, Saadia (1989) "A Lexical Conceptual Structure Editor," Bachelor of Science thesis, Massachusetts Institute of Technology Electrical Engineering and Computer Science Cambridge, MA.

Hutchins, J. W. (1986) *Machine Translation: Past, Present, Future*, Ellis Horwood Limited, Chichester, England

Hutchins, J. W. and H. L. Somers (1992) *An Introduction to Machine Translation*, Academic Press, London, England

Jackendoff, Ray S. (1983) *Semantics and Cognition*, MIT Press, Cambridge, MA.

Jackendoff, Ray S. (1990) *Semantic Structures*, MIT Press, Cambridge, MA.

Johnson, Rod, Maghi King, and Louis des Tombe (1985) "EUROTRA: A Multilingual System under Development," *Computational Linguistics* 11:2–3, 155–169.

Kameyama, Megumi, Ryo Ochitani, Stanley Peters, and Hidetoshi Sirai (1991) "Resolving Translation Mismatches with Information Flow," *Proceedings of the 29th Annual Meeting of the Association for Computational Linguistics*, University of California, Berkeley, CA, 193–200.

Kaplan, Ronald M., Klaus Netter, Jürgen Wedekind, Annie Zaenen (1989) "Translation By Structural Correspondences," *Proceedings of Fourth Conference of the European Chapter of the Association for Computational Linguistics*, Manchester, 272–281.

King, Margaret (ed.) (1987) *Machine Translation: The State of the Art*, Edinburgh University Press, Edinburgh.

Kinoshita, Satoshi, John Phillips, and Jun-ichi Tsujii (1992) "Interaction Between Structural Changes in Machine Translation," *Proceedings of Fourteenth International Conference on Computational Linguistics*, Nantes, France, 679–685.

Levin, Beth (1985) "Lexical Semantics in Review" Center for Cognitive Science, Massachusetts Institute of Technology, Cambridge, MA, Lexicon Project Working Paper 1.

Levin, Beth (1993) *English Verb Classes and Alternations: A Preliminary Investigation*, University of Chicago Press, Chicago, IL.

Levin, Beth and Malka Rappaport (1986) "The Formation of Adjectival Passives," *Linguistic Inquiry* 17:623–662.

Lindop, Jeremy and Jun-ichi Tsujii (1991) "Complex Transfer in MT: A Survey of Examples," Center for Computational Linguistics, UMIST, Manchester, CCL/UMIST Report 91/5.

Lytinen, Steven and Roger C. Schank (1982) "Representation and Translation," Department of Computer Science, Yale University, New Haven, CT, Technical Report 234.

McCord, Michael C. (1989) "Design of LMT: A Prolog-Based Machine Translation System," *Computational Linguistics* 15:1, 33–52.

Maxwell, Dan, Klaus Schubert, and Toon Witkam (eds.) (1988) *Recent Developments in Machine Translation*, Foris, Dordrecht, Holland.

Melby, A. K. (1986) "Lexical Transfer: Missing Element in Linguistic Theories," *Proceedings of Eleventh International Conference on Computational Linguistics*, Bonn, Germany.

Mel'čuk, Igor and Alain Polguère (1987) A Formal Lexicon in Meaning-Text Theory (Or How to Do Lexica with Words)," *Computational Linguistics,* 13:3–4, 261–275.

Meyer, Ingrid, Boyan Onyshkevych, and Lynn Carlson (1990) "Lexicographic Principles and Design for Knowledge-Based Machine Translation," Carnegie Mellon University Pittsburgh, PA, CMU CMT Technical Report 90-118.

Muraki, K. (1987) "PIVOT: A Two-Phase Machine Translation System," *Machine Translation Summit – Manuscripts and Program*, Japan, 81–83.

Nirenburg, Sergei (ed.) (1987) *Machine Translation: Theoretical and Methodological Issues*, Cambridge University Press, Cambridge, England.

Nirenburg, Sergei, and Kenneth Goodman (1990) "Treatment of Meaning in MT Systems," *Proceedings of the Third International Conference on Theoretical and Methodological Issues in Machine Translation of Natural Languages*, Linguistics Research Center, The University of Texas, Austin, TX, 171–187.

Nirenburg, Sergei, and Lori Levin (1989) "Knowledge Representation Support," *Machine Translation*, 4:1, 25–52.

Nirenburg, Sergei and Irene Nirenburg (1988) "A Framework for Lexical Selection in Natural Language Generation," *Proceedings of Twelfth International Conference on Computational Linguistics*, Budapest, Hungary, 471–475.

Nirenburg, Sergei, Victor Raskin, and Allen B. Tucker (1987) "The Structure of Interlingua in TRANSLATOR," in *Machine Translation: Theoretical and Methodological Issues,* Sergei Nirenburg (ed.), Cambridge University Press, Cambridge, England, 90–113.

Nirenburg, Sergei, Jaime Carbonell, Masaru Tomita, and Kenneth Goodman (1992) *Machine Translation: A Knowledge-Based Approach*, Morgan Kaufmann, San Mateo, CA.

Noord, Gertjan van, Joke Dorrepaal, Doug Arnold, Steven Krauwer, Louisa Sadler, and Louis des Tombe (1989) "An Approach to Sentence-Level Anaphora in Machine Translation," *Proceedings of Fourth Conference of the European Chapter of the Association for Computational Linguistics*, Manchester, 299–307.

Noord, Gertjan van, Joke Dorrepaal, Pim van der Eijk, Maria Florenza, and Louis des Tombe (1990) "The MiMo2 Research System," *Proceedings of the Third International Conference on Theoretical and Methodological Issues in Machine Translation of Natural Languages*, Linguistics Research Center, The University of Texas, Austin, TX, 213–233.

Olsen, Mari Broman (1991) "Lexical Semantics, Machine Translation, and Talmy's Model of Motion Verbs," Northwestern University, Evanston, IL, Linguistics Working Paper, Volume 3.

Pustejovsky, James (1988) "The Geometry of Events," Center for Cognitive Science, Massachusetts Institute of Technology, Cambridge, MA, Lexicon Project Working Paper 24.

Pustejovsky, James (1989) "The Semantic Representation of Lexical Knowledge," *Proceedings of the First International Lexical Acquisition Workshop*, IJCAI-89, Detroit, MI.

Pustejovsky, James (1991) "The Syntax of Event Structure," *Cognition* 41.

Rappaport, Malka and Beth Levin (1988) "What to Do with Theta-Roles," in *Thematic Relations*, Wendy Wilkins (ed.), Academic Press.

Rappaport, Malka, Mary Laughren, and Beth Levin (1987) "Levels of Lexical Representation," Center for Cognitive Science, Massachusetts Institute of Technology, Cambridge, MA, Lexicon Project Working Paper 20.

Sadler, Louisa, Ian Crookston, Doug Arnold, and Andy Way (1990) "LFG and Translation," *Proceedings of the Third International Conference on Theoretical and Methodological Issues in Machine Translation of Natural Languages*, Linguistics Research Center, The University of Texas, Austin, TX, 121–130.

Schank, Roger C. (1972) "Conceptual Dependency: A Theory of Natural Language Understanding," *Cognitive Psychology*, 3: 552–631.

Schank, Roger C. (1973) "Identification of Conceptualizations Underlying Natural Language," in *Computer Models of Thought and Language*, Roger C. Schank and K. M. Colby (eds.), Freeman, San Francisco, CA, 187–247.

Schank, Roger C. (ed.) (1975) *Conceptual Information Processing*, Elsevier Science Publishers, Amsterdam, Holland.

Schank, Roger C. and Robert Abelson (1977) *Scripts, Plans, Goals, and Understanding*, Lawrence Erlbaum Associates, Inc. Hillsdale, NJ.

Shaban, Marwan (1991) "GB Parsing of Arabic," Master of Science thesis, Boston University, Computer Science Department, Boston, MA.

Sharp, Randall M. (1985) "A Model of Grammar Based on Principles of Government and Binding," Master of Science thesis, Department of Computer Science, University of British Columbia.

Siskind, Jeffrey Mark (1989) "Decomposition," Massachusetts Institute of Technology, Cambridge, MA.

Slocum, Jonathan (1988) *Machine Translation Systems*, Cambridge University Press, Cambridge.

Talmy, Leonard (1983) "How Language Structures Space," in *Spatial Orientation: Theory, Research, and Application*, Herbert L. Pick, Jr., and Linda P. Acredolo (eds.), Plenum Press, New York, 225–282.

Talmy, Leonard (1985) "Lexicalization Patterns: Semantic Structure in Lexical Forms," in *Grammatical Categories and the Lexicon*, Timothy Shopen (ed.), University Press Cambridge, England, 57–149.

Thurmair, Gregor (1990) "Complex Lexical Transfer in METAL," *Proceedings of the Third International Conference on Theoretical and Methodological Issues in Machine Translation of Natural Languages*, Linguistics Research Center, The University of Texas, Austin, TX, 91–107.

Tsujii, Jun-ich and Kimikazu Fujita (1991) "Lexical Transfer Based on Bilingual Signs: Towards Interaction During Transfer," *Proceedings of the European Chapter of the Association for Computational Linguistics*, Berlin, Germany, 275–280.

Uchida, H. (1989) "ATLAS: Fujitsu Machine Translation System," *Machine Translation Summit II – Manuscripts and Program*, Japan, 129–134.

Vauquois Bernard (1975) *La Traduction Automatique à Grenoble,* Dunod, Paris.

Vauquois Bernard, and Christian Boitet (1985) "Automated Translation at Grenoble University," *Computational Linguistics*, 11:1, 28–36.

Whitelock, Pete (1992) "Shake-and-Bake Translation," *Proceedings of Fourteenth International Conference on Computational Linguistics,* Nantes, France, 784–791.

Wilks, Yorick (1973) "An Artificial Intelligence Approach to Machine Translation," in *Computer Models of Thought and Language,* Roger C. Schank and K. M. Colby (eds.), Freeman, San Francisco, CA, 114–151.

Zubizarreta, Maria Luisa (1982) "On the Relationship of the Lexicon to Syntax," Ph.D. thesis, Department of Linguistics and Philosophy, Massachusetts Institute of Technology, Cambridge, MA.

Zubizarreta, Maria Luisa (1987) *Levels of Representation in the Lexicon and in the Syntax,* Foris Publications, Dordrecht, Holland/Cinnaminson, USA.

PART VI

Computer models for lexical semantics

Lexical semantics is still in a rather early stage of development. This explains the reason why there are relatively few elaborated systems for representing its various aspects. A number of semantic aspects can be straightforwardly represented by means of feature-value pairs and by means of typed feature structures. Others, such as the Qualia Structure or the lexical semantics relations are more difficult to represent. The difficulty is twofold: (1) there is first the need to define appropriate models to represent the various levels of semantic information, including their associated possible inference systems and their properties (e.g., transitivity, monotonicity, etc.) and (2) there is the need to develop complex algorithms that allow for as efficient as possible treatments from these models. The first chapter of this section tackles the first point and the second one addresses some algorithmic problems.

"Introducing Lexlog" by J. Jayez, is a set of specifications for constructing explicit representations for lexical objects in restricted domains. Lexlog offers two types of functions: control functions to formalize representations and updatings on these representations in a controlled way, and expression functions to express different semantic operators and to tailor these operators with syntactic operators, for example, the trees of the Tree Adjoining Grammar framework. The discussion ends with a detailed presentation of the implementation in Prolog.

The last chapter, "Constraint propagation techniques for lexical semantics descriptions," by Patrick Saint-Dizier, addresses the problem of the propagation in parse trees of large feature structures. The motivation is basically to avoid computations of intermediate results which later turn out to be useless. This chapter introduces some elements of the embedding of constraint resolution mechanisms into logic programming and describes an implementation in Prolog using a meta-interpretor.

19   Introducing LexLog

JACQUES JAYEZ

19.1   Introduction

LexLog is not a lexical theory, but a package of logical specifications for constructing explicit representations for lexical items in restricted information domains. We usually call a domain "restricted" in two main cases.

1. The domain is notionally bounded. It is sufficiently simple to be decomposed into an organized finite set of notions, which might be enriched, if necessary, by applying a finite number of explicit combination rules. Metaphorically, one could say that the domain has been "axiomatized". A clear example of this situation can be found in Palmer (1990).
2. The domain is lexically bounded. The representations to be constructed apply to a finite set of lexical items, and not to the whole of a language, or to an indefinite set of terms.

While they are often associated, neither of these properties strictly implies the other. For example, although the use of a statistical tool like PATHFINDER (Schvaneveldt, 1990) allows the construction of limited lexical clusters (case 2), their notional homogeneity is not warranted by the clustering procedure. E.g., in a study of the word marriage based on the definitions in the *Longman Dictionary of Contemporary English* (Wilks et al., 1989), the words *marriage* and *muslim* co-occur. Although the religious link is obvious, making precise the amount of knowledge about *muslim* which would be relevant to *marriage* is not easy. LexLog is designed only for situations which exhibit the TWO forms of boundedness, that is, it can be of some help only when the domain allows the use of a finite notional and a finite lexical basis. What sort of help does it provide? The two basic functions of LexLog can be shortly described as:

1. control function: LexLog helps a user to keep some control on what she is doing when she introduces or changes representations associated with lexical items,
2. expression function: LexLog offers different sets of semantic operators (classifiers and scriptal predicates), as well as syntactic operators for handling tree adjoining structures for French (Abeillé, 1991).

In this chapter we will illustrate these two functions, focusing on aspects which are sufficiently developed and well understood. To appreciate the general problem, one has to notice that a restricted domain, which is the only sort of domain we will consider, is not necessarily a SMALL domain. First, the number of lexical entries can be large. Second, the complexity of representations can be high (leaving aside the complexity of possible inferential processes). When the limited domain under study is sufficiently large or intricate, it is usually impossible to provide a treatment in a few days. The most probable scenario in this case is that of a stepwise approach, during which we add or retract information, revise our judgments, discover new links or abandon spurious ones, and so on. In short, the image of the domain is an evolving object, which stabilizes only in a gradual fashion. We cannot master all the aspects of such a process, but there are some simple tasks for which an assistance would be welcome; LexLog has been devised to ease two of these tasks, which prove to be major ones: controlling consistency of monotonic hierarchical dependences (which pertain to definitions and semantic classification), enhancing the expressive power with respect to some temporal dependences (which pertain to scripts and similar entities). We will ignore the formal aspects, in order to keep the presentation as intuitive as possible. The reader is referred to Jayez (1992a) for an analysis of these aspects

19.2   Hierarchical dependences: Intuitive motivation

There are two typical situations in which hierarchical dependences should be used.

- The "blueprint task". As already explained, some restricted domains correspond to complex informations. A user might have to begin by sketchy representations, making them more and more precise as she studies the domain further. At each stage it is necessary to check whether the representations which are constructed obey the general specifications contained in the "blueprint", and, if they do not, on which points they depart from it. This presupposes that we are able to express and calculate some simple (hierarchical) dependences between elements of information.
  The classification task. In some other cases, we are interested in devising and testing simple (hierarchical) hypotheses between lexico-semantic facts. Such hypotheses are in fact dependences between semantic aspects.

LexLog is not concerned with the construction of representation or hypotheses from data but rather with their internal dependence structure and the manner in which it fits (or not) new representations or new observations. The typical questions one may ask LexLog are, for example, "does this representation agree with such and such dependence constraint ?", "is this fact compatible with such and such hypothesis?" In this respect, LexLog is not an ambitious system, but rather an inference engine based over a precise logic, all other aspects (detailed implementation, graphic interface, etc.) being important but not essential.

Although the problem of hierarchical dependences is far from simple at a formal level, it has several intuitive forms, which are sufficiently frequent and clear to be understood (and recognized) from examples. Consider a generation system which must decide between using *dans* (*in*) or *sur* (*on*) for place names in French. There is of course a similar problem in English: that of the alternation between *in* and *on*, especially when one considers variations between British English and American English. A simple strategy is to write down a list which, for each item, indicates whether the item prefers *dans*, *sur*, or allows any of the two prepositions. Obviously, the domain of place names is limited, since many names are not place names (e.g. names for time periods or for feelings), yet it is a huge domain because most of the names used for material objects can be considered as names for places: you can say that something is *in a glass* or *on a wall*. Trying to construct such a list, even for a subset of place names, will almost always lead one to ask whether there are rules, regularities, or at least tendencies behind the pairings of names and prepositions. It is apparent from the relevant literature (see Herskovits, 1986, Vandeloise, 1986, Lang et al., 1991, Rauh, 1990, for illustrations) that this last problem is a prototypical example of a hard classification problem on a restricted domain. Let us suppose that we embark on the following program: to enumerate criteria for discriminating place names according to their preference with respect to *dans* and *sur*. Let us review some situations which motivate resorting to the functionalities provided by LexLog.

19.2.1 *Expressing necessary conditions*

The following situation occurs repeatedly: we need to express aspects, features, or, to use an uncommitted term, conditions, which are necessary for a word to prefer or to allow a preposition. For instance, we could hypothesize that using *dans* requires that the name designate an entity with an inside. In a self-explaining notation we should register a dependence of the form: `dans_allowed -> has_inside`, which means, intuitively, "each path from `dans_allowed` is a path to `has_inside`". There is a hidden difficulty even in this seemingly trivial case. A dependence is not a path: it says only that the left term entails the right term, but gives no clue as to the path which leads from the former to the latter. Suppose that *dans* is interpreted in two different ways, which we will label `dans1` and `dans2`. The meaning of a `dans1` *X* phrase is roughly: *inside X*, while the meaning of a `dans2` *X* phrase would be rather: *inside a surface which represents one of the external regions of X*. E.g., *in the cupboard* would correspond to a `dans1` and *in the field* to a `dans2` (at least in some of their interpretations): we know that cupboards are used to put objects inside, and we know that an object *in* a field is not necessarily in the ground (this would be a `dans1` case), but can be on the surface of the field, within its limits. Note that an object may have several "insides"; typically, material hollow objects have insides corresponding to their concavities and a "substantial" inside corresponding to the stuff they are made of: we might say of a worm that it is in the cupboard if it digs into the wood of the cupboard. It is reasonable to declare (in the same self-explaining notation as above): `dans_allowed -> dans1_allowed ∨ dans2_allowed`, which means, intuitively, "each path from `dans_allowed` is a path to `dans1_allowed` or a path to `dans2_allowed`". "Or" is inclusive, that is, a path to `dans1_allowed` and to `dans2_allowed` would be admissible.

What LexLog can do in this case is try to "resolve" the two constraints of form `dans_allowed -> X`; if the user has not provided additional information, LexLog will record the following five possibilities:

1. `dans_allowed -> has_inside, dans_allowed -> dans1_allowed, dans_allowed -> dans2_allowed`
2. `dans_allowed -> has_inside, has_inside -> dans1_allowed ∨ dans2_allowed`
3. `dans_allowed -> dans1_allowed ∨ dans2_allowed, dans1_allowed -> has_inside, dans2_allowed -> has_inside`
4. `dans_allowed -> has_inside ∨ dans2_allowed, has_inside -> dans1_allowed, dans2_allowed -> has_inside`
5. `dans_allowed -> has_inside ∨ dans1_allowed, has_inside -> dans2_allowed, dans1_allowed -> has_inside`

What do these sets stand for? Each of them represents a particular distribution of paths which satisfies the two initial constraints `dans_allowed -> has_inside` and `dans_allowed -> dans1_allowed ∨ dans2_allowed`. The first solution says that any path from `dans_allowed` is a path to any of the other terms. By transitivity, it is clear that solution (2) satisfies the two initial constraints. The other solutions use transitivity and distribution of conjunction and disjunction. Consider solution (5) for instance; it says that any path from `dans_allowed` is a path to `has_inside` or a path to `dans1_allowed`, that any path from `has_inside` is a path to `dans2_allowed`, and that any path from `dans1_allowed` is a path to `has_inside`. By combining conjunctions and disjunctions one can check again that the initial constraints hold in this solution.

It should be apparent from this example that LexLog is a device which controls the consistency of path declarations. As the number of local path declarations rises, the necessity of controlling their compatibility and of exploring their global architecture(s) is stronger, and intuition has to face more and more tangled nets of path relations. So it seems necessary to automate the process, at least partially, and to construct a clear picture of the formal properties which are involved.

19.2.2 Sufficient conditions

We may be briefer here since sufficient conditions form the dual case of the last one. Informally, Y is a sufficient condition of X if the information associated with Y is sufficient to determine the information associated with X. In a conjunctive-disjunctive structure (and/or structure) this means that, when Y is true, X is true. In the path metaphor, this means that when the paths are reversed, some path from Y is a path to X.

In our example domain, it turns out that being a three-dimensional solid object is sufficient to allow the use of *dans*, which we will note: `dans_allowed <- 3d_solid_object`. We find here the same sort of information combination problem as in the previous case; for instance, if we declare `dans_allowed <- dans1_allowed` and `dans_allowed <- dans2_allowed`, we may combine these local path indications in several manners, obtaining "solutions" like:

```
dans_allowed <- dans1_allowed, dans_allowed <-
dans2_allowed, dans1_allowed <- 3d_solid_object, or
```

```
dans_allowed <- 3d_solid_object, 3d_solid_object <-
dans1_allowed, dans_allowed <- dans2_allowed.
```

19.2.3 *Negative conditions*

Sometimes it is useful to *forbid* some relation rather than to declare it. Typically, this kind of negative constraint works as a reminder or a *caveat* to oneself, to mark a problematic (set of) item(s). E.g., words and expressions constructed from *route* (*road*) prefer *sur* when an entity is supposed to be located on the surface; one may not use *dans la route* for a car if it just runs on the road. This example (and others) suggest that the `dans2` reading is not automatically accessible even in cases where it seems admissible: every "simple" three-dimensional object, such as a sphere or a simple polyhedron, has an external region. If a road is seen as a parallelepiped, it has faces, and one of its faces constitutes the visible part of the road. A way of preventing *route* from giving access to `dans2_allowed` would be to declare `dans2_allowed <-/- "route"`, which means, intuitively, "when the paths are reversed it is not true that some path from "route" is a path to `dans2_allowed`". Like the two previous forms of constraint, this one can be checked. For instance, a construction where the following constraints occur would violate the negative constraint.

```
dans_allowed <- dans1_allowed, dans_allowed <-
dans2_allowed, dans2_allowed <- 3d_solid_object,
3d_solid_object <- "route"
```

This is so because, by transitivity, some path from "route" leads to `dans2_allowed`.

19.3 The general approach

For such simple examples the path metaphor is sufficient. For the general case it is misleading and leaves unspecified what we can do and what we cannot. We have no proof that the approach we took would still be correct for examples with different, possibly more complex, structures. The Appendix shows the dependence system for data pertaining to the `dans1/dans2` distinction. Although some information is omitted, the overall structure is complex and information modification could result in changes unpredictable for intuition. A general approach, with a formal specification, is needed at this stage.

19.3.1 *An informal presentation of the formal framework*

In this chapter we use a simple language, which will be sufficient to demonstrate the essential features of the dependence approach in LexLog. We consider finite acyclic logic programs using only positive literals (so, we use no special negation operator). We choose the logic programming framework because it combines in a natural way techniques from reduction systems and model-theoretic semantics (Padawitz, 1988), a feature of special importance for capturing definitional knowledge (Nebel, 1990): a definition has a *definiendum* (a *goal* in logic programming) for which the *definiens* consists in an and/or tree of terms which can be primitive terms or new *definienda*. Roughly speaking, logic programs make apparent the kind of hierarchical semantics we need. Consider the following program *P1*:

```
/* program P1 x,y local */
salaried worker(x) <- person(x) pay(x,y)
pay(x,y) <- salary(x,y)
salary(x,y) <- regular(y) fixed(y)
```

The text between /* and */ is a comment. The comment gives the name of the program and reminds us that the terms x and y are local to *P1* (they cannot be freely equated with other terms x and y occurring in another program). The main part of *P1* intends to convey the following meaning: a salaried worker is a person whose pay is a salary, that is, something fixed and regular. This is exactly the sort of information one would expect from a sketchy (and admittedly imperfect) definition for the word *salaried*. One of the most frequent operations carried out with logic programs is checking whether some goal holds in the program. E.g., one could ask whether salaried worker(x) holds. The answer would be negative in the traditional closed-world assumption: for salaried worker(x) to hold it is required that person(x) hold, for instance, but we have no way of proving it in *P1*. This kind of question will be meaningful as soon as we have some semantics for logic programs. One can observe that, even in this trivial case, this question "contains" other, more primitive questions: if we want to prove salaried worker(x) in *P1*, which other goals must we prove or which other goals is it sufficient to prove? In other terms, on which goals does the satisfaction of salaried worker(x) in *P1* DEPEND?

The overall picture is slightly complicated by unification problems. In fact, dependences hold between literals with particular "structures" of arguments. This is illustrated by *P2*.

```
/* program P2 x,y local */
praises(x,y) <- admires(x,y)
admires(x,x) <- boastful(x)
admires(x,y) <- loves(x,y)
```

By choosing to identify x and y or to keep them distinct one obtains different interpretations (and executions of the program). To express dependences properly, it is necessary to relativize them to substitutions. Let *P* be a program and *V* a denumerable set of new variables not occurring in *P*. Let *G* be a goal occurring as the head of a clause in *P*. Informally, we may construct the different dependences associated with *G* in the following manner:

- First, we replace each variable in *G* by a variable in *V* and make the implied replacements in the tail of the clause whose *G* is the head. We repeat the same substitution process, with the same variables, in any clause which allows it.
- Second, for each such clause we choose a set of substitutions based on *V* so that all the resulting clauses contain only variables in *V*.
- Third, for each of those literals which match the head of a clause, we repeat the same operation as in step 1 on this clause, unifying its head with the literal.
- The process goes on until there is no clause to transform or a contradiction (of form $x = v_j$ and $x = v_k$) appears.

Thus we have obtained a family of substitutions (ignoring alphabetic variants). Dependences are relativized to the members of this family, as *P3* illustrates.

```
/* program P3 x...s local */
p(x,y) <- q(z,w)
q(w,w) <- r(w,s)
```

Let $s1 = \{x = v1, y = v2, z = v3, w = v4, w = v5, s = v6\}$ and $s2 = \{x = v1, y = v2, z = v3, w = v3, w = v3, s = v6\}$ be two substitutions. If we consider *s1*, there is a path from $p(v1,v2)$ to $q(v3,v4)$ and a path from $q(v5,v5)$ to $r(v5,v6)$, but there is no path from $p(v1,v2)$ to $r(v5,v6)$, because the transitivity is broken by the difference between $q(v3,v4)$ and $q(v5,v5)$. In the case of *s2* the transitivity obtains: we have a path from $p(v1,v2)$ to $r(v3,v6)$. In this chapter, we will use examples in which the transitivities hold in any substitution; so we may ignore the substitutional structure and define our relations in general. However, the reader should bear in mind that this choice is a simple matter of convenience, which does not reflect the logical properties. In some cases it is necessary to use equational constraints on variables in different clauses; the substitutional structure is then useful and we will use special variables of form v_i to indicate a coreference. E.g., the two clauses P(x) <- Q(v1) and R(x) <- S(v1,x) are to be interpreted only in models which instantiate the two occurrences of v1 in the same way, and the dependences are defined accordingly. We will call such coreferences examples of external sharing (because the sharing occurs between different clauses), other coreferences, inside clauses, being examples of internal sharing.

19.3.2 *Basic definitions for dependence*

It is well known that logic programs can be described as and/or graphs according to the equivalence ($\equiv$) scheme:

```
goali <- subgoall ... subgoaln
            ≡
[goali ⊂ (subgoall ∧ ... ∧ subgoaln)]
goali <- subgoall.........goali <- subgoaln
            ≡
[goali ⊂ (subgoall ∧ ... ∧ subgoaln)]
```

Usually the execution of a logic program runs through several subgoals (think of the WAM goal stack for a concrete illustration); we call *target* the goal which the program tries to satisfy. A goal is *activated* in an execution if (i) it is not the target and (ii) the program tries to satisfy it (for checking the target). At this stage, it seems that a straightforward dependence notion is at hand. For instance, in the conjunctive case, we could use the following definition:

In a logic program P, considered as a closed area (encapsulation), a given goal G ∧-depends on a given subgoal G' iff any execution of P where G is the target activates G'.

But this is not the policy endorsed in LexLog. To see why, let us consider *P1* again, and suppose that salaried worker(x) is the target of an execution EX; the virtual dependences will vary according to the process model of EX: e.g., in a PROLOG-style execution (depth-first and left to right), EX will never activate pay(x,y), because the subgoal person(x) fails. LexLog is not concerned primarily with program satisfaction, but only with definitional dependence structure. So the notion for ∧-dependence runs as follows in LexLog:

> <u>df 1</u>
> Let P be a logic program. G ∧-controls G' in P iff:
> - there is exactly one clause of form G <- ... G' ... in P, or,
> - there is exactly one clause of form G <- ... G'' ... in P and G'' ∧-controls G' in P, or
> - there are exactly k clauses of form G <- $G11$ ... $G1n$, ..., G <- $Gk1$ ... Gkn, in P and in each of these clauses, some Gij is G' or ∧-controls G' in P.

G ∨-controls G' in P is defined dually. We use ∧-cont and ∨-cont for abbreviating ∧-controls and ∨-controls. Since our program is finite and acyclic, we can start from some literal and enumerate all the literals which are accessed when running through the clauses. These literals form the *content* of the former literal, which is said to *contain* them.

In *P1*, the following cont-relations are satisfied:

```
salaried worker(x) ∧-cont person(x), pay(x,y), salary(x,y),
   regular(y), fixed(y),
pay(x,y) ∧-cont salary(x,y), regular(y), fixed(y),
salary(x,y)∧-cont regular(y), fixed(y),
salary(x,y) ∨-cont pay(x,y).
```

The content of salaried worker(x) is simply the set of literals in *P1*.

Inspecting a program and listing the cont-relations which hold in it is a descriptive use of definition 1. There is also a prescriptive use, according to which one declares the cont-relations which MUST hold in an otherwise uncompletely specified program. For instance, we could impose to salaried worker(x) to ∧-cont a certain goal. Let us suppose that we want to express the fact that the salary of a salaried worker is regular. We declare salaried worker(x) ∧-cont regular(y). When presented with the following program *P4*, LexLog will accept it:

```
/* program P4 x...w local */
salaried worker(x) <- paid_worker(x) regular(v1)
paid_worker(x) <- work(x,y) pay_for(y,v1)
```

P4 says that a salaried worker is a worker with a pay, i.e., somebody who does some work (y) and who receives a pay (v1) for this work. According to the first clause, this pay must be regular. Note that the substitutional coreference of the first argument is regular() and the second argument in pay_for() is forced by the use of the special variable v1. This illustrates external sharing.

19.3.3 *Hierarchical positive shadows*

By considering the prescriptive use of constraints, we have surreptitiously introduced a new problem. In our first example of classification we had all the predicates at our disposal, and our task was to express relations in a closed universe. In the present case we might have no precise idea about which predicates will occur in our programs. In addition to "normal" (explicit) literals we may use "variables" for literals in LexLog, in the three following ways.

1. We may simply declare that we do not know the arity of a predicate whose label is still explicit. E.g., we declare *salary<x,y>*, which means that *salary* must have at least the two variables x and y (but it might have some more variables).

2. We may declare *?k<u1 . . . un>*, which means something like: " we need some unknown predicate, referenced as *?k*, having at least the variables *u1 . . . un* in its scope (in any order)". E.g., if we declare *?1<x>* LexLog will consider that any form *P(. . . x . . .)* is a correct instantiation of this declaration.

3. A less simple mechanism is predicate contraction. If we declare *??k<u1 . . . un>*, it means that there is a single predicate *?k* as in the preceding case, OR that there is a sequence of literals which uses at least all the variables in {*u1 . . . un*} (but which might use some more variables).

An example will probably be welcome at this stage. Let us suppose we want to express the following information. A worker works for some entity (person, institution, company, etc.) (idea 1) and does some job in exchange for a remuneration (idea 2) which is a function of the job according to some rules of proportionality. The aspects relevant to these rules are the regularity of the job, its nature and its "quantity" (a function of difficulty and duration) (idea 3). Ignoring the cont-relations for the moment, let us focus on the predicates themselves. If we want to express idea 1, we might use an indication like:

```
{... ?1<y> ...
?1<y> v-cont person(y), institution(y), company(y) ...}
```

LexLog would then accept clauses like:

```
worker(x) <- works_for(x,y) possible(works_for,y) ...
possible(works_for,x) <- person(x)
possible(works_for,x) <- institution(x)
possible(works_for,x) <- company(x)
```

Here we see that ?1<y> has been instantiated as possible(works_for,y).
  If we had declared something like:

```
{... ?2<z>,remuneration(w), nature(w,w1), quantity(w,w2),
    regularity(w,w3),
  nature(z,z1),quantity(z,z2),regularity (z,z3),??3<w1,w2,w3,
    z1,z2,z3> ... }
```

LexLog would have accepted the following program:

```
worker(x) <- ... job(x,z) ... remuneration(w) nature(w,w1)
    quantity(w,w2)
regularity(w,w3) nature(z,z1) quantity(z,z2)
    regularity(z,z3)
combination_of(w1,w2,w3,u) combination_of(z1,z2,z3,u')
    depends_on(u,u')
```

We can note how the two predicates combination_of and depends_on are used to "split" the unknown entity ??3<w1,w2,w3,z1,z2,z3>. The variables u and u' did not occur in our specification.
  More generally, we may declare a finite set of cont-relations of form *goal c-cont goal'*, where $c = \wedge$ or $\vee$. Identical variables in the set but not in V (that is, variables which have not the form v_i) are interpreted as coreferential in any program compatible with the set. Variables in V must occur without change in any program compatible with the set. Such a set is called a hierarchical positive shadow. It is hierarchical because, when there is no variable, all constraints in the set are purely hierarchical. It is positive because all constraints determine what must be the case. It is shadowy since it only "delineates" possible programs but gives no detailed information on their structure. This is due to the non-local character of the hierarchical relations $\wedge$-cont and $\vee$-cont, but also to the use of literal "variables". The interaction between these two aspects is governed by the following rules:

- a form X $\wedge$-cont *?k<x1 . . . xn>* means that X $\wedge$-cont any literal substituted for *?k<x1 . . . xn>*,
- a form *?k<x1 . . . xn>* $\wedge$-cont X means that any literal substituted for *?k<x1 . . . xn>* $\wedge$-cont X,
- a form X $\wedge$-cont *??k<x1 . . . xn>* means that X $\wedge$-cont any of the literals which constitute the construct substituted for *?k<x1 . . . xn>*,

- a form *?k<x1 . . . xn>* ∧-cont *X* means that at least one of the literals which constitute the construct substituted for *?k<x1 . . . xn>* ∧-cont *X*,
- a form *X* ∨-cont *?k<x1 . . . xn>* means that *X* ∨-cont any literal substituted for *?k<x1 . . . xn>*,
- a form *?k<x1 . . . xn>* ∨-cont *X* means that any literal substituted for *?k<x1 . . . xn>* ∨-cont *X*,
- a form *X* ∨-cont *??k<x1 . . . xn>* means that *X* ∨-cont at least one of the literals which constitute the construct substituted for *?k<x1 . . . xn>*,
- a form *??k<x1 . . . xn>* ∨-cont *X* means that any of the literals which constitute the construct substituted for *?k<x1 . . . xn>* ∨-cont *X*.

In the worker example, we could write the following hierarchical positive shadow:

```
/* shadow for worker(x) */
{worker(x) ∧-cont works_for(x,y),?1<y>,?2<z>,
   remuneration(w) nature(w,w1)
quantity(w,w2),regularity(w,w3),nature(z,z1),quantity(z,z2),
   regularity
{z,z3},??3<w1,w2,w3,z1,z2,z3>
?1<y> ∨-cont person(y), institution(y), company(y)}
```

the literal `worker(x)` ∧-cont many things, in particular the three variables constructs `?1<y>`, `?2<z>`, and `??3<w1,w2,w3,z1,z2,z3>`. The first two cases imply simply that `worker(x)` must ∧-cont any literal substituted for `?1<y>` and `?2<z>`. The last case implies that `worker(x)` must ∧-cont each literal which is used to construct the value of `??3<w1,w2,w3,z1,z2,z3>`. The following program *P5* satisfies the requirements of the shadow:

```
/* program P5 x...u' local */
worker(x) <- works_for(x,y) possible(works_for,y) job(x,z)
   exchange(x,y,z,w)
remuneration(w) nature(w,w1) quantity(w,w2)
   regularity(w,w3) nature(z,z1)
quantity(z,z2) regularity(z,z3) combination_of(w1,w2,w3,u)
combination_of(z1,z2,z3,u') depends_on(u,u')
possible(works_for,x) <- person(x)
possible(works_for,x) <- institution(x)
possible(works_for,x) <- company(x)
```

Note that the literal `exchange(x,y,z,w)` did not even occur in the shadow.

19.3.4 *Prescriptive inheritance*

Traditionally, systems which store and handle information (databases, semantic networks, object-oriented libraries, etc.) use *inheritance* as a means of avoiding redundancies: an entity A can inherit from an entity B, which limits repetition since the information associated with A is propagated to B. We do not intend to discuss inheritance in general – the interested reader is referred to CL (1992),

Lenzerini et al. (1991), Dugerdil (1988) for various approaches – but only to make precise the role of inheritance in the present framework. Monotonic inheritance, that is, inheritance in which information associated with A is preserved for B, can be used in LexLog via a declaration of the form: *X inherits_from Y*, where *X* and *Y* may be literals or variables for literals. The general constraint is: if *X* inherits from *Y* anything which is entailed by *Y* must be entailed by *X*, and anything which entails *X* entails *Y*. Practically, inheritance holds in the four following cases (besides simple identity of *X* and *Y*) or in any combination of them:

- some literals ∧-controlled by *X* are not ∧-controlled by *Y*.
- some literals ∨-controlled by *Y* are not ∨-controlled by *X*.
- *X* contains some literals which exhibit internal sharing, while the corresponding literals in *Y* do not.
- *X* contains some literals which exhibit external sharing, while the corresponding literals in *Y* do not.

If we surmise that a salaried is a worker who has entered into a contract with an organization about her job and her remuneration, we can readily reuse the shadow for worker(x), by declaring:

```
/* shadow for salaried worker(x) */
{inherits_from(worker(x))
salaried(x) ∧-cont contract_with_about(x,y,z,w)
?1<y> ∨-cont institution(y), company(y)}
```

salaried(x) adds to worker(x) the information relevant to contract, but simplifies the ∨-control for ?1<y> by removing the person(y) literal (according to this definition, a person cannot be the salaried of another person). In the *dans* distribution shown in the Appendix, the categories 1 to 6 inherit from the category 7: this is intuitively sound, since the categories 1 to 6 refer to different forms of boundedness, while the category 7 refers to boundedness in general.

19.3.5 *Negative shadows*

We have noted that some constraints have a negative effect: they are declared to prevent some situations from taking place. In general negative constraints are more complex than the positive ones we encountered in the previous examples. This is so because they tend to mention SETS of literals instead of isolated literals. These sets are in fact conjunctions of literals which, taken together, form a possible "solution" of a goal in a given program. The formal definition is:

df 2
Let *P* be a logic program. *X* ∧-controls1 *Y* in *P* iff:
- there is exactly one clause of form *X* <- . . . *Y* . . . in *P*, or,
- there is exactly one clause of form *X* <- . . . *G* . . . in *P* and *G* ∧-controls1 *Y* in *P*, or

- there are exactly k clauses of form $X <- Gl1 \ldots Gln, \ldots, G <- Gk1 \ldots Gkn$, in P and $Y \in \{Z1 \vee \ldots \vee Zk: Zi \in \{Gi1 \ldots Gin\}$ or $\exists Hi\ (Hi \in \{Gi1 \ldots Gin\} \wedge Hi \wedge\text{-controls1 } Zi)$, for $1 \leq i \leq k\}$

The conditions for X ∨-controls1 Y are dual. We use ∧-cont1 and ∨-cont1 as abbreviations.

For ∨-cont1, this definition enumerates, for some goal X, all the conjunctions Y of goals which it would be sufficient to prove for proving X in the given program P. It is often useful to restrict the cont1-relation to "terminal" goals, that is, goals which are not heads of clauses in the program. E.g., in *P5* for worker(x) we have:

```
worker(x) v-cont1 works_for(x,y) ∧ job(x,z) ∧
exchange(x,y,z,w) ∧ remuneration(w) ∧ nature(w,w1) ∧
quantity(w,w2) ∧ regularity(w,w3) ∧ nature(z,z1) ∧
quantity(z,z2) ∧ regularity(z,z3) ∧ combination_of(w1,w2,
w3,u) ∧ combination_of(z1,z2,z3,u') ∧ depends_on(u,u') ∧ X,
```

where X can be person(y), institution(y), or company(y).

In the distribution of the Appendix we have a set of ∨-cont relations, between categories and words, and between prepositional constructions and words. E.g., the word *jardin* leads to the category 1, and the same word leads to the category of words which allows the use of *dans* to describe the position of an object "inside" them (*dans le jardin* is roughly translatable as *inside the garden*). Let us suppose we construct a directed acyclic and/or graph, whose leaves are the words, roots the prepositional constructions, and intermediate nodes the categories. The aim of such a graph would be to classify sets of categories (intermediates nodes) according to their preferences for prepositional constructions (roots). The feasibility of such a classification would be controlled by the words: if two words leading to the same set of categories lead to different sets of roots, that will mean that the classification is not coherent. In this context negative shadows can be used to formulate hypotheses. For instance if we think that words partially similar to mass terms cannot be used with the dans2 construction, we might forbid any link between the category and the construction by declaring that dans2_allowed ∨-cont1 (X ∧ 10), where X is any conjunction of categories, must not be satisfied. This will prevent situations in which 10 is sufficient by itself to access dans2-allowed (X is the null set), as well as situations in which 10, with other categories mentioned in X, leads to dans2_allowed. Checking the validity of a negative constraint in a classification amounts, then, to testing a particular form of negative dependence hypothesis.

19.4 Temporal dependences

Up to now, we have considered only hierarchical dependences, which are, in some respects, comparable to decompositional relations in definitions. These dependences were, so to speak, "void of content", since it is the reponsibility of the user to define precisely the items between which she posits dependences. Yet, there are some dependences between lexical elements which seem to imply time and which are not reducible to hierarchical ones. In order to preserve some homogeneity, we shall illustrate LexLog functionalities by choosing examples in a uniform domain where we have put it to use, that of car accidents declarations. Our aim was to construct a prototype for an "intelligent" archiving system, which could help the user to store representations of accidents, as evidenced by the participants'declarations, for future retrieving and comparative analysis. It was part of a more global project which aimed to assess the feasibility of automatic understanding for such declarations (see Kayser, 1992; Jayez, 1992b). However we want to avoid the impression of an ad hoc system, devised for dealing with a very particular domain. So we will provide some different introductory examples to show that the problems are in fact general.

19.4.1 *Examples*

Associations

Consider the two words *buy* and *price*. They exhibit a kind of dependence which is analogous to those studied by Mel'čuk (Mel'čuk, 1982; DEC, 1984, 1988; Steele, 1990), who developed lexical functions to relate lexical items by means of functions picked out from a small finite basis (about 60 functions for English and French). Using the terminology presented in Steele (1990, p. 59) we might say that *price* is the typical noun for the fourth actant of the keyword (*buy* in this example). If S_i designates the lexical function which returns the i-th actant we have:

$S_1(buy) = buyer$, $S_2(buy) = merchandise$, $S_3(buy) = seller$, $S_4(buy) = price$.

There are other examples which do not seem to be amenable to this procedure. They generally correspond to "loose" domain-driven associations of the type studied in Morris and Hirst (1991), like the associations between *traffic lights* and *to stop, post office* and *stamps, doctor* and *appointment,* etc.

Scales

Let us consider a sentence like *The boy is clever but the problem is hard.* This kind of linking by *but* has been the subject of thorough investigations (see Anscombre, 1989; Ducrot, 1980; Jayez, 1989). Although the linguistic and formal descriptions which have been proposed are complex, one can extract from them two essential ideas:

- there is a semantic dependence between *clever* and *problem,* which can be glossed by a comment like "being clever allows an intelligent being to solve problems",
- there is some scale-phenomenon involved in such sentences: the more clever an "intelligent" being is, the more he can solve problems (and more and more complex ones).

Here again we find some "loose" dependence, which seems to relate two scales in an intuitive way.

Aspect

In Pustejovsky (1988) it is argued that the contrast between *Mary threw the ball to John* and *Mary dragged the box to John* amounts to a difference in agent's influence; while it is exerted only at the beginning of the whole episode in the former case, it is (roughly) continuous in the latter. Such differences must be representable at some level (and Pustejovsky offers a general aspectual format to this effect). Note that this example and similar ones point at the general problem of causality (see Croft, 1991, for a review).

19.4.2 *The practical problem*

It should be useful (and in many cases pleasant) to be able to express these relations in a uniform and orderly way, for example, to fulfill the following tasks:

- improving the listings which are to be found in thesauri (such as Roget, 1977, or Delas and Delas-Demon, 1989) by adding temporal (scriptal) dependences when relevant, e.g., by specifying that an appointment is a precondition to being examined by a doctor,
- providing better descriptions of a dispositional term (like *clever*) by indicating their causal import, for generation or understanding systems,
- providing better descriptions of aspectual features in verbal structures for studying thematic structure, polysemy, etc.

Here again, our aim was not to replace detailed studies, since this is obviously an unrealistic aim, but rather to offer a general framework to make quick prototyping easier.

19.4.3 *Temporal entities*

Since LexLog is not a lexical theory, choosing among the tremendous amount of theories of tense and aspect (Binnick, 1991) was not even considered. Rather, we tried to provide general tools which seemed acceptable for most parties. For expository purpose, we will present these tools incrementally, pausing at every stage to provide some illustration.

The basic temporal entities are time points and time intervals (in the sense of Allen, 1984), with relations defined on them. We adopted the version of Meiri, 1991). The basic qualitative relations are Allen's relations augmented with point-to-point (pp) relations, namely, $<$, $=$, $>$, and point-to-interval (pi) or interval-to-point relations, namely, $<$, starts, during, finishes, $>$. pi relations are exactly as expected: they are really relations between a point and the endpoints of an interval; e.g., for an interval $[I\text{-},I\text{+}]$ we have the equivalences between $p < [I\text{-},I\text{+}]$ and $p < I\text{-}$, $during(p,[I\text{-},I\text{+}])$ and $I\text{-} < p < I\text{+}$, etc. The quantitative relations can express durations by means of constants or variables. The basic construct is a constraint network, whose nodes are intervals or points of time at which (boolean combinations of) propositions hold, and arcs are disjunctive temporal constraints in set form. At this level already, one can choose between an interval-based approach for time (see Dowty, 1986, for a systematic exposition) or a davidsonian approach (event-based), as advocated in Parsons (1990). This choice will be embodied in a shift from intervals to points or from points to intervals. Since most representation problems tend to occur when intervals, rather than points, are used, we will focus on interval-based procedures in what follows.

Systems which resort to temporal analysis (like PUNDIT, see Passonneau, 1988) must define various kinds of (families of) intervals, which can readily be defined in Meiri's system, without any particular problem. For instance, one can create and handle closed-bounded intervals, open-bounded intervals, unbounded "intervals" (family of intervals around some point or some interval), and so on. For simplicity we will consider mainly intervals (not families of them). LexLog supplements these Allen-style mechanisms with the two notions of *transition* and of *scale*.

A *transition* is a change whose orientation is undefined. An action of dragging, for instance, presupposes that at each moment the position of some object is changed, but does not presuppose that this change causes a motion with some specified direction: one can drag an object in several successive directions. An action of running does not presuppose that the runner is running somewhere, while it entails that, at each moment, the position of the runner's body is modified.

A *scalar transition* is a transition based on a *scale*, that is, an ordered sequence of degrees for some (combination of) qualities. If we add to the pure process of dragging some telic information, as in the example of Pustejovsky, *Mary dragged the box to John*, we transform the transition into a scalar transition because the degree of proximity to John is continually increased in the process. The relevance of scalar transitions to motion verbs is obvious when some destination is given, but these transitions are also connected with rate verbs, like *accélérer* (*to speed up, to accelerate*) or *ralentir* (*to slow down*). As a simple illustration of the introduction of scalar transitions into Meiri's notational framework, consider the representation proposed in Jayez (1992b) for *accélérer*:

```
<duration(i,alpha)> duration(j,beta)
<starts_pi(p1,i) finishes_pi(p2,i)> starts_pi(p3,j) fin-
ishes_pi(p4,j)
<meets_ii(i,j)>
<during(i,vel_rate(a,r1))> during(j,vel_rate(a,r2))
<sup(r2,r1)> sup(r2,0)
```

There are two interpretations of these declarations, depending whether parentheses around clauses are taken into account. Ignoring them, we have two intervals i and j, with respective durations alpha and beta and respective endpoints p1-p2 and p3-p4. These indications are useful for the chaining of episodes but are not connected with the meaning of *accélérer*. During i the velocity rate of a vehicle a is r1 while it is r2, superior to r1, during j. The velocity rate represents the variation of velocity; it can be positive, negative or null. When r1 is null a has a constant velocity over i and an increasing velocity over j (since r2 > r1). When r1 is negative or null, r2 is positive (it cannot be null) and a still increases its velocity over j. Note that we do not require for *accélérer* that the velocity of a be constant over i (that is, we do not require r1 = 0), because we do not feel intuitively that it is a necessary condition. Users with different intuitions might of course declare r1 = 0. The two intervals i and j *meet*, in the sense of Allen: no interval can be found between them. This a general feature of the approach: when some change is defined over a sequence of intervals, they meet because any intervening interval would not be relevant to the definition of the change. The main point here is that we have no telicity: there is not explicit limit for the velocity. The representation imposes only a continuous increase via the information r2 > 0.

When parentheses are introduced, corresponding clauses are ignored. In this case the vehicle a increases its velocity over j without any comparison to another interval. The selection of the first or the second option depends on the situation which must be coded.

When information concerning the origin or the culmination of the scalar transition is available, the representation must be different. E.g., if one wants to provide a counterpart for sentences like *la voiture a accéléré jusqu'à 50 à l'heure* (*the car speeded up to 30 mph*), it is possible to add to the previous declaration the clause at(p4,vel(a,50)). The final speed is declared to be reached at p4, the end of the interval j. A symmetric declaration would handle the case of an initial speed at p3. In general, for a predicate *pred* which attributes some value v_i to a set of parameters $t_1 \ldots t_n$, we have the following possibilities over an interval.

```
/* starts_pi(p1,i), finishes_pi(p2,i) */
/* state */
during(i,pred(t1 . . . tn,v))
```

pred defines a state for t1 . . . tn over i: the value of pred for the parameters is constant over i.

```
/*starts_pi(pj,i) ∨ finishes_pi(pj,i) ∨ during_pi(pj,i),
   starts_pi(pk,i) ∨ finishes_pi(pk,i) ∨ during_pi(pk,
   i), pj<pk, ¬∃p(during_pi (p,i) ∧ (pj < p < pk))*/
         /* transition*/
IF (at(pj,pred(t1 ... tn,vj)) AND at(pk,pred(t1 ...
   tn,vk))) THEN vj ≠ vk
```

pred defines a transition for t1 ... tn over i: for any two contiguous points on i the value of pred for t1 ... tn is different. Notice that the condition does not prevent pred to have the same value for t1 ... tn at two non-contiguous points on i. E.g., a sequence of loops (considered as a motion) corresponds to a transition; yet the same point may be reached several times during the loops.

```
/*starts_pi(pj,i) ∨ finishes_pi(pj,i) ∨ during_pi(pj,i),
    starts_pi(pk,i) ∨ finishes_pi(pk,i) ∨ during_pi(pk,
    i), pj < pk */
/* transition + increasing scalarity*/
IF (at(pj,pred(t1 ... tn,vj)) AND at(pk,pred(t1 ...
    tn,vk))) THEN vj < vk
```

Here `pred` defines a scalar increasing transition for `t1 ... tn` over `i`: for any two points on `i` the value at the second point is superior to the value at the first. Notice that the two points are not necessarily contiguous. Predicates with a rate suffix, like `vel_rate` above, are typical scalar predicates: when a declaration of form `pred_rate(t1 ... tn,v)` is used over an interval and `v` is not null, it is assumed that pred defines a scalar transition for `t1 ... tn` over `i`. This transition is increasing if `v` is positive, and decreasing if `v` is negative. If `v = 0`, it is assumed that pred defines a state for `t1 ... tn` over `i`.

In some cases we would like to indicate that some given predication is a state, a transition, or a scalar transition without using specialized predicates. This is required notably when we use shadowy predicates (in the form `?k<x1 ... xn>`) which are embedded in the temporal operator `during()`. We may then resort to more precise forms for this operator: `during_state()`, `during_trans()`, `during_sctrans()`.

A scalar dependence between parameters `a1` and `a2` over a set of values `V` is an expression `sc_dep(a1,a2,V,sign,sign)` where `sign` is + or -. A scalar dependence `sc_dep(a1,a2,V,+,+)` means that if `a1 = x` and `a2 = y`, then if `a1 = x'` > `x` then, if `a2 = y'`, `y'` must be > `y`. In other terms, if `a1` increases so does `a2`. Other combinations for other values of signs are defined accordingly. The predicate `during_sctrans` mentioned above is a special case of scalar dependence, a form `during_sctrans(i,pred(t1 ... tn,v))` entails `sc_dep(duration ([x,p2]),v,-,+)` or `sc_dep(duration(x,p2),v,-,+)`, where `x` is a point ranging from the beginning of `i` to its end (`p2`): as `x` comes closer to `p2`, the value `v` increases or decreases. It is important to note that culminating processes and scalar items give rise to analogous phenomena; one can put on a par two sentences like *John is clever but the problem is hard* and *John was dragging the box to Mary but he fell*: in the two cases the first proposition makes possible a virtual inferencing, from cleverness to solving ability and from motion to position, based over a global orientation of the scales toward the points where the inferenced proposition would become true: if John became more and more clever he would perhaps solve the problem; if he dragged the box during a sufficiently long time he would perhaps carry it to Mary (see Ducrot, 1980, and Jayez, 1989, for discussions).

The general syntax for prototyping temporal dependences in LexLog (illustrated by the previous examples) uses expressions which can be:

1. many-sorted literals (Walther, 1987), of form $F(t1^{s1} \ldots tn^{sn})$, where F is a n-ary functor and the ti^{si} are sorted terms of sort si,
2. any boolean combination of expressions,

3. any predicate intends(t,e) or believes(t,e) where t is a sorted term and e an expression,
4. any predicate at(tp,e), during(ti,e), during_state(ti,e), during_trans(ti,e), during_sctrans(ti,e), where tp is a time-point, ti a time-interval, and e an expression.

Usually we do not indicate the sorts, which are implicit from the context.

19.4.4 *Scriptal dependences: A simple example*

The domain of car accidents offers numerous examples of scriptal dependences (essentially causal ones), whose main factors are path shapes (curvatures), velocity, attentional and intentional states of drivers, and legal rules. Among these dependences, some pertain to mundane knowledge in the domain of traffic events, others correspond more precisely to lexical items. The problem of drawing a limit between world knowledge and "pure" lexical information is invoked repeatedly in the works of linguists and computational linguists. Interesting as they are, discussions of this problem should not hide the practical requirements: in most domains, it is necessary to describe lexical contents AND chunks of world knowledge, and the main difficulty is then to provide a smooth transition from one source of information to the other.

Reviewing briefly the articulation between verbs and domain dependences, we find the following cases to be the most frequent:-

- some verbs mention velocity and velocity variations; the dependences bear on trajectories, durations, and relative positions of vehicle;
- some verbs mention directions, direction changes, or, more generally, trajectory shapes; the dependences bear on trajectories;
- some verbs mention mental states of the driver; the dependences bear on trajectories and, more generally, any form of motion control.

For nouns, we find that they mention most often parts of the vehicles, regions of the pathways, and signals. The relevant dependences bear on positions of the vehicles involved in the accident, as well as topological and legal constraints. The archiving task consists essentially in constructing a network of intervals by combining and enriching a small subset of ready-made mini-networks corresponding to scripts attached to verbs and nouns. We give a simple example of these mini-networks, referring the reader to Jayez (1992b) for other illustrations.

The example is associated to the noun *feu rouge* (traffic lights) and to other nouns of the same semantic class (*feu tricolore, feu*). It tries to capture the following description: when a vehicle is going to pass some traffic lights it must (legally) stop if the red is on, it must stop as far as possible if the yellow is on, but it may proceed if no time is left for stopping before passing the traffic lights; in any other case it may go on (other things being equal). The representation for the red-is-on case is indicated here:

```
EVENTS AND INTERVAL RELATIONS
during(i,*see(driver t1)) = 1, during(j,believes(driver,
    *red(t1))) = 2,
starts(p1,i), finishes(p6,k), starts(p1,m), finishes (p6,m),
*front(t1,ft1), *back(t1,bt1), *direction(ft1,bt1,d),
during(k,*brakes(driver)) = 3, during(k,*vel_rate(car,
    vr) = 4,
rough(vr,negative) = 5, at(p6,not(*moving(car))) = 6,
    at(p6,*loc(car,1)) = 7,
*proj(1,<d,ft1>,1'), *before_pp(1',ft1,on(<d,ft1>))
meets_ii(i,j), during_ii(j,k), during(m,knows
    (driver,rule_of_the_road)) = 8,
during(p,intends(driver,obey(driver,rule_of_the_road))) = 9,
during(j,intends(driver,6 ∧ 7)) = 10,
                    DEPENDENCES
cause_of(1,2), cause_of(3,4 ∧ 5), cause_of(4 ∧ 5,6 ∧ 7),
    precondition_of(8,9), cause_of(9, 10), cause_of(10,3),
```

The starred predicates are specific to the archiving domain (traffic accidents). The others are standard predicates in LexLog; among them, the temporal predicates have been introduced in the last section. The new predicates cause_of, intends and believes are dependence predicates which express relations between (finite conjunctions of) predicates holding over some time interval or at some time point. The previous complex declarations form what we call a mini-script, describing the normal behavior of a driver seeing a red light. During a first interval (i) the driver notices the traffic light (t1) which is a cause for believing it is red. This belief and her knowledge of traffic regulations (which spans the whole episode) motivate an intent to stop before the front part of the traffic lights. This intent in its turn causes a braking action, which causes the decreases of velocity rate, which determines (via a scalar transition) the ultimate position of the car. Note that the domain-specific predication proj(1,<d,ft1>,1') means that the orthogonal projection of 1, the final position of the vehicle, on a line of direction d crossing the front of the traffic lights (ft1) is 1'.

In addition to cause_of we use the two predicates precondition_of and applic_cond _of. The precondition_of predicate corresponds to the *enablement* conditions in Pollack (1990): conditions which are necessary for some event to happen, but which do not constitute the production of the event, such as looking for a phone number (precondition) in order to give a call (event). The applic_cond_of predicate corresponds to the *applicability* conditions of Allen and Perrault [1980]: conditions which give its meaning to the event but do not contribute to its validity, e.g., not knowing a phone number (applicability condition) and searching a directory for it (event).

19.4.5 *Scriptal dependence: The problem(s)*

Time is an essential component of description: every static situation or action is located in time. Although it might not be apparent from this kind of example, since traffic accidents obviously involve time, resorting to time is in fact an effect of using dependence predicates. Such predicates have formed the basis of planning (see Allen et al., 1991, for a recent survey), but their role within lexical representation has generally been underestimated. Some approaches have developed advanced practical techniques to enrich the set of relations for analyzing dictionary definitions (Calzolari & Zampolli, 1991; Velardi et al., 1991), but it is unclear at this stage how they could be used to take scriptal relations into account. We already mentioned the work of Morris and Hirst on Roget's thesaurus. The authors note that words "tend to occur in similar lexical environments because they describe things that tend to occur in similar situations or contexts in the world" (Morris & Hirst, 1991, p. 22). We claim that there is more to this problem than simple situational clustering. In many cases things tend to occur "together" because they are physically connected (part_of relations could then be used), or because they are functionally related: they are members of a more or less complex functional chain which involves rules, physical causality, intentions and plans. The fact that physical properties and scriptal properties (origin and destination) have been appealed to in Pustejovsky (1991) to provide a semantic structure for nouns is not very surprising, when we realize that these are precisely the two kinds of properties which really "define" objects in the world, at least in languages like English and French. To contribute the construction of scriptal relations, LexLog has a small (expandable) database of dependencies in the five following domains: perception, physical process (what happens to material entities), emotions, communication, and conventions. The information registered in LexLog is not, of course, a list of scripts for situations in each domain, because thousands of such scripts would be necessary, and we would be anyway unable to determine the level of accuracy which is the most efficient for each script. LexLog has just a list of dependence schemas between the main roles in the five domains. Let us have a look at the perception example.

```
/* Domain: perception, base: perceptual transition of form
during(',perceives(perceiving_mode,perceiver,perceived)) */
/* states and processes */
during_state(i,f(',perceived)) = 1, during_trans(j,y(',
    perceiver)) = 2,
during_state(k,c(',perceiver)) = 3, during(l,perceives
    (perceiving_mode,perceiver, perceived)) = 4,
during_state(m,believes
    (perceiver,belief))= 5
/* temporal dependences */
precondition_of(1,4), precondition_of(2,4),
    precondition_of(3,4), cause_of(4,5),
```

```
precondition_of(1,5), precondition_of(2,5),
    precondition_of(3,5)
overlaps_ii(i, 1), overlaps_ii(j,1), overlaps_ii(k,1),
    overlaps_ii(1,m),overlaps_ii(i,m), overlaps_ii(k,m),
overlaps_ii(k,m)
```

These dependences say that states of the perceived, states or transition processes affecting the perceiver, can influence the possibility of the perception event as well as its belief result. For the corresponding intervals, it is just required that they have a non-empty intersection (overlapping). In addition to these dependences, there are typical names for roles, corresponding to Mel'čuk actants in situations. For instance, a sign is something which, typically, would be a filler for the role perceived, in a perception event. There are also typical names for events themselves, which can designate transitory processes, like see, which would be the value of perceiving_mode for a seeing-event, or stable states like faculty names (vision, audition) which would replace the anonymous predicate c in the above declarations. Note that in this case overlaps_ii(k,1) and over-laps_ii(k,m) could be replaced by during_ii(1,k) and during_ii(m,k), since a faculty is likely to extend beyond the limits of the perception events to which it gives rise. In the other domains we find similar dependences: states or processes affecting the agent or the object can influence the possibility, nature or result of the state or process constituting the core of the situation. Note that the result of the core (a belief state in the example of perception) can be an action. The distinction between casual factors (occasional states of agents) and general trends of behavior (due to individual or general dispositions) spreads over the different domains. To construct the various relations we selected intuitively in a French dictionary of synonyms (Bertaud du Chazaud, 1989) all nouns, verbs, and adjectives which clearly behaved as "controllers" in the sense of Brennenstuhl (1982). This procedure warrants that the relations are not fancy ones, and that they correspond to lexical items, but, of course, it does not provide much information on their content. Conventional relations raise difficult problems. The fact that a human being adapts her behavior to a convention implies that (1) she knows the convention, (2) intends to obey it, (3) interprets the situation in such a way as the convention is applicable to it, (4) finds a way of satisfying the convention in a particular context. All these elements must be mentioned in a script schema. We use the next one.

```
/* Domain: convention, base: any script schema */
/* states and processes */
during_state(i,knows(x,convention)) = 1,
    during_state(j,intends(x,obey(x, convention))) = 2,
    during_state(k,believes(x,y)) = 3,during_state(1,
intends(x,z)) = 4
/* temporal dependences */
precondition_of(1,2), cause_of(2,4), precondition_of(3,4)
```

```
during_ii(j,i), during_ii(k,i), during_ii(l,i),
    overlaps_ii(j, k),
intersection(j,k,m), l = m
```

Note that intersection of two overlapping intervals is defined by case, according to the respective positions of their endpoints. The script schema says that the knowledge of some convention, associated with the desire to respect it and the belief that the applicability conditions of the convention are satisfied motivate some particular intent. The duration of this intent is exactly the duration of the period during which the motivating desire and belief overlap.

19.5   Conclusion

The implementation of LexLog raises two main problems, which we will mention briefly to summarize this discussion. Although the formal model behind LexLog appeals to Horn clauses, we did not use PROLOG to build the first prototype for hierarchical dependences management. The different consistency checks (especially when they concern substitutions and negative shadows) can be VERY costly for complex objects, such as long, intricate programs. It seems necessary in these cases to avoid blind backtracking, which often results into repeating the same calculations at different moments. Unfortunately, standard PROLOGs are not equipped with tools allowing us to stop or control efficiently this repetition. We are currently studying data structures in C, in order to keep the process within tolerable time limits. The problem is complicated because we need to trace the multiple dependences, to make local revision possible. For instance it might be interesting to know on which cont-relations a given cont-relation depends; in fact, if the user wants to revise the dependence structure, it is not enough to deduce the relation without giving any information as to the deductive structure itself. Another problem has to do with the handling of dependences in general; while working in a traditional editor window is perfect for testing the functionalities, graphic helps seem necessary to create and adjust hierarchical dependences or scripts. For the time being we have not attacked this problem, which we expect to be difficult.

Appendix

We present here some data from French. Recall that a form X dans1 Y means that X is located in some "inside" of Y, that is, in most cases, inside Y or in some concavity associated with Y, such as the inner part of a container. We count the position of an object inside some substance as a dans1 case. X dans2 Y means that X is inside a bounded external region of the object associated with Y. The numeric labels are explained in the following:

1:   the expression denotes a region with 3-dimensional bounds, such as those delineated by a wall or a fence.

2: the expression denotes a region which has only partial 3-dimensional bounds, but the global shape can be easily recovered from the visible parts. This happens when the delineating object is interrupted (this is typically the case in France for roundabouts, since circular shape is apparent only from solid portions, generally curbstones or earth).

3: the expression denotes a region with complete 3-dimensional bounds along some dimension(s) only. E.g., a street has a physical delineation over its length.

4: the expression denotes a region with visible bounds (1 entails 4). The bounds must be visible only "in principle". So, 4 is true even for very large regions (e.g., a desert).

5: the expression denotes a region with partially visible bounds, but the global shape can be recovered as in 2 (2 entails 5).

6: the expression denotes a region with totally visible bounds over some dimension(s) only (3 entails 6).

7: the expression denotes a bounded region (1–6 entail 7).

8: the expression denotes an enclosing region in genitive constructions. *Règion* is such an expression: *la région du lac* (*the lake region*) designates an area surrounding the lake.

9: the expression denotes a "matching" region in genitives constructions; by this we mean that the region must match exactly the object which occupies this region. *L'endroit du lac* (*the lake place*) designates the area which is occupied by the lake.

10: the expression is a mass term (at least in some of its uses).

11: the object associated with the expression has some material 3-dimensional extension (e.g., a road). ∨

5 ∨-cont 2 1 ∨-cont "enclos", "jardin"

2 ∨-cont "rond-point"

3 ∨-cont "rue", "allée", "canal", "sentier"

4 ∨-cont 1, "désert", "plaine", "prairie", "pelouse", "terre", "gazon", "herbe", "alpage", "champ", "herbage", "potager", "lande", "pré", "savane", "steppe", "toundra"

6 ∨-cont 3, "route", "pont", "autoroute", "piste", "promenade", "quai", "rocade", "chemin", "boulevard", "cours", "artère", "avenue", "ligne droite", "virage", "courbe"

7 ∨-cont 1, 2, 3, 4, 5, 6, "surface", "zone", "secteur", "région", "espace", "territoire", "endroit"

8 ∨-cont "zone", "secteur", "région", "territoire"

```
 9  v-cont "espace", "surface", "endroit"
10  v-cont "terre", "terres", "terrain", "gazon", "herbe"
11  v-cont "enclos", "jardin", "rue", "allée", "canal", "pla-
    ine", "champ", "pré", "route", "pont", "autoroute",
    "piste", "promenade", "quai", "rocade", "chemin",
    "boulevard", "cours", "artère", "avenue", "sentier", "rond-
    point", "carrefour", "terres", "terrain", "prairie",
    "pelouse", "terre", "gazon", "herbe", "alpage",
    "champ", "herbage", "potager", "lande", "pré", "savane",
    "steppe", "toundra", "ligne droite", "côte", "pente",
    "descente", "virage", "courbe"

    dans1_allowed v-cont "enclos", "jardin", "rue", "allée",
    "canal", "surface", "zone", "secteur", "région", "espace",
    "désert", "plaine", "territoire", "champ", "pré", "route",
    "pont", "autoroute", "piste", "promenade", "quai",
    "rocade", "chemin", "boulevard", "cours", "artère", "ave-
    nue", "sentier", "rond-point", "carrefour", "terres", "ter-
    rain", "prairie", "pelouse", "terre", "gazon", "herbe",
    "alpage", "champ", "herbage", "potager", "lande", "pré",
    "savane", "steppe", "toundra"

    dans2_allowed v-cont "enclos", "jardin", "rue", "allée",
    "canal", "désert", "plaine", "territoire", "champ", "pré",
    "chemin", "artère", "avenue", "sentier",
    "rond-point", "prairie", "alpage", "champ", "herbage",
    "potager", "lande", "pré", "savane", "steppe", "toundra",
    "ligne droite", "côte", "pente", "descente", "virage",
    "courbe"

    dans1_dubious v-cont "bifurcation", "croisement",
    "embranchement", "intersection", "ligne droite", "côte",
    "pente", "descente", "virage", "courbe"
```

References

Abeillé, Anne. (1991). *Une grammaire lexicalisée d'arbes adjoints pour le français. Application à l'analyse automatique.* Thèse de Doctorat de Linguistique. Université Paris 7.

Allen, J. F. (1984). Towards a general theory of action and time. *Artificial Intelligence*, 23, 123–160.

Allen, J. F., Perrault C. R. (1980). Analyzing intentions in utterances. *Artificial Intelligence*, 15, 143–178.

Allen J. F., Kautz, H. A., Pelavin, R. N. Tenenberg, J. D. (1991). *Reasoning about Plans.* San Mateo, Morgan Kaufmann.

Anscombre, J. C. (1989). Théorie de l'argumentation, topoï et structuration discursive, *Revue Québecoise de Linguistique,* 18, 13–56.

Bertraud de Chazaud, H. (1989). *Dictionnaire des Synonymes.* Paris, Les Dictionnaires ROBERT.

Binnick, R. I. (1991). *Time and the Verb. A Guide to Tense and Aspect.* Oxford, Oxford University Press.

Brennenstuhl, W. (1982). *Control and Ability. Towards a Biocybernetics of Language.* Amsterdam, John Benjamins.

Calzolari, N. & Zampoli, A. (1991). Methods and Tools for Lexical Acquisition. In Filguerias, M., Damas, L., Moreira, N. & Tomas, A. P. (eds). *Natural Language Processing. EAIA '90*. Berlin, Springer-Verlag, 4–24.

CL. (1992). *Computational Linguistics*, 18, 2, & 18, 3 (special issues on inheritance).

Croft, W. (1991). *Syntactic Categories and Grammatical Relations. The Cognitive Organization of Information*. Chicago, The University of Chicago Press.

DEC. (1984, 1988). *Dictionnaire Explicatif et Combinatoire du Français Contemporain I et II*. Montréal, Presses de l'Université de Montréal.

Delas, D., Delas-Demon, D. (1989). *Dictionnaire des Idées par les Mots*. Paris, Les Dictionnaires ROBERT.

Dowty, D. (1986). The effects of aspectual classes on the temporal structure of discourse: Semantics or pragmatics. *Linguistics and Philosophy*, 9, 37–61.

Ducrot, O. (1980). *Les Echelles Argumentatives*. Paris, Editions de Minuit.

Dugerdil, P. (1988). *Contribution à l'Etude de la Représentation des Connaissances fondée sur les Objets. Le langage Objlog*. Thèse de Doctorat en Sciences, Luminy, Université d'Aix-Marseille II.

Herskovits, A. (1986). *Language and Spatial Cognition. An Interdisciplinary Study of Prepositions in English*. Cambridge, Cambridge University Press.

Jayez, J. (1989). The use of an inference mechanism based over partiality to supplement fuzzification. *Communication, Cognition and Artificial Intelligence*, 6, 265–280.

Jayez, J. (1992a). LexLog, version 0. Formal Aspects. EHESS-CELITH Research Report, June 1992.

Jayez, J. (1992b). Some problems about hybrid symbolic representations based on French motion verbs. To appear in *Proceedings of 4th European Workshop on Semantics of Time, Space, Movement, and Spatio-Temporal Reasoning*, Bonas, 4–8 September 1992

Kayser, Daniel. (1992) (ed.). Rapport d'activité du groupe 'Sémantique des langues naturelles', Programmes de Recherches Coordonnées Intelligence Artificielle et Communication Homme-Machine. LIPN, Université Paris 13.

Lang, E., Carstensen, K. U., & Simmons, G. (1991). *Modelling Spatial Knowledge on a Linguistic Basis*. Berlin, Springer-Verlag

LDOCE. (1984). *Longman Dictionary of Contemporary English*. Harlow, Longman.

Lenzerini, M. Nardi, D., Simi, M. (eds.) (1991). *Inheritance Hierarchies in Knowledge Representation and Programming Languages*. Chichester, Wiley.

Mel'cuk, I. A., (1982). Lexical functions in lexicographic descriptions. *Proceedings of the 8th Annual Meeting of the Berkeley Linguistic Society*, Berkeley, 427–444.

Meiri, I. (1991). Combining qualitative and quantitative constraints in temporal reasoning, AAAI 91, 260–267.

Morris, J. & Hirst, G. (1991). Lexical cohesion computed by thesaural relations as an indication of the structure of text. *Computational Linguistics*, 17, 21–48.

Nebel, B. (1990). *Reasoning and Revision in Hybrid Representation Systems*. Berlin, Springer-Verlag.

Padawitz, P. (1988). *Computing in Horn Clause Theories*. Berlin, Springer-Verlag.

Palmer, M. S. (1990). *Semantic Processing for Finite Domains*. Cambridge, Cambridge University Press.

Parsons, T. (1990). *Events in the Semantics of English*. Cambridge (MA), MIT Press.

Passonneau, R.J. (1988). A computational model of the semantics of tense and aspect. *Computational Linguistics*, 14, 44–60.

Pollack, M. E. (1990). Plans as complex mental attitudes. In Cohen, P. R., Morgan, J., Pollack, M. E. (eds.), *Intentions in Communication*. Cambridge (MA), MIT Press, 77–103.

Pustejovsky, J. (1988). The geometry of events. In Tenny, C. (ed.), *Studies in Generative Approaches to Aspect*. Lexicon Project Working Papers 24, MIT.

Pustejovsky, J. (1991). The generative lexicon. *Computational Linguistics*, 17, 409–441.

Rauh, G. (ed.) (1991). *Approaches to Prepositions*. Tübingen, Gunter Narr Verlag.

Roget, P. (1977). *Roget's International Thesaurus*. London, Harper and Row.

Schaneveldt, R. W. (ed.) (1990). *Pathfinder Associative Networks. Studies in Knowledge Organization*. Norwood, Ablex Publishing Corporation.

Steele, J. (ed.) (1990). *Meaning-Text Theory. Linguistics, Lexicography, and Implications*. Ottawa, University of Ottawa Press.

Vandeloise, C. (1986). *L'Espace en Français*. Paris, Seuil.

Velardi, P., Pazienza, M.T., Fasolo, M. (1991). How to encode semantic knowledge: a method for meaning representation and computer-aided acquisition. *Computational Linguistics*, 17, 153–170.

Walther, C. (1987). *A Many-Sorted Calculus Based on Resolution and Paramodulation*. London, Pitman.

Wilks, Y., Fass, D., Guo, C.-M., McDonald, J., Plate, T., Slator, B. (1989). A tractable machine dictionary as a resource for computational semantics. In Boguraev, B., Briscoe, T. (eds.), *Computational Lexicography for Natural Language Processing*. London, Longman, 193–228.

20 Constraint propagation techniques for lexical semantics descriptions

PATRICK SAINT-DIZIER

20.1 Introduction

Recent works in Computational Linguistics show the central role played by the lexicon in language processing, and in particular by the lexical semantics component. Lexicons tend no longer to be a mere enumeration of feature-value pairs but tend to have an intelligent behavior. This is the case, for example, for generative lexicons (Pustejovsky, 1991) which contain, besides feature structures, a number of rules to create new (partial) definitions of word-senses such as rules for conflation and type coercion. As a result, the size of lexical entries describing word-senses has substantially increased. These lexical entries become very hard to be used directly by a natural language parser or generator because their size and complexity allow a priori little flexibility.

Most natural language systems consider a lexical entry as an indivisible whole which is percolated up in the parse/generation tree. Access to features and feature values at grammar rule level is realized by more or less complex procedures (Shieber, 1986; Johnson, 1990; Günthner, 1988). The complexity of real natural language processing systems makes such an approach very inefficient and not necessarily linguistically adequate. In this document, we propose a dynamic treatment of features in grammars, embedded within a Constraint Logic Programming framework (noted as CLP hereafter) which permits us to access a feature-value pair associated to a certain word-sense directly into the lexicon, and only when this feature is explicitly required by the grammar, for example, to make a check. More precisely, this dynamic treatment of features will make use of both constraint propagation techniques embedded within CLP and CLP resolution mechanisms. Very roughly, the former will dynamically propagate feature-value pairs while the latter will be in charge of the management of the propagation system, namely, head chaining.

We would like to thank Nabil Hathout and Guy Lapalme for discussions and suggestions while elaborating on this system. We are also indebted to Pierre Zeigenbaum for his detailed comments on this text. This work was partly supported by the GDR-PRC Communication Homme-Machine of the French Ministry for Research and Space.

The motivations for this approach are twofold. The first motivation is obviously efficiency. When parsing or generating a sentence, only small portions of the lexical entries corresponding to the words of the surface sentence being processed are used. Here are a few illustrative examples:

1. in the rule (for French):

VP --> V, NP.

no agreement in gender and in number is required between the verb and the object NP, whereas such an agreement is required between the NP subject and the verb. Thus, gender and number need not be present at this level.

2. The verb *penser* (to think) has a number of associated subcategorization frames, e.g.:

> *Jean pense à Marie. (John thinks to Mary)*
> *Jean pense que Marie arrive. (John thinks that Mary is coming)*
> *Jean pense efficacement. (John thinks efficiently)*
> *Jean pense à rentrer. (John thinks of coming back). etc. . . .*

To process the verb *penser* in a given sentence, it is not necessary to percolate up in the proof tree all these frames. It is preferable to delay this global percolation and to extract only the relevant information when, for example and roughly speaking, the verb's governing domain has been identified and processed.

3. Generative lexicons (Pustejovsky, 1991) allow a treatment of metonymy by means of coercion rules applied on a Qualia structure. Metonymy is not found in all sentences; as a consequence, it seems appropriate to make reference to and thus to percolate in the proof tree the Qualia structure when the standard subcategorization frames cannot be used.

The second motivation to our approach is linguistic adequacy. Most of the information conveyed by features is often linguistically relevant (and thus used) very locally in a parsing/generation tree. Furthermore, the presence of certain features at certain syntactic nodes is linguistically irrelevant. For example, in:

> *John opened the door.*

the aspectual value of the verb to open is relevant only at the level of the VP category, i.e., the level of the maximal projection of the category. There is no reason to have a more or less specified aspectual feature at lower levels, e.g., V^1 and V^0 in the X-bar system. The same remark can be made at sentence level, when there is a temporal adverbial as in:

> *John opened the door every day for 3 years.*

The same remark can also be made concerning the argument structure of the verb which is relevant only at, depending on the linguistic approach, VP, I' or S level.

We now present a dynamic treatment of feature passing. The next section introduces a re-structuring of lexical entries in order to allow for an easier dynamic treatment of features in grammars. Section 20.3 presents the general framework of CLP for lexical semantics, Section 20.4 introduces a dynamic treatment of features, expressed within a CLP framework, which confers all its power to this treatment. Section 20.5 discusses implementation issues and alternative practical solutions, involving, for example, partial evaluation techniques.

20.2 Structure of lexical items

In the previous versions of our parsing/generation system (Saint-Dizier, 1991a,b), lexical and grammatical representations had a uniform representation based on a hierarchy of lexical and syntactic types as defined in Login (Aït-Kaçi and Nasr, 1986). In Login, the syntactic representation of a structured term is called a y-term. It consists of:

1. a *root symbol,* which is a type constructor and denotes a class of entities,
2. *attribute labels,* which are record field symbols. Each attribute denotes a function in extenso, from the root to the attribute value. The attribute value can itself be a reference to a type. And
3. *coreference constraints* among paths of labels, which indicate that the corresponding attributes denote the same function. They are indicated by variables. Here is an example:

```
person( id => name(first => string,
                    last => X: string),
        born => date(day => integer,
                     month => monthname,
                     year => integer),
        father => person( id => name(last => X ))).
```

In this example, the root symbol is *person; id, born* and *father* are three sub-ψ-terms which have either constants or types as values. *X* indicates a coreference. All different type structures are tagged by different symbols. Notice also that in the latter field only relevant information about person is mentioned. Infinite structures can also be specified by coreference links. Variables are in capital letters, constants in small letters. Here now is a simple lexical entry for the verb *to give:*

```
x0( cat => v, word_sense => give,
    passive => yes,
    subcat => [xp( cat => n, string => S1, role => patient ),
               xp( cat => p, string => S2, role => recipient) ] ).
```

This entry says that *give* is a verb which subcategorizes for an np with role patient and a pp with role recipient. The type constructor associated to the lexical entry is a terminal type x0, while the type constructors associated to the phrasal np and the pp are non-terminal types xp.

Lexical entries are reformulated so that feature structures are visible from outside the word-sense they are related to. By visible, we mean directly accessible by the program: feature labels are directly functor names. The basic idea is to index lexical entries by means of feature labels rather than by means of the words themselves, as is usually the case. A very simple reformulation consists in defining an operator ft (for feature_of) such that:

A ft WS.

which means that A is a feature structure for the word-sense WS. The above example would be reformulated as follows:

```
cat => v ft give.
passive => yes ft give.
subcat => [xp( cat => n, string => S1, role => patient ),
  xp( cat => p, string => S2, role => recipient) ] ft give. etc...
```

In a first step, to make the general process easier to understand, we will assume that features are referred to by their absolute address, i.e., from their upper-most label to their value.

This reformulation, where feature-value pairs are made visible, has a certain psychological justification. We often access a word-sense (or a concept) not in an abstract way but by having in mind some of its properties, probably the most typical ones, with respect to the domain being treated. Besides this justification, this approach also permits better structure features, in particular for those having an order or a hierarchical relation on the domain of their values. It is indeed of much interest for both linguistic adequacy and efficiency to structure the values of a given feature label whenever possible, for example by means of trees or graphs. Then, it is possible to associate to each node of that structure the set of those word-senses for which the feature considered bears that value. This point is of much interest, but it will not be further developed here because it is not central to the system we present here.

20.3   Constraint Logic Programming for lexical semantics

Several types of lexical semantics information can be represented with a gain in expressivity within the Constraint Logic Programming framework (CLP). The definition of a constraint consists in two aspects:

- the definition of the domain of the constraint (e.g., booleans, rational numbers, finite list of semantic features, thematic roles, finite set of coercion rules, finite set of lexical redundancy rules); these objects are postulated to be the basic entities on which constraints can apply;
- the definition of an operator and its properties on the domain defined; the operator will be the constraint itself (e.g., > or < for rationals, which is a transitive operation).

Finally, CLP involves 2 types of treatments: the resolution of the constraint step by step throughout the whole execution of a program and techniques for the dynamic propagation of information based on consistency techniques which use CLP. This latter point will be illustrated in detail in Section 20.4.

In the following section, we briefly present CLP and then introduce the different domains of constraints of interest within lexical semantics.

20.3.1   *Introduction to Constraint Logic Programming*

The general form of a rule with constraints is the following:

Head :- Body, { Constraints }.

The resolution mechanism is similar to Prolog except that at each stage of the process, Constraints are added to the previous set of constraints and have to form a coherent set:

CLP Abstract Machine:

(1)   stage i:
       { W , t1 t2 t3 . . . . . . tn , S }

W is the set of variables present in the original query (and which appear in the result of the proof procedure), the ti denote the current set of terms to prove (i.e., the current resolvent) and S is the current satisfiable set of constraints.

(2)   selection of a clause in the programme:
       p :- q1 q2 . . . qm, R.

(3)   stage i+1:
       { W , q1 q2 . . . qm t2 t3 . . . . . . tn , S ∪ R ∪ (p = t1) }
       provided that: S ∪ R ∪ (p = t1) is coherent;
       constraint resolutions and simplifications occur on this set of constraints.

CLP allows us to:

1. *improve efficiency* of the current system; whereas Prolog uses the constraints according to the "generate and test" schema, CLP systems use them to reduce the search space a priori, i.e., before the generation of the values. The CLP approach usually proposes a single (or a very small number of) response(s) to a query; this response being a set of constraints, it potentially contains the different possible solutions to a query, thus avoiding duplication of solutions.

2. *improve expressivity* since active constraints have a different, more general semantics. CLP introduces *new computation domains* (i.e., boolean domain, arithmetic domain, finite domains . . .) besides the usual Herbrand's one. We thus can directly describe the objects and their properties in the discourse domain. We do not have to encode them as Prolog terms or predicates, which results in a saving of naturalness and thus of efficiency. Moreover, we can represent these properties intensionally.

3. *improve genericity and reusability* of the tools developed for language processing so that they can be used for different subareas and purposes.

We now introduce the major aspects of active constraints of the constraint logic programing framework (Jaffar and Lassez, 1987; Dincbas et al., 1988; Colmerauer, 1990) which constitutes the kernel of our proposition. Constraints are such that:

- their coherence is checked at each step of the proof construction;
- they are kept active throughout the whole proof construction process until they can be adequately resolved;
- they are resolved as soon as there is sufficient available knowledge about their variables;
- they introduce a greater modularity since each constraint system is dealt with independently;
- the result of a query is a set of constraints on variables from which it is straightforward to define domains of values for variables; furthermore, constraints cannot be viewed only as coming down to defining domains for variables, because they also express complex relations between variables;
- they are fully declarative and easy to use since they are directly stated;
- and thus, they are fully independent of the way they are used (e.g., for parsing or generating sentences, with a bottom-up or a top-down strategy).

Our constraint system is coherent with the formalism we want to use for lexical descriptions since constraints operate on typed structures (Saint-Dizier, 1991). To compare our approach with the well-known 'parsing as deduction' approach, we can say that using a certain lexical entry, translating a certain construction into another one, etc. . . . , is a constraint satisfaction problem.

20.3.2 *Constraints for lexical semantics*

The domain of constraints in lexical semantics has not yet been explored in depth. It seems that it is a particularly rich area. Among these domains let us mention:

- finite domains of semantic features, these features being structured by, for example, the isa relation,
- finite domains of rules which can be applied on these lexical entries such as coercion rules and lexical redundancy rules,
- finite domains of aspectual values, temporal values, etc. . . .

These domains of constraints are usually treated by a constraint of the form in (X,D) where the variable X denotes a subset of the domain and D denotes a larger subset in which D is supposed to be included. For example, let us suppose that to each lexical entry is associated the (possible) set of coercion rules that may potentially be applied to it. When parsing a sentence, the first element A treated introduces a certain set of coercion rules C1 that may potentially be used to parse the sentence. Next, when a second element B is read, also introducing a certain set of coercion rules C2, the set of potential coercion rules that may be used to parse the sentence is a subset of C1 and C2, containing those rules which are still coherent and appropriate. The process goes on in the same way for the next elements. This process further and further restricts the number of coercion rules which may potentially be applied in a monotonic way.

20.4   A dynamic treatment of feature passing

Most linguistic systems are based on the notion of head categories, possibly modified by a large variety of modifiers, operating at different levels (Gazdar et al., 1985; Pollard and Sag, 1987; Chomsky, 1986). To summarize, these systems show that feature structures are inherited from head to head. This inheritance is not necessarily a direct transfer of feature-value pairs; values can indeed be altered and new features can be created. This is the case when a symbol has several daughters which are heads (as in coordination). The role of modifiers may also have an influence over head feature values.

The dynamic treatment of feature passing is realized by means of a single, simple device: the expression of a chaining between heads in grammar rules. This chaining is managed by a constraint resolution mechanism (Colmerauer, 1990; Dincbas, 1988; Freuder, 1978; Mackworth, 1987) and a constraint propagation technique (Van Hentenryck, 1989). This device permits us to have a direct access to the information stored in the lexical elements.

20.4.1   *Expression of chaining*

To express the chaining between heads in grammar rules, we introduce two operators which will be interpreted as CLP constraints:

```
head(Syntactic_category, Word_sense)
```

which expresses that Word_sense of a certain Syntactic_category is, at this level, a (lexical) head.

```
isa_head(Syntactic_category1, Syntactic_category2)
```

establishes an elementary head chain between Syntactic_category1 and Syntactic_category2, which it immediately dominates. Except for complex phenomena such as those presented in Section 20.4.3, there is a single head chain in each grammar rule. For example, in a simple grammar, we have:

(1)   n --> [house], { head(n, house) }.
          vp --> v, np, { isa_head(v, vp) }.

head and isa_head are given between curly brackets, to indicate that they are treated as active CLP constraints. In the first rule, a constraint specifies that the noun house is a (lexical) head. In the second rule, an elementary chain is established between the V and the VP. If the NP were a head, as specified in:

```
np --> det, n, modifier, { isa_head(n, np) }.
```

then the head-chaining of the noun stops at that level.

It should be noticed that the specification of elementary head chains is a very simple task which can be automated in systems such as the X-bar system or the GPSG grammatical system where a strong emphasis is put on the role of the head (for example via the Head Feature Convention of GPSG). Our chaining system can be used for most current linguistic systems, independently of their complexity. For the sake of clarity, in a simple syntactic tree, chains can be diagrammatically represented as follows:

(2)

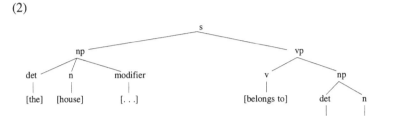

We have three non-elementary chains:

[house] ---> n ---> np
[belongs to] ---> v ---> vp
[community] ---> n ---> np.

The same kind of chaining is recursively repeated in the X-bar system, as illustrated below:

(3)

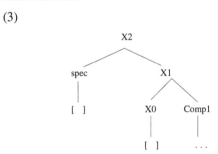

Taking into account the general form of syntactic trees and the role of bounding nodes, it turns out that most chains are short, i.e., of length (2) to (3). This limits the complexity of the system.

Definition 1

In a grammar rule, a symbol is said to be active in a given syntactic tree if there is an uninterrupted chain from that symbol to a lexical head.

In the example (2), at the level of the subtree vp --> v, np, the symbols v and np are active symbols, the det under the np is no longer active. At s level, no more head is active. This approach is independent of the parsing strategy. It is, however, obvious that a bottom-up strategy is much more efficient since chains are established from their starting point, i.e., the lexical head, and not the reverse, which entails freezing controls till terminal elements are reached.

20.4.2 *Management of the chaining*

A simple constraint resolution mechanism manages the chains so that each node in the syntactic tree has a direct access to the corresponding active lexical head. Let us now examine a feature control. In:

```
(4) s --> np( sem => T ), vp( sem_subj => LS ),
      {member_of(T, LS)}.
```

a control expresses (here as a CLP constraint) that the semantic feature T of the subject np has to be included into the list LS of admissible semantic features for the subject of the vp. The feature value T associated to the feature label sem in the np and the feature value LS associated to the feature label sem_subj in the vp are requested to make the control. If they are not accessible now, the control is postponed till they are accessible (this is a classical treatment of contraints). They are accessible if there is a chain from the np to its related head noun and a chain from the vp to its related head verb. The constraint resolution mechanism manages the chains in a such way that lexical heads are directly accessible. Then the access to T and LS is straightforward.

Definition 2

A feature label is said to be active in a grammar rule if it is directly used to make a control in that grammar rule. The management of lexical heads, active features and control specifications is realized by means of a data-structure associated to each node of the parse/generation tree. This data-structure has the following general form:

```
( active head, list of active features, list of controls )
```

where *active head* is defined by a constraint propagation mechanism and a resolution mechanism. In a rule of the form:

```
A --> A₁, ..., Aₙ, { isa_head(Aⱼ, A) }.
```

the field 'active head' associated to A receives the value of the field 'active head' of its daughter A_j. The general form of this field is: head(category, word-sense) as given in Section 20.4.1. At this level, the constraint resolution mechanism which handles the active head-chaining is very simple. More complex cases involving a composition of values from different symbols in the right-hand side of the grammar rule are studied in Section 20.4.3. *Active features* are directly accessible from the grammar rule. For example, in (4) the active features are sem => T for n and sem_subj => LS for v. They are represented in a list with elements of the form:

(6)   active(feature-value, active node involved).

For (4) we would then obtain the list:

(7)   [active(sem => T, n), active(sem_subj => LS, vp)].

List of controls is the set of constraints expressed in the grammar rule. Its execution can be postponed (frozen) if the values of the feature involved are not yet accessible.

At execution time, the system first creates the active head of the father node, then it finds the active features (this can be pre-compiled in the grammar rules) and finally attempts to execute the controls. The values of active features are directly obtained by consulting the lexical entry of the lexical head specified in the grammar symbol involved. As can be noticed, the processing of a sentence amounts to constructing a parse tree which has the form of a context-free skeleton with attached procedures under the form of active constraints associated to each node. This kind of approach has already been used for different purposes outside CLP techniques, for example, in Attribute Grammars and in Restriction Grammars (Hirschman and Puder, 1986).

In the system presented here, the domain of the constraint is a finite set of all possible instantiated data-structures: (`active head, list of active features, list of controls`). The resolution mechanism is based on inheritance. The next section will introduce more complex resolution mechanisms devoted to precise linguistic phenomena.

20.4.3 *Treatment of non-lexical features and chains*

In this section, we address three general situations where feature-value pairs are not accessible at the lexical level. These situations cover: the elaboration of non-lexical features such as aspect, the treatment of coordination and the setting of specific chains for long-distance dependencies such as the pronoun antecedent one. These three classes of situations cover a large spectrum of linguistic phenomena, and they involve a more elaborated resolution mechanism, which maintains in a monotonic way a set of active heads.

The use of Constraint Logic Programming mechanisms at this level is motivated by the following factors:

- at a given syntactic level, all information is not necessarily available to compute a certain feature value. The best strategy is to postpone this computation until enough data is available. CLP handles this in a transparent way, thus allowing a substantial gain in declarativity and expressive power,
- when several values for a given feature can be produced at a certain level, instead of using the Prolog generate and test strategy, CLP permits us to postpone unification and simply reduces the search space a priori,
- in case of ambiguity, CLP permits us to elegantly hypothesize several chainings for a given syntactic level. At later stages, selections will be made between these chainings,
- finally, the constraint resolution mechanisms directly reflect the properties of the linguistic phenomena being treated (e.g., transitivity).

Non-lexical features

Non-lexical features are features elaborated at grammar rule level. In this class fall features expressing aspect and temporal values like iterativity. These feature values are often computed from lexical features in different lexical or non-lexical constituents. For example, in:

John opened the door every Monday for three years.

the construction 'opened the door' has aspectual value event or process (determined from the verb), then its combination with the adverbial modifier 'every monday for three years' because of the quantification introduced by every, which defines a finite set of points over a closed temporal interval of three years, transforms the aspectual value into an iterative process.

An aspectual value is computed by means of a resolution mechanism based on rules expressing the different possible aspectual and temporal combinations. The feature 'aspect' is active at, for example, VP level and the resolution mechanism for computing the aspectual value is activated. This triggers the retrieval of the temporal and aspectual values present in the lexical entries associated to the different constituents being processed, as presented in Section 20.4.2. This can be illustrated by the following diagram:

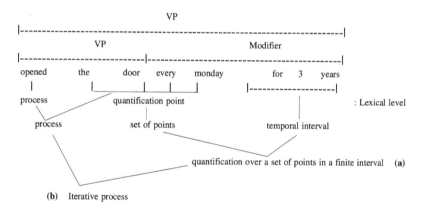

To treat (a) and (b) a new active feature is created and assigned a value. The resolution mechanism treats non-lexical and lexical features in a homogeneous way. The syntactic node temporal_modifier in the parse tree is assigned a feature 'temporal_value' with an appropriate value. It is then treated in a similar way as lexical heads, with respect to the chaining mechanism. The 'active head' field in the data-structure given in Section 20.3.2 becomes a list of lexical and non-lexical active elements. In (a) a non-lexical head of the form:

```
head(temporal_modifier, _ )
```

is added to the current active head (here the noun 'Monday'). We then have the following list of active heads attached to the node 'temporal modifier':

```
[ head(n,Monday), head(temporal_modifier, _ ) ].
```

Then, at a higher level, when searching for a feature-value pair, the system will examine all active heads. Notice that there is no ambiguity in the retrieval of features since lexical and non-lexical feature labels are designed to be disjoint sets. The chaining of non-lexical heads is similar to the chaining of lexical heads. This approach permits us to generalize our system to having chains starting a priori from anywhere in the parse tree. It should be noted that the complexity of the chainings remains limited because most chains are very short.

Coordination

Coordination provokes the modification of lexical feature values but does not create any new feature, a priori. In a rule of the form:

X ---> X1, Conjunction, X2.

the head chains associated to X1 and X2 end at the level of this rule. Appropriate feature and feature values are elaborated by a specific resolution mechanism for X according to the rules of coordination. The features are associated to the node X. X becomes the starting point of a new head chain which is non-lexical. This new chain is processed in a similar way as in the previous section, starting also from a non-lexical symbol.

Chains for long-distance dependencies

For a number of various well-known reasons (dependent on the linguistic phenomenon accounted for) a chain has to be established between two elements forming a long-distance dependency. For example, in:

La personne$_i$ [à laquelle$_i$ Jean parle trace$_i$] . . . (the person to whom John is speaking)

the lexical chain reaching the trace level should be anchored to the pronoun 'à laquelle' and similarly for the antecedent 'la personne' which is related to the pronoun, in order for it to receive the appropriate morphological and case agreements. Elementary chains have to be established from the trace to 'à laquelle' and from the noun 'la personne' to the pronoun.

This treatment can be realized in a straightforward way using the language Dislog (Saint-Dizier, 1989) which allows a simple and declarative way of expressing long-distance relations. A Dislog clause is a finite, unordered set of Horn clauses f$_i$ of the form:

$$(f_1 , f_2 , \ldots \ldots , f_n).$$

The informal meaning of a Dislog clause is: *if a clause f_i in a Dislog clause is used to construct a given proof tree, then all the other f_j of that Dislog clause must be used to construct that proof tree, with the same substitutions applied to identical variables.* Moreover, there are no hypotheses made on the location of these clauses in the proof tree. For example, the following Dislog clause composed of two Prolog facts:

(*arc(a,b)*, *arc(e,f)*)

means that, in a graph, the use of *arc(a,b)* to construct a proof is conditional to the use of *arc(e,f)*. If one is looking for paths in a graph, this means that all paths going through the *arc(a,b)* will have to go through the *arc(e ,f)*, or conversely.

A Dislog clause thus permits us to express the co-occurrence of clauses in a proof tree. The constraint stating that all identical variables in an instance of a Dislog clause must be substituted for the same terms permits the transfer of feature values between non-contiguous elements in a very convenient way. A Dislog clause can be subject to various types of restrictions such as: linear precedence constraints on the f_i , modalities on applications of some f_i and the specification of bounding domains in which a Dislog clause instance must be fully used. From a CLP perspective, the clauses in a Dislog clause may be CLP clauses. On the other hand, Dislog clauses themselves can be interpreted as a kind of meta-constraint on a domain of clauses.

Then, the relation between the pronoun and the noun which is its antecedent is expressed as follows in Dislog:

```
(( np --> np(I), modifier), (Comp --> pro(I), comp )):-
   { isa_head( np(I), pro(I)) }.
```

Similarly, a chain is established between the trace and the pronoun. This chain is less productive, but it mainly permits us to pass the case feature (here accusative) to the pronoun. Notice that the case feature is usually not a lexical feature; it is assigned here at the trace level.

20.5   Architecture and implementation issues

The system presented here has been fully implemented in compiled Sicstus Prolog, using the CLP facilities of the language, in particular the freeze built-in predicate. A meta-interpreter manages calls to rules of the grammar and the data-structure associated to each node of the parse tree. It is also responsible for retrieving the appropriate feature values in the lexical entries. Although this system does not involve complex treatments, the overhead due to the meta-interpreter level is relatively important; but we envisage in the future that this meta-interpreter will be directly encoded in C into the Prolog system. This would then give better efficiency results. It seems to us that this integration should be postponed until there are sufficient basic CLP tools in logic programming languages. This would make our task easier since we will be able to directly use these tools instead of changing procedures in the source code.

The architecture of the system can be summarized as follows:

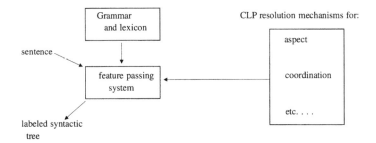

Conclusion

In this short chapter, we have presented a dynamic treatment of feature structures based on CLP and constraint propagation techniques. The main motivations were efficiency and linguistic adequacy since certain features are not relevant to certain syntactic levels.

This system can be used in a number of linguistic and practical approaches. It is indeed not committed to any linguistic approach a priori. It can be used for parsing as well as for generating sentences.

One of our aims is now to include it into a larger constraint system which handles the other aspects of NLP, such as: precedence, long-distance dependencies, inclusion of values, finite domains, etc. . . .

References

Aït-Kaçi, H., Nasr, R. (1986). LOGIN: A Logic Programming Language with Built-in Inheritance, *Journal of Logic Programming,* vol. 3, pp. 185–215.

Chomsky, N. (1986). *Barriers,* Linguistic Inquiry monograph nb. 13, MIT Press.

Colmerauer, A. (1990). An Introduction to Prolog III, *CACM 33-7,* pp. 212–221.

Dincbas, M., Van Hentenryck, P., Simonis, H., Aggoun, A., Graf, T., and Berthier, F. (1988) "The Constraint Logic Programming Language CHIP," *Proceedings of the International Conference on Fifth Generation Computer Systems,* pp. 693–702, ICOT, Tokyo.

Emele, M., Zajac, R. (1990). Typed Unification Grammars, in proc. *COLING'90,* Helsinki, pp. 102–106.

Freuder, E. C. (1978) "Synthetising Constraint Expressions," *Communications of the ACM,* 21:958–966.

Gazdar, G., Klein, E., Pullum, G.K., Sag, I. (1985). *Generalized Phrase Structure Grammar,* Harvard University Press.

Günthner, F. (1988). Features and Values, Research Report Univ of Tübingen, SNS 88-40.

Hirschman, L., Puder, K. (1986). Restriction Grammars, in *Logic Programming and its Applications,* M. van Caneghem et al. eds., Ablex Pub.

Jaffar, J., Lassez, J.L. (1987). Constraint Logic Programming, *Proc. 14th ACM Symposium on Principles of Programming Languages,* pp. 87–102.

Johnson, M. (1990). Expressing Disjunctive and Negative Feature Constraints with Classical First-Order Logic, proc. *ACL'90,* Pittsburgh, pp. 72–77.

Mackworth, A. K. (1987). "Constraint Satisfaction," in Shapiro, ed., *Encyclopedia of Artificial Intelligence,* Wiley-Interscience Publication, New York.

Pollard, C., Sag, I. (1987). *Information-based Syntax and Semantics,* vol. 1, CSLI lecture notes no. 13.

Pustejovsky, J. (1991). The Generative Lexicon, *Computational Linguistics.*

Saint-Dizier, P. (1989). Constrained Logic Programming for Natural Language Processing, proc. *E. ACL-89,* Manchester, pp. 135–143.

Saint-Dizier, P. (1991a). Processing Language with Types and Active Constraints, in proc. *E. ACL 91,* Berlin, pp. 214–220.

Saint-Dizier, P. (1991b). Generating sentences with Active Constraints, in proc. *3rd European workshop on language generation,* Judenstein, Austria, pp. 257–263.

Shieber, S. (1986). An Introduction to Unification-Based Approaches to Grammar, *CSLI Lecture Notes No 4,* Chicago University Press.

Van Hentenryck, P. (1989). *Constraint Satisfaction in Logic Programming,* MIT Press, Cambridge, MA.

Author index

Subject index

activation of concepts, 59, 260
ambiguity, 36
argument structure, 9, 76, 133
argumentative structure, 101
arguments, 80
assertional knowledge, 188
attribute, 168

bridging, 194

case relation, 177
categorial knowledge, 188
cocomposition, 90
cognitive linguistics, 46
collocation, 128
componential semantics, 7
concept, 165, 168
conceptual analysis, 231
conceptual system, 144, 231
connectionism, 255
constraint logic programming, 426, 430
coreferences, 359

default inheritance, 274
discontinuities, 244
discourse knowledge, 188
discourse referent, 187
disjunction of concepts, 176
divergence, 368, 380

encyclopedic system, 144, 304
entailment relation, 178
episodic knowledge, 192
event structure, 24, 76, 131

feature-value structure, 279, 281, 428
frame, 166

generation, 5, 355
generative lexicon, 75, 101, 129, 208, 316
group nouns, 213

inheritance, 212, 273, 400, 409
intensifiers, 243
interlingua, 171

KL-ONE, 166
knowledge acquisition, 342
knowledge representation, 165, 134

lexical access, 4, 50, 58
lexical analysis, 231, 341, 374
lexical conceptual structure, 21, 246, 374, 385
lexical functions, 27, 127, 241, 337, 351, 378
lexical knowledge base, 207, 319
lexical meaning, 193, 198
lexical representation language, 140, 209, 277, 374
lexical semantics relations, 15, 52
lexical signs, 282
linking rules, 382, 401
logic programming, 421, 438

machine readable dictionaries, 220, 253, 319, 340
machine translation, 367
meaning construction, 304
mental lexicon, 50, 317
metonymy, 333

network architecture, 258
neural networks, 257
non-monotonic logics, 282, 303, 402

ontology, 19

polysemy, 33, 321
proper treatment of quantification (PTQ), 142
psycholinguistics, 1, 50

qualia structure, 25, 76, 109, 132, 157, 208

scales, 412, 414
selectional constraint, 190
selectional restrictions (also semantic features), 14, 62, 145
semantic types, 142, 428
semantic value, 282, 303, 326
set of accessible referents, 194
subsumption, 167

term subsumption language, 166
terminological knowledge, 188
troponymy, 177
type coercion, 71, 83, 219

value restriction, 168

world knowledge, 304

For EU product safety concerns, contact us at Calle de José Abascal, 56–1°,
28003 Madrid, Spain or eugpsr@cambridge.org.

www.ingramcontent.com/pod-product-compliance
Ingram Content Group UK Ltd.
Pitfield, Milton Keynes, MK11 3LW, UK
UKHW042138130625

459647UK00011B/1092